D0330759

A TRUE HISTORY

OF THE ASSASSINATION

OF ABRAHAM LINCOLN

AND OF THE CONSPIRACY

OF 1865

A TRUE HISTORY

OF THE ASSASSINATION

OF ABRAHAM LINCOLN

AND OF THE CONSPIRACY

OF 1865

LOUIS J. WEICHMANN

*Chief witness for the Government of the United States
in the prosecution of the conspirators*

EDITED BY FLOYD E. RISVOLD

ALFRED A. KNOPF   NEW YORK   1975

This is a Borzoi Book
published by Alfred A. Knopf, Inc.

Library of Congress Cataloging in Publication Data
Weichmann, Louis J.   A true history of the assassination of Abraham Lincoln
and the Conspiracy of 1865.
Includes 23 letters written by A. C. Richards
to Weichmann from Apr. 1898 to Nov. 1901.
Includes bibliographical references.
1. Lincoln, Abraham, Pres. U.S., 1809–1865—Assassination.
2. Booth, John Wilkes, 1838–1865.
3. United States. Army. Military Commission. Lincoln's assassins. 1865.
4. Weichmann, Louis J. I. Richards, A. C., d. 1907. II. Title.
E457.5.W44   364.1′31′0973   74–21278
ISBN 0-394-49319-2

Manufactured in the United States of America
First Edition

DEDICATED

TO THE MEMORY OF

LOUIS J. WEICHMANN

AND

A. C. RICHARDS

In the middle of the journey of life,
I found myself in a dark wood
for the straight way was lost.

—DANTE, *Inferno, Canto I*

I am anxious before I pass away
to know that this vindication of yourself
has been laid before the country,
and to know further that it has been accepted
as a triumphant response
to the calumnies of the past.

—J. HOLT, May 29, 1893

LOUIS J. WEICHMANN

I have never seen anything like his steadfastness. There he stood, a young man only twenty-three years of age, strikingly handsome, self-possessed, under the most searching cross-examination I have ever heard. He had been innocently involved in the schemes of the conspirators, and although the Surratts were his personal friends, he was forced to appear and testify when subpoenaed. He realized deeply the sanctity of the oath he had taken to tell the truth, the whole truth, and nothing but the truth, and his testimony could not be confused or shaken in the slightest detail.

—MAJOR GENERAL LEW WALLACE,
author of BEN HUR,
from LEW WALLACE: AN AUTOBIOGRAPHY

ACKNOWLEDGMENTS

The editor wishes to express his appreciation to the people who have helped make this publication possible.

First of all, I am indebted to Alma Murphy Halff, the niece of Louis J. Weichmann, to her son, John F. Halff, and to Elizabeth and John Pope III, of St. Louis. I am grateful to Russell W. Fridley of the Minnesota Historical Society for recognizing the historical significance of the manuscript and urging its publication; to Lucile Kane of the Society for reading the manuscript, checking the note format, and smoothing out the wording in my Introduction; to Fleming Fraker, Jr., of Washington, D.C., who helped in the research; and especially to James O. Hall of McLean, Virginia, who made available to this project his extensive records of the assassination—probably the most complete file on the subject in private hands. My thanks, also, to Irving Rothwell Richards of Washington, D.C., the grandson of A. C. Richards, for making available photographs and information pertinent to this publication; to Lloyd Ostendorf of Dayton, Ohio, for making available his great collection of photographs; to Edward L. Wertman of Minneapolis for his generosity in doing research and running down loose ends; to Ms. Bernadette Muck for preparing the index; and, by no means last, to my secretary, Nelda H. Steen, for a tremendous amount of typing in preparing the manuscript for publication.

Among others who have contributed to this work are the following: Senator William G. Kirchner, LuVerne Warnberg, Heidi Fettig, William Laird, Harold Kittleson, and John Parker, all of Minneapolis; Nyle H. Miller, director of the Kansas State Historical Society; Mrs. Kathleen Patterson of Crawfordsville, Indiana; Mrs. Esther Dittlinger of Anderson, Indiana; Elmer O. Parker of Washington, D.C.; Ms. Marion Angus, Pitman Publishing Corporation, New York City; Leonard Fellman of Edina, Minnesota; Mrs. Earl Sanford of Half Moon Lake, Wisconsin; Eugene Becker and Mrs. Roy Ritchie of St. Paul;

Acknowledgments

Henry B. Bass of Enid, Oklahoma; my daughter Mrs. Stephen Pearson of Luck, Wisconsin; Charles Cooney of Washington, D.C.; and Thomas Chowning of Shelburn, Indiana.

The helpfulness of the following institutions has earned my gratitude: Minnesota Historical Society; Library of Congress; National Archives; University of Minnesota Library; Minneapolis Public Library; St. Paul Public Library; Public Library of Anderson, Indiana; General Lew Wallace Library of Crawfordsville, Indiana; and the New-York Historical Society of New York City.

In particular, I wish to thank Mr. Angus Cameron, my editor at Alfred A. Knopf, Inc., for his patience, consideration, and advice in dealing with a tenderfoot, and his staff, including Sally Rogers and Bobbie Bristol; my brothers and partners, Howard and Curtis Risvold, in the firm of O. E. Risvold & Sons; and last, but far from least, my wife, Sophie, who has put up with a man trying to run a business while seemingly living in the America of the nineteenth century.

Truly an experience never to be forgotten.

EDITOR'S INTRODUCTION

When the pistol shot that ended the life of Abraham Lincoln rang out on the night of April 14, 1865, Louis Weichmann was in his room at the boardinghouse of Mary E. Surratt in Washington, D.C. Little then did he realize that he would be caught up in a whirlwind of controversy that would follow him for the rest of his life. Everyone who had an ax to grind, who thought the conspirators, and Mary Surratt in particular, had failed to receive justice and had been railroaded, blamed Weichmann for his testimony at the trial. They called him a liar, a perjurer, and a coward, ignoring the fact that there was another principal witness. According to one of the military judges who presided at the trial, the testimony of John M. Lloyd, Mrs. Surratt's tenant at Surrattsville, was the most damaging and the deciding factor in the verdict. Lloyd lived for twenty-seven years after the assassination and Weichmann for thirty-seven years, but neither one changed his testimony.

After Mary Surratt was hanged, a great cry went up, and ever since that moment on the gallows, some newspapers, historians, and members of the general public have claimed that she was innocent. They have tried to put the blame on the Government, particularly on the military commission that tried her, and on the Government's two principal witnesses, Lloyd and Weichmann. As a result, Weichmann spent the last thirty-seven years of his life defending himself and writing the narrative of his experience as he lived it.

In preparing his narrative of the assassination, Weichmann corresponded with many of the principal characters in the drama, searching for information and advice. Among his correspondents was A. C. Richards, a former major and Superintendent of the Metropolitan Police of the District of Columbia, whose letters appear in the Appendix, along with some correspondence and several newspaper articles that have received little or no attention from historians writing on the subject.

In August 1899, Weichmann informed Nathaniel Wilson, assistant prosecuting attorney at the trial of John H. Surratt, that "the publication of my history is in the future" and that he was not sure whether he would release it during his lifetime or leave it to others as a vindication of himself after he was gone.[1]

Louis J. Weichmann[2] was born of German parents, John C. and Mary Ann Wiechmann, on September 29, 1842, in Baltimore, Maryland. In 1845, they moved to Washington, D.C., where his father carried on the trade of tailoring and Weichmann attended the Washington Seminary. In 1853, the family moved to Philadelphia, where he entered the public schools and graduated from Central High in that city on February 10, 1859.

Weichmann has been described by his contemporaries as tall, broadshouldered, and handsome. He was an exceptional student and is said to have mastered seven languages and the Pitman system of phonography (shorthand). On March 1, 1859, he entered St. Charles College in Howard County, Maryland, to prepare for the Catholic priesthood. In July 1862, he left college because he felt that he was not being advanced to his satisfaction. After leaving college, he went to Washington, D.C., where he taught school at St. Matthew's Institute for

[1] Weichmann Papers, Risvold Collection.

[2] There is some confusion concerning the spelling of Weichmann's name. When he was asked to state his name at the trial of John H. Surratt in 1867, he said, "My name is Louis J. Weichman. Before the trial of the assassins I spelled my name *Wie*. I gave it distinctly to the reporters, as I thought, but they spelled it *Wei*, and since that time I have spelled it that way." Nevertheless, Weichmann's highschool diploma is hand-lettered LOUIS WEICHMANN under date of February 10, 1859, at Central High School, Philadelphia, Pennsylvania. All of his letters in the Risvold Collection, which bear his signature, are signed L. J. Weichmann. Another variant of the spelling uses only one *n*—he always used two *n*'s. When Lloyd Lewis interviewed Miss Tillie Wiechmann in Anderson, Indiana, in 1926, he reported the spelling as *Wei*, but on the headstones in the Catholic cemetery in Anderson all are spelled *Wie*, including Louis'. It could be that the original spelling was *Wie* and that Louis changed it somewhere along the line. On the letterhead of his stationery for the Anderson Business School it was L. J. Weichman— only one *n*—but this was probably a printer's error that Weichmann let pass. His first name was Louis, but it is often spelled Lewis by others. It would appear, then, that the correct spelling of his name is probably Louis J. Weichmann.

It should be noted, however, that when quoting other sources the name will be spelled as quoted. In the case of his father, mother, sister, and brother, it will be *Wie*chmann unless quoted otherwise.

boys. Here he remained until January 1864, when he became a clerk in the War Department, the position he occupied at the time of the assas-sination.

After the trial of the conspirators in 1865 and the trial of John H. Surratt in 1867, Weichmann was employed as a clerk in the Philadelphia Custom House for many years, but political pressure brought on by his persistent persecutors caused him to resign on October 1, 1886. In the same year he moved to Anderson, Indiana, where his brother, Father Fred C. Wiechmann, had a parish. Here he lived in the home of his sister and brother-in-law, Mr. and Mrs. Charles O'Crowley,[3] and established the Anderson Business School, the first institution of its kind in Anderson. While residing in Anderson during the 1890's, he wrote his history of the assassination, telling it in a connected way, as he was unable to do on the witness stand. He always maintained that he would tell the truth as he knew it and would vindicate himself to "all truth-loving people." Weichmann's history of the assassination is the only account left by a participant who was intimately associated with the conspirators. He writes from firsthand knowledge as he relates the events leading up to that tragic night of April 14 and the dramatic days that followed.

Step by step he follows Booth and the conspirators as they weave a web of conspiracy that will end in death for five of them. For the first time he reveals in detail the visit of Superintendent Richards to the Surratt house the night of the assassination and the startling observations made by Richards.

He positively rules out any conspiracy on the part of the Roman Catholic Church or the Confederate Government and leaves little room for argument that Secretary of War Stanton was the mastermind behind the plot to kill Lincoln. Booth and the conspirators stand alone as the plotters and it is doubtful whether future research will produce a "higher unknown." Because of his close association with the conspirators, some observers have felt that he was in on the conspiracy to a greater or lesser degree and that he could easily have been accused and prosecuted. From Weichmann's narrative, supplementary documents, and the editorial notes it would seem that he is telling it as he knows it, so far as his involvement is concerned.

[3] Weichmann had three sisters: Matilda ("Tillie"), who never married; Philomena ("Mina"), Mrs. O'Crowley; and Elizabeth, Mrs. Murphy.

Among the many myths that emerged in the aftermath of the assassination is the story that Weichmann, who died on June 5, 1902, was refused the last rites of the Roman Catholic Church. Nothing could be further from the truth. He was given extreme unction by a priest; his brother, Father Wiechmann, conducted a requiem mass for him in St. Mary's Catholic Church; and he was buried in the Catholic cemetery in Anderson. This unfounded rumor could have been started only by persons who wished to destroy his character—to claim that he had been refused absolution because he had confessed that he had lied at the trial of Mary Surratt.

From his deathbed Weichmann signed a statement in which he maintained that he had told the truth at the great trial and was now ready to meet his God. He had left the Church during his years in Anderson because he believed that certain Catholics were persecuting him for his testimony against Mary Surratt. The cruelest blow of all to Weichmann was the fact that members of his own faith accused him, a devout Catholic, of bearing false witness against another member of the same faith.

To understand better the mood of the conspirators, the very nature of the time and place must be considered. The nation was involved in a great Civil War and Washington, D.C., was a Southern city overrun by soldiers, gamblers, adventurers, and Southern sympathizers. To Booth and the other conspirators, the abduction of Lincoln and his delivery to the Confederates in Richmond would be a patriotic blow for the South. On the other hand, the mood of the victorious North should be taken into consideration in order to understand better the attitude of the Government and the people toward the accused conspirators. Lee had surrendered to Grant and the North was jubilant—then, on April 14, like the explosion of an atomic bomb, John Wilkes Booth murdered the President. The nation was plunged into deep shock and mourning on a scale never known before. On April 19, while the Army was still pursuing Booth, there began in Washington one of the greatest funerals in the history of man. Millions of people marched in it. Millions more witnessed it as the longest funeral procession, before or since, made its 1,700-mile journey to Springfield, Illinois. After this unprecedented outpouring of grief, the nation and the Government were in no mood to coddle anyone associated with the crime. There can be little doubt that the Government planned to mete out severe punishment to anyone convicted, and this was the general feeling of the public, including the press, until after the executions.

It has been established that all of the conspirators knew of the plot to abduct the President, with the possible exception of Mary Surratt and Dr. Samuel A. Mudd, who both maintained that they knew absolutely nothing. In view of the testimony against Mrs. Surratt as presented in Weichmann's narrative and Richards' letters, it is hard to believe that she knew nothing of the conspiracy that was going on in her home.

Weichmann testified at both trials and was subjected to the longest interrogation of any of the witnesses. Although every effort was made by the defense to confuse him and destroy his testimony, the attorneys succeeded only in correcting him on some dates. Because he appeared as a witness for the prosecution, he was the target of attempts at character assassination and he was persecuted by those who were trying to exonerate Mary Surratt and Dr. Mudd.

In 1870, John H. Surratt, in a lecture on the assassination given at Rockville, Maryland, boasted that he had conspired with Booth and others to abduct the President. He claimed that Weichmann knew all about the plan and wanted an active part in it but that he was refused because he could not ride a horse or shoot a gun and because Booth questioned his loyalty. On April 3, 1898, the *Washington Post* published "John H. Surratt's Story," as told to correspondent Hanson Hiss, in which Surratt accused Weichmann of being a coward and a liar and claimed that he had been arrested the morning after the assassination and taken to police headquarters, where "a rope was placed around his neck, the other end of it thrown over a beam, and he was ordered to tell what he knew." This statement was answered in the *Washington Post* on April 18, 1898, by both Weichmann and Richards. In fact, John H. Surratt's part in the whole affair leaves much to be explained. Why did he remain hidden and silent while his mother was being tried for murder, when he might have saved her from the gallows if, as he claims, she was innocent? How can anyone believe John Surratt when he brags about his part in the abduction and then claims he knew nothing about the assassination phase of the conspiracy? From Weichmann's narrative, Richards' letters, and Surratt's allegations in the Hanson Hiss article, it would seem that John Surratt is the liar and not Weichmann.

On June 22, 1898, Weichmann wrote to Ida M. Tarbell, of *McClure's Magazine*: "I am the only one living today to write a real truthful history of the whole affair as it has come to light, with the personality of the parties implicated. John Surratt could do it, but he never will for if he were to speak, and tell all he knows, I believe he would involve himself more deeply than he has done." [4]

Weichmann always felt that he was a victim of circumstance and that fate had placed him in the position he found himself—testifying against the Surratts. On the day after Christmas, 1898, Richards wrote to him in a different vein—that regardless of the personal sacrifice and suffering he had undergone, he felt that "for the sake of justice and in behalf of the murdered Lincoln, I deem it a most fortunate event that *you were there*." [5]

One can only speculate about why neither Weichmann nor his family published the narrative. His intention to do it is clear. In fact, in 1899—three years before his death—he applied to the Library of Congress for information on the copyright and was supplied with the necessary documents. During his lifetime, the delay in publication may have come about because he felt that competition from the many books and articles appearing on the assassination at this time might have hurt the sales of his book. With respect to members of his family, they may have been so wearied by Weichmann's obsession with the subject of the assassination that they would not have welcomed the renewed interest in his role that book publications would have aroused. In any event, the manuscript remained in private hands, unknown to historians writing about the assassination, until now—more than seventy years after Weichmann's death—when it is being published for the first time. With the publication of the narrative, Richards' letters, John Surratt's story by Hanson Hiss, and other related material, historians will be able to take a fresh look at the evidence and write a more definitive account of the assassination.

Weichmann's narrative, acquired by the editor in 1972 with other related papers from Alma Murphy Halff (Louis Weichmann's niece), is in typewritten form and bears corrections and additions which are apparently in the author's hand. The typescript has been printed as it was written, with the exception of some mechanical changes which normally

[4] Weichmann Papers, Risvold Collection.
[5] See Richards' letter of December 26, 1898, below, p. 421. Italics added.

would have been made had the author published the book. In preparing the manuscript for publication, the editor checked all of the quotations used in the manuscript that could be located. Although there are some variances in wording between the originals and Weichmann's renditions, none of them affects basic meaning. The discrepancies are indicated in footnotes, and any words added to the text have been enclosed in brackets. The editor's notes are indicated by numerical superscripts, whereas Weichmann's are denoted by asterisks and other conventional symbols.

The editor is indebted to many people for help in research, preparing the manuscript for publication, and seeing it through the publication process. His greatest debt, however—and a debt now shared by students of the assassination—is to Louis J. Weichmann, who in sorrow and agony of mind wrote his narrative for posterity.

FLOYD E. RISVOLD
Edina, Minnesota
1974

CONTENTS

CHAPTER IV

CHAPTER V

CHAPTER VI

CHAPTER VII

Contents

CHAPTER VIII

CHAPTER IX

CHAPTER X

CHAPTER XI

CHAPTER XII

———

CHAPTER XVII

CHAPTER XVIII

CHAPTER XIX

CHAPTER XX

Contents

CHAPTER XXI

CHAPTER XXII

CHAPTER XXIII

CHAPTER XXIV

CHAPTER XXV

Contents

Contents

ILLUSTRATIONS

(following page 158)

Illustrations

PLATE VII

Booth's escape route

(From Benn Pitman, THE ASSASSINATION OF ABRAHAM LINCOLN
AND THE TRIAL OF THE CONSPIRATORS*)*

PLATES VIII AND IX

The second inaugural of Lincoln

(Photograph by Alexander Gardner, copyright Lloyd Ostendorf)

PLATE X

Lincoln funeral cortege

(Collection of Lloyd Ostendorf)

PLATE XI

Offices of Drs. Brown and Alexander

(Collection of Lloyd Ostendorf)

Howard's stables

(Library of Congress)

PLATE XII

Boston Corbett and Captain Doherty

(Library of Congress)

The Military Commission

(Library of Congress)

PLATE XIII

Wanted poster

(Courtesy of the New-York Historical Society)

PLATES XIV AND XV

The hanging scene

(Library of Congress)

PLATE XVI

The last photograph of Abraham Lincoln

(By Alexander Gardner, Library of Congress)

PRINCIPAL CHARACTERS

THE VICTIMS

ABRAHAM LINCOLN
President of the United States.
Assassinated by John Wilkes Booth.

WILLIAM H. SEWARD
Secretary of State.
Attacked by Lewis Payne and seriously wounded.

THE ASSASSIN

JOHN WILKES BOOTH
Shot and killed at Garrett's farm
near Port Royal, Virginia.

The First Trial

Trial of the Conspirators
before a military commission, 1865.

THE DEFENDANTS

MARY E. SURRATT
Executed July 7, 1865.

LEWIS PAYNE
Also known as Mr. Wood
and Lewis Thornton Powell.
Executed July 7, 1865.

DAVID E. HEROLD
Executed July 7, 1865.

GEORGE A. ATZERODT
Executed July 7, 1865.

DR. SAMUEL A. MUDD
Sentenced to life but pardoned in 1869.

SAMUEL B. ARNOLD
Sentenced to life but pardoned in 1869.

MICHAEL O'LAUGHLIN
*Sentenced to life but died in prison
before he could be pardoned.*

EDWARD SPANGLER
Sentenced to six years and pardoned in 1869.

THE GOVERNMENT'S
PRINCIPAL WITNESSES

JOHN M. LLOYD
*Tenant of Mrs. Surratt's tavern
at Surrattsville, Maryland.*

LOUIS J. WEICHMANN
*Boarder in the house of Mary Surratt
in Washington, D.C.*

The Second Trial

Trial of John H. Surratt in Civil Court, 1867.

THE DEFENDANT

JOHN H. SURRATT
Son of Mary E. Surratt.

*Lloyd and Weichmann
were the principal witnesses
at this trial.*

Trial ended in a hung jury.

A TRUE HISTORY

OF THE ASSASSINATION

OF ABRAHAM LINCOLN

AND OF THE CONSPIRACY

OF 1865

CHAPTER I

The saddest page in American history is that which records the murder of Abraham Lincoln, the first Republican President of the United States, and the author of the Emancipation Proclamation. Not only was it a calamity affecting the North and the entire civilized world, but it was one of untold proportions for the South, in that it removed from the sphere of human action a man who, himself Southern born, had the warmest feelings for his erring brethren, and who would have endeavored to bring them back into the Union by love and kindness. As it was, his assassination carried renewed disaster to the South when it needed all its recuperative powers to build up its waste places and to remove the desolation caused by the Civil War.

Mr. Lincoln was succeeded by Mr. Johnson, who unfortunately was destitute of the wisdom and cool caution so characteristic of his lamented predecessor. His administration resulted in an open rupture between Congress and himself, and precipitated military and "carpet bag" rule in the South. Had Mr. Lincoln been permitted to live, such rule would have had no existence.

Many years, more than the third of a century, have elapsed since his taking off. During all that period, no history has seen the light of day presenting in truthful and succinct narrative the details that preceded its commission, nor have the history and personality of the parties implicated in it been given to the public.

3

It will be my purpose to write such a history. I shall do it fearlessly and truthfully, extenuating nothing, concealing nothing, but rendering equal and exact justice to all. In doing this, I shall present the fullest details, as developed, of the Conspiracy which led up to this event, and to the attempted assassination of the Secretary of State, the Honorable William H. Seward, and the threatened removal of the Vice-President, Mr. Johnson, and of General Grant.

I also write this history as a matter of justice to the great Military Commission of 1865 by which the assassins of Mr. Lincoln were tried and condemned. The officers composing that Commission, ever since the rendition of their verdict, have been ruthlessly pursued, because, on their sworn oaths, they were faithful to duty.[1]

The conclusions reached by them have, with a single exception, stood the test of time, and have been regarded by all fair-minded men as just.[2] With reference to the single exception, the case of Mary E. Surratt, it will be left to the reader, after reviewing the evidence, to determine whether the Commission could have returned a different verdict, had it so desired. The testimony against her was strong, positive, and amply corroborated—evidence unimpeached to the present hour. The chief witness against her was her tenant, John M. Lloyd, to whom she had rented her property at Surrattsville in Prince Georges County, Maryland, in December 1864. That man, and I say it without any fear of contradiction, gave the most direct and positive evidence as to any overt act on the part of Mrs. Surratt in connection with the Conspiracy of any witness in the case; evidence, damning evidence, which carried dismay to the hearts of all who heard it; evidence which for the first time shook my faith in the woman. In spite of all the sensationalism put forth by some newspapers in past years, it is but the simple truth to say that the testimony presented against Mrs. Surratt was stronger, more positive, and more abundant than that against Atzerodt, one of the executed conspirators, and that in all these long years not a fact originally established against her has been put aside, contradicted, or in any manner overthrown, or rendered unworthy of credence. Nor is it possible to overthrow it. The time has come to restate this evidence. I shall do so regardless of all personal consequences, present or future, believing that by so doing I am paying the cause of justice a service long since due.

I write this history also in personal vindication of myself. From the day I gave testimony against the miscreants who robbed Mr. Lincoln of his life, I have been subjected on the part of certain people to an infamous persecution which, if known in all its details, would put American manhood to the blush. One falsehood after another has been uttered against me. Odium has been heaped upon me. Trusting, however, to the healing influences of time to rectify these matters, I have never once stepped aside from the beaten path of duty to notice these falsehoods and slanders nor to correct them.

But now the time has come when further forbearance and silence would be a crime against myself. My reputation and good name are dearer than life, and though I should go down to death as the penalty for placing these pages before the world, yet will I have my say once for all, and yet will I appeal to the great heart of the American people to right the wrong done me. If to speak the truth oblivious of all consequences to myself at a time when red-handed assassination ran riot is a crime, then I am guilty. If faithfulness to a sworn oath, and devotion to the highest interests of the country deserve condemnation, then let me be condemned. But as long as right is right and God is God, I believe there is justice enough in the American people to stand by a man who knows he is right, who has the courage and manhood to stand by the right, and who only asks for fair play and honest treatment.

The assassination of Lincoln was a crime against civilization. It was an event unparalleled in the history of the world. The murder of Caesar by Brutus; of Henry the Fourth of France by Ravaillac; of William the Silent, Prince of Orange, by Balthasar Gérard pale before it in fiendishness of execution and romantic and tragic interest.

Coming at the close of a mighty Civil War when the very heavens were resonant with jubilation and luminous with the fires of patriotic rejoicing over the successes that had crowned the Union cause; when Richmond had fallen, and Lee's army had surrendered; when good men's minds were fraught with high hopes for the future, and when even Lincoln's character was being better understood by friend and foe, this most atrocious crime carried with it a horror and a terror that convulsed the entire world. It was an act hitherto unknown in the annals of the American Republic. Men were struck dumb and with bated breath waited to hear what dreadful crime was yet to come as though they had not reached the end of the chapter of all that was cruel and infamous.

Booth's pistol shot crashed through the brain of one who did not need a tragic end to immortalize him. What the arch-assassin's motives were, whether fame for himself like the "ambitious youth who fired the Ephesian dome," [3] or bloody revenge for the prostrate and bleeding South, no one knows. That is a secret which he carried to the grave, and which only eternity can reveal. But since that event no one in the wide world has dared question the measure of the Emancipator's greatness or his fame. Many of the finest tributes to his character and memory have been paid by those whom he opposed and vanquished.

I saw this kind-hearted, noble man several times during the war. On two occasions I was present at public receptions given by him. Tall in stature, long-limbed, with an honest, homely, and sad face out of which his very soul seemed to speak, he had a kind word and genial smile for all, however lowly, who approached him.

Taking my hand in his with a firm, full grasp, his words were, "How do you do, sir? I am glad to see you." I saw him also when he was being inaugurated for the second time as President of the United States when "with malice toward none and charity for all," he delivered those noble utterances equaled only by his oration at Gettysburg in 1863. Well do I recall how after fervently and prayerfully deprecating a longer duration of the war, he so solemnly said:

"Yet, if God wills that it continue until all the wealth piled up by the bondsman's two hundred and fifty years of unrequited toil shall be sunk, and until every drop of blood drawn by the lash shall be repaid by another drawn with the sword, as was said three thousand years ago, so still it must be said that the judgments of the Lord are true and righteous altogether."

How little did I then realize that in this possible sea of blood which in contemplation spread out before him, his own was so soon to be mingled thus consecrating him as the august martyr of the slaveholder's rebellion, shot from behind, shot in the head, yea, shot by the side of his wife in a public theater, whither he had gone for a few hours of well-earned recreation and amusement.

Few persons are now alive who can realize the extent and scope of the murderous Conspiracy which resulted in Lincoln's death. Booth aimed not only to kill the President, but also the Vice-President, Mr. Johnson; the Secretary of State, the Honorable William H. Seward; and General Grant. Happily he was not successful in all his plans. Payne, the assailant of Mr. Seward, it is true, had almost accomplished his part of the work, but Atzerodt, whom Booth detailed to murder the Vice-President, lost his courage at the supreme moment, and General Grant, instead of going to the theater, fortunately for himself, left during the day for Philadelphia.[4]

Had Booth carried out his nefarious undertaking in its entirety, our government would for a time have been left without a head. The President, the Vice-President, the Secretary of State, and the general commanding the armies would have been removed; the Congress of the United States was not then in session; there was no Speaker of the House of Representatives, and but one frail life, that of the President pro tempore of the Senate,* and he would not have become the actual President, but only Acting President until such time as a President could have been chosen under the due forms of law, would have stood between our government and absolute anarchy or destruction. The human mind recoils in horror at the contemplation of the possibility of the success of such a scheme. Thus Booth would have accomplished by assassination what the Confederates failed to achieve in four years of open warfare—the dismemberment of the Republic. Such a condition of things can be better imagined than described.†

* At that time, the Honorable Lafayette Foster of Connecticut.
† It has always been a mooted question who would have become the constitutional successor to the presidency in such a contingency as has been described in this paragraph. In 1865, the succession, in case of the death of both the President and the Vice-President of the United States, was vested in the President pro tempore of the Senate, and in the event of his death or inability, the Speaker of the House of Representatives.

For the purpose of explicit information upon this subject, I requested one of my friends to address Senator Edmunds, than whom there is no better authority in the United States in relation to this matter.

The succession to the presidency in case of the inability of both the President and the Vice-President to perform the duties of the office is at the present time vested in the Cabinet officers, beginning with the Secretary of State. Senator Edmunds was the author of the act making the change.

The reply of Mr. Edmunds was as follows:

Devon, Pa., June 13, 1896.

Dear Sir:

I have yours of the 5th inst.

The law at the time you mention, in the case of a vacancy in both the offices of President and Vice-President, provided that the President of the Senate should exercise the office; and in case there were no President of the Senate, the Speaker of the House of Representatives. The law made no further provision. Of course, if all these offices were vacant, there would have been a hiatus. Doubtless in such a

At first it was believed that the leaders of the Southern Confederacy had instigated the deed, and heavy rewards were offered by the Government for the apprehension of Jefferson Davis, Jacob Thompson, Clement C. Clay, Beverly Tucker, George N. Sanders, and others, but as time rolled on, it became evident that there was no warrant for such suspicion, and it is a fact to be mentioned to the credit of our American name, and to the glory of our American manhood, that the Confederate Government and the Southern people were in no way mixed up in it.

Nickolay and Hay in their splendid life of President Lincoln when writing upon this subject briefly say:

The charges against [the conspirators] specified that they were "incited and encouraged" to treason and murder by Jefferson Davis and the Confederate emissaries in Canada. This was not proved on the trial: the evidence bearing on the case showed frequent communications between Canada and Richmond and the Booth coterie in Washington, and some transactions in drafts at the Montreal Bank, where Jacob Thompson and Booth kept their accounts. It was shown by the sworn testimony of a reputable witness that Jefferson Davis at Greensboro, on hearing of the assassination, expressed his gratification at the news; but this, so far from proving any direct complicity in the crime, would rather prove the opposite, as a conscious murderer usually conceals his malice.[6]

What these men say is confirmed by John H. Surratt, who in a public lecture delivered in December 1870 in Maryland at a place named Rockville, while disclaiming all knowledge of the assassination plot, stated that the Confederate Government had nothing whatever to do with even the proposed plan of capturing the President,* and this statement is further confirmed by Samuel Arnold in a confession which he has made.†

---

case, the Senate would have assembled on the unofficial call of one or more Senators, and they would have elected a president pro-tem. Mr. Foster, at that time would have exercised the office, but he would not have been President, and would have continued to be the President of the Senate; merely exercising the office of President because he was President of the Senate.

Very respectfully,
Geo. F. Edmunds.[5]

Edgar E. Hendee, Esq.,
Anderson, Ind.

* See below, pp. 129–30.
† See the confession of Arnold, below, Chapter XXXI.

The assassination, however, was the outgrowth of the malevolent doctrines of the Southern pro-slavery Democracy. All those identified with it were impregnated with its teachings, and were sympathizers with the Southern rebellion. They all believed in the divine right of slavery, and the families of some of them—the Surratts, Mudd, and Payne—had held slaves, and others, Arnold and O'Laughlin, had served in the Southern Army.

The assertion, too, has been made that the conspiracy was a Jesuit or Romish conspiracy. Nothing is further from the truth than any such statement. The Catholic Church organization had nothing whatever to do with it. In the famous Conspiracy trial, there was not a single item of testimony on which to rest any such charge, nor was there one Catholic clergyman in the length and breadth of the United States who was directly or indirectly in the remotest degree connected with the affair.

There were ten persons in all who were charged by the Government with being actively implicated in the Conspiracy plot: John Wilkes Booth, Lewis Payne,* David E. Herold, George A. Atzerodt, Mary E. Surratt, Samuel Arnold, Michael O'Laughlin, Samuel A. Mudd, Edward Spangler, and John H. Surratt.

Of these Booth was shot in Garrett's barn in Virginia; Payne, Herold, Atzerodt, and Mary E. Surratt suffered capital punishment; Arnold, O'Laughlin, and Dr. Mudd were sent to the Dry Tortugas for life, and Edward Spangler for six years. John H. Surratt was not apprehended by the Government until November 1866 in Egypt, whither he had fled.

Booth was an Episcopalian; Mrs. Surratt was the only Catholic among those who perished on the scaffold, and she was a convert from the Protestant faith. Payne was a Baptist, and the son of a Baptist preacher. Herold was an Episcopalian; Atzerodt a Lutheran. Of those sent to the Dry Tortugas, Dr. Samuel A. Mudd and Michael O'Laughlin alone were Catholics.[7] John H. Surratt was also a Catholic; he was tried by a civil jury in Washington in 1867, but his trial resulted in a disagreement because his presence in the city of Washington on the day of the murder was not proved to the satisfaction of the jury which tried him.

If the Catholics who were identified with the conspiracy had followed the religious teachings of their church, as I have always understood them, they would never for even one moment have been concerned in the

* The real name of this man was Lewis Thornton Powell.

infamous work with which their names are now and always will be associated.

It is a well-known matter of history that some Catholic clergymen in Canada secreted John H. Surratt in his efforts, after the assassination, to escape from the pursuing hand of justice, and that he was helped on his way to England and France by others, but when finally identified while serving in the Papal Zouaves, in November 1866, he was promptly arrested at the instance of the Holy Father, Pius IX, and of Cardinal [Giacomo] Antonelli for delivery to the U. S. minister at Rome, and this in face of the fact that there was no treaty of extradition between the Papal States and the United States Government in relation to cases of this kind. Indeed, Surratt's arrest was accomplished by the Papal authorities before a demand to that effect was made by the U. S. minister.

And now from all that has been developed and that has come to the surface since the day of the assassination, it can be truthfully said that Booth himself was the author of the whole scheme, both as relates to the plot to abduct, and the plot to assassinate Mr. Lincoln, in the laying of plans, in the securing of accomplices, and in the furnishing of the necessary funds. It was Booth's conspiracy, and that of the foolish young men whom he drew into his schemes along with him. In fact, it may very properly be designated as a conspiracy of foolish and misguided young men.

In a document which he deposited for safe keeping with his brother-in-law, Mr. J. S. Clarke, in Philadelphia in November 1864, Booth announced his purpose to capture the "President" and styled himself "a Confederate doing duty on his own responsibility." * This scheme to capture the President, run him into the Southern Confederacy, and hold him as a hostage for the release of the Confederate soldiers then in Northern prisons was probably Booth's preference, but the other plan, that of assassination, it will be seen as this narrative progresses was in Booth's mind from his first appearance in Washington in the winter of 1864, and appears to have been held as a terrible reserve in case of the failure of the abduction plot. This, as the world knows, was successful.

One of the most unfortunate circumstances connected with the death of the President was that he was not permitted to live long enough to witness the return of the brave Boys in Blue who had battled so nobly for their country's cause, for within six weeks after the fatal day, April

* See below, pp. 49–52.

14, 1865, the review of the Union armies took place in Washington on
May 23 and 24. It was the grandest and most mournful pageant that
ever occurred in the history of the world. For two days the bronzed vet-
erans of Grant's and Sherman's armies swept along the streets of the
capital city with an enthusiasm that can come only to victors. The assembled spectators who lined the sidewalks by the hundreds and thousands rent the welcome with their loud shouts of approval and applause.
Yet over all this display and glory death hung his dark emblems. The
whole city was shrouded in mourning; not a house was left uncovered. As
regiment after regiment passed by, every flag was seen wreathed in
black; the hilt of every officer's sword was wrapped in crepe. Many were
the tears that fell from mortal eyes; it was a time for the angels of
heaven to weep for Lincoln; the great, the noble Lincoln was not there
to hear the glad shouts of his rejoicing countrymen in their hour of
triumph and victory. In his case, the assassin's work was complete.

CHAPTER II

*The writer's early life · Residence in Washington · Removes to Philadel-
phia and is educated in the public schools of that city · Goes to St.
Charles College, Howard County, Maryland · Becomes a student for the
Catholic ministry · Life at the college · Meets John H. Surratt
for the first time in September 1859 · Becomes a teacher
in Washington in January 1863*

Before entering upon the main portion of this history, it will be necessary for me to give some account of my early life and parentage, and
to state briefly in what manner I became acquainted with so many persons who were actively identified with the Conspiracy. It is a noteworthy
fact that out of the ten persons who were charged by the Government as
being principals in and accessories thereto, I was most innocently and

unsuspectingly brought into relation with seven of them, and also with many witnesses for the prosecution and defense in the Conspiracy trial. Indeed, I regret to confess it, a strange fatality seems to have twined itself about my life in this respect. Even as early as 1852, when but a schoolboy, I knew well and familiarly Mr. Petersen, the German tailor, in whose house President Lincoln breathed his last, and it was only seven years from that time that I was fated to meet John H. Surratt in a religious institution to which we were both sent, and under the auspices of the same clergyman, to prepare ourselves for the Catholic ministry. And Dr. J. F. May, who was Booth's physician, and who made a post-mortem examination of his body, was for many years the physician of my father's family.

I was born in the city of Baltimore, Maryland, on September 29, 1842. My father was a Lutheran; my mother a Catholic. In 1843, my father moved his family to the city of Washington, where he carried on the business of merchant tailoring until 1853, when he again changed his abode, this time locating in Philadelphia, Pennsylvania. In politics, he was a Democrat and voted for Stephen A. Douglas in 1860. In 1864 he voted for Abraham Lincoln, and was thereafter a Republican.

In Philadelphia, I was sent to the public schools, and graduated with a two years' course from the high school in February 1859. Like other boys, my troubles began after leaving school. What was I to do to earn a livelihood? What trade or profession should I choose? My preferences were for the drug business, but my mother overruled my predilections in this respect. She was a woman of a pious turn of mind and nothing would satisfy her but that I should enter some Catholic institution as a student for the ministry. My father at this period of his life, in consequence of the death of a dearly beloved child, had embraced the Catholic faith.

I yielded to my mother's wishes although I confess I had but little heart for the profession selected. One of my most revered friends in Philadelphia was an American clergyman by the name of Waldron. He was a man to whom I was deeply attached and who had been my Sunday-school teacher and confessor for many years. He had been the pastor of the Cathedral parish in Philadelphia under the jurisdiction of the Right Reverend John Newman, D.D., but was transferred in 1856 or 1857 to the church of St. Matthew in Washington City, in the Archdiocese of Baltimore. With him I opened correspondence for the purpose of fulfilling my mother's wishes. A number of letters were exchanged. Finally I received the following, which settled the matter and opened to me a new future. A future indeed! How little man knows the ways and dispensations of Providence! Could I have foreseen how much of suffering, of trial, and of persecution this kind letter addressed to me in February 1859 would indirectly cause me, I would a thousand times rather have adhered to my own purpose in life and have followed the calling of my own choosing; for that letter took me to a college where I first met John H. Surratt.

> *St. Matthew's Church, Washington, D.C.*
> *February 14th, 1859.*

Dear Louis:

I enclose to you Bishop McGill's letter, so you can see at once what you have to do. Bishop Newman will no doubt be glad to give you a letter of character and an "exeat."

Then you can enclose them to me and I will hand them to Bishop McGill when he comes here next week.

> Yours faithfully,
> E. Q. S. Waldron.

As a result of this letter, I was ordered to present myself for admission to the preparatory college of St. Charles Borromeo in Maryland, as an ecclesiastical student for the diocese of Richmond, Virginia, whose bishop was the Right Reverend John McGill, D.D.

Preparations at once began; clothes were made ready; a big trunk was packed, and on February 27, 1859, I started southward with my father and uncle for my new home. It was an event in my humble life never to be forgotten. My mother's tearful eyes and heartfelt wishes were the benedictions that accompanied me and lighted my path. After a short stay in Baltimore, I reached St. Charles College on March 1, 1859, and was duly entered as a student for the diocese of Richmond, Virginia.

The college is situated in Howard County, Maryland, about five miles from Ellicott's Mills and about twenty miles from Baltimore. It is a preparatory institution devoted exclusively to the training of young men for the Catholic ministry, and is under the control of the religious order of St. Sulpice, an organization founded in France, having this object in view. The president of the college at the date of my admission was the Reverend Oliver Jenkins, a native of Baltimore, and a very pious man.

The studies at St. Charles were severe, and the discipline was rigid. The young men had no intercourse whatever with the outside world; their only privilege being permission to write letters to their parents and friends. Two months of each year were allowed for vacation, July and August.

In September 1859, among the new arrivals was John Harrison Surratt as a student for the diocese of St. Augustine, Florida, under the Right Reverend Augustine Verot, D.D. The same clergyman, Father Waldron, who had recommended me to Bishop McGill had also recommended Surratt to Bishop Verot.

Father Waldron had written to me about the young man. Consequently I was eager to greet him and make his acquaintance. Well do I recall his first appearance and my impressions of that appearance. He was tall, erect, slender, and boyish, with a very prominent forehead and receding eyes. His nose was sharp, thin, and aquiline; his face bore an unusually keen and shrewd expression. Anyone having seen the portrait of Jefferson Davis can readily recognize his facsimile in John H. Surratt. He was neatly dressed, and I remember he provoked the risibilities of the older students by wearing a white necktie.

During the three years Surratt remained at college he was a very orderly student and one of the best young men I ever knew, and could not have been excelled by anyone. His reputation for conduct and deportment was most excellent. When he left college in July 1862, it was with the determination to abandon a vocation to which he did not feel himself called. Father Jenkins on that occasion said, "Goodbye, Surratt, God bless you; you have been a good student here; we will always remember you." How much better for him had he remained at college and become the humble priest of God!

During my stay at St. Charles very little news was given to us of the mighty events then taking place in the country. We were informed of the execution in 1859 of John Brown and of his men, but not of the causes that led to it.[1] I knew almost nothing of the great presidential contest of 1860, for I was at that time but eighteen years of age. I really did not understand the vital differences between the Democratic and Republican parties, so little was I informed in politics. The only glimpse I had of the great struggle was when I saw a torchlight procession of the Republicans of Philadelphia during the vacation in August 1860. The participants were filled with enthusiasm, singing patriotic songs and carrying large rails on their shoulders. They were called "Wide-awakes" and "Rail-splitters."

It was customary at the college to give us a holiday each week, on Thursday. On these occasions, in the afternoon the students would take long walks into the surrounding country, but always with one of the professors at their head. These rambling excursions were much appreciated and were the only real recreation given us. It was during one of these walks in March 1861 that our professor halted us and, resting by the wayside, read to us the First Inaugural Address of Abraham Lincoln, the President-elect of the United States. Thereafter, we had only occasional snatches of war news. Once in a while, we would see a few soldiers galloping along the Frederick turnpike in front of our school, and at times we could hear the booming of distant guns. That was all. The collegians were divided in their feelings; those from the North generally favoring that section, and those from the South equally pronounced in its support. When the Southern boys in the evenings after supper would sing their songs, the Northern lads would reply with a vigorous chorus of Yankee strains. On our weekly walks, we were sometimes wont to have little sham battles in the woods and along the roads, but it was all in the spirit of fun; no one was ever hurt, and no blood was spilled. The feeling never ran very high; there was no occasion for it. The students were young men destined for missions of mercy and peace, and were to be charged with the salvation of the souls of their fellow men.

John H. Surratt was a pronounced friend of the Southern cause from the start, yet I do not recollect that he ever made himself offensive to anyone by the persistency of his views.

St. Charles College has produced many men eminent for their piety and learning, but none more so than the present Cardinal of the United States, James Gibbons; the Right Reverend John J. Keane, D.D., the first president of the new Catholic University at Washington; and the Most Reverend John J. Kane, D.D., Archbishop of St. Louis.

When I bade goodbye to St. Charles in July 1862, I determined not to re-enter its halls as a student. I felt I had not been treated as fairly or promoted as rapidly as my application warranted. There were others who had been advanced over me and who were selected to enter in September of that year the theological seminary of St. Mary in Baltimore who were not, I felt, as much entitled to it as I was. Returning to my home in Philadelphia, I made application to Father Dubreuil, the president of the seminary in Baltimore, for permission to enter it and thus complete my ecclesiastical studies. I met with a refusal. Father Dubreuil based his action on his inability to hear from my bishop, with whom all communication had been cut off in consequence of the war. In this dilemma, I resolved to devote myself to teaching for a year, or until such a time as the war would be over. Accordingly, I again had recourse to my old friend Father Waldron, then located in Pikesville, Maryland, and from him received the following letter:

Pikesville, Maryland, August 8, 1862.

Dear Friend:

I regret you did not get my letter written some weeks ago. In that letter I encouraged you not to give up a vocation to which I believe you are called. It may be, in your circumstance, no harm to rest off a while, then renew your studies, and enter the larger seminary as soon as possible. Have courage, my dear sir, God, we hope, will not leave your family destitute, and when once ordained you can afford them some aid and help the younger children in getting their education.

In the letter I wrote you, I proposed to you to spend the coming year with me, and to continue your studies and to assist me in teaching my boys. I cannot assist you much in a pecuniary point, but will agree to board you and furnish all expenses here, such as fuel, light, etc., and give you fifty dollars the first year, commencing September 1st and ending July 1st; ten months.

At the end of this time you may be prepared to enter some seminary and I will at once, if you agree with this arrangement, speak with the Archbishop in behalf of your admission to the seminary. Write me at once.

As ever faithfully yours,
E. Q. S. Waldron.

I accepted Father Waldron's offer, but did not remain with him longer than November 1862. From Pikesville I went to a little village on the Northern Central Railroad, in Maryland, called Little Texas, about twenty miles from Baltimore, where a clerical friend resided, named Father William Mahoney. With him I spent my time until December 20, 1862.

In the early part of December, I noticed an advertisement in the *Catholic Mirror* of Baltimore by a clergyman in Washington, the Reverend Charles I. White, D.D., for a teacher for his school. I answered the advertisement, enclosing a letter of recommendation from Father Mahoney.

Dr. White replied as follows:

Washington, December 15th, 1862.

Mr. Weichmann,

Dear Sir:

I have this day received your letter enclosing a note from Rev. Mr. Mahoney. In reply I state that the salary is $38.00 per month. The teacher can have lodging, but not board in the dwelling attached to the institute. For this privilege a slight deduction will be made from salary but no deduction will be made if the teacher will conduct the night school five evenings in the week. There are seventy-six boys in the school at present. I intend to place this school, as well as the other held in the same building, under the charge of the brothers of the Christian schools, but I do not expect their services until next fall, if then. You will please come on immediately if you are willing to accept the post. Otherwise, favor me with an answer without delay.

Yours respectfully,

Chas. I. White, D.D.

I at once accepted Dr. White's proposition and on January 2, 1863, I was installed as the principal of St. Matthew's Institute for boys in the city of Washington.

Thus it was that I came to make my home in that city, the seat of the Federal Government, and then the center of the war operations for the preservation and restoration of the Union.

CHAPTER III

St. Matthew's Institute was situated on Nineteenth Street between G and H. I had a splendid class of boys and found the new position very congenial. Dr. White (now deceased), who had employed me, was one of the most learned of the Catholic clergymen in the United States. He was a very fine French and Spanish scholar, and had translated several works from these languages into English. He was then pastor of St. Matthew's Church, at the corner of Fifteenth and H streets.

I slept at night in the Institute and took my meals at a boarding-house in the neighborhood. Among my earliest callers was John H. Surratt, whom I had not seen since leaving college. He was cordially received, for I was glad to see him. His appearance and manner had considerably changed since his departure from college. He was now more a man of the world, had a brusquer air, and was much bronzed.

We chatted gaily about old times and associates at the college. He was always treated kindly when he came to see me, nor can I complain of a want of civility on his part. There never was the slightest jar between us, and during the entire period of our acquaintance we never quarreled once. So far as one man can judge another, he was a young man of clean habits, upright and moral, and was entirely free of small vices, as smoking, drinking, and chewing.

In those days of 1863 he was accustomed to bring fruits and vegetables from his home in the country to the Washington market to sell. On one of these occasions, in the spring, a short time before Easter, he invited me to accompany him on his return home. I gladly and willingly accepted the invitation.

The place where he lived was called Surrattsville after his father (the name having been changed to Clinton since 1865) and was in Prince Georges County, Maryland, about twelve miles from Washington City. It was directly on the road leading from the capital to Bryantown and to the Potomac River. During the war this road was frequented by thousands who were engaged in running the blockade, spies and go-betweens, and by those who desired to escape from the North to the South to join the Confederate Army. This, too, was the road by which John Wilkes Booth and David E. Herold made their escape from Washington on the night of the assassination of President Lincoln.

Surratt's home was located at the junction of a crossroad and the road to which I have referred. The house was a frame structure. The entrance to it was from the main road to the center of the house. To the right, as you went in, was a parlor and a room in the rear of that. To the left was the country post office with barroom attached, and in the rear of it the dining room. There was a large cellar beneath the house. The second story was used for bedrooms. There was also a farm and a fruit orchard, where the family raised cereals, vegetables, and fruits for their own use, selling the surplus that was not needed. At the date of my visit, a half dozen or more colored people who had been Mrs. Surratt's slaves were still dwelling on the place. Besides this country property Mrs. Surratt owned a valuable house in Washington City, No. 541 H Street.

It was a damp, dark, and murky day when I first visited Surrattsville. It had been raining and the roads were very wet. When I reached his country home, John introduced me to his mother, Mary E. Surratt, and to his sister, Anna. It is needless to say that I met with a kind reception. A cheery fire of wood was blazing on the hearth in the parlor, and the warmth of the room was, indeed, a pleasant contrast to the chilling atmosphere outside.

Mrs. Surratt's family consisted of three children: two sons, Isaac and John Harrison, and a daughter, Anna. Her husband, John H. Surratt, Sr., so I was informed, had died in July 1862.[1]

Her oldest son, Isaac, with whom I have never spoken a word and whom I first saw at the trial of his brother in 1867, was a dark, thickset, powerfully built man, unlike any of the rest of the family. He was a civil engineer by profession and went South to join the Confederate Army at the commencement of the war and did not return home until after the tragic death of his mother. What his movements were during the war I do not know. I was informed that he had left the South and had gone to Matamoros, Mexico, where he found employment in his profession. Further than this I know nothing of him.

Miss Anna Surratt was a tall, well-proportioned, and fair-complexioned young woman of about twenty-six years, possessing many of the features and characteristics of her brother John.[2] She had received a very good education in a Catholic seminary at Bryantown, Maryland, not many miles from Surrattsville. Besides being an accomplished pianist, she was a young woman of much culture. She was the second oldest of the family, John being the youngest.

Mrs. Mary E. Surratt, at the commencement of my acquaintance with her, was about forty-five years of age, of erect bearing, and rather above medium height with a ruddy and fair complexion.[3] Her eye of steel gray was quick and penetrating. Her hair was a dark brown with not a white streak visible in it. Her manner was genial and social and she had the rare faculty of making a stranger feel at home at once in her company. Yet it would not be long before one became conscious that here was a woman devoted, body and soul, to the cause of the South. I never met one in all my experience who so earnestly, and I might add so conscientiously, defended and justified the Southern cause as she. Next to her church and family, her love for the South was her meat and drink. What she lacked in education she made up in force of character, being positive and self-willed. Her affection for her family was a strong and distinguishing trait. Her maiden name was Jenkins. She had been the belle of the town in which she had spent her youth, Uniontown, Maryland, and was married at an early age. Like her husband, she was a Protestant, but not many years after her marriage became a convert to the Catholic faith. Mrs. Jenkins, her mother, was still living in 1865 with her son Zadoc Jenkins, who resided near Surrattsville, and survived the daughter a long time, dying some years ago. Both mother and son were Protestants and remained so.[4] During all my acquaintance with them I never heard any of the Surratt family speak of this old grandmother, and I did not know that there was any such personage living until I read an account of her death in the newspapers.

During the few days I remained at Surrattsville nothing occurred out of the regular order of things to mar my visit. I mingled with the people of the neighborhood and conversed with them when they came to the post office for their mail. It was not long before I discovered that though agreeable and pleasant in social intercourse they were all bitter secessionists.

Mrs. Surratt's country home in those days was the stopping place for many men on their way to the South. Of course, she received pay for her services but I venture to say that, could the history of that home in Prince Georges County from April 1, 1861, to November 1, 1864, when she removed to Washington, be written, such a volume of itself would be of interest as a notable contribution to the war history of the country, and would lead a good many people to entertain a different opinion of her from that which they now hold. The Confederacy had no more active friend in any border state than she was. The character of her home in this respect was known throughout the county in which she resided. It was during all that period a resort for blockade runners, spies, and parties who wanted to cross the Potomac. In fact, it might be called a regular secession headquarters. I did not come into possession of these facts from personal knowledge, but from a number of Union people, white and colored, whom I met at the Conspiracy trial in 1865 and who gave me a full bill of particulars.

As evidence of the hostile feelings of Mrs. Surratt and her son in those days, the following testimony of Mr. John T. Tibbett, a soldier in the Union Army from August 5, 1863, until November 1865, who had known Surratt for more than ten years and who was at one time mail carrier from Washington to Charlotte Hall, Maryland, will be of interest. Tibbett testified at the trial of John H. Surratt that he heard Mrs. Surratt one day in the fall of 1863 say in the presence of her son that she would give anyone a thousand dollars if they would kill Mr. Lincoln. He also stated that whenever there was a victory, he heard Surratt say, "The d——d Northern Army and the leader thereof ought to be sent to hell."

Tibbett said Mrs. Surratt would be continually asking some question about Washington. Every day as he passed backward and forward, they would ask if he had seen blockade runners or something or other. When he would go down from Washington they would ask how times were in

Washington, and when he came up from Charlotte Hall, they would ask if he had heard any news from the South.*

John H. Surratt was at this time postmaster at Surrattsville, and as such had taken the oath of allegiance to the United States. He was appointed September 1, 1862, and continued in office until November 15, 1863, when he was succeeded by Mr. Andrew V. Roby.[5]

The very first morning after my arrival at Surrattsville I was aroused quite early by the sounds of music immediately under the window of the room in which I was sleeping. Surratt called me downstairs. Dressing hastily, I descended and met a number of musicians, a portion of the Marine Band of Washington, who had come down there the previous evening to serenade some of the newly elected county officials. With them was a frowsy-headed youth of sallow complexion and coal-black hair, who seemed to be a kind of hail-fellow-well-met among the whole party. Seeing me, he asked Surratt who I was. Surratt thereupon introduced him to me. His name was David E. Herold. Two years later this young man disgraced himself by becoming one of the active associates of John Wilkes Booth in the Conspiracy. He it was who escaped with Booth from Washington on the fatal night of the assassination, riding down the country road past Surrattsville; who was arrested by the United States soldiers amid the blazing and crackling timbers of the Garrett barn in which Booth was shot and near which his lifeblood ebbed away.

When I left Surrattsville on my return to the city on the following Monday morning, Surratt accompanied me. On reaching the city, he stopped the buggy in front of a drugstore near the Navy Yard. Herold was at that time employed there as prescription clerk. Beyond the compliments of the day I had nothing to say to him. His mother, who was a widow and the parent of a large family of children—this one son and six daughters—resided on Capitol Hill. Herold's father had been in the employ of the United States Government for a long time and had died some years previously. The family was in every sense a very worthy one and in no way responsible for the misdeeds of the scapegrace son who so foully dishonored it.

During this first visit to Surrattsville it was agreed between John and myself that we would make a visit to our alma mater, St. Charles Col-

* *Trial of John H. Surratt*, I, 179. [*Trial of John H. Surratt in the Criminal Court for the District of Columbia* (2 vols.; Washington, D.C.: Government Printing Office, 1867); hereafter referred to as *Surratt Trial*.]

lege, during the coming Holy Week. We arrived there on Thursday, April 2, 1863, and remained two days, leaving on Good Friday. The old students were rejoiced to see us. While here I announced my intention to Surratt to pay a brief visit to my old friend Father Mahoney at Little Texas. This coming to the hearing of Father Denis, one of the professors, the reverend gentleman sought me and said, "Mr. Weichmann, here is an Italian paper" (the *Eco d'Italia*, I believe it was). "Take and give it to a gentleman whom you will meet there, named Mr. Sainte Marie, and who was one of my pupils when I taught in the college at Montreal. Introduce yourself to him, using my name. You will find him a very agreeable person and educated man."

I made my appearance at Little Texas with Surratt on Good Friday, April 3, 1863, and was kindly greeted by Father Mahoney, who introduced me to Mr. Sainte Marie. Surratt did not remain at Little Texas longer than Saturday and returned to Washington without me. Before leaving I had, however, introduced him to Mr. Sainte Marie.

In consequence of the kind words of Father Denis, I took a great liking to Sainte Marie. As this man, later on, will become a prominent character in this history I will state what I learned of him up to the date of the meeting, as he gave it to me. His full name was Henri Beaumont de Sainte Marie.[6] He was born in Canada near Montreal and was educated in the Catholic institutions of that city. After graduating from college he was employed for some time as a clerk in a bank, and afterwards in a store in Montreal until the beginning of the year 1863. Then he conceived a great desire to join the Confederate Army and fight for its cause. He came to New York and sailed from that point on a vessel that intended to run the blockade. The ship, however, was captured by a United States war steamer and Sainte Marie with his fellow voyagers was thrown into Fort McHenry as a prisoner of war. Thence he was released as a British subject through the intervention of the English consul resident in Baltimore.

Sainte Marie's next move was to secure a cheap boardinghouse in the Monumental City and endeavor to obtain employment, as his means were nearly exhausted. One day an old farmer living in the country outside of Baltimore came to his place. To him Sainte Marie narrated his misfortunes and stated his necessities. The farmer had compassion on him and took him to his home. Here Mr. Sainte Marie was compelled to perform menial labor on the farm. It was an occupation for which he was entirely unfitted either by education or by experience, for he was often obliged to feed the cows and pigs. A lady named Miss Maria Padian happened to pay a visit to Sainte Marie's benefactor to collect money for the church at Little Texas. The young Canadian was presented to Miss Padian. She was captivated with his polished manners, good looks, handsome brown eyes, refined conversation, and general education, and listened eagerly to the recital of his adventures, and, hastening back to Little Texas, soon secured for him from Father Mahoney an appointment as teacher in the Catholic parochial school of the village.

And here it was that I met Sainte Marie on Friday, April 3, 1863, and introduced John H. Surratt to him, this being the first occasion upon which they met on United States soil. He could speak French and Italian fluently, touch the guitar lightly, and was a fine tenor singer. He was charming in conversation and had a considerable fund of anecdote. There was an old Italian in the village named Benvenuti, who possessed an excellent bass voice. Sainte Marie and he would occasionally sing a duet. Their voices blended very harmoniously; it was a genuine treat to hear them.

I became interested in the man to such an extent that I promised to help him secure a different position in life from that which he was holding.

I had returned to my post in Washington but a few weeks when I was surprised one day to see Mr. Sainte Marie walk into my school. "Existence any longer in Little Texas," he said, "is impossible. I must get other and more remunerative employment." At that time the post of assistant teacher in St. Matthew's Institute had become vacant and I was successful in getting the place for him.

But this did not satisfy his wishes any more than the place at Little Texas. Little surprised, therefore, was I when waking up one morning about three weeks or a month after acceptance of the position under me to find my friend had left. He had gone, completely gone, with baggage and all. Four long years elapsed before my eyes rested on him again, and then after the most direful tragedy of modern times. In the meantime, after leaving the school he had enlisted as a substitute in the Third Delaware Regiment, Colonel George P. Fisher * commanding. Being sent with his regiment to the front, he seized the earliest opportunity to desert. He was captured by the Confederates, who looked upon him with

* Colonel Fisher subsequently was appointed Judge of the District Court in Washington, and was the one who conducted the trial of John H. Surratt in 1867.

suspicion and sent him to Castle Thunder as a spy.[7] Albert D. Richardson, subsequently shot by Daniel McFarland for the betrayal of his wife, and Junius Henry Browne, both correspondents of the *New York Tribune*, were among his fellow prisoners. It was not long before Sainte Marie discovered the plots of a party of forgers against the Confederate Government and exposed them to the authorities. As a reward for his services he was released from prison and sent to Nassau, at which port he took passage on a vessel bound for England. From this latter country, as soon as his circumstances permitted, he returned to Montreal, where he was when President Lincoln was assassinated. And here I leave him for the present.

I continued to teach in Washington until July 1863, when I returned to my home in Philadelphia for the summer vacation. I renewed my efforts to enter the seminary in Baltimore, but, as will be evident from the following letter, I was again unsuccessful.

> St. Mary's Seminary,
> Baltimore, Md., August 7, 1863.

Dear Sir:

We are very busy with the students retreat and I have only time to say that no letter has yet been received from your Bishop. As soon as any may come to hand I will let you know it.

> Yours very truly,
> F. Paul Dubreuil.

L. J. Wiechmann, Esq.

Once more I had recourse to Dr. White for my position as teacher and from him received the following telegram:

> *Washington, August 28th, 1863.*

L. J. Wiechmann, Philad'a, Pa.

Be here before the first of September.

> Chas. I. White, D.D.

I resumed my task of teaching contentedly and hopefully, hammering away at my boys and glad of the opportunity to instill a little knowledge into their minds.

In January 1864, the wheel of fortune made a sudden and unexpected turn in my favor. A Mr. Grugan, who boarded in the same house with me, informed me of a vacant clerkship in the office in which he was employed, the Commissary General of Prisoners, a bureau of the War Department. I immediately made application for the same, accompanying my letter with the following testimonials:

Washington, June 29th, 1863.

Mr. L. J. Wiechmann having been a teacher in St. Matthew's Institute of this city for the last six months, I take pleasure in stating that he gave general satisfaction in that capacity.

Chas. I. White, D.D.,
Pastor of Saint Matthew's Church.

*Head Quarters Military District of Washington,
Washington, D.C., January 8th, 1864.*

Col. Wm. Hoffman,
Commissary General of Prisoners,

Colonel:

Although my acquaintance with Mr. Louis J. Wiechmann commenced but a few weeks since, it has given me a most favorable impression of him and I cordially bear testimony to his high tone of character and personal worth. I consider him eminently qualified for the position he seeks in your office and entitled to your warmest confidence.

Respectfully,
Your obedient servant,
E. Beatty,
Capt. & A.A.G.[8]

The place was won without much difficulty and early in January 1864 I became a "War Department Clerk." The change was in every sense an agreeable one. My salary was now eighty dollars per month instead of thirty-eight. The work of the office was laborious but there was rich compensation for this in the company of the gentlemanly and kind-hearted clerks who were my associates. John H. Surratt now came to see me frequently, sometimes spending a few days with me at my boardinghouse. He was always welcome; whatever I possessed was his own, as much as mine.

No thought in those days of treason or bloody conspiracy; no plot against the Government or its rulers.[9] Southerner though Surratt was by birth, instinct, and education, he was too fresh from the honorable and sacred teachings of St. Charles College to meditate any such foul designs. He was introduced to all the friends whose acquaintance I had formed in Washington, and a proud and happy reflection it is to me that every such introduction was creditable to him and to me. Several Union officers boarded in the same house where I did and to some of them I presented him. Among others was General Albion Howe of the U. S. Artillery, afterwards a member of the Military Commission which tried Surratt's mother. That gentleman knew what my deportment at this house as a young man was, how kindly I treated Surratt when he came to the table with me, and how honorable my actions were in every particular.

In September 1864, I paid a second visit to Surrattsville. On the Sunday which I spent there I attended service in a little Catholic church at a place called Piscataway, not far from Surrattsville. As fate would have it, here I again saw David E. Herold. He had a companion with him whose name I forget, and had come from Washington on horseback. His trip was, he said, purely one of pleasure and recreation.

During this visit Surratt informed me of a purpose on the part of his mother to lease her country home and occupy her residence in Washington City; the intention being to open a private boardinghouse. In that event I was invited to make my home with the family. Cheerfully did I consent, for I was weary of the loneliness of the large house where I resided. I was then boarding at the corner of Nineteenth Street and Pennsylvania Avenue in a house kept by a colored caterer by the name of Purnell.

I was delighted with the opportunity of being with the friend of my college days, a friend whom I trusted, and honored. Surely, he was the only one among the many thousands in Washington for whom I had an attachment going back to the very beginning of the happiest days of my life, the few brief years I had spent at St. Charles College.

At this time I was a member of the War Department Rifles, a regiment organized from among the clerks of the various bureaus of the War Department for the defense of Washington. It was composed of ten companies fully equipped and ordered into service by the Secretary of War. I was enrolled in Company G. Washington was then being rapidly filled with deserters from the Confederate armies. They came by thousands. On July 19, 1864, Jubal Early made his famous raid on Washington, approaching the city from Hagerstown, Maryland, by way of Seventh Street.[10] Beaten back, he was destined to meet a still more terrific repulse from Sheridan at Winchester in the Shenandoah Valley. All along from this time the clerks of the regiment were compelled to do military duty at night in guarding Government property. It was a serious and dangerous time, and there are now but few who do not appreciate the necessity under which the Government rested to take the greatest precautions to protect these interests in case of a sudden outbreak in the heart of the capital.

On November 1, 1864, I became a boarder in Mrs. Surratt's house, No. 541 H Street, between Sixth and Seventh streets, and agreed to pay her thirty-five dollars per month. John and his sister were there from the very start. Mrs. Surratt, however, did not come until December 1. She, about that date, had leased her property in the country to a man by the name of John M. Lloyd at five hundred dollars per annum. I was a witness to that lease and in that way became acquainted with Lloyd, who was a very plain and unpretentious individual, but abundantly able to run the farm and sell whisky to his neighbors. He was the individual who afterwards gave the very damaging testimony against Mrs. Surratt at the Conspiracy trial, but for which I verily believe she would not have been punished as she was.

A young lady named Honora Fitzpatrick, a friend of Miss Surratt, secured boarding shortly after I did. She roomed with the daughter, Anna, and was in every respect a very good and excellent woman. Later on, Mr. John T. Holohan, his wife, Mrs. Eliza T. Holohan, and their two children also came to board, and still later a little girl of about nine years named Apollonia Dean. Thus the house was well filled almost from the beginning, and was a paying institution.

The dwelling itself was a lead-colored brick, three stories in height with attic. There was a basement on a level with the pavement containing two large rooms, one used as a dining room and the other as a kitchen. In the second story were front and back parlors, the latter being used as a bedroom by Mrs. Surratt. A long flight of wooden steps ran from the pavement to the second story. The third floor contained three rooms; the two front ones were occupied by Mr. Holohan and family, and the back one by myself and by John H. Surratt when in the city. In addition to these rooms there were two large rooms and a small one in the attic. One of these was used by Miss Surratt and Miss Fitzpatrick; the second was a spare room; and the small room was occupied by the servant.

From November 1864 until Christmas time everything went on peacefully and pleasantly in the Surratt home. No one had yet crossed its threshold who breathed treason against the Government, or plotted the death of its honored head. Its peace, however, was short-lived. A fiend with a heart as black as hell was lying in wait on the outside ready to destroy it and to make his own name and the name of Surratt a shame and a hissing reproach for all time throughout the civilized world.

That fiend was John Wilkes Booth.

CHAPTER IV

History brought down to December 1864 · Mrs. Surratt's home in Washington from November to December 1864 · Accountability of Mary E. Surratt and her son · Extract from a lecture by John H. Surratt · Surratt secures employment in the Adams Express Company at Washington · Meeting of Booth, Mudd, and Surratt in Washington, December 23, 1864 · Interview at the National Hotel · Booth's purchase of Mudd's farm · Booth a constant visitor at Mrs. Surratt's house

This narrative has now been brought down to December 1, 1864. I have thus far shown by a series of incidents over which I had not the slightest control how I successively became acquainted with John H. Surratt, his mother, David E. Herold, Henri B. de Sainte Marie, and John M. Lloyd. And certainly up to this time there is not the faintest evidence of any wrongdoing on the part of any of these people, of Mrs. Surratt or any member of her family. Her house during the months of November and December 1864 was just as orderly, decent, and respectable as any home in Washington, and it is only after Surratt and his mother had become acquainted with Booth, Atzerodt, and Payne, and had admitted them to the intimacy and sacredness of their home, and these men made it their headquarters for the accomplishment of their wicked purposes, that the shadows begin to deepen around that home which to mother and son should have been the dearest spot on earth and which should have been guarded at all hazards.

Surratt was now in his twentieth year and was still the slender and erect youth I had known at college. Beyond a slight chin whisker, his features had changed but little. He was to me the same good-natured chum of other days, but utterly without aim or purpose as to his future. He was leading a roving and unsettled life.

Once, so I was informed, he ran the blockade to Richmond. No one knew the people of his own and the adjacent counties better than he. An excellent horseman, a good pistol shot—two points on which he prided himself—he was familiar with every main, cross-, and byroad in Lower Maryland, and was thoroughly posted in all the secret recesses and hiding places of that section.

I cannot give the reader a better idea of the kind of life he was leading at this time than the following extract from a lecture delivered by him at Rockville, Maryland, on December 6, 1870:

At the breaking out of the war I was a student at St. Charles College, in Maryland, but did not remain long there after that important event. I left in July, 1861, and returning home commenced to take an active part in the stirring events of that period. I was not more than eighteen years of age, and was mostly engaged in sending information regarding the movements of the United States army stationed in Washington and elsewhere, and carrying dispatches to the Confederate boats on the Potomac. We had a regular established line from Washington to the Potomac, and I being the only unmarried man on the route, I had most of the hard riding to do. (Laughter.) I devised various ways to carry the dispatches—sometimes in the heel of my boots, sometimes between the planks of the buggy. I confess that never in my life did I come across a more stupid set of detectives than those generally employed by the U. S. Government. They seemed to have no idea whatever how to search men. In 1864 my family left Maryland and moved to Washington, *where I took a still more active part* in the stirring events of that period. It was a fascinating life to me. It seemed as if I could not do too much or run too great a risk.* [1]

* Surratt says he left college in 1861. His sister at the trial of the conspirators testified that he left in 1862, and this is also my recollection.

But this kind of life worried his mother. I have always believed that one of the reasons, if not the chief reason, which influenced her in changing her residence to Washington was that of rescuing her son from the baleful influences and temptations of his country life in those war times, and enabling him to secure some remunerative employment. Her whole heart and soul were wrapped up in her boy. There was no prospect at all for him at Surrattsville. Beyond a bare living, little profit was to be realized out of the farm, tavern, and country post office. In Washington, he would at least have an opportunity; the war would likely come to an end soon and Washington was a growing city.

In pursuance of his mother's wishes, one of John's first moves after his arrival in Washington was to seek employment. The Adams Express Company was then unusually rushed with business. Boxes and packages were pouring in from the North and West by the thousands for shipment to the Boys in Blue at the front. The company was in need of help and Surratt applied for work to the agent, Mr. Charles C. Dunn. In his letter of application he stated that he had "a ready hand and a willing heart," and that he would be faithful in any position given him. Mr. Dunn himself told me during Surratt's trial in 1867 that he was so much pleased with the expression "ready hand and willing heart" that without hesitation he granted him the coveted position. This occurred on December 30, 1864. The sequel will show that he did not retain his place long. Other influences were at work to drag him from his desk—influences which he might and ought to have resisted, had he done his duty as a good man, but which, for reasons of his own, he did not choose to resist.

Prior to December 23, 1864, there is not a scintilla of evidence in existence anywhere that Mrs. Surratt or her son John was acquainted with John Wilkes Booth, had ever heard of him or met him, except what John H. Surratt himself has stated to the contrary.[2]

And let me say by way of preface that in all my intercourse with the Surratt family neither Mary E. Surratt nor her son, nor anyone else, ever intimated to me in any manner in which it is possible to convey human information a knowledge of the existence of any form of conspiracy against Mr. Lincoln, or other United States officers. Had I been placed in possession of such secrets I would have exposed them to the War Department and to the country. My early education, religious training, affection for my parents, ideas of right and wrong, and my whole moral nature would have instinctively rebelled against the conception and execution of such infamous crimes. All that I know—all that I have ever stated anywhere or at any time in reference to the Conspiracy —is purely circumstantial from beginning to end.

On the 23rd of December 1864, two days before Christmas, John H. Surratt for the first time, so far as I know, met his evil genius, John Wilkes Booth, a meeting which in its ultimate results brought ruin to him and to his mother, and which certainly chequered my career and changed my destiny in life.[3]

In the evening after dinner on that day, about six o'clock, while standing on the pavement in front of the Surratt house and having a very pleasant time with John, we agreed to take a stroll along Pennsylvania Avenue. I was anxious to purchase a few Christmas presents for my sisters. We went down Seventh Street together. It was a delightful evening. The store windows looked very gay. Surratt, I am sure, had no expectation of meeting any acquaintance, nor had I. When directly opposite Odd Fellows' Hall someone suddenly called out, "Surratt, Surratt." "John, someone is calling you," said I. My companion, turning around, recognized an old friend from Charles County, Maryland, named Samuel A. Mudd.

"Why, Doctor, how do you do?" said he, grasping him warmly by the hand. "I am so glad to see you, let me make you acquainted with my friend Mr. Weichmann."

"And you, gentlemen, let me present you to my friend Mr. Boone," answered Dr. Mudd, bringing forward his companion. Such was the name my ear first caught. At the first glimpse of Mr. Boone I noticed that he was a young man of medium figure, apparently about twenty-eight years of age. A heavy black mustache rendered the pallor of his countenance very noticeable. He possessed an abundance of black curly hair and a voice that was musical and rich in its tones. His bearing was that of a man of the world and a gentleman. In dress, he was faultless.[4]

His companion, Dr. Mudd, was the very opposite, slender, about six feet in height, with fair and finely cut features. He was not blessed with as much hair as his friend and such as he did have was quite florid in color and straight. His conversation at once betrayed his education and indicated his training and culture as that of a gentleman.

After the etiquette consequent on our meeting, Mr. Boone invited us to forgo our intentions and partake of his hospitality in his rooms at the National Hotel. When we arrived at the hotel, he requested us to be seated, then, pulling a call bell, asked the responsive waiter to serve milk punches and cigars for four. I made some remark about the neatness of the room. Boone replied, "Yes," and added that it had been previously occupied by a member of Congress, Senator Wilkeson. The number of the room at that interview was 84. Taking some documents from the top of a secretary that stood against the wall, Boone remarked, "And what a nice read I will have to myself when left alone." When the milk punches had been sipped, and after some desultory conversation, Dr. Mudd arose, went out into the entry that led past the door, and called Boone out after him. They did not take their hats with them nor did they go downstairs; had they done so I could easily have heard the sounds of their retreating footsteps. In the course of five or six minutes both returned to the door and called out, "Surratt." Then these three men remained in the hall for several minutes longer before returning. When they did so, Dr. Mudd, approaching me, said, "Mr. Weichmann, it is too bad to have left you alone so long, but I hope you will excuse us for the privacy of this conversation; the fact is Mr. Boone has some business with me; between you and me, he desires to purchase my farm but he does not wish to give me enough for it."

Boone made an apology to the same effect, saying that he did intend to purchase lands in the lower part of Maryland, and that he was anxious to secure the doctor's farm.

All this time I was seated on a sofa near a window of the room. Boone, Dr. Mudd, and Surratt then seated themselves around a center table in the middle of the room about six or eight feet distant. They held a private conversation, audible only as to sound, no portion of which I could or did distinguish.

Boone (all this time, I remained under the impression that this was the name of the man) took from his pocket an envelope and made some marks on the back of it, Surratt and Mudd looking on intently. From the motion of the pencil I concluded that the marks were more like straight lines than anything else.[5] I saw enough to know he was not producing written characters.

After about twenty minutes spent in this way the talk was brought to a close. Dr. Mudd invited us to the Pennsylvania House on C Street, where he was staying. At this place I had quite a chat with the doctor. We sat in the public room on a settee apart from Surratt and Boone, who were by themselves near the blazing fire on the hearth. I was dressed in a military suit, wearing blue pants, a short light-blue cloak with cape attached, and regulation U. S. Army cap. It was part of the uniform of the War Department Rifles, the regiment to which I belonged. Dr. Mudd was free and apparently unreserved in his conversation, and was a very pronounced Union man in all his utterances. Not a secesh [6] or disloyal word came to me from him. The other parties, over by the hearth, Boone and Surratt, were meanwhile having a jolly time together, Boone taking letters and photographs from his pocket and exhibiting them to his companion, who, tossing his head in the air, replied with animated laughter. Probably by this time Surratt was duly impressed with the greatness of his new-found friend. Certain it is he acted as if he had known him all his life. What pictures Boone drew before this country boy's vision, what glittering baubles he held out to him, no one knows. Boone, at any rate, found him an easy victim, for from that hour Surratt was his, as completely as Doctor Faust belonged to Mephistopheles.

Boone was the first to bid us good-night at about half past ten o'clock. In a little while Surratt and I parted with the doctor, who said he was going to leave town the next morning. This was the only time I met or saw Dr. Mudd prior to the assassination of President Lincoln, and the only occasion in my life I ever held any conversation with him.

On the return home that night, John Surratt remarked that the brilliant and accomplished young gentleman whom we had met was no less a personage than John Wilkes Booth, the famous actor. When I saw Booth on Seventh Street I did not know that he was an actor nor was I aware that he was John Wilkes Booth until Surratt told me. Surratt further stated that Booth desired to purchase Mudd's farm and that he was to be an agent in its purchase. Some weeks later when I asked Mrs. Surratt what John had to do with Dr. Mudd's farm and whether he had made himself an agent of Booth, she answered, "Oh, Dr. Mudd and the people of Charles County are getting tired of Booth and are pushing him off on John." *

This answer on her and her son's part about Booth's purchase of Dr. Mudd's farm, as developments will show, was pure fiction. Nay, more, it was a falsehood, uttered purposely to deceive me. It was the very beginning of a series of misrepresentations and intrigues practiced on me until Lincoln was laid low. Truth, however, is stranger than fiction. The

* The name Boone, first given me by Dr. Mudd, was, I believe, for the purposes of deception and to conceal Booth's identity.

time came when, with shining lance, she pierced through the mass of trickery and lying and exposed its rottenness to the full gaze of an indignant world.

This introduction to Booth was the very beginning of my acquaintance with him. Thenceforward he was a frequent and welcome visitor in Mary E. Surratt's home, and to her son belongs the sin of introducing the arch-assassin to that mother, to his sister, and to Miss Fitzpatrick.

A thousand times better for himself had he choked the life out of him when he made his proposition of conspiracy. He would have saved his home, himself, and his mother.

Yet, he did not choke the life out of him; on the contrary, he became his principal associate, ally, and fellow conspirator. All this will be shown, not merely by the circumstantial evidence of the case presented before the Military Commission in 1865, and at his own trial in 1867, but by the confessions of Samuel Arnold and George A. Atzerodt, who were associated with him in his criminal purposes, and above all by the hot, self-inculpatory words falling from his own lips in the public lecture delivered by him, from which I have already quoted.

But first of all let us see who John Wilkes Booth was, and what he had been doing up to this date.

CHAPTER V

John Wilkes Booth was an actor and the son of an actor. His father was
the renowned tragedian Junius Brutus Booth, who in his day stood in
the very forefront of his profession. The elder Booth was born in the
parish of St. Pancras, London, on the first day of May 1796. He was
related through his grandmother, Elizabeth Wilkes, to the English agi-
tator and statesman of that name—John Wilkes, in honor of whom his
son John Wilkes was named. He was twice married; his first wife, whom
he deserted after six years of wedded life and from whom he never was
divorced, being a French-Belgian girl, named Christine Adelaide Delannoy. She followed him to this country and confronted him in the
courts of Maryland.[1] Poor, old, and abandoned, she died at the age of
sixty-six on March 8, 1858, and was buried in the old Cathedral Cemetery, Baltimore. The passing visitor who perhaps is filled with curiosity
may there read on a simple tombstone this inscription:

JESUS, MARY, JOSEPH,

PRAY FOR THE SOUL OF

MARY CHRISTINE ADELAIDE DELANNOY,

WIFE OF JUNIUS BRUTUS BOOTH, TRAGEDIAN.[*]

* See *Katy of Catoctin,* by George Alfred Townsend [New York: D. Appleton and
Company, 1886], p. 472.

On January 8, 1821, at the residence of the Honorable Mrs. Chambers, London, he took for his second wife Mary Ann Holmes.[2] Mrs. Chambers was always interested in Booth's career, and on this occasion presented the wife with the well-known jewels which afterwards adorned and sparkled in the crown of Booth's Richard.

In the month of April 1821, with his wife and pony, he sailed for the United States in the *Two Brothers*. After a tedious voyage of forty-four days he landed at Norfolk, Virginia, June 30, 1821. Introducing himself to Mr. Charles Gilfert, the manager of the Richmond Theater, he secured an engagement at once, and on the sixth day of July in the capital city of the Old Dominion State appeared in the character of Shakespeare's Richard III. His success was instantaneous, and thereafter he experienced no difficulty in securing all the engagements he could fill.

While the yellow fever raged at its height in the summer of 1822 and was afflicting the citizens of Baltimore, Mr. Booth purchased a farm in Harford County, Maryland, about twenty miles from the Monumental City. The place was known as "the farm." Here his children—Junius Brutus, Edwin Forrest, Joseph A., John Wilkes, and Asia, wife of the celebrated comedian John S. Clarke, and three other daughters—were born.[3] Here was the tragedian's inevitable resort when, freed from the engagements and worry of his profession, he desired the rest and seclusion of a country life.

"The farm lay in the midst of a dense woodland and was equally distant from the three villages—Bel Air, the county town, Hickory and Churchville."

"The dwelling," as described by the daughter Asia Booth Clarke, in her life of the two Booths, Junius Brutus, Sr., and Edwin Forrest, father and brother, "was a log cabin plastered and whitewashed on the interior; the small square window frames and broad plain shutters, which like the door never knew the innovation of lock or bolt, were painted red. Four rooms besides the loft, and the kitchen, with its Old Dominion chimney, made up a comfortable and picturesque abode, standing in a clearing encompassed by huge oaks, black walnut, beech and tulip trees." [4]

In the year 1822, Mr. Booth welcomed to his home his father, Richard Booth, who there spent the remainder of his days, dying in 1840, aged seventy-six.[5] Booth's last play in the United States was at New Orleans on November 19, 1852, as Sir Richard Mortimer in *The Iron Chest*. Immediately after this engagement he secured passage on the [steamboat] *J. S. Chenoweth* for Cincinnati. He was taken sick during the trip of consumption of the bowels, and died on board the vessel, Tuesday, November 30, 1852.

When the great Rufus Choate heard of his decease, he exclaimed: "There are no more actors."

In the spring of 1858, Mr. Booth was buried in the Greenmount Cemetery, Baltimore.[6] Here a white marble monument, obelisk in form, was erected to his memory by his son Edwin. Three rough-faced huge blocks of granite support the shaft, around the base of which, almost hiding the stone foundation, a mass of creeping ivy clings, springing up from the mound at the foot of the monument. On the front cut in bold relief is the word "Booth," and upon the face of the marble in bas-relief is the medallion head of him to whose memory the stone is erected. Below is the inscription:

BEHOLD THE SPOT WHERE GENIUS LIES,

OR DROP A TEAR WHEN TALENT DIES,

OF TRAGEDY THE MIGHTY CHIEF,

THY POWER TO PLEASE SURPASSED BELIEF.

HIC JACET, MATCHLESS BOOTH.

Upon the face of the shaft to the left are the words:

JUNIUS BRUTUS BOOTH
Born May 1, 1796.

And upon the right face:

Died November 30, 1852.

At the back of the lot on the fourth side of the marble obelisk is the simple announcement:

TO THE MEMORY OF THE CHILDREN

OF JUNIUS BRUTUS AND MARY ANN BOOTH:

JOHN WILKES,

FREDERICK,

MARY ANN,

HENRY BYRON,

JUNIUS BRUTUS, JR.[7]

Of all the sons of Junius Brutus Booth, Sr., Edwin Forrest Booth alone inherited his father's genius and rose to prominence. With his history and great career as an actor, and his reputation as a man, the country is too well acquainted to permit any details here. He was, indeed, the worthy son of his sire.

Junius Brutus, Jr., played in a number of characters, but never at any time came to the front. The closing years of his life were given to the hotel business somewhere in Massachusetts, and there he died.

Joseph A. Booth, unlike any of his brothers, had no taste for the stage, but became a physician, a calling to which he devoted his life. New York City was his home, and the sphere of his work. He died in March 1902, and is also buried in Greenmount Cemetery, Baltimore.

Asia Booth, one of the daughters, was married to Mr. John S. Clarke, the celebrated American comedian, who after the assassination of Mr. Lincoln made his home in England. She, too, is deceased.

Young John Wilkes Booth was born in 1838 and received his school education at St. Timothy's Hall in Maryland, under President Van Bokelin. Among his schoolmates was Samuel Arnold, a Baltimorean, who later in life was one of the first persons whom he induced to join the conspiracy of abducting the President.

At an early age, Booth evinced a great love of sport, became an excellent athlete and a splendid pistol shot. After leaving school he showed a predilection for the stage, and his first employment was at the old Arch Street Theater in Philadelphia, on a salary of about fifteen dollars a week. This was in 1858 and 1859. In politics he was a pronounced pro-slavery man and early espoused the cause of the South.

He traveled through the South in 1859 and in the fall of that year was at Harpers Ferry, and as a member of Militia Company F, Richmond Volunteers, stood to his gun and assisted in the execution of old John Brown, the anti-slavery martyr. Booth refers to this in an exultant spirit in one of his documents, and was evidently proud of his part in the transaction. Thus he not only helped to kill the man who attempted to free the slaves, but afterwards murdered him whose mission it was under God to lead them out of the house of bondage into the broad land of liberty.*

When Booth made his debut in Baltimore, he was hissed. He was playing the part of Arcanio Petruccio and Eliza Wrenn was Lucretia Borgia. When she asked him, "Who art thou?" Booth became so nervous that he forgot his part. He stammered awhile, then broke out impul-

* See below, Chapter VI.

sively, "Who am I anyhow?" He was hissed off the stage and to his dying day felt the rebuke keenly. From Baltimore he went to Richmond, and his successes in that city were remarkable from the start. This generous welcome coming so soon after his rebuff in the Monumental City implanted in his heart a love for Virginia and the South that never wavered. He was the pet of Richmond and led a very wild life there, being allowed to do as he pleased.*

"In 1861, in the spring just after the opening of the war, he again played in Richmond. One night he acted with more than his usual zest, and reaped a rich measure of success and applause. In the audience among those who listened to him was a young Florida soldier by the name of Powell.[8] It was the first play he ever saw, and he was spell bound with the magical influence wielded by the stage over such to whom its tinsel is yet reality. But he was chiefly attracted by the voice and manner of one of the actors—a young man about twenty-five with large lustrous eyes, and a graceful form, features regular as a statue, and a rich voice that lingered in the ears of those who heard him. Although only a private soldier, Powell considered himself equal to any one, and after the play was over, sought and gained an introduction to the actor. Never were two natures thrown together so different, yet so well calculated—the one to rule, the other to be ruled. The soldier was tall, awkward, rough, frank, generous and illiterate. The actor was of delicate mold, polished, graceful, subtle, with a brilliant fancy, and an abundant stock of reading. Each was what the other was not, and each found in the other an admirer of the other's qualities. The actor was pleased to have a follower so powerful in his muscles, and Powell was irresistibly drawn to follow a man so wonderfully fascinating and intellectual. They saw enough of one another to form a close intimacy, and confirm the control of the actor over Powell, and parted not to meet for nearly four years." †

When they met again, it was to confirm Booth's ascendancy over Powell and to enlist him as an active member of the Conspiracy. Thus it was that Booth, the murderer of Lincoln, and Powell, the would-be slayer of Mr. Seward, first began their acquaintance.

Booth, returned to the North, secured all the engagements he could.

* Interview with H. Hunter in the *Indiana Argus*, April 21, 1888, copied from the *Atlanta Constitution*.
† Argument of W. E. Doster, Pitman, pp. 313–14.

His career, however, during the active period of the war was not distinguished by anything unusual. He made some investments in oil stock in Pennsylvania in 1863 or 1864, which he closed out entirely on September 27, 1864, and transferred to his brother Junius Brutus and others. He never realized a dollar from any of his oil interests and his speculations were a total loss.

It has been said that one of the chief reasons for his attachment to the cause of the South was a jealousy of his brother Edwin, who was a good Union man and who cast the first and only vote of his life for Mr. Lincoln. Edwin was very popular with the people of the North, winning praise everywhere.

"On the night of November 25th, 1864, the three Booth brothers appeared in New York City in the play of *Julius Caesar;* Junius Brutus Booth as Cassius, Edwin as Brutus, and John Wilkes as Marc Anthony. The theater was crowded to suffocation, the people standing in every available place. The greatest excitement prevailed, and the aged mother of the Booths sat in a private box to witness the performance. The three brothers received and merited the applause of the immense audience, for they acted well and presented a picture too strikingly historic to be soon forgotten. The eldest powerfully built and handsome as an antique Roman; Edwin with his magnetic fire and graceful dignity; and John Wilkes in the perfection of youthful beauty, stood side by side, again and again, before the curtain to receive the lavish applause of the audience mingled with the waving of handkerchiefs and every mark of enthusiasm." *

This was John Wilkes's last appearance before a New York audience in a theatrical character. In a few weeks he was off for Washington to carry out his part in another tragedy that was then festering in his brain.

Had he lived, Booth would, doubtless, have become one of the greatest actors of the age. He put into all his impersonations the vitality of perfect manhood. To marvellous mental powers, he added a fine physical organization. His Macbeth and Richard were different from any ever witnessed. In the scene in *Macbeth* where he enters the den of the witches, he would not content himself with the usual steps to reach the stage, but had a ledge of rocks some ten or twelve feet high erected in their stead,

* From the life of the Booths by Asia Booth [*The Elder and the Younger Booth*], p. 159.

down which he sprang upon the stage. His Richard was full of marvelous possibilities, and his fighting scene was simply terrific.

Mr. John T. Ford paid him as much as $700 a week, and he could have easily earned $20,000 in a year. He was very fine in *The Apostate*, and his Raphael in *The Marble Heart* was matchless.

When he played in Boston, in 1864, he made the greatest success of any actor of his day. The people waited in crowds after the performance to catch a glimpse of him as he left the theater.

CHAPTER VI

Booth in Meadville, Pennsylvania, in August 1864 · Meets Samuel Arnold and Michael O'Laughlin at Barnum's Hotel in Baltimore in September of the same year · Goes to Montreal, Canada, in October · Vessel containing his wardrobe wrecked at Bic · Deposits $455 in Ontario Bank, Montreal · Seen in company with Martin · Returns to the United States and meets Drs. Queen and Mudd in Charles County, Maryland · Is the guest of Dr. Mudd · Plot to capture the President · Letter in relation thereto

The exact date of the formation on the part of Booth of a purpose hostile to Mr. Lincoln is not known. The writer for more than thirty years has critically watched and examined the periodicals of the country, but has utterly failed to discover a sign of any such purpose prior to August 1864. In that month Booth was playing a theatrical engagement at Meadville, Pennsylvania. He registered at the McHenry House, then kept by a Mr. R. M. U. Taylor. The performance was for one evening only. When it was over, Booth retired alone to his room. The following morning he left the city.

When the servant of the hotel entered the room which had been occupied by the actor, an inscription was found on one of the windowpanes.

It was written in a large, bold hand and was as follows: "ABE LINCOLN departed this life August 13th, 1864, by the effects of poison." The matter caused but slight comment at this time, but when it was ascertained that Booth had killed the President, the circumstances connected with the inscription on the windowpane were recalled. The glass was removed from the window and encased in a wooden frame. A piece of velvet was placed behind it and thus the handwriting was made more distinct. The signature of Booth entered August 13, 1864, was cut from the hotel register, and was pasted on the glass under the inscription. Miss Mary McHenry, daughter of the proprietor of the McHenry House, presented the framed glass to the War Department after the assassination of the President. It is still in the possession of that bureau of the Government. All the circumstances in relation to it and to the visit of Booth to Meadville at that time are certified to by Miss McHenry and other residents of Meadville.*

The handwriting on the windowpane when compared with the signature of Booth on the hotel register is found to be identically the same, and this fact is further verified and strengthened by a comparison with Booth's handwriting in his diary.

There is not the slightest doubt that the writing on the pane of glass is that of Booth, and this goes to show beyond any doubt that as early as August 1864 he had the murder of the President in his mind, especially when this fact is taken in connection with other circumstances taking place after that time.

Although no evidence has ever been presented that Booth was acquainted with David E. Herold in August 1864, yet it is a remarkable fact that at the very time this inscription was cut on the windowpane, Herold, one of the conspirators subsequently identified with Booth, was employed as a drug clerk in the store of Mr. William S. Thompson, Fifteenth Street and Pennsylvania Avenue near the White House, and at this place the presidential family generally purchased their medicines. The employment of Herold at this store at this time would of itself amount to very little, but for the reason that in November 1864 a very important letter was found by a Mrs. Hudspeth in a streetcar in New York.[1] This letter was carried by her to General Dix, and transmitted by him to the War Department. In the letter occurs this expression: "The cup failed us once, and might again." This language would seem

* See *Century Magazine*, April 1896.

to indicate that there had been an effort made to get rid of Mr. Lincoln by poisoning him, but that the attempt had failed.

As a matter of truth, however, it must be said that no direct evidence has ever been found connecting Herold with this effort, and all charges or allegations in reference thereto, so far as he is concerned, are based only on the suspicious circumstances of his having been in the employ of Mr. Thompson at that time.

In the latter part of August or commencement of September 1864, Booth was in Baltimore, and a guest at Barnum's Hotel. One day during his stay there, he sent for Samuel Arnold, who was then living with his parents at Baltimore. Arnold was a Southern man in his political convictions, favored the rebellion, and had been in the Confederate Army. He returned, however, in 1862 to Baltimore, and took the oath of allegiance. At the time of meeting Booth, he was not engaged in any employment, and this bold man found him a pliant tool, an easy victim to his purposes.

Arnold had not seen Booth since 1852 when they were together at Timothy's Hall. Booth's reception of Arnold was extremely cordial. The actor called for wine and cigars, and the two men chatted pleasantly over former times. Soon they were interrupted by a loud knock at the door of the room. The door was promptly opened and the newcomer was admitted. He proved to be Michael O'Laughlin, another Baltimore boy, and also one of Booth's earliest friends and schoolmates. He and his family were then residing in a house owned by Booth's mother. O'Laughlin, too, had been in the Confederate service, had returned, and like Arnold had taken the oath of allegiance to the United States Government. Booth introduced O'Laughlin to his friend Arnold, and then they all went on with their smoking and wine drinking.

Booth, who had previously heard of Arnold's political sentiments, and who knew those of O'Laughlin, now began to speak in glowing terms of the Confederacy. He alluded to the number of Confederates in the Northern prisons, and then made a proposition to his hearers which he thought could be accomplished. He stated that President Lincoln was in the frequent habit of going out to the Soldiers' Home in Washington without any guard. He said that he thought that while on one of these excursions, it would be an easy matter to kidnap the President, carry him to Richmond, and hold him as a hostage for the release of the Confederate prisoners in Federal hands.

Booth claimed to be the originator of the scheme, and requested his two companions to go in with him. After he painted the chances of success in very glittering colors, Arnold and O'Laughlin consented to join him in his purpose. They pledged themselves not to divulge it to a living soul.* [2]

Arnold saw Booth in Baltimore once more after this, and then not again until the following January in Washington.

Booth in a short time after this meeting with Arnold and O'Laughlin went to New York for a few days, then to the oil regions of Pennsylvania, and thence to Boston and finally to Canada.

After Booth's departure, Arnold went to work for a friend named Littleton P. D. Newman, to help him thrash some wheat.[3] During his stay with him, he received a letter which probably came from Booth, for Arnold himself says in his confession that he had received a letter from Booth which he destroyed, in which the arch-conspirator stated that he was laid up with erysipelas, but that he would be with them (Arnold and O'Laughlin) as soon as he was able.

The letter Arnold received while with Newman contained a twenty- or fifty-dollar note. Arnold read the letter, and remarked that he was flush of money. He then handed it to Mr. Newman, who found it very ambiguous in its language and, returning it to Arnold, asked him what it meant. Arnold remarked that "something big will take place one of these days," thus clearly betraying his knowledge of some project evidently then on foot which he did not care to unfold, and which had already as its first fruits brought him this money.

In the latter part of October 1864, Booth was in Montreal, Canada, and was seen in the company of Sanders, Thompson, and others, agents of the Confederacy, appropriately styled "the Canada Cabinet." † [4] He had now given up acting, and one of his first moves in the Conspiracy was to have his theatrical wardrobe sent to Canada.

Several trunks marked "J. W. B., New Providence" were shipped on board the schooner *Marie Victoria* at Quebec. How they reached Quebec, or by whom they were shipped, or where the vessel was bound for, or on what mission, is enveloped in mystery, but the *Marie Victoria* sailed from the port of Quebec without going through the usual formalities of clearing at the custom house; her name does not appear upon

---

* See the confession of Arnold, below, Chapter XXXI.
† General T. M. Harris, *Assassination of Lincoln* [Boston: American Citizen Company, 1892].

the shipping records at that port, thereby giving good grounds for the suspicion that the service she was engaged in demanded secrecy. Subsequent events gave proof of this and led to the belief that she intended to run the blockade of the South, or make for the Bahamas, but the schooner was wrecked at Bic, about 150 miles from Quebec.

From these precautions, it would appear that Booth, in anticipation of his scheme against Mr. Lincoln, sent his theatrical wardrobe through Canada and had it shipped from a Canadian port in expectation of finding it to hand in one of the Southern states when he had succeeded in the object he had in view.

The actor's effects were sold at auction, as appears from the following notice of sale published in the *Quebec Morning Chronicle* of July 19, 1865:

> The theatrical wardrobe of the late John Wilkes Booth recovered about a month ago from the wreck of the schooner [*Marie Victoria*] at Bic last summer, was disposed of by the decree of the Vice-admiralty Court at public auction yesterday afternoon. Among the wardrobe, which unfortunately has been injured by salt water, there was a splendid collection of theatrical clothes in fine silk velvets, silks, ermine and crimson, and also hats, caps, plumes, boots, shoes, etc. In swords and pistols there was a case or trunk packed with a large variety, and there were some very beautifully mounted ones among them. Competition on the whole was very spirited and several articles were sold at high prices. The amount realized for the wardrobe in its damaged state was about $500. The original cost cannot have been less than $15,000.[5]

On the 27th of October 1864, Booth deposited $455 to his own credit with the Ontario Bank in Montreal. This was the same bank in which Jacob Thompson, agent for the Confederacy, kept the funds entrusted to his charge. At the same time Booth purchased from Robert Anson Campbell, teller of the bank, a bill of exchange for sixty-one pounds and some odd shillings, remarking, "I am going to run the blockade, and in case I should be captured, can my capturers make use of the exchange?" Campbell told him they could not unless he endorsed the bill which was made payable to his order. He then said he would take $300 and pulled out that amount in American gold, and a bill of exchange was accordingly made out to him for the amount.[6]

While in Montreal, Booth was frequently seen in the company of a man by the name of [Patrick Charles] Martin, with whom he became very intimate. This Martin came from Lower Maryland, and was concerned in the capture of the steamer *St. Nicholas* very early in the war, and when the leading pirates of the undertaking at Point Lookout had been seized by the Government and put in Fort McHenry, Martin, who had also kept a liquor store in Baltimore with a saloon attachment, slipped off to Canada and there engaged in trading Canadian and American money and in adventuring enterprises for the Confederacy. He finally closed his career by going in with a Scotchman named Alexander Keith to pass a cargo of goods from the St. Lawrence to the Carolinas; the vessel was found in the lower St. Lawrence, a complete wreck, with everything on her lost, including her supercargo and crew.

In the melancholy days of November 1864, Booth made his way to the homes of Dr. [William] Queen and Dr. Mudd in Bryantown, Charles County, Maryland, with a letter of introduction from the Martin above referred to. Dr. Queen's family heard Booth inquire about the price of land and horses in that neighborhood, and say that he was a rich man who had money to put in the county.

"Booth at this time attended St. Mary's Roman Catholic Church near Bryantown, and in a few days after he met Dr. William T. Bowman of Bryantown, asked him if he knew anyone who had any land to sell, and, after getting prices on Bowman's farm, asked him if he had any horses to sell. Mr. Bowman said he could accommodate him, when Booth said he would be down in a couple of weeks and look at the land. Of Mr. John C. Thompson of Charles County at the same time he asked the price of land, and particularly did he inquire about the roads through that part of the country. On this trip he stopped a day or two with Dr. Queen, to whom he had a letter of introduction from a party in Canada. Dr. Queen and his son-in-law, Mr. Thompson, attended church near Bryantown, and Booth sat with them in Dr. Queen's pew. It was here that Booth and Dr. Mudd first met, being introduced by Thompson. Booth again visited this part of the country the following month (December), stopping again with Dr. Queen over night. A few days after this visit Dr. Bowman said to Dr. Mudd: 'I am going to sell my land.' Dr. Mudd asked to whom he expected to sell, and Bowman said: 'To a man by the name of Booth, who said he was coming down soon.' Dr. Mudd then said: 'That fellow promised to buy mine.' Booth had no intention of buying lands; he simply wanted to familiarize himself with the roads, and the people in whom he could trust." * [7]

The actor was subsequently introduced by Dr. Mudd at the village hotel to one Thomas Harbin, a Marylander, who was a signal officer and spy for the rebels in the Lower Maryland counties. Mudd told Harbin that Booth wanted some private conversation with him. Booth then outlined a scheme for seizing Abraham Lincoln and delivering him up the same evening, when captured, in Virginia. He said that he had come down to that county to invite cooperation and to secure partners, and intimated that there was not only glory, but *profit* in the *undertaking*.

During his visit, Booth lodged overnight with Dr. Mudd, and through him procured of George Gardiner one of the several horses which were at his disposal. It was a bay horse, blind in one eye, and was the one subsequently used by Payne in Washington on the night of the assassination.

The plot Booth related to Harbin seems to have been the original and substantial plot; this was to seize the President as he would be driving in his carriage, place two or three of the conspirators beside him and threaten him with instant death if he gave any warning, and then to drive him to the Navy Yard Bridge, and say to the guard there, "This is the President."

Beyond the bridge the horses were to be driven as fast as they could go, and fresh ones substituted halfway down the peninsula, and it was the idea that Mr. Lincoln could be delivered upon the boat at Port Tobacco by eight or nine o'clock at night, if he could be captured about four or five in the afternoon. In another hour he would be in Virginia, within the Confederate lines.†

Further conclusive evidence of Booth's purpose to kidnap President Lincoln is shown by the following verbatim copy of a letter in his own handwriting, furnished to the press by the Honorable William Millward, United States marshal of the Eastern District of Pennsylvania.

It was handed over to that officer by Mr. John S. Clarke, a brother-in-law of Booth, then residing in Philadelphia. The history of it is

* From Oldroyd's history of the assassination, p. 142.

† This statement in relation to Harbin and Booth was made by George Alfred Townsend in the *Cincinnati Enquirer*, April 14–19, 1892. Also see the confession of Atzerodt, below, Chapter XXXI.

somewhat peculiar. In November 1864, the paper was deposited by Booth with Mr. Clarke in a sealed envelope for safe keeping, Mr. Clarke being ignorant of its contents. In January 1865, Booth called at Mr. Clarke's house, asked for the package, and it was given to him. It is now supposed that he, at the time, took out the paper and added to it his signature, which seems to be in a different ink from that used in the body of the letter, and also from the language employed could not have been put to it originally.

Afterwards he returned the package to Mr. Clarke again for safe keeping, sealed, and bearing the superscription "J. Wilkes Booth."

The enclosure was preserved by the family without suspicion of its nature. After the afflicting information of the assassination of the President, which came upon the family of Mr. Clarke with crushing force, it was considered proper to open the envelope. There was found in it the following paper with some seventeen United States bonds and some certificates of shares in oil companies. Mr. Clarke promptly handed over the paper to Marshal Millward.

From a perusal of the document it seems to have been prepared by Booth as a vindication of some desperate act which he had in contemplation and from the language used it is probable that it was the plot to abduct the President and carry him off to Virginia. If this was meditated it failed, and from making a prisoner of the President up to his assassination was an easy step for a man of perverted principles.

—————, *1864.*

My Dear Sir;— You may use this as you think best. But as some may wish to know *when, who* and *why,* and as I know not how to direct, I give it (in the words of your master.)

To whom it may concern,

Right or wrong, God judge me, not man. For be my motive good or bad, of one thing I am sure, the lasting condemnation of the North.

I love peace more than life. Have loved the Union beyond expression. For four years I have waited, hoped and prayed for the dark clouds to break, and for the restoration of our former sunshine. To wait longer would be a crime. All hope for peace is dead. My prayers have proved as idle as my hopes. God's will be done. I go to see and share the bitter end.

I have ever held the South were right. The very nomination of Abraham Lincoln, four years ago, spoke plainly war—war upon Southern rights and institutions. His election proved it. Await an overt act. Yes, till you are bound and plundered. What folly! The South was wise. Who thinks of argument or patience when the finger of his enemy presses on the trigger? In a *foreign war*, I too, could say, country right or wrong. But in a struggle *such as ours* where the brother tries to pierce the brother's heart, for God's sake, choose the right. When a country like this spurns *justice* from her side, she forfeits the allegiance of every honest free man, and should leave him untrammelled by any fealty soever, to act as his own conscience may approve.

People of the North, to hate tyranny, to love liberty and justice, to strike at wrong and oppression, was the teaching of our fathers. The study of our early history will not let me forget it and may it never.

This country was formed for the *white* man and not for the black. And looking upon *African slavery* from the same stand-point as held by the noble framers of our Constitution, I, for one, have ever considered *it* one of the greatest blessings for themselves and for us that God ever bestowed upon a favored nation. Witness heretofore our wealth and power; witness their elevation and enlightenment above their race elsewhere. I have lived among it most of my life, and have seen less harsh treatment from master to man than I have beheld in the North from father to son. Yet heaven knows that *no one* would be more willing to do more for the negro race than I, could I but see a way to *still better their* condition.

But Lincoln's policy is only preparing the way to their total annihilation. The South *are not nor have been fighting for the continuance* of slavery. The first battle of Bull Run did away with that idea. The causes *since* for *war* have been as *noble, and greater far than those that urged our fathers on. Even* though we should allow that they were wrong at the beginning of this contest, *cruelty* and *injustice* have made the wrong become the right, and they now stand before the wonder and admiration of the world, as a noble band of patriotic heroes. Hereafter reading of *their deeds*, Thermopylae will be forgotten.

When I aided in the capture and execution of John Brown who was a murderer on our western border, who was fairly *tried* and *convicted* before an impartial judge and jury, of treason, and who by the way, has since been made a god, I was proud of my little share in the transaction, for I deemed it my duty, and that I was helping our common country to perform an act of justice. But what was a crime in poor John Brown is now considered by themselves as the greatest and only virtue of the Republican party. Strange transmigration. Vice is to become a virtue, simply because *more* indulge in it.

I thought then, *as now*, that the Abolitionists *were the only traitors* in the land, and that the entire party deserved the same fate as poor old Brown, not because they wish to abolish slavery, but on account of the means they have endeavored to use to effect that abolition. If Brown were living, I doubt whether he *himself* would set slavery against the Union. Most, or many in the North do, and openly curse the Union, if the South are to return and attain a *single right* guaranteed to them by every tie which we once *revered as sacred*. The South can make no choice. It is either extermination or slavery for *themselves* worse than death to draw from. I know *my* choice.

I have also studied hard to discover upon what grounds the right of a state to secede has been denied, when our name, United States and Declaration of Independence, *both* provide for secession. But this is no time for words. I write in haste. I know how foolish I shall be deemed for undertaking such a step as this, where on one side I have many friends and every thing to make me happy, where my profession alone has gained me an income of *more than* twenty thousand dollars a year, and where my great personal ambition in my profession has such a great field of labor. On the other hand the South have never bestowed upon me one kind word, a place where I have no friends except beneath the sod; a place where I must either become a private soldier or a beggar.

To give up all the *former* for the *latter*, besides my mother and sisters whom I love so dearly, although they differ so widely in opinion, seems insane; but God is my judge. I love .*justice* more than a country that disowns it; more than fame and wealth; heaven pardon me, if wrong, more than a happy home. I have never been upon the battle field, but, O my countrymen, could all but see the *reality* or effects of this horrid war, as I have seen them *in every state* save Virginia, I know you would think like me, and would pray the Almighty to create in the Northern mind a sense of *right* and *justice* even should it possess no seasoning of mercy, and then he would dry up this sea of blood between us, which is daily growing wider. Alas, poor country, is she to meet her threatened doom? Four years ago I would have given a thousand lives to see her as I have always known her, powerful and unbroken. And even now I would hold my life as naught, to see her what she was. O, my friends, if the fearful scenes of the past four years had never been enacted or if what had been done were but a frightful dream from which we could now awake with over-flowing hearts, we could bless our God and pray for his continued favor. How I have loved the *old flag* can never be known.

A few years since the world could boast of none so pure and spotless. But of late I have been seeing and hearing of the *bloody deeds* of which she has been *made the emblem*, and would shudder to think how changed she has grown. Oh, how I have longed to see her break from the midst of blood and death that circles round her folds, spoiling her beauty and tarnishing her honor! But no; day by day she has been dragged deeper into cruelty and oppression, till now in my eyes her once bright red stripes look *bloody gashes* on the face of heaven.

I look now upon my early admiration of her glories as a dream. My love as things stand to-day is for the South alone. *Nor do I deem it a dishonor in attempting to make for her a prisoner of this man to whom she owes so much misery.*[8] If success attends me, I go penniless to her side. They say she has found that last ditch which the North has so long derided and been endeavoring to force her in, forgetting they are our brothers, and it is impolitic to goad an enemy to madness. Should I reach her in safety and find it true, I will proudly beg permission to triumph or die in that same ditch by her side.

A Confederate doing duty on his own responsibility,
J. Wilkes Booth.[9]

From all this, it is seen that Booth as early as November 1864 had made up his mind to capture the President of the United States. How, when, and where his letter does not indicate.

Booth was not at any time in Washington during the month of October 1864. He always stayed at the National Hotel when in the city, and his first arrival there was on the evening of November 9, 1864, and he was registered as occupying room No. 20. He left on the morning of the 11th, returning on the 14th in the early part of the evening, and left again on the 16th. His appearance in Washington was simultaneous with his visits to Lower Maryland, where, as has been seen, he met about this time Drs. Queen and Mudd, Thomas Harbin, and other prominent Southerners of that section.

He returned to Washington on December 12 and left on the 17th by the morning train. His next arrival was on December 22, leaving again on the 24th, and it was on December 23 he met by appointment Dr. Samuel A. Mudd, who was to introduce him to John H. Surratt, and who did so introduce him.[10]

CHAPTER VII

Mr. Lincoln's attempted assassination in 1861 · In constant receipt of threatening letters · The purpose to capture Mr. Lincoln not a new one · The President informed of such a movement · Interview on the subject with Frank Carpenter, the artist · Remarkable testimony of Samuel Knapp Chester, actor · Booth's plan not limited to abduction · The Charles Selby letter threatening the President's life · It is found in Mr. Lincoln's secret drawer endorsed in his own handwriting · Assassination

Mr. Lincoln from the date of his election and inauguration as President in 1861 was continually subjected to threats of all kinds, especially of assassination, and attempts were made to carry some of them into execution.

The country is still familiar with the attempt to assassinate him in 1861 on his way to Washington and how the scheme was frustrated by the vigilance of Allan Pinkerton, the great detective, Governor [Andrew G.] Curtin of Pennsylvania, and others, and how the President finally reached Washington in safety amid the rejoicings and plaudits of his loyal countrymen.

All along after this period, he was in constant receipt of letters of the most insulting and venomous character; in fact, they became so frequent that they came to have but little value and interest. Mr. Lincoln seemed to be always prepared for the inevitable and was singularly indifferent as to his personal safety. Against the protest of his friends who, by detective means, had obtained from the Southern plotters many of their secrets, he made the Soldiers' Home his summer residence.

Mr. Ward H. Lamon, who for many years was a personal friend of the President and who was United States marshal of the District of Columbia, during his term of office, in some reminiscences published by his daughter, gives an account of an attempt against his life in 1862. The event was related by Mr. Lincoln himself to Mr. Lamon one morning in August of that year.

"Last night," said he, "about eleven o'clock I went out to the Soldiers' Home, riding Old Abe, as you call him"—a horse he delighted in riding—"and when I arrived at the foot of the hill on the road leading to the entrance to the Home grounds, I was jogging along at a slow gait, immersed in deep thought, contemplating what was next to happen in this unsettled state of affairs, when suddenly I was aroused —I may say the arousement lifted me out of my saddle as well as out of my wits—by the report of a rifle, and seemingly the gunner was not fifty yards from where my contemplation ended, and my accelerated transit began. My erratic namesake with little warning gave proof of decided dissatisfaction at the racket and with one reckless bound unceremoniously separated me from my eight-dollar plug hat, with which I parted company without any assent, expressed or implied, upon my part. At a breakneck speed, we soon arrived in a haven of safety." [1]

Another occasion when the vigilance and anxiety of his friends were exercised appears in the following extract from a memorandum written by Robert Lamon, who was deputy marshal of the District of Columbia at the time.

"In the early part of the night my brother (Ward H. Lamon) came to me and asked me to join him in the search for Mr. Lincoln. He was greatly disturbed. We drove rapidly to the Soldiers' Home, and as we neared the entrance to the grounds we met a carriage. Behind it we could see in the darkness a man on horseback. My brother, who seemed unusually suspicious, commanded the party to halt. His order was instantly obeyed. 'Who are you?' he demanded in the same peremptory tone. A voice from within the carriage responded, 'Why do you ask?' The speakers recognized each other. The one in the carriage was Secretary Stanton, and the man behind it was one of his orderlies. 'Where is Mr. Lincoln?' asked Stanton. 'I have been to the Soldiers' Home and he is not there. I am exceedingly uneasy about him. He is not at the White House?' 'No,' said my brother, 'he is not there. I have been looking for him everywhere.' We hurried back to the city. Arriving at the White House before Mr. Stanton, we found Mr. Lincoln walking across the lawn. My brother went with him to the War Department, and from there took him to his (Lamon's) house, where he slept that night and the three or four nights following, Mrs. Lincoln being at that time in New York."

Mr. Lamon's anxiety about Mr. Lincoln that evening grew out of a report of an alarming character made to him by one of his detectives. Stanton had threatening news also, and was therefore excited about Mr. Lincoln's safety.

Mr. Lamon always felt worried about the President, and so far did his anxiety carry him that on the 10th of December 1864, at 1:30 A.M., he addressed the Executive a letter imploring him not to go to the theater unattended, telling him his life was sought after and would be taken unless he and his friends were cautious.

The following story is vouched for by Judge Usher of Lawrence, Kansas:

"About November 1864, Judge Peck went to Mr. Lincoln, who was staying out at the Soldiers' Home, and said: 'Mr. President, General Hunter and I both feel uneasy to have you here without a guard.'

" 'Now, Peck,' said he, 'no one wants to kill me. [Vice-President Hannibal] Hamlin is a great deal worse than I am. He's a black abolitionist. What good would my death do anybody? Besides I can't always be thinking of death. Our soldiers look the grim monster in the face daily; why shouldn't I? Now you want me to ride with six of those tall fellows to the front of me, and six to the rear, like old Frederick, I suppose.'

" 'Yes and six on each side of you, too, for that matter. Now, Mr. Lincoln, if you don't object, we shall place an unobtrusive guard over you.' And it was done." [2]

Threats of the most dangerous character were also made in some of the newspapers, especially those in the South. One of the most prominent effusions of this kind was the following document, which was copied into one of the Washington City newspapers early in 1865.

It was a reproduction from the *Selma Despatch* of Alabama, in which it originally appeared, and was written by one Colonel G. W. Gayle. It is as follows:

> One Million Dollars Wanted to Have Peace by the 1st of March — If the citizens of the Southern Confederacy will furnish me with the cash, or good securities, for the sum of one million dollars, I will cause the lives of Abraham Lincoln, William H. Seward and Andrew Johnson to be taken by the first of March next. This will give us peace, and satisfy the world that cruel tyrants cannot live in a land of "liberty." If this is not accomplished, nothing will be claimed beyond the sum of fifty thousand in advance which is supposed to be necessary to reach and slaughter the three villains.
>
> I will give, myself, one thousand dollars toward this patriotic purpose. Everyone wishing to contribute will address Box X.
>
> Cahawba, Alabama,
> December 1, 1864.[3]

The project of capturing Mr. Lincoln was also not a new one, and does not, so far as has been ascertained, appear to have been confined to Booth.

Mr. Lincoln himself was made cognizant of such a movement. Frank Carpenter, the artist who painted the picture of the Emancipator and who spent several months in the Executive Mansion with the Martyr President, speaks of this in that charming little book of his entitled *Six Months at the White House*. He says:

> A late number of the *New York Tribune* [March 1864] had contained an account from a correspondent within the Rebel lines, of an elaborate conspiracy, matured in Richmond, to abduct, or assassinate—if the first was not found practicable—the person of the President. A secret organization, composed, it was stated, of five hundred or a thousand men, had solemnly sworn to accomplish the deed. Mr. Lincoln had not seen or heard of this account, and at his request, I gave him the details. Upon the conclusion, he smiled incredulously, and said, "Well, even if true, I do not see what the Rebels would gain by killing or getting possession of me. I am but a single individual, and it would not help their cause or make the least difference in the progress of the war. Everything would go right on just the same. Soon after I was nominated at Chicago, I began to receive letters

threatening my life. The first one or two made me a little uncomfortable, but I came at length to look for a regular instalment of this kind of correspondence in every week's mail, and up to inauguration day I was in constant receipt of such letters. It is no uncommon thing to receive them now; but they have ceased to give me any apprehension." I expressed some surprise at this, but he replied in his peculiar way, "Oh, there is nothing like getting *used* to things!" [4]

Further proof of Booth's purpose to capture the President is given in the remarkable testimony of Samuel Knapp Chester, a fellow actor and intimate friend. The following is his sworn evidence before the Military Commission of 1865, and it is so important that it is reproduced almost in full. Said he:

"I am by profession an actor and have known Booth intimately. In the early part of November last—1864—I met him in New York, and asked him why he was not acting. He told me that he did not intend to act in this portion of the country again, that he had taken his wardrobe to Canada and intended to run the blockade.* I saw him again on the 24th or 25th of November, about the time we were to play Julius Caesar in New York, which we did play on the 25th. I asked him where his wardrobe was; he said it was still in Canada, in charge of a friend. I think he named Martin in Montreal.

"He told me he had a big speculation on hand and asked me to go in with him. I met him on Broadway as he was talking to some friends. They were joking with him about his oil speculations. After they left him he told me he had a better speculation than that on hand, and one they wouldn't laugh at. Some time after that I met him again and he asked me how I would like to go in with him. I told him I was without means and therefore could not. He said that didn't matter, that he always liked me and would furnish the means. He then returned to Washington, from which place I received several letters from him. He told me he was speculating in farms in Lower Maryland and Virginia,† still telling me that he was sure to *coin money* and that I must go in with him.

"About the later part of December or early in January, he came to New York and called on me at my house, No. 45 Grove Street. He asked me to take a walk with him which I did. We went into a saloon

* See the previous chapter.
† How like the talk of Dr. Mudd, Chapter IV above.

known as 'The House of Lords' on Houston Street, and remained there perhaps an hour eating and drinking. We afterwards went to another saloon under the Revere House, after which we started up Broadway. He had often mentioned this speculation, but would never say what it was. If I asked him he said he would tell me by-and-by. When we came to the corner of Bleecker Street, I turned and bade him good-night. He asked me to walk farther with him and we walked up Fourth Street, because he said Fourth Street was not so full of people as Broadway, and he wanted to tell me about the speculation. When we got into the unfrequented portion of the street he stopped and told me that he was in a large conspiracy to capture the heads of the Government, including the President, and to take them to Richmond. I asked him if that was the speculation that he wished me to go into. He said it was. I told him I could not do it, that it was an impossibility, and asked him to think of my family. He said that he had *two or three thousand dollars* that he could leave with them. He urged the matter, and talked with me, I suppose, half an hour, but still I refused to give my consent. Then he said to me, 'You will at least not betray me,' then added, 'You dare not.' He said he could implicate me in the affair anyhow. The party, he said, were sworn together, and if I attempted to betray them I would be hunted down through life. He urged me further, saying I had better go in. I told him 'No' and bade him good-night and went home.

"He told me that the affair was to take place in Ford's Theater in Washington, and the part he wished me to play, in carrying out the conspiracy, was to open the back door of the theater at a signal. He urged that the part I would have to play would be a very easy one and that it was sure to succeed, but needed someone connected or acquainted with the theater. He said everything was in readiness and that there were parties on the other side ready to cooperate with him. By these parties I understood him to mean Rebel authorities and others opposed to our Government. He said there were from fifty to one hundred persons in the conspiracy.

"He wrote me again from Washington about this speculation; I think it must have been in January. I did not keep his letters. Every Sunday I devoted to answering my correspondence and destroying my letters. In January I got a letter from him saying that I must come. This was the letter in which he told me his plan was sure to succeed.

I wrote back saying it was impossible and I would not come. Then, by return mail I think, I got another letter with fifty dollars enclosed, saying I must come and must be there by Saturday night. I did not go, nor have I been out of New York since last summer. The next time he came to New York, which I think was in February, he called on me again and asked me to take a walk with him and I did so. He then told me he had been trying to get another party, one John Matthews, to join him, and when he told Matthews what was wanted the man was very much frightened and would not join him; and Booth said that he would not have cared if he had sacrificed him. I told him I did not think it was right to speak in that manner. He said 'No,' but Matthews was a coward and not fit to live. He then again urged me to join and told me I must do so. He said there was *plenty of money* in the affair and that if I joined, I would never *again want for money* as long as I lived. He then said that the President and some of the heads of the Government came to the theater very frequently during Mr. Forrest's engagements. I desired him not to again mention the affair to me, but to think of my poor family. He said he would ruin me in the profession if I did not go. I told him I could not help that and begged him not to mention the affair to me.

"When he found out I would not go, he said he honored my mother and respected my wife, and he was sorry he had mentioned this affair to me, but told me to make my mind easy and he would trouble me no more. I then returned him the money he had sent me. He told me that he would not allow me to do so, but that he was short of funds, and either he or some other party must go to Richmond to obtain means to carry out their designs." [5]

Matthew Canning, another actor, was also very intimate with Booth and had probably as much, if not more, influence over him than anyone else. In an interview with a newspaper reported in Philadelphia, Mr. Canning tells the following story, which goes to show how determined Booth was to have Chester associated with him in the conspiracy:

"Some months before the assassination," said Mr. Canning, "I was in the city of Philadelphia and was told that Booth was looking for me high up and low down. I went to the Continental and there found him. He was very glad to see me, and asked me if I would do him a very great favor. I said, 'Certainly, if in my power. What is it?' He wanted me to promise him in advance of the request. I told him that he ought not to ask me to do anything like that. If it was anything that one man could honorably do for another he needed no such promise, and I could not conceive of him asking anything that was not. He then told me that he wanted me to go and see John T. Ford and get him to give Sam. Chester an engagement. One of Ford's companies was then playing at the Academy of Music, I think, and I replied, 'Why don't you go and see John T. Ford yourself? He will do it as quick for you as for me.' He answered that he and Ford were not just then on good terms and he did not want to speak to him. He also told me that he was about to leave town. I promised to see Ford for Chester, and did so. 'Sam is a clever actor,' was Ford's response, 'and as quick as I can make room for him I will do so.' I wrote to Booth about what he had said and in a few days after left the city on professional business. A week or so later I was in Louisville, and one night I got a dispatch from Washington, signed Booth, saying, 'Hush that matter; don't fail.' I was mystified by it and showed it to Johnny Albaugh. He could make no sense out of it, and handed it back, saying, 'John must be off his base.' It was several weeks later that I learned that the operator had made a mistake in telegraphing the message and that it should have read, 'Push that matter; don't fail.' Meaning Chester's engagement." *

It must be evident to the reader by this time that Booth was fully determined to capture the President; the letter which he had deposited with his brother-in-law, J. S. Clarke, and his attempt to inveigle Mr. Chester into the scheme leave no doubt on that point. Whether his scheme was in any way identified with the conspiracy mentioned by the *New York Tribune*, and referred to by Mr. Carpenter, is not known. It must, however, be apparent from the *Tribune* article that there was a big conspiracy on foot, but whether it embraced the few persons who were subsequently tried and convicted in Washington has not been established.

Booth in the Clarke letter styled himself "a Confederate doing duty on his own responsibility," but stated to Chester that there were from fifty to one hundred persons implicated in the affair; and that everything was in readiness, and that there were parties, the Rebel authorities, on the other side ready to cooperate with him; that there was plenty of money in it, and that the affair was to take place in Ford's Theater in Washington.

In pursuance of these plans, as has been said, he had visited Mon-

* *Philadelphia Evening News*, January 8, 1886.

treal, Canada, had conferred with Martin, and with letters from that individual in his possession had gone down to Lower Maryland and successively met Queen, Mudd, and Harbin. To the strangers who queried him about his business, he said he was there for the purpose of buying lands. To his fellow actors in New York who joked with him, he said he was in the "oil business," when, as a matter of truth and fact, he did not at that time own a dollar's worth of oil stock.[6] But he told Chester that he was in another kind of speculation; a big speculation to capture the President and heads of the Departments. All these expressions about the "oil business" and the "buying of lands" were terms coined and used by him to blind outsiders as to the real nature of his business, and to throw them off their guard. They were employed not only by him but also by his confederates, and there was evidently a preconcerted arrangement and understanding among them about the whole matter.

Booth had two distinct plans for capturing the President; one was to seize him in his box at Ford's Theater in Washington, throw him onto the stage, where Samuel Arnold was to catch him, hurry him to the rear of the theater, and then drive away as rapidly as possible.[7] Another plan was to seize him as he went out riding or driving on his way to the Soldiers' Home. To carry out these plans a large amount of money was spent in the purchase of horses, a buggy, spurs, bowie knives, revolvers, and Spencer carbines. A flat-bottomed batteau was secured through Atzerodt, which lay on the Potomac in the neighborhood of Port Tobacco. It was said to have been capable of holding fifteen persons, and on it the President was to be ferried across the river.*

A road runs down in an almost straight line from Washington to the lower Potomac through two counties, Prince Georges and Charles, in Maryland. On the line of this road was Surrattsville; farther down near Bryantown was Dr. Mudd's farm and residence, thirty miles away from the capital; and still farther was Cox's home.[8] These points were all utilized by Booth and Herold in their bloody flight from justice. There were no two counties in the United States where there existed, during the war, more disloyalty than here. The road referred to was but slightly guarded and during the war was used by blockade runners, dispatch bearers, incendiaries, and murderers, and thousands in this way effected an entrance into the Confederacy. It is astonishing that the Government

* See the confessions of Atzerodt and Arnold, below, Chapter XXXI.

did not find out these things and put a stop to them. The only true friends the Union had down there were the colored people.

The Government at the trial of the assassins ridiculed the idea of abduction and demonstrated its impracticability. Booth's first plan was to capture—that much is certain—and the evidence adduced in these pages proves that fact. It is quite likely that at first he held up his band to this plan without saying anything to them about the murder. Samuel Arnold, John H. Surratt, and George A. Atzerodt have all confessed to a knowledge of and a participation in the plot to capture, but denied any complicity in the assassination scheme. Yet abduction was only a road to assassination, and the man or men who had guilty knowledge of it were morally just as guilty of murder as he who fired the fatal shot which ended Mr. Lincoln's life. Had they done their duty to the Government, they would have exposed the wicked scheme of abduction, and thus saved Mr. Lincoln's life. They preferred the other alternative, kept quiet, went ahead, and then received the pay that always accompanies such work.

Booth's lieutenants in the abduction plot were evidently selected with extreme care for their adaptability to the work in hand. John H. Surratt and David E. Herold were thoroughly acquainted with the geography of Lower Maryland and with every road leading from Washington to the Potomac River. Atzerodt was well posted in the regions bordering on the Potomac and Rappahannock rivers, and was a good boatman, having for some time been engaged in conveying parties over the river from Port Tobacco to the Virginia shore. Payne, Arnold, and O'Laughlin were ex-Confederates accustomed to the handling of firearms, and were well built, muscular men. Payne was a giant in strength, a man of extraordinary sang-froid, and of wonderful self-poise.

If the contemplated abduction of the President could have been carried to a successful issue, such an event would have been hailed by the world as one of extraordinary daring, and the parties concerned in it would have been proclaimed heroes and saviours of their Southern country, but there is no likelihood that it could have succeeded, and the chances are that any such attempt against the President would have been sternly resisted by himself and his attendants. It would have resulted in bloodshed, and it is more than probable that the conspirators themselves always realized that they would have to face just such a contingency.

But did Booth after all intend to confine himself to this chimerical scheme of capturing the President? Did he not have in view at this very time an ulterior and more deadly plan—the assassination of Abraham Lincoln?

A fact comes in play here that throws a world of light on this subject. During his visit to New York in this November of which we have been speaking, a very strange incident occurred which is calculated to expose Booth to the world in his true character as an assassin from the very start of the Conspiracy. The story is best told in the words of Mrs. Mary Hudspeth (afterwards Benson), who narrated the circumstance.

Said she: "In November 1864, after the presidential election, and on the day General Butler left New York, as I was riding on the Third Avenue cars in New York City, I overheard the conversation of two men. They were talking earnestly. One of them said he would leave for Washington the day after tomorrow. The other was going to Newburg, or Newbern that night. One of the two was a young man with false whiskers. This I noticed when the jolt of the car pushed his hat forward, and at the same time pushed his whiskers, by which I noticed that the front face was darker than it was under the whiskers. Judging by his conversation, he was a young man of education. The other man, whose name was Johnson, was not. I noticed that the hand of the younger man was very beautiful, and showed that he had led a life of ease and not of labor. They exchanged letters while in the car. When the one who had the false whiskers put back the letters in his pocket, I saw a pistol in his belt. I overheard the younger one say that he would leave for Washington the day after tomorrow; the other was very angry that it had not fallen to him to go to Washington.

"Both left the car before I did. After they had gone, my daughter, who was with me, picked up a letter which was lying on the floor of the car immediately under the seat where they sat and gave it to me, and I, thinking it was one of mine as I had letters of my own to post at the Nassau Street Post Office, took it without noticing it was not one of my own. When I got to the broker's where I was going with some gold, I noticed an envelope with two letters in it. After I examined the letters and found their character, I took them first to General [Winfield] Scott, who asked me to read them to him. He said he thought they were of the greatest importance and asked me to take them to General [John Adams] Dix. I did so." [9]

One of the letters and the more important was as follows:

Dear Louis: The time has at last come that we have all so wished for, and upon you everything depends. As it was decided before you left, we were to cast lots. Accordingly we did so and you are to be the Charlotte Corday of the nineteenth century.[10] When you remember the fearful solemn vow that was taken by us, you will feel that there is no draw-back—Abe must die and now. You can choose your weapons. The cup, the knife, the bullet. The cup failed us once and might again. Johnson who will give you this, has been like an enraged demon because it has not fallen on him to rid the world of the monster. He says the blood of his noble brother and his grey-headed father calls upon him for revenge, and revenge he will have; if he cannot wreak it upon the fountain head, he will upon some of the blood-thirsty generals. [General Benjamin Frank-lin] Butler would suit him. As our plans were all concocted and arranged, we separated, and as I am writing on my way to Detroit, I will only say that all rests with you. You know where to find your friends. Your dis-guises are so perfect and complete that without one knew your face, no police telegraphic dispatch would catch you. The English gentleman, Harcourt, must not act hastily. Remember he has ten days. Strike for your home — Strike for your country — Bide your time, but strike sure. Get introduced, congratulate him, listen to his stories—not many more will the brute tell to earthly friends. Do anything but fail, and meet us at the appointed place within the fortnight.

Inclose this note together with one from poor Leenea. I will give the reason for this when we meet. Return by Johnson. I wish I could go to you, but duty calls me to the West; you will probably hear from me in Washington. Sanders is doing us no good in Canada.

Believe me your brother in love,
Charles Selby.

The second letter was in the handwriting of a female:

St. Louis, October 21, 1864.

Dearest Husband: Why do you not come home? You left me for ten days only, and you now have been from home more than two weeks. In that long time, only sent me one short note—a few cold words—and a check for money, which I did not require. What has come over you? Have you forgotten your wife and child? Baby calls for papa until my heart aches. *We are so lonely* without you. I have written to you again and again, and, as a last resource, yesterday wrote to Charlie, begging him to see you and tell you to come home. I am so ill, not able to leave my room; if I was, I would go to you wherever you were, if in *this world*. Mamma says I must not write any more, as I am too weak. Louis, darling, do not stay away any longer from your heart-broken wife.

Leenea.[11]

The letter signed Charles Selby was traced directly to Booth. It was shown by the testimony of Mr. David H. Bates, a very competent expert for the Government and a gentleman of unquestioned character and ability, to have been in Booth's handwriting.[12] When a photograph of Booth was handed to Mrs. Hudspeth, she identified it as being the face of the younger of the two persons seen and described by her. A scar had been left upon his neck, the result of an operation performed by Dr. J. F. May sometime prior to the assassination. Mrs. Hudspeth also identified Booth by this scar. The surgeon general of the United States Army, J. K. Barnes, who made the post-mortem examination of Booth's body, also testified to the presence of such a scar.

At the trial of John H. Surratt in 1867, Judge Edwards Pierrepont, addressing the jury and speaking of these letters, said: "There is truth in those letters, gentlemen. And so thought those distinguished and gallant officers, General Scott and General Dix, when they were placed in their hands. General Dix forwarded the letters to Washington and they were finally placed in the hands of Mr. Lincoln. Gentlemen, there is a history about these letters that will never perish. I have shown you Mr. Lincoln's endorsement on the back. Mr. Lincoln had received a great many threatening letters, as had most of the officers of the Government, but had paid no regard to them, considering them as mere threats and no more. When this letter of Booth's was given to him, he went over to the War Department, and into the private office of the Secretary of War.

"After the door had been locked this letter was shown to the Secretary of War and it made a deep and lasting impression on that officer. It was then taken back to Mr. Lincoln. After the President had been shot, and the Secretary was standing by his bedside, the remembrance of the letter flashed across his mind, and it immediately occurred to him that it might have some connection with this murder. He sent Mr. Chas. A. Dana, Assistant Secretary of War, to the Presidential mansion to see if he could get it. It was found in a private drawer of Mr. Lincoln's in this

envelope, and with this endorsement in the President's own handwriting—
'Assassination.' " [13]

CHAPTER VIII

The meeting at the National Hotel on December 23, a conference concerning the Conspiracy · Extract from Surratt's Rockville lecture · Booth enlists Surratt in the Conspiracy to abduct the President · Surratt deserts the Adams Express Company, where he had secured employment · Visits Port Tobacco, the home of George A. Atzerodt · Booth meets Arnold and O'Laughlin in Baltimore the second time · First appearance of George A. Atzerodt, one of the conspirators, at Mrs. Surratt's house

The meeting at the National Hotel on the evening of December 23 between Booth, Mudd, and Surratt was evidently a conference looking to the execution of the Conspiracy. The testimony given by me in relation to it was deemed by the Commission as very important for many reasons. It established the fact of Booth's and Mudd's mutual acquaintance prior to the assassination.

In his Rockville lecture, Surratt uses the following language in reference to Booth:

In the fall of 1864, I was introduced to John Wilkes Booth, who, I was given to understand, wished to know something about the main avenues leading from Washington to the Potomac. We met several times, but as he seemed to be very reticent with regard to his purposes, and very anxious to get all the information out of me he could, I refused to tell him anything at all. At last I said to him, "It is useless for you, Mr. Booth, to seek any information from me at all; I know who you are and what are your intentions." He hesitated for some time, but finally said he would make known his views to me provided I would promise secrecy. I replied, "I will do nothing of the kind. You know well I am a Southern man. If you cannot trust me, we will separate." He then said, "I will confide my plans to you; but before doing so I will make known to you the motives that actuate me. In the Northern prisons are many thousands of our men whom the United States Government refuses to exchange. You know as well as I the efforts that have been made to bring about that much desired exchange. Aside from the great suffering they are compelled to undergo, we are sadly in want of them as soldiers. We cannot spare one man, whereas the United States Government is willing to let their own soldiers remain in our prisons because she has no need of the men. I have a proposition to submit to you, which I think if we can carry out will bring about the desired exchange." There was a long and ominous silence which I at last was compelled to break by asking, "Well, Sir, what is your proposition?" He sat quiet for an instant, and then, before answering me, arose and looked under the bed, into the wardrobe, in the doorway and the passage, and then said, "We will have to be careful; walls have ears." He then drew his chair close to me and in a whisper said, "It is to kidnap President Lincoln, and carry him off to Richmond!" "Kidnap President Lincoln!" I said. I confess I stood aghast at the proposition, and looked upon it as a foolhardy undertaking. To think of successfully seizing Mr. Lincoln in the capital of the United States surrounded by thousands of his soldiers, and carrying him off to Richmond, looked to me like a foolish idea. I told him as much. He went on to tell with what facility he could be seized in various places in and about Washington. As for example in his various rides to and from the Soldiers' Home, his summer residence. He entered into the minute details of the proposed capture, and even the various parts to be performed by the actors in the performance. I was amazed—thunderstruck—and in fact, I might also say, frightened at the unparalleled audacity of this scheme.[1]

Then Surratt, after acknowledging his amazement and fright at the audacity of the project, confesses to the following abject surrender to Booth:

After two days' reflection I told him I was willing to try it. I believed it to be practicable at that time, though I now regard it as a foolhardy undertaking. I hope you will not blame me for going thus far. I honestly thought an exchange of prisoners could be brought about could we have once obtained possession of Mr. Lincoln's person.

Such are Surratt's words. Thus he fell an early and willing victim to Booth's scheme of abducting the President. Out of his own mouth, he stands forever convicted.

Surratt here says that he *first* met Booth in the *fall of 1864.* The suggestion has often been thrown out to me that Surratt knew who Booth was when he met him in my presence on Seventh Street on the 23rd of December 1864. If that be true, then his non-recognition of Booth was a very clever scheme and shrewd trick to hoodwink me. It has always been my firm conviction ever since this introduction of which I speak that Surratt did not know who Booth was until that time.

I have felt that to whatever accountability John H. Surratt and his mother are to be held in the matter of the Conspiracy, that it must be confined to the period between December 23, 1864, and April 14, 1865, and that their connection with it and their fall from the position they had previously occupied in the world must be embraced in the space of those few months.

On the 3rd of April 1898, however, Surratt, then a resident of Baltimore, through a newspaper correspondent,* gave out a statement to the public, in which he denied that I was present when he first met Booth, and said that it was not Dr. Mudd at all who introduced him to Booth.

Here are his words:

(Question by correspondent.) Capt. Surratt, it has been stated in one of the principal magazines that Booth was anxious to get your co-operation on that very account, and that when you were introduced to him in Washington by Dr. Mudd, you thought at first that he was a Union spy. It is stated that you were with Wiechmann.

(Surratt.) Ah! Wilkes Booth. I loathe him. In the first place, Wilkes Booth was never introduced to me by Dr. Mudd on the street or anywhere else. Booth came to me with a letter of introduction from a valued and trusted friend. In the second place, Wiechmann was nowhere near when Booth presented his letter.[2]

I confess my amazement at the statement just quoted. If true, it convicts Surratt, by his own admission, of a degree of perfidy of which I never thought him capable. If he already knew who Booth was on that eventful night of December 23, 1864, when I was a personal witness of the actor's introduction to him by Dr. Mudd, as Mr. Boone, and, for his own reasons, did not wish to recognize him, then he conclusively estab-

* Hanson Hiss, [in an article that appeared in the] *Indianapolis Journal.*

lishes the fact that he was practicing a fraud on me from the very beginning almost of my advent to his mother's home. If he had been introduced to Booth in the fall of 1864, as he stated in his lecture of 1870, and if this introduction was by means of a letter from a trusted friend, as told for the first time in this interview with the correspondent, why did he not recognize Booth when he met him on the night of December 23, 1864, and why does he not tell the world who the trusted friend was that gave him the letter of introduction to Booth?

Ah! Thereby hangs a tale. Let us see. From what Surratt has told us in his public lecture of 1870, he was already at that time, December 23, 1864, a party to the Conspiracy for abducting Mr. Lincoln. Let anyone read that portion of his lecture which I have given at the beginning of this chapter, and he will reach the same conclusion. His non-recognition of Booth at the time was a part of the play just like the talk of some of the other conspirators about being in the "oil business," in "cotton speculation," and in "buying lands in Maryland."

There is not the slightest shadow of a doubt but that John H. Surratt met John Wilkes Booth on December 23, 1864, and was then introduced to him by Dr. Mudd. Let the reader turn to Chapter XXII of this book and read the affidavit of Captain Dutton, who carried Dr. Mudd to the Dry Tortugas, and he will be satisfied of the truth of what I state. And it is quite possible that Dr. Mudd himself did not then know that Surratt was already an acquaintance of Booth, for in this affidavit he states that he came to Washington, at the time referred to by me, to introduce Booth to Surratt.

Shortly after this meeting in December, Surratt stated to me one morning that an elderly gentleman residing in his neighborhood had advanced him three thousand dollars with which to engage in a *cotton speculation;* that he was going to Liverpool and then to Nassau, and thence to Matamoros, Mexico, where he would meet his brother Isaac. I swallowed his story but, like his many other falsehoods, it reacted on him to his eternal disgrace.

Now what was the meeting at the National Hotel on December 23 about? It was conspiracy, and one of the very first things Booth did after it occurred was to rent a frame shanty in the rear of Ford's Theater to use as a stable. It was fitted up with two stalls by Edward Spangler, a carpenter and scene shifter at the theater. The rent was paid monthly to Mr. James L. Maddox for a Mrs. Davis.[3] Booth in all his operations and talk seemed from the start to have Ford's Theater in his mind as an objective point from which to work. At one time he kept two horses in the stable and the buggy in which the President was to be placed in the event of his capture at the theater.

Booth returned to Washington on December 31, and remained until January 10, 1865; he came back on January 12 and left again on January 28.

Surratt, within a very short time after his presentation by the mutual friend, Dr. Mudd, to the arch-conspirator and assassin, is found doing Booth's bidding.*

According to the testimony of Mr. Henry R. McDonough,[4] cashier, he was employed by the Adams Express Company, from December 30, 1864, to January 13, 1865, but received pay for only the last two days of December. Mr. Charles C. Dunn, the Washington agent for the Express Company, stated that Surratt came into his office about two weeks after he had been employed and applied for a leave of absence. Astonishment being expressed that he should make such a request so soon after taking his position, he gave as a reason that his mother was going down into Prince Georges County and he desired to accompany her as her protector. Mr. Dunn informed him that leave of absence could not be granted. He left the office and went back to work. The next morning a lady called at the office who introduced herself as Mrs. Surratt, the mother of the young man of that name in his employ. She asked that he might have a leave of absence to accompany her to Prince Georges County, where she had urgent business. The agent told her he had no reason to change his mind. She urged her application and Mr. Dunn told her that it was impossible for him to yield. Surratt left the office the same day and never returned for duty.†

Now, why did he abandon his desk in the Adams Express Company's office without the permission of Mr. Dunn, never returning to draw the two weeks' pay due him? Why did he falsify his word about going into the country with his mother, and as her protector? Why did Mrs. Surratt falsify her word by stating that she wished him to accompany her into the country as her protector? Why did she personally endeavor by her influence with Mr. Dunn to secure the coveted leave of absence for her son? Ah! The ways of God are passing strange and John Surratt

* See the confession of Atzerodt, below, Chapter XXXI.
† Testimony of Dunn; see [*Surratt Trial*, I, 436].

has found it out. Nearly two years afterwards, about the time of his arrest in Egypt, there fell in Washington from a pocket in a vest which had been worn in life by the assassin, Booth, whose bones had already gone to decay, a little card on which appeared in John Surratt's handwriting these words:

I tried to secure leave but failed.

J. Harrison Surratt.

So testified Charles L. Dawson, the clerk of the National Hotel, who had overhauled Booth's clothing.* The reason for Surratt's falsehood and that of his mother is now as clear as day. It was Booth's affair. It was he who was interested in Surratt's trip to the country and so deeply interested that Surratt on January 13, 1865, left his desk and abandoned his kindly employer without so much as a thank you; taking "French leave" as he called it. His "ready hand and willing heart" were henceforth to be enlisted in another cause.

Surratt went into the country after leaving the Adams Express Company, but without his mother. He rode down to Port Tobacco, a country town in the lower part of Maryland, and what happened there is best told in the words of Mr. Eddy Martin, a witness at his trial in 1867.

Mr. Martin, who was a highly respected gentleman, was at Port Tobacco at that time on important business and with the knowledge of the President of the United States, Mr. Lincoln. He testified as follows:

I remained in Port Tobacco ten days in order to get an opportunity to cross the river. I employed a man by the name of Andrew Atzerodt and paid him to make some arrangements to cross the river. His full name was George A.; he went by the name of Andrew.

This was about the 10th of January, 1865, from the 7th to the 15th. I saw Surratt there on [one] occasion and was introduced to him; it was during the evening.[5] No particular conversation passed between us. I think I told him I was going to cross the river. I remained that night. The next day when he came to supper he had on his leggings. I asked him if he was going to cross the river. He replied that he was going back to Washington; that he was employed in the Adams Express Office; that he had three days leave of absence; that his time was nearly expired and that it was necessary for him to start back that night.

* Testimony of Dawson; see [*Surratt Trial*, I, 337].

I am not positive whether I saw Atzerodt and Surratt speak at all with each other. I had a conversation with Atzerodt the night Surratt left; I was losing confidence in Atzerodt. I thought, although I had been paying him pretty liberally, that he had been throwing off on me. I stayed up pretty late that night. Atzerodt came to the hotel at 11 o'clock. I accused him of intending to cross over that night with other parties; told him I had been paying him all he asked, and that I must cross by the first boat. He denied that any boat was going to cross that night. I reiterated the charge I had made of duplicity on his part. He then made this explanation. He said no one was going to cross that night, but on Wednesday night a large party of ten or twelve persons would cross; that he had been engaged that day in *"buying boats"*; that they were going to have relays of horses on the road between Port Tobacco and Washington. Said I, "What does this mean?" He said he could not tell. After a moment I said, "I suppose that Confederate officers were to escape from prison and that he had made arrangements to cross them over into Virginia." He said, "Yes, and I am going to get well paid for it." *

Well, now, what was the real purpose of the purchase of boats and these relays of horses? It was undoubtedly a part of the program in the contemplated abduction of the President. Why did Surratt return to the city of Washington in the *night?* He said he was going back to the Express Company, but he never did. There was about as much truth in that as there was in his talk of cotton speculation, or Mudd's talk about Booth's purchase of his farm in Maryland. His mission, no doubt, had something more behind it than the retention of a mere fifty-dollar clerkship in the Adams Express Company.

Martin in the foregoing testimony does not show that he at any time saw Surratt and Atzerodt together during his stay in Port Tobacco, but he leaves it to be inferred that they were together. All speculation on this point, however, is set at rest by the admission of Atzerodt which Mr. Doster, his counsel, made for him before the Military Commission. It was to this effect:

> John Surratt and Booth *wanted a man* who understood boating, and could get a boat and ferry a party over on a capture. Surratt knew Atzerodt, and under the influence of the great promises of a for-

* See [*Surratt Trial*, I, 213–16].

tune, the prisoner (Atzerodt) consented to furnish the boat and do the ferrying over.

This statement by Atzerodt when he was on trial for his life is conclusive as to the object of Surratt's visit to Port Tobacco at the time mentioned by Mr. Martin. It shows that it was Surratt who induced Atzerodt under the promises of a big fortune to join the Conspiracy to capture the President. It was Atzerodt who was to secure the boat and do the ferrying over.*

Having had his stable prepared, Booth, who between January 10 and 12 was in Baltimore, again met Samuel Arnold and Michael O'Laughlin. At that time, he delivered to them a trunk in which there were two guns and cap cartridges which were placed in the gun stock. These guns were called Spencer rifles or carbines. The trunk also contained a number of revolvers, knives, belts, cartridges and cartridge boxes, caps, canteens, all equipped for service. They were to be used in case of pursuit by the military. There were also two pairs of handcuffs with which to handcuff the President. Booth's trunk was too heavy to be handled easily and he therefore entrusted the pistols, knives, and handcuffs to O'Laughlin and Arnold to ship or take to Washington.

Booth also purchased in Baltimore a horse, a set of harness, and a buggy, which he left with O'Laughlin and Arnold to drive to Washington. The box containing the handcuffs, knives, and pistols was shipped to Washington by O'Laughlin and Arnold and reached that city about the same time as the men themselves.

When the two Baltimoreans arrived in Washington they met Booth on the street as they were passing Ford's Theater. Booth invited his confederates into a restaurant, where they all had a drink, and then told them that his theater plan had been changed slightly. He had at one time informed them of his design at the theater, in case his plan at the Soldiers' Home should not prove successful.

In the evening the trio went to the theater and Booth posted Arnold and O'Laughlin on all the different back entrances and showed them how feasible was the plan of capturing the President in that place. He also told them that he had bought two horses.

Booth, according to Arnold, at this time always seemed to be pressed with business with a man unknown to him then, but known to him (Ar-

* Argument of Mr. Doster, Pitman, p. 306.

nold) afterwards by the name of John Surratt; most of Booth's time was spent with him.*

On January 17, 1865, I was surprised to receive a letter, via Flag of Truce boat, from my patron, the Right Reverend John McGill, the Catholic bishop of Richmond, Virginia. Ever since leaving St. Charles College in 1862, I had been waiting for an opportunity to resume my studies for the ministry. Before I could do so, it was necessary for me to have the consent of my bishop. I had written to him repeatedly by Flag of Truce boat about the matter in 1863 and 1864, and finally when his permission came, I at once wrote to Father Dubreuil, the superior of the seminary in Baltimore, and communicated to him what was to me very good news. Unfortunately I have lost the bishop's letter, but Father Dubreuil's reply is herewith given.

> *St. Mary's Seminary,*
> *Baltimore, Md., January 19, 1865.*

Dear Mr. Wiechmann:

I am just in receipt of yours and was anyhow going to write to you to-day to inform you that a letter from your bishop has reached me the day before yesterday which I see is of the same date as yours.

You may depend, my dear friend, on my interest in you. All that I could do to make your bishop favorable to you, I have done. Now, I wish to have a talk with you on this matter. Come to Baltimore, at least for a few hours. I think you may have a leave of absence for one day, if necessary.

> Yours affectionately devoted in Christ,
> F. Paul Dubreuil.

I hastened to comply with Father Dubreuil's request and communicated to Surratt my intention to visit Baltimore, but without saying anything about the letters I had received. I merely informed him that I intended to visit St. Mary's Seminary. He then replied that he was also going to Baltimore. Accordingly, we left Washington on the same day, January 21, 1865. We stopped at the Maltby House in Baltimore; our names appear on the register of that hotel as occupying the same room, No. 127.

* See the confession of Arnold, below, Chapter XXXI.

The 21st of January of that year came on Saturday. The following Sunday morning, Surratt called for a càrriage, saying he had three hundred dollars in his possession, and that he intended to call upon some gentleman in Baltimore on private business. He informed me in a sort of a nonchalant way that he did not want me to go along. His language nettled me and I politely answered him that I was not anxious to go with him or know his affairs as I had business of my own to look after. What his private business was with the gentleman whom he was going to see, he did not state to me then or at any subsequent time.

At that period, however, there were residing in Baltimore two of the Booth conspirators, Samuel Arnold and Michael O'Laughlin, and there was boarding at the house of Mrs. Margaret Branson, on Eutaw Street, Lewis Payne, the man who, on the night of the 14th of April 1865, attempted the murder of the Honorable William H. Seward, Secretary of State.

Were any of these the man whom Surratt went to see on private business? Or to whom he was to pay the three hundred dollars? There is no testimony to show that he then met Arnold, O'Laughlin, or Payne, but the inference is that he did.

I visited Father Dubreuil that Sunday morning and made arrangements with him to begin my studies in St. Mary's Seminary on the 1st of September 1865. This was the business that carried me to Baltimore. I returned to Washington the same afternoon, and it is my impression that I went back alone. Surratt, at any rate, was again in Washington in a very short time.

Not long after this in the latter part of the same month, January, on returning one afternoon from my work, I happened to meet a man in Mrs. Surratt's parlor whom John Surratt introduced to me as Mr. Atzerodt. Mrs. Surratt, Miss Fitzpatrick, and Miss Anna Surratt were in the room at the time. The young ladies did not or could not correctly pronounce the man's name, and understanding that he came from Port Tobacco, jestingly styled him Mr. "Port Tobacco," and thus he was known to them and many others afterwards, and thus he will pass into history.

I had never seen the man before. Surratt himself presented him to his mother, to his sister and Miss Fitzpatrick. He looked like a German, spoke broken English, and was of German descent.[6] His complexion was swarthy, his figure low and squat; he had ugly eyes, almost greenish in their expression, and a badly shaped head.

Atzerodt was a wagon maker and smith by trade. For a long time during the war, he ran a boat across the Potomac to help persons escape into the Confederacy. It was in this way, no doubt, that Surratt became acquainted with him. He was a valuable man because of his knowledge of the river and of the adjacent country in Maryland and Virginia. When in Washington, he always put up at the Pennsylvania House (sometimes called the Kimmel House) on C Street between Sixth and Seventh.

If any responsibility is to be attached to Mrs. Surratt for receiving and harboring this man, the full measure of that responsibility must be meted out to her son, who was the means of bringing him there, and introducing him to the inmates of the house.

From this time forward, he was a frequent visitor at Mrs. Surratt's home. Although destitute of learning and not possessed of much refinement, Atzerodt was a man full of fun, country humor, and quaint stories.

John Surratt knew who Andrew Atzerodt was when he came to Washington and to his mother's home, for he had been down to Port Tobacco in the early part of the month, and made arrangements with Atzerodt about securing the boat on which the President was to be ferried over in the event of his capture. The testimony in this respect is positive and absolutely unimpeachable.[7] The Government also knew who Andrew Atzerodt was when it laid its hands upon him and charged him with conspiracy to assassinate Vice-President Johnson.

On the last of January 1865, Booth brought the one-eyed horse, which he had purchased of George Gardiner through the aid of Dr. Mudd, to the stable of William E. Cleaver, on Sixth Street near Maryland Avenue. In about ten days afterwards he brought another horse, a very light bay horse. Booth and Surratt went to the stable quite frequently and generally together, and Booth paid the keep for the horses.

Booth was at the stable on the 27th or 28th of January, and paid the board for one of the horses to February 1. Samuel Arnold was in company with him. Booth told Cleaver, the stable keeper, in Arnold's presence, that he had sold the horse to Arnold, and that he (Arnold) was to pay the board from that time on.

Arnold paid the livery for eight days, to the eighth day of February, when the two horses were taken to Howard's livery stable on G Street near Seventh, almost in the rear of Mrs. Surratt's house, and here they remained until March 31.

On the 25th of January, Surratt was in Cleaver's office for a few minutes. He told Cleaver that he was going down into the country to T.B.[8] to meet a party and help them to cross the river, that he and Booth had some bloody work to do: that they were going to kill Abe Lincoln, the d——d old scoundrel: that he had ruined Maryland and the country. He said that if nobody else did it, he would do it himself, and pulled out a pistol and laid it on the desk. Surratt was under the influence of liquor at the time, so Cleaver stated.*

In harmony with this kind of talk and confirmatory of Surratt's feelings and actions is the following from E. L. Smoot, a citizen of Charles County, Maryland, who was acquainted with Surratt and had known him for three or four years. In January or February he paid Smoot a visit and stayed with him overnight. Smoot was then living in Prince Georges County, a few miles from Surrattsville. Smoot joked his guest about going to Richmond. He never acknowledged to Smoot that he had been to Richmond, but he laughed and said, at the same time raising his hand to his neck in illustration of how the thing was done: "If the Yankees knew what I have done or what I am doing, they would stretch this old neck of mine." †

All these remarks on the part of Surratt indicate how full his mind now was of the ideas and schemes which his newly made friend Booth had evidently planted there.

* [*Surratt Trial,* I, 204–8.]
† [*Surratt Trial,* I, 190.]

CHAPTER IX

No sooner had Surratt returned from Port Tobacco, the home of Andrew Atzerodt, than he found it necessary to go to New York. This was early in February. Here, according to his own words, to me, he called on John Wilkes Booth, and was introduced by him to his mother and to his brother Edwin. He was particularly well pleased with his visit; could never get done talking about the elegant parlors of the Booths, nor of their magnificent home.

Booth, as is shown by the register at the National Hotel, had left Washington on January 28, 1865, and did not return until February 22, at which time he occupied room No. 231 in company with John T. H. Wentworth and John McCullough.[1]

During his absence he was in New York and Baltimore, and Surratt, from his own admissions to me, met him in New York.

Surratt, in fact, at this time, was continually on the go and away from his home much of the time. He was not now busying himself about getting an appointment or securing work. He always appeared to have plenty of money and had the air and actions of a man thoroughly preoccupied with important business affairs.

On the 10th of February, Samuel Arnold and Michael O'Laughlin arrived in Washington and engaged rooms at the house of Mrs. Mary T. Van-Tine, No. 420 D Street. John Wilkes Booth called on them frequently and sometimes in his buggy.

Whenever he found them out he would leave a note for them asking them to come to his stable at the theater. Mrs. Van-Tine once saw in their room a heavy revolver. They were sometimes out all night.

Arnold and O'Laughlin told Mrs. Van-Tine that they were in the "oil business." *

In the early part of January 1865, Lewis Thornton Powell made his appearance in Baltimore. He was the same young Confederate soldier whom Booth had met in the theater at Richmond in 1861, and as he is such a prominent character in the Conspiracy, a short sketch of his history and movements subsequent to 1861 may not prove uninteresting.

"He was the son of Rev. George C. Powell, a Baptist minister, who lived at Live Oak Station on the railroad between Jacksonville and Tallahassee, in the state of Florida, and was born in Alabama in the year 1844.[2] Besides himself his father had six daughters and two sons. He lived for some time in Worth and Stewart Counties, Georgia, and in 1859 moved to Florida. His father was born in Virginia, and was related to Dr. William L. Powell of Alexandria, of that state. The Powell family was one of great prominence and distinction in Virginia.

"At the breaking out of the war, when but a lad, Lewis Powell was engaged in superintending his father's plantation and a number of slaves.

"In 1861 war broke out; —war, the scourge and pestilence of the race. The signal which spread like a fire was not long in reaching Live Oak Station. His two brothers enlisted, and Lewis though but sixteen, became a member of Capt. Stuart's Company in the Second Florida Infantry, commanded by Col. Ward, and was ordered to Richmond. Here, as has been seen, he first met John Wilkes Booth. At Richmond his regiment joined the army of General Lee and was attached to A. P. Hill's corps. With it he shared the fate of the rebel army, passed through the Peninsular campaign, the battles of Chancellorsville and Antietam. At this latter place he heard that his two brothers had been killed at Murfreesboro.

"Finally, on the 3rd of July 1863, in the charge upon the Federal center at Gettysburg, he was wounded, taken prisoner, and detailed as a nurse in Pennsylvania College Hospital.

"From Gettysburg, he was sent to West Building Hospital, Pratt St., Baltimore, and remained there until October 1863, when seeing no

* Testimony of Mrs. Van-Tine, Pitman, p. 222.

hope of an exchange, he deserted for his regiment, and while walking through Winchester, Va., met a regiment of cavalry at Fauquier." *

Powell either attached himself to this independent body of cavalry which operated in the Shenandoah Valley and Piedmont region of Virginia, or organized himself into a command of his own. In this section of the country he soon became known as the boldest of the bold, and the rashest of the reckless. He subsequently became a member of Company B, [General John S.] Mosby's Battalion, and the rolls of that company, if preserved among the Confederate archives at Washington, bear his name. He was a very reserved and silent, but restless man. He was what might be called a "prowler." He rode at night and was almost continually on the go from place to place. One day he dismounted from his horse, shouldered five newly split rails, rode a mile, and then deposited them in the wood yard of a home where he was acquainted.

In Scott's history of Mosby's Battalion the writer, in describing the fight with Captain Blazer, who came to capture Mosby but unfortunately got captured by him, in the Shenandoah Valley in 1864, says: "Captain Blazer do thy speediest, for those are upon thy track who smite and spare not—Syd Ferguson, Cap Maddux and the terrible Lewis Powell."

This would indicate that Powell was acting with Mosby's command, if he was not a member of it, and shows that his reputation had an element of terror in it even at that day. Powell was a good horseman and knew all the byways and highways and short cuts across the fields and through the woods, and he used to say that he could travel from Warrenton to Winchester, or from Fairfax Court House to Port Royal, in a third of the time by his routes than it would take to travel the roads. He would go off alone, penetrate the line of the enemy, and come back with prisoners, horses, and plunder. At one time he had fifteen or twenty horses, all of them branded with "U. S." and the property of the Government at Washington. Powell was with Mosby's men all during the raiding in the rear of General Hunter's army in June 1864, when the celebrated "burning order" was being put in operation. During those raids very few prisoners were taken, but on the contrary it was no uncommon sight to find a dead soldier almost anywhere in the valley with a notice pinned to his back, "Shot for house burning."

* From Doster's argument, Pitman [pp. 308–17].

A great many under pretext were, no doubt, shot who never saw a "house burning"—a pretext which was gladly seized upon as an excuse for their atrocities.

Powell was also one of the men who made the celebrated calico raid in the valley in the fall of 1864, when a train of calico was captured and the calico strewn all over the country for miles around. In retaliation for shooting General Hunter's men, a soldier named Anderson and several others were captured and shot by the Federals at Port Royal. The speed of Powell's mare was all that saved his neck from being stretched on that occasion. He escaped with a number of bullet holes through his clothing. On one occasion the house in which he was stopping was surrounded by the Federals when Powell blacked his face with lampblack and walked out of the house. One of the soldiers remarked: "That is a d—n tall nigger," and let him pass on without molestation.

Among other incidents relating to Powell the following may be mentioned: "During a cannonading at one time between Jackson and Banks across the Shenandoah river, a shell entered the gable end of a house on the Valley pike and exploded. It struck a bureau at which a young lady was dressing her hair in an upper room, chipped off a large wedge-shaped piece of the bureau and drove it into her back under the right shoulder blade. The same day a young Confederate soldier who had been wounded was brought to the house by some of his companions. The name of the girl was Lily Bowie; that of the soldier was Lewis Powell. Miss Bowie was the daughter of a gentleman from Alabama who had married a Virginia lady. Under these singular circumstances these two Southern young people met in Virginia, wounded almost to their death, and formed an attachment for each other which only ended when the one breathed out the last of life upon the scaffold at Washington, and the other returned a broken-hearted woman to her far-away home in the South."

It was said at the time of the assassination trial that Powell could not write, but this was a mistake. He told Major Smith, who arrested him at Mrs. Surratt's, that he could write and he told the truth. It is a matter of fact that Powell had a tolerably good education, as much, perhaps, as usually falls to the lot of Southern youths living in the country, without special educational advantages, at his time of life. He was undoubtedly a man of most respectable birth and family, and possessed qualifications enough to have made a very useful citizen had they been employed in raising cotton and sugar cane instead of killing Cabinets.

The following is a specimen of Powell's work as found in his handwriting in an old docket of a Justice of the Peace, which was used by him as a sort of scrapbook and diary, now in the possession of Miss Lily Bowie, who, however, is Miss Lily Bowie no longer, she having been married since the period of which we have been writing:

In battle, in the fullness of pride and strength, little recks the soldier whether the hissing bullet sings his sudden requiem or the cords of life are severed by the sharp steel.

L. Powell.

Powell continued in this kind of life until about the 1st of January 1865. On that day, according to the testimony of John Grant and wife, he saved the lives of two Union soldiers by rescuing them from a Confederate soldier who had threatened to shoot them.

He now determined to leave Fauquier and make his way North. He therefore bade goodbye to his sweetheart, Miss Bowie. After leaving Fauquier, he went to Noaksville, on the Virginia Midland Railroad, where he left his horse and exchanged his uniform for a suit of citizen's clothes. He then proceeded to walk down the railroad towards Alexandria, near which city he met some Federal pickets and, representing himself as a refugee, was conveyed to Alexandria, where he took the oath of allegiance to the United States Government as "Lewis Payne of Fauquier County, Va.," and was allowed to pass through the lines. Soon he made his way to Baltimore, where he secured board and lodgings in the house of Mrs. Margaret Branson, No. 16 North Eutaw Street, a lady whom he had met in the hospital at Gettysburg in 1863, and here he resolved to wait for the return of peace.

He remained at Mrs. Branson's house six weeks and a few days. During his sojourn there he once asked a negro servant to clean up his room, and she gave him some impudence and said she would not do it. For this he struck her, threw her on the floor, stamped her body and struck her on the forehead, and said he would kill her. The girl had him arrested and brought before the provost marshal, and Powell was ordered north of Philadelphia.*

"While in this pitiable condition he was one day dragging himself along past Barnum's Hotel, Baltimore; a poor creature overcome by destiny. Suddenly a familiar voice hailed him. Looking up the steps he saw the face of the Richmond actor, John Wilkes Booth. The actor on his side expressed astonishment to find him in such a plight, for the light in the eyes of a desperate man needs no translation, and in that distant city. Powell answered him in a few words, 'Booth, I want bread—I am starving.' In ordinary circumstances Booth would have said, come in and eat, but just now he was filled with a mighty scheme for he had been to Canada and was lying in wait for agents. So he did not give him to eat; he did not tell him to go and die, but he seized with eagerness on this poor man's hunger to wind about him his accursed toils, saying, 'I will give you as much money as you want, but first you must swear to stick to me. It is in the "Oil Business." ' An empty stomach is not captious of oaths and Powell then swore a fatal oath binding his very soul to Booth, and went in and feasted. Next morning Booth gave him money enough to buy a change of clothing, and keep him for a week.

"Powell now became anxious to know what plan it was that was to make him rich, but Booth answered evasively that it was in the 'Oil Business.'

"Booth knew full well that he had to do with a desperate man, but he knew also that any proposition of a guilty character might as yet be rejected. He must get full control of this desperate tool and instill into his nature all the subtle monomania of his own. Accordingly he proceeded to secure every thought and emotion of Powell. With a master pencil he painted before the eyes of this boy the injuries of the South and the guilt of her oppressors. He reminded him of the devastated homes, negroes freed, women ravished, the graves of his brothers on a thousand hillsides.

"When his victim was caught and ready, Booth hastened to impart

* The foregoing incidents in relation to the life of Powell (Payne) [pp. 80–83] are taken from an article in *The Philadelphia Weekly Times* of June 3, 1882, written by Mr. Lewis Payne of Fauquier, Virginia, formerly U. S. attorney for Wyoming Territory, whose name Powell assumed.

his mysterious plans for the abduction of the President at the Soldiers' Home in Washington." *

Payne entered heartily into Booth's schemes and became one of his most powerful and trusty lieutenants, and it was not long before he found his way to Washington City, and to Mrs. Surratt's house.

Matters had gone on quietly at this place until the latter part of February, when Powell, alias Wood, alias Payne, who was destined to play so important a part in the great tragedy, unfortunately for the Surratts, made his first appearance at their home.

It was in the evening, I remember the occurrence distinctly. We all had had our dinners and were assembled in the parlor for an evening's enjoyment. Mrs. Surratt, Anna, her daughter, Miss Fitzpatrick, and myself were there, and were having a very pleasant and sociable time together. Sometime during the evening the door bell was rung. Answering the summons, I found standing before me a tall and robust individual with very black hair and ruddy countenance. He was a young man and wore a dark felt hat, rather slouchy, and was clad in a seedy black overcoat. His two hands were buried deep in his overcoat pockets. Looking me full in the face, he asked if Mr. Surratt lived there and if he was at home. I replied that it was Mr. Surratt's home but that he was not in. Then he inquired if Mrs. Surratt was at home, and I told him she was. He thereupon expressed a desire to see her and gave his name as Mr. Wood.

Returning to the parlor, I informed Mrs. Surratt that a gentleman at the front door, who had given his name as Mr. Wood, wished to see her. Without further preliminary she bade me introduce him. Then he was ushered into the room and presented by me to Mrs. Surratt and to the other ladies as Mr. Wood. I had never before seen the man; he was an utter stranger to me. When the introduction was given Mrs. Surratt was seated on the sofa. The man approached her and said something to her which I did not understand. I do not know what was the purport of his remarks, but in a few moments the mistress came to me and remarked, "The gentleman would like to have some supper, and inasmuch as the dining room is disarranged, I will be very much obliged to you if you will take the meal to him in your own room." Of course, I gave my permission, for I was always kind to this woman of whom I never suspected any wrong.

* Argument of Mr. W. E. Doster before the Military Commission.

I sat down while Mr. Wood was eating and watched him intently; he was so silent and uncommunicative. He had the eye of an eagle and was very self-possessed. I asked him whence he came. "I am from Baltimore," was his answer, "and a clerk in the china store of Mr. Parr." Nothing further was said as he continued to devour his food; he ate voraciously as if very hungry. Upon the conclusion of his meal, he said he would like to retire for the night. He was given a bed in the attic. The next morning when I arose he was gone and I did not see him again for several weeks.

How often I have pondered over this event. All unconscious to myself I was entertaining a man then in the service and pay of John Wilkes Booth; one who would ever figure as one of the greatest criminals of the world. Friendly and unsuspicious, in this way, I became an involuntary witness to transactions and events which I regarded at the time as trivial, and occurring only in the ordinary routine of everyday life, but which were destined to become of the greatest importance when the conspirators were placed on trial for their lives, and held to accountability for the murder of Lincoln.

About the 22nd of the same month, a buggy was driven one evening to the house by John H. Surratt with a lady in it. Mrs. Surratt called to me to assist her in getting out, and to bring into the house her trunk, a very small affair, which I did.

The woman was rather diminutive in height, but very active and sprightly in all her movements. She wore what was called in those days a "mask," a kind of short veil, covering the face only as far as the chin. I did not succeed in seeing her face at all, and I believe that it was intended that I should not. She was not introduced to me, but afterwards I ascertained her name to be Mrs. [Sarah Antoinette] Slater, at least that was the name under which she was traveling. She remained in the house only one night, and I gave up my room to her use. I learned subsequently that she was a dispatch bearer, and Mrs. Surratt said that she was a North Carolinian by birth; that she could speak French well, and that if she got into any trouble the French consul could help her out.

After her departure I discovered in the closet of my room a delicate pair of ladies' shoes, evidently belonging to someone who was the owner of a small foot. I laughingly made some remark about this to

Mrs. Surratt, but she grew very angry, and gave me to understand that it was none of my business.

Mrs. Slater at this time had come from Montreal or New York and was on her way to the South. The same evening she came to Mrs. Surratt's house, she met on the pavement in front of the house one Augustus Howell. She was afterwards taken by him to Virginia, and he again met her in Richmond in the latter part of February. Howell himself had been at Mrs. Surratt's before the arrival of Mrs. Slater there. His visit occupied two days and a half. He came about the 20th of February. According to his own statement, he had made the acquaintance of the Surratt family in the latter part of 1863.[3] Before the war he had resided principally in Prince Georges County, Maryland; for about two years he had lived in King George County, Virginia; he had been in the Confederate service up to July 1862.

I knew nothing of him or his antecedents. He was introduced to me by Surratt as Mr. Spencer. I did not know what his business was, but I soon found out that he was in the habit of running the blockade from Maryland into Virginia. I had a good deal of conversation with him, and endeavored to glean from him all the information I could. I resented in my own mind his stay in the house. He taught me a cipher which he said he learned from a magician's book, and had been familiar with for six or seven years.

At the Conspiracy trial, when he was shown the cipher found among the effects of Booth, he said it was the same as he had taught me, and Booth's cipher, by the testimony of Mr. Charles A. Dana, was the same as that used by the Confederates. But I never made any use of it except to translate a few poems into it.

On the 24th of March, Howell was arrested and placed in Old Capitol Prison, and was there when Mr. Lincoln was assassinated. When I heard this I felt satisfied, for I regarded him as an unsafe man, and one who was engaged in an unlawful business.

The second inauguration of the President was now at hand, and Washington in consequence was rapidly filling up with visitors from all sections of the country. The newspapers were alive with accounts of the approaching event, and occasionally some of them would contain some prediction of disaster, or hint at something mysterious that was going to take place. I remember one morning while at breakfast reading aloud from the *Morning Chronicle* the following extract, dated February 27, 1865, copied from the *Louisville Journal:*

> We have reason to say that the rebels are expecting very soon to startle the whole country, and astonish the world. No matter what our reason may be, it is a good one.

This at once arrested Mrs. Surratt's attention, and she remarked that something was going to happen to Old Abe which would prevent him from taking his seat; that General Lee was going to execute a movement which would startle the *whole world*. What that movement was or what she meant by her remark, she never at any time revealed to me. Like her son, she was probably full of Booth's scheme of capturing the President and running him off to Richmond, and it was undoubtedly this which would prevent him from taking his seat.

When the assassination took place, this remark in connection with the quotation from the *Louisville Journal* came back to my mind, and after the trial was over my great interest in the matter led me to examine the files of the *Morning Chronicle* to find, if possible, the article in question, and as is seen I was successful.

CHAPTER X

Booth visits the Capitol on March 3, 1865 · He makes a peculiar remark · Dr. Mudd at the National Hotel · 4th of March 1865 · Reinauguration of President Lincoln · Booth on the grandstand · Probably intended to murder the President at that time · Affidavits as to his actions from several police officers

The evening of March 3, 1865, in Washington was a very joyous and happy one. Numbers of bands of music were on the streets discoursing patriotic airs, and thousands of officers and soldiers in gay uniforms enlivened the scene.

Booth visits the Capitol on March 3, 1865

It was too exciting an occasion for me to remain indoors, and, therefore, after supper I invited John Surratt to take a walk with me down the street to enjoy the sights that were to be witnessed. We went down Sixth Street, and along Pennsylvania Avenue to Eighth Street. Here Surratt left me. In a short time I returned to the house of Mrs. Surratt, a little after seven o'clock. I was surprised to find John Wilkes Booth and John H. Surratt together in the parlor and engaged in an animated conversation. I proposed to them that we should go to the Capitol. The Congress then in session was on the eve of adjournment. We went to the House of Representatives, and while on our way to the gallery a strange circumstance occurred. Booth and I were in the rear of Surratt. A statue of Mr. Lincoln stood in a corner on one of the landings. It attracted the actor's attention. "Who is that?" said he. "That is Mr. Lincoln," was my reply. "What's *he* doing in here before his time?" was the further query. I made no response to this but went on. Surratt did not hear it. This incident has never been given by me to the public, and I have stated it to but one individual.* It was not brought out at either of the trials in 1865 or 1867. Indeed, it only recurred to my mind at some time subsequent to the trial of 1865, when on my way to the House of Representatives, I again beheld this same statue. What Booth meant by the remark, I cannot surmise nor am I able to conjecture, but it certainly revealed a bitter animus towards the distinguished President. Booth in his actions with me was always the gentleman. He had never before spoken to me in an unfriendly manner of Mr. Lincoln.

Dr. Mudd was in Washington on April [March] 3, and at the National Hotel. On this occasion, he stumbled into the room of one Mr. Marcus P. Norton, and then excused himself, saying, "I thought I was in the room of John Wilkes Booth." His manner excited the attention of Mr. Norton, who followed him to the stairs. Mudd looked around and was evidently ill at ease because he had attracted so much notice.[1]

The 4th of March 1865, the day of Mr. Lincoln's reinauguration as President, was a very memorable event. Can they who were in Washington ever forget it? A heavy rain had fallen in the morning and continued until about eleven o'clock. The streets were wet and almost impassable for the mud that lined them, and the inaugural procession

* Mr. Thomas Donaldson of Philadelphia.

was compelled to make its way as best it could through this miry mass.

Just as Mr. Lincoln was about to take the oath of office, the sun shone out and flashed across the portico, and on the Bible in his hand. It was hailed as a bright omen of the future, and an immense shout went out from the throats of the assembled multitude.

John Wilkes Booth was in the crowd that day on the grandstand and witnessed the inauguration. And it has come to be the general belief that he intended to kill the President that morning. Says General Henry L. Burnett, in a paper read at a meeting of the Commandery of the State of New York, Military Order, Loyal Legion, December 5, 1888:

> It was a part of the unwritten history of the time that on the day of President Lincoln's second inauguration, and while he was delivering his inaugural address, Booth sat near and just behind him, with the purpose to stab him then and there, if any fit opportunity should occur, in the press and confusion of the crowd, for him to do the deed, and make his escape; that while the noble Lincoln was uttering those immortal words "With malice toward none, with charity *toward* all," this armed assassin was near his side clutching the knife with which to stab him to death. Another curious fact connected with this event and known to many, was, that Booth secured his ticket of admission to these ceremonies through a United States Senator, one of the most faithful and earnest of the Republican group, and that it was procured through the intercession of his daughter, who, although she had only a casual acquaintance with Booth, had often seen him on the stage, and, like many of the romantic young ladies of our own city and time, had caught the fever of stage-hero worship.[2]

And the Honorable Ward H. Lamon (now deceased), in a lengthy article in the *Philadelphia Times* in 1887, makes a most valuable contribution to history on this point. I here present the most salient portions of his paper and the affidavits in full. The matter is of so much importance that it cannot be left out of this narrative without destroying a good deal of its interest and value.

> A tragedy was planned for that day which has no parallel in the history of criminal audacity, if considered as nothing more than a crime intended. Its consummation would have been immeas-

urably more tragical than the awful scene witnessed at Ford's Theater on the memorable 14th of April following.

Everybody knows what throngs assemble at the Capitol to witness the imposing ceremonies attending the inauguration of the President of the United States. It is amazing that any human being could have seriously entertained the thought of assassinating Mr. Lincoln in the presence of such a concourse of citizens. And yet there was such a man in that assemblage. He was there for the single purpose of murdering the illustrious leader who for the second time was about to assume the burden of the Presidency. That man was John Wilkes Booth. Proof of his identity and a detailed account of his movements while attempting to reach the platform where Mr. Lincoln stood, will be found in the following affidavits:

District of Columbia, county of Washington, ss.

John Plants, being duly sworn, says: That he was a policeman stationed at the east door of the rotunda of the Capitol, near Major B. B. French, the Commissioner of Public Buildings, on the day of the inauguration of President Lincoln in March, 1865. Soon after the President passed out of the door to the platform where the inaugural ceremonies were to be held, a stranger forcibly broke through the line formed by the police to keep off the crowd and endeavored to gain the door where I was stationed and through which the Judges of the Supreme Court and the President had just passed. Lieutenant Westfall [3] seized this man, who seemed to be greatly excited, and after a severe struggle succeeded, with the assistance of others, in forcing him back. After the assassination of the President, affiant was shown a picture of J. Wilkes Booth, which he and others recognized as the man whom Lieutenant Westfall had prevented from getting to the platform on the inauguration day.

John Plants.

Sworn to and subscribed before me this 18th day of March, 1876.

(SEAL)   Jas. A. Tait, Notary Public.

District of Columbia, Washington County, ss.

Charles C. Cleary, of Washington City being duly sworn,

says that he was a policeman employed at the Capitol in March, 1865; that he was present and on duty in the rotunda on the day of the second inauguration of President Lincoln, and was near the east door when he saw J. Wilkes Booth break through the line of policemen and make for the east portico; affiant saw J. W. Westfall seize Booth and after a severe struggle he was forced back into the crowd. Affiant had seen Booth often and states positively that the stranger who broke through the line on that occasion was no other person; affiant thought nothing of it at the time, but afterwards when the President was assassinated, affiant remembers it, and when Booth's picture was shown to Major French he recognized it, and so did other policemen who were present; and affiant has no hesitancy in expressing the belief that Lieutenant Westfall's prompt action on that day saved the life or prevented an attempt to take the life of President Lincoln.

Charles C. Cleary.

Sworn to and subscribed before me this 23rd day of March, 1876.

(SEAL)   John T. C. Clark, J. P.

District of Columbia, County of Washington, ss.

Otis S. Buxton, of the State of New York, gate doorkeeper of the House of Representatives, being duly sworn, says: That he was assistant doorkeeper of the House of Representatives, in 1865 and was in the Capitol during the second inauguration of President Lincoln.

About the time the procession moved to the east door of the Capitol, affiant was walking from the Senate Chamber to the rotunda with a friend, when J. Wilkes Booth passed affiant in great haste, going in the direction of the rotunda. Affiant knew Booth well; had seen him often on the stage and off it, here and elsewhere. Affiant's friend, speaking of Booth who had just passed, said: "That man must be in a hurry." Affiant remarked: "That is Wilkes Booth." Affiant's friend did not know him but said that he had seen his father play. Affiant passed through the rotunda to the House of Representatives and heard shortly afterward that a man had attempted to reach the platform in front of the east door by breaking through the ranks of the policemen, but had been prevented by the prompt action of the Capitol police.

O. S. Buxton.

Sworn to and subscribed before me this 3rd day of April, 1876.

(S E A L)   James A. Tait, Notary Public.

District of Columbia, Washington County, ss.

Robert Strong, a citizen of said county and district, being duly sworn, says: That he was a policeman on the day of the second inauguration of President Lincoln, and was stationed at the east door of the rotunda with Commissioner B. B. French, at the time the President, accompanied by the judges and others, passed out to the platform where the ceremonies of the inauguration were to begin, when a man in a very determined and excited manner broke through the line of policemen which had been formed to keep the crowd out. Lieutenant Westfall immediately seized the stranger and a considerable scuffle ensued.

The stranger seemed determined to get up to the platform where the President and his party were, but Lieutenant Westfall called for assistance. The commissioner closed the door, or had it closed, and the intruder was finally thrust from the passage leading to the platform, which was reserved for the President's party. After the President was assassinated the singular conduct of this stranger on that day was frequently talked of by the policemen who observed it. Westfall procured a photograph of the assassin, Booth, soon after the death of the President, and showed it to Commissioner French in my presence and in the presence of several other policemen and asked him if he had ever met that man. The commissioner examined it carefully and said: "Yes, I would know that face among ten thousand; that is the man you had the scuffle with on inauguration day. That is the same man." Affiant also recognized the photograph. Lieutenant Westfall then said: "This is the picture of J. Wilkes

Booth." Major French exclaimed, "My God! What a fearful risk we ran that day!"

Robert Strong.

Sworn to and subscribed before me this 20th day of March, 1876.

(S E A L)   James A. Tait, Notary Public.

District of Columbia, Washington County, ss.

William J. Belshan, being duly sworn, says: That he was on duty as a policeman in the rotunda of the Capitol on the day of the second inauguration of President Lincoln; that he was stationed about the middle of the line of policemen which was formed from the north to the east door; that he saw a stranger break through the line in a very determined and excited manner and start for the east door through which the Judges of the Supreme Court and the President had just passed. Lieutenant Westfall ordered him back, but he refused to go when he was seized by Westfall and a severe struggle ensued. The east door was closed; assistance came to Westfall and the stranger was forced back into the crowd. The conduct of this man was much talked of by those who witnessed it on that occasion, and after the President was assassinated a photograph of Booth was shown to Major French and he and I and others recognized it as the picture of the man who broke through the lines on the day of the inauguration; and it was believed by us all that Booth attempted to reach the platform to assassinate the President, when he was prevented by Lieutenant Westfall's vigilance on that occasion.

William J. Belshan.

Sworn to and subscribed before me this 20th day of March, 1876.

(S E A L)   James A. Tait, Notary Public.

From these sworn statements it will be seen that Booth's plan was one of phenomenal audacity.[4] So frenzied was the assassin that he determined, if possible, to take the President's life at the certain sacrifice of his own; for nothing can be more certain than this, that the murder of Mr. Lincoln on that public occasion, in the presence of such a vast concourse of admiring citizens, would have been instantly avenged. The infuriated populace would have torn the assassin to pieces, and this the desperate man doubtless knew.

Booth failed to reach the grandstand at the point where the policemen were, but nevertheless he succeeded in getting on the platform. What he failed to accomplish by force, he accomplished, according to General Burnett, by strategy, through the intervention of the card secured from his lady friend.[5]

Booth, too, has put himself on record as to what was in his mind on that day, for on the 7th of April he said to Samuel Knapp Chester, "What an elegant chance I had to kill the President on inauguration day if I wished." [6]

Judge Bingham in his great closing argument before the Military Commission, speaking of this, used the following language:

> It is further in evidence that Samuel A. Mudd was here on the third day of March last, the day preceding the inauguration, when Booth was to strike the traitorous blow; and it was doubtless only by the interposition of the God who stands within the shadow and keeps watch above His own, that the victim of this conspiracy was spared that day from the assassin's hand that he might complete his work and see the salvation of his country in the fall of Richmond and the surrender of its great army.[7]

One of Booth's most intimate friends in his lifetime was an actor by the name of Edwin Hunter. He was with Booth on several occasions in Washington. Once he went out riding with him in the spring of 1865.

Like many other gentlemen, Mr. Hunter has submitted himself to newspaper interviewers, and this is what he said at one time to a reporter of a Southern newspaper:

> Well, Booth had an idea that Lincoln was a personal foe and a menace to the South. About the time Lincoln's first term expired he became very moody. I heard him say one day in Washington:
> "Is there no way to prevent Lincoln's being President again?"
> "No," he was told.
> "He can be President as long as he lives, don't you suppose?"
> "Yes."

Afterwards in speaking of this, he became very much excited. "There is no help that I can see as long as Lincoln lives," he would say. About two months after that I was driving with him on Pennsylvania Avenue. He had sent me a written invitation, and I knew something was wrong. He seemed to be watching for something, and suddenly pointed to a carriage drawn by two gray horses. He said to the driver, "Now follow that carriage."

"Whose carriage is that?" I asked.

"That's Lincoln's," he said.

"Why are you following it?"

"Just to shoot the President," he replied, and laughed.

I never until long afterwards thought that these words might have been spoken in more than jest. Booth turned quickly to the driver, and said: "Now drive towards the Capitol." The President was driving in an opposite direction from that in which he had been driving.*

In the light of all these facts, what now becomes of the allegation that Booth did not conceive the desire to murder the President until after he learned of his intended visit to the theater on the night of the 14th of April? It would probably be nearer the truth to say that murder was in his heart all the time and that he was merely watching his opportunity to do the deed and then escape in safety.

* From the *Atlanta Constitution*, copied into the *Indiana Argus*, April 21, 1888.

CHAPTER XI

Booth remained in Washington from March 1 to March 21 and then left
on the 7:30 P.M. train, north. The first evidence we have after the reinauguration of President Lincoln of his continuance in a plot or conspiracy of some kind is furnished in the subjoined telegram addressed to
Michael O'Laughlin, who, it appears, had returned to Baltimore.

Washington, March 13th, 1865.

To M. O'Laughlin, Esq.,
    No. 57 N. Exeter St., Baltimore, Md.
    Don't fear to neglect your business. You had better come at once.
                               J. Booth.[1]

Booth evidently meant to say, "Don't you fear to neglect your business." The telegram shows on its face that Booth meant business, but
what business? It is a noteworthy fact that coincident with the sending
of this message to O'Laughlin was the reappearance of the bold conspirator, Lewis Payne, alias Wood, at Mrs. Surratt's house. It was his
second visit there and occurred on this very day, March 13. It looked
as if Booth was concentrating his band for some purpose.

As fate would have it, I was again spending the evening in the parlor
of Mrs. Surratt's house when the door bell rang. I again went to the
door. I met the same man whom I had seen some weeks before. His first

visit, however, had produced so little impression on my mind that I had forgotten his name. On my asking it he gave it to me as Mr. Payne. He again inquired for Mr. Surratt, but Mr. Surratt was not at home that evening. I took him into the parlor, where were Mrs. Surratt and the ladies of the house, and said, "This is Mr. Payne," and he seated himself and began conversation with the party. In the course of the talk one of the young ladies addressed him as Mr. Wood, and then I recollected that on the previous occasion he had given the name of Wood. It appeared to run in my mind all the time that the name he had given on his first visit was not that of Payne, but I could not remember what it was until the lady referred to revealed it. My curiosity was aroused and I began to speculate why this man was acting in an assumed character; there was a purpose in it. He was very polite in his actions, and manners; he lifted the piano lid for Miss Surratt and requested her to play for him. Then he sat down to a social game of cards with the young ladies. On this occasion, he was no longer a clerk in a china store but represented himself as a Baptist preacher. He wore a complete new suit of gray and had on a black tie. His baggage consisted of two linen shirts and a linen duster.

"Queer preacher," remarked Mrs. Holohan when she heard of his remarks. "I don't think he will convert many souls."

The following day, March 14, Surratt returned home late in the afternoon. While I was in my room seated at my table, writing, Payne walked in. Surratt at the time was lying on the bed. Payne looked at him and said, "Is this Mr. Surratt?" I answered, "Yes, sir, it is." Payne then observed, "I would like to talk privately with Mr. Surratt." I then arose and left the room.

I have come to regard this performance as part of their work. I have not the slightest doubt that Surratt knew who Payne was when he opened the door and stalked into my room, and that this was another of their tricks to deceive me.

The next day, March 15, on returning from work I found a false mustache on my table. Not thinking much about it, and intending to have a little fun with it, I threw it into a box that stood there.

From the appearance of things I knew that Surratt must be at home. I then ascended to the back attic and as I opened the door I beheld him and Payne seated on a bed surrounded by brand-new spurs, bowie knives, and revolvers. The moment the door was opened they instantly and almost unconsciously threw out their hands as if trying to conceal the articles. When they saw who it was who had entered the room they seemed to regain their equanimity. These things were lying on the bed. There were eight brand-new spurs, two revolvers, and two bowie knives. I at once went downstairs and sought Mrs. Surratt and told her what I had discovered, and that I had seen John and Payne with those weapons, and added, "Mrs. Surratt, I do not like this." She told me I should not think anything of it, that I knew John was in the habit of riding into the country, and that he had to have these things as a protection.

The same evening Surratt showed me a ten-dollar ticket for a private box at the theater that had been given to him by Booth. I playfully wrested the ticket from him and said to him that I was also going. "No," said he, "you are not. I don't want you to go this evening for private reasons." He then playfully struck me and took the ticket from me. He was anxious to have the youngest ladies in the house accompany him. He requested Miss Holohan, a young girl of about thirteen, to go, but she declined. He then took Miss Fitzpatrick and Miss Apollonia Dean. Before leaving, Surratt borrowed my blue military cloak, stating that Payne wanted to wear it, and I have no doubt that it was also Payne's intention to use on that occasion the false mustache which he had unwittingly left on the table in my room, and which I secreted.

The party were driven to the theater in a hack. When the play was over, Surratt and Payne returned to the house. Surratt secured a pack of playing cards and then left the house with his companion. They remained out all night—something I had never known Surratt to do before when in the city.

A few days after this Surratt in conversation with another gentleman, in my presence, made the remark that he had spent the other night (meaning the 15th of March) with a party of sociables at Gautier's saloon, and that he would like to introduce us, but that he could not as it was a private club, or something to that effect.

The box these men occupied at the theater that night was, I believe, the President's box, and I am convinced that Surratt had good reasons for selecting the youngest people in the house to accompany him and for not wishing me to go along.

Little Miss Dean, a few days afterwards while sitting on my knee in the parlor, informed me that the play she had been to see was *Jane Shore*.[2] "And, oh! Mr. Weichmann!" she added. "What do you think; while me and Miss Fitzpatrick were sitting there Mr. Booth came to the box and

called Mr. Surratt and Mr. Payne into the entry, and he was so excited."
This was to me the testimony of an innocent child. I regret that she was
never put on the witness stand that she might have told her story in her
own artless way. The testimony about the visit to the theater was not
fully made public until at John Surratt's trial in 1867, and at that time
Miss Dean was not produced. Miss Fitzpatrick, however, was put on the
stand and testified as follows:

Q. Do you recollect in the month of March going to Ford's Theater,
and if so state in whose company you went?

A. I went with Mr. Surratt, Mr. Wood and Miss Dean.

Q. State in what box of the theater you were seated—whether you
occupied a box or a seat in the orchestra.

A. We occupied a box, sir.

Q. When you say Mr. Surratt you mean John H. Surratt, the prisoner?

A. Yes, sir.

Q. And when you say Mr. Wood you mean Lewis Payne?

A. Yes, sir.

Q. While your party was in the box did you see John Wilkes Booth?
If so state what he did.

A. Mr. Booth came there and spoke to Mr. Surratt. They both
stepped outside the box and stood there at the door.

Q. You mean spoke to the prisoner?

A. Yes, sir.

Q. State if any one else joined them while standing there.

A. Mr. Wood.

Q. Lewis Payne you mean.

A. Yes, sir.

Q. How long were these three men talking together?

A. They remained there a few minutes.

Q. Could you hear what they said?

A. No, sir; I was not paying attention; they were conversing together.

Q. State, if you please, where that box was—in what part of the
theater.

A. I think it was an upper box. I do not remember what side of the
theater it was on.

Q. In what part of the play was this conversation—in the middle or near the end?

A. It was near the last part.

Q. After they separated which way did they go, and which way did your party go?

A. We returned to Mrs. Surratt's house.[3]

The box in which this interview occurred was the President's box. The testimony of Mr. Raybold, the ticket seller at Ford's Theater, settled that. At the trial of Surratt he swore that he had, for ten dollars, sold Booth a box ticket only once during that spring, and that the ticket was for box No. 10, the President's box. Inasmuch as the ticket which Surratt showed me was a box ticket given him by Booth, this testimony leaves no question but that the box occupied on the night of March 15, 1865, by these three men was the President's box.[4]

Now what were these three men after that night that called them to the President's box? What was all the excitement about and what was the meeting later in the night but a gathering of the conspirators? Was this the private club into which Surratt would like to have introduced myself and friend but could not?

Samuel Arnold, one of the conspirators, confessed that a meeting took place about three weeks prior to the 1st of April 1865, and was held at the Lichau House on Pennsylvania Avenue between Sixth and Four-and-a-half streets. Besides himself, John Wilkes Booth, Michael O'Laughlin, George A. Atzerodt, John H. Surratt, and a man with the alias of Mosby (Payne), and another man, a small man (probably Herold), were present.[5]

At this meeting a discussion took place. Booth got angry at something Arnold said. Arnold remarked that if the thing was not done that week he would withdraw. Booth became enraged at this and said that he ought to be shot for expressing himself in that way, or that he had said enough for Booth to shoot him, or words to that effect. Arnold replied that two could play at that game.

Arnold said the purpose of the parties in the Conspiracy at this time was to abduct or kidnap the President and take him South for the purpose of making the U. S. Government have an exchange of prisoners, or something like that. He also said that his part in the plot was to catch the President when he was thrown out of the box at the theater. Booth, he said, furnished the arms for all the men.

These statements of Arnold as to the abduction have been verified by what occurred at Mrs. Surratt's house on the 16th of March. On returning from work on that day I went as usual to my room. Neither Payne nor Surratt was there. I rang the call bell for Dan, a half-witted mulatto who did the chores around the place, and requested him to bring me some water for washing. I asked him where John Surratt was. He replied that Massa Surratt had ridden away from the front of the house in the afternoon about two o'clock with six or seven on horseback. I then requested him to tell me who they were. One, he answered, was Massa Booth, another, John H. Surratt, a third, Payne, then Mr. Port Tobacco (Atzerodt), and Dave Herold. The other two he did not know but they were Arnold and O'Laughlin.* [6]

On the way to dinner, I met Mrs. Surratt in the hall. She was weeping bitterly. "Go down," she said, "Mr. Weichmann, and make the best of the dinner that you can. John is gone away, John is gone away." Here was a distinct avowal on the part of this woman that her son had gone away. Why was she in tears? She certainly must have known and felt that he had departed on some dangerous errand. For my part, I believe she could have nipped the Conspiracy in the bud right then and there, if she had only done her duty as a loyal and Christian woman and a good mother. Is anyone so foolish at this late day as to imagine that she did not see the seven conspirators as they rode away so gallantly from her house, and that she was not aware of the mission upon which they were bent?

Mrs. Surratt did not come to the table that day. Miss Anna Surratt, Miss Fitzpatrick, and I were the only ones there. During the meal, Miss Surratt once grew very excited and, bringing the handle of her knife with great force upon the table, exclaimed, "Mr. Weichmann, do you know that if anything were to happen to my brother John through his acquaintance with Booth, I would kill him (Booth)." I assured Miss Surratt that I did not know what all this business meant, that it was an enigma to me.

After dinner, I returned to my room, and was amusing myself with Dickens' *Pickwick* when to my astonishment at about half past six Surratt burst into the apartment. I looked at him and saw that he was very much excited. His pantaloons were in his boot tops, and he wore spurs. He held a small four-barreled Sharp's revolver in his hand; one that

* See the confession of Arnold, below, Chapter XXXI.

could be easily carried in one's vest pocket. I asked him what was the matter. He leveled his pistol at me and exclaimed, "Weichmann, my prospects are gone; my hopes are blasted; I want something to do; can you get me a clerkship?" I answered him, "You are foolish; why don't you settle down and be a sensible man?"

In about ten minutes more Payne came into the room. He, too, was much excited, and his face seemed to be very much flushed, but he said nothing. Once he pulled up his waistcoat, as if fastening a suspender, and when he did this I noticed a large revolver resting on his hip.

To my increased surprise shortly afterwards Booth came into the apartment. He wore dark clothes; had a riding whip in his hand, and walked excitedly around the room two or three times in a circle before he noticed me. I called his attention and then he said, "Hallo, you here? I did not see you." I saw no arms on him.

Then, at a signal from Booth, the three men went upstairs into the little back attic where Payne slept, and must have remained there, I judge, about thirty minutes. Then they left the house without saying a word to me.[7]

Up to this time, the sudden and extraordinary friendship between Booth and Surratt had not been regarded by me in a serious light. It is true, Booth was not acting and had no visible employment, nor had Surratt, and I used to wonder why this strange intimacy had sprung up between these two men. Why was it? What was at the bottom of it all? I never paid much attention to Atzerodt's visits to the house; he came there often; so did Booth, and they would go off into a room by themselves with Surratt and Payne and have their private talks. And Herold came once in the middle of March, when Payne was staying there, and had a talk with Payne and Surratt. He came on horseback, and left his horse standing in the alley next to the house.

I could not get to the bottom of these proceedings, but now taking into consideration the strange actions of Booth, Payne, and Surratt on this 16th day of March, their sudden and excitable return to the house coupled with what I had seen the previous day in reference to the fire-arms that Payne and Surratt had lying on the bed, and all this taken in connection with the mysterious language and suspicious phrases dropped by Surratt and his mother at different times, the meaning of which I was not shrewd enough to penetrate, but which always seemed to indicate some hidden purpose which they did not wish to reveal, my worst suspicions, for the first time, became fully aroused that something wrong was going on among them.

There was at this time in the same office of the War Department in which I was employed a man by the name of D. H. Gleason, an ex-soldier and a member of the Veteran Reserve Corps. He had been wounded in the war. He was a fellow clerk, and a gentleman with whom I was very intimate. To him I was in the habit of repeating various occurrences which took place at my boardinghouse, and I especially spoke of Booth's frequent visits there. I rather considered it a fine thing to be acquainted with Booth, for he was a leading actor of the day, a good fellow, and a descendant from a most famous family. What I at first told Gleason was more in the nature of gossip, such as was generally indulged in by young men of the age I then was, and was not at all of a suspicious character.

I never could understand the sympathy and affection which existed between Booth and Surratt; they were so dissimilar in their natures, education, and the social position they held in life. Surratt was a young man hardly out of his teens with no experience at all in the active pursuits of life, having spent the greater portion of his brief existence on a small farm.

Booth, on the contrary, was not only an accomplished actor, but a man who could be called a finished scholar in the ways of the world. He had posed on the stage a number of years, and although a young man, had already achieved renown, and was a rising star in his profession. He was familiar with the tinsel and glitter of theatrical life, and was always a boon and welcome companion among his fellow actors. He was a worldly man given to wine, women, and conviviality.

Surratt started out in life with the determination to become a priest, but when the war burst upon the country, he gave up his notion, left St. Charles College, and returned to his home in Prince Georges County to be an emissary and spy in his section of the country for the rebels. The translation from his holy calling was for him an easy and rapid one.

Never were two individuals thrown together so utterly at variance with one another as Booth and Surratt. Booth from the very beginning of their acquaintance seemed to grapple Surratt to his soul with hooks of steel.

Booth was always a welcome guest in Mrs. Surratt's home, visiting it at all hours of the day and evening. There was apparently for him no other feeling on the part of the hostess than respect and friendship. He was never intimate with any of the ladies of the house, and always treated them with the greatest deference and politeness. He took pride and pains in letting it be known that he was paying attention to a most estimable young lady, the daughter of a Republican senator in Washington, and would relate how he was accustomed to send her beautiful flowers, yet at the same time he kept in one of Washington's gilded houses of pleasure a mistress, who on the 15th of April, when she heard of her lover's ruin, attempted with poison to stamp out her own existence.[8] He used the honorable lady as he did everybody else he came in contact with—for the furtherance of his own vile ends.

During the whole period of my acquaintance with Booth, I had no intimacy with him whatever. I never wrote him a letter or exchanged correspondence of any kind with him; I never visited him at his rooms except at the request of Mrs. Surratt. I was friendly with him only because he was the friend of my friend, John H. Surratt, and that was the limit of my friendship for him.

Whenever this man crossed Mrs. Surratt's threshold, he created a fluster among its female inmates. He was so handsome, so fascinating, so winning in his ways, and though he cared but little for Miss Surratt and Miss Fitzpatrick and was content to pay them his respectful salutations, they rushed off to one of the city bazaars and purchased his photograph; thus they would always have his picture in the house and near them.[9]

During the time that I boarded at Mrs. Surratt's I almost always remained at home during the evenings. From the 1st of November 1864 to the unhappy 14th of April 1865, I did not spend four evenings away from the house altogether. I found my companionship in my books, and with those who lived in the house, whom I deemed honest people. I was absent during this time from my position in the War Department only one day, the 11th of April 1865, and that was by special permission of my superior officers. What I saw of the visits and actions of Booth, Surratt, and the rest was generally in the evenings when I returned from my work. As to the events transpiring there in the daytime, these were matters beyond my knowledge.

Mrs. Surratt had but a few acquaintances in Washington, and they came very seldom. The only Catholic clergyman in the city whom she knew well was Reverend Bernardin F. Wigget,[10] who had been a friend of many years' standing to her and her son. He called occasionally, but not often. With Father Jacob Walter, her confessor on the closing days of her earthly life, she had no acquaintance whatever prior to the assassination. I generally accompanied this woman to church on Sundays, and did many little offices of kindness for her in the absence of her son. I do not remember a single time during my stay in her home when her son went with her to church. That seems to have been my function, and I was always happy to be of service to her in this way.

On one occasion I found John Surratt in my room sitting before the fire, looking as if his last friend had deserted him. "What is the matter, John?" said I. "Why are you so dejected?" "Weichmann," was his reply, "I can't tell you; you are a Yankee." Then I informed him that if he did not wish to trust me with his secrets, he had better go to his church, attend to his religious duties, and live as a Christian man should, and all his worriment would cease.

Another time Surratt told me he was engaged in the "oil business," that he had six shares of oil stock. Once he even approached me and requested me to write an article for the newspapers, which I refused to do, to the effect that John Wilkes Booth, the accomplished actor, in consequence of erysipelas in his leg, had retired from the stage and was engaged in the "oil business." He stated that Booth had made quite a fortune out of oil, and had presented his (Booth's) sister with the money.

The Surratts had relatives in Washington, Pennsylvania, by the name of Seaman, who were Republicans and strong Union people. To them John and Anna frequently wrote letters. Here is a copy of one that John addressed in the winter of 1865 to his cousin Bell Seaman. It shows just what he thought of Booth, what a commotion the actor created in his home whenever he went there, and what his feelings were in reference to his own country.

Washington, D.C., February 6, 1865.

Miss Bell Seaman,
Dear Cousin:

I received your letter, and not being quite so selfish as you are, I will answer it, in what I call a reasonable time. I am happy to say that we are all well and in fine spirits.

We have been looking for you to come on with a great deal of impatience. Do come, won't you? Just to think that I have never yet seen one of my cousins. But never fear, I will probably see you all sooner than you expect. *Next week I leave for Europe.* Yes, I am going to leave this detested country, and I think perhaps I may give you a call as I go to New York. Do not be surprised, Cousin Bell, when you see your hopeful cousin. Truly you may be surprised.

I have an invitation to a party to come off next Tuesday night. Anna and myself intend going, and expect to enjoy ourselves very much. I have been to a great many this winter, so they are beginning to get common; but this is something extra, I look forward to it with a great deal of impatience. I wish you were here in order that I might have the pleasure of introducing you to a regular country hoe-down. I know you would enjoy it.

There is no news of importance, except the burning of the Smithsonian Institute which, of course, you have heard of. His Excellency Jefferson Davis and Old Abe Lincoln couldn't agree, as sensible people knew beforehand; and now, I hope, people are satisfied, and I hope they will make up their minds to fight it out to the bitter end.

Show no quarter. That's my motto.

Cousin Bell, try and answer me in a few days at least, as I would like very much to hear from you before *I leave home for good.* I do not know what to think of our mutual friend, Miss Kate Brady.

Byron justly remarks,—

> *"This record will forever stand—*
> *Woman, thy vows are traced in sand."*

I have just taken a peep in the parlor. Would you like to know what I saw there? Well, Ma was sitting on the sofa, nodding first to one chair, then to another, next the piano. Anna sitting in the corner dreaming, I expect of J. W. Booth. Well, who is J. W. Booth? She can answer that question. Miss Fitzpatrick playing with her favorite cat,—a good sign of an old maid,—the detested old creatures. Miss Dean fixing her hair which is filled with rats and mice.

But hark the door bell rings, and J. W. Booth is announced. And listen to the scamperings of the— Such brushing and fixing.

Cousin Bell I am afraid to read this nonsense over, so, consequently, you must excuse all misdemeanors. We all send love to you and family. Tell cousin Sam I think he might write to me at least a few lines.

> Your cousin,
>
> J. Harrison Surratt.

541 H Street between 6th and 7th Streets.[11]

Booth seems to have had a wonderful ascendancy over Surratt, Payne, Atzerodt, and the others of the small band whom he had gathered together. To them he was a young Jove, and his nod and beck were law. He appeared to consult and advise with Surratt more than any of the rest, for next to himself, Surratt was the best-educated and best-informed man among them.

The conspirators were all young men. Booth was only twenty-eight; Surratt, twenty; Payne, twenty-one; Herold, twenty-one; O'Laughlin and Arnold, about twenty-eight; Atzerodt, thirty; and Dr. Mudd, about thirty-five. Mrs. Surratt was at least forty-seven years of age and the oldest of the party.[12] They were all Southerners by birth, with the probable exception of Atzerodt, and all came from respectable families. Some of them, the Surratts and Dr. Mudd, stood high in the social circles in their respective neighborhoods, nor had the names of any of them been sullied by any previous misdeeds or crimes.

What the potent influence was that induced these men and this woman to enlist under Booth's black banner, I cannot comprehend, but in my own mind, I have been satisfied long ago that they were mainly actuated by cupidity—the desire to make money—to gain a large fortune. Indeed, all their talk proves this. When Booth approached Chester, he told him their money was in it, that he could let him have three thousand dollars, and when Surratt induced Atzerodt to join the Conspiracy, and furnish the boat on which the President was to be ferried over the Potomac, it was under the promise of a fortune, and thereafter whenever Atzerodt talked about the scheme, it was always with the idea of making money. Booth himself may have been actuated by what he considered nobler motives, the desire, perhaps, to pose as the Charlotte Corday of the nineteenth century; to gain a name for himself as the avenger of the South, or by his deed to attempt to revive its dying cause; but his followers, it is safe to say, were actuated by no such motives. They were too commonplace and were not of the material out of which heroes are made.[13]

Surratt's mother was in debt and was keeping a boardinghouse to sustain herself and family, but the son when in the city could be often seen with fine gloves and leggings on, riding about on sleek and well-fed horses, and girdled around his waist with a brace of well-loaded revolvers. He kept two horses at Howard's stables on G Street which he claimed as his own, but Brooke Stabler, an employee there, testified that Booth paid for their keeping, and in order that Mr. Atzerodt, the mutual friend of Mr. Surratt and of Mr. Booth, might take an airing occasionally and not weary in well doing, the following note in Surratt's handwriting was sent to the stables by Mrs. Surratt:

Mr. Howard will please let the bearer, Mr. Atzerodt, have my horse whenever he wishes to ride, and also my leggings and gloves, and oblige,

Yours etc.,

J. H. Surratt.[14]

Feb. 22, 1865.

Surratt here calls the horses his own, but he had no more ownership in those horses than he did in the Capitol. Even the arms he carried about with him were paid for with Booth's money. So were the weapons of the others. Each of these men bore a large revolver and a large bowie knife. Besides the knives and revolvers, two handsome Spencer carbines were bought, costing in those days about three hundred dollars; a boat, a buggy, and other things. Booth, no doubt, paid the board of Atzerodt, Payne, O'Laughlin, and Arnold when in the city, and their traveling expenses and those of Surratt, for they were all persons without means or the occupation by which to earn money. Indeed, Booth must have been, judging from all these facts, at an expenditure of several thousand dollars in maintaining his fellow conspirators and carrying out his scheme.

The reader can readily infer how much the events of the 16th of March demoralized and terrified me. During the same evening I sought my friend Captain Gleason to lay everything before him as it had occurred, but he was not in his rooms. I, however, told him my story the next day at the office, and just as it is related here.[15] From what the colored boy, Dan, had said to me it appeared that these fellows must have started out to accomplish some concerted purpose, and had failed in their object. I hastily reached a number of surmises and conclusions. I thought, perhaps, they had been trying to run the blockade, engage in a cotton speculation, or perhaps had attempted to go South. I even said something about capture to Mr. Gleason, and asked him if he thought such a thing could be effected, but this question was not dictated by anything Surratt or any of the conspirators had ever told me. I never for a moment associated them with an attack of any kind on Mr. Lincoln.

Gleason and I talked over the matter a good deal; he told me to keep a watch on them and if anything again occurred of a serious nature we would report in at once to the Secretary of War, and if need be go to General [D. H.] Rucker of the Quartermaster's Department, secure horses, and pursue them wherever they might go. But nothing happened again to command my attention. Payne did not return to Mrs. Surratt's house while I was there, and I did not see him again until he was placed on trial for his life.

Many of my most sincere friends have asked me why I did not leave Mrs. Surratt's house when I began to suspect that there was something wrong going on. My answer invariably has been: "No, in the hour of danger the true soldier does not desert his post, but rather stays and watches the movements of his enemies." I was a sworn officer of the Government, and held a remunerative position under it; so did my father in the United States arsenal in Philadelphia, and I was bound by every consideration of honor to remain where I was, and if anything came up again to renew my suspicions to report it at once to the War Department. My only regret in this whole affair is that when I spoke of the exciting events of the 16th of March to Captain Gleason, he and I did not then go to Secretary Stanton and inform him of the occurrence. Had we done so, these men could have been arrested and placed in separate rooms, and it would not have been long before some one of them would have betrayed the Conspiracy, and thus a life so precious to humanity as was that of Mr. Lincoln, I verily believe, could have been saved, and the awful catastrophe of April 14 with its dire results averted. But no man in my position would have acted differently from what I did; no one would have suspected from the facts stated that these men had that day tried to effect the capture of the President or, that failing, his murder. I always had too high an opinion of John Surratt and his mother to believe them capable of such a crime, but the sad results of the 14th day of April, and the developments growing out of the Conspiracy trial, show how utterly mistaken and deceived I was in them. Their whole course of action towards me from the time they became acquainted with Booth was one of lying, ingratitude, and treachery.

When Lincoln's murder was finally consummated the reader can readily infer the relation in which I stood to Mr. Gleason and can judge his feelings in respect to me. Everything I had ever communicated to him about Booth or the Surratt family returned to his mind and was made known to the authorities. If I had been a disloyal man of the vilest type, if I had been disposed to shield the assassins could I have done so safely, the mere fact that weeks before the 14th of April I had spoken of the events of which I am now writing, to Captain Gleason, not dreaming of any such crime as capture or assassination; these things, I say, required instant and satisfactory explanation from me. And it was given, for I have never for a moment hesitated in my duty in this regard. Even if I had not said a word in advance to Captain Gleason, I would still have considered it my duty, under all circumstances, to have made known these facts to the authorities to aid them in their investigation, and also repeat them under oath when brought face to face with the assassins on their trial.

When the thing was all over and the criminals had gone to their punishment, just what Captain Gleason thought of my services to the Government is evidenced by the following extract from a letter which I received from him November 23, 1865, from Webster, Massachusetts, whither he had gone to reside:

Dear Wiechmann:

Over two months ago, since your welcome letter reached me, and you are deserving of a long apology from me for not writing before . . .

Well, my boy, accept my congratulations, heartily, sincerely, for the manly way in which you discharged your disagreeable duties in regard to the Surratt family. You have done nobly and are deserving of all credit. When I last saw you my feelings were anything but true, friendly ones, as you must know, but the course you pursued, the testimony you gave, which I assure you was critically read by me, has a long time since completely changed my opinion, and I beg your pardon for all unjust suspicions which I have ever entertained toward you . . .

Sincerely your friend,

D. H. Gleason.

I never could understand why John Surratt should have acted in this matter in so reckless and foolish a manner. He was like one who had lost his head. The fact of seven men riding away from the front of his mother's house in full midday, bent on some dangerous and, perhaps, murderous purpose would have been the strongest evidence against him in the event of anything happening to Mr. Lincoln at that time. By this insane act, he exposed his mother and sister, and everyone living in the house, to the greatest possible suspicion and danger.

Now what were those seven men after on that 16th day of March? Has any light been thrown on the errand? Fortunately for the country and all good people there has. Atzerodt, one of the executed conspirators, made a confession before his death to Provost Marshal General McPhail of Baltimore in which he revealed the whole affair. General McPhail assured me over his own signature that the confession was made to him, and that it could be relied upon as truthful. It has been published to the world, and it is given in this book for the purpose of verifying this history.*

The most complete revelation, however, on this point, has been made by John Surratt himself in his lecture of December [6], 1870, to portions of which the attention of the reader has already been called.

Upon one occasion, I remember, we had called a meeting in Washington for the purpose of discussing matters in general, as we had understood that the government had received information that there was a plot of some kind on hand. They had even commenced to build a stockade and gates on the navy yard bridge; gates opening towards the south, as though they expected danger from within, and not from without. At this meeting I explained the construction of the gates, etc., and stated that I was confident the government had wind of our movement, and that the best thing we could do would be to throw up the whole project. Everyone seemed to coincide in my opinion, except Booth, who sat silent and abstracted. Arising at last and bringing down his fist upon the table he said: *"Well, gentlemen, if the worst comes to the worst, I shall know what to do."*

Some hard words and even threats then passed between him and some of the party. Four of us then arose, one saying: "If I understand you to intimate *anything more than the capture of Mr. Lincoln* I for one will bid you goodbye." Every one expressed the same opinion. We all arose and commenced putting our hats on. Booth perceiving probably that he had gone too far, asked pardon saying that he "had drank too much champagne." After some difficulty

---

* See below, Chapter XXXI.

everything was amicably arranged and we separated at 5 o'clock in the morning.

Days, weeks and *months* passed by without an opportunity presenting itself for us to attempt the capture. We seldom saw one another owing to the many rumors afloat that a conspiracy of some kind was being concocted in Washington. We had all arrangements perfected from Washington for the purpose. Boats were in readiness to carry us across the river. One day * we received information that the President would visit the Seventh Street Hospital for the purpose of being present at an entertainment to be given for the benefit of the wounded soldiers. The report only reached us about three quarters of an hour before the time appointed, but so perfect was our communication that we were instantly in our saddles on the way to the hospital. This was between one and two o'clock in the afternoon. It was our intention to seize the carriage, which was drawn by a splendid pair of horses, and to have one of our men mount the box and drive direct for southern Maryland, via Benning's bridge. We felt confident that all the cavalry in the city would never overhaul us. We were all mounted on swift horses, besides having a thorough knowledge of the country, it being determined to abandon the carriage after passing the city limits. Upon the suddenness of the blow and the celerity of our movements we depended for success. By the time the alarm could have been given and the horses saddled, we would have been on our way through southern Maryland towards the Potomac River.

To our great disappointment, however, the President was not there but one of the government officials—Mr. Chase, if I mistake not. We did not disturb him, as we wanted a *bigger chase* (Laughter) than he could have afforded us. It was certainly a bitter disappointment, but yet I think a most fortunate one for us. It was our last attempt. We soon after this became convinced that we could not remain much longer undiscovered, and that we must abandon our enterprise. Accordingly, a separation finally took place, and I never after saw any of the party except one, and that was when I was on my way from Richmond to Canada on business of quite a different nature—about which presently.

Such is the story of our abduction plot. Rash, perhaps foolish,

* March 16, 1865 [March 17, according to Arnold].

but honorable I maintain in its means and ends; actuated by such motives as would under similar circumstances be a sufficient inducement to thousands of southern young men to have embarked in a similar enterprise.[16]

Here we have the whole story of the abduction from the very lips of John H. Surratt. He not only admits that he was a member of the Conspiracy to capture the President, but justifies his connection with it exultingly. He says, "It was our intention to seize the carriage, which was drawn by a splendid pair of horses, and to have one of our men mount the box and drive direct for southern Maryland, via Benning's bridge." But he does not tell us that he was the man selected to mount the box and do the driving. That was left for Atzerodt to reveal in his confession.

There is, however, something else, and more serious, in the quotation just made from Surratt's lecture. He says there was an altercation with Booth at this Lichau House meeting, and that Booth exclaimed, at the same time bringing his fist down on the table, "Well, gentlemen, if the worst comes to the worst, I shall know what to do." Some hard words, and even threats, he said passed between Booth and one of the party, who arose saying, "If I understand you to intimate anything *more than* the capture of Mr. Lincoln, I for one will bid you goodbye." [17]

Now if the avowal of Booth, according to Surratt, that "if the worst comes to the worst, I shall know what to do," and the reply of his fellow conspirator did not mean the assassination, then what did it mean? It was the same in effect as if Booth had said, "Well, if I cannot capture Lincoln, I will kill him." His words are capable of no other interpretation.

This admission from Surratt leaves no possible ground for him to stand upon and convicts him by his own words, if not of actual knowledge of the assassination of Mr. Lincoln, at least of a cognizance of the fact that Booth's thoughts and threats were bent in that direction.

CHAPTER XII

In further corroboration of what has been written in the preceding chapter, the following interview between Mr. Frank A. Burr, journalist, and John Matthews, actor, whom Booth in the fall of 1864 attempted to enlist in the scheme of abducting the President, is given. The interview took place in Baltimore, was written by Mr. Burr, now deceased, but at that time a staff correspondent of the *Philadelphia Press*, and was published in that journal on Sunday, December 4, 1881.[1]

From this report it is clearly evident that Matthews was not only fully cognizant of the attempt to abduct the President at the Soldiers' Home on March 16, which attempt resulted in a fiasco, but that he tried to help it along. From the time of the punishment and execution of the conspirators to this date, the newspapers of the country have teemed with interviews with different parties who were more or less in communication with Booth, and in sympathy with his schemes. John Matthews was one of these men. On several occasions he permitted himself to be interviewed and has never hesitated in freely ventilating his opinions and in giving his knowledge of the Booth business to the public.

"Were Booth and you," queried Mr. Burr, "often together during the winter preceding the murder?"

"A great deal," responded Matthews. "He and I were boys together, you know, having been born and raised in Baltimore. Often during the winter he had talked to me of the feasibility of kidnapping the President, but never confided to me any of his plans. He often seemed to me to be brooding over the war, and to have his heart set upon the relief and exchange of the Confederate prisoners. He once told me that if he could capture the President, carry him within the Confederacy and hold him as a ransom, it would compel the exchange of prisoners, man for man. By man he meant white man for white man, not recognizing the negroes as soldiers. That was his plan and aim until within a few hours of the time he fired the fatal shot."

"Do you know when his plans for the abduction of the President were formed?"

"Yes, sir, very well. The elder Wallack, the late E. L. Davenport and I walked into my room one day and found Booth lying upon my bed studying the part of Marc Anthony in *Julius Caesar*. By-the-by it was in the same room and upon the same bed upon which Mr. Lincoln died. Mr. Davenport and Mr. Wallack began talking about the war. They had been to visit some of the hospitals about Washington and both of them seemed very much affected by the scenes they had witnessed. Booth joined them in the talk about the conflict, and all of them expressed more or less feeling against the war. It was a feeling not of bitterness but of sorrow that brothers should be engaged in killing each other. The pathos and power with which both Davenport and Wallack expressed their desire for peace is beyond description. It made a great impression on my mind as I know it did on Booth's. It had been arranged that Mr. Wallack, Mr. Davenport, myself and some others were to go out to the Soldiers' Home to play for the benefit of the soldiers, and this subject was discussed. Booth made his arrangements to go with us, and he would be one of the audience. He knew that Mr. Lincoln intended to be present, and at once set to work arranging his plans to capture him after the play was over. We played *Still Waters Run Deep*. At the last moment Mr. Lincoln was detained by a pressure of business and did not attend the performance. Booth was very much disappointed, as I afterwards learned. The minuteness with which every detail of Mr. Lincoln's transportation within the Confederate lines had been arranged and the care and attention which Booth intended to bestow upon him after his capture can be read from a transaction with which I had unwittingly to do. A few days before we played at the Soldiers' Home, I was going over to Baltimore, Booth asked me to carry a trunk which he would have at the depot and deliver it to a gentleman living in Baltimore whom I knew. I took the trunk with me to Baltimore and delivered it to the gentleman named by Booth. I did not see him in person and left the following note:

My Dear Sir:————
Please deliver this trunk to Mr. ————, who will see that it is delivered to Mr. ————, who will have it safely shipped to its destination of which he is informed. Be careful.

Very truly,
John Matthews.

"I do not fill the blanks in that note for the reason that the gentleman to whom it is addressed, as well as those who were to handle the trunk, is still living.

"This trunk was filled with potted meats, sardines, the finest kind of crackers, some flasks of brandy and other comforts, even down to toilet articles necessary for a gentleman's use. The trunk was to be shipped to Lower Maryland, where Booth went when he attempted to escape. It was intended for the comfort of President Lincoln on his journey to the Confederate lines. It was Booth's intention to show the President every attention after his capture, for he had a great respect for him notwithstanding he abhorred the manner in which he was forced to use his power."

A very remarkable statement, indeed! It reveals facts and circumstances with which the great mass of the American people are unacquainted. The information contained in this story was not made public until 1881, sixteen years after the murder of the President. What a magnificent and valuable witness Matthews would have been for the Government in 1885! [Weichmann must mean 1865.] At that time, however, he was dumb as an oyster. He preferred to shield his friend Booth to taking a stand in behalf of his own country.

One would have thought with the failure of his plan at the Soldiers' Home, Booth would have given up his designs against Mr. Lincoln. Unfortunately, not so. He went right on as if nothing had occurred to deter him in his mad career. If anything, he seemed to have become more set and determined in his purpose.

When Surratt returned home on the evening of the 16th of March, he was alone. I asked him what had become of his companions, Booth and Payne. He replied that Booth had gone to New York, and Payne to Baltimore. He probably told the truth as to Payne, but not so as to Booth, for Booth did not leave Washington for New York until the 21st of March, returning again on March 25.

Samuel Arnold and Michael O'Laughlin, meanwhile, had also returned to Baltimore. Indeed, it appears from the confession of Arnold that he withdrew at this time from the Conspiracy to abduct the President, and there is no record whatever of his having again returned to Washington. He accepted a position in a store at Fortress Monroe on April 1, was there when Mr. Lincoln was shot, and was arrested at that place.[2]

Here was Arnold's fatal mistake. He should not have contented himself with merely withdrawing, as he alleges he had done, from the conspiracy to abduct, but should have exposed the whole affair to the Government. By doing this he would have brought honor upon himself, and would, no doubt, have averted the great tragedy of the 14th of April, which now so soon followed.

John H. Surratt also claims that he terminated his connection with the Conspiracy at that time—with the failure of the attempted kidnapping at the Soldiers' Home—and that he did not have anything further to do with it. His assertion, however, will bear investigation, for he, Herold, and Atzerodt figured in some proceedings just then which did not look as if the Conspiracy had ended or their connection with it had ceased.

The carbines and some of the other weapons which Booth had delivered into the custody of O'Laughlin and Arnold in Baltimore were now, as appears from the confession of Arnold, conveyed to Herold by Michael O'Laughlin.*

One evening in the latter part of March, about the 20th, Herold arrived at the hotel at T.B., a small place in Maryland about five miles below Surrattsville. It was just at suppertime, and he brought with him two carbines, two guns, a revolver, a huge knife, a sword, a rope, and ammunition. The hotel was run by a man named John C. Thompson, to whom Herold said that he was going duck shooting on the Patuxent. Mr. William A. Norton, an employee at the hotel, carried the articles into the barroom. Herold inquired of both Thompson

* See the confession of Arnold, below, Chapter XXXI.

and Norton if John H. Surratt had been there, and said that he was expecting him.[3]

Herold stopped at the hotel all that night, but Surratt did not appear at that place.

The next morning, when leaving the house, Herold fired off his pistol into the air and started in the direction of Surrattsville, taking the weapons with him. His action in firing off the pistol was perhaps done to notify Surratt and Atzerodt, who were now somewhere on the road, of his own whereabouts, and it was not long before he met these men, and then all three started for the Surrattsville tavern.

John M. Lloyd, who had rented this place from Mrs. Surratt, testified that some five or six weeks before the assassination of the President, John H. Surratt, David E. Herold, and George A. Atzerodt came to his house. Atzerodt and Surratt drove up to the house in the morning first and went toward T.B., a post office about five miles below there. They had not been gone more than half an hour when they returned with Herold. All three, when they came into the barroom, drank, Lloyd thought. John Surratt then called him into the front parlor, and on the sofa were two carbines with ammunition, also a rope from sixteen to twenty feet in length, and a monkey wrench. Surratt asked Lloyd to take care of these things and to conceal the carbines. Lloyd told him there was no place to conceal them and that he did not wish to keep such things. Surratt then took him into an unfurnished room immediately above the storeroom in the back part of the building. He showed him where he could put them underneath the joists of the second floor of the main building. Lloyd put them in there accordingly to his directions. There was also one cartridge box of ammunition. Surratt said he just wanted these articles to stay for a few days, and he would call for them.

The weapons were two fine Spencer carbines, each capable of firing a number of loads in rapid succession without the necessity of reloading. They were enclosed in handsome coverings. They had been carried by the conspirators on their ride on the 16th of March and they were now evidently placed in hiding at Surrattsville for some further purpose. This is fully shown from subsequent developments. It was clearly proved by Lloyd's evidence that Booth, Mrs. Surratt, John H. Surratt, Herold, and Atzerodt knew they had been secreted there and that they would be wanted soon.[4]

The rope that Surratt concealed in Lloyd's house was, in the event of the capture of the President, to have been stretched by the conspirators over some point of the road on which they were making their escape to break the pursuit of any cavalry that might follow. With the aid of the monkey wrench, they intended to remove the wheels of the President's carriage, and set it bodily on the boat on which it was to be ferried across the Potomac River.*

On Saturday evening, March 18, 1865, Booth played in *The Apostate* at Ford's Theater for the benefit of his friend and brother actor John McCullough.[5] He gave Surratt two passes for the play countersigned with his own name. Surratt invited me to accompany him, which I did. On our way to the theater, we met Atzerodt on the street, who was also going to the play. At the theater, we found David E. Herold and Mr. John T. Holohan.

The part that Booth took in the play was that of Pescara, the infamous Duke of Alva. In one of the scenes, a female was dragged on the stage by Pescara and subjected to torture on the wheel. Never in my life did I witness a man play with so much intensity and passion as did Booth on that occasion. The hideous, malevolent expression of his distorted countenance, the fierce glare and ugly roll of his eyes, which seemed ready to burst from their sockets as he seized his victim by the hair and, placing her on the wheel, exclaimed, "Now behold Pescara's masterpiece!" are yet present with me. I cannot use language forcible enough to describe Booth's actions on that night.

At the conclusion of the play, Surratt, Atzerodt, Herold, John T. Holohan, and myself left the theater together. Mr. Holohan, Surratt, and I had gone as far as the corner of Tenth and E streets when Surratt turned around and saw that Herold and Atzerodt were not following us. Surratt requested me to go back and tell them to come to Kloman's saloon on Seventh Street, and partake of an oyster supper. As I entered the saloon, which adjoined Ford's Theater, I saw Booth, Herold, and Atzerodt talking together, as it appeared to me, in a very friendly and confidential manner, near the stove. As I approached them, Booth walked forward and said, "Mr. Weichmann, won't you come and have a drink?" I drank a glass of ale with the party. Herold and Atzerodt then had a further conversation apart with Booth after which they left him and joined Surratt and Holohan at Kloman's saloon. This

* The facts in this paragraph were first made known to me by General Butler.

evidence was important as against Herold because it established the fact of his acquaintance with Booth and Atzerodt prior to the assassination.

John Surratt must have had communication with Payne after that distinguished individual left the city of Washington on the 16th of March for Baltimore, for on the 20th of March I happened on my way home to meet Surratt about half past four o'clock in the afternoon at the corner of Seventh and F streets near the post office. Surratt stepped to the delivery window of the office and inquired for a letter addressed to him under the name of James Sturdy. The clerk handed him such a letter. It was signed "Wood." Surratt foolishly showed me the signature. I saw enough of the letter to recognize that it was in a very bad handwriting though I am ignorant of its contents. On being questioned, Surratt admitted that the "Wood" who wrote was the same man (Payne) who had stayed at his mother's house.

On the 23rd of March I was surprised by a visit to the office of the Commissary General of Prisoners from Mrs. Eliza Holohan. She brought me a telegram which had come from New York. It read:

New York, March 23, 1865.

To ——— Wickmann, Esq., 541 H St.,
    Tell John to telegraph number and street at once.
                J. Booth.[6]

There were two things about this telegram that at once attracted my attention. My first name was omitted and my last name was spelled incorrectly. It was spelled "Wickmann." I knew of no one in New York to send me a telegram. I had no acquaintances there. I opened the envelope and saw that the telegram was from Booth. Why he should address me in that way I could not comprehend. I exhibited the message to the clerks in my room and had a good deal of pleasantry over it.

When I returned to my boardinghouse in the afternoon I gave it to Surratt, saying that I thought it was intended for him, and took occasion to ask him what number and street were meant. His reply was, "Don't be so damned inquisitive."

What Booth's object was in sending the dispatch to me instead of transmitting it direct to Surratt I cannot surmise. There was a purpose in it. My own idea is that Surratt was growing afraid the detectives were after him. In his lecture he admitted as much.[7] For this reason he had his letters and telegrams sent to him under an assumed name, or through other parties, and letters that were intended by him for his own family were often not sent direct to the house at all, but elsewhere in care of a third person, notably Miss Annie Ward.

The meaning, however, of Booth's message soon developed itself. Surratt unintentionally betrayed himself, not knowing that I was watching his movements and drawing my own conclusions.

The same evening he asked me to take a walk with him. The first place he visited was a Catholic school at the corner of Tenth and G streets, and there he called for one of the teachers, Miss Annie Ward. He had some conversation with her, of which I am ignorant. After leaving her he went as far as the corner of Ninth and F streets. Here he went into the Herndon House and I followed him. He called for Mrs. Murray, the mistress of the hotel, and when this lady came to him, he expressed a desire to talk with her privately, but she did not seem to comprehend what he said, being somewhat hard of hearing. Then Surratt spoke out a little more boldly. "Perhaps Miss Annie Ward has spoken to you about a room. Did she not speak to you about engaging a room for a delicate gentleman who was to have his meals sent up to him?" He told her furthermore that he wanted the room for the following Monday, which was the 27th of March 1865. Mrs. Murray then recollected and said such a room had been engaged by Miss Annie Ward, and that it would be ready at that time.[8] Accordingly, on that day, March 27, Lewis Payne returned from Baltimore to Washington and occupied the room at the Herndon House which had been secured for him by the joint efforts of Miss Annie Ward and John H. Surratt. Surratt took good care not to mention to me the name of the individual who was to occupy the room. I was, however, not left long in the dark as to that. Happening to meet Atzerodt on the street one day, curiosity prompted me to ask him, "Is it Payne who is staying at the Herndon House?" He responded, "Yes." I communicated that fact to Mrs. Surratt and she became quite angry that I should have found it out.

And in a very few days Mrs. Surratt herself called on Payne at the Herndon House. I cannot recall the particular evening on which she did so but it was after the 27th of March and sometime during Lent. Mrs. Surratt, Miss Annie Surratt, Miss Olivia Jenkins, a niece of Mrs. Surratt, Miss Fitzpatrick, and myself had been to St. Patrick's Church at the corner of Tenth and F streets. After leaving the church and while on our way home Mrs. Surratt stopped at the Herndon House and remarked that she was going in to see Payne. She left us all on the outside, and in the meantime we took a walk around the square. When we returned to the Herndon House she was descending the front steps, and then we started home together.

I am aware that this portion of my testimony has been questioned, and it has been denied that Mrs. Surratt called on Payne at the Herndon House, but luckily for the truth's sake I am confirmed here by Miss Fitzpatrick, who testified that Mrs. Surratt did go in there on the occasion referred to by me.[9] Mrs. Murray, the landlady, was also put on the stand but swore that Mrs. Surratt did not call upon her at that visit. She was not acquainted with Mrs. Surratt. Whom, then, did she visit if not Payne? There was no one else there that she knew. She seems to have understood every move on the board in this bold play of the conspirators. How she demeaned herself and her womanhood in thus seeking in the evening one of the chief conspirators, the fierce, audacious Payne, at his boardinghouse, where he was in hiding, and afraid to eat his meals at the common table with the other boarders, but had them sent to his room under pretense of being a sick man! Payne was not long in returning the compliment of the woman's visit, and when he again stood before her had almost consummated his part of the scheme of the Conspiracy. Surratt's action in securing a room for Payne does not look as if his connection with the Conspiracy had terminated on the 16th of March, as he said it did.

On the morning after the assassination, April 15, I met in the office of the Superintendent of Police of Washington a young colored waiter who had been employed at the Herndon House. In answer to some questions he told me that he had been in the habit of waiting on Payne, and of carrying his meals to him in his room. "Was he a delicate eater?" I asked. "I should think not," replied the young man with a broad grin on his face. "Why, if I had served a young pig to him he would have eaten it, bones and all."

On Saturday morning, March 25, as I went to breakfast, on looking out of the dining-room window, I beheld in front of the house John Surratt, Mrs. Surratt, and the mysterious Mrs. Slater, who had been at the house in February, all in a four-seated carriage to which was attached a span of white horses. They left the house at about eight o'clock. Where Mrs. Slater came from at this time, or who she was, or how she got there so early, I have never been able to discover. It might have been possible for her to have remained in the house during the previous night without my knowledge. The Government did its best to find out who the woman was but was unable to get any trace of her. She has passed into the future as one of the mysteries of the Surratt house.

In the evening of the same day Mrs. Surratt returned home alone. I did not see the horses brought back. She returned in the Port Tobacco stage—a line that ran from Port Tobacco and Bryantown to Washington, and which delivered its passengers at the Pennsylvania House on C Street. I asked Mrs. Surratt what had become of her son. She said he had gone to Richmond with Mrs. Slater to get a clerkship. This seemed to me a rather queer proceeding; he had never said anything to me about it, and had not even thought enough of me to say goodbye.

The carriage and white horses were returned on Sunday to Howard's stable by Mr. David Barry, to whom Surratt delivered them at Port Tobacco, and the following note from Surratt, given to Mr. Barry, was delivered by him to Brooke Stabler:

March 26, 1865.

Mr. Brooke:

As business will detain me for a few days in the *country* I thought I would send you your team back. Mr. Bearer will deliver in safety and pay the hire on it. If Mr. Booth, my friend, should want my horses let him have them, but no one else. If you should want any money on them he will let you have it. I should like to have kept the team for several days, but it is too expensive, especially as I have women on the brain, and may be away for a week or two.

Yours respectfully,

J. Harrison Surratt.[10]

This letter, too, indicates that Surratt had not lost his interest in his friend Booth, or in what was going on. If the Conspiracy was abandoned, as he claims, why were these horses, to whom he refers, being kept at a big expense to somebody?

Mrs. Surratt had requested me on the previous Saturday evening, March 25, to go to Brooke Stabler and say to him that the white horses and buggy would not be returned until the following Sunday. I made some objection to this. Said she, "Oh, Brooke considers John, Herold, and Atzerodt a party of young sports, and I want him to think so." A queer remark for her to make, but Brooke Stabler and I were not left in ignorance long before we learned to our sorrow what the real characters of Surratt, Herold, and Atzerodt were.

On Sunday, March 26, as I was about to leave the house for morning church service, Mrs. Surratt asked me if I would be kind enough to go to the National Hotel and request Mr. Booth to call on her in the afternoon. On my way down Sixth Street I met Atzerodt, who was also going to see Booth. When we arrived at the National Hotel we met Booth, who introduced us to a fellow actor he had with him, Mr. John B. McCullough. I told him that Mrs. Surratt wanted to see him on private business. Such was her message. Booth came in the afternoon as he promised and Mrs. Surratt had an interview with him near the head of the kitchen stairs. It was about the time that Mr. Barry had returned the white horses and carriage. None of this conversation did I hear nor do I know what it was about.

The last time that I knew of Booth and John H. Surratt having personal communication prior to the assasination was on the 18th day of March, when Booth gave Surratt passes for the play of *The Apostate* at Ford's Theater. After that I have no recollection whatever of having seen or heard of them being again in one another's company. Booth left for New York on the 21st of March, was in that city when he addressed me the telegram of the 23rd, and did not return until the evening of the 25th, stopping on the way at Baltimore. On the morning of that day, however, Surratt had left for Richmond.

On the 27th of March, Booth received the following letter from Samuel Arnold:

Hookstown, Balto. Co., March 27th, 1865.

Dear John:

Was business so important that you could not remain in Baltimore till I saw you? I came in as soon as I could, but found that you had gone to Washington. I called also to see *Mike*, but learned from his mother that he had gone out with you and had not returned. I concluded therefore he had gone with you. How inconsiderate you have been! When I left you, you stated that *we would not meet* in a month or so and therefore I made application for employment, an answer to which I shall receive during the week. I told my parents that I had ceased with you. Can I then, under existing circumstances, act as you request? You know full well that the government suspicions something is going on, therefore the *undertaking* is becoming more complicated. Why not, for the *present*, desist, for various reasons, which if you look into, you can readily see without my making any mention thereof? You nor anyone can censure me for my present course. You have been its cause, for how can I now come after telling them that I had left you? Suspicion rests upon me now from my whole family, and even parties in the country. I will be compelled to leave home anyhow, and how soon I care not. None, no, not one, were more in favor of the enterprise than myself, and today would have been there had you not done as you have. By this, I mean the manner of proceeding. I am, as you well know, in *need*. I am, you may say, in rags, whereas, to-day, I ought to be *well clothed*. I do not feel right stalking about without *means* and more from appearance a beggar. I feel my dependence, but even all this would have been forgotten, for I was *one with you*. Time more propitious will arrive yet. Do not act rashly or in haste. I would prefer your first query, "Go and see how it will be taken in Richmond," and *ere long* I shall be better prepared *to again be with you*. I dislike writing. Would sooner verbally make known my views. Yet your not waiting causes me thus to proceed. Do not in anger peruse this. Weigh all I have said, and, as a rational man and *friend* you cannot censure or upbraid my conduct. I sincerely trust this nor aught else that shall or may occur will ever be an obstacle to obliterate our former friendship and attachment. Write me at Baltimore as I expect to be in about Wednesday or Thursday, or, if you can possibly come on I will Tuesday meet you at Baltimore at B.

Ever I subscribe myself, your friend,

Sam.[11]

The same day, March 27, Booth sent the subjoined telegram to O'Laughlin:

M. O'Laughlin, Esq.,

    No. 57 North Exeter Street, Baltimore, Md.

    Get word to Sam. Come on with or without him Wednesday morning. We sell that day sure. Don't fail.

                                       J. Wilkes Booth.[12]

    It is not known, however, that O'Laughlin responded to this appeal, or that Booth made any efforts to carry out his plan on the Wednesday referred to.

CHAPTER XIII

Mrs. Surratt goes into the country on April 1 · Atzerodt visits her at her request · History of the horses used by the conspirators · The 3rd of April 1865 · Capitulation of Richmond · John H. Surratt returns to Washington · Leaves for Montreal, Canada, which he reaches on April 6, 1865 · Booth visits the Surratt house between April 1 and 10 · The "Lon" letter · Mrs. Surratt again visits Surrattsville on April 11 · Meets her tenant Lloyd on the road · Mysterious conversation about the "shooting irons"

Mrs. Surratt again found it necessary to go into the country on Saturday, April 1. When I left the house in the morning, she was at the breakfast table, and when I returned in the afternoon she was gone. She came back the same evening in a buggy driven by her brother, Mr. Zadoc Jenkins. She told me that she had been to Surrattsville. The buggy was a hired one and was returned with the horse to Howard's stable. Whether Mrs. Surratt went to Surrattsville alone in the morning or was accompanied by someone else I do not know. At any rate the horse and buggy did not belong to Mr. Jenkins, for he returned to his home on foot on the following Monday.

    On Sunday morning, April 2, Mrs. Surratt again requested me to go to the National Hotel for her and see Booth, and if he was not there to go to Atzerodt, and tell either of them that she wanted to see him. I called at the National Hotel but Booth was not there. He had left the hotel and did not return until April 8. Then I went to the Pennsylvania House and directly in front of the hotel stood Atzerodt holding by the bridle two horses, one a very small and the other a very large bay horse, blind of one eye.* Said I to him, "Whose horses are these?" He replied: "One is mine and the other is Booth's." I communicated my message to him and he requested me to mount one of the horses and ride back with him. I refused, stating that I intended to go to church. He then said he would accompany me. Then I mounted the horse and Atzerodt and I rode to Mrs. Surratt's house. Atzerodt dismounted and went in to see Mrs. Surratt, and I remained on the outside taking care of the horses.

The same afternoon Mrs. Surratt said to me that her brother, Mr. Jenkins, was anxious to return home and that she would be thankful to me if I would go to the Pennsylvania House and say to Mr. Atzerodt that he would oblige her very much by letting Mr. Jenkins have one of John's horses—meaning her son's horses. I called on Atzerodt at the Pennsylvania House that afternoon with Mr. Jenkins and stated my message. His reply was that before he could loan Mr. Jenkins one of the horses he would have to see Mr. Payne about it. This answer surprised me and I said to him, "What has Payne to do with the horses? You have stated that one was yours and that the other belonged to Booth, and Mrs. Surratt says that the horses are John's. How is this?" John Surratt himself had told me that the horses were his and had once shown me a receipt for their livery amounting to thirty dollars.

Atzerodt answered that Payne "had a heap to do with them." Mr. Jenkins, Atzerodt, and myself then walked as far as the corner of Ninth and F streets. Atzerodt requested us to wait for him and he went into the house to see about the horses. When he returned he told us that Mr. Payne would not consent to their loan. When I got back to the Surratt house and told its mistress what Payne and Atzerodt had said, she replied that she thought it very unkind of Mr. Atzerodt to refuse her; that she had been his friend, and had loaned him the last five dollars out of her pocket.†

* This was the horse purchased by Mudd and ridden by Payne on the night of the assassination.[1]
† It does not appear that Booth and his fellow conspirators had at any time more than two horses which they owned and which they boarded at Howard's stables.

The 3rd of April 1865 will be remembered as the eventful day on which Richmond capitulated to the successful Union armies. Worn out with the turmoil and excitement of the occasion, I was spending the evening in the parlor of my boardinghouse. At about half past six who should walk into the room but John H. Surratt? I was amazed to see him, for had not his mother told me that he had gone to Richmond to secure a clerkship? I had not seen him since he had left Washington on the morning of the 25th of March. He was very neatly dressed, unusually so. He had on a new suit of clothes. I asked him where he had been. "To Richmond," he answered. I then said, "Richmond is evacuated. Did you not hear the news?" "No, it is not," he said. "I saw Benjamin and Davis in Richmond, and they told me it would not be evacuated." [2] He then went up into my room to put on some clean underclothes. I went upstairs a few minutes after he did. He had very little to say to me. He wanted to exchange forty dollars in gold for greenbacks and he effected the exchange with Mr. Holohan. He showed me at the time nine or eleven twenty-dollar gold pieces and fifty dollars in greenbacks. Where he got the money he did not say nor did I ask him. I expressed a sort of surprise that he should have so much money, and then he said that he had an account in the Bank at Washington, but he did not say that he had received this money from the Bank at Washington. I had seen him before with money. He seemed to be always well supplied although he had no means of livelihood during nearly all the time I boarded in his mother's house. Later in the evening he asked me to walk down the street with him and partake of some oysters. He was dressed in gray clothes and had a shawl thrown over his shoulders. We ate our oysters in a saloon near Four-and-a-half Street and Pennsylvania Avenue. Then we walked back together as far as the Metropolitan Hotel, where he bade me goodbye. He said he was going to Montreal the next morning, and would correspond with me.

That was our final farewell. Little did I realize that evening as I wended my way homeward that we would never speak to one another again in this life; that the next time we met it would be after a period of more than two years, and as accuser and accused; that the Government of the United States would place him on trial as one of the murderers of Abraham Lincoln; that a gulf as deep and wide as an ocean would forever separate us, and that in the bottom of that gulf would lie the dead bodies of his companions, Booth, Payne, Herold, and Atzerodt, and of his own mother—all as the result of this wicked Conspiracy.

The Government at the Conspiracy trial endeavored to prove that Surratt's visit to Richmond was for the purpose of procuring funds to carry on the Conspiracy, but the charge was not sustained. Concerning it Surratt uses the following language in his lecture:

Shortly after our abandonment of the abduction scheme, some dispatches came to me which I was compelled to see through to Richmond. They were foreign ones, and had no reference whatever to this affair. I accordingly left home for Richmond, and arrived there safely on the Friday evening before the evacuation of that city. On my arrival I went to the Spotswood Hotel, where I was told that Mr. Benjamin, the then Secretary of War of the Confederate States, wanted to see me. I accordingly sought his presence. He asked me if I would carry some dispatches to Canada for him. I replied "yes." That evening he gave me the dispatches and $200 in gold with which to pay my way to Canada. That was the only money I ever received from the Confederate government or any of its agents.

It may be well to remark here that this scheme of abduction was concocted without the knowledge or the assistance of the Confederate government in any shape or form. Booth and I often consulted together as to whether it would not be well to acquaint the authorities in Richmond with our plan, as we were sadly in want of money, our expenses being very heavy. In fact the question arose among us as to whether, after getting Mr. Lincoln, if we succeeded in our plan, the Confederate authorities would not surrender us to the United States again, because of doing this thing without their knowledge or consent. *But we never acquainted them with the plan, and they never had anything in the wide world to do with it. In fact, we were jealous of our undertaking and wanted no outside help.* I have not made this statement to defend the officers of the Confederate government. They are perfectly able to defend themselves. What I have done myself I am not ashamed to let the world know.

I left Richmond on Saturday morning before the evacuation of that place, and reached Washington the following Monday at 4 o'clock P.M., April 3, 1865. As soon as I reached the Maryland shore I understood that the detectives knew of my trip South and were on the lookout for me. I had been South several times before for the Secret Service, but had never been caught. At that time I was carrying the dispatches Mr. Benjamin gave me: in a book entitled "The Life of John Brown." During my trip, and while reading that book, I learned, to my utter amazement, that John Brown was a martyr sitting at the right hand of God. I succeeded in reaching Washington safely, and in passing up Seventh street met one of our party, who inquired what had become of Booth.* I told him where I had been; that I was then on my way to Canada, and that I had not heard or seen anything of Booth since our separation. In view of the fact that Richmond had fallen, and that all hopes of the abduction of the President had been given up, I advised him to go home and go to work. That was the last time I saw any of the party. I went to a hotel and stopped over that night, as a detective had been to my house inquiring of the servant my whereabouts. In the early train next morning, Tuesday, April 4, 1865, I left for New York, and that was the last time I ever was in Washington until brought there by the U. S. Government a captive in irons, all reports to the contrary notwithstanding. . . .

Upon arriving in New York, I called at Booth's house, and was told by a servant that he had left that morning suddenly, on the ground of going to Boston to fulfill an engagement at the theater. In the evening of the same day I took the cars for Montreal, arriving there the next day. I put up at the St. Lawrence Hotel, registering myself as "John Harrison," such being my first two names.[3]

I really rejoiced that Richmond had fallen, for I felt that now the war was over, and above all that the friend of my college days would cease his foolish wanderings and settle down to some good business pursuit.

This was my honest feeling in relation to Surratt and one that always controlled my actions towards him. He did not write a single line to me while he was gone.

I saw Booth at Mrs. Surratt's house twice, between the 1st and 10th of April. I remember on one of these occasions, the 10th of April, a letter had been received from Surratt. Booth and Miss Annie Ward, the lady who had secured from Mrs. Murray for John Surratt the room occupied by Payne at the Herndon House, were there. Presently Booth arose and, advancing towards Miss Ward, said, "please let me see the

---

* Atzerodt; see his confession, below, Chapter **XXXI**.

address of *that lady* again." Miss Ward handed him a letter, which he read and then returned to her. When Booth and Miss Ward had departed, Miss Anna Surratt said, "Mr. Weichmann, here is a letter from brother John," and I read the letter which Booth had returned to Miss Ward. No lady's name was mentioned in it and Miss Surratt said it was mean to practice such deception on me. Miss Ward herself had received this letter and brought it to the house.

On this occasion I jested Booth about the fall of Richmond and told him I thought the Confederacy had gone up. "No, it is not gone up yet," he answered excitedly and, pulling a Perrine's war map out of his pocket, began to show the different routes which Johnston [4] would take to the mountains, where, he thought, he could make a stubborn resistance and thus prevent final capture.

I further asked him why he was not playing. He answered he was done playing; that the only play he cared to present was *Venice Preserved*. I did not know what he meant by this; I had never read the play. Years after, however, when I did read it, I found that the whole gist of the play was to assassinate the officers of the Venetian Cabinet in order to save Venice.

A very mysterious letter was delivered at the National Hotel about this time; it was evidently written by someone connected with the Conspiracy and in league with Booth. The letter was placed in the wrong box at the National Hotel, and in this way it failed to reach Booth.

Concerning this document Judge Bingham in his great argument before the Commission spoke as follows:

> One of Booth's conspirators, known as yet only to the guilty parties to the damnable plot and to the Infinite, who will unmask and avenge all blood-guiltiness, comes here to bear witness, unwittingly, against Booth. This unknown conspirator, who dated his letter at South Branch Bridge, April 6th, 1865, mailed and post-marked Cumberland, Md., and addressed to John Wilkes Booth, by his initials, "J.W.B., National Hotel, Washington, D.C.," was also in the "oil speculation." In that letter he says:

> > Friend Wilkes: I received yours of March 12th and reply as soon as practicable. I saw French, Brady and others about the oil speculation. The subscription to the stock amounts to eight

thousand dollars, and I add one thousand myself which is about all I can stand. Now, when you sink your well, go deep enough, don't fail; everything depends upon you and your helpers. If you cannot get through on your trip after you strike oil, strike through Thornton Gap and across by Capon, Romney and down the Branch. I can keep you safe from all hardships for a year. I am clear from all surveillance now that infernal Purdy is beat. . . .

I send this by Tom, and if he don't get drunk you will get it the 9th. At all events it cannot be understood if lost. . . .

No more, only Jake will be at Green's with the funds.

(Signed) Lon.

Who can fail to understand this letter? His words, "go deep enough," "don't fail," "everything depends on you and your helpers," "if you cannot get through on your trip after you strike oil, strike through Thornton Gap," etc., and "I can keep you safe from all hardships for a year," necessarily imply that when he "strikes oil" there will be an occasion for a flight: that a trip or route has already been determined upon; that he may not be able to go through by that route; in which event he is to strike for Thornton Gap, and across by Capon and Romney, and down the Branch, for the shelter which his co-conspirators offer him. "I am clear from all surveillance now" —does anyone doubt that the man that wrote these words wished to assure Booth that he was no longer watched, and that Booth could safely hide with him from his pursuers? Does anyone doubt, from the further expression in this letter, "Jake will be at Green's with the funds," that this was a part of the price of blood or that the eight thousand dollars subscribed by others, and the one thousand additional, subscribed by the writer, were also a part of the price to be paid?

"The oil business," which was the declared business of O'Laughlin and Arnold, was the declared business of the infamous writer of this letter: was the declared business of John H. Surratt; was the declared business of Booth himself as explained to Chester and Payne; was *the business* referred to in telegrams to O'Laughlin, and meant the murder of the President, of his Cabinet and of General Grant.

That this letter is not a fabrication is made plain by the testimony of Robert Purdy, whose name occurs in the letter.[5] He testified that he had been a detective in the Government service, and that he had been falsely accused, as the letter recites, and put under arrest; that there was a noted rebel living at the Thornton Gap; that there was a servant who drank there, known as "Tom" in the neighborhood of the South Branch Bridge; that there is an obscure route through the Gap, and as described in the letter; and that a man commonly called "Lon" lives at South Branch Bridge.

Judge Bingham claimed that if this letter was written by a conspirator every word of its contents was evidence against every other party in the conspiracy.[6]

On the evening of the 10th of April, the day Lee surrendered his forces to General Grant, Mrs. Surratt asked me if I would drive her to Surrattsville on the following Tuesday, April 11. I said "yes." On Tuesday morning she requested me to go to the National Hotel and ask Booth for the use of his horse and buggy. I found Booth in his room and gave him her message. Booth said, "I have sold my horse and buggy but here are ten dollars, go and hire one." I quizzed him about the horses, saying, "I thought they were John Surratt's horses." "No," answered he, "they are mine." I then left the hotel and went to Howard's stables, where I hired a horse and buggy.

The fact of Booth selling his buggy at this time is pretty good evidence that he had given up all thought of capturing the President at the theater.

We left the city about nine o'clock. On the way to Surrattsville we met John M. Lloyd near a small place called Uniontown. Mrs. Surratt had her buggy stopped and requested Mr. Lloyd to come to her. She leaned out of the buggy and spoke to him in such a way that I did not hear what they were talking about. This was the individual to whom Mrs. Surratt had leased her property at Surrattsville.

This is what Lloyd says about the matter:

On the Tuesday before the assassination of the President I was coming to Washington and I met Mrs. Surratt on the road at Uniontown. When she first broached the subject about the articles at my place I did not know what she had reference to. Then she came out plainer and asked me about the "shooting irons." I had myself forgotten about their being there. I told her that they were hid far away back and that I was afraid the house might be searched. *She told me to get them out ready: that they would be wanted soon.* I do not recollect the first question she put to me. Her language was indistinct, as if she wanted to draw my attention to something *so that no one else would understand.* Finally she came out bolder with it and said *they would be wanted soon.* I told her I had an idea of having them buried; that I was very uneasy about having them there.[7]

This evidence on the part of Lloyd shows conclusively that Mrs. Surratt was aware of the fact that the carbines (shooting irons) had been secreted at Lloyd's tavern, and, three days before the murder, she notifies him that they would be wanted soon. What were they to be wanted for?

She desired to meet a Mr. Nothey at Surrattsville, but when we arrived at half past twelve Nothey was not there.[8] She had a messenger dispatched for him with word that he should meet her at two o'clock in the afternoon. We then drove over to Mr. Bennett Gwynn's place, where we took dinner.[9] After dinner Mr. Gwynn, Mrs. Surratt, and I returned to Surrattsville. This time Mr. Nothey was on hand. She transacted her business with him and when it was over got into the buggy again and we returned to the city, which was reached at about six o'clock in the evening.

Atzerodt, who was boarding at the Pennsylvania House at that time, occupied room No. 51 with a party by the name of W. R. Keim, a lieutenant in the United States Army.[10] One day Keim saw a big knife in the possession of Atzerodt, who had arisen in the morning and left it in his bed. Keim arose, secured the knife, and put it under his own pillow. In a few moments Atzerodt returned, went up to his bed, and said, "Have you seen my knife?" Keim replied, "Yes, here it is." Atzerodt then said, "I want that; if one fails, I want the other."

Keim then gave it to him. His pistol and revolver he always carried around his waist.

And now with the conclusion of these events, we are brought face to face with the thrilling occurrences of the 14th of April.

CHAPTER XIV

The fatal 14th day of April · Booth at Ford's Theater in the morning · Is informed of the President's intended visit to the theater in the evening · Grows abstracted · Meets John F. Coyle and makes some significant remarks · Hires a horse from James Pumphrey · Calls at the Kirkwood House and leaves a card for Vice-President Johnson · Visits Mrs. Surratt · Meets John Matthews and delivers to him a mysterious letter · Atzerodt registers at the Kirkwood House · Suspicious actions and movements of Herold · Booth meets Payne and Atzerodt at the Herndon House · At nine o'clock Booth appears on horseback in the alley in the rear of Ford's Theater

The 14th day of April 1865, in Washington, was one of the most perfect days ever witnessed. There had been a slight fog early in the morning but as the day wore on it was dispelled under the influence of a genial spring sun.

It was fully 10 A.M. when John Wilkes Booth entered the dining room of the National Hotel. He was always a late riser and was the last man at breakfast that day. At the same table with him was a Miss Carrie Bean, daughter of a merchant and a very respectable young lady. Those who watched him say that he was as lively, piquant, and self-possessed as ever in his life.

His lady friend [Bessie Hale], who lived with her parents at the hotel, also met him, and with her he had a brief conversation. Then he went to the barbershop. When his toilet had been completed, he passed up Sixth Street to H. Here he went to Mrs. Surratt's house and met that lady.*

* This statement as to Booth's presence at the Surratt house on the morning of April 14, 1865, is confirmed by John T. Ford, in an article in the *North American Review*, April 1889.

From this place he went along H until he reached Tenth, and was seen coming by some attachés of the theater. He was faultlessly dressed in a suit of dark clothes and wore a tall silk hat. He had on a pair of kid gloves of a subdued color, a light overcoat was slung over his arm, and he carried a cane. Harry Ford,[1] who was standing in front of the theater with some other gentleman, first saw him and, turning to his companion, said, "Here comes the handsomest man in the United States."

He came directly to the theater, went to the box office, got his mail, came out, and sat down upon the front steps to read it. One of his letters was a very long one, so lengthy as to attract attention. When he had finished reading it, he arose and, approaching Harry Ford, said, "What's on tonight?"

"*Our American Cousin*, and we are going to have a big night," replied Harry. "The President and General Grant are going to occupy the President's box, and General Lee is going to have the adjoining one," said he by way of chaffing Booth.

"I hope they are not going to do like the Romans—parade their prisoners before the public to humiliate them," bitterly responded Booth.

Harry Ford replied that he was jesting about Lee but that Mr. Lincoln and General Grant would certainly attend the evening performance, that a note had been sent from the White House engaging the box. As Harry said this, the effect on Booth as to the information about President Lincoln and General Grant was apparent. He grew abstracted and soon departed. At last, he was face to face with the opportunity which he had been seeking. Now he could carry out the murderous purpose which had rankled in his brain; now in the theater he could kill the President and avenge the humiliated and conquered South.*

There are those who maintain that the plot to assassinate the President and other officers of the general Government originated with Booth then and there; that all along up to this time he had meditated only the capture of the President; that for its inception and execution he alone was responsible. In behalf of Mrs. Surratt and some of the others, it has been maintained that they knew nothing at all of the plot to assassinate. Indeed, so far as Mrs. Surratt is concerned, it has been alleged time and again that the only knowledge she had of a conspiracy was of the plot to capture the President, and not of Booth's purpose to assassinate him, and that Booth up to the last moment left on her mind the impression

* See *Philadelphia Press*, December 4, 1881.

that he intended only to capture. Well, now, if there were at any time a serious possibility of such an event as running the Chief Executive South and holding him as a hostage for the release of the Confederates in the Northern prisons, that possibility vanished with the evacuation of Richmond and the surrender of Lee's army. Prior to the occurrence of these two great military events, the President, if captured, could, perhaps, have been carried South and kept there, but now there was no South; the entire fabric was falling in pieces and Jefferson Davis himself was running away as fast as he could from the United States authorities. Where, now, could the conspirators have taken Lincoln and secreted him, and for what purpose? Abduction was more than ever an impossibility. It could not have been attempted at any time without probably killing the President, and certainly not now. The great victories won by the Union armies, no doubt, increased the hatred of these men towards Mr. Lincoln and emboldened them to undertake something more desperate and tragic than abduction, but to say that Booth on the very day, nay, the very instant he heard of the intended visit of the President to the theater, changed his plans from capture to murder is the very essence of absurdity.

Much of the testimony taken at the trial of the conspirators in 1865, and of John H. Surratt in 1867, showed that Booth from the start meditated murder; that it was in his heart and brain, and that he was merely waiting for his opportunity to commit the deed. The Charles Selby letter, identified as being in Booth's handwriting, which was dropped in the streetcar in New York City in November 1864; the assassin's actions on the 4th of March 1865, and his subsequent admission on the 7th of April to Samuel Knapp Chester, "What an excellent chance I had to kill the President on inauguration day," are all facts which of themselves wipe out the theory of capture, and show that Booth had it in his heart to kill.

Furthermore, John H. Surratt in his lecture, and the counsel for the conspirators Arnold, O'Laughlin, and Atzerodt admitted in their arguments that their clients had been connected with the plot to kidnap the President at the Soldiers' Home on March 16, 1865, and said the thing had failed. That was, they claimed, the end of the plot to capture, and there is no evidence to be found after that day of a single admission on the part of any of the conspirators that the abduction was ever again attempted.

Now, all this being so, why did Booth bring back Payne from Baltimore on March 27, and keep him in hiding for nearly three weeks at the Herndon House, where Surratt had secured a room for him through the intervention of Miss Annie Ward and where Mrs. Surratt paid him a visit? Why did he continue to keep Atzerodt, alias Port Tobacco, in Washington—a poor man, unemployed, and with no visible means of support? Why was he habitually consorting with Herold? Why did he continue his visits to Mrs. Surratt?

In the light of all that has transpired there is but one answer to all this and that answer can only be read in the President's death.

For the rest of that day Booth's movements were characterized by ceaseless activity; he was, indeed, a very busy man. Going from Tenth Street to Pennsylvania Avenue, he met Mr. John F. Coyle, then one of the editors of the *National Intelligencer*, and his very warm friend.[2]

This was towards noon. Mr. Coyle was accompanied by a friend by the name of Donoho, who had been well acquainted with Booth's father. Coyle shook hands with the actor and introduced his friend.

After some pleasant conversation, Booth expressed a desire to Mr. Coyle to talk with him. Mr. Coyle thereupon excused himself for a few minutes, but soon rejoined Booth and Major Donoho, who then all went to a restaurant in the neighborhood.

When they had consumed their refreshments, Booth spoke very warmly of the treatment of some Southern prisoners a few days before and said, "Suppose Lincoln was killed, what would be the result?" Mr. Coyle replied, "Johnson would succeed." Then he said, "But if he was killed?" "Then Seward," answered Mr. Coyle, and Booth continued, "But suppose he was killed, then what?" "Then anarchy or whatever the Constitution provides," and, laughing, Mr. Coyle said, "But what nonsense: they don't make Brutuses nowadays." Booth shook his head and said, "No—no, they do not." * [3]

This revelation made by Mr. Coyle many years after Mr. Lincoln's death is in itself a complete vindication of the position taken by the Government at the trial of the conspirators that it was Booth's purpose to assassinate not only the President, but other leading officers of the Government.

James Pumphrey, livery-stable keeper, said that about twelve o'clock Booth came in and engaged a horse. The one he hired was a bay with black legs, black mane and tail, with a white star in the forehead. The

* Mr. Coyle's statement was published in the *Washington Post*.

off front foot had white spots. Booth took the horse with him, and placed it in his stable at Ford's Theater. Mr. Pumphrey never saw the horse or rider after that day. Booth also told Pumphrey that he was going to Grover's Theater to write a letter. This was probably the document that later in the day he gave to John Matthews, the actor.[4]

The assassin also called at the Kirkwood House, where Atzerodt had registered in the morning before eight o'clock. The exact time of his visit to the hotel is, however, unknown.

He was evidently anxious to see the Vice-President, Mr. Johnson, but not finding him in, he left a card inscribed as follows: "Don't wish to disturb you, are you at home? J. Wilkes Booth."

This card was placed in the box of William A. Browning, private secretary to the Vice-President. Mr. Browning at first thought the card was intended for him, but when he heard of the assassination of the President he came to a different conclusion.

At three o'clock, he was seen by two colored women, Mrs. Mary J. Anderson and Mrs. Mary A. Turner, standing in the rear door of Ford's Theater in conversation with a woman and pointing down the alley. They remained there quite a while, but who this woman was has never been ascertained.[5]

James P. Ferguson, who kept a restaurant on the upper side of Ford's Theater, testified that he saw John Wilkes Booth between two and four o'clock standing near his place by the side of his horse—a small bay mare.[6] Mr. Maddox was talking with him. Booth remarked, "See what a fine horse I have got; now watch, he can run just like a cat." And striking his spurs into his horse, he went off down the street.

At four o'clock in the afternoon, being yet on horseback, he met John Matthews, the actor, on Pennsylvania Avenue at the triangular enclosure between Thirteenth and Fourteenth streets. What occurred is best told in the words of Matthews himself.

In a communication written by him and published in the *National Intelligencer* under date of July 17, 1867,[7] Matthews says:

> We met, shook hands and passed the compliments of the day. It so happened that the officers of General Lee's Army had just passed up in a body. I asked Booth, "Johnny, have you seen Lee's officers just brought in?" Booth replied, "Yes, Johnny, I have." Then placing his hand on his forehead, he exclaimed, "Great God! I have no longer a country!"

On observing his paleness, nervousness and agitation I remarked, "John, how nervous you are! What is the matter?" To which he replied, "Oh, no, it is nothing," and continued with, "Johnny, I have a little favor to ask of you, will you grant it?" "Why, certainly, Johnny," I replied, "what is it?" He then stated, "Perhaps I may leave town to-night and I have a letter here which I desire to publish in the *National Intelligencer*; please see to it for me unless I see you before ten o'clock to-morrow; in that case I will see to it myself."

At that moment, I observed Grant riding by in an open carriage, carrying also his baggage. Seeing this I called Booth's attention to him and said, "Why, Johnny, there goes Grant. I thought he was going to the theater this evening with the President." "Where?" he exclaimed. I pointed to the carriage, he looked towards it, grasped my hand tightly and galloped down the Avenue after the carriage.

The information imparted to Booth by Matthews was correct. It was, indeed, General Grant who had just passed, and who was on his way to the station to take the train for the North.

General Grant has put himself on record in reference to this incident; what occurred earlier in the day at Willard's Hotel shows that Booth had also intended to kill him, had the opportunity presented itself.

Here is what the General says about it:

Mr. Lincoln had promised to go to the theater that evening and wanted me to accompany him. While I was with the President a note was received from Mrs. Grant, saying that she was desirous of leaving Washington on the same evening on a visit to her daughter at Burlington. Some incidents of a trivial character had influenced this determination, and she decided to leave by the evening train. I was not disinclined, therefore made my excuses to the President, and at the hour determined upon we left home for the railway station. As we were driving along Pennsylvania Avenue, a horseman rode rapidly past us at a gallop, and wheeling his horse, rode back, peering into our carriage as he passed us. Mrs. Grant, with a perceptible shade of concern in her voice and manner, remarked to me, "That is the very same man that sat near us today at lunch with some others, and tried to hear our conversation. He was so rude, you remember, as to cause us to leave the dining-room. Here he is again riding after us." For myself I thought it was only idle curiosity, but learned afterwards that the horseman was Booth. It seemed that I was also to have been attacked, and Mrs. Grant's sudden determination to leave Washington disarranged the plan. Only a few weeks afterwards I received an anonymous letter stating that the writer had been detailed to assassinate me; that he rode in my train as far as Havre de Grace, and as my car was locked he had failed to get in. He thanked God that he had failed. I remember very well that the conductor locked our car door; but how far the letter was genuine I am unable to say. I was advised of the assassination of Lincoln in passing through Philadelphia, and immediately returned to Washington by a special train.* [8]

Booth was seen between four and five o'clock in a restaurant adjoining Ford's Theater in company with Ned Spangler,[9] James L. Maddox, and a young man named John Mouldey, and was drinking with them.

Between five and six o'clock he was seen at the Kirkwood House by one John Deveny, who had met him in Canada in October 1864.[10] Deveny was talking to a young man named Callan. As Booth passed into the hotel, Deveny asked him when he had returned from Canada. Booth replied that he had been back for some time, and that he would see him again.

Deveny said to him, "Are you going to play again?" To this query Booth answered, "No, I am not going to play again; I am in the oil business."

A few moments later he saw Booth going down the street on horseback; he was riding a bay horse; Deveny noticed particularly the kind of harness he had on the horse.

About the same time, according to the testimony of J. C. Burroughs, alias "Peanuts John," Booth returned to the alley at the theater and placed his horse in the stable, and from there he went to the National Hotel.[11]

When Booth handed his key to the clerk of the National Hotel that evening, he asked him, "Are you going to Ford's Theater tonight?" The clerk answered, "No." Booth replied, "You ought to go; there is to be some splendid acting there tonight." †

* This statement is fully confirmed by General Horace Porter in an interesting article in the *Century Magazine,* October 1897, and also by the assertions and confession of Atzerodt. [See below, Chapter XXXI.]

† From Oldroyd's book on Lincoln's assassination, p. 15.

In the meantime where were the other conspirators and what were their movements? That Payne, Herold, Atzerodt, and Mrs. Surratt knew what was going on does not admit questioning. Such of their conversations and actions on that dreadful day as have been preserved prove that fact.

Payne ordered an early dinner from Mrs. Murray, the landlady at the Herndon House, saying he was going to Baltimore. He paid his bill and the dinner was served to him in advance of the other guests. The usual dinner hour at this place was at four o'clock P.M.

Atzerodt had registered and secured a room at the Kirkwood House before eight o'clock A.M. At half past two, with Booth only a short distance away at Mrs. Surratt's house, he was seen endeavoring to get a horse from Brooke Stabler at Howard's stables and when questioned said, "He is going to send for Payne." Being refused by Stabler, he finally secured a bay horse from liveryman Kelleher and paid him five dollars for the hire.[12]

At about a quarter of one o'clock, David E. Herold in company with Atzerodt went to Naylor's stables and engaged of John Fletcher, the hostler, a horse, which he told him to keep, saying he would call for it at four o'clock. He came at a quarter past four, and paid five dollars for the hire. He wanted a particular horse that was there and secured him. A pair of English steel stirrups was given him and also a first-class saddle. He picked out a double-reined bridle. Before he mounted the horse he asked Fletcher how late he could stay out with him. Fletcher answered that he could stay no later than eight or nine o'clock. This horse, like Booth's, was never returned to the stable.[13]

Scipiano Grillo, a musician and keeper of a restaurant adjoining Ford's Theater who resided in the Navy Yard, met Herold on Tenth Street at about five o'clock.[14] Herold asked him if he had seen John Wilkes Booth. Grillo told him he had that morning about eleven o'clock at the theater and again in the afternoon at four o'clock when Booth stopped in his place and got a drink. Herold then said to Grillo, "Do you know that General Lee is in town?" Grillo told him no, he did not know, that he had not heard of it. "Yes," answered Herold, "he is stopping at Willard's." Grillo and Herold then started up the street and when they got to the Kirkwood House they met Atzerodt, who was sitting on the steps. Herold stopped to talk with him for a few minutes, after which he went with Grillo into Willard's Hotel. Here

Herold met two young men and talked with them a while, but Grillo did not hear what they said. As they were in the act of parting Herold remarked, "You are going tonight, ain't you?" One of the young men answered, "Yes." Grillo said that Surratt looked very much like the young man who spoke, but he would not say so positively.

Grillo and Herold then went toward Grover's Theater. Grillo noticed Herold walking a little lame, and said to him, "What's the matter? You are walking lame." He replied, "Nothing, my boots hurt me." When they got behind the little park there, Herold pulled his pants up to fix his boot. Grillo then noticed that he had run down into his boot leg a big dagger, the handle of which was four or five inches above the leg of the boot. Grillo said to him, "What do you want to carry that for?" Herold answered, "I am going into the country tonight on horseback and it will be handy there." Grillo laughed at him and said, "You ain't going to kill anybody with that," and left him.

Of the other conspirators, Arnold was at Fortress Monroe. Dr. Mudd was at his home in the country and O'Laughlin was in Washington. The movements of John H. Surratt will require a separate recital and will be detailed elsewhere.

When it was definitely ascertained that the President would come to the theater, preparations were at once begun towards decorating the box which he would occupy. The exterior was handsomely draped and festooned with flags, some of which were procured from the Treasury Department. The large armchair in which Mr. Lincoln was to sit was brought from Harry Ford's bedroom and placed inside the box during the afternoon. It was stationed next to the audience and railing of the box and farthest away from the stage. Its position seems to have been fixed purposely so as to afford the easiest mode of escape to the assassin. It was the first time it was used in the box during that winter season, and Mr. James L. Maddox, property man at the theater, testified that the last time that he saw it before that afternoon was in the winter of 1863, when it was used by the President on his first visit to the theater.[15]

During the same afternoon, two employees of the establishment, Edward Spangler, scene shifter, and J. C. Burroughs, alias "Peanuts John," bill distributor, were sent by Mr. Harry Ford to the box to remove the partition in it. Mr. Ford told them at the time that the President and General Grant were coming there in the evening. While

Spangler was at work removing the partition, he said to Burroughs, "Damn the President and General Grant." "What are you denouncing that man for—a man who has never done harm to you?" replied Burroughs. Spangler then said, "He ought to be cursed, he got so many men killed." [16]

About this time a man by the name of [Theodore B.] Rhodes, a resident of Washington, made his way into the theater. He was a kind of prying, curious Yankee, a mender of clocks, having a great curiosity to go around into different places and see what he could see, and in his going about he came to the theater and had a curiosity to see it.

He went in merely to see the theater. He went up the steps to the second floor, passed down in front where the circle was, to look upon the stage. While there he saw one of the box doors open a little and shut. He was anxious to see from that point of view, and supposing someone was in there, went down to the box and looked out from that point. As he approached the box, whoever was in there walked out and Rhodes entered and looked from that point onto the stage.

He had been looking but a minute or two when the same person, he supposed, who went out of the box, returned and spoke to him. The man said he was connected with the theater. They then had a few words together, when the attention of Rhodes was again drawn to the scenery on the stage. A curtain was down that had been recently painted and Rhodes stood looking at that. Then he heard this man behind him doing something and turned around to see what he was doing. Rhodes supposed he was looking down and noticed that he had a piece of wood; whether he had it under his coat or was taking it out, he could not say. The piece of wood was about three feet long and about as wide as Rhodes's two fingers, slanting a little towards each end from the center.

As Rhodes turned around, the man said, "The President is going to be here tonight." That was the first intimation Mr. Rhodes had of the expected presence of the President. Rhodes replied, "He is?" The man then said, "We are going to fix up this box for his reception. I suppose there is going to be a big crowd here and we are going to endeavor to arrange it so he won't be disturbed." Some excuse had to be made for these arrangements and this was the excuse given. He then fixed the piece of wood into a hole there as large as his (Rhodes's) thumb.

144

The hole was about one inch or an inch and a half long and about three quarters of an inch wide. The man placed one end of the stick in the hole, and it being a little too large, took a knife and whittled it down a little; he also cut the hole a little larger for the purpose of making it fit. Then he placed it against the panel of the door across to the wall, forming a triangle. The man said, "The crowd may be so immense as to push the door open and we want to fasten it so this cannot be the case." He asked Rhodes if he thought it would hold sufficiently tight. Rhodes answered that he should judge that it would hold against a great pressure; that a hole would be punched through the panel before it would give way. The wood was either of oak or North Carolina pine. Rhodes was rather of the impression that it was North Carolina pine, which is a very tough wood. He thought that it was very singular that the proprietor of the theater could not afford a lock for a box of that kind.

During Surratt's trial the district attorney [E. C. Carrington] put the following questions to Rhodes:

Q. State if this is the man (pointing to the prisoner, John H. Surratt), and whether you saw him there.

A. I should judge that was the man.

Q. Have you any doubt about it?

A. No, sir.[17]

This testimony by Mr. Rhodes has never been contradicted by anyone except Surratt, but whether it was Surratt or someone else who did the work, the facts on this point are very important, for they prove conclusively that there was someone in the theater in the President's box that day who was in active collusion with Booth in the carrying out of his crime. Rhodes not only identified the man as being Surratt, but saw the hole he had made in the wall, and also the piece of wood that was to fit in it.

Thus it will be seen that by nightfall all the arrangements for the approaching assassination had been completed. Four of the conspirators, Booth, Atzerodt, Payne, and Herold, had been provided with horses; that used by Payne, the one-eyed bay, being furnished by Booth himself. The box at the theater was prepared and awaiting its august victim; the hole in the door through which the assassin would sight the President had been bored, and the wooden brace seen by Rhodes, and which was to be fitted in its place in the wall and intended to keep back the outside crowd, was there and ready to do its part in the awful tragedy.

Indeed, everything relating to the execution of the nefarious purposes of Booth appears to have been carried out with marvelous precision and rapidity. Looking back at all these events and considering the amount of detail work necessary to be accomplished before Booth could fire his murderous pistol shot, is it not asking too much of human credulity to have an intelligent people made believe that Booth formed his plan to kill the President only after he had heard of his intended visit to the theater on the night of the 14th of April?

At eight o'clock in the evening Booth met Payne and Atzerodt at the Herndon House. He told Payne the fatal hour had struck, placed in his hands a knife, a revolver, and a bogus package of medicine, told him to do his duty, and gave him a horse with directions to meet him beyond Anacostia Bridge.[18]

Booth, according to Atzerodt, said that he himself should murder Mr. Lincoln and General Grant; that Payne should take Mr. Seward, and Atzerodt, Mr. Johnson. Atzerodt replied that he would not do it; that he had gone into this thing to capture, but was not going to kill.[19]

It is very questionable if this statement of Atzerodt's to the Commission in reference to Mr. Johnson was true, and whether it was not made for the purpose of saving his life. He was seen by John Fletcher, the hostler, to enter the Kirkwood House, where the Vice-President was stopping, about the time the President was shot, and Mr. Seward assaulted; nor did he return the horse which he procured from the liveryman Kelleher until sometime after the assassination. When he left Fletcher, before going into the Kirkwood House, he made this significant expression, "If this thing happens tonight you will hear of a present." Fletcher made some remark about his mare, saying, "I would not like to ride that mare through the city in the night, for she looks so skittish." "Well," said Atzerodt, "she's good upon a retreat." [20]

The room which Atzerodt had secured in the Kirkwood House was directly over that of Mr. Johnson. A guard was stationed at the door of the Vice-President's room, but any evil-disposed person coming downstairs could easily have thrown a handful of snuff into the eyes of the sentry, and thus effected an entrance to the presence of the Vice-President.

A little before nine o'clock Booth, booted and spurred, appeared in the alley and rode up to the rear door of Ford's Theater, fully prepared to commit the deed which for all future time would stand out as the supreme crime of the nineteenth century.

CHAPTER XV

Mr. Lincoln goes to City Point · Enters Richmond after its capture · Returns to Washington · His last address to his fellow citizens · His last day on earth · Interview with Schuyler Colfax · Meets his Cabinet · Takes a drive with Mrs. Lincoln · Goes to Ford's Theater in the evening · Is enthusiastically welcomed · Booth appears on the scene · Calling of the time in front of the theater · Assassination of the President · Booth leaps from the box and makes his escape · His pursuit · Payne enters the Seward house · Attempts to kill Seward · The terrific fighting scene in the sick man's bedroom · Payne makes his escape

"Mr. Lincoln early in April, 1865, went to City Point, Va., and was there when Grant defeated Lee. The day after Richmond was taken, he went to that city, not as a conqueror, but as a deliverer, and was welcomed with acclamation, especially, by the poor negroes, who kissed the hand which had broken their bonds.

"After Lee's surrender he returned to Washington. Here in the evening, in the midst of universal rejoicing, he addressed his fellow citizens, calling upon them to remember Him to whom they owed the preservation of the Union, and the soldiers and sailors who, under God, had won the victory.* He also on this occasion announced his pur-

* President Lincoln addressed the people from his mansion in Washington on the night of April 11, saying, "If universal amnesty is granted to the insurgents, I

147

pose to issue another proclamation to the people of the South in order to hasten the work of restoration.

"On the morning of the 14th, Good Friday, the last day of his life, his son Robert breakfasted with him and received from him all the details of Lee's surrender. The President then spent an hour with Schuyler Colfax, Speaker of the House.[1] The conversation naturally turned upon the immediate future of the nation and every word uttered by Lincoln breathed pardon toward the repentant rebels. After a brief interview with some of his Illinois friends the President met his cabinet between eleven and twelve o'clock. He seemed more joyous than was his wont. General Grant was also present. Then in the afternoon he drove out with Mrs. Lincoln and conversed of the happier days which seemed in store for them. He seemed to be looking forward to four years of peaceful administration and after that to retirement and a quiet conclusion of an eventful life in the midst of old and familiar scenes, but even then the weapon of death in the hands of the assassin was laden with the fatal bullet. A peace such as the world cannot give was nearer to the weary heart of Lincoln than he dreamed.

"In the evening he again met Mr. Colfax with the Hon. George Ashmun, who had presided at the Chicago Convention which had given him his first nomination for the presidency.[2] It was well understood in Washington that the President and General Grant would that evening attend Ford's Theater." *[3] General Grant, however, as already stated, owing to another engagement could not attend, and left for Philadelphia in the afternoon. Mr. Colfax was invited to accompany the party but declined, to his subsequent regret. The President himself was reluctant about going as his mind was on other things, but he was not willing to disappoint the people in their hour of public rejoicing.

---

can not see how I can avoid exacting in return universal suffrage, or at least suffrage on the basis of intelligence and military service."

Booth was standing before Mr. Lincoln on the outskirts of the large assemblage.

"That means nigger citizenship," he said to little Herold by his side. "Now, by God, I'll put him through."

Frederick Stone, counsel for Herold after Booth's death, told Mr. G. A. Townsend this was the occasion of the deliberate murder being resolved upon by Booth, and in the words above. (*Katy of Catoctin*, p. 490.)

* I am indebted to *Harper's* war publication for the introductory to this chapter.

Major [Henry R.] Rathbone and Miss [Clara] Harris, daughter of Senator Ira Harris of New York, joined the President and Mrs. Lincoln and drove with them in the President's carriage to Ford's Theater, reaching there about half past eight.[4]

At the theater, when the presence of the President was known, the actors stopped playing, the band struck up "Hail to the Chief," and the audience arose and received him with cheers and shouts of applause. The party passed to the right into the box, in the second tier, which was on the left of the stage. When the President entered, he turned smilingly to the cheering audience and bowed. He then seated himself in the armchair which had been expressly provided for him that afternoon, and then with his accustomed modesty drew the curtain half across the box. Mrs. Lincoln sat next to the right of the President, and to the right of her, Miss Harris, and almost immediately behind Miss Harris sat Major Rathbone.

The theater was brilliantly illuminated; everybody was happy; the mighty war which had filled the land with desolation and blood was drawing to a close and he, the great chief, who had borne the supreme brunt and burden of it all, and whose kind heart had suffered a thousand agonies, was now in the midst of his beloved people to receive their applause.

"The play for the evening was *Our American Cousin*.[5] The American flag dropped over Lincoln's head, but his thoughts were occupied with a grander drama than that which was presented to the audience. Four years ago the flag had been hauled down from Fort Sumter and on this very day the same old flag had been restored by the hands of Major [Robert] Anderson. It was natural, therefore, that the President's mind should range over the weary years which had intervened and of which he was so great a part. His face wore a happy smile such as had not been there since the beginning of the war.

"Another event, however, was in progress of which neither Lincoln nor the audience knew." [6]

When Booth rode into the alley in the rear of the theater he called for Edward Spangler, an employee of the theater, to hold his horse. Spangler sent a young man named Burroughs, another employee, in his place, telling him that he would take all responsibility.

Booth stepped into the theater through the rear door, and was then overheard by one John Sleichmann, to say to Spangler, "Ned, you will help me all you can, won't you?" to which Spangler replied, "Oh, yes." [7] He now took a brief survey of the house, passed out the same way, and soon after appeared at the front. There he had a private and hurried conversation with two or three persons. One of these persons was a ruffianly-looking fellow. It was then drawing near the end of the second act. Booth then said, "I think he will come out now," referring probably to the President, whose carriage had arrived and was standing in front of the theater. One of the three persons had been standing out on the curb looking at the carriage. Just before ten o'clock Booth went into a saloon near the theater and took a drink of whisky. He then came out and rejoined his confederates, the parties with whom he had been conversing.

He then passed into the passage leading to the stage from the street. At this time, one of his confederates, a neatly dressed man, stepped into the vestibule of the theater, looked at the clock, came out and called the time, started up the street, was gone a few minutes, returned, looked at the clock and called the time again. By this time Booth had reappeared in front of the theater. Presently this same party who had called the time came and looked at the clock and called the time a third time in a loud voice. "Ten minutes past ten." He then started up the street and Booth passed into the theater.

While this scene was being enacted, a young soldier, Sergeant Joseph M. Dye, of Company C, Independent Pennsylvania Artillery, was sitting on a platform in front of the theater, and near the President's carriage.[8] There was also another soldier there, Robert Cooper, a member of the same company, who heard the time called but only for the third time, as he had not always remained in the same place as Sergeant Dye, but had been walking around.

The Government, while conducting its investigation in 1865, confronted Sergeant Dye with a number of persons in the hope of discovering who the man was who called the time, but the sergeant could identify none of these as the guilty person.

At the trial of Surratt in 1867, Dye, when speaking of the man calling the time, said:

"He placed himself in front of the theater, where the light shone clear on his face. There was a picture on that countenance of great excitement, exceedingly nervous and very pale."

Then Judge [Edwards] Pierrepont asked:

Q. Did you see that man distinctly?

A. I did.

Q. Very distinctly?

A. I did very distinctly.

Q. Do you see him now?

A. I do.

Q. Can you tell us where he is?

A. I can.

Q. Tell us where he is.

A. He sits there (pointing to the prisoner Surratt).

Q. Is that the man?

A. It is. I have seen his face often since, while I have been sleeping —it was so exceedingly pale.[9]

Sergeant Dye had been taken to the jail where Surratt was confined, and had identified him there. Speaking of this while under cross-examination by Attorney [Richard T.] Merrick, he said:

"The man I saw in prison I do [can] say positively was the owner of the face I saw in front of Ford's Theater on the night of the 14th of April; and this is the man here. There is no doubt about it." [10]

This was during the second scene of the third act of *Our American Cousin*, then being performed by Laura Keene and her company. Booth passed up to the dress circle to the right and near the President's box, where he stopped a moment and leaned against the wall. He took a small pack of visiting cards from his pocket, selecting one and replacing the others, stood a moment with it in his hand, and then showed it to the President's messenger, who was sitting just below him, and who was thoroughly absorbed in the play of the evening.* Whether the messenger took this card into the box, or after looking at it allowed him to go in, is not known, but Booth went down one step, placed his hands on the door of the passage leading to the President's box with his knee against it, and pushed the door open. Once on the inside, he placed the brace against the door which had been previously prepared for the purpose of preventing an entrance from the outside, passed along the passageway to the door on the left opening into the President's box, stopped and looked through a hole which had been

* This testimony in relation to Booth handing his card to the President's attendant was given by Captain Theodore McGowan. Pitman, p. 78.

bored through the door, to see the President's position, and to observe if his attention was concentrated on the stage, softly pushed the door open and entered, no one observing him, and standing within two or three feet of the President, fired.

The ball entered the back part of the left side of the President's head. The pistol used was a large-sized Derringer, about six inches in length, carrying a large hand-made ball of dense britannia lead,[11] another evidence of the assassin's cruelty. Upon hearing the discharge of the pistol behind him, Major Rathbone, looking around, saw through the smoke a man between the door and the President. At the same time he heard the man shout some word, which he thought was "freedom." Another witness thought he shouted "revenge for the South." Booth, the moment he fired, dropped his pistol and drew a long knife. Major Rathbone instantly sprang upon him and seized him. Booth wrested himself away from the Major's grasp and made a violent thrust at his breast with the knife, which Rathbone parried, receiving a wound in his left arm between the elbow and the shoulder, about one and a half inches deep and several inches in length. Booth then rushed to the front of the box. Major Rathbone attempted to seize him again, but only caught his clothes as he was going over the railing. Holding in his right hand the knife, point downward, Booth leaped over and down to the stage about twelve feet.[12]

As he was descending, the spur in his left boot caught on to the flag which had been draped in front of the President's box, in honor of his presence, and clung to it, causing his left foot to partially turn under him as he struck the stage, and thereby one of the bones of his leg was broken. The height of the box to the stage was twelve feet. Had it not been for this accident, Booth would doubtless have made his escape into Virginia, within the Confederate lines, and possibly out of the country; and thus it was that the national flag was a mute instrument in the vengeance which overtook the President's murderer. Booth, as he fled across the stage, turned partially, faced the audience, threw up his hands, holding aloft the gleaming knife, and exclaimed, "Sic semper tyrannis."

He passed out by the left side of the stage, through the passage, and escaped by the rear door of the theater, which he threw open. In his exit while making towards the door, he encountered but one obstruction in the person of William Withers, Jr., leader of the orchestra.[13]

This gentleman had gone on the stage to see the manager with reference to the singing of a national song. As befitting the occasion he had composed one entitled "Honor to Our Soldiers," and had dedicated it to the President. It was to have been sung between two of the acts by a quartet expressly engaged for the occasion and by the entire company, who were to be attired in American colors.

Mr. Withers had met Booth that evening in front of a saloon which adjoined the theater. It was a sultry night. "Good evening, Billy," said he, "come and have something." As Mr. Withers was leaving to enter the theater, Booth remarked, "I'll witness the performance tonight." Withers noticed nothing strange about his demeanor, and subsequently saw him in the theater as he himself was coming out for the overture.

After the first act J. P. Wright, the stage manager, sent him word that he would be unable to have the special song given at that time, but would try and have it rendered between the second and third acts.

A similar message was sent at the close of the second act, and Mr. Withers became somewhat exercised. As he started to go upon the stage, he saw Booth in the balcony walking down the aisle in the direction of the President's box. He was seemingly attentive to the acting, for the curtain had again gone up. Mr. Withers on the stage encountered Spangler, a scene shifter, whose office he afterwards learned was to turn out the lights in the theater as soon as the shot was fired. This man obstructed the passage of Mr. Withers. "What do you want here?" demanded Spangler. Mr. Withers told him it was none of his business. When Mr. Withers appeared, Spangler left his position on the stage alongside the box in which was the aparatus for illuminating the theater. Mr. Withers closed the lid of the box and sat upon it to talk to the manager, wholly unconscious that he was spoiling the plan of having the lights shut off.

Mr. Wright informed Mr. Withers that the song would be given at the close of the performance, and Miss Laura Keene had sent word to the President requesting him to stay and hear it.

Mr. Withers was about to return to the orchestra when the crack of a revolver startled him. All was quiet instantly, and then he saw a man jump from the President's box to the stage. It was Booth. He ran directly to the door leading into the alley. This course brought him right into the path of Mr. Withers. He had a dagger in his hand

and waved it threateningly. He evidently did not recognize Mr. Withers, for he appeared like a maniac. His eyes seemed starting from their sockets and his hair was disheveled.

With head down, he ran towards Mr. Withers and cried, "Let me pass!" He slashed at him and cut through his coat, vest, and underclothing. The assassin struck again, the point of the weapon penetrating the back of Mr. Withers' neck, and the blow brought him to the floor. Withers saw him make his exit into the alley and caught sight of the horse held by Peanuts John.

What Mr. Withers here says about the turning out of the lights is, no doubt, true. That such was Booth's intention is shown by the confession of Atzerodt, who says that Booth told him an actor was to be the best assistant in the theater, to turn off the gas. Heart-rending as was the scene in the playhouse on that terrible night, had this been accomplished, no one can conjecture what the result might have been in that edifice, crowded as it was with human beings. It is beyond the range of human speculation.*

When the audience discovered that the President had been shot, the greatest commotion arose. Cries of "Stop him!" "Hang him!" "Burn the theater!" could be heard all over the house, and it was with some difficulty that the building was emptied of its treasure of excited men and women.

A gentleman named Joseph B. Stewart was sitting in a front seat of the orchestra on the right-hand side when the President was shot. The noise made by the discharged pistol startled him. He heard an exclamation, and simultaneously saw a man leaping from the President's box. Instantly he jumped on the stage and ran in pursuit of him as quickly as possible, crying out three times, "Stop that man!" He knew Booth and recognized him at once.[14]

Jacob Ritterspaugh, assistant scene shifter at the theater, was the first to pass out of the rear door in the effort to catch Booth, and just as he did so, and before Mr. Stewart reached it, when within twenty-five feet of it, the door was slammed to and closed. Near the door on his right, Stewart saw a person standing who seemed to be

* In the *North American Review* for April 1889, Mr. John T. Ford says, "If the capture was made in the theater, all the lights were to be extinguished by one knowing how to do it." And there is no doubt that the same was to be done in case of assassination, but it miscarried.

in the act of turning and who did not appear to be moving about like the rest. Every other person in the scenes, and there were five or six, was literally bewildered except this man. As Mr. Stewart approached the door, and was only about fifteen feet from it, this person was facing the door. Mr. Stewart testified that he looked more like Edward Spangler than anyone else he knew.

He was satisfied that the person was inside the door, was in a position, and had the opportunity to have interrupted the exit of Booth, and from his manner, he was cool enough to do so. He was nearest the door, and could have opened it and gone out before Stewart did. It was possible for him to slam the door without being noticed. Mr. Stewart was very decided in his opinion that Spangler resembled the person he saw there.

On reaching the door, Stewart pulled it open and rushed out. Booth had just mounted his horse, which Burroughs was still holding, and struck him with the handle of his knife.

The moon was just beginning to rise.[15] The horse was moving with a quick, agitated motion, with the reins drawn a little to one side, and for a moment described a kind of circle from right to left. Stewart ran in the direction in which the horse was heading, and when almost in reach of the left flank, the rider brought him around somewhat in a circle from the left to the right, crossing over, the horse's feet rattling violently on what appeared to be rocks. Stewart crossed in the same direction, aiming to catch the rein, and was now on the right flank of the horse. He could have reached the right flank of the horse when perhaps two-thirds of the way over the alley. Again Booth backed to the right side of the alley, brought the horse forward, and spurred him; at the same time he crouched forward over the pommel of the saddle. The horse then shot forward, and soon swept rapidly to the left of the alley up toward F Street. The assassin now headed for the Anacostia Bridge,[16] on the road beyond which he was to meet Payne and Herold, and was soon out of sight.

When Ritterspaugh returned from the alley to the stage, he encountered Spangler, who struck him on the face with the back of his hand, saying, "Don't say which way he went." Ritterspaugh asked him what he meant by doing that, to which Spangler replied, "For God's sake, shut up." [17]

The scene in the President's box all this time was one of the greatest consternation. Almost as soon as the assassin made his leap, Major Rathbone rushed for the outer door of the passage. He found it barred by the wooden brace, one end of which was secured in the wall, and the other resting against the door. It was so securely fastened that it required considerable force to remove it. Persons on the outside were beating against the door, for the purpose of entering the box. Several gentlemen who represented themselves as surgeons were granted admission.

Miss Laura Keene was one of the first persons to enter the box. She took charge of the President, and his head for a time rested on her lap. An eyewitness who saw her when she made her exit from the box describes her appearance:

"Attired, as I had so often seen her, in the costume in her part in *Our American Cousin,* her hair and dress were in disorder, and not only was her gown soaked in Lincoln's blood, but her hands, and even her cheeks where her fingers had strayed, were bedaubed with the sorry stains! But lately the central figure in the scene of comedy, she now appeared the incarnation of tragedy." *

The President never recovered consciousness after being shot; his head was slightly bent forward, and his eyes were closed. It was first thought that he had been shot through the heart, but when his vest was opened, no wound could be seen in his breast. The surgeons then discovered that he was shot in the head, between the left ear and the central portion of the head.

As soon as the seat of the wound was located, it was determined to remove the President from the theater. He was taken to the house of Mr. [William] Petersen, a German tailor, on Tenth Street directly opposite the theater.[18] He was carried to a small extension room at the end of the hall. The room was plainly furnished and there were some prints hanging on the wall. He was laid transversely across the cottage bedstead, as he was too tall to be placed in any other position. His head was supported upon two pillows and his feet rested against the opposite side of the footboard.

The members of the Cabinet came in one after the other, as soon as they were informed of the terrible deed. Dr. Stone was sitting upon the bed. Secretary Welles occupied a chair, which he did not vacate

---

* Recollections by Seaton Munroe in the *North American Review,* April 1896.

during the entire night. Surgeon General Barnes was sitting in an ordinary chair by the bedside holding Mr. Lincoln's left hand. All the other persons in the room were standing. Senator Sumner and Robert Lincoln were, the greater part of the time, leaning over the headboard.[19]

"From time to time Mrs. Lincoln was brought into the room, but she never remained long. The President's eyes were closed and ecchymose. Below the lids and around the cheekbones the flesh was black. Blood and brain were oozing from the wound in his head upon the uppermost of the pillows which supported it. He had been stripped of all his clothing, and whenever one of the physicians turned down the sheet which covered his person, in order to feel the beatings of his heart, his brawny chest and immensely muscular arms revealed the hero of many a succssful wrestling match in his youthful days at New Salem.

"His breathing was for a long time loud and stertorous, ending in deep-drawn sighs. Except for his respiration and the sobbing of his wife, son, and devoted servant, not a sound was to be heard in that chamber for hours. The dropping of a pin would have been audible.

"What a tragic episode in life's history was this to all there assembled! And not only to them, but to the nation and to the world. His pulse was vacillating all through the night—at times strong and rapid and at others feeble and slow. His vital power was prodigious or he would have died within ten minutes after he was shot." [20]

Surrounding the deathbed of the President were Secretaries Stanton, Welles, Usher, Attorney General Speed, Postmaster General Dennison, M. T. Field, Assistant Secretary of the Treasury, Judge Otto, Assistant Secretary of the Interior, General Halleck, General Meigs, Senator Sumner, F. R. Andrews of New York, General Todd of Dakota, John Hay, private secretary, Governor Oglesby of Illinois, General Farnsworth, Mr. and Miss Kenny, Miss Harris, and Drs. E. W. Abbott, R. K. Stone, C. D Latch, Neal, Hall, and Liebermann. Secretary McCulloch remained until 5 A.M., and Chief Justice Chase, after several hours' attendance during the night, returned again in the morning.[21]

The night wore on, long and anxious, and finally the gray dawn of a dull rainy morning began to creep slowly into the room. And still the martyr lived—if living it could be called.

The town clock struck seven. Almost immediately afterward the character of the President's breathing changed. It became faint and low. At intervals it altogether ceased. And then it would be again resumed. At last, just twenty-two minutes past seven, he ceased to breathe. "Now," exclaimed Stanton, "he belongs to the ages." [22]

When it became certain to all that his soul had taken its flight, the Reverend Dr. Gurley dropped upon his knees by the bedside and uttered a fervent prayer.[23] Never was a supplication wafted to the Creator under more solemn circumstances.

When it was finished most of the persons assembled began slowly to withdraw from the chamber of death. The eyes were completely closed and silver coins placed upon them, and with a pocket handkerchief the jaw, which had already begun to fall, was tied up. Mr. Stanton threw open the windows. Just then Petersen, the owner of the house, entered and, rudely drawing the upper pillow from under the head of the dead, tossed it into the yard. Shortly afterward all retired from the room. Mr. Stanton locked the door and stationed a sentry in front of it. In the front parlor Dr. Gurley was again praying. Mrs. Lincoln was lying upon a sofa mourning and her son Robert was standing at her head. When Dr. Gurley had finished his prayer, Robert Lincoln assisted his mother to rise and walk to the front door. The President's carriage was standing before the house, as it had stood through that terrible night. As Mrs. Lincoln reached the doorstep she cast a hurried glance at the theater opposite and three times repeated, "Oh, that dreadful, dreadful, dreadful house." She was then helped into the carriage, which drove away.

Perhaps the most affecting incident connected with this tragedy occurred an hour later. Mr. Lincoln's body, encased in a plain wooden box around which was draped the American flag, was borne from the house by six private soldiers, then placed in an ordinary hearse, behind which the soldiers marched like mourners, and so carried it to the Executive Mansion.

While Lincoln lay dying in one room of the Petersen house, an important byplay in the tragedy of the assassination was being enacted in another room of the same building. John Matthews was there alone and the chief actor in the scene—the same John Matthews to whom Booth, on the afternoon of the 14th of April, had delivered a letter addressed to Mr. John F. Coyle, one of the proprietors of the *National*

The President's box at Ford's Theater

The conspirators (clockwise from left): John H
Surratt in the uniform
of the Papal Zouaves, 18
David E. Herold, 1865;
Dr. Samuel A. Mudd;
George Atzerodt, 1865;
Edward Spangler, 1865
Michael O'Laughlin, 186
Samuel Arnold, 1865

Left, Mary E. Surratt
Below left, Wanted envelope showing
portrait of Booth and urging his capture;
Lincoln mourning envelope
Below, Lewis Payne
Opposite, John Wilkes Booth,
from a carte de visite

Above, A. C. Richards, 1865; Louis J. Weichmann, 1865
Below, The Navy Yard Bridge, Washington, D. C., on Booth's escape route
Opposite, Booth's escape route, as illustrated in Pitman

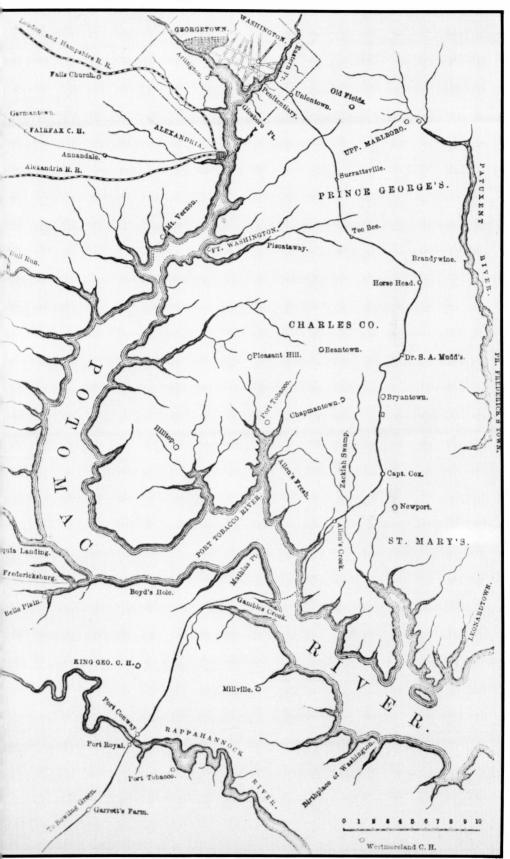

LONDON AND HAMPSHIRE R. R.

Falls Church.

Germantown.

FAIRFAX C. H.

Annandale.

Alexandria R. R.

Bull Run.

POTOMAC

Aquia Landing.

Fredericksburg.

Belle Plain.

KING GEO. C. H.

Port Conway.

Port Royal.

RAPPAHANNOCK

Port Tobacco.

To Bowling Green.

Garrett's Farm.

GEORGETOWN.

Arlington.

ALEXANDRIA.

Mt. Vernon.

FT. WASHINGTON.

WASHINGTON.

Giesboro Pt.

Eastern Br.

Penitentiary.

Uniontown.

Piscataway.

Pleasant Hill.

Port Tobacco.

Hilltop.

PORT TOBACCO RIVER.

Allen's Fresh.

Boyd's Hole.

Mathias Pt.

Gambles Creek.

Millville.

Old Fields.

UPP. MARLBORO.

Surrattsville.

PRINCE GEORGE'S.

Tee Bee.

Brandywine.

Horse Head.

CHARLES CO.

Beantown.

Chapmantown.

Dr. S. A. Mudd's.

Bryantown.

Zachiah Swamp.

Allen's Creek.

Capt. Cox.

Newport.

ST. MARY'S.

PATUXENT RIVER.

PR. FREDERICK'S TOWN.

LEONARDTOWN.

R   I   V   E   R.

Birthplace of Washington.

0 1 2 3 4 5 6 7 8 9 10

Westmoreland C. H.

VII

(1)   *(2)*

(4)

(3)

*Booth himself stated that he had attended Lincoln's second inaugural on March 4, 1865:
"What an elegant chance I had to kill the President on Inauguration Day if I wished."
Some scholars find the other conspirators there, too: (1) Herold; (2) Atzerodt;
(3) Spangler; (4) Payne, in Stetson-like hat; (5) Surratt, in gray suit; (6) Booth.*

Opposite, Lincoln funeral cortege in Philadelphia, April 23, 1865
Above, The offices of Drs. Brown and Alexander, embalmers of Lincoln's body
Below, The stables where Booth hired his escape horse

*Right, Boston Corbett
and Captain Doherty
Below, The Military Commission
(left to right): Col. Clendenin,
Col. Tompkins, Brig. Gen. Harris,
Brig. Gen. Howe, Brig. Gen. Ekin,
Major Gen. Wallace, Major Gen. Hunter,
Major Gen. Kautz, Brig. Gen. Foster,
Judge Bingham, Col. Burnett,
Judge Holt
Opposite, Wanted poster
for Surratt, Booth, and Herold*

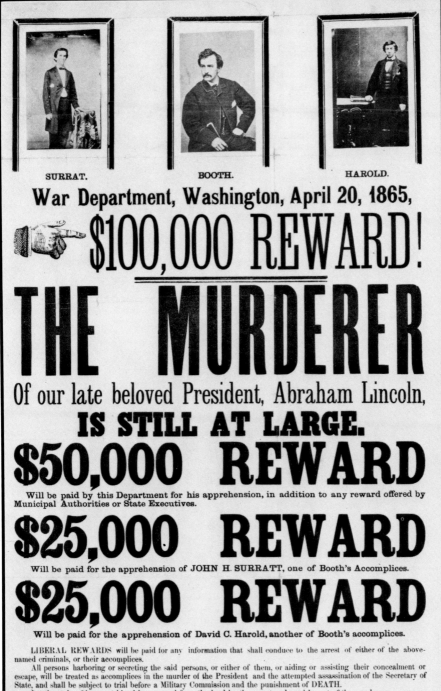

SURRAT.   BOOTH.   HAROLD.

War Department, Washington, April 20, 1865,

$100,000 REWARD!

THE MURDERER

Of our late beloved President, Abraham Lincoln,

IS STILL AT LARGE.

$50,000 REWARD

Will be paid by this Department for his apprehension, in addition to any reward offered by Municipal Authorities or State Executives.

$25,000 REWARD

Will be paid for the apprehension of JOHN H. SURRATT, one of Booth's Accomplices.

$25,000 REWARD

Will be paid for the apprehension of David C. Harold, another of Booth's accomplices.

LIBERAL REWARDS will be paid for any information that shall conduce to the arrest of either of the above-named criminals, or their accomplices.

All persons harboring or secreting the said persons, or either of them, or aiding or assisting their concealment or escape, will be treated as accomplices in the murder of the President and the attempted assassination of the Secretary of State, and shall be subject to trial before a Military Commission and the punishment of DEATH.

Let the stain of innocent blood be removed from the land by the arrest and punishment of the murderers.

All good citizens are exhorted to aid public justice on this occasion. Every man should consider his own conscience charged with this solemn duty, and rest neither night nor day until it be accomplished.

EDWIN M. STANTON, Secretary of War.

DESCRIPTIONS.—BOOTH is Five Feet 7 or 8 inches high, slender build, high forehead, black hair, black eyes, and wears a heavy black moustache.

JOHN H. SURRAT is about 5 feet, 9 inches. Hair rather thin and dark; eyes rather light; no beard. Would weigh 145 or 150 pounds. Complexion rather pale and clear, with color in his cheeks. Wore light clothes of fine quality. Shoulders square; cheek bones rather prominent; chin narrow; ears projecting at the top; forehead rather low and square, but broad. Parts his hair on the right side; neck rather long. His lips are firmly set. A slim man.

DAVID C. HAROLD is five feet six inches high, hair dark, eyes dark, eyebrows rather heavy, full face, nose short, hand short and fleshy, feet small, instep high, round bodied, naturally quick and active, slightly closes his eyes when looking at a person.

NOTICE.—In addition to the above, State and other authorities have offered rewards amounting to almost one hundred thousand dollars, making an aggregate of about **TWO HUNDRED THOUSAND DOLLARS.**

The hanging scene: placing of the hoods

*The last photograph
of Abraham Lincoln
April 10, 1865,
by Alexander Gardner*

Intelligencer. He had been one of the characters—the attorney—in the play of *Our American Cousin* that awful night. He was on the stage when his intimate friend, Booth, shot the President; had heard the report of the pistol and had seen Booth leap out of the President's box, but never made the slightest effort to catch him.

In his excitement he hurriedly left the stage and rushed across to his room in the Petersen house, and there, so he says, the letter which Booth had given him in the afternoon fell out of his pocket. It was addressed, as stated, to Mr. John F. Coyle. No matter, Matthews tore open the envelope and perused its contents, and then, when he was through with it, cast it into the fire and eagerly watched the flames as it was being licked to ashes.

For a long time John Matthews remained silent as to that letter and suffered Mr. Coyle to rest under the darkest suspicion on the part of the Government and of the people. Not a word did he say to the Government of his country that he carried within his bosom the knowledge that Booth, Herold, Payne, and Atzerodt had virtually pledged themselves in writing to assassinate the President.

Matthews told Father John A. Boyle of Washington what he had done and Father Boyle said he had done right in destroying the letter.

Matthews was placed on the stand for the defense during John Surratt's trial in 1867 for the purpose of testifying to the contents of the letter. He stated under oath that he had received it from Booth on the afternoon of the 14th of April. The Government, however, would not permit him to speak of its contents, the letter itself having been destroyed—this in accordance with a well-established principle in law that no one can be permitted to testify as to the contents of any written paper unless the original paper itself is placed in evidence; otherwise, no foundation could be laid to impeach it.[24]

Not being permitted to testify, Matthews rushed into print in the *National Intelligencer*, and this is what he says:

> I desire to state all that did occur in that interview, and also to say that the letter was given with no secrecy of manner, nor were there any remarks made about anything that might occur during the night. The letter was written on a sheet of commercial note paper covering three pages: The first two pages were written in the spirit

and style of the Philadelphia letter and it was only at the concluding paragraph that anything was said bearing upon what had transpired. It was to this effect and in these words, "For a long time I have devoted my energies, my time and money, to the accomplishment of a certain end. I have been disappointed. The moment has arrived when I must change my plans. Many will blame me for what I am about to do, but posterity, I am sure, will justify me. Men who love their country better than gold and life.

John W. Booth, Payne, Herold, Atzerodt." [25]

Upon this portion of the letter the friends of Booth and Mrs. Surratt have rested their claims that it was only at the last hour that Booth changed his plans with reference to the President from abduction to assassination, and this story has been so persistently circulated from one end of the country that many people have been led to believe it.

At precisely the same moment, ten minutes past ten o'clock, when Booth shot the President, Lewis Thornton Powell, alias Wood, alias Payne, made his appearance at the mansion of Secretary Seward, on Lafayette Square, and rang the house bell. On the door being opened, he informed the young colored servant that he wanted to see the Secretary as he had been sent by Dr. Verdi with a package of medicine for him. The servant, suspecting something wrong from the man's appearance, refused him admission, but the powerful ruffian disregarded his wishes, brushed him aside, and made his ascent to the sick man's chamber.[26]

The first person to meet him at the top of the stairway, just outside his father's room, was Frederick Seward, Assistant Secretary of State. Payne told him he desired to see Mr. Seward, as he had medicine for him.[27]

The son went into the chamber of the sick man, but returned with the message that his father could not be seen, as he was asleep, and requested Payne to hand him the medicine. This would not do. "I *MUST* see Mr. Seward." Thereupon Mr. Frederick Seward said, "You cannot see him. I am the proprietor here, and his son; if you cannot leave your message with me, you cannot leave it at all." Payne kept on talking and mumbling some words to himself, but when he saw that Mr. Seward was determined not to let him see his father, started to go down the steps, the young colored servant, Bell, preceding him.[28] Bell had gone down about three steps when he turned to Payne and requested him not to walk so heavily, but by the time he had commenced his descent, Payne had turned around and struck Mr. Frederick Seward on the head twice with the butt of his revolver, saying, "You ————." The Assistant Secretary threw up his hands and fell back into his sister's room, two doors from the Secretary's bedchamber. Bell ran downstairs and out of the front door, hallooing, "Murder!"

Payne, in the meantime, had started for Mr. Seward's chamber, and as George Robinson, who was acting as attendant nurse to the Secretary, and who heard the disturbance in the hall, opened the door to see what the trouble was, Payne was close up to the door.[29] The bold assassin at once struck Robinson with a knife in the forehead, knocking him partially down, and then pressed by him to the bed of Mr. Seward. He jumped on the bed and inflicted with his knife three wounds on the prostrate Secretary, one a very large gash on the right cheek, a cut on his throat on the right side, and one under the left ear. The Secretary's presence of mind, now, prevented any further injury, for he gathered the bedclothes around him and rolled onto the floor.

The case of Mr. Seward shows how sometimes what is considered a misfortune proves a stroke of good luck. He had been out driving a few days before this eventful occasion, and had been thrown from his carriage with great violence, breaking his jaw. The physicians had fixed up a steel mask or frame to hold the broken bones in place while setting. All the family bewailed the accident bitterly at the time it occurred. After that Good Friday night, however, they realized that it was a blessing in disguise. Payne's knife in descending to the Secretary's neck met this steel mask and glanced off. This alone saved the Secretary's life.

Major Augustus Seward now entered the room, sprang on the bed, and immediately clinched Payne.[30] Between him and Robinson they succeeded in getting him as far as the door when Payne unfastened his hands from Robinson's neck and struck him with his fist, knocking him down. While Major Seward was still pushing him, Payne struck him five or six times on the forehead and on the top of the head, and once on the left hand with what was supposed to be a bottle or decanter, seized from the table, repeating at the same time in an intense but not strong voice the words "I'm mad!" Then he broke away from Major Seward and rushed downstairs and out of the house. In his exit he met Mr. Emerick W. Hansell of the State Department, who was coming up the stairs. Payne struck at him with his knife and stabbed him in his right side, inflicting a dangerous wound running from the spine obliquely towards the right side. The wound was three inches deep and nearly one inch wide. In all, he wounded five persons before he left the house.

After Payne's escape, his hat, which had fallen from his head in his desperate encounter with Mr. Seward and the nurse Robinson, and a broken revolver—the one used on Frederick Seward's skull—were found on the floor.

The most intense excitement now raged throughout the Seward house. Dr. Verdi, the Secretary's physician, was at once sent for. On examination of the Secretary's wounds he saw that they were fortunately not mortal. He at once informed the Secretary to that effect, saying, "I congratulate you that the wounds are not mortal." Thereupon, Mr. Seward at once received his family.

Of the others who had been wounded in their encounter with Payne, the condition of the Assistant Secretary, Frederick Seward, was found to be the most serious. His skull was badly fractured in two places, and it required the greatest care and the constant attention of the physicians to save his life. It was, indeed, saved, but for the remainder of his days he was compelled to wear a silver plate over the fractured skull.

Note. Edwin Booth, who was playing in Boston at the time of his brother's crime, addressed the following letter to Mr. Jarrett.

Boston, Franklin Square, April 15, 1865.

Henry C. Jarrett Esq.,
of the Boston Theater.

My dear sir:

With deepest sorrow and great agitation, I thank you for relieving me from my engagement with yourself and the public. The news of the morning has made me wretched indeed; not only because I have received the unhappy tidings of the suspicions of a brother's crime, but because a good man and a most justly honored citizen has fallen in an hour of national joy by the hand of an assassin.

The memory of those who have fallen in the field in our country's defence during this struggle cannot be forgotten by me, even in this most distressing hour of my life. I most sincerely pray that the victories we have won may stay the brand of war, and the tide of loyal blood.

While mourning in common with other loyal hearts the death of the President, I am oppressed by a private woe not to be expressed in words.

But whatever calamity may befall me and mine, my country only, one and indivisible, has my warmest defence.

Edwin Booth.

CHAPTER XVI

Incidents at the Surratt house on April 14 · Mrs. Surratt goes to church in the morning · Booth visits her in the afternoon at two o'clock · She then goes to Surrattsville to meet Lloyd · Story of the "shooting irons" · Return trip to the city · Booth again meets Mrs. Surratt at about nine o'clock · Midnight search of the Surratt house by the detectives · The story of the murder made known to the inmates

The circumstances occurring at Mrs. Surratt's house on the fatal Good Friday of April 1865 in connection with Booth and the murder of Mr. Lincoln in themselves form an interesting chapter.

In accordance with Catholic usage I attended mass in the morning at St. Patrick's Church, and assisted at the veneration of the cross, a ceremony peculiar to Catholics, and calling to mind the tragic death of Him who died to save all men. One of Mrs. Surratt's first acts was to attend divine service and at the very church to which I went. After breakfast I betook myself to the office where I was employed, and remained on duty there until about ten o'clock, when a circular letter from Mr. Stanton was read to the clerks to the effect that all the employees of the War Department desirous of attending religious services could have permission to do so. The letter, however, will tell its own story:

War Department,
Adjutant General's Office,
Washington, April 14th, 1865.

Circular:

All officers and employees of the several bureaus of the War Department who are members of religious denominations that have religious services on this day (Good Friday) are relieved from duty for the day.

By order of the Secretary of War.

(Signed) W. A. Nichols,

Asst. Adjutant General.

If anything were needed to demonstrate the kindness of Mr. Stanton's heart and the nobility of his character, this circular letter furnished it. Brimful to overflowing with gratitude for the Union successes, in the accomplishment of which he bore so tremendous and distinguished a part, he did not forget Almighty God in the hour of victory, and was anxious that his employees should reverently ascribe the credit to Him who holds the nations in the hollow of His hands.

For me it was a very important letter, a document that was unconsciously the arbiter of my fate for the remainder of the day. It was one of those far-reaching things which cannot be understood, but which appear to have come directly from the hand of Providence. Had Mr. Stanton not authorized that letter, I would have remained at my desk until four o'clock in the afternoon, and most certainly I should not have driven Mrs. Surratt into the country, as I did later in the day. But we, poor creatures of circumstance, are often borne silently and smoothly along paths seemingly pleasant and full of flowers, and do not see the thorns, dangers, and crimes laid to entrap us until it is too late.

Availing myself of Mr. Stanton's kind and generous privilege, I went to St. Matthew's Church, where my old friend and employer, Dr. [Charles] White, preached the sermon. At the conclusion of the services, about noon, I bent my steps towards my boardinghouse, meeting a few friends on the way. When I had finished lunch I retired to my room and there indulged in some reading. At two o'clock, or half past two, there was a knock at the door and, on opening it, I beheld Mrs. Surratt with a letter in her hand. "Mr. Weichmann," said she, "I have a letter here from Mr. George Calvert and I find it necessary to go into the country to see about a debt due me by John Nothey. Would you have any objections to driving me down?" Of course, I had no objections. In fact, boy that I was, I was delighted with the opportunity of driving a horse and buggy, and especially on so fine a day. It was my second chance in life to handle a pair of reins and where is the young man who, under such circumstances, would have refused the opportunity? Robert Lincoln, had he been situated as I was, would have done the same thing. "Here are ten dollars," said she, "go you and hire a horse and buggy."

I took the ten dollars which she gave me and went downstairs. Just as I opened the front door I met John Wilkes Booth face to face. He was in the act of pulling the front door bell. Giving me his hand and exchanging a pleasant salutation, he strode into the front parlor.*

I passed down the front steps, then turned to the right to go through an alley to reach the livery stable on G Street. At this place I saw Atzerodt, who was trying to get a horse. The stable keeper refused to let him have one. I asked Atzerodt where he was going, and he said he intended to take a ride into the country, and that he would get a horse and send for Payne.

I secured the horse and buggy for Mrs. Surratt, paying six dollars for their use, and then returned home. Tying the horse in front of the house, I returned to my room for a few necessary articles of clothing, and as I passed the parlor door in coming back I saw John Wilkes Booth and Mrs. Surratt in close conversation near the hearth. Booth's back was towards me and Mrs. Surratt was facing the entry. In a few moments Booth came down the front steps and, seeing me at the curb, waved his hand in token of adieu. This was the last I saw of him, and when I heard of him again he had shot the President, and the next news that came was that he himself had been shot by a Union soldier in the Garrett barn—shot like a dog as he deserved to be.

When Mrs. Surratt herself came down, just as she was in the act of stepping into the buggy she said, "Stop, let me get those things of Mr. Booth." She went into the house and presently returned with two packages in her hand, both done up in coarse brown paper and wrapped with twine. One of these was from six to eight inches in diameter. This she deposited in the bottom of the buggy, remarking that it was glass. She did not say that it was *a* glass nor did I see the contents of that package

* This statement is confirmed by the evidence of Miss Anna Surratt at the Conspiracy trial in 1865. Pitman, p. 131.

until at the trial of John H. Surratt in 1867. It proved to be a magnificent field glass (Booth's) with a screw for marine view and with another for opera. At the time it was placed in the buggy, I had not the slightest idea what the package was. The impression rested on my mind that it contained some articles of glass and crockery ware which Mrs. Surratt, perhaps, intended to give to an old colored servant at Surrattsville of whom she was very fond. She also carried another package, some of her business and legal papers.

A few reflections at this point will not be out of order. What was John Wilkes Booth doing at Mrs. Surratt's house at that time? How did he happen to know that she was going into the country just then? What interest could he have in her visit to Surrattsville that afternoon? [1]

Can Mrs. Surratt's apologists and defenders explain it? It looks to me as if the whole thing had been planned beforehand, and that Booth's visit then was only a coincidence of an earlier visit that he made that day. From a remark dropped by Mrs. Holohan I am convinced that Booth was at that house sometime in the morning. It is very strange that he should have come just at that time in the afternoon. No doubt, he then handed her the field glass which later in the day she delivered to her tenant Lloyd at Surrattsville. This meeting was evidently a preconcerted affair.

On the way to Surrattsville a noteworthy incident occurred which was not stated by me at the Conspiracy trial in 1865, and which, therefore, could have had no weight in determining the verdict in her case, but which I gave to the public in a printed statement in July 1865 and at the trial of her son in 1867. [2]

When about halfway down, we saw a group of cavalrymen to the left, a short distance from the roadside. The soldiers were lolling on the green and enjoying themselves. Their horses were roaming about nibbling grass. Stopping the buggy, Mrs. Surratt hailed an old man, seemingly a farmer, and desired to know what those soldiers were doing there. "They are pickets," he replied. She then asked if they remained out all night, and he stated that they were generally called in at about eight o'clock in the evening. "I am glad to know that," she said, and drove on. That same evening, on our return home, while driving up a steep hill I remember passing between those pickets mounted and bound for headquarters, and I put out my hand and patted several of the horses on the back.

I am very positive in regard to this affair, for it has made a lasting impression on my mind, one which will never be effaced. The circumstances came back to my recollection during the progress of the Conspiracy trial in 1865 after reading the testimony of other witnesses and during the summing up of the lawyers. I then related it to Mr. Benn Pitman, one of the stenographers of the court, who in turn communicated it to General Henry L. Burnett, one of the judge advocates, but the information came too late to be used as evidence by the Government.

The following letter from General Burnett explains itself:

> *Judge Advocate's Office*
> *Department of Ohio*
> *Cincinnati, August 16, 1865.*
>
> Louis J. Wiechmann,
> Philadelphia, Pa.
>
> Dear Sir:
>
> Your published statement contains one inaccuracy. It was not long before the trial that these additional statements were made known to me. They came to me, as you are aware, through Mr. Pitman from your statement to him. This was after the trial had closed as far as the evidence was concerned, and the arguments had been commenced.
>
> Very respectfully,
> Your obedient servant,
> H. L. Burnett,
> Judge Advocate.

I did not at first comprehend the importance of this evidence. I can realize its force now, especially when it is recollected that on that very night Booth and Herold, fresh from their bloody work, dashed down that road past the spot where the pickets had been, on to Surrattsville, on to Bryantown, to the Potomac, to Virginia, and finally to death.

I, at first, thought that Mrs. Surratt's action in reference to the pickets had been prompted by mere curiosity, but I am satisfied now that there was a deeper significance behind it, and that her questions to the old man were dictated by the desire to know if the road would be clear that night for Booth and Herold. Will the friends of Mrs. Surratt say what possible interest this woman could have had in the withdrawal of those pickets?

We arrived at Surrattsville at about half past four o'clock. Mrs. Surratt got out of the buggy and I drove a little while longer through the soft roads of the neighboring country. When I returned to the house she rapped on one of the windows for me. I obeyed her summons, and then she informed me that Mr. Nothey was not there, and that it would be necessary to write to him. Accordingly, at her request, I sat down and wrote this letter:

Surrattsville, Md., April 14th, 1865.

Mr. John Nothey,

Dear Sir:

I have *this day* received a letter from Mr. Calvert intimating that either you or your friends have represented to him that I am not willing to settle with you for the land.

You know that I am ready and have been waiting for these last two years; and now, if you do not come within the next ten days, I will settle with Mr. Calvert and bring suit against you immediately.

Mr. Calvert will give you a deed on receiving payment.

M. E. Surratt,

Administratrix of John H. Surratt.

This letter, written and signed by me with her name, played a most important part in the defense of Mrs. Surratt—perhaps the most important part of any evidence in her behalf. On it she relied mainly to establish the fact that her visit to the country was one of pure business—the collecting of a debt due her by Mr. Nothey to enable her to pay a debt due by her to Mr. Calvert. And yet is it true that such was her real mission? In the foregoing letter to Mr. Nothey I have underscored the words "this day" purposely. Mr. Calvert testified that he had addressed his letter on the 12th of April 1865, and that he resided in Bladensburg, which is about six miles east from Washington.

The letter which Mrs. Surratt had received from Mr. Calvert read thus:

Riversdale, April 12, 1865.

Mrs. M. E. Surratt,

Dear Madam:

During a late visit to the lower portion of the county I ascertained the willingness of Mr. Nothey to settle with you, and I desire to call your attention to the fact in urging the settlement of the claim of my late father's estate. However unpleasant, I must insist on closing this matter, as it is imperative in an early settlement of the estate which is necessary.

You will, therefore, please inform me at your earliest convenience, as to how and when you will be able to pay the balance due on the land purchased by your late husband.

I am, dear madam,

Yours respectfully,

Geo. H. Calvert, Jr.[3]

It has always been to me an inexplicable fact that Mrs. Surratt should have said to me that she did not receive that letter from Mr. Calvert until the 14th day of April. If the letter had been mailed at Bladensburg, where Mr. Calvert resided, on the morning of the 12th, it should have been delivered in Washington before the close of the same day, and certainly on the morning of the 13th at the latest. Mr. Calvert swore that he addressed the letter on the 12th, and the document itself bears that date. Perhaps the most suspicious circumstance in connection with this whole affair, and one which I have never seen explained anywhere, is that instead of going directly to Nothey's place, who lived in Prince Georges County about fifteen miles from the capital, she went only as far as Surrattsville, and then did not meet the man at all, but contented herself with a mere matter of correspondence in reference to the debt.

Again, Mr. John Nothey testified that he had purchased seventy-five acres of land from John H. Surratt, Sr. He said that Mrs. Surratt had sent him word to settle for this piece of land. He owed her a part of the money on it. "*I met her there,*" said he, "*at Surrattsville on Tuesday, April 11th, in regard to it.* On Friday, the 14th of April, Mr. Gwinn [Gwynn] brought me a letter from Mrs. Surratt, *but I did not see her that day.*" [4]

The letter I wrote for her to Nothey was handed to Mr. Bennett

Gwynn, a friend, who was passing Surrattsville in a buggy just at that time, to deliver to Mr. Nothey, and he testified he delivered it the same day.[5]

If Mrs. Surratt had remained in the seclusion of her Washington home on the fatal 14th day of April, she could have transacted all this business in relation to Mr. Nothey for a three-cent postage stamp, an envelope, and a sheet of writing paper. It would not have been necessary to spend six dollars for a horse and buggy. Moreover, there is no evidence in existence anywhere that goes to show that she made an engagement with Mr. Nothey to meet her at Surrattsville on the 14th day of April. He had met her there on Tuesday, the 11th, in relation to this very matter, but he did not see her at all on the 14th, nor had he received any word that he was to meet her at Lloyd's place on that occasion. If she did really intend to see about the debt, why did she not drive directly to Mr. Nothey's house three miles further on? Why alight at Surrattsville, not knowing whether she would meet Nothey there? Why entrust this important business matter to a third party, Mr. Gwynn?

Judge Bingham, in his argument for the Government, did not dwell on these facts at all, as he might have done, but I have pondered them over and over, and the conclusion has fastened itself irrevocably on my mind that all this talk about the Nothey debt was a falsehood fashioned to deceive me as to the real nature and object of the trip. Whenever I think of it, and it is almost incessantly, it is always with feelings of mortification and shame that a woman, having children other than myself, could have so basely and willingly betrayed my confidence, and stooped to actions which have almost ruined my life. It was a vile insult and outrage upon my young manhood. That drive to Surrattsville, and the developments growing out of it, cost Mrs. Surratt her life. She dug a pit for others, but fell into it herself. Certain it is, if she had remained at home and attended to the duties of her boardinghouse, she would, I verily believe, not have been punished as she was.

Mrs. Surratt did not meet Mr. John Nothey that day, but she did meet John M. Lloyd. When she arrived at Surrattsville, Lloyd was not at home but she waited until he came. What followed can best be told in Lloyd's own words. I quote from the record by Benn Pitman, the official stenographer in the case. Lloyd said:

On the 14th day of April I went to Marlboro to attend a trial there; and in the evening when I got home, which I should judge was about five o'clock, I found Mrs. Surratt there. She met me out by the wood pile as I drove in with some fish and oysters in my buggy. She told me to have those shooting-irons ready that night and two bottles of whisky; there would be some parties who would call for them. She gave me something wrapped up in a piece of paper which I took up stairs, and found to be a field-glass. When I drove up to the wood-yard Mrs. Surratt came out where I was. The first thing she said to me was, "Talk about the devil and his imp will appear," or something to that effect. I said, "I was not aware I was a devil before." "Well," said she, "Mr. Lloyd, I want you to have those shooting-irons ready; there will be parties here to-night who will call for them." [6] At the same time she gave me something wrapped up in a newspaper (Booth's field-glass) which I did not undo until I got up stairs.

No portion of this conversation did I hear, nor was I aware that such dangerous articles as "shooting irons" had been secreted in the Sur-rattsville tavern by her son in conjunction with Herold and Atzerodt, until I read Lloyd's testimony in the newspapers.

Mrs. Surratt must have known these weapons were hidden there, for she told Lloyd to have them ready that night. Who told her that these "shooting irons" were secreted in Lloyd's house? Who informed her that they would be called for that night? Who but Booth? To me she said, "I must go into the country to see about collecting a debt which Mr. Nothey owes me." To John M. Lloyd her command was: "Have the shooting irons ready—they will be called for tonight—and two bottles of whisky." Until this testimony of Lloyd's is overthrown, I feel that this woman must stand condemned in the eyes of the civilized world! This was by all odds the main evidence on which she was convicted. It was the chief rivet in the chain which bound her. It was the principal overt act of which she was shown to have been guilty. Up to the moment of Lloyd's testimony, I verily believed that she was an innocent woman, but when I read the story of the shooting irons as related by him, the scales fell from my eyes and I could believe so no longer.[7]

It has been alleged in Mrs. Surratt's behalf that Lloyd had been drinking "right smart" that day.[8] That may have been so and Lloyd himself admits it, but the evidence and the facts show that he was suf-ficiently sober to take the weapons out of their hiding place and deliver them to Booth and Herold—the parties who called for them. In fact, he carried out Mrs. Surratt's orders to the fullest extent, as the sequel will show.

On the return home that evening, I made some remark about Booth, stating that he appeared to be without employment, and asking her when he was going to act again. "Booth is done acting," she replied, and "is going to New York very soon, *never* to return." Then turning around, she remarked, "Yes, and Booth is crazy on the subject, and I am going to give him a good scolding the next time I see him." What that one subject was Mrs. Surratt never mentioned to me. She was very anxious to be at home at nine o'clock, saying that she had made an engagement with some gentleman to meet her at that hour. I asked her if it was Booth. She made no reply, *yes* or *no*.

Now what did this woman mean by telling me all this stuff about Booth? Why should he, a young man, eminent in his calling, beloved by his fellow actors, go to New York and *never* return? What did she mean when she said that he was crazy on one subject, and that she would give him a good scolding the next time she saw him? Why should *she* scold him? What was the necessity on *her part* for doing that? Ah, that to me is one of the many unexplained things of this sad affair. That reply of hers indicated to my mind that she was aware of some purpose on Booth's part that would, indeed, stop his acting, and take him from Washington. Did Booth tell her that he was going to make a prisoner that night of Abraham Lincoln, or shoot him? Which was it? And then, when I asked her if Booth was the gentleman who was to call on her return home, why did she not answer me? Why keep silent, saying nothing?

When about a mile from the city, and having, from the top of a hill, caught view of Washington swimming in a flood of light, raising her hands, she said, "I am afraid all this rejoicing will be turned into mourning, and all this glory into sadness." I asked her what she meant, and she replied that after sunshine there was always a storm, and that the people were too proud and licentious, and that God would punish them.[9]

Just as we drove from New Jersey Avenue past the Capitol into Pennsylvania Avenue, we heard sounds of music in the distance, and then we saw a procession of Arsenal employees passing up Seventh Street and along Pennsylvania Avenue in the direction of the White House.

We arrived home at about half past eight, and then I returned the horse and buggy to the stable. At tea that evening Mrs. Surratt showed me a letter she had received from her son John. It had been brought to the house by Miss Annie Ward, and not by the letter carrier. It was dated Montreal, April 12, 1865.

The Miss Ward here referred to seems to have been a kind of go-between. Three times has she figured in this case to my knowledge. First, when Surratt went to see Mrs. Murray at the Herndon House and said to her, "Did not Miss Annie Ward speak to you about securing a room for a delicate gentleman who was to have his meals served up to him in his room?" Secondly, on the evening of the 10th of March, when Booth said to her in Mrs. Surratt's parlor, "Miss Ward, please let me see the address of *that lady* again." Third, on the evening of the 14th of April, when she brought to the house the letter said to have been from John Surratt in Montreal.[10]

Surratt evidently used her as a tool, and appeared to have adopted the plan of sending his letters in her care instead of forwarding them directly to his own home.

She was a schoolteacher and was employed at the Catholic school at the corner of Tenth and G streets. She found it very convenient not to appear and testify during Surratt's trial in 1867.

Surratt's letter was on general subjects. In it he said he was much pleased with the city of Montreal, and with the French Cathedral; that he had bought a French pea jacket for which he had paid ten dollars in silver; that board was too high, two dollars and fifty cents a day in gold, and that he would probably go to some private boardinghouse, or that he would soon go to Toronto. The letter was signed "John Harrison"—not his full name; his name was John Harrison Surratt.

I believe it was purposely shown to me at that time. A queer circumstance connected with it was that the writer referred to me having driven his mother into the country on the previous Tuesday, April 11. This he did in a jesting manner. Now, the hotel register of St. Lawrence Hall showed that John Harrison Surratt, under the assumed name of John Harrison, arrived there on the 6th of April 1865, left on the 12th for the United States, and returned on the 18th.

Now, how could he in Canada on the 12th of April know about the drive to Surrattsville on the 11th unless he had been informed to that effect by telegraph? That is another of the unexplained circumstances, always an enigma to me.

While yet at supper I heard the footsteps of someone ascending the front steps outside, and then heard the front door bell ring. There was no servant in the house at the time and I remarked to Mrs. Surratt, in all kindness and to befriend her, that I would answer the bell for her, as she must be very tired. She, however, said "No," and insisted on going herself. The front door was opened and I heard the footsteps moving into the front parlor. The gentleman whom she had expected at nine o'clock had arrived. He remained several minutes and then descended the front steps and vanished into the darkness and silence. It was, as I afterwards ascertained, Booth's last visit to Mrs. Surratt and, I believe, the third one on that day.

I have seen it stated several times in the public prints that the man who then called was a Mr. [William W.] Kirby, an old friend of Mrs. Surratt. If that was so, why was not Mr. Kirby placed on the stand? But Mr. Kirby, in court and out of it, since July 1865, when the statement was given to the world by me that it was Booth, has never contradicted the fact as I stated it, nor has he said that it was he and not Booth that called. Mrs. Holohan corroborated the testimony of the writer as to the fact of *some* person coming at that time, but if Mrs. Surratt said to her it was Mr. Kirby, then Mrs. Surratt stated what I believe to be a deliberate falsehood. The words of Mrs. Surratt's daughter uttered on the morning of the 15th prove beyond question that it was Booth.[11]

Moreover, considering all the circumstances surrounding the case, who was more likely to call than Booth? The testimony shows that he had charged Mrs. Surratt, when going to Surrattsville, to deliver his field glass to John M. Lloyd, and to request him to have the two shooting irons that had been concealed there by young John Surratt, Atzerodt, and Herold and the two bottles of whisky ready for that awful night. It was, therefore, very natural for Booth to be anxious to ascertain if his orders had been carried out, and to learn if the road was clear so that he could, after the commission of his crime, escape in safety to the Potomac. And from whom was he more likely to obtain this information than from the woman whom he had chosen to do his bidding?

As soon as I had finished supper I went to the parlor. I was surprised to find that Mrs. Surratt's cheerfulness had left her. She seemed, as I thought, agitated and restless. On asking her what was the matter she replied that she was very nervous and did not feel well. Then, looking at me, she desired to know which way the torchlight procession was going that we had seen on Pennsylvania Avenue. I remarked that it was a procession of Arsenal employees who were going to serenade the President. I knew nothing at all of the President's intention to visit the theater. She said she would like to know, as she was very much interested in it. She had a pair of prayer beads in her hands and once she asked me to pray for her intentions. I answered her by saying that I did not know what her intentions were. She then said to pray for them anyhow. This is a matter essentially Catholic and it is a common thing for Catholic persons to pray for one another's intentions. I myself have often asked my friends to pray for my intentions. Her nervousness finally increased so much that in a playful manner she chased the young ladies (Anna Surratt, Miss Olivia Jenkins, a niece then on a visit, Miss Fitzpatrick) and myself, who were having a good deal of fun and laughter, to our respective rooms.[12]

That night I knelt beside my bed as ignorant of the coming murder as was Mr. Lincoln himself, and I was sound asleep when the fatal shot was fired. Thousands of times have I recalled it, for I was as contented as I could be. My plans for the future had all been laid and I would be in the seminary in Baltimore in the following September pursuing the studies which were so dear to my heart.

My sleep was peaceful; it was the sleep of innocence and of a clear conscience. I had done no wrong and meditated none. I owed no one a dollar, and so far as I knew, in all the world, I had not an enemy.

At about two or half past two in the morning of the 15th of April, I had been up and in the yard. I had returned to my room and was about falling asleep again when I heard the front door bell ring very violently. Hastily drawing on a pair of pantaloons, I went to the front door and, rapping on the inside of it, I asked, "Who is there?" "Detectives," was the reply, "come to search the house for John Wilkes Booth and John Surratt."

"They are not here," I answered. "Let us in anyhow," they said, "we want to search the house." I went to Mrs. Surratt's door and knocked. "Here, Mrs. Surratt," said I, "are detectives who have come to search the house." "For God's sake! Let them come in. I expected the house to be searched," answered she. The men came in; there were four of them, McDevitt, Clarvoe, Bigley, and Kelly, all belonging to the city detective police force.[13] They explored the house from top to bottom, going even into the rooms occupied by the young ladies and looking to see who they were.

When they came into my room, "Gentlemen," said I, "what is the matter? What does this searching of the house mean?" "Do you pretend that you do not know what has happened?" replied Clarvoe. I assured him that I had heard nothing, and that I did not know what had occurred. "Then," said John Clarvoe, "I will tell you. John Wilkes Booth has shot the President and John Surratt has assassinated the Secretary of State," and thereupon he drew forth a piece of black cravat, saying, "Do you see the blood on that? That is the blood of Abraham Lincoln." My feelings can be better imagined than described.

This detective has since this event stated that when he imparted to me the information, I threw up my hands and exclaimed, "My God, I see it all." That may have been so; I do not remember it now, but at any rate, in that instant, the facts of Booth's continued friendship for Mrs. Surratt and her son, his frequent visits to the house, and on the very day of the murder, flashed across my mind, and I realized that every person living in that house would be subjected to a rigid examination in the investigation that would surely be made by the Government.

I now descended with the detectives to the parlor, where we found Mrs. Surratt, who had just come from her bedroom. To her, I myself communicated the awful news which these officers had given me, saying, "Mrs. Surratt, what do you think, Booth has murdered the President." To which she answered, "My God, Mr. Weichmann, you do not tell me so." I did not mention her son's name in connection with the assault on Mr. Seward, out of respect to her feelings.

And yet Mrs. Surratt at that very moment knew that Booth had murdered the President and had been informed of that fact before I communicated to her the news which the detectives had given me, for on that same night, after the young ladies and myself had retired to our respective rooms, when she was alone in her parlor, two Union soldiers, Sergeants Joseph M. Dye and R. H. Cooper, the identical men who had stood in front of Ford's Theater and heard the time called by one of the conspirators, passed along H Street in front of her house on the way to the camp.[14]

Mrs. Surratt was evidently on the "qui vive" for news as she threw up her parlor window and inquired of these men, "What is wrong downtown?" On being informed that the President was shot, she asked who did it, and when informed that Booth did it, inquired of Sergeant Cooper how he knew it, to which he replied, "A man saw him who knew him."

It was then nearly, if not eleven o'clock, and as testified it was very quiet in the neighborhood of her house, for they had not yet met or overtaken anybody until after passing the Surratt house, when they encountered two policemen who had not yet heard of the murder.[15]

Furthermore, Major A. C. Richards, who was then Superintendent of the Washington City Police, had also informed her of the murder before McDevitt and Clarvoe had arrived there. He was the first police officer to enter the house that night, a fact which is now made public for the first time, but I did not see him, for I was asleep. This is what he says, among other things, in a letter addressed to me dated Eustis, Florida, April 29, 1898:

> If I remember rightly the man from whom we got the first information connecting Payne, Herold and Atzerodt with Booth was a saloon keeper under or near the theater, named Ferguson, I think. We soon thereafter obtained information that John H. Surratt was often in company with these men and then that Booth had often visited or called at Mrs. Surratt's house. Those facts led me to pay that house a visit that night at about one o'clock. When I reached the house and had rung the door bell, Mrs. Surratt answered it very promptly. The house was dark so far as I could discover but there was no unusual delay in the response of Mrs. S. to the bell. She appeared dressed as a lady of her station might be expected to dress of an evening. Her hair was not disarranged. She had not time to dress or smooth her hair between the ringing of the bell and her appearance at the door. She had not retired for the night, but was evidently waiting in a dark house for some one to call. When I informed her why I had called after informing her of the assassination she expressed no surprise or regret. In fact she only answered such questions as I asked her in the briefest possible terms—gave me no information in regard to Booth, his visits or the visits of others of the assassins to her house. She seemed entirely self-possessed and did not seem in the least affected when I said to her that President Lincoln had just been assassinated and that Booth and her son were suspected of being implicated in the crime.

In another letter, dated February 22, 1899, from the same place, his home, he confirms the story.

There need be no question in your mind that I visited the Surratt house on the night of the assassination between 12 and 1 o'clock. I am not mistaken as to that point.[16]"

I had told the detectives in my room that I thought it could not possibly be John Surratt who had assassinated the Secretary of State because I had seen a letter from him, that very evening, and that he was in Montreal, Canada. McDevitt asked Mrs. Surratt for the letter but it could not be found; it never was found and was never brought into court as it should have been. There was a purpose in withholding it. Had that letter and envelope been produced it would have settled the fact as to whether it was written by Surratt in Canada on the 12th of April, or elsewhere, and dated back. At any rate it was read to me, at suppertime as I verily believe, for the purpose of deception and, if that was the intention, it succeeded admirably, for it controlled the subsequent movements of the detectives and of myself, and was the means of carrying us to Canada in pursuit of Surratt. When the detectives asked me where Surratt was, I answered, "In Canada," and based my reply on the information obtained from this letter. I also said to the officers that I would go to see them early in the morning, and that I would do all I could to assist them in their investigation. Afterwards I asked McDevitt how it was that they came to Mrs. Surratt's house so soon after the assassination and he informed me that they had come across a man on the street who said to them, "If you want to find out all about this business go to Mrs. Surratt's house on H Street." I have often queried why the officers did not arrest that man.*

When the detectives had gone Mrs. Surratt's daughter, almost frantic, cried out, "Oh, Ma! Mr. Weichmann is right; just think of that man (John W. Booth) having been here an hour before the assassination. I am afraid it will bring suspicion upon us."

"Anna, come what will," she replied, "I am resigned. I think that J. Wilkes Booth was only an instrument in the hands of the Almighty to punish this proud and licentious people."

I returned to my room—no more sleep that night. My God! my God! what agony I endured until the morning light came through the

---

* This statement of McDevitt's is verified by an interview with him reported in the *Indianapolis News,* dated April 14, 1894.[17]

windows. Providence alone is witness. I said to myself repeatedly, "It cannot be that Surratt has been guilty of this crime. Did I not see that letter from him last night in which he wrote that he was in Canada? No, no, it cannot be!"

In those hours I resolved that under all circumstances I would stand by the cause of justice and the Government. I, at least, would do my part, and permit the Government to throw the fullest light of judicial investigation into my life and character, and I was not afraid of the test. I could and would answer truthfully every question put to me, with an unblushing countenance and sinless soul. An upright man never has anything to fear, and I knew that my life had been correct and honest. Nay, more, I determined that I would assist the Government to the extent of my ability in helping to unfold this dark deed, motives are not evidence in law, but such were my motives.

With the early morning I hurried out of the house and purchased a newspaper—the *Chronicle*. Eagerly I read Stanton's dispatches. Booth had indeed murdered the President, but who was the man who had assaulted Mr. Seward? His description ran thus: "Height 6 feet, 1 inch; hair black, thick and full, straight; no beard or appearance of beard; cheeks red on the jaws; face moderately full; overcoat, double breasted; color, mixed of pink and gray spots; voice inclined to tenor."

"Thank God! thank God!" I exclaimed, "that is not John Surratt." I felt grateful for so much, and a heavy weight was rolled from my heart.

Then I went to take breakfast, the last I would ever eat at Mrs. Surratt's table. During the meal I made some remark deploring the great crime, and saying that the repeated visits of Booth to the house would probably cause official inquiry. Anna Surratt answered that there was no use of my going on so, that the death of Lincoln was "no worse than that of the meanest nigger in the army." I told her that I thought she would find out differently.[18]

After breakfast I started for city police headquarters with Mr. John T. Holohan to meet the detectives who had been at the house in the morning. I went without a thought in my mind that the woman left behind was in any way implicated in the atrocious crime, or that she had so basely deceived me. I did not then suspect her any more than I suspected my own dear mother, but I also went with the firm determination to do my whole duty to my country. To me, the murder of the President was a horrible, indescribable revelation, and called aloud in thunder tones for vengeance.[19]

As I turned into Tenth Street from F, I saw six stalwart soldiers bearing on their shoulders a coffin. They had just come out of Petersen's house. The President was, indeed, dead.

CHAPTER XVII

Great excitement in Washington on the morning after the murder · Pursuit of the assassins · Arrest of Samuel Arnold at Fortress Monroe · Arrest of Michael O'Laughlin at Baltimore · History of the escape of Payne · Mrs. Surratt's home is visited and searched · Arrest of Mrs. Surratt · Arrest of Payne · Arrest of Atzerodt in Maryland

The scenes in Washington on the morning of the 15th of April baffle description. Where all had been rejoicing, all was now grief and terror. Excited groups of angry men could be seen everywhere on the streets discussing the terrible calamity. The news boys were unable to hand out the papers fast enough to meet the demands for the latest editions. The poor colored people were especially affected, and the tears rolling down their cheeks were mute witnesses of their sorrow over the loss of their best friend. As rapidly as possible all private residences and public buildings were put in mourning, and before nightfall the whole city was shrouded in black; Lincoln's portrait was placed on many houses and such mottoes as "We mourn our loss," "Our Father," "Our Saviour," were numerous. He who had for years been derided by tongue and pen as a "clown," a "gorilla," and a "negro lover" was now transfigured and became immortal. People could not do enough to show their love for him and their appreciation of his memory. Booth had turned the execration and hatred of many, even of Lincoln's own party, who had been his bitterest political enemies, into the most profound reverence.

The feeling throughout the country, at large, was intense; excitement raged everywhere, and many persons who in an unguarded moment let fall an expression hostile to Lincoln or favorable to Booth were instantly strung up to a lamppost or tree and thus in different sections many lives were lost.

The funeral procession, which took place on the 19th, wending its way to all the large cities, with the body lying in state, added to this feeling.

And now began the hot and angry pursuit of the assassins. It was soon developed that a big conspiracy had been set on foot to assassinate the leading officers of the Government.

Fifty thousand dollars reward was promptly offered by the War Department for the arrest of Booth. Twenty-five thousand dollars for the arrest of each and every accomplice before and after the act. Additional heavy rewards were promised by some of the states and nothing was left undone to stimulate the keen scent of the detectives, citizens, and military, to hunt down the murderous assassins.[1]

One of the first moves of the War Department was to seize Booth's personal effects at the National Hotel. Accordingly, officer William Eaton was ordered thither on the night of April 14 and took possession of his trunk.[2] In it were found a gimlet, a small pair of handcuffs, and a number of other articles. These were the handcuffs which were to have been used on the hands of the President in case of his capture, as originally contemplated.

In the trunk was also found the letter from Samuel Arnold addressed to Booth from Hookstown, Maryland, dated March 27, 1865.[3] This furnished the first and most important clue to the Government and was one of the direct means of unearthing the Conspiracy. It promptly led to the arrest on the morning of the 17th of April at Fortress Monroe of Arnold, who was then employed there in the store of a Mr. John W. Wharton.[4] No sooner had he been taken into custody than he made a clean breast of his connection with the Conspiracy so far as it related to the proposed kidnapping of the President, which purpose he said he had considered impracticable and had abandoned in March. He stated to Mr. Eaton G. Horner,[5] who arrested him, that J. Wilkes Booth, Michael O'Laughlin, George A. Atzerodt, John H. Surratt, a man with the alias of Mosby (probably Payne), and another, a small man (doubtless Herold), whose name he could not recollect, and himself were in the conspiracy to abduct, and were present at a meeting held at the Lichau

House in Washington about two or three weeks before the 1st of April.*

The same day, April 17, Michael O'Laughlin was arrested in Baltimore. These were the two earliest arrests made in connection with the murder. The prisoners were at once taken to Washington and placed in confinement until such time as their trial might take place. Arnold's letter was thus the means of entrapping him and leading to his conviction. It was the most important piece of evidence presented against him, and without which the Government would have had considerable difficulty in finding him guilty.

Young Herold had been stationed at the door of the Seward mansion by Booth to help Payne and act as his guide, but in the excitement and amid the shrieks of murder coming from one of the upper windows, had been frightened and had run away. He was seen about twenty-five minutes after ten o'clock by Fletcher, the hostler at Naylor's stables, of whom he had procured his horse, turning into Pennsylvania Avenue from the direction of the Treasury Department. Fletcher hailed him and told him to get off the horse, that he had had it long enough, but Herold put spurs to it and went as fast as the horse could go up Fourteenth Street, and then turned to the east on F Street.[6]

When the assassin Payne descended from his murderous work in the Seward home he found his companion gone and himself alone. In his desperate encounter with the Sewards and the nurse Robinson, he had lost his hat; his horse, too, was about to break away, but with the agility and spring of an old-time cavalryman, he was soon on his back and rode off through Vermont Avenue. In mounting his steed, his crimsoned knife had fallen into the street. It was found the following morning, and afterwards, in court, its sharp blade bore witness against him in language a thousandfold more damning than words.

Hatless, with his black locks flying in the night wind, he fled like an enraged demon towards Anacostia Creek, expecting to meet Booth as he had been ordered to do, but he lost his way. He rode through the northeastern suburbs of the city and, getting into the old Bladensburg Pike, followed it a considerable distance, and then tumbled into an army road running between two forts. He halted a moment, recognized the fact that he was without his hat, and as he gazed at his overcoat, saw by

* This was undoubtedly on the 15th of March.

the aid of the moon that it was bespattered with blood. He removed it and cast it on the ground. Then from the sleeve of his woolen undershirt he made himself a cap.

He continued his ride; once he had reached the Eastern Branch, which he had to cross, but the voice of the sentries stationed on Anacostia Bridge scared him away. It was midnight. Still he rode on, the roads becoming more mysterious and impenetrable and his horse sinking deeper in the mire. But time was passing, the night was slipping away and daylight would soon appear.

Payne, at one time, thought he heard people moving about; then in the distance he beheld the dome of the Capitol, and at last he saw shining in the dim light the white tombstones of a cemetery. Now, he thought, was his opportunity. The desperate man came down from his horse and then wended his footsteps toward the City of the Dead. The abandoned horse was found early in the morning of the 15th of April at Lincoln Branch Barracks, about three-quarters of a mile east of the Capitol. The sweat was pouring from him and had formed a big puddle on the ground. A sentinel at the hospital had stopped the horse. The poor beast had been ridden almost to death.

In the Congressional Cemetery, for such it proved to be, the burial place of dead heroes and statesmen, and of the common people too, Payne discovered a marble vault which had been built above the ground. He lifted off the slab with his back, and then crept inside, replacing the stone. In this gloomy abode, the companion of worms and dirt, he remained three days and nights, without shelter or sufficient clothing to protect him from the cold. What his thoughts and sufferings were during the terrible ordeal can now only be surmised. If he possessed any conscience at all he must have died a thousand deaths.

On Easter Sunday a funeral came into the graveyard. After the departure of the mourners, Payne noticed that a newspaper had been dropped by one of the attendants. Reaching out, he secured it, and at the same time drew in a pick which lay nearby. In the paper he read the proclamation of Stanton, the Secretary of War. It said:

One Hundred Thousand Dollars Reward!
The murderer of our late Beloved President, Abraham Lincoln, is still at large!

Fifty Thousand Dollars will be paid by this Department for his Apprehension!

Twenty-Five Thousand Dollars Reward for A. Atzerodt, sometimes called "Port Tobacco"!

Twenty-Five Thousand Dollars Reward for David E. Herold!

All persons harboring or secreting the said persons, or either of them, or aiding or assisting their concealment or escape will be treated as accomplices, subject to a trial before a military commission, and the punishment of death!

Let the stain of innocent blood be removed from the land!

Payne was thunderstruck; to his added surprise and consternation he saw that his own name was omitted, and that none of his intended victims had died. He expressed a feeling of gratitude, and inwardly thanked God that his crime had come to naught.[7]

On Monday night, the fourth day after his own assault and Booth's dark deed, the assassin crawled from his gloomy den. He was now weak, trembling, and overcome with the horrid pangs of hunger, having eaten nothing since the previous Friday evening. In his dire extremity he resolved to seek Mrs. Surratt's house. Hers was the only family that he knew in all Washington. There he felt sure that he would find food and shelter. Had he not been there before? And had he not received encouragement and sympathy there? Placing a pick on his shoulders and with the strange woolen cap on his head, at about ten o'clock he started for the widow's home. But the grim vengeance of God had preceded him and was now prepared to seize him. Only a few minutes before the assassin's arrival, some of the military from the War Department had taken possession of the house with instructions to seize all papers and arrest everyone there.

Major H. W. Smith had charge of the arresting party.[8] He went up the front steps and as he rang the bell of the house, Mrs. Surratt came to the window and said, "Is that you, Mr. Kirby?" Officer Smith replied that it was not Mr. Kirby, and to open the door. She did so and then Major Smith said, "Are you Mrs. Surratt?" She replied, "I am the widow of John H. Surratt," and, added the officer, "The mother of John H. Surratt, Jr.?" "I am," was her answer. "Then," said the representative of the War Department, "I came to arrest you and all in the house, and take you for examination to General Augur's headquarters."[9]

Four officers, Major H. W. Smith, Captain R. C. Morgan, Captain W. M. Wermerskirch, and Lieutenant John W. Dempsey, then entered the house and took into custody Mrs. Mary E. Surratt, Miss Anna Surratt, Miss Honora Fitzpatrick, and Miss Olivia Jenkins, the cousin of Miss Surratt.

It was in this disturbed condition of affairs that Lewis Payne mounted the long flight of wooden steps that led to Mrs. Surratt's hallway and parlor.

A knock followed by the ringing of the bell notified those on the inside that there was someone at the front door. Captains Morgan and Wermerskirch stepped forward and opened the door. Payne entered dressed in a gray coat, a gray vest, black pants, and wearing the cap made out of the sleeve of his shirt. As soon as he came in, Morgan shut the door behind him. Seeing the officers, Payne said, "I guess I am mistaken." Morgan asked him, "Whom do you want to see?" "Mrs. Surratt," responded the assassin. "You are right, walk in," said Morgan.

Payne took a seat in the hall and Morgan asked him what he came there at that time of night for, meanwhile taking care to secure his pick.

"To dig a gutter"; Mrs. Surratt had sent for him.

"When?" queried Morgan.

"In the morning," ejaculated Payne.[10]

Being further questioned, he stated that he was a poor man who got his living with his pick; that he sometimes made a dollar or a dollar and a half a day, and that he called at that time of the night to know at about what time he should go to work in the morning; that he had no previous acquaintance with Mrs. Surratt; that she knew he was a poor man and came to him. He gave his age as twenty years and his name as Lewis Payne, Fauquier County, Virginia. He acknowledged that he was from the South, and had taken the oath of allegiance, but said that he would have to go into the army if he remained there, and that he preferred earning his living by the pickaxe.

Major Smith also questioned him in reference to his occupation, and what business he had at the house at that time of night. His response was of the same nature as given to Captain Morgan.

Then Major Smith went to the parlor door and said, "Mrs. Surratt, will you step here a minute?" She came out into the hall in full view of Payne and the officers. Major Smith asked her, "Do you know this man, and did you hire him to come and dig a gutter for you?"

Then, solemnly raising her right hand, Mary E. Surratt declared, "Before God, I do not know this man and have never seen him before, and I did not hire him to dig a gutter for me." [11]

Yet this very man Powell, under the assumed names of Wood and Payne, had been her guest on two different occasions; was seen in her house in company with Booth, Atzerodt, Herold, and her son; had slept in her beds; had eaten at her table, taking his meals at her side for four days; had sat with Miss Fitzpatrick, little Miss Dean, and her son in the murdered President's box on the night of the 15th of March when Booth went there; had ridden away with the other conspirators on the 16th of March from her front door with the determined purpose of capturing the President, and afterwards, when that scheme failed, had been secreted in a room at the Herndon House through the efforts of her son and Miss Annie Ward, where Mrs. Surratt herself had once paid him a visit in the darkness of the evening. Still Mrs. Surratt knew not Lewis Payne! When at the peril of her soul she recorded before God that fearful denial she was face to face with Payne and within three paces of him.[12]

Major Smith and Captain Wermerskirch were witnesses of the scene, and when the day of reckoning came at her trial, repeated the very words she uttered to her shame and condemnation.

Just before leaving the house she requested permission of Major Smith to kneel down and pray. This request was granted. When she arose from her knees, she leaned her head over towards Captain Morgan, and said, "I am so glad you officers came here tonight, for this man came here with a pickaxe to kill us." [13]

A carriage was now called and the women were taken to General Augur's office. After being subjected to a rigid examination they were sent to the Carroll Prison until further inquiry was made into all the circumstances connected with the Conspiracy and the murder.

Mrs. Surratt's room was subsequently searched and in it was found a bullet mold; beneath a picture representing Morning, Noon, and Night was concealed a likeness of John Wilkes Booth, and on another wall, a picture with the coat of arms of the state of Virginia emblazoned thereon, and the motto "Sic Semper Tyrannis" underneath, the very expression that Booth used as he fled across the stage, brandishing his knife in the air.[14]

Payne was also removed to General Augur's headquarters. Here Colonel H. H. Wells took charge of him and subjected him to a most thorough scrutiny. William H. Bell, the colored servant who had admitted him into Mr. Seward's house, and who had witnessed the assault on the Secretary of State, was sent for on the morning of the 18th of April for the purpose of identifying him. Bell was ushered into a room where there were twenty or thirty persons, and was asked if there was anyone present who looked like Mr. Seward's assailant, and he replied, "No."

Then Payne walked into the room with a number of other persons. Young Bell instantly went up to him and, laying his finger on Payne's lip, said, "I know you, you are the man." [15]

The Government was now satisfied that the assailant of Mr. Seward had been caught, and Payne was at once taken and placed on board a monitor.[16]

The next day Colonel Wells removed Payne's coat, shirt, pants, vest, and all his underclothing. He had on a white linen shirt and a woolen undershirt minus one sleeve, a pair of boots with a big ink stain on them on the inside. Spots of blood were found on the inside of his coat sleeve, and also on the white shirt sleeve. Colonel Wells called Payne's attention to this, saying, "What do you think now?" The astonished man could vouchsafe no reply. Then the Colonel asked him about his boots and where he got them. Payne said that he had purchased them in Baltimore, and had worn them for about three months. The officer remarked this was a falsehood, as it was apparent that the boots had been worn but a short time. But Payne made no reply and continued taciturn.

The boots were taken to the Treasury Department, the ink stain was subjected to chemical test, and lo! the name of the President's murderer, J. W. Booth, stood revealed.

Colonel Wells also directed Payne's attention to his overcoat, which had been found at Bunker Hill, and he said, "How did that blood come there?" Payne replied, "It is not blood." Colonel Wells said, "Look and see, and say, if you can, that it is not blood." Payne looked at it and then answered, "I do not know how it came there." [17]

Major Augustus H. Seward also went on board the monitor and identified Payne as the man who had attempted to murder his father.[18]

The chain of evidence against the assailant was now complete; there was no longer any doubt of his identity, and, without further examination, he was held to await the result of his trial. He was placed in irons, manacles on his hands and a heavy ball and chain on his left leg. A padded cap [19] was also placed on his head. He had attempted to butt out his brains by beating his head against the wall of his cell, and the padded cap was used to prevent a repetition of that effort. A sentry was now placed over him and was with him until the end.

When Atzerodt came out of the Kirkwood House, whither he had gone armed with a knife and a loaded revolver, he returned his horse to the stable of liveryman Kelleher. This occurred about eleven o'clock P.M.[20] Then he entered a streetcar going towards the Navy Yard. In it he met Walter Briscoe,[21] an acquaintance who had a store in the Navy Yard. Atzerodt requested permission of him to sleep at his place during the night. This Briscoe refused to let him do. He then returned to the city and about two o'clock in the morning went to the Pennsylvania House. He asked for his old room but could not get it. A man was with him by the name of Thomas, whom he had met on the street. A room was assigned to them jointly. Atzerodt acted all this time in a very nervous and excited manner. Someone asked him if he had heard of the assassination and he said, "Yes, and it was awful news."

On Saturday morning he rose and left the house at five o'clock, not stopping long enough to take his breakfast. He threw his knife into a gutter on F Street near the Herndon House, where it was found by a colored woman. He then found his way to Georgetown, pawned his revolvers, and fled northward into Maryland. He was traced to Montgomery County to the house of Hezekiah Metz on Sunday succeeding the murder, where, as was proved by the testimony of three witnesses, he said that if the man that was to follow General Grant had followed him, it was likely that Grant was shot. To one of these witnesses [Somerset Leaman] he said he didn't think that Grant had been killed; or if he had been killed, he was killed by the man who got on the cars at the same time Grant did, thus disclosing clearly that to one of the conspirators was assigned the task of killing and murdering General Grant, and that Atzerodt knew that General Grant had left the city of Washington.[22]

Atzerodt was arrested on the morning of the 20th of April at about four o'clock at the house of one Hartman Richter.[23] He was in bed at the time. He was at once taken to Washington and also placed on a monitor, the *Saugus*.

In the room, No. 126, which he had engaged at the Kirkwood House, a black coat was found hanging on the wall. In the pocket of the coat there was a bank book on one corner of which was written "J. W. Booth

53," on the inside of the book was "Mr. J. Wilkes Booth, in account with the Ontario Bank, Canada, 1864, October 27—By deposit, credited $455." There was also a map of Virginia, a handkerchief marked "Mary R. Booth," another marked "F. M." or "F. A. Nelson," another with the letter "H" in the corner, a pair of new gauntlets, a colored handkerchief, three boxes of cartridges, a piece of licorice, a toothbrush, a pair of spurs, a pair of socks, and two collars.

Underneath the bolster in the bed, a revolver was found, loaded and capped, and between the sheets and mattress a large knife.

In the same week succeeding the assassination, Edward Spangler, the stage carpenter at Ford's Theater, was arrested at his boardinghouse for complicity in the murder. In his carpet sack a piece of rope eighty-one feet long was found and seized by the Government.

Thus, in a week after the murder, seven of the parties said to be implicated in Booth's crime, Samuel Arnold, Michael O'Laughlin, Mary E. Surratt, Lewis Payne, George A. Atzerodt, Edward Spangler, and Dr. Mudd [24] had been put under arrest. Booth, Herold, and John H. Surratt were, however, still at large, and all the resources of the Government were now being used to run them down.

CHAPTER XVIII

The escape of Booth and Herold into Maryland · Crossing of Anacostia Creek · Scenes at Lloyd's tavern · Arrest of Lloyd · Visit of Booth and Herold at Dr. Mudd's house · Arrival at Samuel Cox's place · Booth and Herold placed in the care of Thomas A. Jones · The assassins are secreted for six days in the pines of Lower Maryland · Flight of the two men across the Potomac River · Booth writes a diary

It soon became known to the Government authorities that Booth and Herold had made their escape into Lower Maryland, and, therefore, the best skill and efforts of the most experienced detectives were concentrated in that direction.

Booth crossed the Navy Yard Bridge over Anacostia Creek at about half past ten o'clock on the night of the murder. To the sentry who hailed him and demanded his name he replied, "Booth." He stated that he was from the city; that he resided in Beantown, in Charles County, and that he was on his way home. The sentry asked him if he did not know that it was the rule to allow no persons to pass after nine o'clock at night. Booth responded that he did not. Thereupon the guard, thinking him a proper person, allowed him to depart.[1]

In a few minutes a second horseman came galloping along who gave his name as Smith. He, too, was on his way home, and stated that he lived at White Plains. He rode a medium-sized roan horse, but was not moving so rapidly as the first horseman. The sentry also allowed this man, David E. Herold, to pass.

Just at what point on the road, after crossing the bridge, Herold joined Booth is not known, but one Polk Gardiner, who was coming to Washington, testified that at about eleven o'clock, when he was on Good Hope Hill about three miles from the city, he met two horsemen, one about half a mile behind the other; both were riding very fast. As the second horseman rode up, a party of teamsters were passing by and Gardiner heard him ask them whether any horseman had passed ahead.[2] This query on the part of Herold proves conclusively that it had been agreed between Booth and himself that they would meet somewhere on the road, and it was not long after the events described by Gardiner before Herold overtook his companion.

Then these two assassins in their mad efforts to escape the avenging justice which would soon overtake them, with the blackest midnight closing around their souls steeped in foul murder, dashed furiously down the Bryantown Road, which they hoped would soon bring them to the Potomac, and to ultimate safety.

The first halting place was Lloyd's tavern at Surrattsville. This they reached at midnight. Lloyd was up and fully prepared to carry out his part of the program. The carbines and whisky ordered by Mrs. Surratt together with Booth's field glass were ready, and awaiting the arrival of the assassins to whom they were to be delivered.

Herold rushed into the house and exclaimed, "Lloyd, for God's sake, make haste and get those things!" Lloyd made no reply but went straight and got the carbines, supposing Booth and Herold were the parties to whom Mrs. Surratt referred.[3] From the way Herold spoke he *must have been apprised that Lloyd already knew what he was to give them.*

Booth did not enter the house; Lloyd was unacquainted with him. Herold procured one of the bottles of whisky which Mrs. Surratt had ordered and took it out to Booth, who drank it while sitting on his horse.

They did not remain at Lloyd's house over five minutes, and on their departure took with them only one of the carbines. Booth said he could not take the other because his leg was broken. As they were about leaving, Booth called out, "I will tell you some news, if you want to hear it." Lloyd answered, "I am not particular; use your own pleasure about telling me." "Well," rejoined Booth, "I am pretty certain that we have assassinated the President and the Secretary of State." [4]

Lloyd was arrested during the following week by detective Joshua A. Lloyd,[5] and was placed in charge of officer George Cottingham at Roby's Post Office, near Surrattsville. When taken he wept bitterly, threw his arms over his wife's neck, and called for his prayer book. For two days he denied knowing anything about the assassination, but Cottingham sprang a trap upon him, and told him he was perfectly satisfied he knew all about it; that he had a heavy load on his mind, and that the sooner he got rid of it, the better. Lloyd then said, "Oh my God, if I was to make a confession, they would murder me!" Cottingham asked, "Who would murder you?" Lloyd replied, "These parties that are in this conspiracy." "Well," said Cottingham, "if you are afraid of being murdered, and let these fellows get out of it, that is your business, not mine." [6]

Lloyd then detailed all the circumstances attending the deposit of the carbines, "shooting irons," at his place by John H. Surratt, Atzerodt, and Herold in March, and stated how Mrs. Surratt came down to his place on the afternoon of the assassination, and ordered them together with two bottles of whisky to be held in readiness, that night, for the parties who would call for them.

All this was told to Cottingham while on the way to Washington with a squad of cavalry. Lloyd commenced crying and hallooing out, "Mrs. Surratt, that vile woman, she has ruined me! I am to be shot! I am to be shot!"

Lloyd stated to Cottingham that the carbine which Booth left behind him was upstairs, in a little room where Mrs. Surratt kept some bags. It was found behind the plastering of the wall. It was in a bag and had been suspended by a string tied around the muzzle of the carbine; the string had broken, and the carbine fallen down.[7]

When the assassins left Lloyd's place they again put spurs to their horses, and at breakneck speed dashed for their second stopping place, the home of Dr. Samuel A. Mudd near Bryantown. The doctor was a notorious Southern sympathizer, and as results proved was himself mixed up in the Conspiracy.

Booth and Herold arrived at Dr. Mudd's farm on the morning of the 15th of April at about half past four, having ridden in all about thirty miles during that eventful and bloody night, and all this time the broken bone in Booth's leg had been terribly lacerating his flesh.

Herold rapped on the door of the house. Dr. Mudd himself opened it and assisted in bringing Booth into the house and in laying him upon a sofa in the parlor. In a short time he was carried upstairs and put on a bed in the front room. Dr. Mudd then examined Booth's leg and found that the front bone of the left leg was broken at nearly right angles, about two inches above the instep.[8] He dressed the limb as well as he was able with the limited facilities at his command and called a young man, a white servant, to make a crutch for him. He also gave Booth a razor, soap, and water. With the aid of these Booth removed his mustache. Thus he tried in every way to conceal his identity so that he would escape recognition.

Herold sat down to breakfast with the Mudd family. When the meal was over he made some remark about the necessity of obtaining a conveyance in which to take away his friend, and accordingly he and the doctor started out of the house for that purpose, but returned in a short time without being able to accomplish anything.

The exact hour of Booth and Herold's departure from Dr. Mudd's house is not known. There is no doubt that when Dr. Mudd found Booth on his hands with a broken ankle, and the soldiery already pouring into Bryantown, he, Booth, and Herold became equally frightened and that sometime early in the evening, the two latter, with a negro for their guide, left by a road to the east for Samuel Cox's farm, several miles distant, and not very far from the banks of the Potomac River. They turned toward Bryantown and there left the road for the north.

Lieutenant Alexander Lovett, with some other officers who were in pursuit of Booth and Herold, arrived at Dr. Mudd's farm on Tuesday, the 18th of April, having tracked the criminals to this point. They subjected Dr. Mudd to a number of interrogations, but he stoutly and persistently denied all knowledge of Booth, saying that he had never met him, that he had heard that there was an eminent tragedian by the name of Edwin Booth, but that he had no knowledge of John Wilkes Booth. He said two men had come to his house, one with a broken leg; that the latter wore a pair of long whiskers and had a shawl thrown over his shoulders; but that these parties were unknown to him. The officers left the house, but returned again on Friday, April 21, for the purpose of searching the house and arresting Dr. Mudd. Then it was that Mrs. Mudd became alarmed. She went upstairs and brought down a long riding boot slit up in front about eight inches. This boot, Mrs. Mudd said, had been left on the bed by the man whose leg had been broken. Mudd said he had cut the boot from the man's leg in order to set it. Officer Lovett then turned down the top of the boot and saw the name of "J. Wilkes" written in it.[9]

Concealment any longer was impossible and Dr. Mudd now, for the first time, admitted that he was acquainted with Booth, that he had been introduced to him in the fall of 1864 by a man of the name of [John C.] Thompson.[10]

He was now arrested and sent to Washington for further examination.

After leaving Mudd's place on the 15th, the Government lost all trace of the two assassins for a period of ten days. Nor was this hiatus fully explained until many years afterwards, when the matter was unraveled in a very able article in the *Century*, April 1884, entitled "How Wilkes Booth Crossed the Potomac." *

Samuel Cox, to whom Booth with his companion fled for protection and assistance after leaving Dr. Mudd, was a prominent and wealthy Marylander who resided in Charles County. He lived in a large two-story house with handsome piazzas in its front and rear; it was located almost directly on the line of the road by which Booth and Herold were attempting to make their escape. It was not far from Pope's Creek on the lower Potomac; and just about six miles south of the village of Port Tobacco. The sympathies of Cox were entirely with the South, and to no one could the fugitives have applied more readily with the sure prospect of being helped than to him. They reached his place at midnight on April 15, 1865.

* By George Alfred Townsend.

He had a foster brother, Thomas Jones, with whom he had been reared. Jones was not only a very courageous and self-collected man, but also one of the most energetic individuals in that region in the cause of the South.

Jones had risen somewhat in the world and had owned a few slaves, he sympathized warmly with the South; he owned a farm right at Pope's Creek, the most eligible situation of all for easy intercourse with Virginia. His house was on a bluff, eighty to one hundred feet high, from which he could look up the Potomac to the west, across Mathias Point, and see at least seven miles of the river way, while his view down the Potomac was fully nine miles.

This man during the war was the principal signal officer for the Confederacy north of the Potomac, and was the agent for the mail that went to and was received from the South by this route and at this place. He was familiar with all the river harbors and localities both on the Maryland and Virginia side of the river in that neighborhood.

On Sunday morning, the 16th of April, about nine o'clock, a young man came from Samuel Cox's place to Jones's farm, situated about two and a half miles back from his old river residence, which Jones had been forced to give up when the Confederate cause was lost.

This young man was told, if stopped on the road, to say that he was going to Jones's to ask if he could let Cox have seed corn, which in that climate is planted early in April. He told Jones that Colonel Cox wished him to come immediately to his house, about three miles to the north, and mysteriously hinted that there were some very remarkable visitors at Cox's the night before.*

What happened subsequently is best told in the words of Jones himself in an interview published in the *New York World* for April 1895. He says:

> It's quite true. John Wilkes Booth, with a broken ankle, sick and suffering the tortures of the damned, was placed in my hands to be spirited across the river, and the $300,000 reward, or even $3,000,000, would not have caused me to turn traitor to the southern Confederacy, the people I loved, and surrender a man whose life was in my keeping, even if I did know he had assassinated Abraham Lincoln.

* See *Katy of Catoctin,* by George Alfred Townsend.

It was on the morning of the 16th of April when friends of Samuel Cox came to my house on Huckleberry farm, Maryland, and told me that Cox wanted to see me at once. I had heard that evening before that Lincoln had been killed. I had a horse saddled and rode over to Cox's, who told me that Booth and David Herold had been there and wanted assistance to get across the river. I was told where the men were—in a pine thicket about a mile and a half from the house.

I was given instructions how to reach them without being shot—certain signs by whistling, etc. Upon reaching the dense pines I met Herold, to whom I explained that I was sent by Cox. I was then piloted to where Booth was. He lay on the ground wrapped in a pile of blankets, and his face bore traces of pain. Booth asked many questions as to what people thought of the assassination. He appeared to be proud of what he had done. I at the time thought he had done a good act, but, Great God, I soon saw that it was the worst blow that ever struck the south!

I did the best I could for the poor fellow. I carried him papers to read and something to eat and tried to keep him in good spirits until I got a chance to send him across the river. The country was full of soldiers and detectives, and I did not know how soon I could get him away. I think it was the following Tuesday I went up to Port Tobacco to see how the land lay, and it was there, in the barroom of Brawner's hotel, that Captain William Williams, chief of the United States secret service, said he would give $300,000 to any man who would tell where Booth was.

("That's true," admitted Captain Williams at the time of the above interview, "and he would have been General Jones instead of a discharged employee from the Navy Yard if he had given the information.")

I did the best I could for Booth and Herold. I did not know them but when Cox put them in my keeping nothing would have tempted me to betray them. I could have placed my hands on Booth, but honor and truth were worth more to me than the entire wealth of the government.

At the expiration of the sixth day I heard the officers give orders for the cavalry to go down in St. Mary's county; that the assassins were there. That was my chance, and I made good time to where

Booth and Herold were concealed. Booth was glad to know that his time to get into Virginia had come.

The night was dark, and Herold and I lifted Booth on to my horse. Our progress was slow. We finally reached my house, and I went in to get them something to eat. We then proceeded to the river. Booth was lifted into the boat and was placed in the stern, while Herold took the oars. I then lighted a candle and showed Booth by his compass how to steer to get into Machodoc creek and gave him directions to Mrs. [Elizabeth R.] Quesenberry's who, I thought, would take take care of him. That was the last I saw of Booth.*

The fugitives, however, were unskilled in navigating and, striking the river at high tide, floated along for several hours; when finally they touched the Maryland shore again, they found themselves at a point about nine miles west of Pope's Creek. Here Herold discovered the residence of one Colonel John J. Hughes, whom he knew. He went to the house and asked for food for himself and for Booth, who, he said, was nearby in a boat in a marsh. Food was given, though reluctantly, the man of the house being much disturbed over Herold's revelation.

Herold again pulled off, and this time successfully made the trip to the Virginia shore, though put back a day and half. On Sunday morning, April 23, the ninth day after the assassination, the wanderers arrived at Mrs. Quesenberry's on Machodoc Creek, and with her they left their boat.

Whether they entered Mrs. Quesenberry's house is not certain, but they soon made their way to the home of a man by the name of Bryan on the next farm, and probably to him they revealed their identity. They remained with Bryan all day Sunday, and on the following Monday morning were taken by him to the residence of Dr. [Richard H.] Stewart, the richest man in King George County. Stewart was much chagrined and enraged to find the assassins of Lincoln on his place. He was just entertaining a number of friends who had returned from the Confederate service. The doctor did not invite Booth or Herold to enter his house, but suffered them to stay outside, in a barn or probably some

---

* Jones subsequently had a position in the Navy Yard at Washington but was dismissed from it through the influence of Republican Congressman [Sydney E.] Mudd for the part he took in Booth's escape. He died in Charles County in 1895 at the age of seventy-four.[11]

negro quarters. Booth was very indignant at the treatment he received at this place.

A conveyance to Port Conway was procured from Dr. Stewart. The vehicle was driven by a negro by the name of Lucas, and thus the Rappahannock River was gained on Monday, April 24, by these men who were so madly and vainly endeavoring to escape from the vengeance which was shortly to overtake them.

During his abode in the Maryland pines, Booth ordered Herold to shoot the two horses on which they had made their escape from Washington. He was fearful lest the neighing of the animals would reveal their hiding place, and moreover, it was becoming a very serious question how they should be fed and cared for. Accordingly, Herold obeyed the commands of his chief, and by means of his revolver ended the lives of these innocent creatures. No trace of them was ever found.

Booth wrote a diary while in the pines which is now in the possession of the national Government. The daily papers, as narrated, were brought to him by Jones, and thus he was made conscious of the fact that there was a reward of $175,000 for his capture, and that the Government was leaving no stone unturned to secure him. He must also have read of the arrests of Mrs. Surratt, Payne, Atzerodt, Arnold, O'Laughlin, and Dr. Mudd, which were all accomplished facts at the time he made his entries in his diary, but he did not give himself the slightest concern about the fate of Mrs. Surratt, although he knew it was through her aid that he obtained the very carbine and field glass which he then carried on his person, and which he was using as a means of escape. Nor was he much troubled about the other conspirators who had stood with him in his crime; nay, he was proud of what he had done and took especial glory in the fact that he had been the means of ridding the world of Abraham Lincoln.[12]

CHAPTER XIX

Meeting of Booth and Herold with three Confederate soldiers at Port Conway · The assassins are taken in charge by them · Crossing of the Rappahannock · Booth and Herold are lodged at Garrett's farm by Captain Jett · Booth's trail struck at last by the Government · Eager pursuit by the soldiers and detectives · Captain Jett is arrested at Bowling Green · Booth and Herold discovered at night in Garrett's barn · Exciting scenes around the barn · Herold surrenders · Booth is shot by Boston Corbett · Return of the pursuing party to Washington on the tug John S. Ide with Herold and Booth's body on board · Identification of the body at Washington · Its burial

At Port Conway, the two assassins met three young men, Major M. B. Ruggles, Lieutenant A. B. Bainbridge, and Captain William Jett, all of whom were arrayed in Confederate uniforms. They were soldiers on their way home.

Port Conway is in King George County, Virginia. The width of the Rappahannock River at that point is about three hundred yards. It is directly opposite Port Royal. The ferry was owned by a man named [William] Rollins, but the scow was pushed across by Peyton Washington, a negro.[1]

As the soldiers rode up, they noticed a wagon with two men—Booth and Herold—in it. To the wagon were hitched two horses. The negro driver, Lucas, had refused to carry the men any further. On beholding the soldiers' approach, Herold went towards them, and finding that they were Confederates, began to talk with them. He gave his name as Boyd, and stated that his brother had been wounded in making his escape from prison, and was anxious to be helped on his way South. The soldiers promised their aid and said they would do for them what they could. While waiting for the scow from Port Royal, Booth got out of the wagon. He walked with the aid of the crutch which his friend Dr. Mudd had caused to be made for him, and was evidently in much pain. He appeared to mistrust Herold, for the first words he uttered on meeting the young Confederates were, "I suppose you have been told who I am." Ruggles, remembering what Herold had told him, answered in the affirmative. Then Booth threw his whole weight on his crutch and, drawing a revolver, exclaimed, "Yes, I am John Wilkes Booth, the slayer of Abraham Lincoln, and I am worth just $175,000 to the man who captures me." [2]

To these defiant words Ruggles answered that though they did not sanction his act as an assassin, they were not men to take "blood money," and that having promised his friend Herold to take them across the river to a place of safety, they would do so. At these words, Booth put up his weapon.[3]

Captain Jett was well acquainted in Caroline County on the Port Royal side of the river, and said to Booth with the approval of his companions, Ruggles and Bainbridge, that he would find a place for them where they would be secure. "God bless you, sir," ejaculated Booth, his face all the time writhing with the pain from his disabled leg.[4]

When Booth realized that he was among friends, he threw off all reserve and became quite communicative. His face was covered with a short, thick growth of hair, and he kept pulling at his mustache, which had somewhat grown in again since his exit from Dr. Mudd's house. He exhibited to Ruggles the initials "J.W.B." done in India ink on his right hand, and said the shawl had done good service in concealing these telltale marks. Over his shoulder was strung a pair of large field glasses; they were attached by a long leather strap, and were the very same field glasses he had given to Mrs. Surratt on the afternoon of the 14th of April which she in turn had delivered to John M. Lloyd, and which Lloyd handed to the assassins when they made their appearance at his house at midnight after the murder. Booth acknowledged that the glasses had not been of much use to him because "he had been forced to keep under cover too much."

When the scow at length arrived, Major Ruggles assisted Booth to mount his (Ruggles') horse and then the whole party started across the Rappahannock for Port Royal. All this time they were very keenly eyed by the dusky ferryman, and very little was said by any of them. When they touched the wharf, Booth lost no time in landing. His spirits seemed to have returned, and he cried out joyously: "I am safe in glorious old Virginia, thank God."

"Now boys," said Jett, "I propose to take our friend, Booth, up to Garrett's house. I think they will give him shelter there and treat him kindly." "I'm in your hands," answered Booth, "do with me as you think best." [5]

A start was then made for Garrett's farm, which was reached after a journey of three miles. Shelter was asked for in behalf of the fugitives and granted. The Garrett house was some distance from the main road and was situated on a hill.

When they arrived at the gate leading into the farm, Herold remained with Bainbridge, and said he would go as far as Bowling Green to buy a pair of shoes. Jett and Ruggles accompanied Booth to the house. Herold and Bainbridge went on to Bowling Green, where they remained all night, stopping at the house of a Mr. Clark. Jett and Ruggles, after seeing Booth disposed of at Garrett's, also went on to Bowling Green and put up at the house of a Mr. [Henry] Goldman, whose daughter was Jett's sweetheart.

When Booth entered the Garrett house, he gave his name as James W. Boyd and stated that he was a Confederate and was wounded at Petersburg, and was trying to get home to his people in Maryland, but that his wound was too painful to allow him to travel.

At that time the Garrett family had not heard of the death of the President. That night at supper, a neighbor came in and told the family of the assassination, and the subject was discussed, the wounded man joining in the conversation. He agreed that perhaps it was only a rumor started by stragglers, but assented when old Mr. Garrett said that, if it was true, it was an exceedingly unfortunate thing for the South. The neighbor stated that there was a big reward offered, $100,000, and one of the Garrett boys said that the assassin had better not come that way, for he would like to make such a sum of money about that time. Boyd (Booth) turned round and said, "Would you betray him for that?" Young Garrett laughed and said, "They had better not tempt me. I've not a dollar in the world." [6]

Booth slept in the house that night (April 24) and there were two of the Garrett boys in the same room with him. Next day he played with the children in the yard. About noon he went into the house and asked young Mr. R. B. Garrett to take down a map from the wall. He put it on the floor and studied it, tracing a line from Norfolk to Charleston by water and from Charleston to Galveston. On being asked where he wanted to go, he answered, "To Mexico." This was the only clue the Garretts had as to his intended escape.

On the morning of Tuesday, April 25, Ruggles and Bainbridge returned to Port Royal together, Herold going with them as far as Garrett's gate, where he left them. He said he was going right up to join Booth and would stick to him to death.

As Ruggles and his companion neared Port Royal, they came across a soldier who had been in Ruggles' command and who advised them, if not paroled, to turn back, "for," said he, "the town is full of Yankees in search for Booth, who, they say, crossed the river yesterday." Ruggles and Bainbridge lost no time in getting back to Garrett's farm. They found Booth lying on the lawn in front of the house. As soon as he recognized them, he arose and hobbled towards them, saying, "Well, boys, what's in the wind now?" He was promptly informed that the enemy was after him, and was urged to seek a shelter in the woods. Bainbridge pointed to a thick piece of woodland at some distance from the house, saying, "Booth, get over there at once and hide yourself." Booth looked around for Herold, but he was not in sight at that time, then straightening himself up, said, "I'll do as you say, boys, right off. Ride on. Goodbye. It will never do for you to be found in my company." Then biting his lips, as if he had conceived a desperate resolve, he said, "Rest assured, good friend, Wilkes Booth will never be taken alive." [7]

Herold soon rejoined Booth. He had been introduced to the Garrett family by Booth as Mr. Harris. They did not know who he was any more than they knew Booth. The two men became very much excited over the information received from Ruggles and Bainbridge. Booth sent R. B. Garrett up to his room for his pistol, which he had left hanging on the bedpost. By the time he had returned, a detachment of troops rode past the house on the road about a quarter of a mile distant. As a matter of fact, they were after Jett, knowing that he had crossed the river with Booth, and supposing that Booth was still with him.

After the troops had passed the house, the two men walked to a piece of woods back of the house and stayed there about an hour, returning to ask one of the Garrett brothers if he would rent them a horse to take them to the nearest railroad station. Garrett refused, having become suspicious of them, but helped them to make a bargain with a colored man who lived nearby. The negro was to call for them the next morning. Mr. Garrett, the father of the family, was not feeling well that evening, and retired early. The men sat out upon the upper gallery of the house and talked until quite late, after which they asked if they might sleep in the barn fifty yards away so as not to disturb the father of the family when they went away in the morning.

This explains why Booth and Herold retired to sleep in the barn.

The information which Ruggles imparted to Booth was, indeed, correct. His trail had been struck at last, and now the detectives and the Union soldiers were after him and his companion in hot haste. Booth's earthly days were but few, and were rapidly drawing to a close.

On the very day, April 24, 1865, on which the fugitives crossed the Rappahannock, and were lodged in the Garrett home, First Lieutenant E. P. Doherty of the 16th New York Cavalry at about 4 P.M., while sitting on a bench in Lafayette Square opposite the White House, received the following official orders through a messenger:

> *Headquarters, Department of Washington,*
> *April 24, 1865.*

Commanding Officer 16th New York Cavalry,

Sir:

You will at once detail a reliable and discreet commissioned officer with twenty-five men, well mounted, with three days' rations and forage, to report at once to Colonel L. C. Baker, Agent of the War Department, at 211 Pennsylvania Avenue.

> By command of General C. C. Augur,
> J. C. Sewell, A. A. A. Gen'l.

In accordance with the foregoing order First Lieutenant E. P. Doherty is hereby detailed for the duty, and will report at once to Colonel Baker, 211 Pennsylvania Avenue. —N. B. Switzer, Colonel, 16th New York Cavalry, Bvt. Brig. U.S.A.[8]

Lieutenant Doherty proceeded to the company barracks, had "boots and saddles" sounded, selected the first twenty-five men in the saddle who reported to him, Sergeant Corbett [9] being the only one of his own command, and in less than half an hour had reported to Colonel Baker.

Photographs of the alleged assassins of President Lincoln were handed him, and he was told that inasmuch as no troops had as yet been in Fredericksburg, he must reach that neighborhood as soon as possible. Colonel E. G. Conger and Lieutenant L. B. Baker [10] of the detective force were assigned to accompany and assist him. Both were good officers and experienced men. Colonel Conger had raided the country in every direction and was valuable on account of his familiarity with the roads and for his undaunted bravery and courage.

The party went on board the tug *John S. Ide,* at the Sixth Street wharf, and steamed down to Belle Plain near the mouth of Acquia Creek. They landed about ten o'clock at night and at once began the search for the murderers. They proceeded directly south until the main road to Fredericksburg was struck. Here a halt was made until four o'clock A.M. on the morning of the 25th of April. A negro informed Doherty that a cavalry regiment had passed to Fredericksburg on the previous evening, going on the north side of the river, and Lieutenant Doherty then determined to go down on the south side.

He halted about six o'clock in the evening within a mile of Port Conway, and ordered his men to unsaddle and feed. Then he rode with his bugler to Port Conway.

In the meantime, Lieutenant Baker, who had been searching the country, came across a man and his wife who were sitting at the front door of their house, which was four or five rods from the ferry. They proved to be the ferryman and his wife. He went to them and asked them if they had seen within a day or two any citizens passing that way; finally, if they had seen a lame man. They answered they had, and from their description, Baker concluded that it must have been Booth. He then took a likeness of Booth from his pocket and asked the ferryman (Rollins was his name) if that picture resembled the lame man. He said it did, except for the mustache, which he said the lame man did not have. He then showed him Herold's picture, and the ferryman replied that he thought it resembled the small man who carried a carbine. Baker then learned that Booth and Herold had come to the ferry about half past nine o'clock on the previous morning, and that they paid the negro Lucas ten dollars for bringing them thus far. They offered Rollins ten dollars in gold to take them to Orange Court House, but Jett, Ruggles, and Bainbridge rode up just at that time, and the result of the meeting was that, as has been seen, the proposed route of Booth and Herold was changed, and they were taken to Garrett's farm.

It was also ascertained that Jett was courting a young lady named Goldman, whose father kept a hotel at Bowling Green, Virginia, and that the party had probably all gone there. Lieutenant Doherty immediately sent his bugler for Sergeant Corbett and the rest of the men. He sent Rollins for a flatboat which was on the other side of the Rappahannock River. By this time the soldiers had ridden up and they were at once ferried across to Port Royal. Several trips had to be made and on the last trip, Rollins, the ferryman, was arrested. This was done at his own request to avoid suspicion.[11] Lieutenant Doherty ordered him to act as guide by the nearest road to Bowling Green, which was fifteen miles away. When they arrived there, all except eight men were left in the outskirts of the town. With this detail Doherty surrounded Goldman's hotel, and there after some delay, at midnight, Captain Jett was arrested. He was in bed at the time, but he arose, dressed, and came out to the officers in one of the rooms. At first, Jett denied all knowledge of Booth and Herold. When, however, Colonel Conger said to him, "Where are the two men who came with you across the river?" Jett went up to him, and said, "Can I see you alone?" Conger replied, "Yes, sir; you can." Lieutenants Doherty and Baker were present at the time. Colonel Conger politely requested them to leave the room. After they were gone, Jett reached out his hand to Conger and said, "I know what you want; I will tell you where they can be found." [12] Conger answered that was what he wanted to know. Jett now said they were at Garrett's house, and that he would accompany them and show them where they were.

Jett was placed on a horse, and the way was at once retraced to Garrett's farm. Rollins rode at the head of the command with Doherty and Jett immediately behind.

At a little after four o'clock in the morning (April 26) the soldiers came in sight of the farm. A short halt was allowed and then a dash was made through the lane in short order and the house surrounded. The officers dismounted, went onto the piazza, and thundered at the door. The old man Garrett threw up the nearest window, and asked in a frightened tone, "What is the matter?" Lieutenant Baker seized him by the arm, and ordered him to unfasten the door and strike a light. In obedience to this demand, Mr. Garrett soon appeared with a tallow candle. Baker took the candle and asked, "Where are the men who are stopping with you?" The old man was very much excited, and he stammered out, "They went to the woods when the cavalry went by." "Don't you tell me that again," replied Lieutenant Baker, "they are here." The sight of a pistol brought one of the young Garretts to the front who said, "Don't injure father, and I will tell you all about it; they are in the barn." [13]

About this time Colonel Conger came on the scene. Young Garrett was taken by the collar and led out on the piazza while the men were being formed to surround the barn. Garrett was then ordered to lead the way, but before reaching the barn, he said, "I have forgotten the key, but my brother who is sleeping in the corn crib has it. We would not let those men sleep in the house, and were afraid they would steal the horses and get away." The brother soon appeared with the key and delivered it to Baker. The barn was now surrounded, and Lieutenant Baker himself unlocked the door. Up to this time Booth and Herold appeared to be asleep, but the noise of the soldiery soon awakened them, and a rustling was heard inside the building, as if the inmates were rousing up. It was agreed between the officers that Garrett should go in, demand their surrender, and bring out their arms. Garrett was, however, reluctant about obeying, and said, "They are desperate fellows and armed to the teeth." Lieutenant Baker seized him, opened the door, shoved him in, and then closed the door. The Lieutenant hailed the assassin and said, "We sent in this young man, in whose custody we find you, and you must surrender your arms to him, or we shall set fire to the barn, and have a bonfire and a shooting match." A low conversation took place inside the barn, and Booth was heard to say to Garrett, "D—n you. You have betrayed me; get out of here or I will shoot you."

Garrett came back to the door, and cried out, "Let me out, Captain. I will do anything for you but I can't risk my life here." The door was opened, Garrett came out with a bound, and then the door was closed again. Lieutenant Baker still had the light in his hand, and young Garrett said, "If you don't put out that light he will shoot every one of you." The light was placed at a short distance from the door, but so as to illumine the whole front of the building, which had once been used as a tobacco house. The light was necessary in case the assassins should make a break for the door and get out. The soldiers were dismounted, but refused to stand in the light, and were allowed to seek a safer position. Lieutenant Baker again demanded their surrender. Booth replied in a clear, ringing tone, "Captain, there is a man here who wishes to surrender very much." At the same time, a conversation took place within, and Booth was heard to say to Herold, "D—n you, leave me, will you? Go, I don't wish you to stay." And in a few minutes Herold rapped at the door, saying, "Let me out; I know nothing of this man." Lieutenant Baker said, "Bring out the arms and you can come." He replied, "I have no arms." The Lieutenant said, "You have a carbine and pistol, bring them out, and we will let you out." Booth then said, "He has no arms; they are mine, and I shall keep them." [14]

While this parleying was going on, everything was being done to keep the men aroused and on the alert, for they had become so exhausted with their ride of two days and two nights, without rest and with but one meal, that it was almost impossible to keep them awake. Strict orders were given not to fire, as it would endanger the lives of the men who surrounded the building. Herold begged and entreated in the most piteous manner to be let out, and he was ordered to put his hands out of the door, which was partly ajar. He did so; one of the officers caught hold of them, pulled him out, and immediately closed the door. Lieutenant Doherty took charge of him, and at once examined him to see if there were any arms on his person, but found none. The only thing he had in his pockets was a piece of a map of Virginia. Herold kept making assertions that he knew nothing about Booth, and Colonel Conger threatened to tie him and gag him if he did not stop his noise. Doherty, then, took him and tied him by the hands to a tree opposite the veranda of the house and within a few yards of the spot where Booth was finally to give out his life.

Another parley with Booth now ensued. Lieutenant Baker again made the demand for his surrender. Booth said, "Who are you and what do you want of me? It may be that I am being taken by my friends." The Lieutenant replied, "That makes no difference; we know who you are and want you. We have fifty men armed with carbines and pistols around the barn and you cannot escape." After a pause he said, "Captain, this is a hard case, I swear. Give a lame man a chance. Draw up your men twenty yards from the door, and I will fight your whole command." The Lieutenant answered, "We did not come to fight, but to take you; have got you, and you had better surrender." Booth replied, "Give me a little time to consider." Baker said, "Very well, take time. You can have five minutes." He was heard to come toward the door or near the door. As he came he said, "Captain, I believe you are a brave and honorable man. I have had a half dozen opportunities to shoot you, and have a bead drawn on you now, but don't wish to do it. Withdraw your forces a hundred yards from the door and I will come out. Give me a chance for my life, Captain, for I will not be taken alive." "We have waited long enough. Now come out or we will fire the barn." Booth then said in his peculiar stage tone, "Well, my brave boys, prepare a stretcher for me, then." After a pause of about half a minute he was heard to say, "One more stain on the glorious old banner." [15]

Just as he ceased speaking Colonel Conger applied a match to some hay which he drew through a crevice, and in an instant the inside of the building was a blaze of light. The door was next opened in order to give Booth a chance to come out, and thus from the outside every movement made by him could be seen. He seemed to be leaning against the haymow supported by his crutch, with his carbine in his hand. He sprang forward toward the fire with the seeming intention of shooting the man who touched the match, but the intense light inside the building prevented him from seeing objects in the darkness without. He then turned and with the aid of his crutch came rapidly in the direction of the door, but halted about the center of the floor. Here he drew himself up to his full height, and seemed to take a survey of the terrible situation. He looked first at the roaring flames, and then his glaring eyes rested on the open door. He resembled an infuriated wild beast at bay. A cloud of smoke rolled to the roof, swept across the room, then came down to the floor on the other side, and he appeared to be standing in an arch of fire and smoke. He remained but an instant in this position, and then dropped his crutch, and with his carbine in one hand and his pistol in the other, dashed for the door. When within ten feet of the opening the crack of a pistol was heard from the rear of the barn. Booth reeled forward, threw up one hand, dropped his carbine, and fell face downward on some hay which was scattered on the floor.

Lieutenant Baker rushed in, followed by Conger, Doherty, and young Garrett. Officer Baker, not knowing how fatal the shot was, seized him by the arms, intending to secure him in case he had only been stunned. On turning Booth over, a pistol was found in his left hand which he still held with a vise-like grip, and it required great strength to wrench it from him. A leather belt was around his body, with a bowie knife and another revolver in it. Lieutenant Baker then accused Colonel Conger of shooting him, which the Colonel denied, and said Booth shot himself. This the Lieutenant claimed was impossible, as he saw him every moment from the time the hay was fired until he fell. Colonel Conger said, "The man who did shoot him shall go back to Washington under arrest." Upon further inquiry it was found that Sergeant Boston Corbett had fired the shot from a navy revolver through a crevice in the rear of the barn. This was a most difficult feat to perform, for the ball struck Booth on the side of the neck a little back of the center, and passed entirely through, breaking the spinal column.[16]

The fire was making such progress that Booth was taken out of the building and carried a short distance and placed under a tree. He began to show signs of life. Water was dashed in his face and a little was poured in his mouth. His lips began to move and he faintly whispered, "Tell mother—tell mother." He seemed to gain further strength and then in a more distinct voice said, "Tell mother I died for my country."

Day was breaking, and the heat from the burning barn was so intense that the wounded man was removed to the piazza of the house. The young ladies brought a narrow straw bed, and on this Booth was placed. A cloth soaked in whisky and ice water was placed in his mouth, which revived him. He opened his eyes, seemed to take in the situation at once, and said, "Kill me, O, kill me quick." Lieutenant Baker said, "No, Booth, we did not want to kill you, and hope you will recover. You were shot against orders." He then was unconscious for several minutes, when he again revived. His chest heaved, his chin dropped; he put out his tongue and seemed to wish to know if there was blood in his mouth. He was assured there was none, and then said, "Tell mother I died for my country. I did what I thought best." He showed no signs of life in his body below the wound with the exception of the action of the lungs. He said, "My hands," when one of his hands was raised so he could see it, and it was bathed in ice-cold water. His hand was placed by his side, and he said, "Useless, useless," which were the last words of the dying assassin. He died a few minutes after seven o'clock.[17]

Thus perished a young man, brilliant, handsome, and accomplished, but rash, misguided, and perhaps (who knows to the contrary?) bereft of a sane mind, who, had he lived and followed the profession he had chosen in early life, could have risen to the very zenith of prominence; but now all was gone—fame, life, and he was only a mangled corpse, a mere shadow and a wreck of his former self. Truly did he exclaim with his last breath, "Useless, useless."

Colonel Conger gave Sergeant Corbett a stinging reprimand, and said to him, "Why did you shoot without orders?" The Sergeant took the position of a soldier, saluted the Colonel, and with right hand pointed upward, said, "God Almighty ordered me to shoot." At this reply the

Colonel mellowed in his manner, and said, "I guess He did," and then dropped the subject.[18]

Before leaving for Washington, Colonel Conger examined Booth's clothing, and took from his person and pocket the following articles: a knife, a pair of pistols, belt, holster, file, pocket compass, spur, pipe, carbine cartridges, bills of exchange, and a diary. On the compass were some candle drippings, and the bills of exchange were the identical ones which he had secured in Montreal, Canada, in October 1864, which he had never used, but which were now here to bear evidence against their owner of his dastardly purpose even at that time. There were also found on him some photographs, a little Catholic medal,[19] which hung around his neck, and a diamond scarf pin, on the gold setting of which was engraved the name of Dan Bryant, which had been given to him by that gentleman. The inscription on the pin read: "Dan Bryant to J. W. Booth."

His diary, which was written after he had committed his awful crime and during the period in which he attempted to make his escape, betrays in every line the terrible remorse and the fearful despair which had taken possession of his agonized soul. He attempted to justify himself, but for such a crime there was none. The diary, however, tells its own story. It will be noticed how he used the words "we" and "our" through it, thus proving almost unconsciously that there were others implicated in the crime of assassination besides himself.

This diary bears the heading "Te amo."

April 13, 14, Friday, The Ides.

Until to-day nothing was ever thought of sacrificing to our country's wrongs. For six months we had worked to capture. But, our cause being almost lost, something decisive and great must be done. But its failure was owing to others who did not strike for their country with a heart. I struck boldly, and not as the papers say. I walked with a firm step through a thousand of his friends, was stopped, but pushed on. A colonel was at his side.[20] I shouted "Sic semper" before I fired. In jumping broke my leg. I passed all his pickets, rode sixty miles that night, with the bone of my leg tearing the flesh at every jump.

I can never repent it, though we hated to kill. Our country owed all our [her] troubles to him, and God simply made me the instrument of his punishment.

The country is not what it was. This forced union is not what I have loved. I care not what becomes of me. I have no desire to outlive my country. This night before the deed, I wrote a long article and left it for one of the editors of the *National Intelligencer*, in which I fully set forth our reasons for our proceedings. He or the gov'r—[south]

Friday 21.

After being hunted like a dog through swamps, woods, and last night being chased by gunboats till I was forced to return, wet, cold and starving, with every man's hand against me, I am here in despair. And why? For doing what Brutus was honored for—what made Tell a hero. And yet I, for striking down a greater tyrant than they ever knew, am looked [up]on as a common cut-throat. My action [act] was purer than either of theirs. One hoped to be great [himself], the other had not only his country's but his own wrongs to avenge. I hoped for no gain[s]. I knew no private wrong. I struck for my country and that alone. A country groaned beneath this tyranny, and prayed for this end, and yet now behold the cold hand they extend [to] me. God cannot pardon me if I have done wrong. Yet I cannot see my [any] wrong, except in serving a degenerate people. The little, the very little, I left behind to clear [bear] my name, the Government will not allow to be printed. So ends all. For my country I have given up all that makes life sweet and holy, brought misery upon my family, and am sure there is no pardon in [the] Heaven for me since man condemns me so. I have only heard of what has been done, (except what I did myself,) and it fills me with horror. God!, try and forgive me, and bless my mother. To-night I will once more try the river with [the] intention to cross, though I have a greater desire and almost a mind to return to Washington, and in a measure clear my name, which I feel I can do. I do not repent the blow I struck. I may before [my] God, but not to man. I think I have done well, though I am abandoned with the curse of Cain upon me, when if the world knew my heart, that one blow would have made me great, though I did desire no greatness.

To-night I try to escape these blood-hounds once more. Who, who read his fate? God's will be done.

"I have too great a soul to die like a criminal. O, may He spare me that, and let me die bravely!"

I bless the entire world. [I] have never hated nor wronged any one. This last was not a wrong, unless God deems it so. And it's with [for] Him to damn or bless me. And for this brave boy with me, who often prays (yes, before and since) with a true and sincere heart,— was it crime in him, if so, why can he pray the same? I do not wish to shed a drop of blood, but "I must fight the course." "T'is all that's left to me." [21]

Booth's remains were sewed up in a saddle blanket by Lieutenant Doherty, placed in a one-horse wagon driven by a negro, and taken across the country to Belle Plain, where the whole party, including Herold, arrived about dark. The tug *John S. Ide* was waiting, Herold and Booth's body were put on board, and she then steamed up the river for Washington. The capital was reached about daylight on the morning of April 27, and the body delivered to Secretary Stanton. It was placed on board the *Montauk*.[22] So, also, was Herold.

A commission composed of Judge Advocate General [Joseph] Holt, Judge [John A.] Bingham of Ohio, General Lafayette C. Baker, and others was convened for the purpose of establishing the identity of the body of the wretched assassin.

Of the witnesses called who had known Booth in his lifetime, one of the most interesting was Charles L. Dawson, clerk of the National Hotel, who had been acquainted with him for some years.[23] This gentleman, when questioned if he knew of any physical mark or peculiarity on the person of Booth, replied that he did, and stated that he had often seen on his right hand near the junction of the thumb and the forefinger the letters "J.W.B." tattooed in india ink. Dawson often noticed this when Booth was in the act of placing his name on the hotel register, and said to him jestingly, "Booth, what a fool you were to disfigure that pretty white hand in such a way."

Dr. J. F. May, who had been Booth's physician, also identified the remains. Sometime before the assassination the doctor had performed an operation on the left side of his neck for the removal of a tumor. The wound had partially healed, but it was afterwards torn open by Charlotte Cushman while playing some part with him in an engagement in Baltimore. The opening finally closed, but a scar was left on the neck and by this scar Dr. May fully recognized the body.[24]

The testimony of these gentlemen settled the question of Booth's identity, but there were others called who had known him and who swore as to the authenticity of the body.[25]

During all this time the body lay on a rough carpenter's bench. His mustache and the curly lock of hair which he wore on his forehead were missing, and had been removed at the home of Dr. Mudd. His foot was covered with an old shoe which replaced the riding boot which had been cut off and also left behind at Mudd's.

An autopsy of the remains was made on deck by Surgeon General Barnes. A portion of the spine and one of the vertebrae, taken from that part of the neck near which he had been shot, were put into small glass bottles and subsequently placed in the Army Medical Museum in Ford's Theater, the scene of his tragedy.

When the Commission adjourned, the body was sewed up in a navy blanket, and was then lowered from the side of the vessel to two men in a small boat. These men had been selected by General Baker for this work. They had strict orders to keep silent and not reveal what they were doing. The vessel was rowed down the Anacostia, and then went around the point in the direction of the old United States Arsenal.

Here in the dead of night in the presence of the military storekeeper, four enlisted men, and Dr. George L. Porter, the only commissioned officer with them, it was hidden in a place so secret that never to this day has it been accurately described.[26]

The body was finally given to the family of the deceased in February 1869.

In this connection the following documents will be found very interesting:

Baltimore, Maryland, February 18, 1869.

Permit 16821.

Mr. J. H. Weaver for J. W. Booth.

For digging one lot 9–10 area Dogwood,	$4.00
250 bricks at $2.00 per 100,	5.00
7 feet stone slab to cover the same,	5.63
Depositing in vault,	5.00
Second bill June 26, 1869,	5.00
	$24.63

Superintendent Greenmount Cemetery
Baltimore, Maryland, May 25, 1892.

The remains of J. Wilkes Booth were interred in this cemetery in February or March 1869,[27] being brought from Washington, D.C., by John H. Weaver, undertaker, since deceased.

(Signed.) Alex. Russell, Foreman.*

Mr. Richard H. Garrett in a letter to the *New York Herald* has given a very interesting and complete account of the time Booth and Herold were with him, their actions, and the subsequent death of Booth; it is as follows:

"On Monday, the 24th of April, 1865, about 4 o'clock P.M., three men rode up to my yard, and when I went out to them I found they were all strangers to me. The one in front introduced himself as Capt. Scott; he then introduced the others to me—one as Lieut. Ruggles and the other as his friend, Mr. Boyd. He stated that Mr. Boyd was a wounded confederate soldier; that he belonged to the former command of Gen. [Ambrose P.] Hill, and that he was wounded before Petersburg just before the close of the war; that he and Lieut. Ruggles were going (as he expressed it) on a little scout towards Richmond, and asked me to keep and take care of his friend Boyd until the next Wednesday morning, as he was suffering too much to travel with them, and that they would call for him at that time.

"As it had always been one principle of my religion 'to entertain strangers, especially any that seemed to be suffering,' I consented that he should remain, and that I would take as good care of him as I could. I did not promise this because he was a confederate soldier, but because he seemed to be suffering. I had before this administered to the wants of about twelve wounded soldiers, who had been captured and brought to my neighborhood in a suffering state, and it was comforting to my feelings to see the gratitude expressed by them to me, and to feel that I had helped to relieve the wants of some of my fellow creatures. Never shall I

* A local undertaker, recently deceased, told this story of his last interview with Edwin Booth. He said: "I had fixed up the Booth lot in Greenmount and took a diagram to Philadelphia to show just what I had done. Mr. Booth was highly pleased; I then asked him what he wished done in reference to the grave of John Wilkes Booth, telling him that I put marks at every grave except his. A shade passed over the face of the tragedian and the struggle of emotion that was going on within him was pitiful to see. Then he turned slowly, and in a low voice said: 'Leave that as it is; place no mark there.'"

forget this circumstance; it is graven deep upon my heart. This man, whom I and all my family looked upon as Mr. Boyd, a wounded confederate soldier, was taken at once into my house. He supped with my family and slept that night in one of my upper rooms, in which my sons, John M. and Wm. H. and two smaller children slept. He breakfasted with my family the next morning and remained in the house and yard, most of the time reclining upon the grass in the yard, my little children being most of the time with him. He had very little to say, and seemed to be suffering, we thought, from his wound. After breakfast, that morning, my eldest son, John M., rode to a shoemaker's, about one mile from my house, to have his boots repaired, and while there, he met with a gentleman of the neighborhood, who had gotten by private means, a newspaper from Richmond, (there being no mails to our section), and this paper had in it, an advertisement offering a large reward ($150,000) I think, for the capture of Booth, the murderer of President Lincoln. After my son's return, and while at the dinner table, he spoke of having seen this paper containing the advertisement. This man, who was at the table, remarked that he would not have been surprised if $500,000 had been offered, but that he had heard, that the man that committed the act, had been arrested between Baltimore and Philadelphia and was now in Washington. He having before this told me that he was a native of Maryland, I then asked him if he had ever seen the man Booth who was charged with the offense. He said he had seen him once, he saw him in Richmond about the time of the John Brown raid. I asked him if he was an old or young man: he said he was rather a young man.

"I had never heard of but one Booth as an actor, and thought it was Mr. Edwin Booth. My younger son, who was a mere youth, remarked, 'I wish he would come this way, so that I might catch him and get this reward.' He turned to him and said: 'If he were to come out would you inform against him?' My son, laughing, said he would like to have the money. The man talked all this time coolly, and showed nothing like excitement upon the occasion, and caused no grounds of suspicion in any of our minds that he was the man who had done the act. Some two or three hours after dinner two men on horseback, with a third man riding behind one of them, rode up to my gate on the main road. The man who was riding behind got down and came to my house, while the other two men rode on towards Port Royal. When this man came to the house the man who was here introduced him to my son, John M., who was in the yard, as Mr. Boyd, his cousin. They walked up the road from my yard, and seemed to be in earnest conversation. Very soon after this the two men who had passed on horseback returned, riding very rapidly—one of them was Lieut. Ruggles—and said to the two men who were here, 'The Yankees are crossing at Port Royal and you must take care of yourselves the best way you can,' and rode off immediately. I was a short distance from my house, where my laborers were at work, and on coming to the house I saw these two men going off towards the woods. Soon after getting to the house one of these men, who proved to be Harold [David E. Herold], returned to my yard. I and my son said to him we should not be surprised if these forces were in pursuit of him and his friend. He said: 'Oh no, we have done nothing to make them pursue us'; but that he had heard that some federal soldiers that were stopping the night before at a place called the Trap, between here and Bowling Green, had their horses stolen, and he expected these forces were sent down from Fredricksburg to endeavor to capture the thieves. Soon after this the federal forces passed the road by my house and went on toward the place at which the horses were said to have been stolen. After the forces passed Harold went to the woods and brought his friend back to the house. They took supper with my family, and, after supper, I, being unwell, went directly to my room, and my sons and these two men went to my front porch. My son said they seemed to be very uneasy and that they said they were anxious to get a conveyance to Orange Court House, at which place they heard there were a good many Marylanders who were endeavoring to get west of the Mississippi river, and that they wished to go with them. They asked my son if he knew of any conveyance they could get that evening to go part of the way. He told them there was a colored man living near by who had a horse and carryall that he hired out at times. They endeavored to get it, but the man was not home. They then offered my son ten dollars to carry them about twenty miles on the way. He told them that he could not go that night, but that if they wished to go next morning he could take them. They proposed sleeping in my house that night, but my son objected, as he thought from their excited manner there was something wrong about them. They then proposed sleeping under my front porch; but he told them we had bad dogs, and they might be annoyed by them. They then asked him if we had an out house in which they could sleep. He told them there was fodder and hay in the tobacco house, and they could go in there and sleep if they liked.

"They went in there, and after they did so my two sons—having heard Harold say, 'We should like to get the horses we saw you riding this evening,' and fearing they might get up in the night and take their horses and go off—concluded to take their blankets and go into a corn-house between the tobacco house and the stable, and guard their horses; and my youngest son, fearing, as these men were heavily armed, that if they attempted to take the horses they might have great difficulty, and might probably get shot, concluded he would take the key to the house and lock the door on the outside, so as to prevent them coming out if they wished it. This is the reason why the door was found locked when the officers went to the house. About two o'clock A.M. I was awakened by the violent barking of my dogs. I arose from my bed and went to the window, and found the house surrounded by armed forces. I drew on my pantaloons, and, without waiting to put on any other dressing, I opened the door to my end porch, and when I did so three men rushed in, and one of them put a pistol to my head and said to me, 'Are there not two men in your house?' I said no; that there were two men here last evening; that they went to the woods when you were passing, and afterwards re-turned and got their supper, and I did not at that time know where they were. I had gone from my supper to my sleeping room, and did not know where they had slept.

"The officer said I was not telling the truth and called for a rope and said they would hang me. Being thus rudely treated, I no doubt appeared scared and affrighted. About this time my son, John M. Garrett, came to the door and said to the men that these men were in the tobacco house, and they put me under guard, and carried my son with them to the tobacco house, and the door opened, and made him go in and try to bring the men out. When he went in he addressed Mr. Booth as Mr. Boyd, as the officers said, and told him there was a large force surrounding the house, and he had better surrender. He ordered my son out, and appeared to be drawing a pistol, and he ran out. The officer then parleyed with the men for some time, when Harold expressed a wish to surrender and Booth said to the officer that the man in here wishes to come out. The officer told him to hand his arms to one of them, I believe to my son at the door, and to come out, Booth said the man had no arms; they were all his, and they would not be delivered up. Harold then came out, and Booth refusing to surrender, Col. Conger ordered the house fired to force him out. When he gave these orders Booth said to him, 'Don't destroy the gentleman's property; he is entirely innocent, and does not know who I am.' The house was then fired, after which Sergeant Corbet[t] shot Booth, and he was brought out and died on my porch. It was not until after Booth was shot that we were told who he was; we had no idea that they were the murderers of the President. When the forces passed my house they went over to Bowling Green and got Jett, the man who brought Booth to my house, and he told them that he left Booth at my house. When he came here I asked him why he brought that man to my house and left him here as a wounded confederate soldier, and had brought so much trouble upon me. He said he wished to get clear of him and left him at the first house he came to after leaving Port Royal; that he had told the officers when they came to Bowling Green, that he had left him with me as a confederate soldier, and that I was not apprised who he was. I told him to make that declaration to an officer in my presence. He made it to Lieut. Daugherty [*sic*], who was the officer in command of the regular forces, Col. Conger being a detective, but in command, I understand, of the expedition. These are the facts of the case; those in regard to the burning of the barn were learned of my sons, who were present. The subject of the murder of the President having been talked of at church the day before Booth came to my house, I condemned it publicly in unmeasured terms.

"Richard H. Garrett." [28]

"Washington, April 2, 1872."

CHAPTER XX

With the death of Booth and the capture of Herold, nearly all the parties who were suspected of being identified with the Conspiracy were safely housed in prisons or on board gunboats. John H. Surratt, however, was still at large, and it was now beginning to look as if he would escape in safety and thus defeat justice.

I have already informed my readers that my first act after taking my last breakfast at my boardinghouse on the morning after the assassination was to proceed to city police headquarters on Tenth Street with Mr. J. T. Holohan. When we arrived there, we for the first time met Major A. C. Richards, the superintendent of the city police, and also again the detective officers who had been at the house of Mrs. Surratt within a few hours after the commission of the murder. After some consultation with the chief and his men, it was decided that we should first go to the Government stables on Nineteenth Street, procure horses, and start in pursuit of Booth and his confederates.

On the way to the stables, it was necessary for us to pass the office of the Commissary General of Prisoners, the bureau in which I was employed. The clerks of the office were all out in front of the building. Among them was my friend Captain [D. H. L.] Gleason. As I approached him, I saw that he was very angry. He wanted to know who those men were with me. I told him that they were detectives, and that we had started out in pursuit of the alleged assassins. He then gave me to understand that he recollected the various conversations I had had with him on several occasions, and in which I had communicated to him my suspicions that everything at the Surratt house was not as it should be. I answered that he need have no fears but that I would assist the Government to the full extent of my ability. This pacified him, and I bade him good-day.

At the stables it was our good fortune to meet Fletcher, who had hired the horse to Herold from Naylor's stables on the afternoon of the 14th of April, and which was never returned. I asked him the name of the party who had procured the horse. He stated it as Herold, and said that he had pursued him as far as the Navy Yard Bridge, but was prevented by the guard from going any farther.

I knew where Herold's family resided in the Navy Yard, and I suggested to the officers that we should go there at once. This was agreed to, but we first returned to Mrs. Surratt's house to see if we could procure a photograph of John H. Surratt. This was done and the desired picture was obtained from his mother with but little persuasion. All this time I had not·the slightest suspicion of Mrs. Surratt's complicity in this terrible affair, nor did I believe that her son, after what I had read in the papers, was the man who had attempted Mr. Seward's life. Hence I felt that it would be a proper and honorable thing to secure Surratt's photograph, give it to the authorities, and in this way it would appear at once if he was really the person who had assaulted the Secretary. I did not believe that he was, and as a friendly act it would tend to establish his innocence.

When we entered the home of Mrs. Herold, we found that good lady greatly disturbed and in tears. There was a kind-hearted man sitting near her who was endeavoring to console her, and who did everything he could to assuage her grief. Upon questioning her, it was learned that her son had not been at home since the evening of the preceding day. This looked very suspicious, and confirmed our impressions that we were on the track of one of the guilty parties at least.

Mr. McDevitt asked permission of Mrs. Herold to examine her photograph album. This was very kindly granted by the grief-stricken mother. I pointed out a good picture of the young man, and at the request of the leader of our party, Mr. McDevitt, she gave it to him.

Officer McDevitt immediately turned over the photographs of Surratt and Herold to the Government authorities, and in twenty-four hours many copies of the likenesses of these two men were struck off and distributed over the country.

With the conclusion of these two episodes, we next determined to make a dash across Anacostia Bridge, and go down the Bryantown road towards Surrattsville. We scoured that section of the country all day, but secured no results of any moment. For some reason, McDevitt turned away from Surrattsville, and went in another direction. We returned to the city about eight o'clock in the evening. That night I slept on the floor of the police station with nothing but a knapsack for my pillow.

The following Sabbath morning, I attended early mass at St. Patrick's Church with Mr. McDevitt.

Later in the day our party went to Baltimore. We had received some clue relative to Atzerodt. We called at the office of Provost Marshal General [James L.] McPhail, but outside of some meager information gained from him, our visit to the Monumental City did not amount to much. We then returned to Washington, and it was now concluded that on the following Monday morning, April 17, we would start for Canada in quest of young Surratt, and accordingly we procured from the War Department the requisite papers:

Headquarters Department of Washington,
Washington, D.C., April 16, 1865.

Special Orders No. 68—Extract.

Special Officers James A. McDevitt, George Holohan [1] and Louis J. Wiechmann are hereby ordered to New York on important government business and after executing their private orders to return to this city and report at these headquarters. The Quartermaster's Department will furnish the necessary transportation.

By command of Major General Augur.

T. Ingraham, Colonel and Provost Marshal
General, Defenses North of the Potomac.

Official,
G. B. Russel,
Captain and Asst. Prov. Mar. Gen'l.
Defenses North of the Potomac.

I was convinced that I was doing the right thing in going to Canada in pursuit of Surratt. I went with the kindest intentions in my heart towards him. I began to realize that his mother and himself were in the greatest possible danger, and I felt that he owed it to her and to his own good name that he should return to the United States, surrender himself to the authorities, and clear himself of all connection with this great crime. He had not been at his home, so far as I knew, since the 3rd day of April, the day I saw him for the last time prior to his own trial in 1867, and I reasoned that if he were in Canada at the time of the murder, he probably knew nothing of it. Of course, when making these conclusions I had no suspicion or information whatever that he had been identified, as he himself has subsequently confessed, with the alleged plot to capture Mr. Lincoln. I only know that so far as my visit to Montreal at this time was concerned I went thither with the best motives, which, I believed, if realized would inure to Surratt's benefit, but the subsequent developments in relation to the Conspiracy, both as to the abduction and assassination plots, show how little I understood the real facts of the case.

How can I ever forget that trip to Canada! Black everywhere. The railway coaches were all heavily draped in morning. Along the lines of travel where a house could be seen, there hung some sable emblem as a mute witness of the great and universal grief under which the land rested.

The great cities of Baltimore, Philadelphia, New York, Albany, and Troy, through which we passed, were one mass of swaying crepe. The heart of the nation was almost ready to burst in its mighty agony; yet, amidst all this woe, strange as it may now appear, there were people who actually rejoiced in the assassination, and were glad that Abraham Lincoln was no more. What a reflection on our poor human nature! Happily that day is forever gone, and many of the unfortunate beings who gave vent to such feelings have lived to repent in sorrow all such sentiments, inhuman as they were. Time sweeps on, and as year after year passes by, the name and fame of Abraham Lincoln grows brighter, so that he now stands as one of the greatest benefactors who ever lived to bless the human race.

Our party arrived at Montreal on the 20th day of April 1865. We made our headquarters at the St. James Hotel, the most noted French hotel of the city. Then we began to lay our plans; the first place visited was St. Lawrence Hall. Here I made a careful examination of the hotel register, and ascertained that John H. Surratt had arrived there on the 6th day of April, and had left on the 12th of the same month for the United States; that he subsequently returned on the 18th, and left immediately on the same evening without stating where he was going. He had registered under the name of John Harrison. Thus we were informed from the very beginning of our visit that he was then in Canada, and it was our purpose now to definitely locate his whereabouts, and, if successful, report our discovery to the United States consul general at Montreal, and have a demand promptly made for his extradition to his native land. Through some source which I cannot now recall, we learned that he had been concealed at the house of a Mr. [John] Porterfield, and had escaped to parts unknown to us. Here our pursuit ended, although we made the most thorough search possible, and ran down every clue that was brought to us. We even went as far as Quebec in the accomplishment of our object, but all to no purpose. We were baffled at every point, and were compelled to return to Washington without our man.

That Surratt was in Montreal during our stay there, and that he knew of our movements, does not admit of any controversy, and perhaps the best thing to be done right here is to place him once more on the witness stand and let him speak for himself. I again quote from his lecture. After stating that he had returned to Montreal at two o'clock on the afternoon of the 18th of April, and had gone to St. Lawrence Hall, he goes on to say:

Soon after I called on a friend, to whom I explained my former connection with Booth, and told him that I was afraid the United States government would suspect me of complicity in the plot of assassination. He advised me to make myself scarce. I immediately went to the hotel, got my things, and repaired to the room of a friend. When my friend's tea-time came I would not go to the table with him, but remained in the room. The ladies wanted to know why he didn't bring his friend to tea with him. He replied that I didn't want any. One of the ladies remarked, "I expect you have got Booth in there." (Laughter.) "Perhaps so," he answered laughingly. That was rather close guessing. (Laughter.) At nightfall I went to the house of one who afterwards proved to be a most devoted friend. There I remained until the evening of the next day [April 19], when I was driven out in a carriage with two gentlemen, strangers to me. One day I walked out and I saw Weichmann on the lookout for me. He had little idea I was so near. One night about 11 o'clock, my friend, in whose house I was, came to me and said, in a smiling way: "The detectives have offered me $20,000 if I will tell them where you are." "Very well," said I, "give me one half and let them know." They suspected this gentleman of protecting me, and they had really made him the offer. One day about 12 o'clock, I was told that they were going to search the house, and that I must leave immediately, which I did. They searched it before morning. This gentleman was a poor man, with a large family, and yet money could not buy him. (Applause.) I remained with this gentleman until I left Montreal, within a week or two afterwards. The detectives were now hunting me very closely, and would doubtless have succeeded in capturing me, had it not been for a blunder on the part of my friend Weichman. He had, it appears, started the detectives on the wrong track, by telling them I had left the house of Mr. Porterfield in company with some others, and was going north of Montreal. Soon that section was swarming with detectives. I was not with that party, but about the same time, I too left Montreal in a hack, going about 8 or 9 miles down the St. Lawrence river, crossing that stream in a small canoe. I was attired as a huntsman. At 3 o'clock Wednesday morning, we arrived at our destination, a small town lying south of Montreal. We entered the village very quietly, hoping no one would see us.[2]

Surratt's remarks in reference to myself in this quotation are entirely gratuitous. His story that I threw the detectives off the track by a blunder is something coined in his own brain, and which has no existence elsewhere. Instead of being in Montreal two weeks after he had left St. Lawrence Hall on the 18th of April, he was there, according to the sworn evidence of Joseph Du Tilly, only until the 22nd day of April, eight days after the murder, when Mr. Du Tilly took him to the home of Father Charles Boucher at St. Liboire.[3] During my own sojourn in Montreal at this time I did not at any time see him, nor did I know where he was secreted; but he, as he says, saw me when he was out walking one day, and that I had but little idea that he was so near. Why then did he not come to me? Why did he not seek to learn something of that home which he had deserted, and which he would never know again? Why, if he was the innocent man that he has declared himself to be, did he not voluntarily return to the United States, and free himself of all suspicion of the crime with which his name was now associated? His mother, his sister, Miss Jenkins—his cousin—and Miss Fitzpatrick had been arrested on the night of the 17th of April, and were now confined in prison, a fact known to the whole world, yet here he was running away as fast as he could and hiding himself. Certainly, during that eventful week when he was in Montreal, and when he alleges he saw me, he must have known all these facts, but he made no move to return, and was only anxious to get away from Washington as far as possible. While in Montreal, I visited a Catholic clergyman, one Father Cleary. I stated to him who I was, and also mentioned the fact that I was in possession of important evidence which the Government at Washington would probably utilize, and asked him what my duty was as a Catholic under the circumstances. He promptly replied to speak the truth in answer to all questions asked me. When in Quebec, I put the same question to the archbishop at that place, and his reply was identical with that of the clergyman in Montreal. Had I felt disposed to remain in Canada, I could have done so very readily, but no such thought ever entered my mind. I was not made of that kind of material. Montreal was then filled with blockade runners, spies, St. Albans raiders,[4] and dangerous characters of every description, and I am now satisfied in the light of all that has happened that could my evidence of a few weeks later have been anticipated, I would not have been permitted to leave Canada alive. Of this I am as firmly convinced as that I am writing these pages. French Canadians, too, in those days had very little use for a Union man, and Surratt received from them as much sympathy in his efforts to escape as did Booth and Herold in making their way through Lower Maryland and Virginia.

Nothing of any moment bearing on the assassination occurred during our return, and we reached Washington on Saturday, April 29, 1865. Our first act was to report to the War Department, and there we gave such information in relation to the trip to Canada as we had obtained. We were then discharged by General [Henry L.] Burnett under orders from the Secretary until further called for. When General Burnett returned to the War Department that night, one of the first officers he happened to meet was Colonel [H. S.] Olcott.

"Burnett," exclaimed Olcott, "Stanton is in a rage over your actions in discharging Weichmann and Holohan. He is furious, and won't accept any excuses."

Burnett at once went to the Secretary's room, but Stanton would listen to no explanations whatever, although Burnett tried his best to say that we had been discharged by the orders of the Secretary himself. The Secretary told the General that if we were not at hand by morning, he might consider himself out of the service.

There was now nothing left for Burnett to do but to go back to his own room. Here, after much and serious reflection, he issued orders to the camps and military stations surrounding Washington that they should take the utmost precautions and see that no two men answering the description of Weichmann and Holohan should be permitted to pass the lines. Mr. Holohan was found with his family and was at once taken into custody and held to await further inquiry.

That night I slept at a private boardinghouse about one half square distant from the War Office, and at breakfast the next morning I had as my right-hand companion at the table young Ulysses Grant, a son of General Grant. When the morning meal was finished, at about nine o'clock, I was taking a walk along Pennsylvania Avenue with a friend named Gilbert Raynor, and when near the War Department, we saw General Henry L. Burnett, who was just crossing the street. He greeted me very pleasantly and shook me by the hand. I then presented my friend to him. The introduction was kindly acknowledged, but the General begged my friend to excuse me, and at the same time, tapping me on the shoulder, said the Secretary of War wanted to see me. We entered the War Department building together, and General Burnett at once reported to the Secretary, informing him of the meeting on Pennsylvania Avenue, and stating that I was now in the building, and was awaiting the further commands of the Secretary.

There was, however, another action which General Burnett performed right there, and that was to tender his resignation as Judge Advocate to Mr. Stanton, reverting to the unkindness the Secretary had visited upon him during the previous evening wrongfully and without cause.

Then Stanton turned to Burnett with tears in his eyes and begged him to desist from any such action, saying that he (Burnett) knew what a great burden rested on his shoulders and how the people of the country were looking to him for sturdy action and justice in this case.

Under such circumstances and with such an appeal coming from the great Edwin M. Stanton, the resignation was at once withdrawn.*

It was immediately after this crisis that I was ushered into the presence of the great War Secretary, the man of iron and blood. I found him to be a sturdy, heavy-set man, about five feet ten inches in height, with iron-gray whiskers. He wore gold-rimmed spectacles. A glance revealed to me at once the man I had to deal with. Bidding me "Good morning," he at once began questioning me. He desired to know all about my antecedents; who my parents were and where they lived; in fact, all possible information I could give in relation to them and myself.

"Mr. Weichmann," now said Mr. Stanton, "I believe you are a clerk in my department; for a year and a half you have had your support and clothing from the Government." I admitted that this was all so, and that I was glad of the opportunity. "That being so," resumed the Secretary, "how in the name of common sense did you come to make your home with that disloyal Surratt family?"

"To that there is but one answer, Mr. Stanton," replied I. "For three years this boy, John H. Surratt, was a college mate of mine, and it was under his influence that I went to board at his mother's house." I further stated to him that when I went there I knew they were Southern people in their feelings, but had no evidence of any disloyal act on their part.

* These facts were first communicated to me by General Burnett in New York City, May 1901.[5]

Then I was asked if I knew John Wilkes Booth; if so, when and where did I first meet him? I informed the Secretary that it was during the winter of 1865, sometime near the 15th of January. He wanted to know how I remembered the date. I stated that I recollected it in connection with an important letter received about that time from the bishop of Richmond, Virginia, in which he authorized me to begin my theological studies at St. Mary's Seminary in Baltimore. He asked me for the letter, and I gave it to him, and then after reading it, he returned it to me. He now requested me to state who had introduced me to John Wilkes Booth. "Dr. Samuel A. Mudd," answered I. "Did you say Dr. Mudd?" queried Mr. Stanton. "Yes, sir." And then I related the story of the meeting of Booth, Mudd, Surratt, and myself as detailed in Chapter IV of this book.

Then Stanton, half rising from his desk, and bringing down his clenched hand on the table with much force, exclaimed with great earnestness to General Burnett, "By God, put that down, Burnett; it is damned important."

I did not understand its importance but soon learned that Booth and Herold's second stopping place on the night of the murder was Dr. Mudd's house; that the doctor had received and harbored them for a whole day and then denied all knowledge of them.

"Have you any weapons on you?" was the next question. "No, sir," was my answer. I could have laughed had it not been for the seriousness of the occasion; I had never carried a revolver in all my life and did not know how to shoot one. That was a part of my education which my father had carefully neglected.

Mr. Stanton now gave me to understand that he would be compelled to put me under lock and key, and hold me until such a time as the Conspiracy should be thoroughly investigated. "All right, Mr. Stanton," was my reply, "but, sir, by the time the trial is over, you will be the first one to recognize the fact that I shall have done my whole duty to the Government." "I hope so," said Mr. Stanton.

Before leaving his presence I made a plea in behalf of Mrs. Surratt, and begged him to be lenient and gentle with her. To this, as I recollect, he answered that he was sorry that she was in such a plight, but that the law must take its course, and that justice must be done. This is substantially my interview with him, as I recollect it.

I was now placed in the custody of General Lafayette C. Baker, chief of the secret service, with whom I went in a streetcar to the Carroll Prison, which was situated in the rear of the Capitol. I was assigned to a room on the third floor of the building, and facing the front street. There were some twenty or thirty other persons in the same room, some of whom I afterwards ascertained were detectives purposely placed there to watch and report what was said and done.

The time of my arrival in this place was about eleven o'clock in the morning. At noon, a bell was rung, and then all the persons who were in the different rooms of the building descended to the prison yard, and I went along with the crowd. The very first man I saw whom I knew was Dr. Samuel A. Mudd. Never did a man's face change its color more quickly than his. It became almost deathlike in its expression, and of a frightful pallor. No attempt at recognition was made, but he gave me a quick, sharp glance which satisfied me that he knew me. This was our second meeting in life. Had he recognized me or spoken to me at that time, he would have given away his whole case, for the place was full of keen officers who were noting the actions and expression of every one in the yard.

Among others whom I saw here were John T. Ford and his two sons [brothers]. Mr. Ford was the proprietor of Ford's Theater. Junius Brutus Booth, a brother of John Wilkes, and John S. Clarke, the distinguished comedian of that name, Booth's brother-in-law, who had married Asia Booth, were also there. So was Zadoc Jenkins, the brother of Mrs. Surratt.

I took a stroll around the prison yard, and then as I came back, on looking up, beheld Mrs. Surratt, her daughter, and Miss Fitzpatrick seated at one of the windows of the adjoining prison, the Old Capitol. They saw me and from their actions it was evident that they recognized me.

That same afternoon, if I remember rightly, about two o'clock, General Baker came to the front of the prison, alone in a two-seated buggy. I could see him from the window where I was. He entered the prison, and in a short time returned accompanied by Dr. Mudd, who now took a seat in the buggy alongside the great detective. Baker was one of the most impassable and imperturbable men I ever saw, and as cool as an iceberg. And it was now evident to all who witnessed this affair that the Government had concluded to hold Dr. Mudd as one of the guilty parties.

On the day following Mudd's removal, General Baker returned to the Carroll Prison [6] in the same conveyance, and took Mrs. Surratt away. This scene was also a silent announcement that the Government had finally resolved to place her on trial, and to hold her responsible for the blood of Abraham Lincoln.

Every witness possessing any important evidence for the Government was locked up, and justly so. At this length of time, these stern measures and precautions may seem to have been harsh, but when it is remembered that the assassin's deadly clutch was at the throat of the Government, that its very existence was imperiled by the deeds of Booth, Payne, Atzerodt, and the others, no action that the War Department took could in my judgment have been too severe.

As to myself, I justify Mr. Stanton's actions. He found me boarding in the Surratt house, and knowing that I was an employee in his department, had the right to demand of me a full account of my stewardship. It was his duty to investigate my life and actions, and see if I was the honest man I claimed to be. As for myself, I never possessed the slightest fear in this matter, for I saw but one line before me—the straight line of truth and honor, and to that I adhered. Moreover, as a protection to the witnesses for the Government, it was better and safer that they should be locked up. The city of Washington was thronged with correspondents from every prominent newspaper in the country, whose quick pencils and sharp ears were ready to gather all the news they could. By Mr. Stanton's course, many a witness was spared from being interviewed and subsequently contradicted from the witness stand as to what he might or might not have said. Then again everybody's blood was at fever heat; there were thousands of returning Confederates on the streets and I really believe that my own life, and that of others who were ready to stand up for the Government, were saved by the wise though stern measures of the War Secretary.

Mr. Stanton was the master genius who conducted and controlled the preliminary investigation to discover the culprits. His great legal mind sifted everything; he arranged, planned, and entered into the minutest details, and left no clue that he did not follow to its legitimate conclusion. His immense experience as one of the foremost lawyers of the country long before he entered Buchanan's Cabinet stood him in good turn, and he went about his business with the twofold purpose of protecting the innocent and punishing the guilty.

The Government now lost no time in preparing for the trial of the conspirators and it was set for the 7th day of May 1865. During the period which intervened between the 30th of April and the time for the commencement of the trial, painful as it is for me to write it, my own life and conduct were under investigation. Because I had loved John H. Surratt, my friend, my schoolmate, with whom I had for three years eaten at the same table, knelt around the same altar, partaken of the same Holy Communion, and prayed to the same God, in whose family I hoped to find what I believed would be a pleasant home, and which was, indeed, such a home until the murderous conspirators entered its doors—I found myself subjected to the gravest suspicion.

Every letter that I had received for seven years I had kept. The box containing them was seized by the War Department officials, and the letters were read. Captain Gleason now came to the front and told all about my conversations with him at different times. The men with whom I had walked and mingled in daily life were interrogated to see if I had let fall some expression in an unguarded moment which could be twisted into a knowledge, on my part, of this great and awful crime. My father's home in Philadelphia was visited and searched, so also was the table at which he worked in the United States Arsenal, but nothing was found to cast the slightest stain on my character.

One day while in prison, I was called downstairs by the superintendent, and was ushered into a room where there were three or four army officers. With them was a heavy-set man (who I subsequently ascertained was Sergeant Joseph Dye). As soon as I entered the room one of the officers said to this man, "Is this the person who called the time in front of the theater on the night of the assassination?" "No, sir," said Mr. Dye, "that is not the man who called the time."

During my trip to Canada in search of Surratt, my father, who was ignorant of my whereabouts, left his home in Philadelphia for Washington, and in this way endeavored to secure some information in relation to me. When he arrived in the capital city, his first act was to go directly to the Surratt house. He rang the door bell, and the officers of the War Department who were in charge answered the call. My father stated who he was and what he wanted. He was at once taken in charge by the military, who had been ordered to arrest everyone approaching the house, and taken to the War Department. He was led to one of the offices, I think that of General Augur. As soon as he entered the room he was ordered to stand erect, and then, quick as a flash, a camera was opened upon him, and his features were photographed.

He was now permitted to seat himself at one of the tables, and was subjected to a rigid questioning. His replies were given forcibly and without equivocation. One of the officers during this colloquy happened to make a remark very derogatory to myself. Then Father, seeing at a short distance from himself a penholder, nervously reached for it, at the same time excitedly exclaiming, "Gentlemen, give me that pen, and if you can prove that my boy has had anything to do with this awful crime, I will be the first to sign his death warrant."

The feelings of the officers were much moved, and some of them gave way to tears. It is needless to add that Father was instantly released and allowed to return to his home.

Mr. Benn Pitman, chief official stenographer of the trial of the conspirators, in a contribution to the *Phonographic Magazine* of Cincinnati, Ohio, under date of August 15, 1893, relates the following story in relation to myself at this time:

A dramatic incident connected with this memorable trial in which phonography figured as a prime element, has never yet been told. Among the seizures of property that had been made at the house of Mrs. Surratt was a carpet sack belonging to one of her boarders, who was a friend and had been a fellow student of John H. Surratt. The conduct and character of the young gentleman who owned the sack were subjected to a most careful investigation, as were all those who resided in the house. With other like matters the carpet sack came to me for safekeeping, examination and report. In this sack to my surprise, I found copies of my manual and *Reporter's Companion*, together with a quantity of phonographic exercises. I particularly noticed that the exercises were carefully written and were dated continuously up to the time of the great tragedy. These were significant facts in favor of the young man. I could not believe that a student who had recently left college and who was pursuing a study like phonography, could in any way be cognizant of a conspiracy so dangerous.

I soon had an opportunity of making the acquaintance of the gentleman and found him to be a young man of prepossessing appearance, with clear and placid eye, and a countenance indicative of intelligence, modesty and conscientiousness. I communicated the fact to the judge-advocates and laid stress upon the fact that the study of phonography without a teacher, save the books, required considerable application and necessarily demanded the time, interest and energy of the student, and that such a one would be a very unlikely person to have anything to do with such a conspiracy. My suggestions received a most careful consideration. The gentleman appeared as a witness in the case, was on the stand three days and passed through a most trying ordeal unscathed.[7]

Such was the penalty I was compelled to pay because of my friendship for John H. Surratt and his mother; such the ordeal through which I had to pass because I lived in their home, and gave them of my earnings to help them in their worldly struggle. In those trying hours, however, the blameless life which I had always led, coupled with the facts that weeks before the assassination I had communicated my suspicions to Captain Gleason that something was wrong, and that when I was informed by officers Clarvoe and McDevitt of the murder, I voluntarily sprang to their help, went with them to Canada in search of Surratt, then returned to the United States, and of my own free will placed myself in the custody of the Government to do with me what was just and right, were proofs as strong as Holy Writ of my absolute innocence of any wrongdoing.

When the ordeal was over, Edwin M. Stanton, who had sternly called me to account, became my friend and protector, and was only too glad to accord me the justice which I had won by my conduct, and which was my due.

Time and again in the years that are passed have my actions during this eventful period been called into question and misrepresented, but no honest-minded man who reads the subjoined letters which close this chapter will for a moment question my courage and my loyalty to duty and my country at that time.

Eustis, Florida, Dec. 26, 1898.

L. J. Weichmann,
Anderson, Ind.

Dear Sir:

I have your letter of the 16th of December, 1898, and in reply, I take much pleasure in giving you the information you desire.

You did report to me about eight o'clock on the morning of April

15th, 1865, and you communicated to me such facts as had come to your knowledge at that time. You acted as a special officer with my men, going with them to lower Maryland, Baltimore, and finally to Canada in pursuit of some of the alleged guilty parties.

In no instance, was any statement made by you in relation to the conspiracy found to be false or incorrect, and very many of your assertions were subsequently corroborated by undoubted testimony of which you did not know the existence. No threats or undue influences of any kind were resorted to by any of us to control your actions.

You performed a manly part all the way through, and did your duty in such a manner as to challenge the admiration of all lovers of the truth.

Let me add that the fact that you were a boarder at Mrs. Surratt's house may have been to you the cause of much personal sacrifice in your worldly prospects, and of much suffering; but for the sake of justice and in behalf of the murdered Lincoln, I deem it a most fortunate event that you were there.

Trusting that this will be sufficient for your purposes, I am,

Respectfully yours,

A. C. Richards.

(Superintendent of Police, Washington, 1865.) [8]

New York, April 13, 1898.

L. J. Weichmann, Esq.
Anderson, Ind.

Dear Sir:

I am in receipt of your favor of the 8th inst. in which you say "You were the Judge-Advocate on the part of the Government in the collation of the testimony and examination of witnesses prior to the great conspiracy trial of 1865. You have no doubt seen the recent story of John H. Surratt, as published in the newspapers, and I will now ask you to state as a matter of justice to me and to my honored name, if the charges of unkind and inhuman treatment and threats, as alleged upon the part of the War Department or any of its officers are true."

In response I beg to say that by order of the Secretary of War early in April, 1865, I was assigned to the duty of investigating the facts as to the assassination of President Lincoln, and the attempted assassination of Secretary Seward and others, and arranging the order of the testimony for the trial of the conspirators. For that duty I was assigned an office in the War Department. There was taken in my presence and under my supervision by my stenographer, Mr. Benn Pitman, when you returned from Canada, on April 29, 1865, the first statement made by you, I believe, of the facts within your knowledge; and I have to say that no threat or inducement of any kind was made to you on my part, or on the part of any official of the Government so far as I have ever had hint or information, to make such a statement. You were simply appealed to to state the facts within your knowledge bearing upon the assassination of the President, and throughout the trial you conducted yourself and made your statements and gave your testimony in a manner that commended you to me as a truthful and upright man.

Very respectfully yours,

Henry L. Burnett.

CHAPTER XXI

Trial of the conspirators · Charge and specification against them · Opinion of the Attorney General · Triable by Military Commission · Composition of the court · The prisoners select their counsel · Plead Not Guilty to the charges against them

Within three weeks after the death of Mr. Lincoln, the Government authorities were prepared to proceed with the trial of the conspirators, and the Arsenal building, situated at the foot of Four-and-a-half Street on the banks of the Potomac River, was selected as the place for holding it. As a result of the preliminary investigation by the War Department, the following persons were held as principals and accessories for the murder of the President and the attempted assassination of the Honorable William H. Seward and others: David E. Herold, George A. Atzerodt, Lewis Payne, Michael O'Laughlin, Edward Spangler, Samuel Arnold, Mary E. Surratt, and Samuel A. Mudd.

It was a matter of much discussion and speculation as to how the accused parties should be tried, whether by Military Commission or by civil court. The subject was referred by President Johnson to the Attorney General of the United States, the Honorable James Speed, for decision, and that high official, after due consideration of the question, gave it as his opinion that the conspirators were subject to the jurisdiction of and lawfully triable by a Military Commission.

Thereupon the President issued the following proclamation:

Executive Chamber,
Washington City, May 1, 1865.

Whereas, the Attorney General of the United States hath given his opinion:

That the persons implicated in the murder of the late President, Abraham Lincoln, and the attempted assassination of the Honorable William H. Seward, Secretary of State, and in an alleged conspiracy to assassinate other officers of the Federal Government at Washington City, and their aiders and abettors, are subject to the jurisdiction of and lawfully triable before a Military Commission:

It is ordered: 1st. That the Assistant Adjutant-General detail nine competent military officers to serve as a commission for the trial of said parties, and that the Judge Advocate General proceed to prefer charges against said parties for their alleged offences, and bring them to trial before said Military Commission; that the said trial or trials be conducted by the said Judge Advocate General, and as recorder thereof, in person, aided by such Assistant and Special Judge Advocates as he may designate; and that said trials be conducted with all diligence consistent with the ends of justice: the said Commission to sit without regard to hours.

2nd. That Brevet Major-General Hartranft be assigned to duty as Special Provost Marshal General, for the purpose of said trial, and attendance upon said Commission, and the execution of its mandates.

3rd. That the said Commission establish such order and rules of proceeding as may avoid unnecessary delay, and conduce to the ends of public justice.

(Signed.) Andrew Johnson.[1]

The Commission so appointed under orders of the President of the United States was composed of the following officers: Major General David Hunter, U. S. Volunteers; Major General Lewis Wallace, U. S. Volunteers; Brevet Major General August V. Kautz, U. S. Volunteers; Brigadier General Albion P. Howe, U. S. Volunteers; Brigadier General Robert S. Foster, U. S. Volunteers; Brevet Brigadier General James A. Ekin, U. S. Volunteers; Brigadier General T. M. Harris, U. S. Volunteers; Brevet Colonel C. H. Tompkins, U. S. Army; Lieutenant Colonel David R. Clendenin, Eighth Illinois Cavalry; Brigadier General Joseph Holt, Judge Advocate and Recorder.[2]

The Judge Advocate General introduced as his assistants—Special Judge Advocates—the Honorable John A. Bingham and General Henry L. Burnett.

The officers of the Commission were men who had rendered eminent service to the country during the war of the rebellion; some of them were excellent lawyers, and all in their personal characters were above reproach. They were an exceedingly fine-looking body of men, and made a good impression on all who visited the court during the hot and exciting days of the trial.

General John F. Hartranft, the marshal of the court, had achieved great fame for himself in the closing days of the rebellion as the "hero of Fort Stedman." He was tall, erect, and handsome, but these fine qualities were transcended by his kindness of heart, and by his gentle dealings with the unfortunate prisoners placed in his charge.

Joseph Holt, the Judge Advocate General of the United States Army and Recorder of the court, was a Kentuckian by birth, and was then about fifty-eight years of age. He was one of those brave sons of the South who had remained true to his country when millions faltered. Not only was he a man of great legal attainments, of fine culture, of splendid appearance, but also of consummate judgment. During Buchanan's administration he had been Postmaster General, and in its closing days when treason raised its slimy head, and disloyal men were trying to destroy the Government, he and Stanton by their steadfast devotion to the Union rendered a service to the country so conspicuous and exalted that it will never be forgotten by the people as long as the Republic stands.

Abraham Lincoln had appointed him to be the Judge Advocate General of the United States Army, a position which he filled with credit to himself, and glory to the nation. In his own person, he brought a dignity and lustre to that office until then unknown. No finer tribute was ever paid to anyone than that which James G. Blaine gave to him in his funeral oration over Garfield when speaking of the approval which Garfield had won (by his service on courts-martial) from the Judge Advocate of the Army. Said Mr. Blaine:

"This of itself was warrant to honorable fame, for among those great men who in those trying days gave themselves, with entire devotion, to the service of their country, one who brought to that service the ripest learning, the most fervid eloquence, the most varied attainments, who labored with modesty and shunned applause, who in the day of triumph sat reserved and silent and grateful—as Francis Deak in the hour of Hungary's deliverance—was Joseph Holt, of Kentucky, who in his honorable retirement enjoys the respect and veneration of all who love the Union of the States."

The Honorable John A. Bingham, one of the Special Judge Advocates, was from the state of Ohio. In selecting him as Special Judge Advocate, Judge Holt chose the right man. No better lawyer could have been selected, and in the two months of fierce legal battle which awaited him, he was equal to every emergency, physical or mental, which presented itself.

General Henry L. Burnett, also Special Judge Advocate, and like his legal brother, Bingham, a native of Ohio, was equally well equipped for the fray. During the war he had rendered great service to the Government as Judge Advocate in connection with several of the treason trials of the West, notably in the Bowles and Milligan case, and for that reason had arrested the attention of the Secretary of War and the Judge Advocate General. When the President was struck down, he was one of the first men summoned to Washington to serve the Government in its dire extremity. Upon him principally devolved the detail work, the preparation, collecting, and sifting of the great mass of evidence the Government would use, and nobly and loyally did he perform his part of the work.

The room in which the prisoners were tried was about twenty-five feet wide and thirty long, the entrance to which was from the end opposite the penitentiary. Lengthwise it was divided into two sections, that on the right being taken by the court, who sat around a long green-covered table, while Judge Advocate General Holt with his assistants

236

was at the left end. A portion of the room was set aside for the use of spectators, all of whom had to be admitted on a pass countersigned by General Hunter, the president of the court. The official reporters had a space to themselves near the witness box in the center of the room.

At the farther end of the apartment behind a wooden railing on an elevated platform, the accused were seated, all in a row. First at the left came Mrs. Surratt, then Herold, Payne, Atzerodt, O'Laughlin, Spangler, Mudd, and Arnold. Next to Mrs. Surratt was a stout iron door which led into a corridor where the cells of the prisoners were. All of them with the exception of Mrs. Surratt were handcuffed, and to the left leg of each male prisoner was attached a thirty-two-pound ball and chain. When not in court, the prisoners wore padded caps so that they could not butt out their brains, as one of them had attempted to do.[3] An armed sentry sat between every two prisoners during the hearing of the court.

On the 9th day of May 1865, all the members were present, the Commission proceeded to the trial of the accused, who were brought into court, and were asked if they had any objection to any member of the Commission, to which all replied severally that they had none.

The members of the Commission were then duly sworn by the Judge Advocate General, in the presence of the accused.

The Judge Advocate General, and Assistant Judge Advocates, the Honorable John A. Bingham and Brevet Colonel H. L. Burnett were then also duly sworn by the President of the Commission, in the presence of the accused.

Benn Pitman, R. Sutton, D. F. Murphy, R. R. Hitt, J. J. Murphy, and Edward V. Murphy were duly sworn by the Judge Advocate General, in the presence of the accused, as reporters to the Commission.

The accused were then severally arraigned on the following Charge and Specification:

CHARGE.— For maliciously, unlawfully and traitorously, and in aid of the existing armed rebellion against the United States of America, on or before the 6th day of March A.D. 1865, combining, confederating, and conspiring together with one John H. Surratt, John Wilkes Booth, Jefferson Davis, George N. Sanders, Beverly Tucker, Jacob Thompson, [William C. Cleary,] Clement C. Clay, George Harper, George Young, and others unknown to kill and murder within the Military Department of Washington, and within the fortified and intrenched lines thereof, Abraham Lincoln, late, and at the time of said combining, confederating, and conspiring, President of the United States of America, and Commander-in-Chief of the Army and Navy thereof; Andrew Johnson, now Vice-President of the United States aforesaid; William H. Seward, Secretary of State of the United States aforesaid; and Ulysses S. Grant, Lieutenant-General of the Army of the United States, under the direction of the said Abraham Lincoln; and in the pursuance of and in prosecuting said malicious, unlawful, and traitorous conspiracy aforesaid, and in aid of said rebellion, afterward, to-wit, on the 14th day of April A.D. 1865, within the Military Department of Washington aforesaid, and within the fortified and intrenched lines of said Military Department together with said John Wilkes Booth and John H. Surratt, maliciously, unlawfully, and traitorously murdering the said Abraham Lincoln, then President of the United States and Commander-in-Chief of the Army and Navy of the United States as aforesaid; and maliciously, unlawfully, and traitorously assaulting with intent to kill and murder, the said William H. Seward, then Secretary of State of the United States as aforesaid; and lying in wait with intent maliciously, unlawfully, and traitorously to kill and murder the said Andrew Johnson, then being Vice-President of the United States; and the said Ulysses S. Grant, then being Lieutenant-General, and in command of the Armies of the United States, as aforesaid.[4]

SPECIFICATION.—In this: that they, the said David E. Herold, Edward Spangler, Lewis Payne, Michael O'Laughlin, Samuel Arnold, Mary E. Surratt, George A. Atzerodt, and Samuel A. Mudd, together with the said John H. Surratt and John Wilkes Booth, incited and encouraged thereunto by Jefferson Davis, George N. Sanders, Beverly Tucker, Jacob Thompson, William C. Cleary, Clement C. Clay, George Harper, George Young, and others unknown, citizens of the United States aforesaid, and who were then engaged in armed rebellion against the United States of America within the lines thereof, did in aid of said armed rebellion, on the 6th day of March 1865, and on divers other days and times between that day, and the 15th day of April A.D. 1865, combine, confederate, and conspire together at Washington City within the Military Department of Washington, and within the intrenched fortifications and military line of the United States, there being, unlawfully, maliciously, and traitorously to kill and murder Abraham Lincoln, then President of the

United States aforesaid, and Commander-in-Chief of the Army and Navy thereof; and unlawfully, maliciously, and traitorously to kill and murder Andrew Johnson, now [*sic*] Vice-President of the United States aforesaid, upon whom, on the death of said Abraham Lincoln, after the 4th day of March A.D. 1865, the office of President of the said United States, and Commander-in-Chief of the Army and Navy thereof would devolve; and to unlawfully, maliciously, and traitorously kill and murder Ulysses S. Grant, then Lieutenant-General, and, under the direction of the said Abraham Lincoln, in command of the Armies of the United States aforesaid; and unlawfully, maliciously, and traitorously to kill and murder William H. Seward, then Secretary of State of the United States aforesaid, whose duty it was, by law, upon the death of the President and Vice-President of the United States aforesaid, to cause an election to be held for electors of President of the United States; the conspirators aforesaid designing and intending, by the killing and murdering of the said Abraham Lincoln, Andrew Johnson, Ulysses S. Grant, and William H. Seward, as aforesaid, to deprive the Army and Navy of the said United States of a constitutional Commander-in-Chief; and to deprive the Armies of the United States of their lawful commander; and to prevent a lawful election of President and Vice-President of the United States aforesaid; and by the means aforesaid to aid and comfort the insurgents engaged in armed rebellion against the said United States, as aforesaid, and thereby to aid in the subversion and overthrow of the Constitution and laws of the said United States.

And being so combined, confederated, and conspiring together in the prosecution of said unlawful, malicious, and traitorous conspiracy, on the night of the 14th day of April A.D. 1865, at the hour of about ten o'clock and fifteen minutes P.M. at Ford's Theater, on Tenth Street, in the City of Washington, and within the Military Department and military lines aforesaid, John Wilkes Booth, one of the conspirators aforesaid, did, then and there, unlawfully, maliciously, and traitorously, and with intent to kill and murder the said Abraham Lincoln, discharge a pistol then held in the hands of him, the said Booth, the same being loaded with powder and a leaden ball, against and upon the left posterior side of the head of the said Abraham Lincoln; and did thereby, then and there, inflict upon him, the said Abraham Lincoln, then President of the said United States, and Commander-in-Chief of the Army and Navy thereof, a mortal wound, whereof, to-wit, on the 15th day of April A.D.

1865, at Washington City aforesaid, the said Abraham Lincoln died; and thereby, then and there, in pursuance of said conspiracy, the said defendants, and the said John Wilkes Booth and John H. Surratt, did unlawfully, maliciously, and traitorously, and with intent to aid the rebellion, as aforesaid, kill and murder the said Abraham Lincoln, President of the United States, as aforesaid.

And in further prosecution of the unlawful and traitorous conspiracy aforesaid, and of the murderous and traitorous intent of said conspiracy, the said Edward Spangler, on said 14th day of April A.D. 1865, at about the same hour of that day aforesaid, within said Military Department and military lines aforesaid, did aid and assist the said John Wilkes Booth to obtain entrance to the box in said theater, in which said Abraham Lincoln was sitting at the time he was assaulted and shot as aforesaid, by John Wilkes Booth; and also did, then and there, aid said Booth in barring and obstructing the door of the [box of] said theater, so as to hinder and prevent any assistance to or rescue of the said Abraham Lincoln against the murderous assault of the said John Wilkes Booth; and did aid and abet him in making his escape after the said Abraham Lincoln had been murdered in manner aforesaid.

And in further prosecution of said unlawful, murderous, and traitorous conspiracy, and in pursuance thereof, and with the intent thereof as aforesaid, the said David E. Herold did, on the night of the 14th of April A.D. 1865, within the Military Department and military lines aforesaid, aid, abet, and assist the said John Wilkes Booth in the killing and murder of the said Abraham Lincoln, and did, then and there, aid, abet, and assist him, the said John Wilkes Booth, in attempting to escape through the military lines aforesaid, and did accompany and assist the said John Wilkes Booth in attempting to conceal himself and escape from justice, after killing and murdering said Abraham Lincoln as aforesaid.

And in further prosecution of said unlawful and traitorous conspiracy, and of the intent thereof, as aforesaid, the said Lewis Payne did on the same night of the 14th of April A.D. 1865, about the same hour of ten o'clock and fifteen minutes P.M., at the City of Washington, and within the Military Department and the military lines aforesaid, unlawfully and maliciously make assault upon the said William H. Seward, Secretary of State, as aforesaid, in the dwelling house and bed chamber of him, the said William H. Seward, and the said Payne did, then and there, with a large knife held in his hand, unlawfully, traitorously and in pursuance of said conspiracy, strike, stab, cut, and attempt to kill and murder the said William H. Seward, and did thereby, then and there, and with the intent aforesaid, with said knife, inflict upon the face and throat of said William H. Seward divers grievous wounds. And the said Lewis Payne, in further prosecution of said conspiracy, at the same time and place last aforesaid, did attempt with the knife aforesaid, and a pistol held in his hand, to kill and murder Frederick W. Seward, Augustus H. Seward, Emrick W. Hansell, and George F. Robinson, who were then striving to protect and rescue the said William H. Seward from murder by the said Lewis Payne, and did, then and there, with said knife and pistol held in his hands, inflict upon the head of said Frederick W. Seward, and upon the persons of said Augustus H. Seward, Emrick W. Hansell, and George F. Robinson, divers grievous and dangerous wounds, with intent, then and there, to kill and murder the said Frederick W. Seward, Augustus H. Seward, Emrick W. Hansell, and George F. Robinson.

And in further prosecution of said conspiracy and its traitorous and murderous designs, the said George A. Atzerodt did, on the night of the 14th of April A.D. 1865, and about the same hour of the night aforesaid, lie in wait for Andrew Johnson, the Vice-President of the United States aforesaid, with the intent unlawfully and maliciously to kill and murder him the said Andrew Johnson.

And in further prosecution of the conspiracy aforesaid, and of its murderous and treasonable purposes aforesaid, on the night of the 13th and 14th of April A.D. 1865, at Washington City, and within the Military Department and the military lines aforesaid, the said Michael O'Laughlin did, then and there, lie in wait for Ulysses S. Grant, then Lieutenant-General and Commander of the Armies of the United States, as aforesaid, with intent, then and there, to kill and murder the said Ulysses S. Grant.

And in further prosecution of said conspiracy, the said Samuel Arnold did, within the Military Department and the military lines aforesaid, on or before the 6th day of March A.D. 1865, and on divers other days and times between that day and the 15th day of April A.D. 1865, combine, conspire with, and aid, counsel, abet, comfort, and support the said John Wilkes Booth, Lewis Payne, George A. Atzerodt, Michael O'Laughlin, and their confederates in said unlawful, murderous, and traitorous conspiracy, and in the execution thereof as aforesaid.

And in further prosecution of said conspiracy, Mary E. Surratt did at Washington City, and within the Military Department and military lines aforesaid, on or before the 6th day of March A.D. 1865, and on divers other days and times between that day and on the 20th day of April A.D. 1865, receive, entertain, harbor, and conceal, aid, and assist the said John Wilkes Booth, David E. Herold, Lewis Payne, John H. Surratt, Michael O'Laughlin, George A. Atzerodt, Samuel Arnold, and their confederates, with the knowledge of the murderous and traitorous conspiracy aforesaid, and with intent to aid, abet, and assist them in the execution thereof, and in escaping from justice after the murder of the said Abraham Lincoln as aforesaid.

And in further prosecution of said conspiracy, the said Samuel A. Mudd did, at Washington City, and within the Military Department and military lines aforesaid, on or before the 6th day of March A.D. 1865, advise, encourage, [receive,] entertain, harbor, and conceal, aid, and assist the said John Wilkes Booth, David E. Herold, Lewis Payne, John H. Surratt, Michael O'Laughlin, George A. Atzerodt, Mary E. Surratt, and Samuel Arnold, and their confederates, with the knowledge of the murderous and traitorous conspiracy aforesaid, and with the intent to aid, abet, and assist them in the execution thereof, and in escaping from justice after the murder of the said Abraham Lincoln, in pursuance of said conspiracy in manner aforesaid.

By order of the President of the United States.

J. Holt.

Judge Advocate General.[5]

Charge and Specification indorsed:

Copy of the within Charge and Specification delivered to David E. Herold, George A. Atzerodt, Lewis Payne, Michael O'Laughlin, Samuel Arnold, Mary E. Surratt, and Samuel A. Mudd, on the 8th day of May 1865.

(Signed.)

J. F. Hartranft.
Brev. Maj.-Gen. and Spec. Prov. Mar. Gen.

To the Specification, all the accused severally pleaded, Not Guilty

To the Charge ....Not Guilty [6]

The Commission then considered the rules and regulations to govern its proceedings, which being adopted, an adjournment was had until the following day.

On Thursday, May 11, the Commission met pursuant to adjournment. Samuel A. Mudd now applied for permission to introduce Frederick Stone, Esq., and Thomas Ewing, Esq., as his counsel.

Mary E. Surratt applied for permission to introduce Frederick Aiken, Esq., and John W. Clampitt, Esq., as her counsel, which applications were granted; and the aforesaid counsel, having first taken in open court the oath prescribed by act of Congress, approved July 2, 1862, accordingly appeared.

The accused George A. Atzerodt applied for permission to introduce William E. Doster and Walter S. Cox as his counsel which was granted.

Edward Spangler by permission introduced General Thomas Ewing as his counsel.

At the session of the 12th day of May, David E. Herold applied for permission to introduce Frederick Stone, Esq., as his counsel.

Samuel Arnold and Michael O'Laughlin applied for permission to introduce Thomas Ewing and Walter Cox as their counsel, which applications were granted.

Mary E. Surratt applied for permission to introduce the Honorable Reverdy Johnson as additional counsel for her, which application was also granted.

The accused now withdrew their pleas of Not Guilty heretofore filed and then they severally filed a plea to the Commission denying its jurisdiction to try their cases.

To this the Judge Advocate General filed a replication maintaining that the Commission had the jurisdiction to try and determine the matters in the Charge and Specification alleged and set forth against said defendants.

The court was then cleared for deliberation, and on being reopened, the Judge Advocate announced that the pleas of the accused had been overruled by the Commission.

Thereupon, each one of the accused made an application to be tried severally, which application was also denied.

The accused then severally pleaded:

To the Specification: "Not Guilty."

To the Charge: "Not Guilty."

The two attorneys, Aiken and Clampitt, who had been employed to defend Mrs. Surratt were from Washington, in which city they enjoyed a large and lucrative practice, and were good lawyers. Reverdy Johnson was at that time a senator from Maryland, and a man of distinguished national reputation. He was regarded as a great jurist, and had won renown in his profession. He did not worry himself much with the details of the case, the examining of the witnesses, but devoted himself chiefly to the denying of the jurisdiction of the Commission to try the accused. This he did in a lengthy argument which was replied to with much force by Judge Advocate Bingham.

General Thomas Ewing was one of the best advocates employed by the defense, and did harder and more effective work than any of them. He labored incessantly in behalf of his clients. He was a member of the famous Ewing family of Ohio, was a brother of Mrs. General Sherman, and a cousin of the Honorable James G. Blaine.

The other attorneys, Messrs. Stone, Cox, and Doster, were all able men and rendered their clients the best service of which they were capable. Stone was a Marylander, Cox a resident of Washington, and Doster a Pennsylvanian. He was an officer of the Army, and had won the title of colonel.

With the conclusion of the foregoing preliminaries, the trial was now fairly under way, and the taking of testimony began.

CHAPTER XXII

Interesting details of the great trial · Testimony against Herold, Payne, Atzerodt, Dr. Mudd, Arnold, O'Laughlin, and Spangler

The Military Commission that was convened for the trial of Mr. Lincoln's assassins in the city of Washington was one of the most extraordinary bodies that ever assembled in the history of this country, but it was justified fully by the circumstances in which the Government found itself and which called it into being. The war was not yet over, Johnston's army had not surrendered, and other bodies of troops were still fighting at different points in the South. Washington City was yet a fortified camp, and the headquarters for directing the operations of the Army and Navy of the United States. The Commander in Chief of all its forces had been slain in the very center of its military lines.

Under these circumstances it was justifiable that the Government should put forth its whole strength, and assert its right to try the alleged assassins by Military Commission. Had the assassination, however, occurred sixty days later than it did, every one of the parties implicated would have been tried in the civil courts.

The Honorable James Speed, Attorney General of the United States under Lincoln and Johnson, who had rendered the opinion that the assassins of Lincoln were triable by Military Commission, many years after the Conspiracy trial was over, wrote an able review of the case which was published in the *North American Review* for September 1888. In this article among other things he says:

Mr. Lincoln was assassinated April 14, 1865. A few days before this General Lee had surrendered the army of Northern Virginia. But the war was not over by any means at that time. For more than a month afterwards, armies of the Rebellion were still in the field, and for many months the angry billows of the war did not entirely subside. For four years the sulphuric atmosphere of actual war had hung over the country. At the national capital no other air was breathed. Four years of fierce, bloody conflict raging all around, within sight and hearing, and almost up to its very gates, had constituted Washington practically a military camp. The city was policed by soldiers. The public buildings were guarded by soldiers. The army was the protector as well as defender of the Capitol. This condition of affairs perfectly answered Lord Coke's definition of war:

"So when by invasion, insurrection, rebellion or the like, the peaceable course of justice is disturbed and stopped, so the courts of justice be as it were shut up, *et inter arma leges silent*, then it is said to be time of war."

It was in the midst of such a disturbed state of affairs that the assassination took place. The dreadful event, of course, intensified those conditions. The assassins were taken and held to answer for the awful crime. The question arose, should they be tried by civil or military courts? The victim was not an ordinary citizen. He was the Commander-in-Chief of the Armies of the Union, which at that time numbered more than a million men. The crime was most extraordinary. The times were equally so. Every substantial consideration of justice and fairness and common sense demanded that the military arm of the government should try the case and deal with them according to the facts.[1]

The trial began on May 9. Sessions of the court were held daily, Sundays excepted, from 10 A.M. until late in the afternoon. It was conducted with the utmost celerity, consistent with justice, on the part of the Government. No time at all was lost.

The Government witnesses who had been detained in custody were brought to the Arsenal in conveyances under the protection of armed guards, and were returned to their quarters in the same way. Every possible safeguard was thrown about them by the Government to protect its interests, and to take care that they should not be tampered with by outsiders.

Three hundred and forty witnesses were examined, of whom one hundred and eighty were for the prosecution and one hundred and sixty for the defense.[2]

The legal contests between the counsel on opposing sides was sometimes very exciting and often acrimonious. The lawyers for the defense were constant in their objections, to the admission of much of the testimony, denying its applicability to the case.

It was Judge Bingham's province to meet these objections as they arose. Every inch of disputed ground was fought by him, ably, forcibly, and with dignity. He was on his feet almost constantly, parrying the thrusts of his opponents and driving home his own point and arguments with terrific force and effect. To great activity, he added the courage of a lion. In the conduct of this case, Judge Bingham, in every way, proved himself a great lawyer and patriot.

The case presented by the Government against Herold was very strong. By the testimony adduced, it was shown that he was acquainted with John H. Surratt as far back as April 1863; that in March 1865 he had visited Surratt's home, leaving his horse standing in the alley next to the house, and had met Booth and Payne there; that he was in the restaurant adjoining Ford's Theater on the evening of March 18, 1865, when Booth played Pescara, and was seen in the company of Booth and Atzerodt on that occasion, acting in a suspicious manner. It was also shown that he was one of those who had ridden from Mrs. Surratt's house on the 16th of March, when the President's capture was contemplated,[3] but above all his conduct on the day of the assassination was of the most damaging and compromising nature. His meetings with Booth and with Atzerodt at the Kirkwood House, where he left his overcoat in Atzerodt's room, were proved. Again, he was seen in the evening by Fletcher, of whom he had procured his horse at Naylor's stables, coming from the neighborhood of the Seward home about the time of Payne's assault and Booth's awful deed; his flight along F Street, then across the Eastern Branch Bridge;[4] his subsequent meetings with Booth and his actions at Surrattsville (Lloyd's tavern), where he called for the carbines (shooting irons), which he about March 20 had helped to deposit at that place with Surratt and Atzerodt, and which Mrs. Surratt on the very afternoon of the murder had ordered to be delivered to the parties who would call for them that night; his flight to Dr. Mudd's house on the night of the murder; and his subsequent capture in the barn at Garrett's farm— were all events and facts proved and established in such a manner as to leave no possible chance for him to escape from the awful peril into which he had plunged.

For him there was no defense; it was almost ridiculous to attempt one, yet his friend and counsel, Mr. Frederick Stone, did everything for him that was possible to save a fellow being's life. Not a single fact, however, brought by the prosecution against him was set aside or discredited, and up to the present day the case of the Government against him remains uncontradicted and unimpeached.

The only defense made in his behalf was that his previous reputation in life had been good, and that he had always been a weak, simple-minded youth without much force of character—light and trifling. One of his witnesses said he was like a boy only eleven years of age. This was his only plea to the tremendous crime with which he was charged, and it was so feeble and insignificant that it had no weight at all with the Commission in determining his fate.

Anyone who could have seen him from day to day as he sat in the court room with his life hanging in the balance, and watched the play of his countenance, would have considered him a weak and foolish boy.

How such an insignificant and puny character could have mustered courage enough to nerve himself for his terrible deeds is to those who knew him best and who saw him in the court for nearly sixty days utterly incomprehensible.

Payne was too poor to employ counsel. In his extremity, he had no friends, and possessed not a dollar in the world. So the Government whose president and chief officers he had conspired to murder, at its own expense, assigned to him as counsel Colonel William E. Doster, a brave Union soldier. No better selection could have been made, and earnestly and enthusiastically did Mr. Doster apply himself to the difficult task of defending his wretched client. Never did a man enter more courageously upon an undertaking apparently so hopeless.

Judge Bingham in presenting the evidence against this man left for him no ground of hope upon which to stand. Payne's course from the time of his arrival at Mrs. Branson's house in Baltimore, in January 1865, until he forced his way into Mr. Seward's room, on the night of the 14th of April, was a merciless array of facts. It was shown how in his coarse brutality he had knocked down a colored servant at the Branson house during his abode there and then trampled upon and kicked her. His appearance at the Surratt house, in February, when he called himself Wood, and said he was a clerk in a china store in Baltimore; his reappearance there three weeks later under the name of Payne, and styling himself a Baptist preacher; his presence on a bed with Surratt, handling the weapons of death; his visit to Ford's Theater on the evening of March 15, where he was seen holding a conference with Booth and Surratt in the President's box; his association with the other conspirators on the 16th of March in the effort to capture the President—were all minutely described. Then after that wild attempt, which resulted in failure, it was shown how John H. Surratt and Miss Annie Ward, at a time when Surratt said he had abandoned his connection with the abduction plot, secured a room for him at the Herndon House, where he remained in hiding until he emerged therefrom amid the awful shadows of that April night when he would, as his share of the vile work, attempt to stab a high officer of the Government to death. The fact of his acquaintance with Booth, Mrs. Surratt, John Surratt, Atzerodt, and Herold was thoroughly established.

William H. Bell, the colored servant at the Seward house, stated how the bold ruffian had forced his way into Mr. Seward's house against his protest under the plea that he had a package of medicine for the sick man from his physician. His assault on the Honorable Frederick Seward, and the crushing blow delivered to that gentleman's skull with the butt end of a revolver; the battle in the sick man's chamber; how he threw himself on his bed, and stabbed him right and left; his scuffle with the nurse [George] Robinson and Major Augustus Seward—were graphically narrated.

The officers who arrested Mrs. Surratt on the night of the 17th of April related under oath how with woolen cap, made from the sleeve of his undershirt, and with pickaxe on his shoulder, he had mounted the front steps of her house in the dead hour of night, saying that she had sent for him to dig a ditch, and when she was brought face to face with him, with uplifted hand and sworn oath, denied ever having seen him.

The gleaming knife with which he had attempted to kill Mr. Seward was brought into court to cry out against him, and as he gazed upon it, his eyes lighted up with a sudden and wild flash almost demoniacal in its expression. The very boots he had worn were summoned, and as the top of one of them was turned down, the name of the President's murderer, Booth, was revealed.[5] His shirt, undershirt, and overcoat, still red with the drops of blood, all testified against him in language that could not be refuted. Once the court compelled him to stand up, clad in this overcoat, with the cap on his head, and repeat the words, "I am mad! I am mad!" uttered by him as he fled from the Seward house, and by those words the colored servant identified him. Those who witnessed that scene can never forget it.

Doster's argument for Payne was a sublime effort. It reads like an epic poem and is one of the finest productions in the English language. During its delivery, the audience sat as if entranced with the orator's thrilling utterances. He accepted all the testimony offered by the Government against his unfortunate client as the truth, nor did he in any manner assail and vilify the Government witnesses, who, he knew, had spoken the truth.

When Mr. Doster made the following statement in his plea, he gave away his whole case and showed that there was but little hope for his charge:

> There are three things in the case of the prisoner, Payne, which are admitted beyond dispute.
> 1. That he is the person who attempted to take the life of the Secretary of State.

2. That he is not within the medical definition of insanity.

3. That he believed what he did was right and justifiable.[6]

The story of Payne's early life on the farm of his father in Florida; his enlistment in a Florida regiment; his visit to the Richmond theater in 1861 where he first met Booth and fell a victim to the fascinating genius of that bad man—were depicted with a master hand. Then he informed his hearers of Payne's history in the war, told of the death of his two brothers at Murfreesboro in 1862. He spoke of the part he took in the battle of Gettysburg in 1863 and how he became a prisoner of war and was sent to West Hospital, Baltimore. His subsequent life in that city, his return to the Southern army, joining a cavalry regiment at Fauquier Court House, Virginia, were also detailed.

Payne remained with this arm of the service until January 1, 1865; on that day, according to farmer [John] Grant, he saved the lives of two Union prisoners. Then, according to Doster, he went to Alexandria, Virginia, took the oath of allegiance, and came North. He found board with Mrs. Margaret Branson, the lady already referred to, who lived on Eutaw Street in Baltimore.*

About the end of January or the middle of February the second meeting between Booth and Payne took place. It occurred in front of Barnum's Hotel. Of this meeting Colonel Doster spoke in the most feeling and eloquent manner, portraying Booth as taking advantage of Payne's hunger and necessities, in his efforts to enlist him in the "oil business"— the scheme of capturing the President and telling him there was a fortune in it. Doster alluded to his connection with the effort to kidnap the President, and then passed on to the occurrences of the 14th day of April. He pictured the scene in Payne's room at the Herndon House on the evening when Booth gave him the bogus package of medicine and bade him go and kill the Secretary, Mr. Seward.

I have asked him why he did it, said Mr. Doster. His only answer is, "Because I believed it my duty."

Doster's argument may justly be termed "Payne's confession," for such it was. All the way through, it was an open and candid admission of the prisoner's guilt; indeed, the argument is more than a confession, it is an attempt at a justification of his deed by this cold-blooded man.

During the delivery of the argument, Payne sat stolid and indiffer-

* See above, Chapter IX.

ent; not a muscle in his face moved, and his stout frame exhibited no signs of emotion or fear. He was apparently the most unconcerned and the bravest man in the court room.

The defense of George A. Atzerodt was as hopeless as that of Herold and Payne. He was the most wretched and woebegone-looking prisoner among them all. From the commencement of the trial, dark despair seemed to settle on his soul; not a ray of hope illumined his countenance. It was painful to look at him. He appeared to realize the enormity of his crime and it looked as though he was continually praying to his God to afford him some means of escape.

Colonel W. E. Doster was also his attorney, and was assigned to him by the Government, for Atzerodt was as poor as Payne. Inasmuch as the part he took in the Conspiracy has been already set forth in these pages, the following extract from Mr. Doster's argument is given for the benefit of my readers. Said Mr. Doster:

What is, then, the plain unvarnished truth of Atzerodt's part in this conspiracy? I will briefly relate it. During the latter part of February, John Surratt and Booth wanted a man who understood boating, and could both get a boat and ferry a party over the Potomac on a capture. Surratt knew Atzerodt, and under the influence of great promises of a fortune, the prisoner consented to furnish the boat, and do the ferrying over. The plot was attempted the 18th of March and failed.* Booth, however, kept his subordinates uninformed of his plans, except it was understood that the President was to be captured. Meanwhile, everybody was waiting for Booth. On the 18th of March, Atzerodt went to the Kimmel House. On the 1st of April he talked of future wealth. On the 6th he spoke to Lieut. Keim, over their liquor, of using one, if the other failed.[7] On the 12th he stayed at the Kirkwood, and tried to sell the bay horse at Pope's. On the 14th Booth unfolded his plans at the Herndon House, and Atzerodt refused. From the Herndon House he went to Oyster Bay and took drinks until ten. At ten he took a drink with Fletcher at the Union; at ten minutes after ten he took a drink at the Kirkwood; at twenty minutes after ten he took a drink at the Kimmel House and rode about the city. At eleven, he returned his horse; at twelve he was at the Navy Yard; at two he went to bed. Next morning at five he got

* Mr. Doster is mistaken. It was the 16th of March.

up and went to Georgetown, pawned his pistol, and went to Mr. Metz's. On the 16th (Sunday) he took dinner at Metz's. On Sunday evening he went to Hartman Richter's. On the 19th he was arrested. Thus ends this history, which under a greater hand, might have become a tragedy, but with the prisoner has turned into a farce.[8]

The prisoner, by his counsel, submitted the following statement to the court:

I am one of a party who agreed to capture the President of the United States, but I am not one of a party to kill the President of the United States, or any member of the Cabinet, or General Grant, or Vice-President Johnson. The first plot to capture failed; the second—to kill—I broke away from the moment I heard it.

This is the way it came about: On the evening of the 14th of April, I met Booth and Payne at the Herndon House, in this city at eight o'clock. He (Booth) said he himself would murder Mr. Lincoln and General Grant, Payne should take Mr. Seward, and I should take Mr. Johnson. I told him I would not do it; that I had gone into the thing to capture, but I was not going to kill. He told me I was a fool; that I would be hung anyway and that it was death for every man who backed out; and so we parted. I wandered about the streets until about two o'clock in the morning, and then went to the Kimmel House, and from there pawned my pistol at Georgetown, and went to my cousin's house, in Montgomery County, where I was arrested, the 19th following. After I was arrested, I told Provost Marshal Wells and Provost Marshal McPhail the whole story; also told it to Capt. Monroe, and Col. Wells told me if I pointed out the way Booth had gone, I would be reprieved, and so I told him I thought he had gone down Charles County in order to cross the Potomac. The arms which were found in my room at the Kirkwood House, and a black coat, do not belong to me; neither were they left to be used by me. On the afternoon of the 14th of April, Herold called to see me, and left the coat there. It is his coat, and all in it belongs to him, as you can see by the handkerchief marked with his initial, and with the name of his sister, Mrs. Naylor. Now I will state how I passed the whole of the evening of the 14th of April. In the afternoon, at about two o'clock, I went to Kelleher's stable, on Eighth Street, near D, and hired a dark bay mare, and rode into the country for pleasure, and on my return put her up at Naylor's stable. The dark bay horse which I had kept at Naylor's before, on or about the 3rd of April, belonged to Booth, also the saddle and bridle. I do not know what became of him. At about six in the evening, I went to Naylor's again, and took out the mare, rode out for an hour, and returned her to Naylor's. It was then nearly eight, and I told him to keep the mare ready at ten o'clock in order to return her to the man I hired her from. From there I went to the Herndon House. Booth sent a messenger to the "Oyster Bay," and I went. Booth wanted me to murder Mr. Johnson. I refused. I then went to the "Oyster Bay," on the Avenue, about Twelfth Street, and whiled away the time until nearly ten o'clock. At ten I got the mare, and having taken a drink with the hostler, galloped about town, and went to the Kimmel House. From there I rode down to the depot, and returned my horse, riding up Pennsylvania Avenue to Kelleher's. From Kelleher's, I went down to the Navy Yard to get a room with Wash. Briscoe. He had none, and by the time I got back to the Kimmel House it was nearly two. The man Thomas was a stranger I met on the street. Next morning, as stated, I went to my Cousin Richter's, in Montgomery County.

George A. Atzerodt.[9]

What Atzerodt's object was in making this statement to the Commission cannot be surmised. It certainly convicts him of a guilty knowledge beforehand of the intended murder of President Lincoln, General Grant, and Secretary Seward, although he, as he says, refused to murder Mr. Johnson. His idea was, probably, to secure a mitigation of sentence —imprisonment—but if such was his intention, it failed. Furthermore, he says the plot to kill was only formed on the night of the 14th of April.

In view of the fact of Booth's extensive preparations at the theater on that day, and also that a room had been secured for Atzerodt at the Kirkwood House that morning at eight o'clock, and that Booth and Herold called on him during the day, such a pretense and defense vanish into thin air. If they did not intend to kill Johnson, why was a room secured at all at the Kirkwood House for such a personage as Atzerodt?

Dr. Samuel A. Mudd in his efforts to escape conviction made the most strenuous and bitter fight of all the prisoners. In his attorney, General Thomas L. Ewing, he had a gentleman who left no stone unturned to free him. Dr. Mudd's complicity in the Conspiracy lay not so much in what he did before the crime as what he did after it—shielding and har-boring Booth and Herold when escaping from justice.

Could the fact be once successfully established by the Government that he had known these men before the murder of Lincoln, and had met them, then, in the eye of the law, it rendered him a dangerous accom-plice and co-conspirator after the fact. And such was the case. It was demonstrated by the Government that he had met Booth in Maryland in 1864 in November, in his own neighborhood, and that Booth, according to Samuel Arnold, had come with letters of introduction to him and to Dr. Queen from one Martin in Montreal, Canada; that he had lodged with Mudd one night, and that, at this time by his agency and help, Booth procured from one Polk Gardiner the one-eyed bay horse which was used by Payne on the night of the assassination.

The strongest evidence against him as to his acquaintance with Booth before the assassination was given by me (the writer). I have already related the circumstances of the accidental meeting on Seventh Street in the early winter of 1864–1865 between Mudd, Booth, Surratt, and my-self, and the subsequent interview at the National Hotel. I have described this affair at length in Chapter IV of this work, and it is not necessary to repeat it here. At first at the trial of the conspirators in 1865, I tes-tified that the meeting, according to the best of my recollection, took place on or about January 15, 1865, and I associated the date of the meeting with an important letter received about that time, from the bishop of Richmond. I subsequently became convinced that I was mis-taken as to the date, and I accordingly testified at the trial of John H. Surratt in 1867 that it occurred on the 23rd of December 1864, and gave my reasons for changing it.

Dr. Mudd fought my evidence on this point bitterly, as though his very existence depended upon it, bringing witness after witness to prove that he was not in Washington on the occasion referred to by me, but he was unsuccessful. His attorney hammered away at me, denouncing me in harsh language, and casting out all sorts of slurs and innuendoes, even denouncing me as a co-conspirator, but all his work and talk failed to shake my testimony in the least. He was endeavoring to save the life of his client, and if he could do it by destroying my character, what mattered it to him so long as he could gain his point?

Judge Bingham, when speaking to this point, frankly admitted that I was probably in error as to the time of the meeting, but not as to the fact that such meeting had taken place. His keen analysis of my evidence in respect to this interview of which I am now writing was most powerful, and will, no doubt, be of much interest here. He says:

Some time in January last, it is in testimony that the prisoner Mudd introduced Booth to John H. Surratt and the witness Weichmann; that Booth invited them to the National Hotel; that when there in the room to which Booth took them, Mudd went out into the passage, calling Booth out, and had a private conversation with him, leaving the witness and Surratt in the room. Upon their return to the room, Booth went out with Surratt, and upon their coming in, Booth, Surratt, and Samuel A. Mudd went out together and had a conversation in the passage, leaving the witness alone. Up to the time of this interview, it seems that neither the witness nor Surratt had any knowledge of Booth, as they were then introduced to him by Dr. Mudd. Whether Surratt had in fact previously known Booth, it is not important to inquire. Mudd deemed it necessary, perhaps a wise precaution, to introduce Surratt to Booth; he also deemed it necessary to have a private conversation with Booth shortly afterward, and directly after that to have a conversation together with Booth and Surratt alone. Had this conversation, no part of which was heard by the witness, been perfectly innocent, it is not to be presumed that Dr. Mudd, who was an entire stranger to Weichmann, would have deemed it necessary to hold the conversation secretly, nor to have volunteered to tell the witness, or rather pretend to tell him, what the conversation was; yet he did say to the witness, upon their return to the room, by way of apology, I suppose, for the privacy of the conversation, that Booth had some private business with him and wished to purchase his farm. This silly device, as is often the case in attempts at deception, failed in the execution; for it remains to be shown how the fact that Mudd had private business with Booth, and that Booth wished to purchase his farm, made it all necessary or even proper that they should both volunteer to call out Surratt, who up to that time was a stranger to Booth. What had Surratt to do with Booth's purchase of Mudd's farm? And if it was necessary to withdraw and talk by themselves secretly about the sale of the farm, why should they disclose the fact to the very man from whom they had concealed it?

In the light of other facts in this case, it must become clear to the Court that this secret meeting between Booth, Mudd, and Surratt was a conference looking to the execution of this conspiracy. It so impressed the prisoner, it so impressed his counsel, that they deemed it necessary and absolutely essential to their defense to attempt to destroy the credibility of the witness Weichmann.

I may say here in passing that they have not attempted to impeach his (Weichmann's) reputation for truth by the testimony of a single witness, nor have they impeached his testimony by calling a single witness to discredit one material fact to which he has testified in this issue. Failing to find a breath of suspicion against Weichmann's character, or to contradict a single fact to which he testified, the accused had to fly to the last resort, an alibi, and very earnestly did the learned counsel devote himself to the task.

It is not material whether this meeting in the hotel took place on the 23rd of December or in January. Weichmann, I repeat, is not positive as to the date, he is only positive as to the fact; and he disclosed voluntarily to this court, that the date could probably be fixed by a reference to the register of the Pennsylvania House.[10]

The testimony of Marcus P. Norton as to the presence of Mudd in the National Hotel on March 3, 1865, when he asked for Booth, also bore heavily against the prisoner.[11] A strong effort was made to destroy Mr. Norton's evidence by bringing two witnesses to swear that he was an unreliable man and could not be believed even under oath.

The Government in its turn produced four witnesses, among them General Horatio King, who had been Postmaster General under Buchanan's administration, all of whom said that Mr. Norton was a man of good character, of excellent business habits, and that there was no reason why his word could not be depended upon under all circumstances.

His testimony stood, as did also that of the Rev. William A. Evans, who swore that about the 1st or 2nd of March, certainly before inauguration day, he saw Dr. Mudd driving to Washington City and that he passed him on the road.[12] He also testified that at one time during the winter he saw Dr. Mudd going into Mrs. Surratt's house just as a man named [James] Judson Jarboe was coming out.[13] He also stated that at one time, about a year before the assassination, he had seen David E. Herold and Dr. Mudd coming to town together in a buggy, thus proving that Mudd was acquainted with Herold at least one year prior to the taking off of Mr. Lincoln.

A number of witnesses, some of them being Dr. Mudd's slaves, were introduced, who testified to his acquaintance with Surratt, and how he had secreted him and a number of other rebels in the woods near his house during 1864, when they were continually making secret trips over the river into the South. One colored man [Elzee Eglent] testified that Dr. Mudd had shot him at one time.[14] Abundant evidence was given to thoroughly establish Mudd's character as a disloyal man.

All the foregoing facts having been successfully established and the fact of the acquaintance of Booth, Surratt, Herold, and Mudd being proved beyond contradiction, it will be readily seen what a tremendous fact the visit of Booth and Herold to Mudd's house on the morning of the 15th of April within a few hours after the murder became against him. No wonder that he prevaricated to the detectives and others and denied for a time knowing who the murderous outlaws were, but the truth was mighty and prevailed.[15] The very boot which Mudd had removed from the assassin's foot was brought into court, and when the name at the top on the inside of it was examined, as in the case of the boots given to Payne, the name of Booth was blazoned forth.

Dr. Mudd was convicted and sent to lifelong imprisonment, and when he was on board the gunboat on his way to his future home, when perhaps his conscience reasserted itself, and he began to realize the great wrong his counsel had done me, he made the following statement:

Camp Fry, Washington, D.C.
August 22, 1865.

Brig.-Gen. Joseph Holt,
Judge Advocate General U.S.A.

Sir: I am in receipt of your communication of this date, in which you request information as regards the truthfulness of certain statements and confessions reported to have been made by Dr. Mudd while under my charge, *en route* to the Dry Tortugas.

In reply, I have the honor to state that my duties required me to be constantly with the prisoner, and during a conversation with Dr. Mudd on the 22nd of July, he confessed that he knew Booth when he came to his house with Herold, on the morning after the assassination of the President; that he had known Booth some time but was afraid to tell of his having been at his house on the 15th of April fearing that his own and the lives of his family would be endangered thereby. He also confessed that he was with Booth on the evening referred to by Weichmann in his testimony; that he came to Washington on that occasion to meet Booth by appointment who wished *to be introduced* to John Surratt; that when he and Booth were *going* to Mrs. Surratt's house to see John Surratt, they met on Seventh Street, John Surratt was introduced to Booth, and they had a conversation of a private nature; I will here add that Dr. Mudd had with him a printed copy of the testimony pertaining to his trial, and I had a number of times referred to the same. I will also state that this confession was voluntary, and made without solicitation, threat or promise, and was made after the destination of the prisoners was communicated to them which communication affected Dr. Mudd more than the rest; and he frequently exclaimed, "Oh, there is now no help for me." "Oh, I cannot live in such a place."

Please acknowledge receipt of this letter.

I am, General, very respectfully,

Your obedient servant,

George W. Dutton.

Capt. Co. C. 10th Regt. V.R.C.; Com'dg Guard.

Sworn and acknowledged at Washington D.C., this 23rd of August 1865 before me,

G. C. Thomas,

Notary Public.[16]

I was in Philadelphia when the wires flashed the news of this confession across the country. The reader can picture to himself the feeling which filled my heart. It was not only a complete vindication of the only portion of my testimony for which I had been most bitterly assailed, by General Ewing, Mudd's counsel, but it was a notice to the world that the Commission had done their duty in Mudd's case for shielding, secreting, and helping Booth and Herold when they rode down to his house with the red blood of Abraham Lincoln on their hands and souls.

The testimony against Arnold and O'Laughlin in reference to their connection with the assassination was not so pronounced as against some of the other conspirators. It was shown by the confession which Arnold made to Eaton G. Horner on April 17 that he and O'Laughlin were active members of the Conspiracy to abduct the President, but they always maintained that they had no knowledge or connection with the plot to assassinate.[17]

The abduction plot, Arnold said, was attempted in March [on the 17th] at the Soldiers' Home, but failed of execution. Arnold then claimed to have returned home to Baltimore on March 21, 1865, and that since that time had not been in Washington City. On the 1st of April he went to Fortress Monroe, where he obtained employment in the store of a man named John W. Wharton, and was there on the night Booth shot President Lincoln and was arrested there.[18]

Judge Bingham used the "Sam" letter found in Booth's trunk against Arnold with great effect. He employed the following language in relation to it:

> Here is the confession of the prisoner Arnold that he was one with Booth in this conspiracy; the further confession that they are suspected by the Government of their country, and the acknowledgement that *since they parted*, Booth had communicated among other things a suggestion which leads to the remark in this letter (Sam) "I would prefer your first query, 'Go and see how it will be taken at Richmond,' and ere long I shall be better prepared to *again be with you*." This is a declaration that affects Arnold, Booth and O'Laughlin alike, if the court are satisfied on the subject, that the matter to be referred to Richmond is the matter of the assassination of the President and others, to effect which these parties had previously agreed and conspired together.[19]

The Government in this trial always scouted the idea of capturing the President, ridiculed it, and would not for a moment admit the possibility of its execution. The accomplished fact was the death of the President, not his capture.

Judge Bingham on this point spoke as follows:

> The letter (Sam), therefore, of his co-conspirator, Arnold, is evidence against O'Laughlin because it is an act in the prosecution of the common conspiracy, suggesting what should be done in order to make it effective, and which suggestion, as has been stated, was followed out. The defense has attempted to avoid the force of this letter by reciting the statement of Arnold, made to Horner at the time he was arrested, in which he declared, among other things, that

the purpose was to abduct President Lincoln and take him South; that it was to be done at the theater by throwing the President out of the box upon the floor of the stage, when the accused was to catch him. The very announcement of this testimony excited derision that such a tragedy meant only to take the President and carry him gently away! This pigmy to catch the giant as the assassins hurled him to the floor from an elevation of twelve feet! The court has viewed the theater and must be satisfied that Booth, in leaping from the President's box, broke his limb. The court cannot fail to conclude that this statement of Arnold's was but another silly device, like that of the "oil business," which, for the time being, he employed to hide from the knowledge of his captor the fact that the purpose was to murder the President. No man can for a moment believe that any one of these conspirators hoped or desired by such a proceeding as that stated by the prisoner, to take the President alive in the presence of thousands assembled in the theater after he had thus been thrown upon the floor of the stage, much less carry him through the city, through the lines of your army, and deliver him into the hands of the rebels. I shall not waste a moment more in combatting such an absurdity.

Arnold does confess that he was a conspirator with Booth in this proposed murder; that Booth had a letter of introduction to Dr. Mudd; that Booth, O'Laughlin, Atzerodt, Surratt, a man with an alias, "Mosby," [20] and another whom he does not know, and himself were parties to this conspiracy, and that Booth furnished them all with arms. He concludes this remarkable statement to Horner with the declaration at the time, to-wit, the first week of March, or four weeks before he went to Fortress Monroe he left the conspiracy, and that Booth told him to sell his arms if he chose. This is sufficiently answered by the fact that four weeks *afterward* he wrote his letter to Booth, which was found in Booth's possession after the assassination, suggesting to him what to do in order to make the conspiracy a success, and by the further fact that at the very moment he uttered these declarations, part of his arms were found upon his person, and the rest not disposed of, but at his father's house.

A party to a treasonable and murderous conspiracy against the Government of his country cannot be held to have abandoned it because he makes such a declaration as this when he is in the hands of the officer of the law, arrested for his crime, and especially when his declaration is in conflict with and expressly contradicted by his written acts, and unsupported by any conduct of his which becomes a citizen and a man.

If he abandoned the conspiracy, why did he not make known the fact to Abraham Lincoln and his constitutional advisers that these men, armed with the weapons of assassination, were daily lying in wait for their lives? To pretend that a man who thus conducts himself for weeks after the pretended abandonment, volunteering advice for the successful prosecution of the conspiracy, the evidence of which is in writing, and about which there can be no mistake, has, in fact, abandoned it, is to insult the common understanding of men. O'Laughlin, having conspired with Arnold to do this murder, is, therefore, as much concluded by the letter of Arnold of the 27th of March as is Arnold himself.

It was further shown in evidence that O'Laughlin was in Washington on April 1. He was seen at that time by a man named Street,[21] who knew him. Booth and a third man were talking together whom Street did not know. Street wanted to talk with Booth, and then O'Laughlin called Street to one side, and told him Booth was busily engaged with his friend—was *talking privately* to his friend.

On the 13th of April, O'Laughlin again came to Washington. According to the prosecution, on the same evening he was seen at the house of the Secretary of War, making some inquiries about General Grant. Of this incident the able prosecuting attorney for the Government spoke in these words:

> On the evening preceding the assassination—the 13th of April— by the testimony of three reputable witnesses, against whose truth- fulness not one word is uttered here or elsewhere, O'Laughlin went to the house of the Secretary of War, where General Grant then was, and placed himself in position in the hall where he could see him, having declared before he reached that point, to one of these witnesses, that he wished to see General Grant. The house was bril- liantly illuminated at the time; two, at least, of the witnesses con- versed with the accused, and the other stood very near to him, took special notice of his conduct, called attention to it, and suggested

that he be put out of the house, and he was accordingly put out by one of the witnesses.

These witnesses are confident, and have no doubt, and so swear upon their oaths that Michael O'Laughlin is the man who was present on that occasion. There is no denial on the part of the accused that he was in Washington during the day and during the night of April 13th, and also during the day and during the night of the 14th; and yet, to get rid of this testimony, recourse is had to that common device—an alibi; a device never, I may say, more frequently resorted to than in this trial. But what an alibi! Nobody is called to prove it, save some men who by their own testimony were engaged in a drunken debauch through the evening. A reasonable man who reads their evidence can hardly be expected to allow it to outweigh the united testimony of three unimpeached and unimpeachable witnesses who were clear in their statements—who entertain no doubt of the truth of what they say—whose opportunities to know were full and complete, and who were constrained to take special notice of the prisoner by reason of his extraordinary conduct.

These witnesses describe accurately the appearance, stature, and complexion of the accused, but because they describe his clothing as dark or black, it is urged that as part of his clothing, although dark, was not black, the witnesses are mistaken.

O'Laughlin on the morning of the 14th of April called on Booth at the National Hotel. He was in the city on the night of the murder, and did not return home until the afternoon of the following day.

Spangler's conduct in aiding Booth in his escape before and after the assassination was shown. The testimony against him was not so strong as against the others, but it was sufficient to insure his conviction.

CHAPTER XXIII

The case against Mary E. Surratt · The story of the "shooting irons" ·
Return of Payne to her home · Testimony of clergymen in her behalf ·
Letter No. Five · Remarks of Jefferson Davis
at Greensboro, North Carolina

Of all the cases on trial before the Commission, that of Mrs. Mary E. Surratt excited the greatest attention, not only because of her sex, but because of her age and her standing in life. She was the oldest of all those connected with the Conspiracy, and at the time of her trial must have been about forty-seven years of age.

Throughout the conduct of her case, it was plainly evident to a careful observer that Judge Bingham's heart and feelings were not enlisted in the prosecution of this woman, and all his actions and arguments against her can be regarded as made only in the strict line of duty, and in vindicaton of the murdered President.

The evidence against her was very strong; more so than against Atzerodt, Arnold, O'Laughlin, Mudd, and Spangler. It extended from the date of her son's meeting with Booth and Mudd on December 23, 1864, to the date of her arrest on April 17, 1865. The visits of Booth, Atzerodt, Payne, Herold, and Dr. Mudd (once) to her house were shown. Her intimate acquaintance with Booth during that period was well established. Her own daughter, Miss Fitzpatrick, Mr. and Mrs. John T. Holohan, and myself testified to the presence of Payne in her house on two different occasions, giving his name as Wood on his first visit, and taking his meals, and making his home there for four days, on his second visit.

All this and much other matter in relation to her alleged connection with the Conspiracy prior to April 14, however, would have counted for but little, had it not been for her doings on the day of the murder itself. It was shown that Booth came to her house at two o'clock in the afternoon: that she then had a private conference with him in her parlor, and that immediately thereafter, with his field glass in her possession, she had driven into the country under pretense of collecting a debt, and that when she arrived at Surrattsville, she gave Lloyd, her tenant, orders to have the two carbines concealed there, which she called "shooting irons," to be held in readiness for some parties who were to call for them *"in the night."* She also delivered to Lloyd the field glass which Booth had given her. By her language to Lloyd, it was proved that she knew the "shooting irons" had been secreted at his place, and that they would be wanted that fatal Friday night after Booth had shot the President to facilitate his escape and that of Herold from their pursuers.[1]

When this evidence was given, it sent a thrill of indignation and horror through the court room. It was past comprehension how an honorable woman could, nearly eight hours before the murder, leave the sacred precincts of her home, and undertake such an errand as that. The fact of her giving the order for the delivery of the carbines was held to be conclusive proof of her knowledge of their deposit at that place, and of what was going on the day of the assassination.

This evidence of Lloyd was supplemented by that of the officers of the War Department—Major H. W. Smith, Captain R. C. Morgan, and Captain W. M. Wermerskirch—who arrested her on the night of April 17. These men all testified how Payne climbed the front door steps of her house on that night with pickaxe on his shoulder and asked for her, stating that she had sent for him to dig a ditch, and when she was confronted with him, denied ever having seen him. The testimony of every boarder in the house proved the falsity of this, and it was positively shown that he had been her guest on two occasions, giving the names Wood and Payne.[2]

These two bits of evidence on the part of Lloyd and the War Department officers were, I firmly believe, and I say it deliberately, the main testimony which resulted in her conviction. Had it not been for them, the death sentence, in my judgment, would not have been imposed upon her. The testimony of myself and the other boarders as to the frequent visits of Booth and the others to her house; the evidence which I gave about the occurrences on the 16th of March when the seven conspirators rode from her front door with the avowed purpose of capturing the President as shown by Arnold's confession—were, indeed, very important, yet insufficient to convict her, but all this matter became of the greatest weight when taken in connection with her conduct on the day of the assassination, with the important evidence of Lloyd and with that of the War Department officers. A chain was thus formed about her from which it was impossible to escape.

Although I have many times in the newspapers been styled the chief witness against Mrs. Surratt, yet anyone who will take the pains to read my testimony in 1865 will discover that there is not a line, not a word in it on which of itself there was the least possible chance to secure this woman's conviction.

Everything I said was purely circumstantial, and the most important statement in her defense in reference to her trip to Surrattsville was when I swore that she told me she was going down there to see about a debt due her by Mr. Nothey. The letter I wrote for her to Mr. Nothey was what she and her counsel relied on chiefly to prove that the purpose of her visit to Surrattsville was an innocent one. The simple truth is that I was not the principal witness against her. The chief witnesses to that effect were John M. Lloyd, the officers of the War Department who arrested her, and the silent carbines which lay on the table of the Commission, and which she had ordered her tenant, Lloyd, to deliver to the parties who would call for them.

An effort was made by her counsel to disparage the testimony of Lloyd on the ground of intoxication. A number of witnesses were introduced who swore that he had been drinking, and he himself admitted that he had taken considerable liquor. It was held that for this reason his testimony was unreliable and ought not to be taken into account against the prisoner.

At this, Judge Bingham sprang to his feet, and with his whole frame quivering with emotion, seized one of the carbines lying on the table before him, and raising it aloft, eloquently and forcibly exclaimed, "Gentlemen, they say that Lloyd lies and that he was drunk, but these carbines, these mute witnesses were not drunk and they do not lie. Where did Booth get them? One was found at Lloyd's tavern, and the other its mate was taken from the body of the dying assassin in Garrett's barn." [3]

Judge Bingham's terrific words had such force that all opposition in that direction was at once squelched.

The defense made by Mrs. Surratt through her counsel, taken in its entirety, was very weak. Not one of the facts in regard to the visits of the conspirators to her house, nor any of their acts bearing against her, and in which she was personally concerned, was disproved. In reference to the visit of Payne to her house after the assassination a strong attempt was made to prove that her eyesight was defective, and that she did not recognize the assassin when he stood before her in his blood-bespattered garments. This also failed.

In speaking of the visit of Payne, at this time, Judge Bingham in his argument used the following language:

But there is one other fact in this case that puts forever at rest the question of the guilty participation of the prisoner, Mrs. Surratt, in this conspiracy and murder; and that is that Payne, who had lodged four days in her house—who during all that time had sat at her table, and who had often conversed with her—when the guilt of his great crime was upon him, and he knew not where else he could so safely go to find a co-conspirator, and he could trust none that was not like himself, guilty, with even the knowledge of his presence—under cover of darkness, after wandering for three days and nights, skulking before the pursuing officers of justice, at the hour of midnight, found his way to the door of Mrs. Surratt, rang the bell, was admitted, and upon being asked, "Whom do you want to see?" replied, "Mrs. Surratt." He was then asked by the officer, Morgan, what he came at that time of night for? To which he replied, "To dig a gutter in the morning; Mrs. Surratt had sent for him." Afterwards he said, "Mrs. Surratt knew he was a poor man and came to him." Being asked where he last worked, he replied, "Sometimes on 'I' Street"; and where he boarded, he replied, "he had no boardinghouse, and was a poor man who got his living with the pick," which he bore upon his shoulder, having stolen it from the intrenchments of the Capitol. Upon being pressed again why he came there at that time of night to go to work, he answered that he simply called to see what time he should go to work in the morning. Upon being told by the officer, who fortunately had preceded him to this house, that he would have to go to the provost marshal's office, he moved and did not answer, whereupon Mrs. Surratt was asked to step into the hall and state whether she knew this man. Raising her right hand, she exclaimed, "Before God, sir, I have not seen this man before; I have not hired him; I do not know anything about him." The hall was brilliantly lighted.

If not one word had been said, the mere act of Payne flying to her house for shelter would have borne witness against her, strong as proofs from Holy Writ. But when she denies, after hearing his declarations, that she sent for him, or that she had gone to him and hired him, and calls for God to witness that she had never seen him, and knew nothing of him, when, in point of fact, she had seen him for four successive days in her own house, in the same clothing which he then wore, who can resist for a moment the conclusion that these parties were alike guilty? [4]

A number of witnesses were introduced to prove her good character, prior to the commission of Lincoln's murder, notably the following Catholic clergymen: Rev. Francis E. Boyle, Rev. Chas. H. Stonestreet, Rev. B. F. Wigget, and Rev. D. N. Young, all of Washington, and Rev. Peter Lanihan of Maryland. All these gentlemen were in accord in what they said, and spoke exceedingly well of her.

Some witnesses were also called who testified that they had heard her give utterance to Union sentiments, and that she, on several occasions, had been kind to Union soldiers, and had given them food. This was met by the Government, who presented other witnesses who testified that she was a disloyal woman.

The most important evidence in relation to her character, however, was given by me when examined by her very able counsel, the Honorable Reverdy Johnson.[5] I was rejoiced to be able to give it, and to say all that I conscientiously could in her behalf. The following is the testimony to which I make allusion:

Cross-Examination by Mr. Johnson.

Q. During the whole of that period, you never heard him (Booth) intimate that it was his purpose, or that there was a purpose to assassinate the President?

A. Never, sir.

Q. You never heard him say anything on the subject, or any body else during the whole period from November until the assassination?

A. No, sir.

Q. During the whole of that period what was her (Mrs. Surratt's) character?

A. It was excellent; I have known her since 1863.

Q. You have been living in her house since November?

A. Since November.

Q. During the whole of that time as far as you could judge, was her character good and amiable?

A. Her character was exemplary and lady like in every particular.

Q. Was she a member of the church?

A. Yes, sir.

Q. A regular attendant?

A. Yes, sir.

Q. Of the Catholic Church?

A. Yes, sir.

Q. Are you a Catholic?

A. Yes, sir; I am a Catholic.

Q. Have you been to church with her?

A. I generally accompanied her to church every Sunday.

Q. As far then, as you can judge, her conduct in a religious and in a moral sense was altogether exemplary?

A. Yes, sir. She went to her religious duties, at least, every two weeks.

Q. Then, if I understand you, from November up to the 14th of April, whenever she was here, she was regular in her attendance at her own church, and apparently, as far as you can judge, doing all her duties to God and to man?

A. Yes, sir.

By Doster.

Q. You do not know of any conversation that passed between Atzerodt and Booth, or between Atzerodt and Payne having reference to a conspiracy?

A. No, sir.

Q. Have you ever heard any conversation having reference to Payne's assignment to the assassination of the Secretary of State?

A. No, sir.

By Aiken.

Q. What was your object in being so swift to give all this information?

A. My object was to assist the Government.

Q. Were any threats ever made to you by any officer of the Government in case you did not divulge?

A. No, sir; no threats at all.

Q. Any inducements?

A. No, sir; no inducements at all. I myself had a great deal to fear, being in this house where these people were, I knew that I would be brought into public notice, but as for myself being cognizant of anything of this kind, I had no fears at all, for I was not cognizant.

When I surrendered myself to the Government, I surrendered myself because I thought it my duty. It was hard for me to do so situated as I was with Mrs. Surratt and her family, and with John Surratt, but it was my duty, and my duty I have always regarded it since. I had not a word of private conversation with these people which I would not be willing to have the world hear.

Q. You state that all the prisoners at the bar were free and unreserved in your presence in their conversation?

A. They spoke in my presence on general topics, and so on; but as to their private conversation they never spoke to me.

Q. Do I understand you as stating to the court that in all your conversation with them, you never learned of any intended treasonable purpose or act or conspiracy of theirs?

A. No, sir.

Q. You never did?

A. No, sir.

Q. You were not suspicious of anything of the sort?

A. I would have been the last man in the world to suspect John Surratt, my schoolmate, of the murder of the President of the United States. I looked upon Atzerodt as did every one in the house as a good-hearted countryman.

Q. And did you still profess to be a friend of his (J.H.S.) at the time you were giving this information to the War Department that you speak of?

A. I was a friend as far as he himself was concerned; but when my suspicions as to the danger of the Government in any particular, were concerned I preferred the Government to John Surratt. I did not know what he was contemplating. He said he was going to engage in cotton speculation, he was going to engage in oil.

Q. If you did not know what he was contemplating, how could you forfeit your friendship to him? What is the rationale of that?

A. I never forfeited my friendship to him; he forfeited his friendship to me.

Q. Not by engaging the cotton speculation?

A. No, sir, by placing me in the position in which I now am—testifying against him.[6]

This evidence of mine absolutely exonerated Mrs. Surratt and her son from any knowledge of the abduction or assassination plot, as far as I knew, and it gave her the best character of any witness before the court in her behalf.

Many times during the years that are gone, have I been denounced as an untruthful man, but no friend of the Surratts who reads this evidence will dare say that I did not speak the truth as to the questions asked. If then I could speak the truth when the character of the Surratts was at stake, how could I as an honest man falsify my word in relation to the other facts about which I gave evidence?

The Conspiracy—the association of these people with one another for the purpose of murdering the President—was clearly proved. The knives and revolvers which they carried, the boots and clothing they wore, their telegrams and letters, the carbines deposited at Lloyd's, the horses which they had ridden, were all placed in evidence against them.

Booth's field glass had not yet been recovered by the Government, and therefore could not be utilized, nor was his diary brought forth at this trial, for important reasons. A mysterious passage in it, in which he stated that he had sent a letter for publication addressed to the *National Intelligencer* on the 14th of April, caused the Government to withhold it, as the authorities were eager to ascertain who the individual was to whom the letter in question had been delivered. This fact did not come to the surface until at the trial of John H. Surratt in 1867, when the party proved to be John Matthews, the actor, whose story in connection therewith has already been told.

Among the curious documents which came into the possession of the Government was one which was written after the assassination. It was dated at Washington. It was in cipher and was found floating in the water at Morehead City, North Carolina, by a Mr. Charles Duell. The envelope was addressed "John W. Wise." The letter was as follows:

Dear John:

I am happy to inform you that Pet has done his work well. He is safe and old Abe is in hell. Now, sir, all eyes are on you.

You must bring Sherman—Grant is in the hands of old Gray ere this. Red Shoes showed lack of nerve in Seward's case, but fell back in good order. *Johnson* must come. Old Crook has him in charge.

Mind well that brother's oath, and you will have no difficulty; all will be safe and enjoy the fruit of our labors.

We had a large meeting last night. All were bent in carrying out the programme to the letter. The rails are laid for safe exit. Old ——— always behind, lost the pop at City Point.

Now, I say again, the lives of our brave officers, and the life of the South depend upon carrying the programme into effect. No. Two will give you this. It's ordered no more letters shall be sent by mail. When you write, sign no real name, and send by some of our friends who are coming home. We want you to write us how the news was received there. We receive great encouragement from all quarters. I hope there will be no getting weak in the knees. I was in Baltimore yesterday. Pet has not got there yet. Your folks are well and have heard from you. Don't lose your nerve.

C. B.   No. Five.[7]

This letter was undoubtedly written by some party who was connected with the Conspiracy, but whose identity up to the present time stands unrevealed.

A vast amount of testimony was taken by the Commission which had no relation to the prisoners on trial, but which was introduced for the purpose of showing the animus of the Southern rebellion.

Many horrible facts were brought out in relation to plots for the destruction of steamers and gunboats; plot to burn New York City; introduction of yellow fever pestilence into Northern cities; starvation of Union prisoners; mining of Libby Prison, etc.[8] The bank account of Jacob Thompson, Confederate agent in Canada, was introduced and showed the expenditure of a large amount of money in that section of the country in behalf of the rebellion. This was the same bank in which Booth had deposited his funds when in Canada.[9]

Some evidence was also presented in relation to Jefferson Davis by Mr. Lewis E. Bates, who resided in Charlotte, North Carolina, and at whose house Mr. Davis stopped while on his way South making his escape. He made an address to the people from the steps of Mr. Bates's house. While he was talking a telegram from John C. Breckinridge was handed him. It was as follows:

Greensboro, April 19, 1865.

His Excellency President Davis:

President Lincoln was assassinated in the theater in Washington on the night of the 14th inst. Seward's house was entered on the same night and he was repeatedly stabbed, and is probably mortally wounded.

In concluding his speech, Jefferson Davis read the dispatch aloud, and according to Bates, made this remark: "If it were to be done, it were better it were well done." A day or two later, Jefferson Davis and John C. Breckinridge were in conversation at Mr. Bates's house, and were discussing the subject. Mr. Breckinridge remarked to Davis that he regretted it very much; that it was very unfortunate for the people of the South at that time. Davis replied, "Well, General, I don't know, if it were to be done at all it were better that it were well done; and if the same had been done to Andy Johnson, the beast, and to Secretary Stanton, the job would then be complete." [10]

When the arguments of counsel had all been made, the Commission adjourned for the purpose of deliberating upon the evidence in the case of the accused.

CHAPTER XXIV

---

*Final meeting of the Commission to determine the verdict in the case of the
accused persons · David E. Herold, George A. Atzerodt, Lewis Payne, and
Mary E. Surratt are found guilty and sentenced to be hanged · Michael
O'Laughlin, Samuel Arnold, and Samuel A. Mudd are found guilty and
sentenced to the Dry Tortugas for imprisonment for life · Edward
Spangler found guilty and sentenced to imprisonment at the Dry Tortugas
for six years · A majority of the Commission recommend that the
sentence of Mrs. Surratt be commuted to imprisonment for life · The
President disregards the petition · Issuance of a writ of habeas corpus in
the case of Mrs. Surratt · Its suspension by the President · The
sentences of the Commission are carried into effect*

On June 29 and 30, 1865, the Commission met with closed doors pursuant to adjournment.

All the members were present; also the Judge Advocate General Holt and the Assistant Judge Advocates, Bingham and Burnett.

The Commission proceeded to deliberate upon the evidence in the case of each of the accused.[1]

David E. Herold

After mature consideration of the evidence adduced in the case of the accused, David E. Herold, the Commission find the said accused—

Of the Specification .... Guilty.
Except "combining, confederating, and conspiring with Edward Spangler"; as to which part thereof .... Not Guilty.
Of the Charge .... Guilty.
Except the words of the charge, "combining, confederating, and conspiring with Edward Spangler"; as to which part of the charge—Not Guilty.

And the Commission do, therefore, sentence him, the said David E. Herold, to be hanged by the neck until he be dead, at such time and place as the President of the United States shall direct; two thirds of the Commission concurring therein.

George A. Atzerodt

After mature consideration of the evidence adduced in the case of the accused, George A. Atzerodt, the Commission find the said accused—

Of the Specification .... Guilty.

Except "combining, confederating, and conspiring with Edward Spangler"; of this .... Not Guilty.

Of the Charge .... Guilty.

Except "combining, confederating, and conspiring with Edward Spangler"; of this .... Not Guilty.

And the Commission do, therefore, sentence him, the said George A. Atzerodt, to be hanged by the neck until he be dead, at such time and place as the President of the United States shall direct; two thirds of the Commission concurring therein.

Lewis Payne

After mature consideration of the evidence adduced in the case of the accused, Lewis Payne, the Commission find the said accused—

Of the Specification .... Guilty.

Except "combining, confederating, and conspiring with Edward Spangler"; of this .... Not Guilty.

Of the Charge .... Guilty.

Except "combining, confederating, and conspiring with Edward Spangler"; of this .... Not Guilty.

And the Commission do, therefore, sentence him, the said Lewis Payne, to be hanged by the neck until he be dead, at such time and place as the President of the United States shall direct; two thirds of the Commission concurring therein.

Mrs. Mary E. Surratt

After mature consideration of the evidence adduced in the case of the accused, Mary E. Surratt, the Commission find the said accused—

Of the Specification .... Guilty.
Except as to "receiving, sustaining, harboring, and concealing Samuel Arnold and Michael O'Laughlin," and except as to "combining, confederating, and conspiring with Edward Spangler";
of this .... Not Guilty.

Of the Charge .... Guilty.
Except as to "combining, confederating, and conspiring with Edward Spangler"; of this .... Not Guilty.

And the Commission do, therefore, sentence her, the said Mary E. Surratt, to be hanged by the neck until she be dead, at such time and place as the President of the United States shall direct; two thirds of the members of the Commission concurring therein.*

Michael O'Laughlin

After mature consideration of the evidence adduced in the case of the accused, Michael O'Laughlin, the Commission find the said accused—

Of the Specification .... Guilty.
Except the words thereof, "And in the further prosecution of the conspiracy aforesaid, and of its murderous and treasonable purposes aforesaid, on the nights of the 13th and 14th of April 1865, at Washington City, and within the Military Department and military lines aforesaid, the said Michael O'Laughlin did there and then lie in wait for Ulysses S. Grant, then Lieutenant-General and Commander of the Armies of the United States, with intent there and then to kill and murder the said Ulysses S. Grant"; of said words Not Guilty; and except "combining, confederating, and conspiring with Edward Spangler";
of this .... Not Guilty.

Of the Charge .... Guilty.
Except "combining, confederating, and conspiring with Edward Spangler"; of this .... Not Guilty.

The Commission do, therefore, sentence the said Michael O'Laughlin to be imprisoned at hard labor for life, at such place as the President shall direct.

* I was informed by General Ekin in November 1865 that the vote in the case of Mrs. Surratt and the others who were sentenced to death was unanimous.

Edward Spangler

After mature consideration of the evidence adduced in the case of the accused, Edward Spangler, the Commission find the accused—

Of the Specification .... Not Guilty.

Except as to the words, "the said Edward Spangler, on said 14th day of April A.D. 1865, at about the same hour of that day, as aforesaid, within said Military Department and the military lines aforesaid, did aid and abet him (meaning John Wilkes Booth) in making his escape after the said Abraham Lincoln had been murdered in the manner aforesaid"; and of these words .... Guilty.

Of the Charge .... Not Guilty.

But of having feloniously and traitorously aided and abetted John Wilkes Booth in making his escape after having killed and murdered Abraham Lincoln, President of the United States, he, the said Edward Spangler, at the time of aiding and abetting as aforesaid, well knowing that the said Abraham Lincoln, President as aforesaid, had been murdered by the said John Wilkes Booth, as aforesaid.................Guilty.

The Commission do, therefore, sentence the said Edward Spangler to be imprisoned at hard labor for six years, at such place as the President shall direct.

Samuel Arnold

After mature consideration of the evidence adduced in the case of the accused, Samuel Arnold, the Commission find the said accused—

Of the Specification .... Guilty.

Except "combining, confederating, and conspiring with Edward Spangler"; of this .... Not Guilty.

Of the Charge .... Guilty.

Except "combining, confederating, and conspiring with Edward Spangler"; of this .... Not Guilty.

The Commission do, therefore, sentence the said Samuel Arnold to imprisonment at hard labor for life, at such place as the President shall direct.

Samuel A. Mudd

After mature consideration of the evidence adduced in the case of the accused, Samuel A. Mudd, the Commission find the said accused—

Of the Specification .... Guilty.

Except "combining, confederating, and conspiring with Edward Spangler"; of this .... Not Guilty.
and excepting "receiving, entertaining, and harboring and concealing said Lewis Payne, John H. Surratt, Michael O'Laughlin, George A. Atzerodt, Mary E. Surratt, and Samuel Arnold";

of this .... Not Guilty.

Of the Charge .... Guilty.

Except "combining, confederating, and conspiring with Edward Spangler"; of this .... Not Guilty.

The Commission do, therefore, sentence the said Samuel A. Mudd to be imprisoned at hard labor for life, at such place as the President shall direct.

Prior to the adjournment of the Commission, at the suggestion of General James A. Ekin, a memorial was prepared and signed by five members of the court, a majority, addressed to the President of the United States, recommending that on account of the age and sex of Mrs. Surratt, the sentence which the Commission was constrained to render in her case from the testimony presented, be commuted from death to imprisonment for life if the Chief Executive, in considering the case, could, in his judgment, so determine.

The petition was worded as follows:

To the President: The undersigned, members of the military commission appointed to try the persons charged with the murder of Abraham Lincoln, etc., respectfully represent that the commission have been constrained to find Mary E. Surratt guilty, upon the testimony, of the assassination of Abraham Lincoln, late President of the United States, and to pronounce upon her, as required by law, the sentence of death; but, in consideration of her age and sex, the undersigned pray your Excellency, if it is consistent with your sense of duty, to commute her sentence to imprisonment for life in the penitentiary.[2]

It was signed by Generals Hunter, Kautz, Foster, Ekin, and Colonel Tompkins. Four members of the Commission declined to sign it.

This memorial, copied in the handwriting of General Ekin, was before the dissolution of the court attached to its official proceedings and forms a part of the record on file in the Judge Advocate General's office.

When the record was received at the Bureau of Military Justice the recommendation to mercy in the case of Mrs. Surratt was upon the last leaf of the mass of foolscap, and when Judge Holt made his report to the President, which was not long, it followed after.

Judge Holt himself carried the entire record to the President, including the recommendation for commutation of sentence.

The President, after due consideration of the important matter laid before him, issued the following order in approval of the sentences as promulgated by the Commission, and directing them to be carried out:

Executive Mansion, July 5, 1865.

The foregoing sentences in the cases of David E. Herold, G. A. Atzerodt, Lewis Payne, Michael O'Laughlin, Edward Spangler, Samuel Arnold, Mary E. Surratt, and Samuel A. Mudd are hereby approved, and it is ordered that the sentences of said David E. Herold, G. A. Atzerodt, Lewis Payne, and Mary E. Surratt be carried into execution by the proper military authority, under the direction of the Secretary of War, on the 7th day of July 1865, between the hours of 10 o'clock A.M. and 2 o'clock P.M., of that day. It is further ordered that the prisoners, Samuel Arnold, Samuel A. Mudd, Edward Spangler, and Michael O'Laughlin be confined at hard labor in the Penitentiary at Albany, New York, during the period designated in their respective sentences.

Andrew Johnson,
President.[3]

Thereupon, in accordance with the President's order, the following instructions were issued by the War Department:

*War Department, Adjutant General's Office,
Washington, July 5, 1865.*

To Major-General W. S. Hancock, United States Volunteers, commanding the Middle Military Division, Washington, D.C.

Whereas by the Military Commission appointed in paragraph 4 Special Orders No. 211, dated War Department, Adjutant General's Office, Washington May 6, 1865, and of which Major-General David Hunter, United States Volunteers, was President, the following persons were tried, and, after mature consideration of evidence adduced in their cases, were found and sentenced as hereinafter stated, as follows:

(Here follow the findings and sentences in the case of David E. Herold, George A. Atzerodt, Lewis Payne, and Mary E. Surratt.)

And whereas, the President of the United States has approved the foregoing sentences: (Here follows the executive order above given.)

Therefore, you are hereby commanded to cause the foregoing sentences in the cases of David E. Herold, G. A. Atzerodt, Lewis Payne, and Mary E. Surratt, to be duly executed in accordance with the President's order.

By command of the President of the United States.

E. D. Townsend,

Assistant Adjutant General.[4]

On the morning of July 7, 1865, Messrs. Aiken and Clampitt made application to the Supreme Court of the United States for a writ of habeas corpus in behalf of Mrs. Surratt as follows:

Washington, D.C., July 6 [7], 1865.

To the Hon. Andrew Wylie, one of the
    Justices of the Supreme Court
    of the District of Columbia:

The petition of Mary E. Surratt, by her counsel, F. A. Aiken and John W. Clampitt, most respectfully represents unto your Honor, that on or about the 17th day of April, A.D. 1865, your petitioner was arrested by the military authorities of the United States, under the charge of complicity with the murder of Abraham Lincoln, late President of the United States, and has ever since that time been and is now confined on said charge, under and by virtue of the said military power of the United States, and is in special custody of Major-General W. S. Hancock, commanding Middle Military Division; that since her said arrest your petitioner has been tried, against her solemn protest, by a Military Commission, unlawfully and without warrant, convened by the Secretary of War, as will appear from paragraph 9, Special Orders, No. 211, dated War Department, Adjutant-General's Office, Washington, May the 6th, 1865, and by said Commission, notwithstanding her formal plea to the jurisdiction of the said Commission, is now unlawfully and unjustifiably detained in custody and sentenced to be hanged on to-morrow, July 7, 1865, between the hours of 10 A.M. and 2 P.M.; your petitioner shows unto your Honor that at the time of the commission of the said offense she was a private citizen of the United States, and in no manner connected with the military authority of the same, and that said offense was committed within the District of Columbia, said District being at the time within the lines of the armies of the United States, and not enemy's territory, or under the control of a military commander for the trial of civil causes. But, on the contrary your petitioner alleges that the said crime was an offense simply against the peace of the United States, properly and solely cognizable under the Constitution and laws of the United States, by the Criminal Court of this District, and which said court was and is now open for the trial of such crimes and offenses. Wherefore, inasmuch as the said crime was only an offense against the peace of the United States, and not an act of war; inasmuch as your petitioner was a private citizen of the same, and not subject to military jurisdiction, or in any wise amenable to military law; inasmuch as said District was a peaceful territory of the United States, and that all crimes committed within such territory are, under the Constitution and laws of the United States, to be tried [only] before its criminal tribunals, with the right of public trial by jury; inasmuch as said Commission was a Military Commission, organized and governed by the laws of military court-martial, and unlawfully convened without warrant or authority, and when she had not the right of public trial by jury as guaranteed to her by the Constitution and laws of the United States, that, therefore, her detention and sentence are so without warrant against positive law and unjustifiable; wherefore, she prays your Honor to grant unto her the United States' most gracious writ of *habeas corpus*, commanding the said Major-General W. S. Hancock to produce before your Honor the body of your said petitioner, with the cause and day of her said detention, to abide, etc., and she will ever pray.

Mary E. Surratt.

By Fredrick A. Aiken, John W. Clampitt.

Indorsed.—Let the writ issue as prayed, returnable before the Criminal Court of the District of Columbia now sitting, at the hour of 10 o'clock A.M. this 7th day of July, 1865.

Andrew Wylie,
A Justice of the Supreme Court of the
District of Columbia, July 7, 1865.[5]

This writ was served by U. S. Marshal David Gooding on General W. S. Hancock, Commanding Middle Military Division, who at half past eleven o'clock on the morning of the 7th of July, accompanied by Attorney

General Speed, appeared before Judge Wylie in obedience to the writ, and made the following return:

> *Headquarters Middle Military Division,*
> *Washington, D.C., July 7, 1865.*

To Hon. Andrew Wylie, Justice of the
Supreme Court of the District of Columbia:

I hereby acknowledge the service of the writ hereto attached and return the same, and respectfully, say that the body of Mary E. Surratt is in my possession, under and by virtue of an order of Andrew Johnson, President of the United States and Commander-in-Chief of the Army and Navy, for the purposes in said order expressed, a copy of which is hereto attached and made part of this return; and that I do not produce said body by reason of the order of the President of the United States, indorsed upon said writ, to which reference is hereby respectfully made; dated July 7th, 1865.

> W. S. Hancock.
> Maj.-Gen. U. S. Vols., Commanding Middle Division.

> *Executive Office, July 7, 1865, 10 A.M.*

To Major-General W. S. Hancock,
Commander (etc.):

I, Andrew Johnson, President of the United States, do hereby declare that the writ of *habeas corpus* has been heretofore suspended in such cases as this, and I do hereby especially suspend this writ, and direct that you proceed to execute the order heretofore given upon the judgement of the Military Commission, and you will give this order in return to the writ.

> Andrew Johnson, President.

The court ruled that it yielded to the suspension of the writ of habeas corpus by the President of the United States.[6]

This action on the part of President Johnson, in suspending the writ of habeas corpus issued in behalf of Mrs. Surratt, terminated all legal proceedings in her case, and nothing now remained but an appeal to the heart and tender mercies of the President.

During all this time Miss Anna Surratt had made most strenuous efforts in behalf of her mother. On the morning of the day fixed for the execution, accompanied by a gentleman friend, she called on General Hancock at his hotel, and asked him what she could do to save the life of her mother, to which the General replied that there was but one way left and "that was to go to the President, throw herself upon her knees before him, and beg the life of her mother."

Miss Surratt then hastened to the Executive Mansion, but the President was inexorable, and had given the sternest commands that he would not be interviewed by anyone in behalf of the condemned. He did not and would not see Miss Surratt.

Father Jacob Walter, Mrs. Surratt's confessor, also made an effort to get the ear of the President, but was equally unsuccessful.[7]

When Miss Surratt found that she could not have access to President Johnson, she endeavored to have General Mussey, his private secretary, secure an audience for her. That gentleman received her most courteously, but gently informed her that it was impossible for him to do anything with the President, as he had given positive orders not to admit anyone to his presence.

Miss Surratt spent the night before the execution with her mother in her cell, and the final separation between them on the following morning was very sad and affecting.

Two of Herold's sisters, on the same day, went to the office of the Bureau of Military Justice, waited until Judge Holt arrived, and then pleaded earnestly with him to save their brother's life. He told them that it was out of his power to interfere, and referred them to the President. They left the office weeping bitterly, and then the Judge took his departure and did not return during the day.

The place fixed for the execution was in the old Arsenal grounds. On the top of the wall, at the right of the enclosure, in which the scaffold had been erected, a single sentinel paced back and forth, his gun and equipment glistening in the sunlight. The day was excessively hot and those who had been permitted to attend waited patiently until the last religious services with the condemned persons should be concluded.

At length there was a stir in the building where the accused were, and then the procession came out and slowly made its way to the scaffold, which was ascended, and the condemned were placed in the following order: Atzerodt on the extreme left, then Herold, next Payne, and lastly Mrs. Surratt. Atzerodt was accompanied by Rev. J. George Butler, pastor of St. Paul's Lutheran Church of Washington, Herold by Rev. Mr. Olds of the Episcopal Church, and Payne by Rev. Dr. Gillette of the Baptist Church.

Mrs. Surratt was attended by Father Walter and Father Wigget of the Catholic Church, who stood on either side of her and held a crucifix, which she kissed. She was so weak that a chair was placed for her.

Payne looked bold and defiant. The closely fitting sailor suit he wore set off his robust figure to advantage. Herold seemed thoroughly dazed by the situation, while Atzerodt was absolutely quaking with fear.

There were not many spectators present, the number of passes being limited, and these were mostly confined to army officers and representatives of the press. Of all those who were present there was scarcely a single individual, with perhaps the exception of the officers who had charge of the execution, who did not believe or hope that a reprieve would come for Mrs. Surratt.

Every moment heads were turned to the rear as if expecting to see a messenger with an order for a stay of execution in her case. General Hancock had caused couriers with relays of swift horses to be stationed between the White House and the Arsenal so that if the President would relent, the news could with the greatest speed be brought to him, but the President was as firm as the hills.

The execution and all its details were under the direction of General Hancock, who had ordered General Hartranft to carry them into effect.

When the supreme hour arrived, both these officers stood in front of the scaffold. After the President's order for the execution had been read by General Hartranft the clergymen left Mrs. Surratt, the chair was taken away.

General Hartranft then gave the final signal, there was a moment of painful silence on the part of those assembled, broken only by the blows of the soldiers underneath the scaffold, as they knocked the pin from the trap, and then, at [1:26] P.M.,[8] four bodies swung into the air and the law was vindicated. Only one attempted to say anything and that was Atzerodt. Just before the trap was sprung he cried out: "Gentlemen, take war—" Probably he intended to say "take warning," but the sentence was finished in eternity.

The bodies remained suspended thirty minutes, were then cut down, and buried in the penitentiary grounds. Here they remained until February 1869, when by an order of the Executive they were given over to the families of the deceased. Booth's body was taken to Baltimore and interred in Greenmount Cemetery, and Mrs. Surratt's remains were laid to rest in Mount Olivet at Washington, the burying grounds of the Catholics of that city.

After the execution the remaining conspirators, Dr. Mudd, Arnold, O'Laughlin, and Spangler, were placed on board a gunboat destined for the Dry Tortugas. This barren island, situated off the southwestern coast of Florida, was reached in the latter part of July 1865.[9]

CHAPTER XXV

The conclusions of the Commission endorsed by the people · Exception to the verdict against Mrs. Surratt · Persecution of members of the Commission in consequence · The suicide story in relation to Mr. Stanton · Assails on Generals Hancock and Hartranft · Important letters from General Hartranft and Frederick Aiken · Careers of Judge Advocates Bingham and Burnett

The verdict of the Commission against the conspirators was accepted as an eminently just one by the people everywhere, a fact that has only been strengthened by the course of events since the close of the great trial.

There was, however, a very notable exception in the case of Mrs. Surratt. No sooner had the decree of the Commission with reference to her been carried into effect by the approval and order of the President than a great outcry was raised in Washington and other sections of the country by those sympathizing with the rebellion and by certain elements in the church of which she was a member, that the Government had executed an innocent woman. Everyone who had in any way been connected with the case—the President, Andrew Johnson, the Secretary of War, Edwin M. Stanton, the Judge Advocate General, J. Holt, the two assistant Judge Advocates, Bingham and Burnett, the Marshal of the

Court, General John F. Hartranft, the commandant of the Middle Division of the Army, General W. S. Hancock, the members of the Commission, the witnesses for the prosecution—were all denounced in the most violent language and characterized as perjurers, murderers, and executioners.

For several years in many of the states, notably in the South, severe resolutions were passed by the Democratic party in its conventions denouncing trial by military commission and reprobating the use of the military power, in such cases.

It appears that Mrs. Surratt, just before leaving her cell, when the soldiers came to take her away for the final scene, had turned to Father Walter and is alleged to have said, "Father, I wish to say something." "Well, what is it, my child?" "That I am innocent." [1]

On these words, and they are the only ones she is said to have left behind her, the whole fabric of her alleged innocence has been constructed, and from this has sprung a persecution which for falsehood, abuse, invention, and slander has not had its counterpart in American history.

It will not be inappropriate in the closing pages of this book to review this phase of her case and to prove the utter falsity of the allegations made in her behalf. The very fact that her friends and defenders have been compelled to resort to such arguments and assertions is in itself the fullest exposure of the weakness of her cause. Failing utterly to destroy the strong array of facts proven against her by sworn testimony, which has never been impeached, they have endeavored to accomplish their purpose by mendacious statements of the most infamous nature, and by the defamation of the characters of honorable men.

As time wore on, every now and then a report would appear in certain newspapers that some member of the Commission had died of some dread disease, or had come to a sudden and ignoble end. The reverse of all this is true. It is a remarkable fact that there was not an officer who was connected with the Commission who has not lived to a ripe old age, and whose career in life has not been covered with honor, and, in some instances, with world-wide fame. General David Hunter, the President of the Court was the first to pass away; he died in Washington in 1887 at the advanced age of eighty-two.[2] The second officer to answer the final roll call was General James A. Ekin in Louisville, Kentucky, in 1891 at the age of seventy-two.[3] Then followed General A. V. Kautz [4] and Colonel David R. Clendenin,[5] as they were verging toward their seventieth year, and General A. P. Howe, the great artillery officer, paid his final debt to nature in Cambridge, Massachusetts, in the spring of 1897, in his seventy-ninth year.[6]

Of the other officers of the Commission, General T. M. Harris of Harrisville, West Virginia, still abides in the land of the living and is in his eighty-fourth year.[7] It has been his good fortune to write a history of the assassination of Lincoln which should command the perusal of every loyal American citizen.

General Lew Wallace, the hero of two wars, Mexico and the Great Rebellion, has passed his seventieth milestone, and is fast approaching the great and final boundary line.[8] This distinguished man, as the author of *Ben Hur* and other writings, has attained a fame second to none. His memory will last as long as the noble English language, the language of Milton and Burke, shall be spoken. When President Garfield selected him as his minister to Turkey, before giving him his commission, as a testimony of his own warm feeling, he wrote across the face of it in bold letters "Ben Hur." The general is now passing his old age in happiness and contentment, at his beautiful home in Crawfordsville, Indiana.

General R. S. Foster, another veteran, was for many years U. S. marshal of Indiana and resides at Indianapolis in that state; he is still actively engaged in business and has the esteem and love of all his fellow citizens and of those who knew him best.[9]

Colonel C. H. Tompkins makes his home in Washington. He is on the retired Army list. His record in the Army during his term of service has always been a distinguished and honorable one.[10]

President Johnson, although he had signed Mrs. Surratt's death warrant, and had been vigorously denounced by the Democratic party in all sections of the country for his action, was by that same party elected United States senator from Tennessee, which position he held until his death in Greenville, Tennessee, in 1874.[11]

The Secretary of War, Mr. Stanton, was in December 1869 nominated by President Grant to be one of the justices of the Supreme Court. When this occurred, he was confined to his home by sickness. On the day before Christmas, he died.[12] Straightway from the same sources which had traduced the Military Commission, the story was started that he had committed suicide because of remorse for the punishment of Mrs. Surratt. This was published and circulated from one end of the country to the other, and by none with greater pertinacity than by James Mc-Masters of the New York *Freeman's Journal*. In a Catholic paper published in Cincinnati, Mr. Stanton was styled "Maledictus" Stanton, accursed Edwin Stanton.

This slander about suicide had a run of ten years, and it was given out with such an assurance of truth that many people came to believe it, and only after the beloved partner of his life and his eldest son had gone to their last rest, then and not until then, did Surgeon General Barnes, whose hand rested on Stanton's heart, and who had felt the last throb of the great Secretary's blood, put a quietus to the infamous story and squeezed the life out of it forever.

In 1879 in answer to a letter from Mr. Edwin McPherson, the editor of the *Philadelphia Press*, General Barnes wrote as follows:

Washington, D.C. April 16th, 1879.

Hon. Edwin McPherson, Philadelphia.

Dear Sir: In reply to your inquiry, the late Mr. Edwin M. Stanton was for many years subject to asthma in a very severe form, and when he retired from the War Department, was completely broken down in health. In November of 1869 the "Dropsy of Cardiac Disease" manifested itself (after a very exhausting argument in chambers, in a legal case), and from that time he did not leave the house, rarely his bed. For many days before his death I was with him almost constantly, and at no time was he without most careful attendance by the members of his family or nurses. On the night of December 23rd the dropsical effusion into the pericardium had increased to such an extent, and the symptoms were so alarming, that the Rev. Doctor Starkey, rector of the Epiphany, was summoned and read the service appointed for such occasions; he, with Mrs. Stanton, Mr. E. L. Stanton, the three younger children, Miss Bowie, their governess, myself and several of the servants were by his bedside until he died at 4 A.M. December 24, 1869. After the pulse became imperceptible at the wrist I placed a finger on the carotid artery, afterwards my hand over his heart, and when its action ceased I announced it to those present.

It is incomprehensible to me how any suspicion or report of suicide could have originated, except through sheer and intentional malice, as there was not the slightest incident before, or during, his long sickness, indicative of such a tendency, nor a possibility of such an act. Fully aware of his critical condition, he was calm and composed, not wishing to die, while unterrified at the prospect of death. During the lifetime of his widow and his son, Mr. E. L. Stanton, I did not feel called upon to make any written contradiction of the infamous and malignant falsehood you allude to; but now, in view of your letter of April 14th, and in behalf of Mr. Stanton's minor children, I do most emphatically and unequivocally assert that there is not any foundation whatever for the report that Mr. Edwin Stanton died from other than natural causes, or that he attempted or committed suicide.

Very respectfully yours,

Jos. K. Barnes, M.D.

And thus the suicide story passed to the region of infamy where it belonged and in which it had its birth.

General Hancock was for many years after the execution of the conspirators comparatively free from criticism and attack for the part he took in the affair, but when in 1880 he became the nominee of the Democratic party for the presidency of the United States, the floodgates of abuse were at once opened upon him. The charge was made that he had been guilty of cruelty to Mrs. Surratt, to her daughter, Anna, and to Father J. A. Walter, her spiritual adviser and confessor, in preventing them from seeing the President.

It was said that rather than have obeyed the order of the President in suspending the writ of habeas corpus and assisting in the execution, he should have taken his sword, broken it in twain, and resigned his position in the Army. These stories were retailed with great persistency and cruelty, and were probably the cause of the loss of many votes to General Hancock among the members of his own party.

The charges, however, were shown to be false and by the very parties most interested and incessant in their allegations that Mrs. Surratt was an innocent woman.

In a letter written by Mr. J. W. Clampitt, one of Mrs. Surratt's counsel, and the sole survivor, at the present writing, at Highland Park, Lake County, Illinois, dated July 22, 1880, and addressed to the Honorable W. T. Bartlett, Washington, D.C., that gentleman, after reviewing the order constituting the Military Commission, its findings, approval thereof, and subsequent suspension of the writ of habeas corpus in the case of Mrs. Surratt by President Johnson, says, among other things: *

"From the official proceedings it will be observed that General Hancock had nothing whatever to do with the organization of this Military Commission, nor was he in the slightest degree responsible for its organization, or the execution of its mandates; nor did he possess any discretion in the matters relating thereto in any degree whatsoever.

"It is true that the order of the President directing the execution of the condemned parties was transmitted through the commandant of the military post of Major-General Hartranft, who had been designated by the President in Executive Order, dated May 1, 1865 (as a special Provost Marshal), for the purpose of said trial and attendance upon said commission and the execution of its mandates. It could have not been otherwise in feature and form, from the very nature of the military organization of the government and its regulations and rules of procedure.

"General Hancock was in command of a geographical Military Division, comprising several states, of which Washington City, where his headquarters had been located by the President's order, was a part at the time Mrs. Surratt was sentenced to death. Being chief in command of that Military Division, the order of the President, through the War Department, had inevitably to pass through him for the transmission to the officer designated by the same authority (Ex Order, May 1, 1865) to execute the mandates of the Commission that condemned Mrs. Surratt to death.

"It is a notable fact that Brevet Major-General Hartranft and not Major-General Hancock, gave the verbal order of execution, after first reading, while standing on the platform beside the prisoners, the findings of the Military Commission and the President's order of approval. In this General Hartranft performed his duty as the subordinate officer of the President from whom he had derived his powers as Provost Marshal. The functions of General Hancock were purely ministerial as the 'Commandant of the Miltary Post' etc., and not judicial, and he took no part in the execution. The act, which was performed in obedience to an order of the President, was not Hancock's act, but the act of his superior having power to command.

* The letter referred to was published in full in a campaign life of General Hancock by Mr. Bartlett.

"It has been suggested that General Hancock should have resigned rather than have been the passing medium through which the order for the execution was transmitted. There can be no weight in that suggestion. He was in command of the post, and had many diversified duties and responsibilities to perform; and no soldier, no citizen in fact, can properly avoid the performance of his duty by deserting the post to which that duty belongs, on account of the order of a superior over whom he has no control.

"No officer of the army has the right to resign his commission at his own pleasure, as every intelligent citizen knows. He may tender it but it remains with the government to accept, when, and how it pleases. The 24th paragraph, Art. 5, of the United States Army Regulations, says:

'That any officer, who, having tendered his resignation, shall, prior to due notice of the acceptance of the same by the proper authority, and without leave, quit his post, or proper duties, with the intent to remain permanently absent therefrom, shall be registered as a deserter and punished as such.'

"In this instance, General Hancock retained his post and performed his duty.

"As the counsel of Mrs. Surratt, I can testify of my own knowledge, that he was deeply moved in her behalf, and distressed on her account.

"As to the point, whether, on the morning of the execution of Mrs. Surratt, he refused the privilege of having the spiritual consolation of her religion, by denying her the assistance of a priest, this charge I know to be untrue and it is effectually refuted by the testimony of the Rev. J. A. Walter, her spiritual adviser, which has come to my knowledge. This testimony is in the form of a letter addressed by Father Walter to General Hancock, dated Washington, Nov. 14th, 1879, which has been published, in which he completely refutes the charge. I quote that portion of his letter as follows:

'I am at loss how to account for this malicious report. I have always believed you to be too much of a Christian and gentleman to suppose for a moment that you would interfere with one's religious feelings, much less in the case of the unfortunate lady for whom you showed much sympathy. Duty which I owe to truth, and in strict

290

accordance and justice to you, compel me to deny these false charges, and exonerate you from all blame.'

"As to the charge that General Hancock refused to obey the writ of habeas corpus, sued by me as the counsel of Mrs. Surratt before Judge Wylie, I know this to be wholly groundless. The records of the Court show that on the morning of the execution, upon proper application at the early hour of two o'clock, Judge Wylie with characteristic firmness issued the writ of habeas corpus, ordering the Commandant of the Military District in which she was confined to produce the body of Mrs. Surratt in his court at ten o'clock (the hour of execution having been named in the order as between ten A.M. and two o'clock P.M.). This writ was handed me by the Marshal of the District of Columbia, at a very early hour in the morning. It is a fact sustained by the records of the Court, that General Hancock appeared in obedience to that summons before his Honor Judge Wylie accompanied by the Attorney-General of the United States, who, as the representative of the President, presented to Judge Wylie the executive order suspending the writ of habeas corpus.

"It is thus seen that the charge that General Hancock refused to obey the writ issued by Judge Wylie was false. The very reverse is the truth. Not only did he obey the writ, so far as he was permitted to do so, thus subordinating the military to the civil power of the government, but so prompt and clear was the performance of his duty, in the estimation of the Court, that Judge Wylie complimented him on his ready obedience to the civil authority, and discharged him from the process because of his own inability to enforce the order of the Court.

"The question asked in newspaper discussions, why General Hancock was present at the Arsenal on the morning of the execution, is easily answered. The application for a pardon for Mrs. Surratt was expected to be renewed that morning, and that on his own suggestion; and he deemed it proper to be at a convenient place to afford his aid in case of a pardon.

"The facts show that so deeply was General Hancock moved in the matter, that his feelings led him to believe it possible for the President to relent at the last moment; and should the President so act, that the reprieve might not arrive too late, but be borne swiftly on its mission of mercy, General Hancock had couriers stationed at points from the White House to the Arsenal, in order that if a pardon or respite should be issued by the President, at the last moment, it should reach its destination promptly and before the execution. This is the evidence of Gen. W. G. Mitchell, Chief of General Hancock's staff.

"This evidence is corroborated by the sworn testimony of Mr. John P. Brophy, now at St. Louis College, N.Y., and at the same time a resident of Washington City. Mr. Brophy was a friend of the family and after the imprisonment of the mother he be-friended the daughter, Anna. On the morning of the execution he met her at the Executive Mansion in the hope of seeing the President, whither she had gone at the suggestion of General Hancock to beg the life of her mother.[13] Mr. Brophy, who did all in his power to befriend the helpless girl in her sorrowful condition and who is a gentleman of high character, testified, under oath, as to the humanity displayed by General Hancock towards the unfortunate mother and daughter, on the morning of the execution. The following are extracts from Mr. Brophy's sworn statement:

" 'On our way from the White House to the Arsenal, I noticed mounted soldiers at intervals along the route.' These were the couriers, stationed by order of General Hancock, to convey to him any notice of reprieve by the President. At the Arsenal gate, he, accompanying Anna Surratt to bid her mother farewell, met General Hancock, who spoke to Anna, and, in a voice of subdued sadness, told her that he feared there was no hope of Executive clemency.

"Mr. Brophy further states that he is 'impelled by a sense of duty to add his testimony to others in vindication of one who has been assailed for alleged misconduct of which no brave man could be guilty. That he is not a politician, but loves justice, and feels that he has done an act of simple justice to as knightly a warrior as ever saluted with his spotless sword the sacred majesty of the law.' "

General Hancock was not elected President, but he received the full vote of his party; in fact, a larger vote than heretofore received for the same high office by any candidate of the Democratic party. He died at Governor's Island, New York, in 1887.[14]

General [J.] F. Hartranft was another officer who was destined to experience, in his own person, the indignity and horror of this most atrocious persecution. Shortly after the trial, he resigned his position in the Army and returned to private life in his native state, Pennsylvania. In the fall of 1865 he was nominated and elected by the Republicans as their choice for state auditor. He was renominated in 1868 and re-elected. In 1871, the nomination of governor was conferred upon him, and he was successful at the polls by a tremendous majority. This was repeated in 1874. In all these campaigns, he was bitterly assailed for the part he took in the trial and execution of the assassins, and especially of Mrs. Surratt. He was denounced in the most outrageous and malignant manner, but what the people of Pennsylvania thought of him was shown in the splendid vote and majorities which they gave him whenever a candidate for their suffrages.

In 1876, he was presented by his party in the National Convention held at Cincinnati as its candidate for the nomination for President of the United States.

Upon the expiration of his term as governor of Pennsylvania, he was appointed Postmaster of Philadelphia, and subsequently Collector of Customs in that city. This latter position he held until relieved by President Cleveland in 1885.

His life was always full of honor to himself and credit to his country. He died in 1890, and a beautiful monument now rests over his remains at his home in Norristown, Pennsylvania, as a mute and eloquent tribute of the love and esteem in which he was held by his fellow citizens and by his state.[15]

A vile story was put into circulation that Mrs. Surratt during her trial had been treated unkindly and inhumanly, in fact, had been tortured and manacled. This slander was even repeated in so respectable a journal as the *New York Tribune* in September [2,] 1873, in a communication addressed to that paper by Mr. John T. Ford, proprietor of Ford's Theater, under the caption of "Truth." It met with a prompt response on the part of Judge Holt on September 9, 1873, who submitted the following letter from General Hartranft as full and authentic information on the subject:

Executive Chamber,
Harrisburg, Penn., Sept. 4, 1873.

Gen. Joseph Holt, Washington, D.C.—Dear Sir: My attention having been directed to a letter dated Washington, Aug. 29, 1873, and signed "Truth," that appeared in the *New York Tribune* a few days since, I think it proper, in justice to you, to declare publicly that its statements, so far as they relate to occurrences within my own observation, are absolute falsehoods.

As Marshal of the Court before whom the conspirators were tried, I had charge of Mrs. Surratt before, during and after the time of her trial, in all a period of about two months; during which she never had a manacle or manacles on either hands or feet; and the thought of manacling her was not, to my knowledge, ever entertained by any one of authority.

During the pendency of the trial I made application to the Secretary of War for permission to remove her from the cell to a comfortably furnished room adjoining the court-room, and for her daughter Anna to occupy the room with her, that she might attend to her wants. This request was granted. She was so removed; her daughter occupied the room with her, and Mrs. Surratt was fully provided for according to her needs and tastes.

A few days after her death, Miss Anna Surratt, by letter, thanked me for the kind treatment her mother and herself had received from myself and officers.

You will perhaps remember the name of the young priest who visited Mrs. Surratt so frequently, and which has escaped me. He will certify to her proper treatment and to the falsity of the statements of "Truth."

I have the honor to be your obedient servant,

J. F. Hartranft.

As illustrating still further the malicious misrepresentation in reference to this matter, the following letter from one of Mrs. Surratt's counsel which was brought out by the *Washington Chronicle* in answer to some statements put forth by one Mrs. Swisshelm in the *New York Tribune* of September 16, 1873, is also given:

Washington, D.C., 1047 F. St.,
September 17, 1873.

To the Editor of the Chronicle:

I have your letter of this date, enclosing the letter of Jane G. Swisshelm, published in the Tribune (N.Y.), the 16th inst., and asking me, "Is her statement true that Mrs. Surratt was manacled during her trial?" Without reference to any other fact or to any of the details of the case of that most unfortunate lady, I have to say in reply that at no time during her unlawful trial was Mrs. Surratt manacled, either on her wrists or her ankles, while in the presence of the Court. I not only speak from my own absolute knowledge, but from recollection of Mrs. Surratt's oft-repeated statements to me that she was not manacled.

Yours very truly,

Frederick A. Aiken.[16]

Judge Bingham, the able Special Judge Advocate of the Commission, also came in for his share of abuse and persecution, but was always, to any issue growing out of the case which confronted him, able to defend himself. His whole career subsequent to the trial of the assassination is filled with renown and lustre. For a number of years he was representative in Congress from his district in the state of Ohio. When President Johnson was impeached, he was chosen chairman by the managers who had been selected by the House of Representatives to present to the Senate the case of the people against the President. When his service in Congress had ceased, he was appointed by General Grant as United States minister to Japan, which position he filled with much credit, and which he retained until the accession of Mr. Cleveland to the presidency. He is now spending in happy repose the evening of an honored and well-spent life at his home in Cadiz, Ohio, at the advanced age of eighty-two years.[17]

General H. L. Burnett, the junior Judge Advocate of the court, after the trial was ended, returned to his home in Cincinnati, Ohio, but subsequently moved to New York City, where he established a lucrative business in the law and was for a long time the head of one of the largest law firms in that city. He is now the United States District Attorney for the Southern District of New York.[18]

CHAPTER XXVI

THE CONTROVERSY
BETWEEN PRESIDENT JOHNSON AND JUDGE HOLT

A paper read by General Henry L. Burnett, late U.S.V., at a Meeting of the Commandery, State of New York, Military Order, Loyal Legion, April 3, 1889 [1]

Perhaps no incident connected with the trial of the assassins of President Lincoln created more general interest—was so much discussed and commented upon by the public press, or aroused deeper feeling of antagonism and bitterness between two public men—than the charge by President Johnson that the Judge-Advocate-General, Judge Holt, had withheld or suppressed the recommendation to mercy of Mrs. Surratt signed by five members of the commission, when he presented to him, the President, the record for his official action. While this charge had circulation and was asserted in the press during the time Mr. Johnson was occupying the presidential office, Mr. Johnson never openly made the charge until after his term had expired, some time in 1873.

No graver charge could be made against a public officer than this against Judge Holt, and, if true, no more cruel and treacherous betrayal of a public trust was ever committed by a man in high official position. It would be murderous in intent and effect. This charge rested, so far as human testimony went, upon the solemn assertion alone of President Johnson, and, if untrue, was one of the most cruel wrongs ever perpetrated by one man against another. I propose to give a brief abstract of the testimony produced by Judge Holt to disprove this charge, and also a statement of my connection with, and what little personal knowledge I had of, the matter.

In a communication addressed to the *Washington Chronicle*, dated August 25, 1873, Judge Holt gives a copy of a letter addressed by him to the Secretary of War, on the 14th of that month, in which he sets forth evidence tending to disprove the charge originating with Andrew Johnson, of his suppression of the petition, signed by five of the nine members of the commission, recommending, in consideration of her age and sex, a commutation of the death sentence of Mary E. Surratt to imprisonment for life in the penitentiary. The petition read as follows:

> To the President: The undersigned, members of the military commission appointed to try the persons charged with the murder of Abraham Lincoln, etc., respectfully represent that the commission have been constrained to find Mary E. Surratt guilty, upon the testimony, of the assassination of Abraham Lincoln, late President of the United States, and to pronounce upon her, as required by law, the sentence of death; but, in consideration of her age and sex, the undersigned pray your Excellency, if it is consistent with your sense of duty, to commute her sentence to imprisonment for life in the penitentiary.

In a letter dated February 11, 1873, addressed to Hon. John A. Bingham, one of the special Judge Advocates during the trial, Judge Holt states:

> In the discharge of my duty when presenting that record to President Johnson, I drew his attention to that recommendation, and he read it in my presence, and before approving the proceedings and sentence. He and I were together alone when this duty on his part and on mine was performed. . . . The President and myself having, as already stated, been alone at the time, I have not been able to obtain any positive proof on the point, although I have been able to collect circumstantial evidence enough to satisfy any unbiased mind that the recommendation was seen and considered by the President, when he examined and approved the proceedings and sentence of the Court. Still, in a matter so deeply affecting my reputation and official honor, I am naturally desirous of having the testimony in my possession strengthened as far as practicable, and hence it is that I trouble you with this note. While I know that the question of extending to Mrs. Surratt the clemency sought by the petition was considered by the President at the time mentioned, I have, in view of its gravity, been always satisfied that it must have been considered by the Cabinet also; but from the confidential character of Cabi-

net deliberations I have thus far been denied access to this source of information.

He then proceeds to inquire whether or not he (Judge Bingham) had any conversation with Secretary Seward or Mr. Stanton in reference to this petition, and if so to please give him as nearly as he (Judge Bingham) could, all that Secretary Seward or Mr. Stanton had said upon the subject.

Judge Bingham replied under date of February 17, 1873, and among other things said:

Before the President had acted upon the case, I deemed it my duty to call the attention of Secretary Stanton to the petition for the commutation of sentence upon Mrs. Surratt, and did call his attention to it, before the final decision of the President. After the execution, the statement that you refer to was made that President Johnson had not seen the petition for the commutation of the death-sentence upon Mrs. Surratt. I afterward called at your office, and, without notice to you of my purpose, asked for the record of the case of the assassins; it was opened and shown me, and there was then attached to it the petition, copied and signed as hereinbefore stated. Soon thereafter I called upon Secretaries Stanton and Seward and asked if this petition had been presented to the President before the death-sentence was by him approved, and was answered by each of those gentlemen that the petition was presented to the President, and was duly considered by him and his advisers before the death-sentence upon Mrs. Surratt was approved, and that the President and Cabinet, upon such consideration, were a unit denying the prayer of the petition; Mr. Stanton and Mr. Seward stating that they were present. . . .

Having ascertained the fact as stated, I then desired to make the same public, and so expressed myself to Mr. Stanton, who advised me not to do so, but to rely upon the final judgment of the people.

In replying to this letter, Judge Holt very justly remarks:

It would have been very fortunate for me indeed could I have had this testimony in my possession years ago. Mr. Stanton's advice to you was, under all the circumstances of the case, most extraordinary. . . .

This asking you "to rely upon the final judgment of the people," and at the same time withholding from them the proof on which the judgment—to be just—must be formed, was a sad, sad mockery.

The next is a letter from ex-Attorney General Speed, dated March 30, 1875, in which he says:

After the finding of the military commission that tried the assassins of Mr. Lincoln and before their execution, I saw the record of the case in the President's office, and attached to it was a paper, signed by some of the members of the commission, recommending that the sentence against Mrs. Surratt be commuted to imprisonment for life; and, according to my memory, the recommendation was made because of her sex.

I do not feel at liberty to speak of what was said at Cabinet meetings. In this I know I differ from other gentlemen, but feel constrained to follow my own sense of propriety.

So that it is most clear from this statement of Attorney General Speed, unless he without interest or motive stated a most deliberate falsehood, that Judge Holt did *not* "withhold" or "suppress" the recommendation to mercy, but carried it with the record and *"attached to it,"* as Mr. Speed says, and delivered it in the President's office. Certainly every intelligent mind will concede that this testimony of Mr. Speed utterly disposes of the charge of Andrew Johnson that Judge Holt "suppressed" or "withheld" this recommendation to mercy. If Mr. Johnson did not see it or read it when in his office, that was his neglect, his failure to perform a solemn official duty. But on this question of his having *read* and *considered* it, how stands the evidence? Judge Holt states that he drew his attention to it, and that Mr. Johnson read it in his presence. Judge Bingham says both Mr. Stanton and Mr. Seward stated to him that this petition had been presented to the President and was duly considered by him and his advisers before the death sentence upon Mrs. Surratt was approved. Under date of May 27, 1873, James Harlan,[2] a former member of Mr. Johnson's Cabinet, addressed a letter to Judge Holt, in which he said:

After the sentence and before the execution of Mrs. Surratt, I remember distinctly the discussion of the question of the commutation of the sentence of death pronounced on her by the Court to imprisonment for life and by members of the Cabinet in presence of President Johnson. I cannot state positively whether this occurred at a regular or a called meeting, or whether it was at an accidental meeting of several members, each calling on the President in relation to the business of his own department. The impression on my mind is, that the only discussion of the subject by members of the Cabinet which I ever heard occurred in the last-named mode, there being not more than three or four members present—Mr. Seward, Mr. Stanton, and myself, and probably Attorney-General Speed, and others —but I distinctly remember only the first two. When I entered the room, one of these was addressing the President in an earnest conversation on the question whether the sentence ought to be modified on account of the sex of the condemned. I can recite the precise thought, if not the very words, used by this eminent statesman, as they were impressed on my mind with great force at the time, and I have often thought of them since, viz.: "Surely not, Mr. President, for if the death-penalty should be commuted in so grave a case as the assassination of the head of a great nation, on account of the sex of the criminal, it would amount to an invitation to assassins hereafter to employ women as their instruments, under the belief that if arrested and condemned, they would be punished less severely than men. An act of executive clemency on such a plea would be disapproved by the Government of every civilized nation on earth."

Judge Harlan adds that he made inquiry at the time, and "was told that the whole case had been carefully examined by the Attorney-General and the Secretary of War, and that the only question raised was whether the punishment shall be reduced on account of the sex of the party condemned. I do not remember that any differences of opinion were expressed on that point."

This is indirect but very conclusive evidence that the petition was attached to the record submitted to the President and examined by the Attorney General and Secretary of War; and that the subject of the mitigation of Mrs. Surratt's sentence was considered by the President and these members of his Cabinet, because in no part of the record was there the slightest allusion to the question of clemency to Mrs. Surratt, or to any of the other convicted persons, except in the petition signed by the five members of the Court.

The next is a letter from the Reverend J. George Butler, pastor of St.

Paul's Church, Washington. Under date of December 5, 1868, in describing an interview he had with President Johnson, he says:

> The interview occurred during a social call upon the family of the President in the evening, a few hours after the execution.
>
> I had been summoned by the Government, I then being a hospital rhaplain, to attend upon Atzerodt, and was present at the execution.
>
> Concerning Mrs. Surratt the remarks of the President, by reason of their point and force, impressed themselves upon my memory. He said, in substance, that very strong appeals had been made for the exercise of executive clemency; that he had been importuned; that telegrams and threats had been used; but he could not be moved, for, in his own significant language, Mrs. Surratt *"kept the nest that hatched the eggs."*
>
> The President further stated that no plea had been urged in her behalf, save the fact that she was a *woman*, and his interposition upon that ground would license female crime.

This harmonizes entirely with the "thought" which Secretary Harlan heard uttered with so much force by a member of the Cabinet in Mr. Johnson's presence—either Mr. Stanton or Mr. Seward—and from his language, "this eminent statesman," I take it to have been Mr. Seward.

The Reverend Mr. Butler adds: "I feel it due to a Christian soldier and personal friend (General Ekin) to make this statement showing clearly that at the time of the execution the President's judgment wholly accorded with the judgment of the military commission; and that no appeals could then change his purpose to make 'treason odious.'"

General R. D. Mussey, under date of August 19, 1873, writes to Judge Holt:

> In a few days after the assassination I was detailed for duty with Mr. Johnson and acted as one of his secretaries, and was an inmate of his household until sometime in the fall of 1865.
>
> About the time the military court that tried Mrs. Surratt concluded its labors, I was, if I remember aright, for some days the only person acting as private secretary at the White House, my associate being absent on a visit.
>
> On the Wednesday previous to the execution (which was on Fri-

day, July 7, 1865), as I was sitting at my desk in the morning, Mr. Johnson told me that he was going to look over the findings of the Court with Judge Holt, and should be busy and could see no one. I replied, "Very well, sir, I will see that you are not interrupted," or something to that effect, and continued my work. I think it was two or three hours after that that Mr. Johnson came out of the room where he had been with you, and said that the papers had been looked over and a decision reached. I asked what it was. He told me, approval of the findings and sentence of the Court; and he then gave me the sentences as near as he remembered them, and said that he had ordered the sentence where it was death to be carried into execution on the Friday following. I remember looking up from my desk with some surprise at the brevity of this interval, and asking him if the time wasn't very short. He admitted that it was, but said that they had had ever since the trial began for "preparation"; and either then or later on in the day spoke of his design in making the time short, so that there might be less opportunity for criticism, remonstrance, etc. I do not pretend to use his precise language as to this, but the purport of it was that "it was a disagreeable duty, and there would be endeavors to get him not to perform it, and he wished to avoid them as much as possible." . . . I am very confident, though not absolutely assured, that it was at this interview Mr. Johnson told me that the Court had recommended Mrs. Surratt to mercy on the ground of her sex (and age, I believe). But I am certain he did so inform me about that time; and that he said he thought the grounds insufficient, and that he had refused to interfere; that if she was guilty at all, her sex did not make her any the less guilty; that about the time of her execution, justified it; that he told me there had not been women enough hanged in this war.

This evidence would seem to establish most conclusively that the "petition" was not only attached to the record, and delivered by Judge Holt at the President's office in the Executive Mansion, but that he read the same and afterward considered and discussed it with at least three members of his Cabinet; and intelligent charity can reach no further than to say that President Johnson, when he charged Judge Holt with having withheld this recommendation to mercy when he delivered the record of the trial at the Presidential Mansion, made a cruel and untruthful charge; and that when he asserted in 1873 that he had not seen, read, or heard of this recommendation to mercy, at the time he approved the sentences of the 5th of July, 1865, had forgotten the facts —that his "forgettery" was much better than his memory.[3]

One of the main points in President Johnson's response to this evidence was that in the published volume of the record of the trial of the assassins, prepared by Mr. Benn Pitman, of Cincinnati, under my official supervision, this recommendation to mercy does not appear. There is no force in this. The petition or recommendation to mercy constituted properly no part of the official record of the trial. Mr. Pitman, who had his desk and place in my office at the War Department, was one of the official stenographers of the court, and had special charge and custody of the record from day to day. The other reporters sent in to him their portions of the testimony as they were written up, and thereafter he was responsible for them. My recollection is also that as the testimony was written up a press copy was made of it, which he (Mr. Pitman) took with him to Cincinnati, and used, after he had received permission from the War Department to publish.

The commission met with closed doors at 10 A.M. on the 29th of June to consider its findings, and continued and concluded its labors with closed doors on the 30th. From these meetings all the stenographic reporters were excluded. The findings and sentences, when finally made and recorded, were handed to me to be attached to the record, or to go with the record to the Judge-Advocate-General's office, as was then the course of procedure. By the oath administered all the members of the commission, as well as the Judge Advocates, were bound not to reveal those findings and sentences. I therefore retained them in my possession instead of passing them on to the stenographers. When the recommendation to mercy was drawn and signed by five members of the commission, that was also handed to me to accompany the findings.

Mr. Pitman never saw, I presume, either the original findings or the recommendation to mercy, and the first knowledge he had of the former doubtless was after they were promulgated by the Adjutant-General on the 5th day of July. This is evidenced by the fact that the Adjutant-General, in promulgating the proceedings, took Mrs. Surratt's name from the position it occupies in the records, and placed it next to that of Payne, evidently for the purpose of grouping together the four persons condemned to death. Mr. Pitman gives the findings and sentence in the order promulgated by the Adjutant-General—that is to say, he places the findings and sentence in Mrs. Surratt's case next after that of Lewis Payne, while the Court, in making up its findings, followed the order named in the charge and specifications, where Mrs. Surratt's name follows that of Samuel Arnold.

When I reached my office at the War Department on the 30th—possibly on the morning of the 1st of July—I attached the petition or recommendation to mercy of Mrs. Surratt to the findings and sentence, and at the end of them, and then directed some one—probably Mr. Pitman—to carry the record of the evidence to the Judge-Advocate-General's office. I carried the findings and sentences and petition or recommendation and delivered them to the Judge-Advocate-General in person or to the clerk in charge of court-martial records. Before leaving the War Department I may have attached these findings and sentences and petition to the last few days of testimony, and carried that to the Judge-Advocate-General's office. I never saw the record again until many years after—I think in 1873 or 1874.

I left Washington several days before, and was not there on the day of the execution. My recollection is, that I left there either on the evening of the 5th or on the morning of the 6th of July. On the 5th day of July, when Judge Holt had his conference with President Johnson over the record and proceedings of the military commission, when the President considered and passed upon the findings and sentences of the accused persons, after that interview Judge Holt came directly to Mr. Stanton's office in the War Department. I happened to be with Mr. Stanton as Judge Holt came in. After greetings the latter remarked, "I have just come from a conference with the President over the proceedings of the military commission." "Well," said Mr. Stanton, "what has he done?" "He has approved the findings and sentences of the Court," replied Judge Holt. "What did he say about the recommendation to mercy of Mrs. Surratt?" next inquired Mr. Stanton. "He said," answered Judge Holt, "that she must be punished with the rest; that no reasons were given for his interposition by those asking for clemency, in her case, except age and sex. He said her sex furnished no good ground for his interfering; that women and men should learn that if women committed crimes they would be punished; that if they entered into conspiracies to assassinate, they must suffer the penalty; that were this not so, hereafter conspirators and assassins would use women as their instruments; it would be mercy to womankind to let Mrs. Surratt suffer the penalty of her crime." After some further conversation, and after making known to Mr. Stanton that the President had fixed Friday the 7th as the day of execution, Judge Holt left. In giving the above conversation I cannot say that I have given the exact words; but the substance of what Judge Holt said I know I have given. It is indelibly impressed upon my memory. This conversation, while it does not constitute legal evidence of the fact of President Johnson's consideration of the recommendation to mercy, has always been a circumstance strong and convincing to my mind that President Johnson's charge was totally false. It showed that Mr. Stanton had knowledge of the recommendation—probably had examined the record in the four or five days which had intervened since the trial. As Secretary of War he was at one [that] time daily—almost hourly—in consulation with the President over the disbandment of the military forces; the occupation by the army of the rebel States; the powers and duties of officers there, and the innumerable questions semi-military in character arising out of the chaotic political and social condition of the rebel States, and they could hardly have come together at that time without the question of the conviction and execution of the assassins coming up. The circumstances of the assassination, the plot or conspiracy to assassinate President Lincoln and his Cabinet, the Vice-President himself, and General Grant; who were concerned in it; the evidence submitted to the Court, the weight given to it by the Court, and the conclusions reached by the Court—were matters in which the President and the Secretary of War could not fail to take, and, as is well known, did take the deepest possible interest. It is past human credulity to believe that they would thus come together during the time intervening between the conclusion of the trial on the 30th day of June and the execution of the sentences on the 7th day of July, and the result of the trial, together with the recommendation to mercy, not to be discussed between them. It is inconceivable to me that Judge Holt, even if he were so malicious and murderous in purpose, could be so reckless and foolish in execution of such purpose as to withhold from and try to conceal from President Johnson this recommendation to mercy, when the fact of its existence was made known to Mr. Stanton, and was so certain to be made known to the President by him, and its contents discussed between them.

The historian in passing judgment upon this event, and in weighing the evidence as to the truth or falsity of this charge made by President Johnson, will take into consideration the mental characteristics and moral fiber of the two men, and what adequate motive there was actuating one occupying the exalted position of President Johnson to make the charge, or of Judge Holt to commit so wicked and cruel a wrong.

Andrew Johnson's mental make-up is well known to the officers of the old Union army, and to the American people. His life, his acts, and his speeches are still remembered, and the public judgment formed and registered. I do not propose here to-night to take your time in going into a statement or discussion of this subject. It is sufficient to say that he was endowed by nature with more than ordinary intellectual abilities, and that he had risen from the lowest walks of life by the vigor of his own will, energy, and mental power, through many intermediate places of honor and trust to the second place in the [gift] of the American people—the Vice-Presidency of the United States. He was a man of controlling prejudices and strong personality. He was ambitious, bold, hot-tempered, obstinate, and in the achievement of the ends and aims he sought—right ends and aims he may have thought them—he was unscrupulous in the means he used. This is well illustrated in the instance given by General Sheridan in his memoirs of President Johnson's treatment of him while he was in command in New Orleans in 1866.

You will recall the intense feeling aroused throughout the country by the wanton and bloody massacre of the convention assembled at New Orleans on the 30th of July that year to remodel the Constitution of the State. General Sheridan had been absent several days in Texas, and was returning, when the riot occurred. He reached New Orleans August 1st, made an investigation, and on the same day sent the following telegraphic report to General Grant:

You are doubtless aware of the serious riot which occurred in this city on the 30th. A political body, styling themselves the Convention of 1864, met on the 30th, for, as it alleged, the purpose of remodeling the present Constitution of the State. The leaders were political agitators and revolutionary men, and the action of the convention was liable to produce breaches of the public peace. I had made up my mind to arrest the head men, if the proceedings of the convention were calculated to disturb the tranquillity of the department, but I had no cause for action until they committed the overt act. In the meantime official duty called me to Texas, and the mayor of the city, during my absence, suppressed the convention by the use of the police force, and in so doing attacked the members of the convention and a party of two hundred negroes with fire-arms, clubs, and knives, in a manner so unnecessary and atrocious as to compel me to say that it was murder. About forty whites and blacks were thus killed, and about one hundred and sixty wounded. Everything is now quiet, and I deem it best to maintain a military supremacy in the city for a few days, until the affair is fully investigated. I believe the sentiment of the general community is great regret at this unnecessary cruelty, and that the police could have made any arrest they saw fit without sacrificing lives.

> P. H. Sheridan,
> Major-General commanding.

General Sheridan adds:

On receiving the telegram, General Grant immediately submitted it to the President. Much clamor being made at the North for the publication of the dispatch, President Johnson pretended to give it to the newspapers. It appeared in the issues of August 4th, but with this paragraph omitted, viz:

"I had made up my mind to arrest the head men, if the proceedings were calculated to disturb the tranquillity of the department, but I had no cause for action until they committed some overt act. In the meantime official duty called me to Texas, and the mayor of the city, during my absence, suppressed the convention by the use of the police force, and in so doing attacked the members of the convention and a party of two hundred negroes with fire-arms, clubs, and knives, in a manner so unnecessary and atrocious as to compel me to say that it was murder."

General Sheridan adds:

Against this garbling of my report, done by the President's own order, I strongly demurred, and this emphatic protest marks the beginning of Mr. Johnson's well-known personal hostility toward me.

It will be observed that the omission of this portion of the dispatch— this "garbling" done by President Johnson's own order—changes its whole tenor and meaning; made General Sheridan say exactly contrary to what he did in fact say. Omitting the part struck out, and connecting the two sentences that come together, the President made the dispatch read: "The leaders were political agitators and revolutionary men, and the action of the convention was liable to produce breaches of the public peace. About forty whites and blacks were thus killed, and about one hundred and sixty wounded."

Observe—this makes General Sheridan say that the action of the convention was liable to produce breaches of [the] public [peace], and thus, in this wise, about forty whites and blacks were killed and about one hundred and sixty wounded. General Sheridan said nothing of the kind— nothing in the whole dispatch had any such implication or meaning. What he did say was that the mayor of the city "suppressed the convention by the use of the police force, and in so doing attacked the members of the convention and a party of two hundred negroes with fire-arms, clubs, and knives, in a manner so unnecessary and atrocious as to compel me to say that it was murder"; and "thus" by this means, by this mayor and his police, about forty whites and blacks were killed and about one hundred and sixty wounded.

Is it too much to say that a man who could do this wrong to General Sheridan—could mutilate and corrupt a dispatch so as to cause him to make a false report about a people over whom he was placed in Government; to cause him to state falsely the facts and circumstances about an event in which forty persons had lost their lives, and one hundred and sixty had been grieviously wounded—would hesitate to state a falsehood about Judge Holt? It it too much to say that a man who could do this, and then try to mislead and deceive the people of the United States as to this tragic event, about which they were clamoring to know the truth, perpetrating a lie upon them by mutilating and corrupting a dispatch and promulgating it as a true one, would hesitate to deceive the people about the fact as to whether he did or did not see the recommendation to mercy of Mrs. Surratt? Is it not fair to say that he was of such mental structure and moral fiber as to do this wrong?

And now the motive:

It is known of all men that Andrew Johnson had only fairly settled himself in the presidential chair of the great Lincoln, before he began to dream, to scheme, and to intrigue for an election by the people to that office.

The presidential bee was buzzing under the accidental presidential hat. The Southern leaders, clever diplomats and long-headed politicians as they are, soon took the measure of the man, and began to consider how best they could use him and his ambition for their own purposes. It was noticed that Andrew Johnson had not been many months in the White House before there was a decided change in the style and type of visitors passing in and out under the great white portico. The men of the North—the old "Union Republican group" of the House and Senate that were daily visitors there in the days of Lincoln—began to find the atmosphere of the White House less kind and congenial; there was a lack of warmth in the welcome, and a constraint in talk and exchange of ideas, progressing gradually to actual antagonism over the questions of amnesty, reconstruction, and constitutional guarantees to the freed-[men.] Then the Northern men dropped away, seemed not to go there any more. Men from the South who but lately had borne arms against the Government, and who had not yet taken the oath of allegiance, were found plentiful about the White House, and apparently basking in the sunshine of presidential favor, as in the rays of a southern sun. It became the reign of the unreconstructed and unreconciled. Somebody had whispered loud enough for Mr. Johnson to hear—perhaps the bee buzzed it—that if the Southern States could be reconstructed previous to the presidential convention of 1868, and he (President Johnson) should be found friendly and faithful to the South in that work, there were fifteen Southern States whose electoral votes might be found solid for him as the Democratic nominee, and he would only need the votes of two or three Northern States in addition to carry off the nomination. You know how the poison took—how from the most radical of Union Republicans he became the most extreme—the leader—of the "strictest sect" of the Democrats; how the words "treason should be made odious"— "traitors should take back seats"—"a few traitors should be hung," with which his mouth was filled when elected, and were still sounding in the air when he sat down in Lincoln's vacant chair, had hardly died away before he had turned against and upon all those who had upheld the Union cause—all his old Union friends; how he fought the Congress with a bitterness and a boldness unparalleled in history. He took issue [with] every measure by which the Congress sought to fix in statute and in the fundamental law what the sword had achieved, what war had enacted. Thus he stood.

And now turning to Mrs. Surratt and her case. Over her execution a great clamor was raised throughout the country, not only by those who were lately in the rebellion, and those in the North who were in sympathy with the rebellion, but almost universally by the Roman Catholics of the country, she being a member of that Church, they believing her innocent and a martyr. Mr. Johnson heard this clamor, and "his startled ambition grew sore afraid." He bethought himself of some means to turn this wrath away from himself. The press kept referring to the fact that a recommendation to mercy had been signed by a majority of the Court; and his new friends and allies were calling upon him with a loud voice to know why he had not heeded the appeal for mercy, and save this hapless woman. His fears whispered that the storm might grow so fierce and strong as to sweep away his carefully constructed political fabric. How could he turn away this wrath and clamor; how turn the fury of the storm? Were here not motive and interest enough? He doubtless remembered that, when he examined the record, he and Judge Holt had been alone. How easy to shift the blame, to turn the storm of wrath and execration upon another head by having it circulated that the recommendation had been suppressed by Judge Holt, and that he had never seen or heard of it up to the time of the execution! Here was a sufficient motive—the motive of ambition—the motive, which as we have seen, changed the whole nature of the man—changed his political thought and attitude—spoiled the purpose of his life.

Of Judge Holt's life little need be said. Born and reared in Kentucky, of the best blood of the State, he had achieved fame and stood in the front rank with the great lawyers and orators of that State, before the rebellion began, and before he was called to the Cabinet of James Buchanan, first as Postmaster-General, and afterward as Secretary of War, to fill the place made vacant by the retirement of the traitor John B. Floyd.[4] Judge Holt was a man of collegiate education, a student and scholar of wide and varied reading, and a rhetorician and logician second to few men in the country. Of the next generation after Henry Clay, he was of the time and type in intellectual grasp and power of the Marshalls, the Breckinridges and the Crittendens of that State. He breathed in the spirit of loyalty, patriotism, and love of the Union of Clay, and never doubted, never swerved in giving all his powers—in dedicating his life to the work of saving the Union. It is related by the historian that at one of the Cabinet meetings of President Buchanan, when several of the Southern Secretaries were still occupying their places and were boldly demanding that the forts at Charleston should be evacuated, and Mr. Buchanan was too weak to take a position against them, Mr. Stanton, who had been called to fill the office of Attorney-General, sprang to his feet and said, "Mr. President, it is my duty, as your legal adviser, to say that you have no right to give up the property of the Government, or abandon the soldiers of the United States to its enemies, and the course proposed by the Secretary of the Interior, if followed, is treason, and will involve you and all concerned in treason!" For the first time in this Cabinet treason had been called by its true name. Floyd and Thompson, who had had everything their own way, sprang fiercely to their feet, while Mr. Holt sprang to Mr. Stanton's side indorsing his utterances and ready to uphold him in any struggle. Mr. Buchanan begged that there would be no violence, and for the gentlemen to resume their seats. Thus bolstered by Mr. Stanton and Judge Holt, the President determined not to withdraw Major Anderson. Soon after this meeting Floyd resigned, and Judge Holt was appointed Secretary of War in his place.

Save this charge of Andrew Johnson, no stain or blot, nor the least spot or soilure, has ever reacted upon the fair name and fame of Joseph Holt. For the last year or two of the war I was brought in close official and personal relations with him. I learned to know him well. He was most refined and sensitive in his nature, gentle and kindly in his intercourse and in all his relations with those about him, pure in his private life, exalted in his ideas, dignified, and courtly in his bearing, yet always thoughtful, considerate, and courteous. He had travelled much, read much, and held as his friends strongly attached to him the best men of the land. I can now as little associate him in my mind with the commission of a dishonorable action as any man I have ever known.

One of the interesting episodes connected with this charge against Judge Holt is his appeal to Mr. Speed, Mr. Lincoln's Attorney-General, to "speak out" and state the fact whether or not the recommendation to mercy was before President Johnson and his Cabinet and considered by them. The correspondence between Judge Holt and Mr. Speed is published in the *North American Review* for July 1888. It will be remembered that Mr. Speed, in his letter to Judge Holt of March 30th, 1873, had said:

> After the finding of the military commission that tried the assassins of Mr. Lincoln, and before their execution, I saw the record of the case in the President's office, and attached to it was a paper,

signed by some of the members of the commission, recommending that the sentence against Mrs. Surratt be commuted to imprisonment for life; and according to my memory the recommendation was made because of her sex.

As I have heretofore stated, this settled, so far as the testimony of James Speed could settle it, that the charge of Andrew Johnson that Judge Holt had withheld the recommendation to mercy was false. It settled the fact that previous to the execution the recommendation to mercy was in the President's office, and was attached to the record. But in this letter Mr. Speed added: "I do not feel at liberty to speak of what was said at Cabinet meetings. In this case I know I differ from other gentlemen, but feel constrained to follow my own sense of propriety."

Judge Holt had learned, through statements of Mr. Seward and Mr. Stanton to Judge Bingham, that the recommendation to mercy had been presented to the President, and had been considered by him and members of the Cabinet before the execution. But when this information came to him, both Mr. Seward and Mr. Stanton were dead, and the statement of Judge Bingham of what they told him was secondary evidence; and Judge Holt was anxious, therefore, to get the direct evidence of Mr. Speed that this recommendation was, to his personal knowledge, before Mr. Johnson and his Cabinet and considered by them. His appeals to Mr. Speed are pathetic in the earnestness and depth of feeling they reveal. What could be more profoundly sorrowful or touching than this, in his letter of April 18, 1883: [5]

Allow me to add that we are now, each of us, far advanced in years, so that whatever is to be done for my relief should be done quickly. While, however, it is sadly apparent that I can remain here but a little while longer, I have not been able to bring myself to the belief that you will suffer the closing hours of my life to be darkened by a consciousness that this cloud, or even a shred of it, is still hanging over me—a cloud that can be dissipated at once and forever by a single word spoken by yourself in defense of the truth and in rebuke of a calumny, the merciless cruelty of which none can better understand than yourself. I make this final appeal to your honor as a man to do me the simple justice which, under the same circumstances, I would render to you at once and joyfully.

But Mr. Speed would not speak—finally saying, in his letter of October 25, 1883, "After very mature and deliberate consideration, I have come to the conclusion that I cannot say more than I have." Neither would he enter into consideration or discussion of his determination not "to speak of what was said at Cabinet meetings." It seems to me that Judge Holt was right and Mr. Speed was wrong in their relative positions upon this question. In his letter of April 18, 1883, addressed to Mr. Speed, to which I have referred, Judge Holt forcibly presents his view:

You were a member of his (President Johnson's) Cabinet, and I have the strongest reasons for believing that this atrocious accusation is known to you to have been false in its every intendment. It originated with President Johnson, and for years was industriously circulated by his unscrupulous abettors, though he did not dare to make open proclamation of it until he felt assured, through your letter of the 30th of March, 1873, that no damaging disclosures were to be apprehended from yourself. . . . The question whether a President of the United States, as a craven refuge from accountability for official action, did seek to blacken the reputation of a subordinate officer holding a confidential interview with him, is in no just sense a private question; it is essentially a public one, which concerns the whole country, and one of which the country may well expect you to speak, seeing that you were a member of that President's Cabinet at the time of this disgraceful transaction. Your unwillingness thus to speak of it in 1873 seemed to have arisen from an exaggerated estimate of a rule which once prevailed with regard to the inviolability of Cabinet councils and secrets. But whatever may have been in the remote past, the recognized force of this rule, the frequent and conspicuous disregard of it during the last two decades, by statesmen of the highest probity and rank, leaves the impression that the rule itself has lived its day and is now practically dead and inoperative. Waiving, however, this view, it is clear to me that, were the rule accepted as now binding in its utmost rigor, it could have no application to this case. I cannot be misled in supposing that the relations between the President and his Cabinet are relations of honor, and that, therefore, they cannot be held to oblige any member of his Cabinet to protect, by his concealment, and thus become a moral accomplice in it—any criminal or wrongful act into which the President may be drawn by a guilty ambition, or by any other unworthy passion or purpose. In a word, the rule never has been and never should be so construed as to become a shelter for perjury or crime. . . .[6]

Your associates in the Cabinet—Messrs. Seward and Stanton—condemning the rule by which I have been so long victimized, declared the truth fully to Judge Bingham, as he has so forcibly set forth in his letter to which you are referred.

But, as I have said, Mr. Speed would not speak. I can only account for it by the life circumstances and education of the man. In the old slave States, in the antebellum days, there existed many of the ideas, traditions, and rules of personal conduct of the feudal times. Things touching personal honor, or trusted to it, or that partook of the knightly and chivalrous, were esteemed above common right, common honesty, or common sense. Restrained by these limitations of birth and tradition, and controlled by his chivalrous idea of not revealing what he regarded as Cabinet secrets, Mr. Speed would not speak, even to save a public officer from a great wrong, or his personal friend from a calumny which he knew would walk beside him shadowing and embittering a life, noble and void of wrong, down to its close. In this I think the judgment of mankind will be that he erred. He knew that this charge of Andrew Johnson was a cruel falsehood. Not only what he said, but what he refuses to say, proves this. His letter of March 30, 1873, states that he saw the record, with the recommendation attached to it, in the President's office before the execution. Judge Holt did not, therefore, "withhold," as the President alleged. But, stronger than this, and conclusive, I believe, in the mind of every honest and unprejudiced man, were Mr. Speed's utterances less than two years ago at a meeting to the Loyal Legion at Cincinnati. Mr. Speed read a paper at the meeting of this society, held there on the 4th of May, 1887, in which he said: "Only the group of fiends who stilled the pulsations of Lincoln's great heart paid the penalty of the crime. A maudlin sentiment has sought to cast blame on the officials who dealt out justice to these. One in particular is my distinguished friend the then Judge-Advocate-General of the army. Judge Holt performed his duty kindly and considerately. In every particular as was just and fair. This I know; but Judge Holt needs no vindication from me nor any one else. I only speak because I know reflections have been made, and because my position enabled me to know the facts, and because I know the perfect purity and uprightness of his conduct." Could any words say in stronger form, he knew that in this matter Judge Holt did his whole duty, and that President Johnson's charges were false? Could he have said, "In every particular he was just and fair, this I know," if he did not *know* and intended to say that he knew Judge Holt did his whole duty and had presented this recommendation to mercy to President Johnson? But what he refused to say is as strongly convincing to my mind of the fact that the recommendation to mercy was, to his knowledge, duly brought to the President's attention, and was read and considered by him and members of his Cabinet, as anything he has affirmatively stated.

He was asked by Judge Holt to state whether this paper was or was not before President Johnson and his Cabinet. He refused to answer, because he did not feel at liberty to speak of what was said at Cabinet meetings. If nothing was said about the recommendation, if no such paper ever came before the Cabinet, might he have not so stated; might he not have said, "No such matter ever came before the Cabinet"? This would not reveal any Cabinet secret, would come nowhere near the limitations he had prescribed for himself "not to speak of what was said at Cabinet meetings."

Is it not the inevitable logical conclusion that it was because of this knowledge that this recommendation had been before and had been discussed by the President and his Cabinet, and his determination "not to speak of what was said at Cabinet meetings," that he would not speak?

But finally, my friends, has not the faith of Judge Holt been realized? Has not time caused the truth to shine forth and his innocence to appear? In 1873 he said: "An abiding faith, however, remains with me that the public will do these witnesses justice, and myself also; and that if truth has power to disarm the cloud of calumny of its lightnings, that then, standing in their presence and under their shelter, I may well feel that for the future this cloud can have no terrors for me."

Saith the old poet:

> *. . . I have ever thought*
> *Nature doth nothing so great for great men*
> *As when she's pleased to make them lords of truth.*
> *Integrity of life is fame's best friend,*
> *Which nobly beyond death shall crown the end.*

CHAPTER XXVII

Important paper by the Reverend J. A. Walter in relation to the case of Mrs. Mary E. Surratt

On May 25, [1891,] a period of more than twenty-five years from the date of her execution, Father J. A. Walter,[1] the confessor of Mrs. Surratt, for the first time made public a written statement in relation to his penitent, in which he distinctly proclaims her innocence, and charges that the Government had punished her wrongfully. His statement was read before United States Catholic Historical Society of New York, and was placed among the archives of that association, probably to be used at some future day.*

Reverend Walter's Statement

Among the open letters of last April (1891) of the *Century*, I find one referring to the priest who attended Mrs. Mary E. Surratt. As I am the priest alluded to in this article, I must positively deny that I prohibited Mrs. Surratt from asserting her innocence.

The object of this article is to make manifest the truth in this case and thus vindicate the innocence of Mary E. Surratt.

Time alone could quiet the deep feeling embittered against every one who might have been suspected of having anything to do with the crime. Amidst all this excitement, I had determined in my own mind to wait twenty-five years before I would give to the public a clear and full statement.

The public mind has had time to quiet down, and men can now calmly listen to reason. Very few persons at this date believe that Mary E. Surratt knew anything about the plot to assassinate the President.

* Printed in the *Catholic News* of New York City.

Now as to the facts of the case—President Lincoln was assassinated at Ford's Theater, on the 14th of April (Good Friday) about 10 o'clock P.M. It was, in my opinion, the act of an insane man, and no friend of the South.

Mary E. Surratt, whose name has been associated with this awful tragedy, was a quiet, amiable lady. She had removed from the country a few months previous to the murder of the President, resided on H near Sixth Street northwest, and was in St. Patrick's parish. I was not acquainted with her, and never spoke to her until the eve of her execution. I received a letter from her dated Sunday, April 23, 1865, asking me to come and see her. She was then in Carroll Prison. I went on Tuesday morning, April 25th, but she had been removed to the penitentiary, and I was told by those in authority at Carroll Prison that no one would be allowed to see her. On Wednesday, July 5th, 1865, I learned that the trial was over. On Thursday at 10 o'clock A.M. I went to the War Department and asked Colonel Hardie for a pass to visit Mrs. Surratt, who had requested me to visit her when in Carroll Prison some three months previous. Colonel [James A.] Hardie [2] told me that Secretary Stanton was not in, and asked me if I was in a hurry about it; I told him I was not. He then replied that he would let me have a pass in a few hours. When I returned home, and whilst at dinner, an orderly came with a pass signed by Colonel Hardie. I gave the usual receipt for the same, and going to the door with the orderly, I remarked to him, "You cannot make me believe that a Catholic woman would go to Communion on Holy Thursday and be guilty of murder on Good Friday." Shortly after the orderly had left, Mr. John F. Callan and Mr. Holohan, a boarder at Mrs. Surratt's house, called and informed me that the execution of Mrs. Surratt was to take place the next day. To act so hastily in a matter of this kind was certainly strange on the part of the Government. Whilst talking to these two gentlemen, Colonel Hardie came in and seemed much excited; I requested him to walk into the parlor, leaving the two gentlemen standing in the hall. He then said to me: "Father Walter, the remarks you made to that young man," meaning the orderly who brought me the pass, "have made a deep impression on him; I was afraid that the pass I sent you would not answer, so I have brought you one from Secretary Stanton, but I want you to promise me that you will not say anything about the innocence of Mrs. Surratt." I replied: "Of course I cannot let Mrs. Surratt die without the sacraments, so if I must say yes,

I say yes." He then gave me the pass signed by Secretary Stanton. This was about 2:30 P.M. Thursday, July [6], 1865. That afternoon I went to see Mrs. Surratt to make arrangements to give her Communion next morning. I also called to see the President, having Annie, Mrs. Surratt's daughter, with me. On entering the gate at the President's house I met Hon. Thomas Florence, ex-member of Congress from Pennsylvania. He remarked, "Father Walter, you and I are on the same errand of mercy. The President must not allow this woman to be hanged." We went into the Executive Mansion and upstairs to a room next to the one occupied by the President, Andrew Johnson. There I met General Mussey, secretary of the President, Preston King, and one other person [Senator James Lane of Kansas]. I requested General Mussey to go in and ask the President if he would see me. He returned and said the President would not see me. Again, at my request, General Mussey went in, telling the President that I would not detain him more than five minutes. This was denied me. I made another attempt, and told General Mussey to say to the President that I did not ask for pardon or commutation of sentence, but asked ten days' reprieve to prepare Mrs. Surratt for eternity. This reasonable request was also refused. Annie, Mrs. Surratt's daughter, was in like manner refused an interview with President Johnson. The President sent me word to go to Judge Holt. I went with Annie to see this man, but it was perfectly useless. He had no more feeling for the poor daughter than a piece of stone; he referred her to the President. The poor child, with eyes streaming with tears, was left without any sympathy from this cold, heartless man.

This was Thursday afternoon, the day before the execution. On the following morning I went at 7 o'clock, carrying with me the Holy Communion, which I gave to Mrs. Surratt in her cell. I remained with her until the time of her execution, which was about 2:30 P.M. I can never forget the scene witnessed on that sad occasion. Poor Mrs. Surratt had been sick for several weeks and was quite feeble; she was lying on a mattress laid on the bare brick floor of her cell. Shortly before the hour of her execution, Mrs. Surratt was brought out of her cell and was sitting on a chair at the doorway. It was at this time that she made clearly and distinctly the solemn declaration of her innocence. She said to me in the presence of several officers: "Father, I wish to say something."

"Well, what is it, my child?" "That I am innocent" were her exact words. These words were uttered whilst she stood on the verge of eternity, and were the last confession of an innocent woman.

When the time arrived for the execution, she was carried to the scaffold by two soldiers, because she was too weak even to stand on her feet. I went immediately to see Annie and try to give her some consolation. When I told her that it was all over she gave way to her intense feelings, but one word was sufficient to calm her.

Some time after the execution of Mrs. Surratt an article appeared in the *New York Tribune* accusing Secretary Stanton of refusing me a pass to visit Mrs. Surratt unless I would promise to say nothing regarding her innocence. It seems that at this time Horace Greeley and Secretary Stanton were not on good terms. Mr. Forney, editor of the *Philadelphia Press* and *Washington Chronicle*, denied the charge that Secretary Stanton had refused me a pass on terms as above stated. Two reporters of the *Tribune* called on me to ascertain the truth of the matter; I told them what had occurred between Colonel Hardie and myself in relation to the pass. Of course they drew their own conclusions from what I told them. I said to them that I wished to have nothing to do with the quarrel. The next day they published verbatim what had passed between Colonel Hardie and myself. Colonel Hardie thought proper to write an article in the *National Intelligencer,* calling me some harsh names and saying I was not a proper person to have attended Mrs. Surratt.[3] I paid no attention to this article, but attended to my duties as if nothing had happened. Some friends met me on Pennsylvania Avenue on the morning of the publication and asked me what I was going to do about the article. I simply told them I would do nothing.

I would here state that General Hancock was simply commander of the military division comprising the District of Columbia, and General Hartranft was the officer in charge, and superintended everything. Evidently some one at the War Department must have been alarmed, for Major-General Hancock was telegraphed to go and see Archbishop Spalding, so as to prevent me from asserting the innocence of Mrs. Surratt. I received a telegram from the Archbishop's secretary, asking me to keep quiet, and saying that the Archbishop would write me a letter by the evening mail. The letter came. It was no order, but simply a request that I should keep quiet in regard to the innocence of Mrs. Surratt.[4] My answer was, that what he requested was hard to comply with, but I would try to do so. Archbishop Spalding told General Hancock that he also believed Mrs. Surratt was an innocent woman. At the present time I think there are few persons in this country who are not of the same opinion. Let any one quietly and calmly sift the evidence given in this trial and the same conclusion will be reached. Let us examine this evidence.

Mrs. Surratt's guilt could only be in consequence of her son John H. Surratt's guilt. She was concerned in the conspiracy to murder President Lincoln only inasmuch as he was one of the conspirators. Now, John H. Surratt had nothing whatever to do with the conspiracy to murder President Lincoln; in fact, he knew nothing about it. He came to Washington on the 4th of April, took supper at home, changed his clothes, and left for Elmira the next morning. The testimony of Susan Jackson, Mrs. Surratt's servant, was correct as to facts, but she mistook the date, saying it was April 14th. It was ten days previous to the 14th of April. It is strange that the hotel register in Elmira could not be found, some one had made away with it. Whoever it was, he did not know that John H. Surratt had telegraphed to New York to know where Booth was. I saw the telegraph register in Mr. Bradley's office on which his name, John Harrison, the name he assumed, appears on the date of April 14th. If he were one of the conspirators he certainly ought to know where the chief conspirator, Booth, was, and it was his business to have been on hand in Washington and not in Elmira, N.Y., some 400 miles distant. When he read the account of the assassination of President Lincoln on the morning of April 15th, he was utterly astounded when he saw his name in connection with the plot, and supposed it must have been done by some parties of whom he had no knowledge. He immediately left for Canada and remained concealed there several months. He has been accused of deserting his poor mother. This is not true. He sent a person to Washington, furnished him the means, and was ready to give himself up in her defence. This friend saw the counsel of his mother. They advised the friend to return and tell John H. Surratt to remain in Canada, for there was no danger that his mother would be convicted. Everyone knows that had he come to Washington he would have been placed in the docks with the other prisoners and condemned with them. Prudence and common sense demanded the course he followed. Now, John H. Surratt being in Elmira, how was he to be transported these 400 miles so as to be in Washington in time for the assassination of the President? Mr. DuBarry, master of transportation of the Northern Central Railroad, proved that there were no trains running on that day by which he could possibly have reached Washington.

Again, a handkerchief of John H. Surratt's was found in a car going North after the 14th of April, and this fact was adduced as evidence that he was escaping from Washington on his way to Canada. This handkerchief was lost by Mr. Holohan, who boarded at Mrs. Surratt's, and it had by mistake been placed in his bureau drawer. He was on his way to Canada with Detective McDevitt to try to find Surratt and lost it out of his pocket.

Again, John T. Ford testified that no one knew that the President was to be at the theater before 12 o'clock, yet Mrs. Surratt had ordered a carriage at 10 o'clock (two hours previous) to take her to Surrattsville. She went down there to attend some business in connection with her husband's estate. She was coming out of the house about 2 o'clock in the afternoon when she met Booth, who requested her to take two packages wrapped in newspaper, one containing a bottle of whiskey and the other a spy-glass, and give them to Mr. Lloyd at Surrattsville. She went down to this place, did not see Lloyd, but gave the packages to his sister-in-law. What this poor lady did anyone would have done, without suspecting any harm was intended; she thought she was simply doing an act of kindness and nothing more. The fact of her ordering her carriage at 10 o'clock shows that it had no connection whatever with the assassination of the President.

Every trivial circumstance was brought forward as positive evidence of guilt, when there was not the slightest ground for such a conclusion. I am convinced that if President Johnson had given me a hearing on the day preceding the execution he would not only have saved the life of an innocent woman, but would have prevented a blot that will forever remain as a stigma on the Government of these United States.

This would have given ample time to examine the evidence on which she was convicted, and this examination would have proved her innocence.

Of all the documents that have been presented to the public in this long controversy in relation to Mrs. Surratt, this paper by Father Walter is certainly the most noteworthy. It is the only written statement which has been given out by him in which he affirms the innocence of Mrs. Surratt, and charges the Government with her wrongful and illegal execution. Inasmuch as he was her confessor in the closing hours of her earthly life, and was thus brought into closer relation with her than anyone else, his assertions are entitled to the closest scrutiny and the most careful consideration.

Although living in Washington in 1863, 1864, and the first six months of 1865, I had never met Father Walter, and was therefore an entire stranger to him. I had seen him often, and had frequently worshipped in his church. He was the pastor of St. Patrick's congregation, at the corner of Tenth and F streets. He was a man well liked by his people, and possessed great influence in the religious circle in which he moved. Of his political feelings and convictions, I knew nothing whatever. He was a graduate of St. Charles College, the same religious institution in which Surratt and I had spent so many pleasant days together.

Father Walter in his statement says that he was unacquainted with Mrs. Surratt prior to the afternoon of Thursday, July 6, 1865, when he met her for the first time; that he had previously received a letter from her dated Carroll Prison, April 23, 1865, asking him to visit her; that he had applied to the War Department for a pass to enable him to do so, but that he did not then succeed in getting one.

This much is correct; he had not yet met her, none of the prisoners were permitted to receive visits from clergymen or anyone else, except immediate family relations, during the period in which the War Department was conducting its preliminary investigation or during their trial.

Then he goes on to tell us that he applied to the War Department for a pass on the morning of the 6th of July, and that one was subsequently sent to him signed by Colonel Hardie. He informs us of his remarks to the orderly who brought it, and how this was the means later in the day of bringing Colonel Hardie to him who handed him another pass, in place of his own, signed by Secretary Stanton.

With the Father's colloquy with Colonel Hardie, we have nothing to do; it is not at all pertinent to this issue, but when he alleges that Secretary Stanton would not give him a pass to attend to Mrs. Surratt, until he had first promised that he would not say anything about her innocence, he not only attempts to cast the greatest discredit on Mr. Stanton, but absolutely stultifies himself. Is there a man with a spark of reason about him who, for a moment, would believe that Mr. Stanton would require any such pledge before granting the necessary pass? That was not Mr. Stanton's way of doing business. He was too good a lawyer, and too great a man, to prostitute his manhood to any such requirement as that.

How did Father Walter know that Mrs. Surratt was innocent when he made his statement to the orderly who brought him the first pass? He had not met her, had not spoken to her, and yet with a single asser-tion he brushes aside the vast array of testimony against her, and says he believes her to be an innocent woman. Then he visits her that same evening and hears her confession, and prepares her for the reception of Holy Communion the next morning, Friday, July 7.

Ah, Father Walter, why did you not proclaim the innocence of your penitent on the very evening you heard her confession? With her consent, you could have caused it to have been published to the world through the Associated Press, and it would have been read in every prominent news-paper in the United States the next day. Why did you not do it? Through you she could have, if innocent, explained away all the evidence against her, but you permitted her to do nothing of the kind, and suffered her to go down to her grave, without one word in explanation of all that had been testified against her. Had you insisted on a public confession, you might have saved her from a disgraceful death. The theological teachings of the Catholic Church gave you the right to interrupt your penitent just as soon as she told you she was not guilty, and in order to save her life, you should have insisted on her making a public confession. You could then have proclaimed her innocence even from the very thresh-old of the scaffold. Father Walter, why did you not do this? You had on the evening of the 6th of July pronounced over her the sacred words of absolution prescribed by the church, and you gave her Holy Communion on the morning of the 7th of July, and yet you wait more than twenty-five years before you in your priestly character announce her innocence.

But there is another phase of this matter, generally unknown, and a very serious one. Father Walter says that Mrs. Surratt's exact and only words to him were: "Father, I am innocent." In his own written, and published article, he does not say that he made any reply to her, nor does he say that she used any additional words other than those he gives. Now, right here comes a very astounding disagreement between the utterances of Father Walter and Mr. John W. Clampitt, Mrs. Surratt's only surviving counsel! In a paper given out to the public in March 1894 by Mr. Clampitt in relation to this incident, the attorney says that the following interview took place between Father Walter and Mrs. Surratt, and that he had obtained his information from the lips of the Father himself: Mrs. Surratt asked, "Holy Father, can I not tell these people before I die that I am innocent of the crime for which I have been condemned to death?" To this Father Walter is said to have replied, "No, my child, the world and all that is in it have now receded forever; it would do harm, and it might disturb the serenity of your last moments." Now who is right in this matter, Father Walter or Mr. Clampitt? If Mr. Clampitt is right, then Father Walter has done wrong in not giving us the entire and precise language said to have been used by Mrs. Surratt and himself on this occasion. The reader is left to explain this difference between these two men, if he can, and draw his own conclusions; I cannot.

Again, when Father Walter attempts to review the evidence in the case of Mrs. Surratt and characterizes it as insufficient to convict, he makes assertions which are utterly out of harmony with the truth.

He says: John T. Ford testified that no one knew that the President was to be at the theater before twelve o'clock on the 14th of April, yet Mrs. Surratt had ordered a carriage at ten o'clock, two hours previous, to take her to Surrattsville.

In contradiction of this it must be said that John T. Ford, the proprietor of the theater, was not in Washington at all on that day, but had gone to Richmond, and was there when the President was murdered. He never gave any evidence of the kind that Father Walter says he did. His son,[5] James R. Ford, testified that he was first apprised of the intended visit of the President to the theater on Friday morning at half past ten o'clock, and another son, H. Clay Ford, testified that he first heard of the President's visit at about half past eleven o'clock, and that he saw Booth about half an hour after this or about twelve o'clock.

When Father Walter says that Mrs. Surratt had ordered a carriage two hours earlier, or about ten o'clock, he betrays a recklessness of statement or want of knowledge of the true facts of the case which are amazing. I know from my own personal knowledge that his statement in this particular is not true; for I am the person who drove Mrs. Surratt into the country on that day, and I know that this took place about two o'clock. At that time she gave me ten dollars, asking me to go and hire a buggy for her, and stating that she was going into the country to see one Mr. Nothey on a matter of business, and she placed no restrictions upon me as to where I should get the buggy, which she would have done had it been ordered in advance, at ten o'clock, as Father Walter says it was.

How the reverend gentleman could make any such statement as that is utterly past comprehension; it is so false, so utterly at issue with the actual facts as not to be entitled to a moment's serious consideration.

Again, he says, as she was coming out of her house at two o'clock she met Booth, who requested her to take two packages wrapped in newspaper, one containing a bottle of whisky, and the other a spy glass, and give them to Mr. Lloyd at Surrattsville.

It is not true that she met Booth as she was coming *out* of the house; he had gone into the house and she met him in her parlor, was alone with him, and then he left her house before she got into the buggy.

Father Walter, however, makes a very important admission, and one that is of great weight against Mrs. Surratt when he says that she *saw* Booth at *two o'clock*. That is true, very true; her own daughter saw him, and I saw him. He also states the truth when he says that Booth gave her a spy glass (field glass) and this is another fact of tremendous importance against Mrs. Surratt; but when he says Booth gave her a bottle of whisky wrapped up in paper he does not know what he is writing about. Why should she carry whisky to Surrattsville? Lloyd kept a tavern at that place, and Booth could get all the whisky he wanted there.

Then he says that when Mrs. Surratt arrived at Surrattsville, she did not see Lloyd at all, but gave the packages to Mrs. Offutt, his sister-in-law. What a prevarication! What a disregard of facts! Mr. Lloyd himself testified under oath in 1865 and at John Surratt's trial in 1867 that Mrs. Surratt came down to his place; told him to have the "shooting irons" and two bottles of whisky ready for that night, and that she herself gave him a package which, on opening, he found to contain a field glass, and which she requested him to give to the parties who would call for them in the night.

How Father Walter can overcome Lloyd's evidence, and reconcile it with his own untruthful statement, is more than I am able to fathom.

Father Walter also says that Mrs. Surratt went down to Surrattsville on business connected with the real estate affairs of her deceased husband. Why then did she not drive directly to Mr. Nothey's place, the man who had purchased the real estate in question, and who owed her the money on it? She did nothing of the kind; she could have remained at home, as I have before said, and through the mails transacted all the business that really took place, with Mr. Nothey.

The reverend father also expresses himself to the effect that: Mrs. Surratt could only have been a conspirator in so far as her son was a conspirator, and that she could have only been guilty as he was guilty, and that because, as he alleges, her son was not in Washington on the day and night of the murder, and in fact did not know anything about it, she could not have been guilty.[6]

In making this assertion, Father Walter again lays himself open to the severest criticism. Taking it for granted that John H. Surratt was not in Washington on the day of the assassination, but in Elmira, New York, where he says he was, four hundred miles distant, how does that excuse the actions of his mother? How does that account for her trip to Surrattsville in relation to the delivery of the shooting irons, or how does that explain her meeting with Booth, both before and after this trip? Even if Booth had conceived the plan to shoot Mr. Lincoln only after he heard of his intended visit to the theater that night, which is very doubtful, that does not exonerate Mrs. Surratt, who, as the evidence before the Military Commission proved, carried out Booth's behests to the letter and was one of his most active assistants in the events of that day. Such a plea may afford a quasi defense to John H. Surratt, but it certainly does not exculpate his mother.

Finally, Father Walter informs us that John H. Surratt, during the trial of the conspirators, sent a person to Washington, furnished him the means, and was ready to give himself up in the defense of his mother. This friend saw the counsel of his mother. They advised the friend to return, and tell John H. Surratt to remain in Canada, for there was no danger that his mother would be convicted.

This part of the reverend gentleman's statement, I believe to be measurably true. I myself was approached by Mr. Fredrick Aiken of Mrs. Surratt's counsel, at one time, during the trial and informed by him that John H. Surratt would return to the United States, if certain stipulations, which I do not *fully* remember, could be secured from the

Government. One of these stipulations, however, was that he should be used as a witness against Jefferson Davis.

When the trial of the conspirators was over, I wrote to the Judge Advocate General, Judge Holt, about the proposition to have Surratt returned, but was assured by him that he had heard nothing of it.

My criticism of Father Walter's paper is now at an end. It has been made by me regretfully, painfully, and only from the sincere desire to have the people become acquainted with the whole truth in this matter. It is after all with the people that the final decision in this controversy must rest, and when they shall have once fully investigated it, the cause of truth and justice will, I feel, have no reason to fear their verdict.

CHAPTER XXVIII

Author's return home · Is appointed to a position in the Philadelphia Custom House · Is discharged · Whereabouts of John H. Surratt · Significant letter from Judge Holt · Career of Surratt after the assassination · His secretion in Canada by Fathers Boucher and LaPierre · Departure from Canada in the steamer Peruvian *· His meeting with Dr. McMillan, the surgeon of the vessel · His astounding revelations to him*

In the chapter detailing my interview with Mr. Stanton on April 30, I have told how I was placed by him in the custody of the Government. On the 14th day of May, Judge Advocate General Holt addressed a letter to the Secretary in which he recommended my release from custody, saying I had faithfully given my testimony in the cases then on trial before the court. I was accordingly released on May 29, but gave my parole to report daily to the War Department until further ordered.[1] On June 29, I was finally discharged from further service, and at once started for my home in Philadelphia. Never before in my life had I realized so fully what home meant. It was indeed "home, sweet home" to me. My parents received me with open arms, and their long-pent-up anxiety gave way to grateful tears.

I shall not say much of the weeks of worriment, suffering, and sickness that overtook me; that is now in the past. When kind nature, however, had reasserted herself and I had recovered, I began to look around for employment. I was in humble circumstances and could not afford to remain idle. I was determined not to abandon the religious calling which had been marked out for me in life, and I made application in August to the Catholic bishop of Richmond, Virginia,[2] for his permission to begin my theological studies in the seminary at Baltimore, but he took no notice of my letter, and it remained unanswered. He even visited Philadelphia, and I endeavored to have an interview with him, but was repulsed. Soon the true condition of affairs dawned on my mind, and I was compelled to face the bitter truth that I need not now look for sympathy or friendship to the clergy of my church; that they were opposed to me. It was a sad revelation in my life for which I was wholly unprepared, but under God, I resolved to bravely meet it and every emergency which might thereafter confront me. In this desperate situation, I applied to the Government for protection and employment. Secretary Stanton and Judge Holt at once took charge of my case, and in December 1865, I was appointed to a clerkship in the Philadelphia Custom House.[3] This was a most grateful action on the part of those in authority, for it not only provided me with the means of earning a livelihood, but it was also a notice to my vilifiers and traducers that the Government of the United States had believed me, and now stood behind me in my dire necessity.

I retained this position until November 1866, when, through the successful efforts of my enemies, I was discharged. Andrew Johnson, the President, was no longer a Republican, but had gone over to the other side, and nearly every Republican in the country holding official position under him was left out in the cold. Under such circumstances as these, a very bitter fight was made on me, and I was compelled to leave the service and once more face the sharp winds of adversity.

During all this interval since the assassination of the President, and the close of the Conspiracy trial, where was John H. Surratt? What had become of him? Was he in Washington on the night of the murder, and if so, how did he make his escape? These were questions I often addressed to myself. I began to think that he was probably in some monastery in a distant portion of the world, that he was in all respects dead to the world, and would never more be known among living men; but an event took place in May 1866 which set my wits to work, and caused much thought and speculation. It was in the shape of a letter from the Judge Advocate General, as follows:

Washington, D.C., May 19, 1866.

Mr. Louis J. Weichmann,
Philadelphia, Pa.

Dear Sir:

In your testimony on the trial of the assassins you speak of a "Ste. Marie," as an acquaintance of yours, probably at college. Will you be so good as to inform me what has become of this man, and of what country he is a native?

Did you hear anything of him in Canada, or, have you heard of him since?

Very respectfully,
Your obedient servant,
J. Holt,
Judge Advocate General.

Judge Holt's letter was answered very fully and all the desired information given him, and I was not left long in suspense as to the meaning of his communication. A few months rolled by, and then the news was flashed across the ocean by lightning, one of the first messages over the new, great Atlantic cable,[4] that John H. Surratt had been arrested in Italy, while serving in the Papal Zouaves, and that his discoverer was Henri B. de Sainte Marie, whom I had introduced to him at Little Texas, Maryland, on Good Friday, April 3, 1863.

Here was, indeed, a tremendous revelation! How truly inscrutable the ways of Providence!

I immediately wrote to the Judge Advocate General in relation to the news and from him received this reply:

Washington, Nov. 28, 1866.

Dear Sir:

In answer to your inquiry of the 21st inst., I have to state that since last winter it has been known here that John H. Surratt was at Rome in the Papal service. The late telegram by the cable which you have seen proves that the information previously received by the Government was correct.

Very respectfully,

Your obedient servant,

J. Holt.

Thereupon feeling that it was a duty that I, of all men, owed to the Government, if there was any doubt as to the identity of the individual arrested, I made a proposition to the Judge Advocate General to be permitted to go to Europe and identify him myself. To this Judge Holt answered:

Washington, Dec. 8, 1866.

Dear Sir:

In reply to your favor of the 5th., inst., I have to say from all I can learn, the Government is so well satisfied as to the identity of the party arrested, as to dispense altogether with the step you suggest. He is understood to be now on his way to the United States, and may arrive by the close of the month.

The proposition you make is one that does you much credit as a citizen and a patriot, and but for the action already taken, as mentioned, I should at once have presented it for the consideration of the proper authorities here.

Very respectfully,

Your obedient servant,

J. Holt.

The career of Surratt from the time of his departure from Washington on April 4, 1865, until his final arrest in Egypt, November 27, 1866, constitutes one of the most thrilling episodes in history. It reads more like fiction than reality, and rivals in interest and daring the attempted escape of Booth and Herold.

Surratt, as I have already related, bade me goodbye on the night of April 3, 1865. He remained at the National Hotel in Washington until the morning of the 4th, and then took the train for New York City, which he reached on the same day. On the morning of the 5th, he called, according to his own statement, at the Booth residence, but did not find John Wilkes at home. He then started for Montreal, Canada, where he arrived on the 6th of April at 10:30 A.M. He went to St. Lawrence Hall, the leading hotel of the city, and registered himself as "John Harrison," omitting his last name. Here he remained until the 12th of April, when he left for the United States. From this time until his return to Canada, his actions and whereabouts are enveloped in the deepest doubt and mystery. He himself claims to have gone under orders to Elmira, New York, for the purpose of making a sketch or map of the camp then located there for the detention of Confederate prisoners of war, and that he was in that city on the 14th of April, the day on which Booth murdered the President.

The Government of the United States, on the other hand, while admitting that he was in Elmira on the 13th of April, contended that he was in Washington on the day and evening of the murder, and produced a large number of witnesses in support of its assertion. This feature of the case, however, will be treated at length in another place. Suffice it at present to say that Surratt had returned to Montreal on the 18th of April at 12:30, and had again registered at St. Lawrence Hall as "John Harrison." Finding that he was suspected and pursued, he took his departure from the hotel almost immediately and was for a brief period secreted in the house of one Porterfield of Tennessee, a man of some prominence and an agent in Canada for the Confederacy.

About the 22nd of April, he was taken out of Montreal by one Joseph Du Tilly, and conveyed to the home of Father Charles Boucher, a Catholic priest and a French Canadian, who then resided at St. Liboire, forty-five miles distant from Montreal. Here Surratt dwelt for nearly three months, remaining for the greater part of the time in his room, and whenever an opportunity offered going hunting with the priest and other parties who came from Montreal, conspicuous among whom was Father LaPierre of Montreal. When Surratt was first presented to Father Boucher, it was under the name of Charles Armstrong. This deception he kept up about two weeks when, the priest becoming suspicious of his identity, the supposed Armstrong made known his true name as that of John H. Surratt. He remained with Father Boucher until the latter part of July, when the priest found it necessary to have him removed because the people of his parish became suspicious as to the character of his mysterious guest, and his continued abode in his home. He was now taken back to Montreal by Fathers Boucher and LaPierre, and secreted at the home of the father of Reverend LaPierre on Old Cemetery Street, a very narrow thoroughfare and running directly in the rear of the bishop's residence. The LaPierre house itself was situated very close to the episcopal palace.

Surratt's sojourn at this place was maintained with the greatest secrecy. He very seldom went out on the streets, and when he did so, it was generally at night. But this condition of affairs could not last long, and it soon became apparent to the two priests who were shielding and harboring him, and to those who visited him, that other and safer quarters must be provided. Accordingly, after much consultation and deliberation, it was determined to send him out of the country, to Rome, where he could, perhaps, enter some monastery or educational institution or, that failing, the Papal army, and preparations were now actually made for that purpose. Through the exertions of his two clerical friends, passage was secured in the steamer *Peruvian* of the Montreal Ocean Steamship Service, which was marked for sailing from Quebec on September 16, 1865.

One day early in the month, Father LaPierre happened to meet on the street a young officer who was connected with the ship in the capacity of surgeon. His name was Lewis J. A. McMillan,[5] and he was a Canadian by birth. Father LaPierre was well acquainted with Dr. McMillan. He told him that he had a friend by the name of McCarty who was going over in the same vessel as the doctor, and that he would like to introduce him to this friend. McMillan said it was all right, and it was accordingly arranged that they should meet on the steamer *Montreal,* which would leave for Quebec on September 15.

The meeting, as stipulated, took place, and the first thing Father LaPierre did was to take Dr. McMillan up to a state room on the steamer of which he had the key. He unlocked the door and introduced a man (J. H. Surratt) who was in there to the young surgeon under the name of McCarty. McMillan did not suspect in the least who the man was and passed the evening and most of the night with him and a third party besides the priest who was going all the way to Quebec. McCarty at this time wore green spectacles.

The *Montreal* reached Quebec the following Saturday morning between five and six o'clock. When McMillan first observed his guest in the light of day, to his surprise he saw that, in addition to the spectacles which he wore, his hair was dyed dark brown, and was cut short.

Breakfast was had on board the steamer between seven and eight o'clock. Between nine and ten, the steamship company sent a tug to take the passengers and their luggage on board the *Peruvian*. Father Boucher had also gone to Quebec to see off his friend, but was for some reason not permitted to go on board the *Peruvian*.

When McMillan and his friends had arrived on board the steamer, Father LaPierre said to the doctor that he desired him to let Mr. Mc-Carty remain in his room until after the departure of the steamer. This was done, and Father LaPierre now returned on shore. In another half hour, the steamer was gone.

From this time, McCarty, whenever the opportunity presented itself, sought the company of McMillan, with whom he became very intimate, and indulged in a series of conversations and revelations which were not only very damaging to himself, but subsequently became of the highest value to the Government.

On the very same day on which McCarty had embarked, he approached Dr. McMillan, after lunch or dinner, and pointing to one of the passengers, asked if he knew who that gentleman was. The answer came that he did not, but that he was probably a passenger like himself. McCarty then replied that he thought the man was an American detective, and that he was after him. McMillan said that he did not believe anything of the kind. "What," said the doctor, "have you done that you should be afraid of an American detective?"

To this McCarty replied that he had done more things than the doctor was aware of, and that very likely, if he knew all, it would make him stare or something to that effect.

McMillan then told him that he should not be afraid of an American detective; that he was on board a British ship in British waters, and that if an American detective had been after him, he would have tried to arrest him before he left port.

Then McCarty retorted that he did not care if the man was a detective, that if he tried to arrest him, this would settle him—and in saying so he put his hand into his waistcoat pocket, and drew a small four-barreled revolver.

McCarty now informed McMillan that he had been in the habit for some time during the rebellion of going to Richmond with dispatches, and bringing them back to Washington, and also to Montreal. He stated that at one time he was told in Montreal that he would meet a lady in New York, and that he did meet her in that city; that he went to Washington with her; from Washington he started for Richmond with the lady in question and four or five others; that after a great deal of trouble they managed to cross the Potomac; that when they got south of Fredericksburg, they were drawn or pushed on a platform car by negroes. As they were moved along, they saw some five or six men coming towards them. It was ascertained that they were Union prisoners or soldiers escaped from Southern prisons; they were, according to McCarty, nearly starved to death. The woman who was with the men said, "Let's shoot the damned Yankees." She had hardly uttered the words when they all drew their revolvers and shot them, and then went right along, paying no more attention to them.

At another time, he told McMillan that there were several of them crossing the Potomac in a boat; it was in the evening, when they were perceived by a gunboat and hailed. They were ordered to surrender, or else they would be fired upon. They immediately said they would surrender. The gunboat sent a small boat to them; they waited until the boat came alongside, then fired right into them, and escaped to the shore.

McCarty also said that he was with a regiment of rebel soldiers one evening; that after sunset he and some others went into an orchard or garden close by to pick some fruit; that while sitting on the ground they heard the ticking of a telegraph, or what they supposed to be a telegraphic machine; that they went down to the headquarters of the regiment and reported the fact; that the party in command ordered some soldiers to go to the house connected with the orchard and search it; that in the garret of the house in a closet, a Union soldier was discovered; that they found he had an underground wire, and was working a telegraph. They took him down and shot or hung him.

In reference to his visit to Richmond before the fall of that city, McCarty told McMillan that he had seen the Secretary of State, Mr. Benjamin, several times, and that he had received two large sums of money from him, respectively $30,000 and $70,000.

In talking of the mere possibility of his being arrested in England, he said he would shoot the first officer who would lay his hand on him. On being told that if he did so, he would be shown very little leniency in England, his reply was, "I know it, and for that very reason I would do it, because I would rather be hung by an English hangman than by a Yankee one, for I know very well if I go back to the United States I shall swing."

Among other things revealed (by Surratt) to McMillan was the fact that he had been concerned in the plan for carrying off President Lincoln from Washington; that it was entirely concocted by John Wilkes Booth and himself; that he was in Montreal during the week prior to the assassination; that he had during that period received a letter from John Wilkes Booth, dated "New York," ordering him immediately to Washington, as it had been necessary to change their plans, and to act promptly, and that, thereupon, he started at once for Washington. He said that on his way back, he stopped at Elmira, in the state of New York, and that while there he telegraphed to John Wilkes Booth in New York City, and that the answer came back that Booth had already started for Washington.

Concerning his escape from the United States after the assassination, McCarty said that he arrived at St. Albans a few days after the assassination; that the train was delayed there some time, and that he took advantage of it to go to the village to get his breakfast; that while sitting at the public table with several other persons he saw that there was a great deal of talking and excitement among those who were at the same table with him. He asked his neighbor, an old man, what the talk was about. The man replied, "Why, don't you know that Mr. Lincoln has been assassinated?" McCarty answered, "Oh, the story is too good to be true."

The man whom he had addressed then handed him a newspaper, which he opened, and said that among the names of the assassins, he saw his own. This so unnerved him at the moment that he dropped the paper in his seat, and that was the last of his breakfast.

He arose from the table, walked into another room, and just as he was passing from it, he heard a party rushing in, say that Surratt must have passed, or must then be in St. Albans, as his handkerchief had been found in the street with his name upon it. Then without thinking he clapped his hands on a courier bag in the outside pocket of which he was always in the habit of carrying his pocket handkerchief, and he found out that he had really lost it.* [6] Then he concluded it was time to make himself scarce, and he made for Canada as soon as possible. When he arrived in Montreal he went to the house of one Mr. Porterfield, a Confederate agent. Realizing that he was being pursued by the detectives, even in that city, it became necessary for him to leave there. Accordingly, one evening two carriages were driven to the Porterfield residence. McCarty and another party dressed nearly as he was came out at the same time, and got one into one carriage, and the other, into the second. The carriages were then started, the one being driven one way, and the other in an opposite direction. The carriage in which Mc-Carty (Surratt) was went to the foot of the island of Montreal, about ten miles from the city. A man there had been engaged previously to take him across the river, and did so in a small canoe during the night. He was carried to the southern shore of the St. Lawrence. From this point he was guided across the country to a village on the Grand Trunk Railroad named St. Liboire. Here he was put in charge of the priest of the parish, Rev. Charles Boucher, and made his abode with him.

In describing this place, McCarty said to McMillan that between the bedroom and sitting room, there was a hole cut in the partition for a stove; that under the stove there was a vacant space about six or eight inches high; that one day while the priest was absent, he was lying on the sofa in his bedroom when a female servant, desirous of knowing who was in the priest's house, put her head under the stove so as to see in the room. He saw her face as it came under the stove, and scared her away by jumping suddenly at her. The story was immediately circulated around the village that the priest had a woman in his room hiding. Then the priest told McCarty that he could keep him no longer, and that he must find other quarters. He was now returned to Montreal, and secreted in the home of Father LaPierre.

On the last day of his stay on board the *Peruvian*, which was Sunday, September 24, in the afternoon he approached Dr. McMillan and desired to converse with him. They went behind the wheel house. Here he told his listener many things. Among others he said, pointing to the coast of Ireland, in sight of which they were then sailing, "Here is a foreign land at last. I hope I shall be able to return to my country in two

* This statement is fully corroborated by the testimony of the witness Blinn, who found the handkerchief.

years. I hope to God"—at the same holding in his hand a revolver—"I shall live to see the time when I can serve Andrew Johnson as Abraham Lincoln has been served."

As the hour approached when he would have to leave the steamer, McCarty asked McMillan what he would advise him to do, to land in Ireland, or go down to Liverpool, but McMillan told him that he would give him no advice whatever; that he might do just what and land where he pleased.

McCarty then said, "Well, I believe I will go down to Liverpool with you." McMillan was somewhat surprised, therefore, when on reaching the Irish coast he met his acquaintance in the after square of the vessel, and saw him all prepared to leave.

"Hello," exclaimed the doctor, "are you going ashore? I thought you were going to Liverpool." McCarty answered, "I have thought over the matter, and I believe it is better for me to get out here. It is now dark, and there is less chance of being seen."

Then McMillan said, "You have been telling me a great many things about what you have done, and seen, and I believe the name under which you travel is not your name. Will you please give me your name?"

McCarty looked about to see if anyone was near, and then whispered in McMillan's ears, "My name is Surratt."

Then Surratt requested McMillan to get him some liquor to drink. All this time he appeared to be very much excited. The required liquor was secured, and Surratt took three drinks of raw brandy.

By this time the vessel had arrived at the place where the mails and passengers are taken off the steamships. McMillan, seeing the half-intoxicated condition in which his friend was, called for the chief officer at the gangway, and asked him to lead Surratt down by the arm. This was done and Surratt was accordingly landed in Ireland. On the following Wednesday, he called on Dr. McMillan at his boarding place in Birkenhead, and asked to be directed to a certain house in Liverpool. Birkenhead is directly opposite Liverpool. A cab was called for, and after going a certain distance with him, McMillan left the cab, and requested the driver to take Surratt to the house to which he desired to go. Surratt had letters from his Canadian friends to clergymen and others in England.

Before meeting Surratt at Birkenhead, McMillan had gone to the American consul at Liverpool, and made affidavit as to Surratt, and the information he had imparted to him on the *Peruvian*. McMillan returned to Canada, and then on his return met Surratt once or twice again. Surratt had entrusted him with some messages to his friends in Canada, and this was the last Dr. McMillan saw of Surratt until he confronted him as a witness at his trial.

CHAPTER XXIX

Surratt tarries for a time in England · Goes to France · Arrives at Rome · Enters the English College · Enlists in the Papal Zouaves · Is discovered by Sainte Marie, who reports the fact to the American minister · Steps taken for Surratt's capture · Interview with Cardinal Antonelli · Surratt is arrested · His escape · Leaps into a yawning chasm · Makes his way to Naples · Sails for Alexandria, Egypt · His recapture · Placed on board the gunboat Swatara · Starts homeward · His arrival in Washington in February 1867

After a brief sojourn in England, during which he visited London, Birmingham, and Liverpool, Surratt took his departure for France. In this country, his stay was of but short duration, and as soon as possible he made his way to Rome, Italy, which he reached in November or December 1865. While in Canada, he had procured letters for some parties in Rome, amongst others the Reverend Dr. Neane, rector of the English College. Being detained for some days at Civita Vecchia, and having no money to pay his expenses there, he wrote to Dr. Neane, from whom he received fifty francs.

On his arrival at Rome, he went to the English College, where he lived for some time. His assumed name was now John Watson. The College, too, did not afford him a safe retreat, for he began to grow uneasy and to suspect that he was being pursued, and, therefore, as a final resort he made up his mind to enlist in the Papal Zouaves. This he did in January 1866, and was enrolled as John Watson in the 3rd Company of Volunteers, stationed at [Sezze], about forty miles distant from Rome.

Alas, even here, amid the vine-clad hills of sunny Italy and among a foreign soldiery, thousands of miles away from his native land, John H. Surratt was not secure. A grim Nemesis was ever on his path and destined to overtake him. One day in one of his walks he was halted by a dark-eyed, sun-browned young man who stepped up to him and said, "What is your name?" "My name is John Watson," replied Surratt. "No, your name is not John Watson, your name is John H. Surratt, and you were introduced to me by Louis J. Weichmann at Little Texas, Maryland, in 1863," answered the young man.

It was, indeed, Henri B. de Sainte Marie who now stood face to face with him and who identified him.

Surratt at once acknowledged to Sainte Marie that he was right in his assertion, and begged him for God's sake to keep the matter secret, and to let bygones be bygones.

Sainte Marie, however, lost no time in communicating his discovery to the American minister, General Rufus King, then resident at Rome. In fact, he had been laboring for months towards the accomplishment of this end. He was in Canada when Lincoln was assassinated. When Surratt left for Europe, through some means he became possessed of that information. He then resolved to pursue him, and accordingly tracked him through England and France, and finally found him serving in the Papal Zouaves, in which organization he himself enlisted.

As soon as General King had heard Sainte Marie's story, he at once, under date of April 23, 1866, wrote to Mr. Seward, Secretary of State, at Washington as follows:

Sir:

On Saturday last, 21st instant, a private in the Papal Zouaves, giving his name as H. B. St. Marie, and claiming to be Canadian by birth, called upon me for the purpose, as he said, of communicating the information that John H. Surratt, who was charged with complicity in the murder of President Lincoln, but made his escape at the time from the United States, had recently enlisted in the Papal Zouaves, under the name of John Watson, and was now stationed with his company, the 3rd, at [Sezze]. My informant said that he had known Surratt in America; that he recognized him as soon as he saw him at [Sezze]; that he called him by his proper name, and that Surratt, taking him aside, admitted that he was right in the guess. He added that Surratt acknowledged his participation in the plot against Mr. Lincoln's life, and declared that Jefferson Davis had incited or was privy to it. St. Marie further said that Surratt seemed to be well provided with money, and appealed to him as a comrade not to betray his secret; and he expressed an earnest desire that if any steps were taken towards reclaiming Surratt as a criminal, he, St. Marie, should not be known in the matter. He spoke so positively in answer to my questions as to his acquaintance with Surratt, and the certainty that he was the man, and there seemed such entire absence of motive for any false statement on the subject, that I could not very well doubt the truth of what he told me. I deemed it my duty, therefore, to report the circumstance to the Department and ask for instructions.

I have the honor to be, with great respect, your obedient servant,

Rufus King.[1]

Upon receipt of General King's letter at Washington, the information it contained was promptly communicated to the Secretary of War, and by that officer referred to the Judge Advocate General, Holt, for report.

General Holt replied as follows:

Bureau of Military Justice,
Washington, May 19, 1866.

Respectfully returned.

It is recommended that the American Minister at Rome be urged to procure without delay, if possible, a full statement of John H. Surratt's confession to H. B. St. Marie, verified by oath, which could probably be obtained through assurances that St. Marie should in no matter be compromised thereby. This man, there is reason to believe, is the same referred to by one of the witnesses on the trial of the assassins of the President.* He was represented to have been engaged in school teaching in Maryland, at a village called Ellangowan, in the year 1863. Afterwards he came to Washington, and was for a short time employed by Father Wigget.† He stated that he had come from Montreal, Canada, where he

* Myself. [Weichmann.]
† Dr. White, and not Wigget.

had sold his farm, the proceeds of which he had lost in this country. He spoke French, Italian, and English fluently, and was known as Henri de St. Marie. The American Minister has no doubt written it "B" instead of de St. Marie.

The particulars above given will make it easy to ascertain if this is the person mentioned in the despatch to the Secretary of State. If he is, it is believed that it can be shown here that he is a man of character and entitled to credit in his statements. It may be added that in his despatch the American Minister has slightly mistaken Surratt's name. It is not John S., as he supposes, but John H.

J. Holt,
Judge Advocate General.[2]

Also this letter:

Bureau of Military Justice,
[Washington, D.C.,] May 22, 1866.

Mr. F. W. Seward,
Asst. Sec'y. of State.

Dear Sir:

Referring to your conversation of this morning, I have the honor to state that the full name of the person supposed to be alluded to in the despatch of the American Minister at Rome is now ascertained to be Henri Beaumont de St. Marie. He is represented to be about five feet eight inches in height, thirty years old, of a very dark complexion, and black hair, with sharp piercing eyes. Should he make a statement in regard to Surratt's confession, there should be embodied in it his entire name, together with the circumstances of his sojourn in the United States; if he was here, mentioning dates, places, etc., as well as the names of some persons with whom he was associated. This will make the question of identity of easy solution.

Very respectfully, your obedient servant,
J. Holt.[3]

Much further correspondence now took place between General King and Secretary Seward in relation to the matter, covering a period of several months, which is not material to reproduce here. During all this time Surratt was at his ease in the Zouaves, and was leading a pleasant life, utterly unsuspicious of the fate in store for him.[4]

Among the questions to arise now was that of extradition in the event of the United States Government demanding his arrest and surrender by the Papal authorities. There was no treaty of extradition in force between the two countries, and it became a matter of serious comment how the Holy Father, Pius IX, would act when the case would be called to his attention. The Government at Washington, however, was not long left in the dark as to the position of both Cardinal Antonelli and the Pope. Their action when appealed to was so high-minded and honorable that it should forever endear them to all Americans who revere the name of Lincoln, and should for all time set at rest the silly story that the Catholic Church in any way rejoiced at his death or was privy to it.

The following correspondence in relation to this point will be of great interest:

Rome, August 8, 1866.

Sir:

I availed myself of the opportunity to repeat to the Cardinal the information communicated to me by St. Marie in regard to John H. Surratt. His Eminence was greatly interested by it, and intimated that if the American Government desired the surrender of the criminal there would probably be no difficulty in the way.

I am, sir, very respectfully, your obedient servant,

Rufus King.[5]

To Mr. Seward.

In reply to this communication, Mr. Seward, under date of October 16, 1866, among other things wrote to Minister King:

Extract.

3. Seek an interview with Cardinal Antonelli, and referring to an intimation made by him to Mr. King in a conversation which took place on the 7th of August last (as reported in Mr. King's No. 62), namely, "that if the American Government desired the surrender of the criminal (Surratt) there would probably be no difficulty in the way," ask the Cardinal whether His Holiness would

now be willing, in the absence of an extradition treaty to deliver John H. Surratt upon an authentic indictment, and at the request of this department, for complicity in the assassination of the late President Lincoln, or whether, in the event of this request being declined, his Holiness would enter [into] an extradition treaty with us, which would enable us to reach the [his] surrender.

4. Ask as a favor to this Government that neither St. Marie nor Surratt be discharged from the guards until we shall have had time to communicate concerning them after receiving a prompt reply to this communication from you.[6]

To this Mr. King made answer as follows:

Rome, November 2, 1866.

Sir:

I hasten to acknowledge your despatch No. 43, marked "confidential," under date of October 16th, in reply to my private letter of September 12th from Hamburg, and conveying instructions upon the subject therein referred to. I lost no time in seeking an interview with the Cardinal Secretary of State, as directed to do in the aforesaid despatch; and with that view proceeded this morning to the Vatican, accompanied by Mr. Hooker, acting as secretary, as well that he should hear the conversation between the Cardinal and myself, as that he should repeat to His Eminence in Italian what I proposed saying to him in French, relative to the wishes and expectations of our Government in reference to Surratt. We were fortunate in finding the Cardinal alone and disengaged, and I proceeded to state at once the business upon which we had called. His Eminence was greatly interested in the matter, the more so as I showed him the portraits of the "conspirators" contained in the volume published by "Benn Pitman," and entitled "Assassination of President Lincoln." [7] He remembered very well our previous conversation on the same subject (referred to in my despatch No. 62 of August [8]), and the intimation he then gave me as to the disposition of the Papal authorities to surrender Surratt, should he be claimed by the American Government; and in reply to my question whether, upon authentic indictment or the usual preliminary proof, and at the request of the State Department, he would be willing to deliver up John H. Surratt, frankly replied in the affirmative. He added that there was, indeed, no extradition treaty between the two countries, and that to surrender a criminal, where capital punishment was likely to ensue, was not exactly in accordance with the spirit of the Papal Government; but that in so grave and exceptional a case, and with the understanding that the United States Government, under parallel circumstances, would do as they desired to be done by, he thought the request of the State Department for the surrender of Surratt would be granted. I then requested, as a favor to the American Government, that neither Surratt nor St. Marie should be discharged from the Papal service until further communication from the State Department, and His Eminence promised to advise with the minister of war to that effect. I thanked His Eminence for his prompt and frank replies to my queries, and assured him that they would give great satisfaction to our Government. . . .

I have the honor to be, very respectfully, your obedient servant,

Rufus King.[8]

Also the following from Mr. King to Mr. Seward:

Rome, November 10, 1866.

Sir:

In my despatch No. 65, under date of November 2nd, I mentioned the result of the interview I had had with the Cardinal Secretary of State on the subject referred to in your "confidential" communication of October 16. I had occasion yesterday to call again upon His Eminence, with the view to ascertain, if possible, the truth of the widely prevalent rumor, that the Pope intended leaving Rome and seeking a refuge in the island of Malta. Before, however, I had the opportunity of making this inquiry, the Cardinal apprised me that John Watson, alias John H. Surratt, had been arrested by his orders, and that while on his way to Rome had made his escape from the guard of six men in whose charge he had been placed. At the same time His Eminence handed me the official documents, copies of which I herewith transmit, relating to the arrest, the escape, and the subsequent pursuit. As Veroli is close to the frontier, it is not at all unlikely that Surratt will make good his escape from his Zouave pursuers into the Italian Kingdom. I thought it well, therefore, to send a confidential person at once to Florence to lay the whole case before the American Minister, and solicit his aid and that of the Italian Government in the recapture; for I did not feel at all sure that either a message by telegraph or a letter by mail to Mr. Marsh would, under the circumstances, escape the surveillance or possible interruption of the Papal authorities. I hope to have a report from my messenger within two or three days, and as Surratt was in his Zouave dress when he effected his escape, I think the chance a fair one that he will be retaken. I trust that the course which I have pursued in the premises will meet the approbation of the Department. I feel bound to add that, incredible as the details of the story appear, the Cardinal spoke of them as verified beyond all question, and expressed very great and apparently sincere regret at Surratt's escape.

I have the honor to be, very respectfully, your obedient servant,

Rufus King.[9]

(Order.)

November 6, 1866.

Colonel:

Cause the arrest of the Zouave Watson, and have him conducted under secure escort to the military prison at Rome. It is of much importance that this order be executed with exactness.

The General, pro: minister, Kanzler

To Lieut. Col. Allet.

Pontifical Zouaves.

Velletri, November 7, 1866.

General:

I have the honor to inform you that the Zouave John Watson has been arrested at Veroli, and will be taken to-morrow morning, under good escort to Rome. While he was searched for at Trisulte, which was his garrison, he was arrested by Captain De Lambilly, at Veroli, where he was on leave. I have the honor to inform you that his name is not Waston but Watson.

I have the honor to be, general, your excellency's very humble and obedient servant,

Lieut. Col. Allet.[10]

Pontifical Telegraph

(Presented at Velletri, 8th of November, 1866, at 8:35 A.M.
Received at Rome, 8th November, 1866, at 8:50 A.M.)

His Excellency, the General, Minister of War, Rome.

I received the following telegram dated ———— from Captain Lambilly:

At the moment of leaving the prison, surrounded by six men as guards, Watson plunged into the ravine, more than a hundred feet deep, which defends the prison. Fifty zouaves are in pursuit.

I will send your Excellency the news which I shall receive by telegraph.

Lieut. Col. Allet.[11]

Pontifical Zouaves.

Velletri, November 9, 1866.

My Dear General:

Following out your Excellency's orders, I sent this morning, to Veroli, Lieutenant de Farnel, to make examinations into the escape of Zouave Watson. I have learned some of the details of this unfortunate business. Watson at the moment when he was arrested must have been on his guard, having obtained knowledge of a letter addressed to Zouave St. Marie, which concerned him probably. This letter, sent by mistake to a trumpeter named St. Marie, was opened by him and shown to Watson, because it was written in English. I have sent [it] to your Eminence, with the report of Captain Lambilly.

I am sure that the escape of Watson savors of a prodigy. He leaped from a height of 23 feet on a narrow rock, beyond which is a precipice. The filth from the barracks accumulated on the rock [and in this manner the fall of Watson was broken], and in going farther he would have fallen into an abyss.

I am, with respect, my general, your Eminence's very humble subordinate.

Allet.[12]

To Minister of War Roux.

Veroli, November 8, 1866.

My Dear Colonel:

I regret to announce to you that, notwithstanding all my precautions, I learn Watson has succeeded in escaping. To carry out the orders received, I had sent Sergeant Halyerid and six men to Tresulte, where this zouave was on duty. They did not find him there, for on that day Watson had asked leave to go to Veroli. I charged the corporal of the 3rd Company, Vanderstroeten, to take him and turn him over to the post corporal, Warrin, to whom I had already given all my instructions on this subject.

All the measures ordered were carried out from point to point; two sentinels with loaded arms were placed, one at the very door of his prison, with orders to prevent any communication of the prisoner with persons outside, and the other at the door of the barrack. The prison, the doors and windows, etc., had been inspected in the minutest details by the locksmith of the commune. There was, therefore, nothing to fear in that quarter. All passed off well until this morning at four o'clock.

Then the prisoner was awakened, arose, put on his gaiters, and took his coffee with a calmness and phlegm quite English. The gate of the prison opens on a platform which overlooks the country; a balustrade prevents the promenaders from tumbling on the rocks, situated at least thirty-five feet below the windows of the prison.

Beside the gate of the prison are situated the outhouses of the barracks; Watson asked permission to halt there. Corporal Warrin, who had six men with him as guards, allowed him to stop, very naturally nothing doubting, either he or the zouaves present, that their prisoner was going to escape at a place which it seemed quite impossible to us to clear. This perilous leap was, however, to be taken, to be crowned with success. In fact, Watson, who seemed quiet, seized the balustrade, made a leap, and cast himself into the void, falling on the uneven rocks, where he might have broken his bones a thousand times, and gained the depths of the valley. Patrols were immediately organized, but in vain. We saw a peasant, who told us that he had seen an unarmed zouave who was going towards Casa Mari, which is the way to Piedmont.

I address you herewith the report of the corporal of the post, besides two letters which are not without importance. They may be of some use to the police.

Lieutenant Mously and I have been to examine the localities, and we asked ourselves how one could make such leaps without breaking arms or legs.

Please, my colonel, to receive the assurance of my request [respect].

De Lambilly.

I have sent the description of this zouave to the gens. d'armerie.[13]

Surratt when he struck the ledge of rocks was knocked senseless. In the meantime what a scene of confusion and what a babel of voices there was above! The lieutenant in command wrung his hands in anguish and swore in choice, musical Italian. His break had been so sudden that every man was taken completely by surprise. Running to the side of the precipice, they looked over the wall. They immediately began firing down on him. He was brought back to his senses by the reports of their rifles from above, and the bullets flattening themselves on the bare rock unpleasantly near his head. Dizzy and sick and shaken, he managed to gather himself together and crawl out of danger and gradually made his way down the side of the mountain to the little town which nestled at its base. Hurrying along the main street of the town, he ran directly into the arms of a detail of Zouaves. They were as much surprised as he, but he had the advantage of being on the alert. With him it was almost a matter of life or death. Doubling quickly on his tracks and expecting every moment to be hit by some of the bullets which were flying around his head, he ran like a frightened deer. Through alleys, down dark streets, and across lots he sped, and managed to elude his pursuers. In the meantime the entire town was in an uproar. Everyone had the alarm and all the gates were guarded. Selecting a good point, he managed to get over the wall and headed down the white Italian road towards the coast. All this took place during the early hours of the morning. By the time he had left the town a few miles in the road, the sun was high in the heavens, and he was congratulating himself on his escape, when he was suddenly startled by the sharp command:

"Halt! Who goes there?"

"Friend," he answered in his best Italian, recognizing that he had run into a Garibaldian camp. Glancing at his Papal uniform, the outpost was by no means reassured. In the meantime, Surratt raised his hands above his head. Bringing his rifle to his shoulder, the guard was pressing the trigger unpleasantly hard. Raising his hands even higher in the air, Surratt sang out to him, "Lower your rifle, man; can't you see my hands are up?" Still covering him with his rifle, the guard ordered him to advance within a few paces of him and called out lustily for the corporal of the guard. That officer came on the run, and seeing Surratt's rig, called for the sergeant of the guard, who no sooner caught the glimpse of his dress than he called the officer of the guard. To make a long story short, Surratt was soon surrounded by a mob of Garibaldians of all ranks and sizes. When he told them that he was an American, a deserter from the Guard, and wanted to get to the coast, they treated him with the greatest kindness.

As he was passing under English passports, Surratt went direct to the English consul and told him who he was. Glancing with unmingled surprise at his red fez, baggy trousers, and leggings of the Papal Zouaves, he said to him, "Do you realize for a moment, man, the risk you run? Don't you know that Naples is in the hands of the Garibaldi, and that you might have had a knife run in your back at any moment?"

Surratt told him that the Garibaldians were the very best friends he had—the only friends, in fact, and that the money he had in his pocket was given him by them.[14]

Surratt's stay in Naples was limited to nine days—from the 8th of November to the 17th, when he took the steamer for Alexandria.

In the meantime the following correspondence in relation to his escape had been submitted to Mr. Seward by General King.

Sir:

I had hoped ere this to have been able to announce to the department the fact of the recapture of John H. Surratt, whose arrest and subsequent escape were mentioned in my last despatch; but I regret to say that thus far all our efforts to apprehend the fugitive have proved fruitless. Mr. Marsh, our Minister at Florence, will no doubt report to the Government the steps he may have seen fit to take in the premises. I shall therefore, content myself with a brief recital of what was done here.

On Friday last, November 16, General Kanzler, the Papal Minister of War, called to inform me of a rumor which had reached him that Surratt had been received, wounded into a military hospital at Sora, a few miles beyond the Papal frontier. I instantly telegraphed this information to Mr. Marsh, and in a few hours received a reply from him to the effect that he had made the necessary application to the Italian Government. Regarding, however, the identification and apprehension of Surratt as of the first importance, I despatched Mr. Hooker, acting secretary of Legation, by the earliest train to Sora, furnished with all the necessary documents and a photograph of Surratt, and also with instructions, if he found Surratt there, to ask, in the name of the American Government, that he should be held in close custody until a proper demand could be made upon the Italian authorities for his surrender as a fugitive from justice. Mr. Hooker executed his mission with intelligence and despatch. Arriving at Isoletta, the frontier station, and communicating by telegraph with the commanding officer at Sora, he ascertained that one of the Pontifical zouaves, calling himself Watson, of Richmond, United States, twenty-two years old, tall, fair complexion, blue eyes, high forehead, reddish (sandy) hair, moustache and goatee, had passed Sora for Naples, on the 8th instant, the same day that he escaped from Veroli, only a few miles distant. Mr. Hooker at once telegraphed this intelligence to our Consul at Naples. The officer in charge at Isoletta did the same to the Neapolitan chief of police. Both asked that Surratt should, if possible, be arrested. I received a prompt reply from Mr. Swan at Naples, acknowledging receipt of Mr. Hooker's telegram, and stating that they were on the lookout for Surratt. Our hopes were strong, therefore, that we should succeed in catching him somewhere in the vicinity of Naples. But yesterday a second despatch from Mr. Swan apprised us that Surratt had left the preceding day, November 17th, for Alexandria, by a steamer which stopped at Malta to coal, and that he had telegraphed the facts to our Consul at that point. I also immediately telegraphed to Mr. Winthrop at Malta, urging the arrest of Surrat, but up to the moment of closing this despatch I have received no reply from Mr. Winthrop. The probabilities I fear, are, that Surratt will make good his escape.

Some surprise perhaps may be expressed that Surratt was arrested by the Papal authorities, before any request to that effect had been made by the American Government. This was alluded to in the conversation I had on the subject with Cardinal Antonelli and the Minister of War, on Friday last. Both gave me to understand that the arrest was made with the approval of his Holiness, and in anticipation of any application from the State Department, as well as for the purpose of placing Surratt in safe custody, as with the view to show the disposition of the Papal authorities to comply with the expected request of the

American authorities. I have no reason to doubt the entire good faith of the Papal Government in the matter.

I enclose for the information of the Department, copies of one or two additional reports upon the facts connected with Surratt's arrest and escape.

I have the honor to be, with great respect, your obedient servant,

Rufus King.[15]

To Mr. Seward.

Mr. Frank Swan was the U. S. consul in those days at Naples, and in his letter to Mr. Seward, he tells the story of Surratt's movements while in Naples, and of the steps he took which resulted in his recapture at Alexandria, Egypt.

United States Consulate,
Naples, November 21, 1866.

Sir: On Sunday morning, November 19, I received a despatch from Hon. Rufus King, minister at Rome, of which the following is a copy: "Surratt, conspirator against Lincoln, under the name of Watson, went to Naples the 8th. Arrest him if possible." I immediately went to the quistore here, and at three o'clock learned from him, through the police, that Surratt had sailed the evening before by the English steamer for Alexandria, touching at Malta. I immediately telegraphed to our consul at the latter port, informing him of the fact.

Since that time I have learned the following: Surratt came here about the 8th, dressed in the uniform of the Papal zouaves, having no passport, but stating that he was an Englishman who had just escaped from a Roman regiment. He stated that he had no money, and the police being somewhat suspicious of him, gave him (at his own request) lodgings in the prison, not exactly as a prisoner, but holding him for three days in surveillance, and questioning him as opportunity offered. He stated that he had been in Rome two months, that being out of money he had enlisted in the Roman zouaves, and was put in prison for insubordination, from which he escaped by jumping from a high wall, or window, in doing which he hurt his back and arm, both of which were injured. On the third day he asked to be taken to the British consulate, to which place one of the police went with him, when he complained of his confinement, stating that he was a Canadian, and the consul claimed his release as an English subject. In the meantime the police had found that he had twelve scudi with him, and on asking him why he went to prison, he replied that he wished to save his money. He remained there till Saturday, giving them some trouble at the English Consulate, and exciting sympathy by his position of a young man of good appearance, without means, they not knowing of the money which the police had found. He expressed at the consulate the greatest desire to return to Canada, and through the influence of the consul he obtained passage on the steamer to Alexandria, some English gentlemen paying for his board during the voyage, and giving him a few francs. He still wore his uniform when he sailed.

The steamer left here Saturday [evening] at nine o'clock, clearing for Alexandria but not having time to coal here, the captain intended to stop at Malta to do so, which would detain him all day Monday. The following is a copy of the despatch which I sent to our consul at Malta:

Sunday afternoon at three o'clock—"Surratt, one of the conspirators against Lincoln left here last evening on the steamer Tripoli for Alexandria, under the name of Waters or Watson. He has on the uniform of the Papal States. The steamer stops at Malta to-morrow to coal. Have him arrested. If you do not receive this in time, telegraph the consul at Alexandria." As there is a quarantine between Naples and Malta, he could not land there.

Signore La Cava, the quistore of Naples, exercised the greatest promptness in finding Surratt's whereabouts, sending word immediately to all the neighboring towns.

I have the honor to be, very truly

Frank Swan, Consul.[16]

What took place when the vessel arrived at Alexandria is fully told in the annexed dispatch sent to Mr. Seward by Consul General [Charles] Hale:

Agency and Consulate General of the United States of America, Alexandria, Egypt, November 27th, 1866.

Sir: I have the honor to report that in the consequence of a telegram received via Constantinople, from Mr. King, United States minister at Rome, and of several letters received from Mr. Winthrop, United States consul at Malta (the Mediterranean wire being, unfortunately, broken between Malta and this place), I have this day arrested a man calling himself Walters, dressed in the uniform of a zouave, who arived at Alexandria on the 23rd instant, in the steamship Tripoli, from Naples, and who is believed to be John Harrison Surratt, one of the conspirators of the assassination of President Lincoln.

The telegram and some of the letters being delayed in transmission, I was fortunate in finding the man still in quarantine among the third class passengers, of whom there is no list whatever. It is easy to distinguish him among seventy-eight of these by his zouave uniform, and scarcely less easy by his almost unmistakable American type of countenance. I said at once to him, "You are the man I want; you are an American." He said, "Yes, sir; I am." I said, "You doubtless know why I want you. What is your name?" He replied promptly, "Walters." I said, "I believe your true name is Surratt," and in arresting him mentioned my official position as United States consul general. The director of quarantine speedily arranged a sufficient escort of soldiers, by whom the prisoner was conducted to a safe place within the quarantine walls. Although the walk occupied several minutes, the prisoner, close to my side, made no remark whatever, displaying neither surprise nor irritation. Arriving at the place prepared, I gave him the usual magisterial caution that he was not obliged to say anything, and that anything he said would be at once taken down in writing. He said, "I have nothing to say, I want nothing but what is right." He declared that he had neither Passport, nor money except six francs.

His companions confirm his statements in this respect. They say he came to Naples a deserter from the Papal army at Rome. I find that he has no papers, and no clothes but those he is wearing.

The appearance of the prisoner answers very well the description given by Weichmann, at page 116 of Pitman's Report, officially sent to me by the government, and is accurately portrayed in the likeness of Surratt in the frontispiece of the same volume. Mr. King and Mr. Winthrop speak in confident terms of the identity of the zouave Walters with Surratt, and after seeing the man I have not the slightest doubt of it.[17]

On December 24, 1866, General Hale sent the following cablegram to Washington:

To Seward:

I delivered Surratt on board Corvette Swatara twenty-first (21st.) December. No trouble.

Hale, Alexandria.[18]

The vessel was at once started homeward and reached Washington about the middle of February 1867.[19]

Surratt was now placed in the custody of the United States marshal;[20] he had been away from his country more than twenty-two months.

His indictment and trial soon followed.

CHAPTER XXX

Trial of John H. Surratt · Judge George P. Fisher · The Honorable Edwards Pierrepont, the Honorable A. G. Riddle, Edward C. Carrington, Esq., and Nathaniel Wilson, Esq., counsel for the Government · Surratt selects Joseph H. Bradley, Sr., Richard T. Merrick, and Joseph H. Bradley, Jr., as his attorneys · Testimony as to Surratt's presence in Washington on the evening of April 14, 1865 · Argument of counsel · Case goes to the jury · Disagreement and discharge of the jury · Surratt remanded to jail · His final release

The 10th of June 1867 was fixed as the time for holding Surratt's trial. During all this period of over three months, from the time of his delivery to the authorities at Washington, he remained in jail.

His friends and counsel, however, had free access to him, and helped him to prepare his case.[1]

On the abolishment of the old circuit and criminal court of the District of Columbia, and the creation of the Supreme Court by the act of Congress of March 3, 1863, the Honorable George P. Fisher was appointed one of the four justices of the new tribunal. Having recently completed a five-year term as attorney general of his native state—Delaware—his colleagues thought it best that he should take the laboring oar of holding the criminal court. It fell to his lot to hold the March term of that court, 1867, during which Surratt was indicted and arraigned, and the day of his trial set. The case was conducted on the part of the Government by U. S. District Attorney Edward C. Carrington,

Esq., with whom were associated the Honorable Albert G. Riddle of Washington, the Honorable Edwards Pierrepont of New York, and Nathaniel Wilson, Esq., assistant district attorney, and on the part of the prisoner by his counsel, Joseph H. Bradley, Sr., Richard T. Merrick, and Joseph H. Bradley, Jr.

In justice to Judge Fisher it ought, perhaps, to be stated that during the trial of the other conspirators he never visited the military court, and not only refrained from reading any of the testimony adduced before it, but also declined to hear any conversation on the subject, for the reason that John H. Surratt was still at large—and that in all probability it would become his duty to preside at the trial, whenever he should be captured. He felt that he ought to avoid the possibility of allowing his mind to be affected by anything like bias or prejudice in the case. Moreover, that whatever bias he had, if any, was in Surratt's favor, as he had heard that he was brought up on a farm, and at the outbreak of the war had entered a college for the purpose of being educated for the Catholic priesthood, and he could scarcely conceive how one so young, and who had been reared under these influences, could at one bound descend to such a depth of criminal infamy.

Messrs. Wilson and Bradley, Jr., were bright young members of the Washington bar; Mr. Carrington was quite an experienced practitioner, a fluent speaker, and had been for six years the prosecuting attorney for the District of Columbia; Mr. Merrick was in the prime of manhood, a ripe scholar and highly cultured rhetorician; Mr. Pierrepont had acquired celebrity at the New York bar, and the elder Mr. Bradley had been in full practice in Washington City for about forty years or more. He, like Mr. Riddle, was a man of great legal ability—one of the very best Nisi Prius lawyers in the country; he always had his cases well in hand, and fought them with audacity from start to finish. To see him engaged in a trial, one could not help being reminded of the description given by a single line in *Ars Poetica*, by Horace, of the character of Achilles: "*Impiger, iracundus, inexorabilis, acer*" ("Impetuous, irascible, inexorable, bitter").

On the day for which Surratt's trial was set, immediately upon the calling of the case, the U. S. district attorney filed an affidavit sworn to and subscribed by Samuel E. Douglass, Register of the District of Columbia, setting forth that on or about the 1st day of February 1865, he had deposited in a box kept for that purpose, four hundred names of persons written on separate and similar slips of paper, each slip being carefully rolled and tied, as a part of the names from which jurors for that term of court were to be selected to serve during the term; that the clerk of the corporation of Georgetown had in like manner deposited in said box eighty names, and the clerk of the Levy Court of the county of Washington had deposited in said box the names of forty persons resident in the rural portion of the said county; that the qualifications and selection of these four hundred persons whose names were so deposited by him were passed upon by Mr. Douglass alone, without any consultation with any of the aforesaid clerks or either of them, and that each of the said clerks alone passed upon the qualifications and selection of the persons whose names were deposited as aforesaid by them respectively, and that neither of these officers communicated to either of the other two any of the names so deposited by him in said box, and that after the names of the persons written on said slips had been so deposited in the box as aforesaid, box was sealed not by register or by either said clerks, but was delivered by them or one of them unsealed, to the clerk of the court, who sealed it as he supposed.

Upon this affidavit the district attorney grounded a motion to quash the array of jurors; to this motion the counsel for the prisoner demurred, averring that the said motion was bad in law and in substance and that the facts stated therein did not constitute any ground in law for a challenge to the array; in which demurrer issue was joined by the U. S. and argued by counsel at great length and with much ability.

By the law as it stood prior to the passage of the act of Congress of the 16th of June 1862, both grand and petit jurors were selected and summoned by the marshal of the District. This act abolished the power of the marshal to select, and made it the duty of the Register of Washington City and the respective clerks of the city of Georgetown and the Levy Court of Washington County to select the jurors, both grand and petit, in the following manner:

Section 1 provides that "It shall be the duty of the Register of Washington City and of the respective clerks of the City of Georgetown and the Levy Court of Washington County in the District of Columbia within one month after passage and on or before the first day of February in each year thereafter to make a list of such of the white male citizens, tax payers, residing within their respective jurisdictions as they shall judge best qualified to serve as jurors in the courts of the said district in which lists may be included, in the discretion of the officer making the same, the names of such qualified persons as were on the list of the previous year, but did not serve as jurors; and the lists thus made by the Register and the clerks aforesaid shall be kept by them respectively and be delivered over to their successors in office."

Section 2 provides that "the officers aforesaid shall select from the list of the Register of Washington City the names of four hundred persons; from that of the clerk of Georgetown, eighty persons, and from that of the clerk of the Levy Court forty persons, which proportion after the year 1863 may be varied from year to year according to the increase or decrease of population in the respective jurisdictions, by order of the judges of the Circuit Court of Washington County."

These two first sections are quoted in their entirety.

Section 3 provides what persons shall be exempt from jury service.

Section 4 provides "that the names selected from said lists shall be written on separate and similar pieces of paper which shall be so folded or rolled up that the names cannot be seen and be placed in a box to be provided by the Register and clerks aforesaid; which box shall be sealed and after being thoroughly shaken shall be delivered to the clerk of the Circuit Court of Washington County for safe keeping."

The contention of the Government was that it was the duty of the Register and clerks, 1st: to make a list of each one for himself of the names of persons who were taxpayers, and who were also residents in his own jurisdiction as provided in Sec. 1 of the act of Congress aforesaid; 2nd: that then the three should meet together, each with his own list and that all three acting jointly should make selections from the Register list of four hundred names, from the list of the clerk of Georgetown, eighty names, and from the list of the clerk of the Levy Court, forty names, and 3rd: that these names (aggregating five hundred and twenty) should by the joint judgment of these three officers be selected and written on separate and similar slips of paper and deposited in the jury box, which box after such deposit should be sealed and delivered to the clerk of the Supreme Court for safe keeping and that the petit jurors for the March term of the criminal court, 1867, should be drawn therefrom by the clerk of the Supreme Court as provided in the fifth section of said act of Congress, whereas in truth and fact the Register of Washington never saw the names or passed upon the fitness of any of the persons named on the list either of the Georgetown clerk, or the clerk of the Levy Court, nor did either of these clerks see the names or pass upon the fitness of any of the persons upon the list of either of the other selecting officers, and that the box was not sealed by either of them, nor were the jury for said term of the criminal court drawn out of said box by the clerk of the Supreme Court. 4th: that the provisions of law in these respects were mandatory and not merely directory.

The discussion of this question lasted till the close of the second day of the trial; and on the morning of the third day, the judge, Fisher, decided that the Register of Washington, the clerk of Georgetown, and the clerk of the Levy Court not having selected, in their joint capacity, the five hundred and twenty names in the manner prescribed by the statute, the panel of jurors already in attendance was not a lawful panel, and ordered that the same should be quashed; and directed the marshal of the District of Columbia to summon twenty-six talesmen, in pursuance of the provisions of the act aforesaid.

There was great difficulty in obtaining a jury out of these twenty-six talesmen so summoned in obedience to this order; a large number were excused for good and sufficient reasons; several failed to appear, and others were summoned in their places, causing further delay. Upon the completion of the panel of twenty-six, by the appearance of the talesmen brought in on the second summons, the panel was at length completed, whereupon the prisoner's counsel filed in writing a challenge to the new array; but inasmuch as the question of the legality of the new panel had been virtually decided in the quashing of the first array, no argument was had upon this challenge, and after conference held between the counsel on both sides twelve jurors were selected by them from the new general panel, and it was agreed that these twelve need not be put on their voire dire in respect to previously formed opinion or conscientious scruples against capital punishment; but these twelve gentlemen appeared to be not so willing to serve on the trial as were the counsel to have them, and so forthwith began to make excuses which could not be ignored, and it became necessary to summon other talesmen to make up the twenty-six, which was done. Many of these last, on coming into court, declared that they had formed and expressed an opinion as to the guilt or innocence of the prisoner; others entertained conscientious scruples against rendering a verdict of guilty, in a case where the punishment was death, even though the evidence might be sufficient to satisfy them as to the guilt of the prisoner, and others still were invalids, unable to endure the continuous confinement of a long trial, such as Surratt's would probably be; so that only three out of the twenty-six were accepted and sworn.

Believing that it would be better to summon at once another and a much larger number of talesmen, by consent of counsel on both sides an order was made by the judge for the summoning of one hundred, from which to make up the panel of twelve acceptable jurors on the next day and proceed with the hearing of the evidence on that day, if possible.

By act of Congress of 1854 one term of the court could not be extended into another term, except in the event of a case happening in which the jury had already been empaneled—that is to say, the entire twelve men sworn and put in charge of the case; and some doubts were also expressed as to whether the March term would terminate on Saturday, the 15th of June, at midnight, or at ten o'clock on Monday morning, the 17th.

On Thursday night, the 13th of June, Judge Fisher was seized with a severe chill, and was unable to attend court on that day or on Saturday, and Associate Judge [A. B.] Wylie held court on those days, in his stead. The hundred talesmen, or nearly all of them, were in attendance and shortly before midnight on Saturday, the panel to try Surratt was completed and put in charge of the case. It consisted of the following jurors: William B. Todd, Robert Ball, J. Russell Barr, Thomas Berry, George A. Bohrer, Christian G. Schneider, James Y. Davis, Columbus Alexander, William McLean, Benjamin F. Morsell, Benjamin E. Gittings, and William W. Birth.

The indictment, upon which the prisoner had been arraigned earlier in the term, was then read to the jury by the clerk, who after reading it, addressed to the jury, according to the usual form, the following words, to-wit: "To this indictment the prisoner at the bar pleads not guilty and puts himself upon his country, which country you are. You will stand together and hear the evidence."

Mr. Merrick, for the prisoner, then proposed that the jury be allowed to separate until Monday morning at ten o'clock, to which proposition the counsel for the Government signified their assent.

Judge Wylie then ordered the clerk to make entry upon the record that "By consent of the counsel on both sides, the jury is permitted to separate," and to the jury said, "Be here, gentlemen, on Monday morning at ten o'clock. I do not know that I shall have the pleasure of seeing you. You are admonished to avoid conversation with anybody on the subject of this case. If you are approached, you shall regard it as a personal indignity. I am inclined to think that under the Act of Congress this term is extended. I shall not, therefore, adjourn in course, but adjourn until Monday morning at ten o'clock." [2]

Feeling somewhat better on Monday morning, Judge Fisher repaired to the City Hall, resumed his place on the bench, and caused the court to be opened at the hour to which it had been adjourned; the jurors empaneled on Saturday night being all present, promptly responded to the call of their names.

Mr. Bradley, Jr., then presented and read the following petition:

To the Honorable, the Justice of the Supreme Court
of the District of Columbia
holding the criminal court for the March Term 1867:

The petition of John H. Surratt shows that he has now been upon his trial in this court in a capital case; that he has exhausted all his means and such other means as have been furnished him, by the liberality of his friends, in preparing for his defence, and he is now unable to procure the attendance of his witnesses. He therefore, prays your honor that process may issue to summon his witnesses, and to compel their attendance at the cost of the government of the United States, according to the statute in such case made and provided.

(Signed.) John H. Surratt.[3]

Sworn to in open court this 17th day of June 1867.

Test: R. J. Meigs, Clerk.

This application was subsequently granted, and the names and residences of the witnesses being furnished from time to time, as needed, witnesses numbering in the aggregate over one hundred were brought into court at the cost of the Government to testify for the prisoner.

Mr. Wilson then proceeded to address the jury, stating the nature of the offense charged in the indictment and the proofs by which the Government proposed to support the charge. The counsel for the prisoner reserved their opening until the Government should conclude its testimony in chief.

Eighty-five witnesses were produced by the counsel for the Government to deliver that testimony, which was not concluded until the 5th day of July, although begun on the 17th of June.

There were in all three hundred and one witnesses examined during the trial; eighty-five as witnesses in chief for the Government; ninety-seven in chief for the prisoner; ninety-six in rebuttal for the Government, and twenty-three in surrebuttal for the defendant.

Judge Pierrepont was a rather diminutive man with a decidedly phlegmatic, sallow countenance. He was cool and self-possessed in his bearing, and never permitted himself to be caught or thrown off his guard by his antagonists. Such a thing as passionate excitement was unknown to him. In these attributes he was the very opposite of Judge Bradley. He conducted the examination of the witnesses for the Government with dignity and ease, and in this way secured all the information he was anxious to obtain.

Judge Bradley cross-examined the Government witnesses on behalf of the defense. This he did with a master mind, for there is no doubt that he was a great lawyer. He was a large man with ruddy countenance, but he was very readily disconcerted, and this several times happened to him in his encounters with Judge Pierrepont, who was always like an iceberg, while Judge Bradley often resembled a furnace full of a seething hot fire.

Occasionally attorney Merrick would take hold for the defense in the cross-examination of witnesses, but he was entirely too vindictive and revengeful, and carried into all his actions the spirit and feelings of his client. He was from the beginning to the end of the case a bitter partisan and never lost the opportunity when it presented itself of venting his spite and of betraying his political animus.

The first witness called for the prosecution was Surgeon General Barnes of the United States Army, who testified that he had been summoned to attend the President on the night of the assassination after he had received his death wound. He described its nature and location, and stated that he had made a post-mortem examination of the body, and that he had removed the ball from the brain of the President. The ball was exhibited and identified by him. General Barnes said that in his judgment the President came to his death from the effects of this gunshot wound.

The Surgeon General was followed by a Mr. [William F.] Kent, who stated that he had entered the box occupied by the President after he had been removed to Petersen's house, and that he had picked up from the floor a pistol which was the one with which Booth shot the President.[4]

Witness after witness was now called and examined in rapid succession. Nearly all those who had testified at the Conspiracy trial in 1865 were recalled and many new ones, Tibbets, Smoot, Rhodes, Cooper, McMillan, Sainte Marie, and others came to the front and gave very important information, connecting the prisoner with the Conspiracy and all of which has been incorporated into the present narrative in its proper place.

I was on the stand for three days. I repeated the testimony which I gave in 1865 with many additional facts which had come to my mind since that time. I also made some corrections in my evidence, notably in relation to the time when I met Dr. Mudd, and stated my reasons for so doing. Mr. Bradley in his cross-examination was very severe, and pressed me very hard; he tried his best to confuse me and make me contradict myself, but his efforts all came to naught.

Dr. L. J. A. McMillan, the young surgeon who had crossed the ocean with Surratt on the steamer *Peruvian,* was also placed on the witness stand. He was a small man, with a quick, bright eye, florid complexion, and wearing side whiskers. He was very polite and quiet in his actions, and was a man of good education.

The story of Surratt's voyage across the ocean and of his almost daily revelations to him were told in an effective manner. The spectators in the court room listened to his recital with rapt and eager attention. McMillan's evidence has never been contradicted; in fact, there was no one who could do so, and it remains unshaken on the legal record of the country. The defense attempted to impeach his character, but in this they failed utterly.

The point of greatest interest in Surratt's case centered in his doings and whereabouts on the 14th of April. The defense endeavored to show that the prisoner was in Elmira, New York, on the day and evening of the assassination; and that in consequence of the interruption of travel by reason of severe floods causing heavy washouts in the railorads, it was utterly impossible for him to get from Elmira to Washington by the 14th of April, but this impossibility seemed to vanish in the light of the evidence given by the officers of the railroad companies. The Government maintained that he came to Washington by the way of the Northern Central Railway, passing through Williamsport, Sunbury, Harrisburg, and Baltimore; they said he left Elmira, New York, on a special train over this route at 10:30 on the morning of April 13, and that he arrived in Washington at 10:25 A.M. on Friday, April 14. At Williamsport, he approached conductor Ezra B. Westfield[5] and desired to know about the trains leaving for Sunbury. Westfield did not give him much satisfaction and looked upon him as a spy. When asked in court if Surratt looked like the man who had approached him, he said he believed him to be the man.

In consequence of the storms already referred to, the only connection with Sunbury on April 13 was by means of a rope ferry. This was operated by a man by the name of Martin Drohan,[6] who testified that he carried a man across the ferry that day between noon and two o'clock; that he collected from him when in the middle of the river (the Susquehanna) one dollar for his services. Drohan positively identified Surratt as the man whom he had ferried across to Sunbury.

Moreover, it appeared utterly out of the question to get rid of the testimony of more than a half dozen respectable persons, mostly residents of Washington, some of whom had known him from his boyhood, and whose evidence was positive, emphatic, and beyond the possibility of impeachment either by cross-examination, by their manner of testifying, or by attacks upon their character for veracity, who declared on oath in the strongest manner that they saw him here at that time. In addition to this, his confessions to Sainte Marie, his comrade in the Papal army, acknowledged his presence in Washington on the memorable 14th of April, by admitting that he escaped from there on the night of that day, or the morning of the next, disguised as an Englishman.

Sainte Marie was the man who identified him while serving in the Papal Zouaves. After referring to some conversation he had with Surratt one day while on a walk with him at Velletri in April 1866, about the 14th, he gave the following testimony:

Q. Did the prisoner tell you at this time anything about his disguises? If so, what?

A. Yes, sir; I asked the prisoner how he got out of Washington; if he had a hard time in escaping. He told me he had a very hard time.

Q. How did he say he got out of Washington?

A. He told me he left that night.

Q. What night?

A. The night of the assassination, or the next morning, I am not positive.

Q. What was the disguise, if any, he told you he had?

A. He told me he was so disguised that nobody could take him for an American; that he looked like an Englishman; that he had a scarf over his shoulders. He did not mention any other disguise that I remember.[7]

Surratt was seen in the forenoon of April 14th by barber Wood, who shaved him at Booker and Stewart's shop, near Grover's Theater, on E Street; he came into the shop with Booth and was travel-worn and dusty.[8]

Mr. D. C. Reed, who had known him since his early childhood, swore positively to meeting him on the same day; Mr. Benjamin Rhodes testified to seeing him about noon in the President's box, actually engaged in the act of adjusting the piece of wood in the wall that was to be used by Booth that night.[9]

Benjamin W. Vanderpoel, a lawyer of New York, who happened to be in Washington on business with the Paymaster of the Army, also testified in the most positive manner that he saw Surratt and Booth together about the middle of the afternoon, at a drinking saloon on the south side of Pennsylvania Avenue and, though very sharply and shrewdly cross-examined, could neither by his manner nor by contradicting himself be made to waver or detract from his statement, that he identified Surratt beyond a doubt, as the man whom he saw with Booth on that afternoon in the saloon, and he insisted that he was just as certain the prisoner was the man as that he was looking at Mr. Bradley, to whom he was making reply.[10]

Dr. William E. Cleaver, a veterinary surgeon who had known Surratt for some time, testified to seeing him on H Street in the afternoon about four o'clock, on horseback, and that he bowed to him.[11]

Sergeant Joseph M. Dye identified him without any equivocation or hesitation in his manner, as the man who called the time in front of the theater, and Susan Ann Jackson, the servant at his mother's house, stated that he came to the house that night, after his mother had returned from the country, changed his clothes, ate his supper, and then left, and that all this occurred without my knowledge, and during my absence in another part of the house.[12]

All this evidence was met by the defense bravely and with no fear. Three witnesses, Joseph Carroll, F. C. Atkinson, and Charles B. Stewart, residing in Elmira, New York, and connected with the clothing establishment of Stewart and Ufford in that city, all testified that they had seen Surratt in Elmira between April 13 and 15, 1865. One of these, Mr. Carroll, stated that he saw him on April 13 and 14 in the store in which he was employed, but the other two could not and did not state that they had seen him on the 14th, but they were sure of having seen him on the 13th in their place of business. These gentlemen were all good citizens, and in good standing in the community in which they lived.[13]

One witness, Dr. Augustus Bissell, was produced, who swore positively that he had met Surratt in the Brainard House in Elmira in the forenoon of April 14, and that he had held a conversation with him. The statements of this man, however, were so full of prevarications and contradictions that but little faith was placed in what he narrated. Judge Pierrepont tore his assertions all to pieces and said there was not a word of truth in anything he said. In addition to this, the Government placed on the stand a great number of witnesses who swore that the doctor could not be believed under oath and that he was a man utterly devoid of character.[14]

The fifth and strongest witness was a Mr. [John] Cass, who testified that he saw Surratt in Elmira on the morning of the 15th of April. He said news of the death of Abraham Lincoln had been received about nine o'clock. At that time he was standing at the front of his store. He then noticed a gentleman coming across the street whom he thought from his dress was a friend of his from Canada. That was his first idea when he saw him, but he soon saw it was not, and then he turned and started to go back into the store. He had probably not gone more than ten feet, when this party whom he had observed came in. He inquired for some white shirts. He asked for a particular make which Mr. Cass did not keep, and he told him so, and proceeded to show him some other descriptions of white shirts. He examined them, but said he would rather have those of the make which he had been accustomed to wear. At that time Mr. Cass made a remark that some very sad news had been received. He asked, "What?" Cass said, "Of the death of Abraham Lincoln."

The party made an answer to the remark of Mr. Cass, which at first he took to be a little disrespectful, and he felt rather incensed, but before he concluded he was satisfied that no disrespect was intended. Mr. Cass thought he was a Canadian and had no sympathy with our people.

The following questions were asked Mr. Cass:

Q. Have you ever seen that man since?
A. I have.
Q. Look at that man (pointing to Surratt) and state if he is or is not the man.
A. That is the man I saw there.[15]

An attempt was made to introduce the register of the Webster Hotel of Canandaigua for April 15 showing that Surratt had arrived there on the evening of that day, and had registered under the name of "John Harrison." The handwriting was identified as that of Surratt by Miss Olivia Jenkins, his cousin, and by Mr. David Bates, an expert in handwriting, who had also appeared during the trial as a witness for the prosecution. The name John Harrison appeared midway on the page, and there were a number of signatures before and after it.

The admission of this register in evidence was sternly resisted by Judge Pierrepont, who spoke of it as follows:

> This was the first time he had ever heard a person who claimed to be educated as a lawyer, get up in a court of justice and seriously argue that a man could make evidence for himself, and then bring it in for the purpose of securing his acquittal: that it was the same thing when a man undertook to bring in his own writing, his own acts, as when the Government undertook to bring such against him. Anybody who had the slightest particle of common sense in his head knew perfectly well that if that entry could be introduced in evidence, as in the prisoner's handwriting, every word that it should say could be introduced.
>
> Suppose then, there stood on that register such an entry as this: "John Harrison Surratt, Washington City. Wilkes Booth murdered the President. I thank God I never had anything to do with it, and never heard of it." Such would have to be admitted if the name could be. See what the effect would be. If such were allowed, any murderer, any assassin, could acquit himself. Test the case. This murder oc-

curred on the 14th of April, 1865, and, from the testimony in the case, the prisoner at the bar had never left this country until the 17th of September, 1865. From April to September, five months after the murder, did he remain in this country in his various disguises. He knew that his mother had been tried; he knew that his co-conspirators had been tried; and he knew, as the proof is, that some of them had been executed; and he lay on the border, within twelve hours' ride of Canandaigua, these whole five months, while these things were going on, and he shrinking from the investigation. [Why should not he be preparing to defend himself?] Why should not he come down in his disguises and make this entry there for the purpose of raising the presumption, if he should be seized and brought to trial, that he was there at the time now claimed? As the court would see, on looking at the register, that there were five or six blank lines on each page, and from the easy access which was had to the book, he could very easily, in his disguise, have gone and made this entry there. He had ample opportunity to do it. If he was not an idiot he would be fixing up such testimony as would help him in his defense when he should be tried, which he anticipated would come.[16]

Judge Fisher, on Monday, July 15, 1867, refused to admit the register in evidence, in the following language:

The register of the Webster House, Canandaigua, offered in evidence when we took a recess on Saturday, cannot be allowed to go to the jury at present. It was proved by the proprietor of the house, who kept it on the 15th of April, 1865, to have been the register used by him and turned over by him on Monday, April 17th, 1865, to his successor, who swears that he kept the same book lying open on his counter until all the blank leaves were filled up, and then placed it under the counter, where it could have been, without his knowledge, used for any purpose, whether honest or fraudulent. This is just precisely one of the cases which the ancient and well-established rule of evidence, that a prisoner shall not be allowed to manufacture evidence for himself, was intended to meet. It is said that the name "John Harrison," standing on that register for the 15th of April, 1865, having been sworn to by Miss Jenkins as the handwriting of Surratt, it ought to be admitted as evidence tending to prove that he was present at Canandaigua at that date. But, as I have said, it is evidence made by himself, and, although it might be put in evidence against him if in his handwriting, yet it cannot be used as evidence in his favor, just as any diary which he may have kept in his handwriting might be produced against him, but could not be produced in evidence in his behalf.

Besides, the fact, if established beyond all peradventure, that the name "John Harrison" is in the prisoner's handwriting, does not tend to show that he was in Canandaigua on the 15th of April, 1865. The name could as well have been written by him in Canada, or Rome, or Egypt, as in Canandaigua. The book has been at the mercy of everybody for more than two years. It could have gone to Canada and back a hundred times; or the prisoner, during his stay there in Canada, could have gone to the book just as often. The entries below the name of "John Harrison," as well as that entry itself, may as well have been made at any other time as on the 15th of April, 1865. It is to guard against just such contingencies as this that the rigid rule of evidence to which I have alluded was established.

If the defense had proved by any credible witness that the entry of the name of "John Harrison" had been made at the hotel in the regular course of business, on the 15th of April, by a person passing under that name, the book might go in evidence as a memorandum of a fact made at the time of its occurrence, and thus prove that the entry was in Surratt's hand would tend to show he was there at the time. It is only as a memorandum, so made, that it is allowed to speak at all, and it cannot take the character of such memorandum until it be shown that it was so made at the time and place of which it is desired to speak.

Let the principle become established that such evidence as this register as it now stands is admissible and the proof of an alibi will be the easiest thing made that could possibly be conceived of. A crime may be committed here, the guilty party may escape to Canada, registering himself in an assumed name wherever he may stop, and will only have to travel back again, write his true name at or near the bottom of the appropriate page of the hotel register wherever he stops on his return, with one or two friends to write their names under his, and the defense of the alibi is complete.[17]

The first point at which the Government located Surratt in his alleged escape from Washington after the assassination of Mr. Lincoln had been effected, was Burlington, Vermont. A man named Charles H. Blinn, who was employed as night watchman in the passenger depot of the Vermont Central Railroad Company, stated that on Monday night, April 17, when the boat, which was some hours late, arrived from Whitehall, New York, among the passengers were two men, one tall and the other short.[18] The taller of the two approached Mr. Blinn and said as he did not wish to go to a hotel, he would request permission for himself and his companion to lie on one of the benches in the depot until the arrival of the train which would carry them to St. Albans and Montreal. To this Mr. Blinn made no objection. The train left for St. Albans at 4:30 on Tuesday morning, April 18. About two hours after its departure, the night watchman found a handkerchief under the head of the bench which had been occupied by the taller of the men. On it was written the name "J. H. Surratt, 2." Mr. Blinn did not at first notice the name, but discovered it during the course of the day, and spoke of it to some fellow officers. Two days afterwards he had it washed and then handed it to a detective officer named [George] Chapin, who placed it in the possession of the Government.[19]

The defense attempted to prove by Mr. John T. Holohan that he had lost the handkerchief, and he so swore, but when he rose in court at the request of Judge Pierrepont, Mr. Blinn said Holohan was not one of the men who came into the depot at the time mentioned by him. As stated, the handkerchief was found by Mr. Blinn on the night of April 17. At that time Holohan was in Philadelphia with officers Bigley, McDevitt, and myself, where we remained nearly all day of the 18th. We did not reach New York City until the morning of the 19th, and did not arrive at Burlington until early on the morning of the 20th, so that taking all these points into consideration, the very strong probabilities are that the handkerchief was really lost by Surratt, and that he was really at Burlington at that time. Indeed, he so stated this fact in his talks with McMillan.

And all of this is supported by what occurred subsequently. When the train on which the tall man and his companion arrived at Essex Junction, about 103 miles from Burlington, it was necessary to change cars to reach Montreal. The new train on which they embarked was under the direction of a conductor by the name of Carroll Hobart and arrived at Essex Junction at 5 A.M. Tuesday morning. Mr. Hobart said after the train got started he was going through the cars and found, between the passenger and the baggage cars, two men standing on the platform of the passenger car, one on each side of the door. He spoke to them and asked them for their tickets. They said they had none, that they had no money and had been unfortunate. One of the men was tall, rather slim, and had on a close-fitting skull cap and a peculiar coat; his vest was opened down low and his scarf came from under his collar and stuck in his vest. The other man was short, thickset, with sandy hair and whiskers, and he wore a slouch hat; he was a rough-looking man.[20]

The conversation Mr. Hobart had was with the tall man; he told him to go into the car, and put his hand on his shoulder. The man went in and then said that three of them had been to New York. They were Canadians and had been at work in that city; that they had received some money two nights before and had gone to Boston, and that the other party who had been with him got up in the night and took all the money they had and left them in a destitute condition. He said that they wanted to get to their home and friends in Canada, where they would get plenty of money and would remit him the fare.

Mr. Hobart then told them that he could not carry them through free, and said they would have to leave at the next station, Milton, between Essex Junction and St. Albans. However, he was so busy when he got there with the train that he forgot them. After leaving Milton, on going through the train, he found them in the rear end of the car. The conductor again asked them for money and again they said they had none. They said they must get to St. Albans and that when they arrived there they could foot it. They inquired how far it was to Franklin and he told them the distance was about four miles from the Canadian line. The tall man did all this talking and he tried to use broken language, as if he were a Canuck, but once in a while he would grow earnest for fear he would be put off and then he would drop his Canuck and speak good, square English. This aroused Mr. Hobart's suspicion that things were not all right. Hobart looked at the hands of the tall man and he said they were not at all like those of a laboring man, or one who had been used to hard work, they were white and delicate.

The conductor took them to St. Albans, where he left them. When he was asked if he had seen anybody who looked like the tall man, Surratt was directed to stand up in court. Mr. Hobart said, "The man that stood up before me resembles the man I saw, very much. I should not recognize his face, he had at that time a moustache with no whiskers on his chin and wore a cap."

In an interview with a correspondent signing himself "Pilgrim" and published in the *Philadelphia Times*, October 4, 1885, Surratt admitted that the circumstances as told in Hobart's testimony were in the main correct.

He said he was at the moment without means and that his companion was equally poor, and was never identified. They got out of St. Albans on foot and walked across the line to Franklin, a place twelve or fifteen miles northeast, and were for the moment safe and in funds at once, and that he, Surratt, reached Montreal that same day, April 18.

All this testimony on the part of the Government in its allegation that Surratt was in Washington City on April 14, 1865, and the counter allegation on the part of the defense that he was in Elmira, New York, on that day and evening, and the morning thereafter, although so many years have intervened since the death of the dear President, still fills my mind with doubt and confusion. I know not what to believe. Knowing this young man as intimately as I did, and he always presented to me only the honorable side of his character, I cannot reconcile myself to the belief that he was the man who stood in front of Ford's Theater, as narrated by Sergeant Dye, and called out the time when Booth would enter the theater and do his murderous deed, nor can I believe that it was he who at midday, as told by Mr. Rhodes, was in the President's box and prepared the wooden bar which Booth would use that night. Still less can I entertain the story as told by Susan Mahoney [21] that he entered his mother's house that night, partook of supper, changed his clothing and then left. I was in the house during the whole of that time after eight o'clock, and there was not the slightest indication to satisfy my mind that Surratt was there at that time.

I remember how Mr. Merrick shook his clenched hand at me once during the course of the trial, denounced me as a friend, and said that if I had ever spoken the truth it was when I said that Surratt was not in Washington City on the day of the murder. Now I said nothing of the kind: I did say that the last time I saw him in Washington, prior to the murder, was on April 3, 1865, which was the truth: yet, it was very possible for him to have been in Washington on the 14th without any knowledge whatever on my part as to such presence.

This matter always presents a great perplexity to me; the trend of my own thoughts has always led me to the conclusion that Surratt was not there, yet this whole case from the beginning to the end has been to me so full of surprises, and deceptions on the part of Surratt and his mother, that it may be proved ultimately that even my own feelings are doing me a gross injustice.

So eager and earnest has been my quest for the truth in this affair that some years ago I ventured to address a letter to General Burnett in relation to it, and I now for the first time, with his consent, make public his reply.

New York, March 2, 1892.

L. J. Weichmann, Esq.,
Anderson, Ind.

Dear Sir:

I beg to acknowledge receipt of your favor of the 25th inst., and in response to your request have this day mailed you two copies of the pamphlet to which you refer.

From the investigations which I made at the time and from all that I have read since, I am convinced that John H. Surratt was not in Washington on the 14th day of April, 1865.

Very truly yours,
Henry L. Burnett.

Surratt, too, has spoken of this feature of his case in his lecture, and for his benefit, and that of my readers, I again quote him. Referring to his trip to Montreal, he says he carried dispatches to one General Edwin G. Lee, then in Montreal, and then goes on to say:

In accordance with Gen. Lee's order, I went to Elmira, arriving there on Wednesday, two days before Mr. Lincoln's death, and registered at the Brainard House, as usual, as "John Harrison." The following day I went to work, and made a complete sketch of the prison and surroundings. About ten o'clock on Friday night I retired, little thinking that on that night a blow would be struck which would forever blast my hopes, and make me a wanderer in a foreign land. I slept the night through, and came down the next morning little dreaming of the storm then brewing around my head. When I took my seat at the table about 9 o'clock A.M., a gentleman to my left remarked: "Have you heard the news?" "No, I've not," I replied.

"What is it?" "Why President Lincoln and Secretary Seward have been assassinated."

I really put so little faith in what the man said that I made a remark that it was too early in the morning to get off such jokes as that. "It's so," he said, at the same time drawing out a paper and showing it to me. Sure enough, there I saw an account of what he told me, but as no names were mentioned, it never occurred to me for an instant that it could have been Booth or any of the party, for the simple reason that I had never heard anything regarding assassination spoken of during my intercourse with them. . . . I was pretty sure it was none of the old party. I approached the telegraph office in the main hall of the hotel for the purpose of ascertaining if J. Wilkes Booth was in New York. I picked up a blank and wrote "John Wilkes Booth," giving the number of the house. I hesitated a moment, and then tore the paper up, and then wrote one "J.W.B.," with directions, which I was led to do from the fact that during our whole connection we rarely wrote or telegraphed under our proper names, but always in such a manner that no one could understand but ourselves. . . .

I telegraphed Booth thus:
"J.W.B., in New York:

"If you are in New York, telegraph me.

"John Harrison, Elmira, N.Y."

The operator, after looking over it, said, "Is it J.W.B.?" to which I replied, "Yes." He evidently wanted the whole name, and had scarcely finished telegraphing when a door right near the office, and opening on the street, was pushed open, and I heard some one say, "Yes, there are three or four brothers of them, John, Junius, Brutus, Edwin, and J. Wilkes Booth." The whole truth flashed on me in an instant, and I said to myself, "My God! What have I done?" The dispatch was still lying before me, and I reached over and took it up for the purpose of destroying it, but the operator stretched forth his hand and said, "We must file all telegrams." My first impulse was to tear it up, but I pitched it back and walked off. The town was in the greatest uproar, flags at half mast, bells tolling, &c., &c. Still I did not think I was in danger, and determined to go immediately to Baltimore to find out the particulars of the tragedy. But here I wish to say a few words concerning the register of the Brainard House.

When my counsel, by my own direction, went to seek that register, it could not be found. Our inability to produce it on the trial naturally cast a suspicion over our *alibi.* For weeks, months, did we seek to find its whereabouts, but to no purpose. Every man who was connected with the hotel was hunted up and questioned. Every register of the hotel before and after the one which ought to contain my name was to be found, but the most important one of all was gone. Now the question is what became of that register? The U. S. Government, by one of its witnesses, Doctor McMillan, knew in November, 1865, that I was in Elmira at the time of the assassination. They knew it, and they naturally traced me there to find out what I was doing. . . .

The dispatch I sent to Booth also from Elmira it was impossible to find. We had the operator at Washington during my trial, but he said the original was gone though he had a copy of it. Of course we could not offer this copy in evidence, because the original alone would be accepted, and that had been made away with. So sure was the Government that they had destroyed all evidence of my sojourn in Elmira, that in getting me in Washington in time for Mr. Lincoln's death they brought me by way of New York City, but so completely were they foiled in this that in their rebutting testimony they saw the absolute necessity of having me go by way of Elmira, and they changed their tactics accordingly. That was enough to damn my case in any man's mind. This is a strange fact, but nevertheless true that the Government having it in its possession this hotel register as well as my dispatch to Booth and knowing moreover by one of its witnesses that I was in Elmira, yet tried to prove that I was in Washington on the night of Mr. Lincoln's death, giving orders and commanding in general as they were pleased to say. The gentlemen in Elmira, by whom I proved my *alibi,* were men of the highest standing and integrity, whose testimony the United States Government could not and dare not attempt to impeach. I left Elmira with the intention of going to Baltimore. I really did not comprehend at that time the danger I was in. As there was no train going South that evening I concluded to go to Canandaigua, and from there to Baltimore, by way of Elmira and New York.

Upon arriving at Canandaigua on Saturday evening I learned to my utter disappointment that no train left there until the Monday following, so I took a room at the Webster House, registering myself as "John Harrison." The next day I went to church, I remember it being Easter Sunday. I can here safely say that the United States Government had not the remotest idea that I stopped anywhere after I left Elmira. They thought, when I left there, I went straight through to Canada. It was a very fortunate thing for me that I could not leave Canandaigua. . . .

On Monday when I was leaving Canandaigua I bought some New York papers. In looking over them, my eye lit on the following paragraph which I have never forgot, and don't think I ever will. It runs thus: "The assassin of Secretary Seward is said to be John H. Surratt, a notorious secessionist of Southern Maryland. His name, with that of J. Wilkes Booth, will forever lead the infamous roll of assassins." I could scarcely believe my senses. I gazed upon my name, the letters of which seemed sometimes to grow as large as mountains and then to dwindle away to nothing. So much for my former connection with him I thought. After fully realizing the state of the case, I concluded to change my course and go direct to Canada.

I left Canandaigua on Monday, 12 M., going to Albany arriving there on Tuesday morning in time for breakfast. When I stepped on the platform at the depot at St. Albans I noticed that one of the detectives scanned every one, head and foot, myself as well as the rest. Before leaving Montreal for Elmira, I provided myself with an Oxford cut jacket and a round-top hat, peculiar to Canada at that time. I knew my trip to Elmira would be a dangerous one, and I wished to pass myself off as a Canadian, and I succeeded in so doing, as was proved by my witnesses in Elmira. . . . Of course I was obliged to talk as loud as anybody about the late tragedy. After having a hearty meal I lighted a cigar and walked up town. One of the detectives approached me, stared me directly in the face, and I looked him quietly back. In a few moments I was speeding on my way to Montreal, where I arrived at two o'clock in the afternoon, going again to the St. Lawrence Hotel.[22]

There probably never was a jury trial in which partisan feeling was so much excited. President Johnson had returned to the Democratic fold, and though he, perhaps, did not desire to encourage the secession sympathizers in Washington, or elsewhere, to revive the smouldering embers of their hatred for the Government that had destroyed slavery, yet there were hundreds of them at the capital who construed his tergiversation to mean that those whom he had formerly denounced as traitors and determined should take "back seats," might now venture to occupy the amen corner of the political church. Many of these people, as soon as Surratt had been arrested, were active in their endeavors to create sympathy for him by talking of the murder of his mother by the Military Commission. Every low instinct and passion of human nature was appealed to. The court room was daily filled with his friends from Lower Maryland, and with the disloyal element of Washington City who espoused his cause. So pronounced was this that the Government was compelled in a quiet way to interfere in behalf of its witnesses, and use whatever means at its command for their protection.

One day, I was waited on by two ladies, Mrs. Griffen and Mrs. Thomas L. Tullock, representing a committee of the loyal ladies of Washington, who stated that they had come to me from Secretary Stanton to say that I should in no way feel alarmed during my attendance at court; that the Secretary had taken the precaution to have a number of colored men in the court room every day who would take care that the Government witnesses should not be insulted or subjected to bodily harm.

This wise precaution of Mr. Stanton was an actual fact; there were three rows of benches which were occupied as long as the trial lasted by colored men. They were always orderly and polite in their behavior, but their presence was a great restraint on the element which sympathized with Surratt, and, I believe, was often the means of checking an outbreak in the court room.

The religious feeling was also called into play, and worked to its best advantage. Some of the priests of Washington, Father Jacob Walter, Father L. Roccofort, and others were almost constant in their attendance on court, and were continually hobnobbing with the lawyers for the defense, thus showing which way their feelings ran.

Father Roccofort, a member of the Society of Jesus, was put on the stand, and the question was asked him if I had stated to him outside of the confessional that I was employed in an office of the War Department and engaged to send information to the Southern Confederacy. This was objected to by the prosecution, and no answer was permitted by Judge Fisher. The witness was thereupon dismissed from the stand.[23]

Of all the assaults made on my character during Surratt's trial, I pronounce this the most infamous. There was not a word of truth in what he was asked. I had never had any communication at any time with him on any such subject. Father Roccofort was a man to whom I frequently went to confession. The tribunal of penance has always been regarded in the Catholic Church as of divine institution, and it is the custom of all good Catholics to have stated recourse to it. Yet here was a man who was ready to pervert his holy office and to make it appear to the jury that I had really made such a statement to him. His action was made with the view of influencing the Catholics on the jury and I believe it had its effect. It could have been done for no other reason.

On one occasion about twenty students from St. Charles College, the institution where Surratt and I had studied, with the Reverend John B. Menu, one of the professors and my former father confessor, at their head, came into court. All of them were permitted, by the marshal of the court, to approach the prisoner and to shake hands with him, and this in the presence of the jury. Father Menu sat in the court room during the entire day, right by the side of Surratt as much as to say: "Gentlemen of the jury, I am a Catholic priest, you can see where my sympathies are."

Not one of these men came to me, and gave me his hand, or showed me the slightest recognition. Their feelings were all on the side of the man who was on trial, and who had been charged by his country with the murder of Abraham Lincoln.

Out of such actions as these, and out of the doings of Fathers Boucher and LaPierre, who secreted Surratt in Canada and who arranged and facilitated his escape to Europe, coupled with the fact that some of the priests and other prominent Catholics in Washington, have persistently and unscrupulously maligned the Government, the Military Commission, the witnesses for the prosecution, because of the verdict in Mrs. Surratt's case, more than from any other circumstances, has grown the charge that the assassination was the outcome of a Catholic plot.[24]

In fact, nothing else has been developed that could lead to a suspicion that could in any way inculpate the authorities of the Catholic Church. But the charge is too ridiculous for a moment's consideration. What these men did was in their individual capacity, and they are responsible to their consciences and God; the Church can in no wise be held accountable for their deeds.

But for me there was a precious balm for all this contumely, and one that I did not dream of. Not long after this incident was over, when I was alone in one of the anterooms of the court house, I was approached by a young lad apparently about fifteen years of age, who seated himself on my knees and, placing his arms around my neck, kissed me on one of my cheeks, saying, "I desire to thank you, sir, for your testimony in behalf of my murdered father." "Who are you, sonny?" asked I. "My name is Tad Lincoln," was his answer.

This kind action on the part of the son whom the President loved so well, I can assure my readers, has always been a bright spot in my life.

When the testimony had all been taken, the arguments of the attorneys to the court began on July 27. General Carrington opened for the prosecution and spoke at length and with much force on his side of the case. His arguments were listened to with much attention and he did his best to help bring about a conviction.[25]

He was followed by Judge Merrick, who spoke for the defense.[26] His remarks took up an entire day. He was very eloquent and showed great mastery of his subject. He was very impassioned and from the beginning to the end of his speech his language was like a succession of strong hammer blows in favor of his client. He made every available use of the facts at his command, and if the prisoner was not acquitted it was due to no effort on the part of Mr. Merrick.

Judge Pierrepont closed for the Government and his talk consumed the best portion of two days. The judge spoke calmly, but his whole argument was a terrible array of the evidence against the prisoner linked together in such a way as had never been done before. It may be in fact called the first complete history of the Conspiracy up to that time. He handled his case without gloves. He was evidently a very conscientious man and seemed to be seriously impressed with the guilt of the prisoner.[27] When he had finished, Judge Fisher made his charge to the jury. This was a very lengthy paper, and there is too much of it to reproduce here.[28]

The jurors at 11:30 A.M., Wednesday, August 7, retired to their chamber, accompanied by two bailiffs; the latter had instructions to notify Judge Fisher of the fact as soon as they had agreed on their verdict. The judge remained in or near the court room till late in the afternoon that day, fully persuaded that a verdict would be reached before sunset; he also attended there on Thursday and Friday. During each of these last days he received a communication from the foreman of the jury advising him that it was impossible for them to agree, and on receipt of the second message he came to the conclusion to call them into the court room on Saturday, and if there should be no prospect of their agreeing, to discharge them. He reached the court house on Saturday morning between eleven and twelve o'clock. One of the bailiffs placed in his hands a note signed by each of the jurors stating that they stood precisely then as when they first balloted on entering the chamber, nearly equally divided, and that they were firmly convinced that they could not possibly reach a verdict, and that in view of their private affairs and of the fact that the health of several of their number had become seriously impaired under their protracted confinement, they desired to be at once dismissed. The judge subsequently learned that they stood eight in favor of acquittal and four for conviction, but he did not know positively that such was the fact. On receiving this note he sent a bailiff to notify the counsel on either side that he would call in the jury at precisely twelve o'clock. Whereupon Messrs. Bradley, Sr., and Carrington came into the court and, after Judge Fisher had read the note aloud, were asked if anything was to be said while the jury should be discharged. Mr. Bradley said that the prisoner gave no consent to any discharge of the jury, and that if they were discharged, he desired it to be understood that it was against his will and protest. Mr. Carrington expressed his willingness to leave the matter entirely to the discretion of the court, believing there was no possibility of an agreement as to the verdict. Judge Fisher thereupon discharged the jury and remanded the prisoner to the custody of the marshal.

CHAPTER XXXI

*Confessions of Arnold and Atzerodt · Full account of their connection
with the Conspiracy · History of the abduction plot · Booth the
owner of the revolvers and carbines used by the conspirators*

The following confession of Samuel Arnold was made in the office of Marshal McPhail of Baltimore on the 18th of April 1865 immediately on his being brought to that city from Fortress Monroe. He sat down and voluntarily wrote it without any questioning. It was first published in the *Baltimore American* of January 19, 1869. The reason of its being withheld from the public notice for so long a period was because, it was thought, it could be used at the trial of John H. Surratt.

The confession is very important; it exposes the whole plot of capturing the President, and shows John H. Surratt's connection fully with the same. It also gives a complete account of the carbines and other matters.

The Confession of Samuel Arnold

To Whom It May Concern:— Know that I, Samuel B. Arnold, about the latter part of August or the first part of September, 1864, was sent for by J. Wilkes Booth, who was a guest at Barnum's Hotel, in the city of Baltimore, Md., to call to see him. I had not seen the same J. Wilkes Booth since 1852, when we both were schoolmates at St. Timothy's Hall, President L. Van Bokelin then having said Hall as a place of tuition. His reception of me was warm. Calling for wine and cigars, we conversed a while on our former school-boy days. We were interrupted by a knock at the door, when Michael O'Laughlin was ushered in. After a formal introduction, we sat sipping our wine, and all three smoked a cigar. During smoking, he having heard previously of my political feelings or sentiments, spoke in glowing terms of the Confederacy and the number of surplus prisoners in the hands of the United States. Then ensued the proposition of J. Wilkes Booth, and which he (Booth) thought could be accomplished, viz: of kidnaping President Lincoln, as he frequently went unguarded out to the Soldiers' Home; and he thought he could be picked up, and carried to Richmond, and for his exchange produce the exchange for the President of all the prisoners in the Federal hands.

He, J. Wilkes Booth, *the originator of the scheme,*[1] asked if we would enter into it. After painting the chances of success in such glowing colors, we consented, viz: Michael O'Laughlin and myself. We were bound not to divulge it to a living soul. I saw him once more in Baltimore, and then he (J. Wilkes Booth) left to arrange his business up North, first to New York, thence to the Oil Regions, and from there to Boston and finally to Canada. He was to be back in a month. I received a letter which I destroyed, stating he was laid up with erysipelas in his arm, and he did not make his appearance until sometime in January. In his trunk he had two guns, cap carriages, which were placed in the gun stock—Spencer rifles * I think they were called, revolvers, knives, belts, cartridge boxes, cartridges, caps, canteens, all fully fixed for service—which were to be used in case of pursuit, and two pairs of handcuffs to handcuff the President. His trunk being so heavy, he gave the pistols, knives and handcuffs to Michael O'Laughlin and myself, to have shipped or bring to Washington, to which place he had gone, bought a horse, harness and buggy wagon, leaving the team, etc., with us to drive on to Washington. We started from Baltimore about twelve or one o'clock after having shipped the box containing the knives, handcuffs and pistols, arriving in Washington about seven or half past seven the same evening. We met him on the street as we were passing the theater. We alighted, took a drink, and he told us of the theater plan slightly, saying he would wait till we put the horses away, and tell us more fully. He had previously, as I now remember, spoken of the chance at the theater if we could not succeed in the other plan at the Soldiers' Home. We went to the theater that night, he (J. Wilkes Booth) telling us about the different back entrances, and how feasible the plan was. He had rented a stable in the rear of the theater, having bought two horses down in the country. One was in the stable behind the theater, the other at the livery. Met him next day;

* These were the carbines subsequently deposited at Surrattsville by John Surratt, Atzerodt, and Herold, and which on the order of Mrs. Surratt were delivered to Booth on the night of the assassination.

went together to breakfast with him. He was always pressed with business with a man unknown to us then, by the name of John Surratt: most of his (Booth's) time was spent with him. We were left entirely in the dark.

Michael O'Laughlin and myself rented a room on D St., No. 420, and obtained meals at the Franklin House, on the corner on D and 8th Sts. We thus lived for nearly two months, seeing him perhaps three or four times during the week, and, when seen, always but for a short time, having still pressing business on hand, viz: to see John Surratt. Michael O'Laughlin and myself drove out occasionally, the horse liveried at Mr. Naylor's stable. We drove always (but once) in the city and Georgetown; the once excepted, across the Eastern Branch Bridge, when we went upward of five miles, I suppose, and returned. This was the only time I ever went over the bridge. How often J. Wilkes Booth crossed I cannot state, but from his own words, often. Thus was Michael O'Laughlin's and my time spent for the most part—down at Rullman's Hotel (now Sinclair House) on Pennsylvania Avenue and Louisiana Ave., in drinking and amusements, with other Baltimoreans besides ourselves congregating there, all of whom knew nothing of our business but that of selling oil stock. Oil stock was the blind for them as well as for my family. During the latter part of March, whilst standing on Rullman's porch, between eleven and twelve o'clock P.M., a young man—name unknown,* as I cannot remember names—about five feet, five or six inches high, thick set, long nose, sharp chin, wide cheeks, small eyes (gray) I think, dark hair, and well-dressed—color I do not remember—called Michael O'Laughlin aside, and said J. Wilkes Booth wished to see us both at Gautier's saloon, on the avenue. I was then, for the first time, introduced to him, but forget his name. We walked up together. Michael O'Laughlin, this unknown and myself were ushered into the presence of J. Wilkes Booth, who introduced me to John Surratt, Atzerodt, alias Port Tobacco—alias Mosby †—making in all seven persons.‡ J. Wilkes Booth had sent word to Michael O'Laughlin to bring me up in good humor (still always in the dark). Then commenced the plan of seizing the President. Each had his part to perform. First, I was to rush into the

* David E. Herold from the description given.
† Payne.
‡ This was the exact number of persons that rode away from Mrs. Surratt's house on March 16, 1865.

private box and seize the President, whilst Atzerodt, alias Port Tobacco, and J. Wilkes Booth were to handcuff him and lower him on the stage, whilst Mosby was to catch him and hold him till we got down. Surratt and the unknown were to be on the other side of the Eastern Branch Bridge to facilitate escape. It was afterwards changed to Mosby and Booth to catch him in the box and to lower him to me on the stage. O'Laughlin and the unknown were to put out the lights, and Surratt and Atzerodt, alias Port Tobacco, to be on the other side of the bridge. I was opposed to the whole proceeding and said that it could not be accomplished. If ever, which was an impossibility, we could get him out of the box and to the bridge, we would be stopped by the sentinel. "Shoot the sentinel," said Booth. I said that would not do, for if an alarm was given there the whole thing was up, and, as for me, I wanted the shadow of a chance for escape and success. Michael O'Laughlin wanted to argue the same way, whereupon J. Wilkes Booth said, "You find fault with everything concerned about it." I said no; that I wanted to have a chance, and I intended to have it; that he could be the leader of the party, but not my executioner. Whereupon J. Wilkes Booth remarked in a stern, commanding voice, "Do you know that you are liable to be shot? Remember your oath." I told him the plan or basis had changed, and a compact on the part of one broken is broken by all. If you feel inclined to shoot me, you have no further to go; I shall defend myself. This, if I remember aright, was on Friday, or maybe on a Thursday night, when I said: "Gentlemen; if this is not accomplished this week, I forever withdraw from it." I stayed up till 6 or 7 o'clock the next morning, Friday or Saturday, and then went to bed. I remained indoors until 12, when I arose and went to get my breakfast. Michael O'Laughlin and myself roomed together; both arose at the same time, and were always in a measure together. Went to bed that evening about 7:30 o'clock. This day that I went to bed so early we met about 2 or thereabouts; told me I spoke angrily the night of meeting; said I had been drinking. I told him no; I was in my sober senses, and meant every word I said; if not accomplished this week I withdraw. Next Monday the thing was to be accomplished on the 7th street road and failed.* On Sunday I stayed in Washington, and on Monday or Tuesday, I returned to the city of Baltimore, and thence to Hookstown. J. Wilkes Booth in the meantime went to New York, and returned to Baltimore during the week, on Saturday, I think.

* See above, Chapter XI.

He said he wished to see me on very urgent business and my father sent for me. I came from the country and he had gone to Washington, whereupon I wrote him the letter which was found in his trunk.* The Richmond authorities, as far as I know, knew nothing of the conspiracy. The letter was written after my return to the country, after finding that he could not wait to see me in Baltimore. During the week I came to the city and met Michael O'Laughlin who asked me to go to Washington with him to arrange his affairs. I went in the morning—Friday, I think—and returned that same evening home, having cut loose forever from it. Next day I received a letter from J. W. Wharton, at Fortress Monroe, giving me employment. Went to the country, and on Saturday, the 1st of April, left Baltimore for Fortress Monroe, at which place I have remained never corresponding with Booth or seeing him from the above named date to the present writing. The groundwork was to kidnap the President, without violence. He never to me said that he would kill him. Further than this I know nothing, and am innocent of having taken any active part in the dark deed committed.

Samuel B. Arnold.

The Plan of Escape was to place Mr. Lincoln in the buggy purchased for that purpose, and cross Eastern Branch Bridge. Surratt and Atzerodt and alias Port Tobacco were to follow them to where they had a boat concealed; turn the horse loose, place the President in the boat, and cross the Potomac to the Virginia shore, and thence to make our way to Richmond. Surratt knew the route and was to act as pilot.

Samuel B. Arnold.

A box painted black, like unto a sword-box, was sent by Booth from the hotel, by the porter there in our room. The next day it was transferred in a wagon, O'Laughlin acting as pilot, to some place. I was not present. After giving the box to the driver, went to Georgetown, and O'Laughlin had full charge of it. Mr. O'Laughlin said he took it to Mr. Heard's,† and from thence the unknown carried it home. Took the guns out and carried them to Pedee.‡ This latter clause Booth told me.

Samuel B. Arnold.

* Letter signed "Sam."
† This was no doubt David Herold.
‡ T.B. instead of Pedee.

Witness:— V. Randall, E. G. Horner, Baltimore, April 18th, 1865.

Note:— Besides this written statement of Arnold, he verbally communicated the fact that Booth was the correspondent of Doctors Mudd, Garland and Queen. This was told the Secretary when I presented him Arnold's statement.

J. L. McPhail.

The Confession of Atzerodt

The confession of Atzerodt was made in his cell at Washington, on the night before his execution. He asked for paper and it was written with a lead pencil, the disconnected manner of it indicating the state of mind of the prisoner. It was as follows:

I had not seen John Surratt for about eight days before the murder. Booth told me a few days before the murder that he was in Washington. Kate Thompson, alias Brown, came from Richmond with John Surratt about the time that Richmond fell. He had come previously with Gustavus Howell, now in the old Capital Prison. Kate Thompson stopped at Mrs. Surratt's and also at the National and Kimmel Hotels. This woman was about twenty-one years of age, spruce and neat, medium size, black eyes and fair complexion. She had a sister in New York who, it is said, was a widow. Surratt was made known to her in New York by a signal conveyed by a small switch with a waxed end and a piece of red ribbon on the butt, handled horizontally through the fingers. This signal was given on a hotel pavement on Broadway. He went with her South, and hired a horse at Howard's stables for the purpose.*

Harold [David E. Herold] came to the Kirkwood House and left the knife, pistol and coat, on the evening of the murder about half past six o'clock, as I was about leaving, I having told the clerk to tell whoever might call that I was gone out. This was before Harold came in. Harold and I then went to the Herndon House, Mrs. Murray's, corner of Ninth and F Street. It was then about eight o'clock, and I saw Booth, Wood or Payne in Wood's room. Here the proposed murder was first mentioned. I refused to take part in it when Booth said,—Then we will do it, but what will become of you? You had better come along and get your horse. I then left them and went to the Oyster Bay on the evening and stayed

---

* This was probably the mysterious Mrs. Slater, with whom he left his home on the morning of March 25, 1865. See above, Chapter XII.

385

some time; then to the stable and got my horse and went up D Street. This was about ten o'clock. I called at the Kimmel House and got a drink. I saw none of the party after we separated about nine o'clock that evening. I then went out C Street toward the Baltimore depot; went between the old and new Capitol, came on the Avenue again, and concluded to come back. I rode down the Avenue and the cavalry were dashing by me. This was the first I heard of the murder. I then went up Eighth St., left the horse at the stables opposite the Franklin House, and then went to the Herndon House, and heard a little boy talking about the murder. I then took a car and went towards the Navy Yard. This was about eleven o'clock, and I met two young men named Briscoe and Spates, with whom I had some talk. After walking some distance I took a car to the corner of Sixth St. and Pennsylvania Avenue. Here I met a man inquiring for a place to sleep at. I took him around to the Kimmel House, and we retired to one room with six beds in it. I left early next morning, and passed through Georgetown on my way to Montgomery County. No one left the hotel with me.

I saw Mike O'Laughlin about a week before the President was killed. I never wanted O'Laughlin and Arnold's aid; met O'Laughlin once or twice at Southard's, and a few times in the street.

When we were at Murray's on the night of the murder, Harold said he had a letter from a printer to Andy Johnson. He said he was going to give it to him, and he wanted me to give him the key of my room, which I refused to do. Previous to the arrangement for the murder Booth heard that the President was to visit a camp.* The coach was to be taken out Seventh St. Surratt was to jump on the box as he was the best driver, and drive through Old Fields to the Long Bridge. This was about the middle of March. O'Laughlin, Samuel Arnold, Payne, Surratt, Booth, Atzerodt and Harold went to the Long Bridge with two carbines, and were to wait for us. They did so until midnight and returned to Washington next morning. This failed. All was quiet then for some time. Booth went to New York, Arnold to Baltimore, O'Laughlin, also, and Payne left for New York. After this Howell brought a woman across the Potomac. Howell was made prisoner, and Surratt took her North about a week before the murder. Booth told me that Surratt was in the Herndon House on the night of the murder, the 14th of April, we were not all together at the Herndon House. Booth told me that Surratt was to help

* The Soldiers' Home, March 16.

at the box, that he expected others in the box. Booth went from the Herndon House down Ninth St. The words of Booth were: "I saw Surratt a few moments ago." [2] All the parties seemed to be engaged at something that night, and were not together. Booth appointed me and Harold to kill Johnson; in going down the street I told Booth we could not do it. Booth said Harold had more courage, and he would do it. Harold and I were on Pennsylvania Avenue together. I told him I would not do it, and should not go to my room for fear he would disturb Mr. Johnson. He left me to go for Booth. This was after nine o'clock. I went to the Oyster Bay, and Harold came in and said that Booth wanted to see me. Harold left me here. I promised to get my horse and come. I was not at the Kirkwood House after two o'clock. I have no recollection of being there after that. I had nothing to say at any of the meetings. One of the attempts was at the theater; *the gas was to be put out,* etc.—etc. No discussion was had about failure, and what to do in that case. The coil of rope at Lloyd's was to stretch across the road to trip the cavalry. I know nothing about Spangler's rope; I believe him innocent. Booth told me an actor was to be the best assistant in the theater to turn off the gas. Arnold and O'Laughlin were to grab the President and take him off; and Booth said, when applied to for money, he would go to New York and get some, as he had it there. Mrs. Surratt, Mrs. Slater, Major Banon, and John Surratt left Washington together; got horses at Howard's. Mrs. S. stopped at Surrattsville. John Surratt and Mrs. Slater crossed, and Banon and Mrs. Surratt came back. Banon was in the Rebel army. I don't think Banon knew anything about the conspiracy. I sold a horse for Booth and thought the affair was about over. The murder was broached first on the 14th, at night, when Harold came for me. I did hear Booth say Lincoln ought to be killed. A widow woman was living near Mr. Seward's, and Booth said by her influences he could get entrance to Seward's house; through her influences with the chamber-maid and house servant. The girl at the house was good looking and knew the widow. Harborn was into it first; he came to Port Tobacco with John Surratt for me during the winter. The boat was at the head of Goose Creek and moved to Nanjemoy Creek. It was a lead-colored, flat-bottom boat, and will carry fifteen men. This boat was bought of Jas. Brawner, the old man. Mrs. Slater went with Booth a good deal. She stopped at the National Hotel.

CHAPTER XXXII

[The beginning of this chapter (one or two pages) is missing and must be presumed lost. The remainder of the chapter begins with Weichmann's discussion of Dr. Mudd's part in the Conspiracy.]

. . . the President. He never made the slightest efforts to apprehend the assassins. Thus he became a strong accessory after the fact.

There is much evidence to show that he knew of the scheme to abduct, and that he was one of the parties to help it on.

Says Mr. Oldroyd in his book:

> I have it from unquestionable authority that Dr. Mudd acknowledged a short time before his death that he was connected with the original plan of kidnapping the President. The plan was to take Lincoln across the Potomac at Port Tobacco Creek and Mudd was in readiness at any time to assist the work. Various plans were talked over at his own house. My informant feels very positive that the Doctor would not have entered into the plan to murder the President, and was horrified at the deed done by Booth; but as Booth came to his house a wounded man, he felt it to be his duty to dress his broken leg and get him out of the way as quickly as possible.*

There is also sufficient evidence that before Booth left his house he knew that he [Booth] had murdered the President.

Says Mr. Samuel Cox, Jr.:

> In 1877 Dr. Samuel A. Mudd and myself were the Democratic candidates for the legislature from Charles County, and on frequent occasions during the campaign, when we were alone together, Mudd would talk about the assassination and the part for which he was tried and convicted and sent to the Dry Tortugas. He had been pardoned by President Andrew Johnson, and had been at home several years when these conversations took place. He told me that he had

---

* Oldroyd, p. 260.

never admired Booth, who had forced himself upon him twice before he came to his house the morning after the assassination; that several years before he had refused to be introduced to Booth in Washington, and that, after his refusal, Booth had introduced himself to him on Pennsylvania Avenue; that months afterward Booth came to the Roman Catholic Church at Bryantown, of which Dr. Mudd was a member; that seeing Booth there he had spoken to him, and studiously avoided inviting him to his house, but that when going home from church Booth had followed him uninvited; that he never saw him again until the morning of the 15th of April, 1865, when Booth came to him with a broken leg, and told him he and Herold had just come from across the Potomac, and that soon after leaving the river his horse had fallen and broken the rider's leg; that he believed the statement, and knew nothing different while he was ministering to Booth's sufferings; that after he had made Booth as comfortable as he could, he left him and rode to Bryantown to mail some letters, and when he arrived within half a mile of the village he found the place surrounded by soldiers, and was stopped by a sentry, by whom he was told of the assassination of the President the night before, and that Booth was the assassin. He then said his first impulse was to say, "Come with me and I will deliver him to you." But instead he rode back home with the full determination to warn Booth and upbraid him for his treachery and the danger he had placed him in; that he felt outraged at the treatment he had received at the hands of Booth, and that he did threaten to deliver him up. He then said Booth, in a tragic manner, had appealed to him in the name of his mother not to do so, and he yielded to the appeal, but made them leave his premises forthwith. This statement was made to me by Dr. Samuel A. Mudd several years after he had been released from the Dry Tortugas, when he could have had no motive in telling me what was untrue as to his part in assisting Booth. From statements made to me I believe Mudd was aware of the intention to abduct President Lincoln, but am confident he knew nothing of the plan of assassination.*

Again between four and five o'clock on Saturday afternoon April 15 he called at the house of Francis R. Farrell, who lived half way between Dr. Mudd's and Bryantown, a short distance off the road. During this

* Oldroyd, p. 268.

389

visit of not more than fifteen minutes, Dr. Mudd said that the President had been assassinated by a man by the name of Booth. When Dr. Mudd was asked whether it was the Booth who was down there the fall before, he replied that he did not know, for there were three or four men by that name; but if that was the one he knew him. He made no allusion to the two men that spent the day at his house.* [1]

Dr. Mudd died at his home on January 10, 1883, and sleeps in the little Catholic cemetery a few feet from St. Mary's Church near Bryantown. He was preceded on February 27, 1875, by Spangler, whom he took with him on his release from the Dry Tortugas, and to whom he gave employment and shelter for the remainder of his days. In doing this, Dr. Mudd evinced a kindness of character of which the world has utterly failed to take note. Spangler died in 1875 and was buried in the graveyard at St. Peter's Church, about two miles from Dr. Mudd's house.[2]

For Dr. Mudd I have the sincerest feelings of regret and pity that he should in any way have allowed himself to have been placed under the influence of John Wilkes Booth. I met him but once in my life, and my recollections of him are that he was a gentleman in his intercourse with me. He never did me any wrong, but rather the highest service, when even after conviction, he acknowledged that the testimony which I gave against him was the truth.

In relation to Spangler, it was not shown that he was a party to either the conspiracy to abduct or kill, and the evidence against him was limited, but his actions on the night of the murder at the theater, when he for the first and only time appears on the scene, condemned him.

Michael O'Laughlin while serving his sentence died of yellow fever on September 23, 1867. His remains were subsequently delivered to his mother, who caused them to be brought North.

Samuel Arnold is also dead and is buried near Baltimore.[3]

Boston Corbett, the slayer of Booth, is still alive, and is now about sixty-three years of age. His real name was John Corbett, and he was a hatter by trade. In 1860 in Boston, where he then resided, he experienced religion at a revival, and thereafter out of gratitude to the city in which this event occurred, he assumed the name of Boston and was ever afterwards known as Boston Corbett. Early in the war, he enlisted as cavalryman in the service of the Government. Corbett was a strange

* Oldroyd, p. 145.

and very eccentric fellow and much given to moody silence, followed by periods of religious fervor and ranting. After the shooting of Booth, he made his home for a time in Camden, New Jersey, and then went to Boston, and subsequently emigrated to Kansas. He spent the first winter of his residence in that state in the city of Topeka, and was a constant attendant at the Salvation Army meetings. He had a farm or claim about eighteen miles from Concordia in Cloud County. His home while at Concordia is thus described by a correspondent:

We found him at home in his dugout, a kind of a hole in a steep hill with a brown stone front, a roof of brush, clay and clapboards. There was but one room, and the furniture in it was an old stove, a table, a chair, a homemade bed, a trunk, a box or two, a well worn Bible and a variety of firearms. Mr. Corbett had received a pension of several hundred dollars a short time before, and invested in a flock of sheep what he had not given away to others that he thought might be needing money. A herd of Antelopes would have served him just as well—he had no practical knowledge of the use of sheep. He was very hospitable, told us much of his history and readily consented to deliver a lecture on the capture of Booth and his experience in Andersonville. A packed house greeted him on the night set. By way of introduction, the choir sang a song. Some sentiment of the song set him off on a regular sermon and for nearly an hour he talked, but failed to either capture Booth or to get to Andersonville. At last, the preacher reminded him that he was to talk of Andersonville and Booth. He apologized for his forgetfulness, and in about a dozen words told that he was captured and landed safe inside the walls of Andersonville prison. The first man he met was an old acquaintance, who told him that over in a certain portion of the prison they were holding a prayer meeting. He went directly to it. Then he talked for about a half hour about the prayer meeting which, as far as his description went, might have been held in Cloud County or the back woods of Arkansas. Being reminded again that he was forgetting all about Booth, he apologized and said in substance:

"We surrounded the barn in which he had taken refuge. We demanded that he surrender, but he refused. We then set fire to the barn. By the light he saw one of our men and raised his revolver to shoot him. I was peering through a crack, saw him raise his arm, and to keep him from killing one of our men, I fired and killed him. The bullet went into his head in nearly the same place as his bullet had entered Lincoln's head."

This is as full a history as he saw fit to give of an incident, that had called forth many long articles during the past years, and of which none knew more than our neighbor, Boston Corbett.[4]

Corbett never married and lived alone on his claim in a miserable shack. He always went well armed because of a delusion that the members of the Booth family were upon his trail.

In 1878, through the influence of some friends, because of his army record he was sergeant at arms of the House of Representatives in the Kansas Legislature. He had charge of the ladies' gallery. One morning after the roll call he appeared there with a large revolver in each hand. He began shooting and gesticulating wildly and incoherently and the House had an immediate adjournment, without a dissenting voice.

Corbett was finally arrested and committed to the Kansas State Asylum at Topeka. From here he subsequently escaped and went to Texas.

Nothing further was seen of him until within the past five years, when he was resurrected. He had during that period been a traveling salesman for W. W. Gavitt & Co. of Topeka, a proprietary medicine concern. He lives and travels through Oklahoma Territory and Texas and for a long time had his quarters at Enid, Oklahoma. He has relatives living at Boston and Hyde Park.[5]

Petersen, the German tailor in whose house the President died, committed suicide. His body, full of laudanum, was found in the grounds of the Smithsonian Institution.[6]

John T. Ford, proprietor of Ford's Theater, died in 1894 in Baltimore, and Father Walter, Mrs. Surratt's confessor, passed away on the 5th of February in the same year in Washington.[7]

John M. Lloyd, who leased the tavern at Surrattsville, and who delivered the carbines to the assassins Booth and Herold on the night of the murder, died in Washington in 1892.[8]

Sainte Marie, the discoverer of Surratt, died in Philadelphia in 1873 in extreme poverty, and is buried in the Potter's Field of that city.[9]

He was awarded $10,000 for his services by special act of Congress, the largest sum, but one, given to any one of those identified with the capture of any one of the conspirators.

But strangest of all, Ford's Theater, in the summer of 1893 fell to the ground with a heavy crash, burying in its ruins some eighteen or twenty Government clerks, and on the very same day when the remains of Edwin Booth were being laid to rest in Boston.[10]

The expense incurred by the Government in bringing the culprits to justice, including the two trials of 1865 and 1867, the rewards offered for the taking of the assassins, the pay of the witnesses, attorneys, and detectives, with a vast array of other necessary expenses, probably aggregated in the neighborhood of one million dollars.

In the payment of rewards for the capture of Booth and Herold:

Colonel E. J. Conger received	$15,000.00
Lieutenant Doherty, commander of the Cavalry,	5,250.00
General Lafayette C. Baker,	3,750.00
Luther Baker, detective,	3,000.00
James R. O'Beirne, detective,	2,000.00
George Cottingham, Alexander Lovett, and H. H. Wells, each $1,000.00,	3,000.00
The two sergeants, the seven corporals, and the seventeen privates, each $1,653.85,	43,000.00
	$75,000.00

Amount paid for capture of Payne:

Major H. W. Smith,	$1,000.00
Richard C. Morgan, Eli Devore, Charles W. Rosch, Thomas Sampson, W. M. Wermerskirch, detectives, each $500.00,	2,500.00
J. N. Kimball, citizen,	500.00
P. M. Clark, citizen,	500.00
Susie Jackson, colored,	250.00
Mary Ann Griffin,	250.00
	$5,000.00

Amount paid for capture of Atzerodt:

Major E. R. Artman, 213 Pennsylvania Infantry,	$1,250.00
Sergeant Z. W. Gemmill, 1st Delaware Cavalry,	3,598.54
Christopher Ross, David H. Baker, Albert Bender, Samuel J. Williams, George W. Young, James Longacre, privates 1st Delaware Cavalry, and James W. Purdman, citizen, each, $2,878.78,	20,151.46
	$25,000.00 [11]

The disastrous effects of the assassination were not confined to Lincoln and Seward, for it was only a short time after Mr. Lincoln's death that Mrs. Seward and Miss Fannie Seward, wife and daughter of the Secretary, passed away, both victims of the dire tragedy.[12]

Mrs. Lincoln herself survived the crime several years, but her mind was always in a shattered condition; she was never the same happy woman she had once been and was the constant object of the care and sympathy of her dearest friends until she was finally laid to her rest.[13]

Major Rathbone, who was in the President's box with Miss Harris on the night of the assassination, subsequently made this lady his wife. He was a gentleman of means, position, and culture. He went abroad to reside in Germany. There he became a raving maniac, and while in this unhappy condition, murdered his wife. He is now confined in an asylum in Germany, still a madman.[14]

The revolver and ball with which Booth shot the President, the knife with which he attacked Major Rathbone, the carbines and field glass delivered to him by Lloyd, the compass used in steering himself in his boat with the drippings of the candle still on it, the diary he wrote in the pines of Maryland, the revolver and the knife used by Payne in his attack on Secretary Seward, his overcoat with the blood stains still on it, with his woolen cap and other clothing, the boot which Mudd cut from Booth's foot, the bloody weapons of death carried by the other conspirators, Atzerodt, Herold, Arnold, O'Laughlin—are yet all in the possession of the Government, and some day, when the actors of the present generation are asleep, will perhaps be exhibited in its National Museum as grim reminders of that awful night in 1865 when a few rash, misguided young men attempted to subvert this Government, and destroy liberty in our favored land.

In 1893, after a lapse of twenty-eight years, Dr. J. F. May, Booth's physician, published a statement to the world, that he was insane when he murdered the President, and in a lengthy article endeavored to maintain his position. This was the first announcement of the kind by anyone, and especially by one occupying the high medical standing of Dr. May. To me, who knew Booth well, who saw him often, and heard him talk, the thought never came that he was insane. Dr. May's statement was made at too late a period in life to change public opinion or to have any effect whatever.

When I returned to my home in Philadelphia at the conclusion of the trial of John H. Surratt in 1867, I found such employment as came to my hands, and in 1869, with the advent of General Grant to the presidency, I was appointed on the reommendation of Secretary Stanton and Judge Holt to a position in the Philadelphia Custom House. This I retained until October 1886, when I resigned.

During much of this period, when the feelings engendered by the punishment of Mr. Lincoln's assassins had not yet subsided, I was often in the newspapers, the subject of misrepresentation and slander. For the purpose of correcting this, and of showing the esteem in which I was held by the Commission and high officers of the Government, I publish the following letters at the conclusion of this history.

I shall let the words that these gentlemen have written in my behalf plead for me. Their words are more potent and eloquent than any I can frame. If they are not sufficient to place me right in the estimation of all good people, then naught that I can do will be of avail.

The first is a letter of recommendation from Judge Holt to the Honorable William D. Kelley, M.C.

Washington, March 30, 1869.

Hon. Wm. D. Kelley,

Dear Sir: Referring to our conversation this evening in regard to Mr. Louis J. Weichmann, a constituent of yours, I write to say that ever since this young man gave his testimony on the trial of the assassins of the President he has been subject to the most malignant proscription and persecution of the part of those sympathizing with the rebellion and its crimes, chief among which was the murder of the President. In giving his testimony on that occasion, which I verily believe he did with entire truthfulness, he performed a public duty imposed on him with a conscientious faithfulness which entitles him to support of the government and to the commendation of all loyal and honorable men, yet because of his fidelity and of his ardent loyalty he was, under Johnson's administration, driven from a position in the custom-house in Philadelphia, and has been left without employment and shelter from the malice and the obloquy of his enemies. His restoration to the public service would be in my judgment an act of simple justice on the part of those now in power, and is called for as some indemnity to this young man for what he has suffered in aiding to maintain the law and the highest interests of the country, and as an expression of that confidence in his integrity and veracity which the government has heretofore felt and declared, and which events occurring since the memorable trial referred to have served but to strengthen and confirm.

He has fine intelligence and culture, and sustains an irreproachable character, and is in every way worthy of that kindly consideration which I venture to invoke from you in his behalf. You are too just and too generous not to appreciate in their full force the circumstances on which I shall comment.

If you will lend the influence of your name in supporting the appeal which Mr. Weichmann now makes for a return to the public service, it will be to me a source of great gratification. Very respectfully, your obedient servant,

J. Holt.

Fortieth Congress United States, March 31, 1869.

My Dear Moore (then Collector of the Customs in Philadelphia): I invite your special attention to the enclosed letter from Hon. Joseph Holt, the Judge Advocate General of the United States Army. I know Mr. Weichmann. He resides in the Fifteenth Ward, and has fairly earned the profound interest Judge Holt feels in him. I hope you will not fail to restore him to the desk from which he was expelled because he testified to the truth against the murderers of Lincoln.

The other matter has my approval, but it is less important.

Yours very truly,
William D. Kelley.

Washington, March 30, 1871.

Col. John W. Forney, Collector, Philadelphia, Pa.
Dear Sir: I think I have heretofore spoken to you of Mr. Louis J. Weichmann now a clerk in the custom-house at Philadelphia. In a letter to Judge Kelley, I bore testimony to his fine qualifications, but more especially to the eminent services which he rendered to justice and to the country on the trial of the assassins of the President. He spoke, I firmly believe, the truth, and rendered himself conspicuous by his fearless faithfulness on that occasion. This has subjected him to continual defamation and persecution.

It is my judgement, the solemn duty of the government to protect this man, and to express that confidence in him of which he is in every way worthy. The government believed him, and it would dishonor itself were it to allow him now to be sacrificed by any clamor, which, under the promptings of his enemies, may be raised against him. I commend him to your kind consideration, and feel sure that your just, generous and loyal nature will not deny him that shelter in the public service which he seeks.

Very sincerely yours,

J. Holt.

Washington, April 3, 1871.

Hon. John A. Bingham:

Dear Sir: You will remember Louis J. Weichmann, who was so prominent a witness in the trial of the assassins of the President, and you may know something of the persecution to which he has since been subjected because of the courage and faithfulness with which he performed his duty to the country on that occasion. He is now a clerk in the customhouse at Philadelphia, and fears that amid the changes taking place he may be displaced through the intrigues of his enemies. Cannot you address a letter to Col. Forney, the collector, in his behalf, expressing your estimate of him and his claims to the kindly consideration and protection of the government?

Sincerely yours,

J. Holt.

Indorsement—

Respectfully forwarded to Col. Forney with request that he consider the suggestions of Mr. Holt regarding Mr. Weichmann, in which I fully concur, but have no doubt that you will do what is just and proper in the premises of your own accord.

April 11, 1871.   John A. Bingham.

Washington, Nov. 8, 1865.

Friend Weichmann: Please accept my regards and consider me as your friend.

Lew Wallace, Major General.
Jeffersonville Depot of
Quartermaster's Department.

Jeffersonville, Ind., June 7, 1877.

Mr. Louis J. Weichmann, Philadelphia, Pa.

My Dear Sir: Your letter of June 2, has been received. It affords me great pleasure to bear testimony to your integrity and character. It was never questioned by me, and you were on several occasions favorably mentioned in conversation by the late Secretary Stanton and Gen. Joseph Holt.

During the memorable trial of the conspirators, your testimony was considered by the court as conclusive and clear, and your evidence was regarded as truthful in every particular. It stood the test of cross-examination and remained unshaken on the record.

I have understood that the duties with which you were charged in the Philadelphia custom-house have been performed with fidelity and efficiency and I trust that you may not be disturbed in the position which you have occupied for the past eight years.

You are authorized to use this letter in any manner that shall be to your advantage. I am, respectfully and sincerely, yours,

James E. Ekin.

Deputy Quartermaster General of the United States Army.

Headquarters Eighth United States Infantry,
Angel Island, Cal., April 27, 1885.

Dear Sir: In reply to your request of the 6th instant, I will state that it is my recollection that you were the most important witness before the Commission on the part of the prosecution to show the nature and extent of the conspiracy that resulted in the assassination of President Lincoln. I have no recollection that your testimony was invalidated in the slightest degree, and it certainly impressed me, and also as far as I am able to judge, the other members of the Commission as sincere and truthful. I cannot now recall any impression made upon my mind unfavorable to you as a witness, or that you made any other than a good impression on the Commission as a whole. I have no knowledge of you in any other capacity, except as a witness on that occasion.

Very respectfully,

August V. Kautz,

Colonel Eighth Infantry, Brevet Major General,

United States Army.

Office of the United States Marshal,
District of Indiana,
Indianapolis, Ind., July 30, 1885.

Louis J. Weichmann, Esq., Philadelphia, Pa.

My Dear Sir: Your letter under date of the 27th instant came duly to hand, contents carefully noted. I am glad to hear from you. I remember you very well, and have often referred to your testimony in that eventful trial. I do not wonder that you are the target for the venom of the unreconstructed. You did your duty and deserve and have the respect of all lovers of justice and right. You were placed at that time, as I now remember, in a very delicate and trying position. Your evidence was of great value to us in determining the guilt of those parties. You were unimpeached, and came off the cross-examination leaving the conviction in our minds that you had told the truth. I am respectfully,

R. S. Foster,
United States Marshal.

Washington, March 10, 1869.

To His Excellency, Gen. U.S. Grant, the President of the United States.

Sir: I understand that Louis J. Weichmann, of Philadelphia, will apply for some place under the government. In his behalf, I beg to say that I made his acquaintance while acting as counsel for the United States in the trial of John H. Surratt in 1867.

Mr. Weichmann was so situated in reference to the case that he was compelled to act a very conspicuous, delicate, and painful part, and one which severely tried his mental and moral qualities. He acquitted himself in an admirable manner, which gained him the entire confidence of both Judge Pierrepont and myself, and aside from testifying, his services in other respects were valuable to us.

I think him entitled to the most favorable consideration of the government.

Very respectfully,
A. G. Riddle.

Treasury Department,
Office of the First Auditor,
Washington, D.C., February 3, 1892.

L. J. Weichmann, Esq.

My Dear Sir: Your letter of the 12th ultimo was duly received in which you request from me an opinion as to your testimony and conduct in the trial of John H. Surratt for the murder of Abraham Lincoln. I have no hesitation in saying that your conduct on the witness stand all through on that occasion was that of a perfectly honest and truthful witness.

Yours very truly,
George F. Fisher.

And General Harris, a member of the Commission, and author of a history of the assassination of Lincoln, has this to say of me in reviewing the trial of John H. Surratt:

> Weichmann stood the test of every effort and came out unscathed from a bitter and most hostile cross-examination that occupied a day and a half. Every effort was made to make him contradict himself as to his present testimony-in-chief, and also as to his testimony two years before at the military trial, but without avail. No false witness could possibly have come out of such a fiery ordeal unscathed.

> After every effort was made that could be devised by the ingenuity of man, Weichmann stood before the court, the jury, and the country as an honest, conscientious, truthful man. He was also a man of superior talent, education, and intelligence. In short, he established a character that must challenge the admiration of every candid man.[15]

It has been customary to describe the parties who were with Booth in his plot as depraved characters. Such, at least, was not the case with them in early life. Leaving Booth out of the question, although descended from a great family, the Surratts, mother and son, had always been honest people, and were respected; Herold came from a very respectable family, his mother, a widow, hard-working, conscientious, striving to support in comfort her large family; Payne, when a boy, converted to religion and the son of a man who had consecrated his life to the winning of souls to Christ; Atzerodt, an honest German, the pride and love of his mother.

Dr. Mudd was of the oldest and best Maryland blood, and his family name ranked high in the community in which he lived; his brother, Mr. George Mudd, was always a staunch supporter of the Union.

O'Laughlin and Arnold were Baltimore boys of good repute. Arnold's father was a baker and enjoyed the trade and confidence of his neighbors.

Of Spangler little can be said, except that he was more than anyone else Booth's dupe.

Such was the party that the chief assassin had gathered together to do his bidding, and it is incredible that he should have succeeded.

Booth had a wondrous power of fascination, and it was probably to this, and to his promises, that so many fell from the honorable path which had once been theirs. On one occasion, during the Conspiracy trial, O'Laughlin asked leave to introduce evidence to show the extraordinary power Booth had over others, with his fine command of language and word painting, but the request, of course, was denied. Nevertheless, it was probable in this way that O'Laughlin was influenced to leave the sacred path of right.

APPENDIXES

SELECTED BIBLIOGRAPHY

NOTES

INDEX

OBITUARY OF LOUIS J. WEICHMANN

In 1926 the late Lloyd Lewis interviewed Weichmann's sisters, Mrs. Charles O'Crowley and Miss Tillie Weichmann, at Anderson, Indiana. They told Mr. Lewis that when their brother realized that he was about to die, he asked them to take down the following statement, which he signed: "June 2, 1902; This is to certify that every word I gave in evidence at the assassination trial was absolutely true; and now I am about to die and with love I recommend myself to all truth-loving people." [1] The original signed statement has never been produced and must be presumed lost. However, this statement is supported by the long obituary in the *Anderson* (Indiana) *Herald* of June 6, 1902 (printed below), which states that H. J. Creighton was called to his bedside, but that Weichmann was too weak to talk, so he wrote on a piece of paper that while on the witness stand at the great trial he had "told the truth and nothing but the truth." (Hugh J. Creighton was the owner of the Perfection Magneto Company.)

Weichmann's death certificate gives June 5, 1902, as the date of his death and "Cardiac Asthma" as the cause—not "extreme nervousness" as reported by Lewis in *Myths After Lincoln*.

L. J. WEICHMAN GOES TO REST

PASSED AWAY LAST NIGHT AT O'CROWLEY HOME

MADE DYING STATEMENT

SAID HE TOLD ONLY TRUTH IN THE GREAT TRIAL

Man with a National History · Had Many Friends in This City ·
Arrangements for Funeral will be Made Today

Lewis J. Weichman died at 7:45 o'clock last night at the home of his sister, Mrs. Charles O'Crowley, at Eighth and Henry streets, after an illness of several months. He was surrounded by his brother and sisters and a few friends. While he has been in ill health for many months he has not been confined home much of the time, having been up town less than a week ago. During the afternoon, Mr. Weichman realized that he must die. There seemed to be something on his mind which worried him. He called H. J. Creighton to his bedside and undertook to talk to him but was too weak. He wanted to talk about the assassination of Abraham Lincoln and

1 See Lloyd Lewis, *Myths After Lincoln*, p. 267.

the part he had taken as a witness in the trial of the conspirators. After a time he wrote on a piece of paper. He said that he realized that he was about to pass out of this world and was about to face his God in another world and he wished the people of this country to understand that in the great trial, and while on the witness stand, he told the truth and nothing but the truth.

Educated for Priesthood

Prof. Weichman was among the best known men in Anderson to the younger people, having been for many years a teacher of a business college. Mr. Weichman was born in 1842 at Baltimore of German parents, the mother being a strong Catholic and the father a Lutheran. He was graduated from the high school in 1859, after which it was decided by his parents that he should become a student for the Catholic priesthood. Accordingly he was sent in March, 1859 to St. Charles, Md., twenty-five miles from Baltimore. He left college in 1862 and returned to his home in Philadelphia and in the fall of that year he became a teacher in the schools at Little Texas, Md. The school house burned the following December and he went to Washington, D.C., where he taught a year. In January, 1864, Mr. Weichman was appointed a clerk in the war department at Washington and in August of that year he became a member of the War Department Rifles, a body of men composed of clerks, whose purpose was to defend Washington from invasion. After the war Mr. Weichman returned to Philadelphia where he became connected with the custom house and remained twenty years.

Many Years a Teacher

Mr. Weichman came to Anderson in 1886 soon after his brother, Father Weichman was assigned to Anderson. It was not long until he opened a business college, where bookkeeping, stenography and other courses for a business life were taught. It was the first school of the kind ever in Anderson. Mr. Weichman was successful in his undertaking. He has had the school in operation almost continuously until a few weeks ago, when he was compelled to give up on account of ill health. Almost all the young people in business, either for themselves or for others attended his school. Mr. Weichman was a highly educated man, being able to talk a number of different languages.

Mr. Weichman was a brother of Father Weichman of the Catholic church of Gas City and chaplain of the Marion Soldiers' Home. He was a brother-in-law of Charles O'Crowley of this city and besides Mrs. O'Crowley he leaves another sister. Miss Nellie Weichman.

His Part in Great Trial

Lewis J. Weichman was a man of more than local interest. He was a character of national interest. This is because of the fact that he was one of the main characters in connection with the trial of the accomplices to the assassination of Abraham Lincoln by John Wilkes Booth. He was the most important witness in the trial and it is said that it was [by] his testimony that Mrs. Mary E. Surratt, George A. Atzerodt, David E. Harrold and Lewis Payne, were convicted by the court and sentenced to be executed. It was in the fall of his first year at St. Charles College that Mr. Weichman met John H. Surratt, the son of Mrs. Surratt, age sixteen years. They became intimate friends and college mates. In 1864, John Surratt learned that Weichman was in Washington and the college acquaintance was renewed and Weichman was taken to the Surratt home. It was the next morning at a band concert, Weichman met through Surratt, John E. Harrold, one of the conspirators and the one who escaped with Booth on the night of the shooting. Weichman and Surratt met Dr. Mudd who in turn introduced them to Booth.

On the night of the tragedy, Mr. Weichman was at his home and knew nothing of the assassination until the detective came the next morning to search his home. Mrs. Surratt was placed under arrest, but Weichman was allowed to go, yet he was under surveillance for a long time.

Mr. Weichman testified to the number of meetings which the conspirators held at the Surratt home. He knew nothing of what was going on at the meetings. One of the main things he testified to was that Dr. Mudd was an intimate friend of Booth. When the latter denied it, Judge Bingham, one of the judges who tried the conspirators said of Prof. Weichman, "I may say in reference to the witness that they have not contradicted a single fact to which he has testified in this issue, nor have they found a breath of suspicion against his character."

Ungrounded Fear

Because of the fact that four of the conspirators were members of the Catholic church, Mr. Weichman believed that there was a conspiracy against him and for many years he lived in fear. There was no ground for fear, however. The Catholic people at large were anxious to see the guilty parties punished and they have borne no ill feeling to Mr. Weichman. He left the church and was not connected with it any time until Wednesday morning, when it was thought he was going to die. The priest at the hospital was called and anointed him. Mr. Weichman after that until his death was more cheerful than he has been in a long time and he smiled more than has been noticed for some time. He seemed more cheerful and talked and joked with members of the family.

NOTICE OF WEICHMANN'S FUNERAL [2]

The funeral of the late Lewis J. Weichman will take place this morning at 9 o'clock, at St. Mary's Church, and the interment will be at the Catholic cemetery. Mass will be conducted by Father Weichman.

[2] From the *Anderson Herald*, June 7, 1902.

LETTERS OF A. C. RICHARDS
TO LOUIS J. WEICHMANN

Almarin Cooley Richards was born in Cummington, Massachusetts, on December 24, 1827, the seventh child of Nehemiah Richards, Jr., and Betsey Packard Richards. His name was Almarin Nehemiah, but later in life he changed it to Almarin Cooley.

About 1833, he moved with his parents to Chester, Ohio, where he attended the public schools and eventually was graduated from Western Reserve Teachers' Seminary at Kirtland, Ohio. In 1851, he left for Washington, D.C., where he joined the Union Academy as a teacher. On September 5, 1859, he established the Prescott High School as the proprietor and principal, but with the outbreak of the Civil War he accepted a position in the Washington post office as a financial clerk. In 1862, he was elected an alderman to the third ward and took an active part in the civic and political affairs of the city.

At the time of Lincoln's first inauguration, Richards volunteered as a deputy marshal and rode at the right wheel of Lincoln's carriage in the parade from the old Willard Hotel to the Capitol. With the outbreak of the war the Government took over the administration of the municipal affairs of the city to guard against any disloyalty in the local administration. In 1864, Lincoln was submitted a list of persons being considered to head the city police force. Seeing Richards' name, he remembered him as one of the guards at the first inaugural and appointed him as Superintendent of the Metropolitan Police on December 1, 1864, a position he held until 1878. He entered this office during a very trying period when the city was overrun with soldiers, adventurers, gamblers, Southern sympathizers, and representatives of some of the worst elements of society.

Four months and fifteen days after becoming Superintendent of the Metropolitan Police, Richards became officially involved in the most momentous event to take place in the history of the local police and perhaps in the history of our nation—the assassination of Abraham Lincoln.

Only brief mention of Richards as head of the police force has been made in the numerous books written on the assassination. He did not give testimony at the trial of the conspirators in 1865, and if he had appeared at the first trial as a witness and given the testimony he writes Weichmann about, it could only have tightened the noose around the neck of Mary E. Surratt.

On April 3, 1898, the Washington Post *published "John H. Surratt's Story" under the name of Hanson Hiss, in which Surratt gives Weichmann a rough going over—calling him a liar and accusing the police of threatening to hang Weichmann unless he told them what they wanted to know. Both Richards and Weichmann responded to this article, and their responses were published in the* Washington Post *on April 18, 1898. Richards was a subscriber to the paper and had seen the article; the* Post *had written to Weichmann on April 6, 1898, offering him the courtesy of its columns "for any response you would like to make to John H. Surratt's Story, and furthermore would make the writing of a good historical story worth your while." As a result of the* Post *article, Weichmann located Richards in Eustis, Florida, in April of the same year, and began a correspondence with him about the assassination and the book he was writing. In all, Richards wrote twenty-three revealing letters on the assassination to Weichmann, and they are printed here for the first time.*

In 1874, Richards was appointed to the Board of Trustees of the Public Schools, a position which he held for several years. In 1882, Richards was graduated from the National University Law School and practiced in the courts of the District of Columbia until 1893, when he moved with his family to Eustis, Lake County, Florida, where he owned and operated the Lochmead Orange Groves.

Richards passed away at Eustis, Florida, on February 17, 1907. His remains were returned to Washington and buried alongside his wife's in Rock Creek Cemetery on February 22, 1907.

The following group of twenty-three letters was written by Richards to Weichmann during a period beginning in April 1898 and ending in November 1901. From Richards' first letter, dated April 26, we learn that Weichmann opened the correspondence on April 22. This would indicate that contact between Richards and Weichmann was made after the April 18, 1898, reply to "John H. Surratt's Story" in the Washington Post. *In other words, there could not have been any collusion on the part of either party in regard to this article. All of the letters are on the subject of the assassination of Abraham Lincoln and the events that followed in Ford's Theater on the night of April 14, 1865. These letters, published here for the first time, provide the eyewitness account of Richards, who was in the theater and heard the pistol shot that ended Lincoln's life. Richards gives a detailed description of the assassination as he witnessed it from his seat in the dress circle, which is in conflict with the testimony given by Joseph B. Stewart.[1] From Richards' letters it would seem that Stewart had let his imagination run away with him. He reveals in detail for the first time his visit with detectives to the Surratt house and it is significant that he should point the finger of suspicion at Mrs. Surratt. That she had been sitting in a darkened house "waiting for someone" becomes evident from these letters. It is also significant that Richards places Mrs. Surratt second only to John Wilkes Booth in the Conspiracy and assassination, while Weichmann apparently thinks that her son John H. Surratt was second.*

Richards describes the effort to procure cavalry horses to mount twelve detectives to pursue Booth and Herold when two men were reported to him to have passed the guard at the Navy Yard Bridge heading into Maryland. It was eleven o'clock the next morning before he was able to get the required horses and follow

[1] See Pitman, p. 79.

a cold trail. If the horses had been available when first called for, it might have resulted, he thinks, in the capture of the fugitives.

Some have claimed that the assassination was advocated by the Catholic Church and was a Roman conspiracy. Although four of the conspirators were of the Catholic faith and John H. Surratt was concealed from the law by some Catholic officials in Canada, Richards rules out the possibility of a Catholic conspiracy. He is surprised that Weichmann, a Catholic, handles Father Walter "without gloves" in regard to the confession of Mrs. Surratt just before her execution. Richards heard the shots that killed two Presidents—Lincoln and Garfield—and lived to read about the shot that killed President McKinley. He was near the railroad depot when he heard the shot that killed President Garfield. In one of his last letters, he makes note of this and recommends that the Government acquire an island in mid-ocean where all professed anarchists could be sent to establish "a community based on their own ideas."

These letters are all informative and give solid documentation by the top police official of Washington, D.C. In these letters, he vindicates the action, purpose, and character of one of the Government's chief witnesses, Louis J. Weichmann. He indicates that he has read most or all of the chapters of Weichmann's narrative and approves the historical content, narration, and literary style and urges its publication.

[*April 26, 1898*]

It gives me much pleasure to acknowledge the receipt of yours of the 22d-inst. It came to hand this morning. I have often wondered where you were and now am glad to be assured you are alive. I hope you are doing well.

Your letter as published in the Washington Post is an admirable refutation of the dastardly and scandalous attack upon your character by John H. Surratt under the cognomen "Hanson Hiss." [2] The *"hiss"* part of the cognomen is appropriate. In it I note the sinnous course of a serpent and fancy I can hear his "hiss." Your letter is entirely appropriate and well conceived and the testimonials you submit are of the best and are conclusive.[3] In my opinion Surratt had better have kept out of this last conspiracy to defame you. You will be fully justified in revealing the entire plot for the assassination of the Noble Lincoln with all its attendant incidents and circumstances as you related them to me. It is your duty to vindicate your character and standing as a man and a citizen by unveiling the truth. Truth is the unassailable vindicator. You know, of course, that at the trial of the conspirators, as a witness you could not give all the facts in your knowledge, nor narrate incidents and circumstances as they transpired. In your proposed history of that vile tragedy give everything—withhold nothing—Let the blow fall—Surratt essays a self vindication at your expense and tries to make a victim of you. Of course it is a senseless attempt on his part yet it leaves you free to speak.

I hope to hear from you again soon. . . . With highest regards, I am . . .

[2] See Hanson Hiss article, below, p. 441.
[3] See above, p. 395.

[April 29, 1898]

My Dear Sir:

Yours of the 25th inst. to hand. I answered your former letter the day after its receipt, but it did not reach the post office for a day or two thereafter, as my home is some 3 miles from the office. I also received a day or two since a copy of the Phono[g]raphic Magazine. This is now my home—have res[i]ded here since 1893. Am not here for my health. That is good. I have an orange grove here of 25 acres, and also have charge of another grove of 120 acres belonging to a Co. of Washington people. The great freezes of 1894 & 1895 killed all the orange trees to the ground but they are now sufficiently rehabilitated to bear some fruit. Bigley (the detective) became insane—was sent to St. Elizabeth Asylum and died there some twenty or more years ago. McDevitt is yet in W[ashington] and is a private detective and doing very well I think. I think he could give some points of interest relative to the incidents of the night of the assassination. He was very active that night and gave me many items of information that night. He, with others, went with me to Mrs. Surratt's house that night. It was McDevitt who took me to Laura Keen[e] within an hour or less, perhaps, after the assassination. Then she (Laura Keen[e]) told me that the man who jumped from the theatre box, in which the President was witnessing the play was Wilkes Booth. She did not know whether he shot the President or not. I do not recall the name Gleason now. If I remember rightly the man from whom we got the first information connecting Payne, Harold and Atzerot with Booth was a saloon keeper under or near the theater, named Ferguson, I think. We soon thereafter obtained information that John H. Surratt was often in company with these men and then that Booth had often visited or called at Mrs. Surratt's house. Those facts led me to pay that house a visit that night at about one o'clock.[4] When I reached the house and had rung the door bell, Mrs. Surratt answered it very promptly. The house was dark so far as I could discover but there was no unusual delay in the response of Mrs. S. to the bell. She appeared dressed as a lady of her station might be expected to dress of an evening. Her hair was not disarranged. She had not time to dress and smooth her hair between the ringing of the bell and her appearance at the door. She had not retired for the night, but was evidently, waiting in a dark house for some one to call. When

---

[4] On May 12, 1865, Richards wrote a notarized letter to Stanton in which he stated that the Surratt house was searched by detectives Clarvoe and McDevitt, previous to the hour of two o'clock on the night of the murder, but makes no mention of his earlier visit the same night.

He further stated to Stanton that Weichmann was "put under arrest by McDevitt by my orders and held under arrest until orders were received from you to deliver him at the War Department, which was done as soon as he could be brought from Canada." (*National Archives*, Microfilm 619, Reel 456, Frames 0566-7-8.)

Richards was at loggerheads with the War Department and had been severely reprimanded by Stanton for sending Weichmann to Canada. It would appear that he wished to disengage himself from any further confrontation with Stanton and thus made no mention of his earlier visit to the Surratt house the night of the assassination. (*Why Was Lincoln Murdered?*, p. 198. See also below, Richards' letters of May 7, 1898, and September 18, 1899.)

His statement regarding Weichmann's arrest seems to have the same implication. At the Surratt trial Richards stated that while Weichmann was under arrest, it was more like protective custody of a witness and that Weichmann was not aware of this. (*Surratt Trial*, II, 987-9.)

I informed her why I had called after informing her of the assassination she expressed no surprise or regret. In fact she only answered such questions as I asked her in the briefest possible terms—gave me no information in regard to Booth, his visits or the visits of others of the assassins to her house. She seemed entirely self-possessed and did not seem in the least affected when I said to her that President Lincoln had just been assassinated and that Booth and her son were suspected of being implicated in the crime. No doubt that you are correct in your statement that you first called at my office on Saturday morning instead of Sunday morning as I wrote. My statements were from memory only. I had no memoranda—I recollect that you called quite early and I also remember that I did not get home that night until daylight which led me to conclude that I did not go back to my office again that morning in time to see you so early. It must be I did not remain at home long. I have not time to write more just now. This is writtin in great haste. If you can communicate with McDevitt it is probable he can give interesting particulars. If you think of any points which I may be informed upon let me know. I hope to hear from you further in relation to this matter. Give me the "interesting" points you refer to in your last.

[*May 7, 1898*]

Your two letters of the 2d-inst. came to hand yesterday. I will be glad to see the article you send out to the papers for which Hiss is a correspondent and in which his Surratt "vindication" was published. Also I hope to receive the matter you intimate you will soon send. I will write to McDevitt and get from him whether he was with me the night I called at Mrs. Surratts house. I am strongly impressed that he was. Clarvoe, Bigley and Kelly are all deceased. It is my present impression that on that night during my conversation with Mrs. Surratt that either myself or McDevitt intimated that we would like to look through the house to see who was there, and that McDevitt did go through the house to some extent at least. I remember I think that McDevitt seemed to be somewhat acquainted with Mrs. Surratt and her family. Hence I left the examination to him. If I remember rightly he found Holehan (I think that the name) and two young ladies there. Miss Surratt and another. If I remember rightly I remained at the front door while McDevitt went through the house with Mrs. Surratt. Of course you will bear in mind that up to the visit in question, and not until after I had conversed with you next day did I have the remotest conception or suspicion that Mrs. Surratt was to any extent implicated in the plot to assassinate Mr. Lincoln. Even after our suspicious file on John H. [Surratt], through finding that he had been seen in company with Booth the winter previous many times, we did not realize that Mrs. Surratt was one of the conspirators. It is possible that McDevitt paid a second visit to that house that night. I know he was very active and efficient in developing the plot. You will remember that in two or three days after the assassination the authorities were being urged through newspapers & otherwise to offer rewards for the capture of Booth and others and that large rewards were offered. After that all information securred was kept close by the detectives of the War Department. Persons who had information were given to understand that they had better divulge only to certain persons.

[*May 9, 1898*]

Yours of the 4th inst. to hand. You request of me a statement of the fact you reported to me on Saturday April 15th 1865 and subsiquently. I recall, generally that you reported very important facts in relation to your being present on occasions when Booth met Surratt, Dr. Mudd, Payne and others at hotels, on the street and at Mrs. Surratt's house. Also that you observed several movements of these conspirators that satisfied you that they, sometime in March I think, made an abortive attempt to capture and abduct the President to Virginia.[5] Also I recall your statements in relation to your trip to Surrattsville with Mrs. S (Surratt) on Friday the 14th of April I think it was etc. etc., but just at that time I was getting so many reports from different persons that I fear I might confound reports made by you with those made by others. I kept no memoranda of those events and must rely entirely on memory. Thirty-three years is a long time to retain particulars. Now I wish you would write me giving a statement of what you did report to me. Such a statement will refresh my memory and enable me to segregate your statement from those made by others. Also indicate the ground you want covered by my statement. On receipt of that I will prepare such a paper as will meet your desires probably. I have written to McDevitt for certain facts and ought to hear from him soon. He is a little slow sometimes in answering letters.

[*May 16, 1898*]

Responding to yours of the 10th inst. I have to say that in April 1865 I was Major and Superintendent of the Metropolitan Police of the District of Columbia. It so happened that I was in Ford's Theatre on the night of April 14th 1865 at the time of the assassination of President Lincoln. It became my duty at once to seek to ascertain the identity of the President's assassin. Within a short time—less than an hour—I had positive and undoubted information that the man who had been seen to vault from the box occupied by the President and others was Wilkes Booth. Very soon thereafter I was authentically informed that Booth had been frequently seen in the company of John H. Surratt and others during the then preceeding few weeks, and that Booth and others then not known by name to me were known to have frequently visited the house of John H. Surratt's mother. Between the hours of 12 and 1 o'clock that night, in company with several of my officers I visited the house of Mrs. Surratt and saw and conversed with her, giving her as I then presumed, the first information she had received of the assassination of the President. You were sleeping in Mrs. Surratt's house that night and one of my officers reported to me that he had seen you in your room, & at that hour I had no grounds for suspecting that Mrs. Surratt was implicated in the conspiracy to assassinate the President. She was not arrested. A guard of police officers was left to observe

[5] The "horseback ride," March 16–17, 1865.

who came to or left the house, when I left for other duties. At about half past eight the next (saturday April 15th) morning, very soon after I reached my office you came in and, introducing yourself, stated that you were and had been for sometime a boarder at Mrs. Surratt's house and that in view of the assassination and developments that had come to your knowledge within a few hours, believed that you were in possession of facts and, a knowledge of circumstances that would materially aid in developing the fact that a band of men had for some time previous been concocting a plot to assassinate the President. You then and there narrated many facts and incidents you had observed, together with meetings at Mrs. Surratt's house, on the street and at hotels, of the men you believed had compassed the plot for the assassination of the President and other principal officers of the government. You gave names, dates, incidents and circumstances connected with the plot. All the names of men you gave were subsequently proven to have been implicated in the conspiracy. Many of the incidents and circumstances you narrated were afterwards established as correctly stated by you. In no instance was any statement made by you subsequently discredited or you shown to be in error in any manner. The course you pursued immediately after the assassination was of the utmost value in aiding in establishing the fact of a conspiracy and convicting the conspirators. No one rendered greater aid. Now as to threats to you, cruelty or unkind treatment—You came to my office early Saturday morning April 15th, 1865, voluntarily and unattended by any one.[6] You proceeded to make your statement without hesitation or solicitation on my part. It must have been the first statement you made in regard to your knowledge in the premises—You came to and went from my office for some days as and when you pleased—aided my officers effectively to the extent of your power and information. At my request you accompanied my officers to Montreal Canada in pursuit of John H. Surratt and returned with them. At no time during a period of two weeks subsequent to the assassination were you under arrest, restraint or threats in any manner whatever. If at any time up to the 29th of April following the assassination, you were treated harshly, unkindly or were the subject of threats I must have been the author or instigator of the same. I saw you daily except while on your trip to Montreal. I pronounce any statement intended to countervail the above as to your treatment as without the slightest foundation and false.

While I have not seen you for more than thirty years, nor heard from you until recently during the same period of time, I cheerfully and out of a sense of justice to you make the foregoing statements.

[*May 24, 1898*]

I have yours of the 18th inst. Whether McDevitt or myself was first at the Surratt house on the night of the assassination I cannot say. I had always supposed, or presumed rather, that McDevitt accompanied me to that house on the night in question for the reason that he was with me much of the time that night. Now McDevitt writes me that he thinks I did not visit the house that night and that

---

[6] Holohan went with Weichmann to the police station.

he was the first one to enter the house. I have written McDevitt that he was never more mistaken in his life than in supposing I did not visit the house that night. I am not certain that the hour of the visit was one o'clock, but I do not think it could have been as late as two o'clock. I did not enter the house, as I have before stated, but remained at the front door in conversation with Mrs. Surratt a part of the time, while officers entered of whom I supposed McDevitt was one. I did not go there to search the house, but to ascertain from Mrs. S. (Surratt), if I could, who the parties were that Booth called to see at her house. I knew at the time that Booth was the assassin of the President, but had not learned who the other conspirators were. I had then learned of the attempted assassination of Secretary Seward and had reports of other attempts or plans of assassination viz: Vice President Johnson, Gen. Grant, Secretary Stanton and perhaps others. At the hour of my said visit I had not the remotest idea that Mrs. Surratt could have been in any way privy to the plot and hence sought her for information. The only recollection I have of Clarvoe that night is, that at about 11 o'clock I had information that two mounted men had passed the military guard at the Navy Yard bridge and that from statements made by that guard I suspected that those two mounted men might be the assassins. Very soon thereafter I directed Clarvoe to assemble 12 good riders from the force and be prepared to follow those men into Maryland as soon as I could procure horses to mount the men.[7] Presuming that I could get a dozen cavalry horses from the thousands then in corrals about Washington I sent an officer to secure such mounts. After considerable delay the officer reported that after being sent from one officer of the Army to another he finally found one who promised to send the horses at once. From that hour until about 11 o'clock next morning Clarvoe was waiting at headquarters, or within call, to head his expedition as above indicated, as the horses did not arrive at headquarters until the last above named hour. For the reasons above stated I cannot see how Clarvoe could have been at Mrs. Surratts house at 2 o'clock on the night in question. Are you positive in your mind that Clarvoe was at the house at 2 o'clock that morning? Are you also positive that you let McDevitt in at the *front* door that morning? If you are then there must have been two visits to the house that night, the first of which you were unaware of. Did you impart any information to McDevitt at that visit of his? Did you call at my office next morning at McDevitt's suggestion or was it of your own motion? Am I not correct in stating that you came unattended by any one? I am unable to make it clear to my own mind that it was Saturday morning when you first called. I know I did not get home until sometime after daylight that morning. My family had not learned of the assassination when I reached home. I remained home to breakfast which was usually at 8 o'clock so that it must have been 9 o'clock or after when I reached the office. I remember of noticing the crowd about the theatre and opposite as I went down towards my office and that I remained there for a while. Now it seems to me that you called at my office quite early—as soon as 8½ o'clock. I do not recall that you referred, in our first interview, to any visit to Mrs. Surratt's house the night previous. It

[7] Weichmann was one of the twelve who rode into Maryland in pursuit of Booth and Herold.

seems to me that you believed you were in possession of information which after reading the morning papers and from other sources, you deemed important that I should also possess. It also seems to me that when you called it was quiet about my office. No one in at the time. That could hardly have been the case on saturday morning. It is the conditions above named that led me to believe it was Sunday morning that you first called more than a distinct remembrance of the day of the week. Of course I cannot explain why when you informed Mrs. S. (Surratt) of the assassination after Clarvoe had told you that she should have expressed surprise and astonishment. Was not Mrs. S. (Surratt) *"acting"* a part at that time. When I said to her that the President had just been assassinated and that Booth who had been known to be a frequenter of her house was his assassin she expressed no surprise or astonishment. When I went to the house it was dark so far as I could see throughout the house. I know I was surprised that she answered my ring at the bell so promptly and that she should be dressed and hair in perfect order. I now account for this on the presumption that Mrs. Surratt at the hour of my visit was expecting a call from some other person and had been waiting in a darkened house for a call prearranged and anticipated but in which she was disappointed. My call was a surprise to her of course and she had not then considered the part she should enact. When you first saw her that night she had had time for reflection as to the position she might be placed in. Evidently she and the others had not proceeded upon the possibility that their plot would misscarry in any manner as it did to a large extent. They had presumed upon dismay and confusion as well as disorganization and immobility on the part of the government and its officers for a time at least. During this presumed confusion and alarm the conspirators had satisfied themselves that they could meet some where prior to making their escape. If so many of the leading officials of the government as were included in their plot had been killed they had good grounds to presume that alarm, anarchy and confusion would exist for awhile. Circumstances and faint hearts of actors prevented the realization of their preconceived expectations of the course of events immediately following the denouement. The above are thoughts that have possessed my mind for a long time.

I shall be glad to respond further to any suggestions you may make, for in this reminiscence we both want matters as clear as possible.

[*June 2, 1898*]

I received, yesterday, chapters 1 to 6 inclusive of your proposed book relative to the assassination of President Lincoln and have read the same carefully. Your narrative is deeply interesting to me and will be equally so to others who may read your book I doubt not. Your references to John H. Surratt are in good taste and breathe a spirit of magnanimity on your part in his behalf. I cannot agree with you that next to Booth John H. Surratt was the archconspirator. I think Mrs. Surratt, next to Booth was the moving spirit. See that the book is well advertised and it will command a wide circulation.

I observe that in chapter 1 p. 8 you state that Surratt was captured in Italy while serving in the Papal Zouaves. My recollection is that he escaped or left that service and fled to Egypt and was there captured. In this I may be in error as I write from memory only. I am quite sure that the accounts published of his capture at about the time it occurred located his arrest in Egypt. And I so understood the fact to be when I recovered Surratt at the Washington Navy Yard from the hands of the chief officer of the U.S. vessel that brought him to Washington. I took charge of Surratt at the Navy Yard and conveyed him to the City Hall where I handed him over to the U. S. Marshall.

I note nothing to criticise in the chapters read. You handle the subject in a judicious and attractive manner.

I hope to see succeeding chapters as you have opportunity to send them.

Do you get anything satisfactory from McDevitt? He has written me twice on the subject. His letters are very brief and general in statements. His letters though over his signature are evidently prepared by some other persons—possibly his type writer. Is McDevitt under any local influence that you know of that would restrain free utterances on his part?

[*June 10, 1898*]

Your letters of the 3d & 6th inst. to hand as are also the two registered packages of matter for your forthcoming book. These packages I will return in a day or two either by registered mail or by express. Have you received the first package you sent and which I forwarded to you by registered mail some days ago?

I fully agree with you in your statement that there were at the time, and are now, no grounds for the assertion, or suspicion even, that assassination of President Lincoln was compassed in any way whatever by Catholic or Romish effort, influence or approval. Insinuations that the plot had such an origion or was furthered in the remotest manner by the Authorities of the Catholic Church are preposterous and seem silly to one who was familiar with the circumstances attending the consumation of the plot and with the character, personnel and church bias of the conspirators. I have had occasion more than once to express my views as above to friends who have inquired and whose minds had been disturbed by lectures by a certain renegade Catholic Priest some years ago.[8]

Allow me to suggest that you review the rules of law in regard to the production of evidence where you state that at the trial of the conspirators the contents of the destroyed letter that Booth put into the hands of Matthews was not allowed to be proven for the reason that said letter had been destroyed as I understand you to say. As I remember the law is as a preliminary step to the introduction of parole testimony relating to the contents of papers in writing the loss or destruction of such papers must be shown. I understand you to say that as it appeared in trial that said letter had been destroyed Matthews was not allowed to testify as to its contents. Before you publish look that matter over. If a written statement

---

[8] Father Chiniqui, a former Catholic priest, author of *Fifty Years in the Church of Rome* (London: Robert Banks & Son, 1886). Father Chiniqui claimed that the plot to assassinate originated with the Catholic Church in Rome.

is produced in trial it would not be necessary to prove its contents by parole. The paper itself would be admitted as the *best* evidence. That letter, or its contents, must have been ruled out on other grounds than those you state I think.

On page eight, chapter XV you refer to the testimony of Joseph B. Stewart. What you state on that page and following as to Stewart's operations that night I presume you take from Stewart's testimony as published in the record of the trial. I suggest that you make it clear that those statements are Stewart's and not from your own personal knowledge. I say this for the reason that Stewart drew largely upon his imagination when he gave his testimony as to what transpired immediately after the shot was fired. When the fatal shot was fired I was sitting in the dress circle of the theater and near the center of the circle in company with Capt. Reed, then Inspector of Police. As soon as I realized that some one had been shot in the President's box, I sprang from my seat, rushed down the stairs, through the crowd in the orchestra circle and upon the stage. Of course I had seen a man vault from the box and cross the stage. When I got upon the stage I found Stewart already there and no other person then in sight on the stage or among the curtains. I must have been upon the stage within two minutes from the time the shot was heard. Stewart had had no time to make any explorations of the stage when I reached him. I knew him and he knew me. Together we searched among the scenery and finally found the door from the stage leading into the alley open. It was quite dark both among the scenery on the stage and in the alley. As we stepped out into the alley I saw a man (Peanut John I think) standing there and heard the rattling of a horse's feet moving rapidly down the alley but not in sight. The man found there on demand explained that the footsteps of the horse we heard were those of one he had been holding for a man whom he claimed he did not know and said that the man had had some difficulty in mounting his horse and so on. No such scene as you describe as part of Stewart's testimony occurred there. The statement is apocryphal and imaginary. The gyrations Stewart describes as having participated in could not have taken place as there was no horse and rider then there and in sight. Stewart and I soon went back into the theater and upon the stage by the rear door. There I lost sight of him. What transpired after we seperated I do not know so far as he was concerned. Stewart had not recognized Booth as the man who jumped from the box up to the time we seperated as above stated, or if he had done so, he concealed that recognition from me. We both tried to ascertain the identity of the man who mounted the horse from the man we found in the alley. None of the scenes Stewart describes had transpired up to the time we returned to the stage from the alley. I do not think they occurred afterwards for when we got back upon the stage there were a number of people there. Probably you did not know Stewart. I did. His career as a lawyer had been somewhat shady. Months before the scenes he de[s]cribes are said to have been participated in by him I had caused his arrest in connection with a large amount of R.R. bonds—some $200,000 in W. & T. Bonds. However no serious charge in connection with said bonds was sustained. The transaction was somewhat shady that is all as I remember it. I recall reading in the newspapers at the time of the trial of the conspirators a synopsis of the testimony Stewart gave then and that it struck me then as an exaggeration of actual facts, but I then presumed the reporters were responsible for errors in statement. I have now read an official report of his testimony on the trial. If I had read these imaginary accounts before I now see them in your narrative I do not think I would have publicly controverted them as they have no material bearing upon the matter of the identity or guilt of Booth or others. Stewart's testimony in no way affected the interests of the defendents in the trial. The identity & guilt of Booth were overwhelmingly established irrespective of Stewart's testimony. At most his statements were only cumulative. Now if what you write is based on the official report of the trial do not change it but make it clear that you are sustained by said official report and do not claim to speak from personal observation or knowledge. About the time Stewart and I parted on the stage after going to the alley I was called to the box where the President was and aided somewhat in his removal from the theater. While in the box there was handed to me the pistol with which the President was shot, his hat and one or two other articles picked up from the floor in the box. I have now the receipt for the pistol which I took when I turned it over to the military authorities. But I must stop here. This letter is too long already. Some day I may write out for publication my version of the scenes and incidents in question as well as some that followed soon after the foul assassination, but not now. I have read so much romance claimed to have been actual occurrences connected with this the greatest tragedy of the century that I recoil from entering the lists of "eye witnesses" to that event. Yet I may overcome my hesitation.

To me the chapters of your proposed book are very interesting and I have no doubt will be equally attractive to others who may read the book. The matter is well arranged and the facts and events marshalled in due order. If judiciously advertised the book will be in demand. People must know of the book if expected to purchase it. I hope to be able to get a copy as soon as published.

McDevitt maintains a continued reticence as to this particular matter that I do not comprehend.

[June 20, 1898]

I enclose herewith the 3 chapters of your book sent me under date of the 8th inst. I have read the same with deep interest. I note no hiatus of interest in the manner in which you unfold the scheme & consumation of the plot for assassinating the chief officers of our government as well as the pursuit capture and punishment of the chief operators in the tragedy. It may be that I take a deeper interest in your book, on account of my personal connection with some of the events narrated, than would others not so associated, yet I do not see how any intelligent American Citizen can fail of a desire of being fully informed as to the inception, progress and outcome of this nefarious attempt to wreck our government. As I have before stated to you it is my opinion that the book when published and for sale will meet with a great demand from the reading public. Although numerous episodic accounts have been written and published relating to this supreme crime of the age. Yet all that I have seen have been but partial with no attempt, even, to give a full and chronological history of that event. Yet however interestingly you may have presented the subject the reading public must *know of the existance* of the book and the historical importance of its contents if it is to be in demand. I do not know how you propose to place the book before the public but I do know that its success as a publication will depend very largely upon the manner in which it is brought to the attention of the public. You have my best wishes for success in your enterprise.

[*July 3, 1898*]

Yours of the 27th ult. to hand. I trust you may be successful in getting your book placed before the public by a good publisher. Don't fail to send me the photograph you refer to.[9] I will return the compliment if I can put my hand on some photos I had printed years ago. I have some I think somewhere. I hope to see the succeeding chapters of your book in due time. Of course I know nothing of the course of Father Walter and other Washington Catholics towards you relating to Mrs. Surratt and the conspiracy. I do know however that I would rather stand in your place in relation to that matter than in that of those who are seeking to make it appear that Mrs. Surratt was innocent of the crime with which she was charged and for which she forfeited her life. The fact that certain prominent Catholics in Washington have so persistently persecuted you and others who were prominent in bringing her and the other conspirators to justice has done more to lead many people to believe that the assassination was the outcome of a Catholic plot than any or all other circumstances. In fact there is nothing else developed that could lead to a suspicion that could in any way inculpate any one of the authorities of that church. Mrs. Surratt was privy to the assassination of Abraham Lincoln, President of the United States and justly expiated her offence upon the gallows. Whether she should have had Executive clemency extended to her is quite another question.

[*July 31, 1898*]

Yours of the 26th inst. also yours of the 12th and also your photo are before me. I plead guilty of unwarranted delay in responding to yours of the 12th as also to the receipt of the photo. Thirty years had effaced from my mind considerably your personal appearance but with my first view of the photograph all came back to me. It was the letting in of sunlight upon the gathering shadows of years. I thank you very much for the picture. I would much like to meet you once more.

Please find enclosed herewith the newspaper slip relative to "Billy Williams." Much that is stated therein is apocryphal. I knew of Williams for some years in Washington as passing as a detective then largely engaged in looking up evidence in divorce cases. I hardly ever saw him. Never knew of his doing any real detective work. Nor did I ever hear of his being connected with any work in the great

[9] This photograph, which Weichmann sent to Richards, is now in the possession of his grandson, Irving Rothwell Richards. It has been reproduced in the illustration section of this book.

conspiracy trial. Neither in ability or personal appearance was Williams a man who would command respect. He was a very ordinary appearing man. This article is simply an attempt of some friend of his to give him a posthumous reputation as a detective. Since reading John H. Surratt's "vindication" by "Hiss" and your response to the same I have read J. B. Stewart's testimony on the trial of the assassins as published in the official record of the trial. I do not understand why he gave his imagination such full play in embelishing the part he performed that night. I note also that his testimony in some minor particular does not harmonize with that of certain other witnesses. I have heard nothing from McDevitt recently. He is not much of a letter writer however good a detective he may be.

My health is good. There is not much money made here since the freezes of 1894–5, but trees are getting back where they will soon fruit again.

[*Dec. 26, 1898*]

I have your letter of the 16th of December, 1898, and in reply, I take much pleasure in giving you the information you desire.

You did report to me about eight o'clock on the morning of April 15th, 1865, and you communicated to me such facts as had come to your knowledge at that time. You acted as a special officer with my men, going with them to lower Maryland, Baltimore, and finally to Canada in pursuit of some of the alleged guilty parties.

In no instance, was any statement made by you in relation to the conspiracy found to be false or incorrect, and very many of your assertions were subsequently corroborated by undoubted testimony of which you did not know the existence. No threats or undue influences of any kind were resorted to by any of us to control your actions.

You performed a manly part all the way through, and did your duty in such a manner as to challenge the admiration of all lovers of the truth.

Let me add that the fact that you were a boarder at Mrs. Surratt's house may have been to you the cause of much personal sacrifice in your worldly prospects, and of much suffering; but, for the sake of justice and in behalf of the murdered Lincoln, I deem it a most fortunate event that you were there.

Trusting that this will be sufficient for your purposes, I am,

[*February 22, 1899*]

I was glad to receive yours of the 16th inst. and shall certainly be glad to read over the portion of your history of the great Tragedy which you propose to send me to peruse.

There need be no question in your mind that I visited the Surratt house on the night of the assassination between 12 and 1 o'clock. I am not mistaken as to that point. I am not sure who I took with me. The only reason that led me to suppose McDevitt was with me is that I was with him at the Theater earlier that night. He (McDevitt) told me that Laura Keen[e] had told him that it was Wilkes Booth who vaulted from the box the President occupied. Soon thereafter it came to my knowledge that Booth and young Surratt had several times been in each others company the latter part of the preceeding winter. That information led me to seek Mrs. Surratt's house in search of Booth, or to learn something definite about him and his intimates. Not for one moment then suspecting that Mrs. Surratt was implicated in the assassination. The more I study over this matter the more convinced I am that McDevitt was not with me the night of the murder but that he reported to me the next (saturday) morning, that he had visited that house the night previous and that he had seen you at the house. And further that you would call at my office that morning. I do not recall much about Clarvoe's operations that night. I know he was about for I detailed him to take charge of a squad of mounted men to visit lower Maryland that night as soon as horses could be obtained. This duty he executed the next morning as there was delay in procuring horses.

I hope to hear from you again soon.

[March 19, 1899]

Yours dated the 6th inst. with enclosure did not reach me until yesterday.

I have read over the matter enclosed very carefully and with much interest. I can see no grounds for criticism. Chapter twenty seems to me to be in the nature of a self vindication of the course you persued in relation to the Surratt family subsequent to the assasination of the President which I do not think you need, yet the chapter is very interesting and, historically, valuable as any incident connected with the most fiendish crime of the age must be. The only circumstance connected with the plot to murder the President that with some might seem to involve you unfavorably is the fact that you, an officer of the government in the War Department were a boarder in the Surratt house and on intimate terms with that family. It seems to me that your statement will allay any unfavorable impression that would arise in the mind of a reasonable person. As the scheme of your proposed book is not only to give an inside historical account of matters and incidents that came to your personal knowledge relative to the conspiracy, but also to repell unkind and malicious attacks that the Surratts and their sympathizers have made upon you from time to time since the closing scenes of that greatest of tragedies in the history of the world. I can perceive of no impropriety in the publication of the matter contained in chapter twenty. In fact your book would not be complete without it.

Hoping that you are well and that I may soon have the pleasure of again hearing from you, I am,

[September 18, 1899]

Yours of the 7th inst. came duly to hand as also did chapters of your book per express some days later. I am reading the chapters and find them intensely interesting both in matter and literary style and conception. I cannot but believe that your book will prove a financial success if duly placed before the public. I note that in the matter of the writ of habeas corpus sued out by Mrs. Surratt you state in one place that the writ was issued out of the Supreme Court of the U.S. instead of D.C. Yet the matter following shows that the writ was issued out of the Supreme Court D.C.

I sent the letter you forwarded to me some months ago to the newspaper correspondent designated endorsed to be returned to me if not called for at the P.O. It has not been returned. So of course it was duly received. No response has come to me to that request. Of course the writer of the article is one of the Washington party who are creating sympathy for the Surratts so far as they can. I am also inclined to think they have captured McDevitt. I am led to this view from the fact that in the last letter I had from McD. he indicated a doubt that I visited Mrs. Surratt's house on the night of the assassination. While he (McD.) might not have been with me at that visit I know that I spoke of incidents connected with my visit immediately thereafter not only to him but to others about police headquarters, as well as to people not connected with the police force. You know that within a day or two subsequent to the assassination large rewards were offered by the government for the capture of the assassins. From that moment onward Baker and others connected with the War Dept. undertook to monopolies all movements and information regarding the assassins. I know that on the Sunday morning following the assassination Baker called at my office and with considerable swagger demanded that I turn you over to him as the representative of the War Dept. Also a similar demand was made upon me for the hat, pistol and some other articles of the President's that were handed to me in the theater box that night. You may remember that at about 11 o'clock on the night of the assassination I sent to the War Dept. for a detail of a dozen cavalry horses to mount a squad of my men to send down into Md. (Maryland) to pursuit of some persons whom we had learned from the guard at the Navy yard bridge had crossed into Md. (Maryland) soon after 11 o'clock that night. After being baffled for an hour or two my officer was told that the horses would be sent to my office at once. As a matter of fact it was 11 o'clock next morning when they were delivered to me. I think Clarvoe had charge of the squad I sent. There is a strong probability that had the horses been furnished promptly Booth and Herold would have been overtaken on their way to Dr. Mudds. When will your book be published? I want a copy when it is issued.

We had no floods here. In fact we have not had much of the usual rainy season. The freeze of Feb. 13th last cut down my orange trees again, but they are coming on again. Prior to 1886 there was a period of 51 years without serious freezes in this part of Fla. but since that time including that year we have had three winters when trees were badly killed down.

[October 5, 1899]

Yours of the 28th ult. to hand. When I last wrote you I was greatly pressed for time so that I simply restricted myself to a letter of transmittal. I may now say however that the manner in which you handled Father Walter's relations to the case against Mrs. Surratt surprised me. Knowing as I do that you are a Catholic and Father Walters being a Catholic priest I naturally did not expect you to handle him "without gloves" as you do in the chapter relative to his methods. You proclaim to the world his, to say the least, very questionable conduct. He has exhibited a recklessness in his statements of facts sufficient to put truth to a blush. You call him down by pointedly and justly giving the historic account without fear or favour leaving him to his conscience and his God. It has been claimed by some people not familiar with the history of the assassination of President Lincoln that it was a Catholic plot. I have had occasion to denounce that charge as unfounded and unjust more than once. The only circumstances that give color to such a charge against Catholics is the course that has been pursued by Father Walters and a few other prominent Washington Catholics who take their cue from that priest as I understand his relations to Washington Catholics. If it could be established that Father Walters by his course has the support of leading Catholics then I would conclude that the assassination savors of a Catholic plot. But so far as I know or have reason to suspect Father Walters is not sustained outside of the few Catholics I have indicated. You as a Catholic by your unvarnished statements do much to vindicate the Catholic church from the unwarrantable charge of complicity in that great crime.

After reading your presentation of the trial of John H. Surratt I am led to more than suspect, in fact to almost believe, that he was in Washington on the night of April 13th, 1865. Discretion rather than criminal valor may have guided his operations that night.

[*July 1, 1900*]

A few days since I received four numbers of the Saturday Evening Post of Phila. Pa. which you kindly sent me containing a serial story of an imaginary attempt to kidnap President Lincoln. I read the story with considerable interest. It was suggested, no doubt, by Booth['s] attempt at abduction. I thank for sending me the papers.

What progress are you making with your proposed book giving an account of the assassination of Lincoln?

I trust that you are well and doing well. My health is good. For a few days we have had warm weather. It is too hot to write much today. The rainy season is at hand with more or less rain almost daily.

[*August 5, 1900*]

Yours of the 26th ult. with enclosure came duly to hand. Of course I was somewhat interested in the Rev. Porter's narrative, but I realize the fact that he is not in the article stating facts in the main of which he has personal knowledge. Simply reiterates what he has heard from others although he writes as if he were stating matters he had witnessed in person. You know the papers have been publishing for years statements in which the writers conveyed the idea that they were giving to the public that of which they knew personally. Some have claimed personal knowledge when their statements showed conclusively that they were romancing. Of course you will point out a number of errors into which this doctor of physic and doctor of divinity has fallen. This class of men are usually very dogmatic in reiterating as facts matters which they learn from third persons. I recognize the face you send as that of a person I used to see often in Washington but did not personally know. He has made an issue of fact with Miss Ida M. Tarbell. Let them settle the matter. I do not think this man's statement that he was the only "Commissioned" officer present at the disposition of Booth's body by any means proves that non commissioned officers and others have not spoken the truth.[10] A "Commission" adds little sanctity in my mind to statements made by its bearer for I have known some very vile men to hold commissions.

I am doing the best I can towards reproducing my orange groves so seriously injured by freezes of the last four or five years and will soon have five groves again barring further freezes. These freezes have injured me to the extent of several thousands of dollars and yet I am fighting on with the hope of milder winters as was the case years ago. I hold property interests in Washington yet and a son and daughter reside there. My wife died here some four years since. I trust you are financially, as well as otherwise, prosperous. I conclude that Anderson is a lively and pushing city. Let me hear from you again soon.

[*December 24, 1900*]

Yours of the 17th inst. as, also, Gen. Burnett's pamphlet, duly received. Although I had read some prior papers from Gen. Burnett I have read this pamphlet with much interest and thank you for forwarding it to me. I return it under separate cover by this mail.

It surprises me somewhat that Gen. Burnett should state that it was not until April 19th following the assassination that it became "absolutely certain" that Wilkes Booth was implicated in that crime. The fact is that it was well and certainly known that Booth was the assassin of Lincoln before 12 o'clock midnight of the day of the assassination as it ever became known subsequent to that hour. Laura Keen had stated before that hour that while she did not know who had shot the President but that the man who jumped from the President's box on that night was J. Wilkes Booth. While there seemed to be a peculiar hesitancy on the part of the theater people on that night to disclose information relating to the tragedy yet Miss Keen did not hesitate to state as above indicated. It was information that I had that Booth had been an associate of John Surratt's for a few weeks prior to the assassination that led me to visit Mrs. Surratt's house soon after midnight on that night. No doubt Gen. Burnett did not get his information prior to the date he states but what ever facts he learned were filtered through Baker's mind before

[10] Probably Dr. George L. Porter.

they were revealed to Burnett. Baker was scheming for rewards. His plan was that information should reach officials of the War Dept. only through himself.

I am well and trust that you are. The weather here is simply delightful.

[August 25, 1901]

Yours of the 16th inst. came duly to hand as did the copy of the N. Y. Sun containing Judge Harris's article. Judge Harris states the case of Mrs. Surratt strongly —conclusively, as it seems to me vindicating the position you assumed, i.e. that you had no animus in the case and only sought to do your duty to your country and yourself. But you need no vindication. I do not think there is a living person who comprehends the facts and circumstances leading to the assassination of the lamented Lincoln, who is not consumed by prejudice, or some sinister motive, who does not regard your course highly honorable and patriotic. It has long seemed to me that the man who has done most to keep up this persecution of you is the Rev. Father Walter. His meddling in the matter of the "recommendation of mercy" by the commission was unbecoming in him to say the least. His whole course since the execution of Mrs. Surratt and the other assassins as being such as to lead many unthinking people, especially the adherants of his church, to believe that Mrs. Surratt was not implicated in the scheme of the assassination. That is the class of people who are seeking to heap contumely upon you. Next to Booth Mrs. Surratt was the chief conspirator and ninety nine people out of every one hundred so regard her. Even McDevitt formerly so regarded her, but I fear has been won over to lead people to think otherwise. If Father Walter had simply confined his office towards Mrs. S. to spiritual ministrations, in accordance with the mandates of the Catholic Church, as I understand them, persecutions based upon false statements would not have followed you. They all originate in Washington and are inspired, if not actively, yet approvingly, by Father Walter. What do you think as to his course. I trust you are well.

[January 30, 1901]

Yours of the 24th inst. with enclosure to hand. In response I have to say that I prefer not to place my signature to the enclosed letter to the Sec. of War inquiring as to the final disposition of the remains of J. Wilkes Booth by the War Department. I presume that if the remains were turned over to Edwin [Booth] there was no agreement or understanding that the arrangement should not be divulged to the public as otherwise it would have long ago been reported what had been done with the body. The note would seem to put me in the position of seeking the information in question from a mere desire to gratify curiosity which I do not entertain. I would gladly comply with your request could I feel justified in so doing. I am glad to be able to state that I am well and that we are having a very pleasant winter. As yet we have had but one frost—a white frost that did no damage whatever to growing trees (orange). Yet I shall not feel that were entirely free from danger from a blizzard for two weeks yet. Orange trees have not started to grow as yet and of course are in a dormant condition and able to withstand ten or twelve degrees of freezing without much injury. It is the cold that strikes them after the sap commences to flow that does the damage, but this does not often occur. The past three or four have been exceptions to the general rule in this regard. I hope you are well and doing well.

[*October 1901*]

Yours of the 21st ult. with newspaper clippings enclosed, came duly to hand and was read with pleasure as all your letters are. I was also interested in reading the clippings.

Enclosed herewith please find one dollar for the book you refer to and which I shall be glad to see. By the way have you yet published your book relative to the Lincoln Assassination. I have he[a]rd shots that killed two Presidents (Lincoln & Garfield) and now a third President is added to the list of martyred Presidents.[11] I hope the government will acquire an island somewhere in mid ocean, if we have not one there already, to which shall be sent all or any professed anarchists and there kept and not allowed to depart. There let them establish a community based on their own ideas without any interference on the part of our government save to confine them to the island. I would have the government furnish them food and clothing until they shall have time to provide for themselves. Then let them "paddle their own canoe" and put their ideas of life into practical operation. The establishment of the fact that a person is a professed anarchist of the kind that approve of murder of our Rulers should be all the proof required for their conviction and deportation. In fact such a course on the part of our government should be welcomed by them. If we are to wait for the commission of overt acts of violence and undertake to punish only such as are guilty of such acts on proof of the same we will never get rid of anarchists. Those fellows will face death for the notoriety they may gain by the murder of our Presidents and other. Under their training they nerve themselves for the ordeal they must meet when selceted to murder one in authority.

[*November 17, 1901*]

Yours of the 27th ult. came duly to hand. How that letter got away from me without the enclosure of one dollar I do not know. Please find it enclosed herewith.

I would have responded to your last sooner but have not been well. I think the mosquitoes must have inoculated me with malaria. I am all right again now I think. I read Gen. Harris' article and was very much interested in it. He always seems to make strong points. It seems to me Clampitt [12] is hardly worthy of his attention. I had not heard or thought of Clampitt for years before reading your

[11] William McKinley, the twenty-fourth President, was shot by Leon Czolgosz, an anarchist, on September 6, 1901, and died on September 14.
[12] Attorney for Mary E. Surratt.

letter. When I knew him in Washington he was little more than a big mouthed political rounder—certainly had no standing as a lawyer, or otherwise, except as a rebel sympathizer without the courage of his opinions.

THE ROCKVILLE LECTURE

On Tuesday, December 6, 1870, John H. Surratt gave a lecture at Rockville, Mary-land, on the Conspiracy and the assassination of Abraham Lincoln. Surratt attempts to vindicate himself of any complicity in the assassination, but on the other hand he boasts about his part in the Conspiracy to abduct the President, and gives Weichmann a rough going over in the process.

In this lecture Surratt makes two important statements. One that he met Booth in the fall of 1864 and not two days before Christmas, and second, that Booth in-timated drastic action at the March 15 meeting of the conspirators. (See above, page 113.)

Although Weichmann uses portions of this lecture in his narrative, it is repro-duced here in full as published in the Evening Star, *Washington, D.C., December 7, 1870. Weichmann's quotations from this lecture are out of context and not always word for word, but with no loss of meaning. Also reproduced is the editorial com-ment on the lecture, by the same newspaper, which was published nine days later.*

A REMARKABLE LECTURE!

JOHN H. SURRATT

TELLS HIS

STORY.

*A Vivid Narrative · History of the Abduction Plot · Surratt's
Experience with J. Wilkes Booth · Booth Hints at the Murder of
Lincoln · The Other Conspirators Threaten to Withdraw · The
Assassination · Surratt's Escape to Canada · He Implicates
Weichmann in the Abduction Plot · He Denounces Weichmann,
Judge Fisher, and Edwin M. Stanton · "John Harrison" · Surratt
and the Confederate Government · Why Surratt Did Not Come
to the Aid of His Mother.*

"What, go twenty miles for an item?" Well, you'd have thought so if you had seen the *Star* reporter making the dirt fly last night on the Rockville turnpike. And this is what called the *Star* reporter to Rockville last night—the following announce-ment in the Rockville paper.

Lecture by John H. Surratt

On Tuesday evening, December 6th, 1870, John H. Surratt, will deliver a Lec-ture, in the court-house, in Rockville, on "His introduction to J. Wilkes Booth— The Plot for the abduction of President Lincoln—Its Failure and Abandonment

—His trip to Richmond and from thence to Canada—then by orders to Elmira; and what was done there—His hearing of the Assassination of President Lincoln —His escape back to Canada, and concealment there—The efforts of Detectives to arrest him, and means used to baffle them—His final departure for Europe."

Doors open at 6½ o'clock, and Lecture commences at 7. Admittance, 50 cents, Children, half price.

John H. Surratt—everybody knows who he is, and of his alleged connection with the conspiracy of 1865, his escape, capture, and subsequent trial and discharge in this city, over a year since. Since then, he has spent a portion of his time in Lower Maryland, been in the commission business in Baltimore, and now has turned up a school teacher in Rockville, where he has availed himself of leisure hours to prepare, in the shape of a lecture, a history of the events which brought him so prominently before the public. The lecture took place in the courthouse, a quaint old building, but roomy and comfortable. The village looked deserted of everything save horses and empty vehicles of all kinds, from a sulky to a cord wood wagon, the occupants of which had passed into the court room, the scene of the lecture. A curious spectacle was presented within. The bar was occupied by the ladies in large numbers, while without and high up around the walls, on criers' bench, etc., men and boys held every available spot. At 7 o'clock Surratt entered and passed up the side platform in unceremonious style to the judge's desk. He was unattended, wore a mixed grey suit, and with the exception of having grown much stouter, looks the same as during his trial here. He has rather a mild and pleasant face, and a decidedly intellectual head; and does not look like the sort of stuff for a performer of desperate deeds.

On his entrance the Rockville Cornet Band in attendance struck up a lively air. Surratt then threw off his overcoat, revealing a manuscript book, which he drew from under his arm and laid open on the desk before him. He referred to it but little, however, having his lecture well in his memory. Without any introduction he was on, speaking very rapidly but distinctly for an hour and a quarter. He has a good voice and easy delivery, to which he occasionally added great warmth of feeling, particularly when he referred to his mother, and his alleged desertion of her in her darkest hour.

He spoke as follows:

Ladies and gentlemen:— Upon entering that door a few moments ago the impression on my mind was so strong as to vividly recall scenes of three years ago. I am not unacquainted with court room audiences. (Sensation.) I have stood before them before; true, not in the character of a lecturer, but as a prisoner at the bar, arraigned for the high crime of murder. In contrasting the two positions I must confess I felt more ease as the prisoner at the bar than I do as a lecturer. Then I felt confident of success; now I do not. Then I had gentlemen of known ability to do all my talking for me; now, unfortunately, I have to do it for myself, and I feel illy capable of performing the task; still I hope you will all judge me kindly. I am not here to surprise you by any oratorical effort—not at all—but only to tell a simple tale. I feel that some explanation, perhaps, indeed, an apology, is due you for my appearance here this evening. In presenting this lecture before the public I do it in no spirit of self-justification. In a trial of sixty-one days I made my defense to the world, and I have no need or desire to rehearse it; nor do I appear for self-glorification. On the contrary, I dislike notoriety, and leave my solitude and obscurity unwillingly. Neither is it an itching for notoriety or fame. My object is merely to present a simple narrative of events as they occurred. I stand here through the force of that which has obliged many other men to do things quite as distasteful—pecuniary necessity, for the supply of which no more available channel presented itself. This is a reason easily appreciated. So you will take it kindly, I trust, and the ground we will have to go over together will guarantee sufficient interest to repay your kind attention. In this my first lecture I will speak of my introduction to J. Wilkes Booth, his plan—its failure—our final separation—my trip from Richmond, and thence to Canada—then my orders to Elmira—what was done there—the first intimation I had of Mr. Lincoln's death, my return to Canada and concealment there, and final departure for Europe. At the breaking out of the war I was a student at St. Charles College, in Maryland, but did not remain long there after that important event. I left in July, 1861, and returning home commenced to take an active part in the stirring events of that period. I was not more than eighteen years of age, and was mostly engaged in sending information regarding the movements of the United States army stationed in Washington and elsewhere, and carrying dispatches to the Confederate boats on the Potomac. We had a regular established line from Washington to the Potomac, and I being the only unmarried man on the route, I had most of the hard riding to do. (Laughter.) I devised various ways to carry the dispatches—sometimes in the heel of my boots, sometimes between the planks of the buggy. I confess that never in my life did I come across a more stupid set of detectives than those generally employed by the U. S. Government. They seemed to have no idea whatever how to search men. In 1864 my family left Maryland and moved to Washington, where I took a still more active part in the stirring events of that period. It was a fascinating life to me. It seemed as if I could not do too much or run too great a risk.

In the fall of 1864 I was introduced to John Wilkes Booth, who, I was given to understand, wished to know something about the main avenues leading from Washington to the Potomac. We met several times, but as he seemed to be very reticent with regard to his purposes, and very anxious to get all the information out of me he could, I refused to tell him anything at all. At last I said to him, "It is useless for you, Mr. Booth, to seek any information from me at all; I know who you are and what are your intentions." He hesitated some time, but finally said he would make known his views to me provided I would promise secrecy. I replied, "I will do nothing of the kind. You know well I am a Southern man. If you cannot trust me we will separate." He then said, "I will confide my plans to you; but before doing so I will make known to you the motives that actuate me. In the Northern prisons are many thousands of our men whom the United States Government refuses to exchange. You know as well as I the efforts that have been made to bring about that much desired exchange. Aside from the great suffering they are compelled to undergo, we are sadly in want of them as soldiers. We cannot spare one man, whereas the United States Government is willing to let their own soldiers remain in our prisons because she has no need of the men. I have a proposition to submit to you, which I think if we can carry out will bring about the desired exchange." There was a long and ominous silence which I at last was compelled to break by asking, "Well, Sir, what is your proposition?" He sat quiet for an instant, and then, before answering me, arose and looked under the bed, into the wardrobe, in the doorway and the passage, and then said, "We will have to be careful; walls have ears." He then drew his chair close to me and in a whisper said, "It is to kidnap President Lincoln, and carry him off to Richmond!" "Kidnap President Lincoln!" I said. I confess that I stood aghast at the proposition, and looked upon it as a foolhardy undertaking. To think of successfully seizing Mr. Lincoln in the capital of the United States surrounded by thousands of his soldiers, and carrying him off to Richmond, looked to me like a foolish idea. I told him as much. He went on to tell with what facility he could be seized in various places in and about Washington. As for example in his various rides to and from the Soldiers' Home, his summer residence. He entered into the minute details of the proposed capture, and even the various parts to be performed by the actors in the performance. I was amazed—thunderstruck—and in fact, I might also say, frightened at the unparalleled audacity of this scheme. After two days' reflection I told him I was willing to try it. I believed it practicable at that time, though I now regard it as a foolhardy undertaking. I hope you will not blame me for going thus far. I honestly thought an exchange of prisoners could be brought about could we have once obtained possession of Mr. Lincoln's person. And now reverse the case. Where is there a young man in the North with one spark of patriotism in his heart who would not have with enthusiastic ardor joined in any undertaking for the capture of Jefferson Davis and brought him to Washington? There is not one who would not have done so. And so I was led on by a sincere desire to assist the South in gaining her independence. I had no hesitation in taking part in anything honorable that might tend towards the accomplishment of that object. (Tremendous applause.) Such a thing as the assassination of Mr. Lincoln I never heard spoken of by any of the party. Never! (Sensation.) Upon one occasion, I remember, we had called a meeting in Washington for the purpose of discussing matters in general, as we had understood that the government had received information that there was a plot of some kind on hand. They had even commenced to build a stockade and gates on the navy yard bridge; gates opening towards the south as though they expected danger from within, and not from without. At this meeting I explained the construction of the gates, etc., and stated that I was confident the government had wind of our movement, and that the best thing we could do would be to throw up the whole project. Everyone seemed to coincide in my opinion, except Booth, who sat silent and abstracted. Arising at last and bringing down his fist upon the table he said: "Well, gentlemen, if the worst comes to the worst, I shall know what to do."

Some hard words and even threats then passed between him and some of the party. Four of us then arose, one saying, "If I understand you to intimate anything more than the capture of Mr. Lincoln I for one will bid you goodbye." Every one expressed the same opinion. We all arose and commenced putting our hats on. Booth perceiving probably that he had gone too far, asked pardon saying that he "had drank too much champagne." After some difficulty everything was amicably arranged and we separated at 5 o'clock in the morning. Days, weeks and months passed by without an opportunity presenting itself for us to attempt the capture. We seldom saw one another owing to the many rumors afloat that a conspiracy of some kind was being concocted in Washington. We had all arrangements perfected from Washington for the purpose. Boats were in readiness to carry us arcoss the river. One day we received information that the President would visit the Seventh Street Hospital for the purpose of being present at an entertainment to be given for the benefit of the wounded soldiers. The report only reached us about three quarters of an hour before the time appointed, but so perfect was our communication that we were instantly in our saddles on the way to the hospital. This was between one and two o'clock in the afternoon. It was our intention to seize the carriage, which was drawn by a splendid pair of horses, and to have one of our men mount the box and drive direct for southern Maryland via Benning's bridge. We felt confident that all the cavalry in the city could never overhaul us. We were all mounted on swift horses, besides having a thorough knowledge of the country, it being determined to abandon the carriage after passing the city limits. Upon the suddenness of the blow and the celerity of our movements we depended for success. By the time the alarm could have been given and horses saddled, we would have been on our way through southern Maryland towards the Potomac river. To our great disappointment, however, the President was not there but one of the government officials—Mr. [Salmon P.] Chase, if I mistake not. We did not disturb him, as we wanted a bigger *chase* (Laughter) than he could have afforded us. It was certainly a bitter disappointment, but yet I think a most fortunate one for us. It was our last attempt. We soon after this became convinced that we could not remain much longer undiscovered, and that we must abandon our enterprise. Accordingly, a separation finally took place, and I never after saw any of the party except one, and that was when I was on my way from Richmond to Canada on business of quite a different nature—about which, presently. Such is the story of our abduction plot.

Rash, perhaps foolish, but honorable I maintain in its means and ends; actuated by such motives as would under similar circumstances be a sufficient inducement to thousands of southern young men to have embarked in a similar enterprise. Shortly after our abandonment of the abduction scheme, some dispatches came to me which I was compelled to see through to Richmond. They were foreign ones, and had no reference whatever to this affair. I accordingly left home for Richmond, and arrived there safely on the Friday evening before the evacuation of that city. On my arrival I went to [the] Spotswood Hotel, where I was told that Mr. Benjamin, the then Secretary of War of the Confederate States, wanted to see me. I accordingly sought his presence. He asked me if I would carry some dispatches to Canada for him. I replied "yes." That evening he gave me the dispatches and $200 in gold with which to pay my way to Canada. That was the only money I ever received from the Confederate government or any of its agents. It may be well to remark here that this scheme of abduction was concocted without the knowledge or the assistance of the Confederate government in any shape or form. Booth and I often consulted together as to whether it would not be well to acquaint the authorities in Richmond with our plan, as we were sadly in want of money, our expenses being very heavy. In fact the question arose among us as to whether, after getting Mr. Lincoln, if we succeeded in our plan, the Confederate authorities would not surrender us to the United States again, because of doing this thing without their knowledge or consent. But we never acquainted them with the plan, and they never had anything in the wide world to do with it. In fact, we were jealous of our undertaking and wanted no outside help. I have not made this statement to defend the officers of the Confederate government. They are perfectly able to defend themselves. What I have done myself I am not ashamed to let the world know. I left Richmond on Saturday morning before the evacuation of that place, and reached Washington the following Monday at 4 o'clock P.M., April 3d, 1865. As soon as I reached the Maryland shore I understood that the detectives knew of my trip South and were on the lookout for me. I had been South several times before for the secret service but had never been caught. At that time I was carrying the dispatches Mr. Benjamin gave me: in a book entitled "The life of John Brown." During my trip, and while reading that book, I learned, to my utter amazement, that John Brown was a martyr sitting at the right hand of God. (Uproarious laughter.) I succeeded in reaching Washington safely, and in passing up Seventh street met one of our party, who inquired what had become of Booth. I told him where I had been; that I was then on my way to Canada, and that I had not seen or heard anything of Booth since our separation. In view of the fact that Richmond had fallen, and that all hopes of the abduction of the President had been given up, I advised him to go home and go to work. That was the last time I saw any of the party. I went to a hotel and stopped over that night, as a detective had been to my house inquiring of the servant my whereabouts. In the early train next morning, Tuesday, April 4, 1865, I left for New York, and that was the last time I ever was in Washington until brought there by the U. S. Government a captive in irons, all reports to the contrary notwithstanding.

The United States, as you will remember, tried to prove my presence in Washington on the 15th of April, the day on which Mr. Lincoln met his death. Upon arriving in New York, I called at Booth's house, and was told by the servant that he had left that morning suddenly, on the ground of going to Boston to fulfill an engagement at the theater. In the evening of the same day I took the cars for Montreal, arriving there the next day. I put up at the St. Lawrence Hotel, registering myself as "John Harrison," such being my two first names. Shortly afterwards I saw General Edward G. Lee, to whom the dispatches were directed, and delivered them to him. Those dispatches we tried to introduce as evidence on my trial, but his Honor Judge Fisher ruled them out, despite of the fact that the government had tried to prove that they had relation to the conspiracy to kill Mr. Lincoln. They were only accounts of some money transactions—nothing more or less. A week or so after my arrival there, General Lee came to my room, and told me he had a plan on foot to release the Confederate prisoners then in Elmira, N.Y. He said he had sent many parties there, but they always got frightened, and only half executed their orders. He asked me if I would go there and take a sketch of the prison, find out the number of prisoners, also minor details in regard to the number of soldiers on guard, cannon, small arms, etc. I readily accepted these new labors, owing to the fact that I could not return to Washington for fear of the detectives. The news of the evacuation of Richmond did not seem to disturb the General much in his plan, as he doubtless thought then that the Confederacy wanted men more than ever, no one dreaming that it was virtually at an end. I was much amused at one expression made use of by an ex-reb with regard to the suddenness of its demise: "D—n the thing, it didn't even flicker, but went right out." (Laughter and applause.) In accordance with Gen. Lee's order, I went to Elmira, arriving there on Wednesday, two days before Mr. Lincoln's death, and registered at the Brainard House, as usual, as "John Harrison." The following day I went to work, and made a complete sketch of the prison and surroundings. About ten o'clock on Friday night I retired, little thinking that on that night a blow would be struck which would forever blast my hopes, and make me a wanderer in a foreign land. I slept the night through, and came down the next morning little dreaming of the storm then brewing around my head. When I took my seat at the table about 9 o'clock A.M., a gentleman to my left remarked: "Have you heard the news?" "No, I've not," I replied. "What is it?" "Why President Lincoln and Secretary Seward have been assassinated." I really put so little faith in what the man said that I made a remark that it was too early in the morning to get off such jokes as that. "It's so," he said, at the same time drawing out a paper and showing it to me. Sure enough, there I saw an account of what he told me, but as no names were mentioned, it never occurred to me for an instant that it could have been Booth or any of the party, for the simple reason that I had never heard anything regarding assassination spoken of during my intercourse with them. I had good reason to believe that there was another conspiracy afloat in Washington, in fact we all knew it. One evening, as I was partially lying down in the reading-room of the Metropolitan Hotel, two or three gentlemen came in and looked around as if to make sure that no one was around. They then commenced to talk about what had been done, the best means for the expedition, etc. It being about dusk, and no gas light, and partially concealed behind a writing desk, I was an unwilling listener of what occurred. I told Booth of this afterward, and he said he had heard something to the same effect. It only made us all the more eager to carry out our plans at an early day for fear some one should get ahead of us. We didn't know what they were after exactly, but we were well satisfied that their object was very much the same as ours. Arising from the table I thought over who the party could be, for at that time no names had been telegraphed. I was pretty sure it was none of the old party. I approached the telegraph office in the main hall of the hotel for the purpose of ascertaining if J. Wilkes Booth was in New York. I picked up a blank and wrote "John Wilkes Booth," giving the number of the house. I hesitated a moment, and then tore the paper up, and then wrote one "J.W.B.," with directions, which I was led to do from the fact that during our whole connection we rarely wrote or telegraphed under our proper names, but always in such a manner that no one could understand but ourselves. One way of Booth's was to send letters to me under cover to my quondam friend, Louis J. Weichman.

Doubtless you all know who Louis J. Weichman is. They were sent to him because he knew of the plot to abduct President Lincoln. I proclaim it here and before the world that Louis J. Weichman was a party to the plan to abduct President Lincoln. He had been told all about it, and was constantly importuning me to let him become an active member. I refused, for the simple reason that I told him he could neither ride a horse nor shoot a pistol, which was a fact. (Laughter.) These were two necessary accomplishments for us. My refusal nettled him some; so he went off, as it afterwards appeared by his testimony, and told some government clerk [Captain Gleason] that he had a vague idea that there was a plan of some kind on hand to abduct President Lincoln. This he says himself: that he could have spotted every man on the party. Why didn't he do it? Booth sometimes was rather suspicious of him, and asked me if I thought he could be trusted. Said I, "Certainly he can. Weichman is a Southern man," and I always believed it until I had good reason to believe otherwise, because he had furnished information for the Confederate government, besides allowing me access to the government records after office hours. I have very little to say of Louis J. Weichman. But I do pronounce him a base-born perjurer; a murderer of the meanest hue! Give me a man who can strike his victim dead, but save me from a man who, through perjury, will cause the death of an innocent person. Double murderer!!!! Hell possesses no worse fiend than a character of that kind. (Applause.) Away with such a character. I leave him in the pit of infamy, which he has dug for himself, a prey to the lights of his guilty conscience. (Applause.)

I telegraphed Booth thus:

"J.W.B., in New York:

"If you are in New York telegraph me.

"John Harrison, Elmira, N.Y."

The operator, after looking over it, said, "Is it J.W.B.?" to which I replied, "Yes." He evidently wanted the whole name, and had scarcely finished telegraphing when a door right near the office, and opening on the street, was pushed open, and I heard some one say, "Yes, there are three or four brothers of them, John, Junius Brutus, Edwin, and J. Wilkes Booth." The whole truth flashed on me in an instant, and I said to myself, "My God! What have I done?" The dispatch was still lying before me, and I reached over and took it up for the purpose of destroying it, but the operator stretched forth his hand and said, "We must file all telegrams." My first impulse was to tear it up, but I pitched it back and walked off. The town was in the greatest uproar, flags at half mast, bells tolling, &c., &c. Still I did not think that I was in danger, and determined to go immediately to Baltimore to find out the particulars of the tragedy. But here I wish to say a few words concerning the register of the Brainard House. When my counsel, by my own direction, went to seek that register, it could not be found. Our inability to produce it on the trial naturally cast a suspicion over our *alibi*. For weeks, months, did we seek to find its whereabouts, but to no purpose. Every man who was connected with the hotel was hunted up and questioned. Every register of the hotel before and after the one which ought to contain my name was to be found, but the most important one of all was gone. Now the question is what became of that register? The U. S. Government, by one of its witnesses, Doctor McMillan, knew in November, 1865, that I was in Elmira at the time of the assassination. They knew it, and they naturally traced me there to find out what I was doing. That some of the government emissaries abstracted that register I firmly believe, or perhaps it is stored away in some of the other government vaults, under charge of some judge high in position, but this is only a surmise of mine. But the circumstance involves a mystery of villainy which the All Seeing God will yet bring to light. The dispatch I sent to Booth also from Elmira it was impossible to find. We had the operator at Washington during my trial, but he said the original was gone though he had a copy of it. In telegraph offices they are compelled to keep all dispatches filed. Of course we could not offer this copy in evidence, because the original alone would be accepted, and that had been made away with. So sure was the government that they had destroyed all evidence of my sojourn in Elmira, that in getting me in Washington in time for Mr. Lincoln's death they brought me by way of New York City, but so completely were they foiled in this that in their rebutting testimony they saw the absolute necessity of having me go by way of Elmira, and they changed their tactics accordingly. That was enough to damn my case in any man's mind. This is a strange fact, but nevertheless true that the government having in its possession this hotel register as well as my dispatch to Booth and knowing moreover by one of its witnesses that I was in Elmira, yet tried to prove that I was in Washington on the night of Mr. Lincoln's death, giving orders and commanding in general as they were pleased to say. The gentlemen in Elmira, by whom I proved my *alibi*, were men of the highest standing and integrity whose testimony the United States government could not and dare not attempt to impeach. I left Elmira with the intention of going to Baltimore. I really did not comprehend at that time the danger I was in. As there was no train going South that evening I concluded to go to Canandaigua and from there to Baltimore by way of Elmira and New York. Upon arriving at Canandaigua on Saturday evening I learned to my utter disappointment that no train left until the Monday following, so I took a room at the Webster House, registering my self as "John Harrison." The next day I went to church, I remember it being Easter Sunday. I can here safely say that the United States government had not the remotest idea that I stopped anywhere after I left Elmira. They thought, when I left there, I went straight through to Canada. It was a very fortunate thing for me that I could not leave Canandaigua. Now mark, ladies and gentleman, if you please, my name was signed midway of the hotel register, with six other parties before and after. There was no doubt as to the genuineness of my signature, because the very experts brought by the United States to swear to my signatures in other instances, swore also that that was my handwriting. After all this the register was ruled out by Judge Fisher, because he was well aware if he admitted it my case was at an end. I could not be in two places at once, though they tried to make me so. Listen to his reason for so ruling: "The prisoner might have stepped down from Canada to Canandiagua during his concealment and signed his name there for the purpose of protecting himself in the future." It was a likely idea that the proprietor of a hotel would leave a blank line in the register for my especial benefit. Need I say that the ruling was a most infamous one, and ought to damn the Judge who so ruled as a villain in the minds of every honest and upright man. (Loud and prolonged applause.) Had Judge Fisher been one of the lawyers for the prosecution, he could not have worked harder against me than he did. But, thanks to him, he did me more good than harm. His unprincipled and vindictive character was too apparent to every one in the court room. I could not help smiling at the time to think of the great shrewdness and foresight he accorded me by that decision. At times, really, during my trial, I could scarce recognize any vestige of my former self. Sometimes I would ask myself, "Am I the same individual? Am I really the same John H. Surratt?" When that register was produced in court, the Hon. Judge Pierrepont, the leading counsel for the United States, became exceedingly nervous, especially when Mr. Bradley refused to show it to him, and he tore up several pieces of paper in his trembling fingers.

He evidently saw what a pitiful case he had, and how he had been made the dupe of his precious, worthy friend, Edwin M. Stanton. At the time of my trial the proprietor of the Webster House, in Canandaigua, could not find the cash book of the hotel, in which there should have been an entry in favor of "John Harrison" for so much cash. When he returned to Canandaigua, my trial being then ended, he wrote Mr. Bradley that he had found the cash book, and sent it to him. It was then too late. My trial was over. If we had had that cash book at the time of my trial it would have been proved beyond a doubt that I was in Canandaigua and not in Washington city.

On Monday when I was leaving Canandaigua I bought some New York papers. In looking over them, my eye lit on the following paragraph which I have never forgot, and don't think I ever will. It runs thus: "The assassin of Secretary Seward is said to be John H. Surratt, a notorious secessionist of Southern Maryland. His name, with that of J. Wilkes Booth, will forever lead the infamous roll of assassins." I could scarcely believe my senses. I gazed upon my name, the letters of which seemed to sometimes to grow as large as mountains and then to dwindle away to nothing. So much for my former connection with him I thought. After fully realizing the state of the case, I concluded to change my course and go direct to Canada. I left Canandaigua on Monday 12 M., going to Albany arriving there on Tuesday morning in time for breakfast. When I stepped on the platform at the depot at St. Albans I noticed that one of the detectives scanned every one, head and foot, myself as well as the rest. Before leaving Montreal for Elmira, I provided myself with an Oxford cut jacket and a round-top hat, peculiar to Canada at that time. I knew my trip to Elmira would be a dangerous one, and I wished to pass myself off as a Canadian, and I succeeded in so doing, as was proved by my witnesses in Elmira. I believe that costume guarded me safely through St. Albans. I went in with others, and moved around, with the detectives standing there most of the time looking at us. Of course I was obliged to talk as loud as anybody about the late tragedy. After having a hearty meal I lighted a cigar and walked up town. One of the detectives approached me, stared me directly in the face, and I looked him quietly back. In a few moments I was speeding on my way to Montreal, where I arrived at two o'clock in the afternoon, going again to the St. Lawrence Hotel. Soon after I called on a friend, to whom I explained my former connection with Booth, and told him I was afraid the United States government would suspect me of complicity in the plot of assassination. He advised me to make myself scarce. I immediately went to the hotel, got my things, and repaired to the room of a friend. When my friend's tea-time came I would not go to the table with him, but remained in the room. The ladies wanted to know why he didn't bring his friend to tea with him. He replied that I didn't want any. One of the ladies remarked, "I expect you have got Booth in there." (Laughter.) "Perhaps so," he answered laughingly. That was rather close guessing. (Laughter.) At nightfall I went to the house of one who afterwards proved to be a most devoted friend. There I remained until the evening of the next day, when I was driven out in a carriage with two gentlemen, strangers to me. One day I walked out and I saw Weichman on the lookout for me.

He had little idea I was so near. One night about 11 o'clock, my friend, in whose house I was, came to me and said, in a smiling way: "The detectives have offered me $20,000 if I will tell them where you are." "Very well," said I, "give me one half, and let them know." They suspected this gentleman of protecting me, and they had really made him the offer. One day about 12 o'clock, I was told that they were going to search the house, and that I must leave immediately, which I did. They searched it before morning. This gentleman was a poor man, with a large family, and yet money could not buy him. (Applause.) I remained with this gentleman until I left Montreal, within a week or so afterwards. The detectives were now hunting me very closely, and would have doubtless succeeded in capturing me, had it not been for a blunder on the part of my friend Weichman. He had, it appears, started the detectives on the wrong track, by telling them that I had left the house of Mr. Porterfield in company with some others, and was going north of Montreal. Soon that section was swarming with detectives. I was not with that party, but about the same time, I too, left Montreal in a hack, going some 8 or 9 miles down the St. Lawrence river, crossing that stream in a small canoe. I was attired as a huntsman. At 3 o'clock Wednesday morning, we arrived at our destination, a small town lying south of Montreal. We entered the village very quietly, hoping no one would see us.

It has been asserted over and over again, and for the purpose of damning me in the estimation of every honest man that I deserted her who gave me birth in the direst hour of her need. Truly would I have merited the execration of every man had such been the case. But such was not the case. When I left Montreal there was no cause for uneasiness on my part, and upon my arrival in the country I wrote to my friends in Montreal to keep me posted in regard to the approaching trial, and to send me the newspapers regularly. I received letters from them frequently, in all of which they assured me there was no cause of anxiety; that it was only a matter of time, and it would all be well. After a while papers did not come so regularly, and those that did, spoke very encouragingly. A little while afterwards, when they came, sentences were mutilated with ink and pen.

I protested against such action, and for some time I received no papers at all. I became very uneasy, and wrote for publication an article signed by myself, which I sent to Montreal to be forwarded for publication in the New York *World*. It is needless to say it never went. Things continued in this way for some time, until I could stand the suspense no longer. I determined to send a messenger to Washington for that purpose, and secured the services of an intelligent and educated gentleman. I started him off immediately, I paying all expenses. I gave him a letter to a friend of mine in Washington, with instructions to say to him to put himself in communication with the counsel for the defense, and to make a correct report to me as to how the case stood; if there was any danger; and also, to communicate with me if my presence was necessary, and inform me without delay; with an urgent request that he would see and inquire for himself how matters stood. He left me, and God alone knows the suspense and anxiety of my mind during the days of his absence. I imagined and thought all kinds of things; yet I was powerless to act. At last he returned, and so bright and cheerful was his countenance that I confess one-half of my fears were dispelled. He represented everything as progressing well, and brought me the message from the gentleman in Washington to whom I had sent him:

"Be under no apprehension as to any serious consequences. Remain perfectly quiet, as any action on your part would only tend to make matters worse. If you can be of any service to us, we will let you know; but keep quiet."

These were the instructions I received from my friend in Washington, in whom I felt the utmost reliance, and who I thought would never deceive me. He also sent me copies of the *National Intelligencer,* containing evidence for the defense. I certainly felt greatly relieved, though not entirely satisfied. This news reached me some time in the latter part of June, just before the party of gentlemen of whom I have spoken arrived. They, too, assured me there was no cause for fear. What else could I do but accept these unwavering assurances? Even had I thought otherwise, I could not have taken any action resulting in good.

Just on the eve of my departure to join a party of gentlemen on a hunting excursion, while I was waiting at the hotel for the train, the proprietor handed me a paper, and said: "Read that about the conspirators."

Little did the man know who I was, or how closely that paragraph bore upon me or mine. That paper informed me that on a day which was then present, and at an hour which had then come and gone, the most hellish of deeds was to be enacted. It had been determined upon and carried out, even before I had intimation that there was any danger. It would be folly for me to attempt to describe my feelings. After gazing at the paper for some time I dropped it on the floor, turning on my heel, and going directly to the house where I had been stopping before. When I entered the room, I found my friend sitting there. As soon as he saw me, he turned deadly pale, but never uttered a word. I said, "You doubtless thought you were acting a friend—the part of a friend—towards me, but you have deceived me. I may forgive you, but I can never forget it."

"We all thought it for the best, Charley," he commenced to say, but I did not stay to hear more. I went to my room, remained there until dark, and then signified my intention to leave the place immediately. I felt reckless as to what should become of me.

After visiting Quebec and other places, with the reward of $25,000 hanging over my head, I did not think it safe to remain there, and so I concluded to seek an asylum in foreign lands. I had nothing now to bind me to this country, save an only sister, and I knew she would never want for kind friends or a good home. For myself, it mattered little where I went, so that I could roam once more a free man. I then went on a venture, and now, ladies and gentlemen, I go forth again on a venture. Gladly would I have remained hidden among the multitude, but the stern necessities arising from the blasting of my earthly prospects have forced me to leave my solitude and to stand again before the public gaze as the historian of my own life. One mitigation to its distastefulness in this and my first attempt, however, is the kindness with which I have been received, and the patience with which I have been listened to, for which I return you, ladies and gentlemen, my sincere and heartfelt thanks. (Applause.)

The lecture concluded, the band played "Dixie," and a concert was improvised, the audience not separating till a late hour, during which time Surratt was quite a lion among the ladies present.

EDITORIAL: SURRATT [1]

John H. Surratt is denounced in various quarters for appearing as a lecturer, and with singular vehemence by the New York *World*, a paper deemed so friendly to him that he proposed, while in Canada, to send to it his defence to be published. Surratt is out in a card in the New York papers stating that the reason of the *World*'s assault is that the Democracy of New York, as he is assured by a friend "who stands high in the political arena," is so rotten and in such a critical condition that it is obliged to repudiate him to save itself. In conclusion, Surratt says that he will not be deterred from his course "by the howlings and carpings of those who would be my friends if they dared." *The good taste of portions of Surratt's lecture may be questioned, and especially his tirade against the Judge* [2] *who tried*

[1] From the *Evening Star* (Washington, D.C.), December 16, 1870.
[2] Judge George P. Fisher.

him, and the flippancy with which he dwells upon his love adventures in Canada in the same breath with his reference to his mother's death upon the gallows, but it is difficult to see the reason for the furious outburst against him of the World, the Cincinnati Enquirer, and some other papers of like party affiliations. Really the serious defect in the Surratt lecture was not what he said, but what he failed to say. He, if anyone, was in a position to clear up his mother's memory and establish her innocence, if that were possible, and it would have seemed a filial and creditable act in him to have appeared before the public in her defence. But it will be noticed that throughout his lecture he is silent in regard to the part she took or did not take in the plottings of the conspirators. He thus puts himself in the attitude of making an egotistical defence of himself and of leaving her memory to take care of itself; and at the same time an impression is conveyed to the public adverse to her innocence.[3]

THE HANSON HISS ARTICLE

This newspaper interview which John H. Surratt gave to Hanson Hiss has had little or no attention since it was published in the Washington Post, *April 3, 1898. Oldroyd mentions the "Hanson Hiss" article in his book* Assassination of Abraham Lincoln *in relation to Surratt's meeting with Booth in the National Hotel, but that is all.*

Surratt again attempts to vindicate himself but with more detail than in the Rockville lecture. He continues his attack on Weichmann—calling him a liar and a perjurer—and blames him for the misfortunes that have befallen the Surratt family. Here again he claims he met Booth before that fateful December 23, 1864, meeting in the National Hotel. Surratt states that he was never introduced to Booth by Dr. Mudd "on the street or anywhere else."

In his flamboyant style he describes his adventures in Canada, his flight to Europe and eventual escape from the Papal authorities. He brags about giving himself up after checking into a hotel in Alexandria, Egypt. Actually the ship that brought Surratt to Egypt was held in quarantine and the U. S. consul, Charles Hale, arrested him on board that vessel November 27, 1866. He was held at the quarantine station until November 29, when he was transferred to the prison of the local government. On December 21, 1866, Surratt was delivered on board the U. S. corvette Swatara *and returned to the United States. It is doubtful if Surratt ever walked the streets of Alexandria or saw the inside of a hotel in Egypt.*

On April 18, 1898, the Washington Post *published Weichmann's and Richards' response to the Hanson Hiss article under the title "Pursued by His Foes," in which Richards leaves little doubt as to who is telling the truth.*

John H. Surratt in later years was freight auditor for the Baltimore Steam

[3] The italics are the editor's.

Packet Company and died in Baltimore, April 21, 1916. See Baltimore Sun, *April 22 and 23, 1916. Rumor has it that he had written his biography but destroyed it before his death.*

JOHN H. SURRATT'S STORY

His Connection with the Plot to Abduct President Lincoln Told for the First Time

Special Correspondence of The Post
Baltimore, April 2.
Thirty-three Easter Sundays have come and gone since Abraham Lincoln was shot to death by John Wilkes Booth, in the old Ford's Theater, Washington, and of the eleven individuals who were connected, directly or indirectly, with that tragic and unhappy event, but two are yet living. One of these is Lewis J. Weichmann, now a resident of Philadelphia, whose testimony was the foundation stone on which the government rested its hopes of convicting Mrs. Mary E. Surratt and her son, John H. Surratt, and on which history, and the light of subsequent events, have since cast a grave shadow. The other living actor in that famous tragedy is John Harrison Surratt, a resident of this city, a trusted and honored official in the Old Bay Line of Chesapeake steamers, whose life-story, from the time he ran away from school as a mere lad of sixteen and joined the Secret Service Bureau of the Confederacy, until the last day of his lengthy and highly sensational trial, reads like a fairy tale, and is but another evidence of the oft-proven adage that "truth is stranger than fiction."

For a third of a century prominent writers for newspapers and magazines, in every section of the Union, have realized that could John H. Surratt be induced to tell his story, freely, unreservedly, and fully, it would rival in romantic interest and dramatic detail anything hitherto published concerning the landmarks of the war between the States. Countless efforts—over a thousand, in fact—have been made to get him to tell his story and make a statement of his true relations with Wilkes Booth, Weichmann, Dr. Mudd, and the other actors who figured in that long train of stirring events which culminated in the assassination of Abraham Lincoln and the execution of his mother, but prior to the three interviews granted me for The Sunday Post, in which he told me every detail of his life, he has returned but one answer to all. The wound was too deep and rankling to tear open at this late day and expose to the critical gaze of an unsympathetic public.

He feels now, however, that after a lapse of a third of a century the bitterness of feeling, rancor, and hate engendered by four long years of internecine strife has passed away and given place to a more fair and liberal feeling concerning his reputed connection with an event which shocked the world and thrust a nation into mourning. "I feel that I owe it to those who have passed away, as well as to myself, to make a statement concerning what I know of that event," he said.

Capt. Surratt is very different from the ignorant and bloodthirsty Southerner pictured by an angry press during his trial. On the contrary, he is refined, highly educated, and polished. His manners are stately and dignified. He is a brilliant talker, and every word he utters conveys the exact meaning he intends. He is above the medium height, straight and slender, and has iron gray hair and mustache, and two piercing gray eyes set deep in his head beneath heavy eye brows. He talks in a low tone of voice, never hesitates for a word, and only twice during my talks with him did he become excited, although dwelling for the first time in over thirty years on matters which must have stirred his feelings to their core. Once was when he spoke of Wilkes Booth, and the other time was during his terrible arraignment of Weichmann. He is only fifty-five years old, although he looks seventy. He told me he lived fifty years from the time he entered the Southern Army until he was liberated on bail after his two months' trial. As the substance of this interview is of considerable historical importance, in that it is the first purely voluntary statement of any one who had aught to do with Wilkes Booth, I will give his statement, word for word, as they left his mouth, merely preserving historical sequence:

When the war broke out I was a small boy of sixteen, studying at St. Charles' College, in Carroll County, Md., and like all Southern boys at that time, I was a red-hot rebel, and dearly loved my native State. At the college it was strictly against the rules to discuss, even in the most casual manner, any of the political questions, then agitating the country. I remember one afternoon we were all on the campus, which directly faced Charles Carroll of Carrollton's beautiful estate, Dourehegan Manor, when there issued from the main driveway opposite a troop of Confederate cavalry on their way to join the Army of Northern Virginia. The troop had been recruited and was led by young Charles Carroll. They were a magnificent set of young men, full of fire, dash, and vim, and presented a splendid appearance. I was fired with martial ardor at the sight, and tossing my cap into the air, I cheered and cheered again. In fact I cheered myself hoarse.

When the troop had disappeared behind a cloud of dust my comrades assured me that I would certainly be expelled, and taking the bull by the horns, as it were, I went direct to the principal and told him what I had done. He was very angry at first, but finally softening, said it might prove a good thing after all, adding: "We may have use for those young men yet." It was at this college that I first met Lewis J. Weichmann, my Nemesis, a man who has done more than any one living or dead to bring disgrace on me and my family. He is a living proof that the child is father to the man.

Followed the Confederacy

After staying at the college a few months, I became convinced that my place was in the ranks of the Southern Confederacy, and, suiting the action to the thought, I went direct to Richmond and entered the Secret Service Bureau, under Gen. Wilder, one of the finest Americans that ever lived. It would take every column of space in the paper you represent to detail all my experiences. I had innumerable hairbreadth escapes. When I look back on the risks I ran and the desperate chances I took, I fail to see how I could have been so foolhardy. I walked in and out of the lines of the two armies, entered and left Washington, went from Richmond to New York, to London, returned to Washington, and elbowed the Union Generals, all the while gathering valuable information for the service. I knew every cross road, bypath, and hiding place in Northern Virginia and Southern Maryland.

Capt. Surratt, it has been stated in one of the principal magazines that Booth was anxious to get your co-operation on that very account, and that when you were introduced to him in Washington by Dr. Mudd, you thought at first that he was a Union spy. It is stated that you were with Weichmann.

Ah! Wilkes Booth. I loathe him. In the first place, Wilkes Booth was never introduced to me by Dr. Mudd on the street or anywhere else. Booth came to me with a letter of introduction from a valued and trusted friend. In the second place, Weichmann was nowhere near when Booth presented his letter. I looked upon Booth from the start as a hot-headed, visionary man, and the moment he broached his wild scheme to me of abducting Lincoln I simply laughed at him.

His Interview with Booth

"It is utterly impracticable," I said to him. "In the first place I know Northern Virginia and Southern Maryland by heart."

"It is on that very account that I have come to you for your assistance, co-operation, and advice," said Booth.

"And it's on that very account that I tell you that the idea is not feasible," I replied. "In the second place, you do not realize the danger."

"I don't consider that for a moment," said Booth.

"Nor I," I replied, "but it must be considered. After leaving Washington, provided we are able to leave with President Lincoln—which I doubt—we will have to drive over one hundred miles before we can cross the Potomac. After having crossed that in safety we will have to drive from one end of Midland Virginia to the other. Don't you know that that section is simply swarming with Yankees? I do, because I have just come through there. Granted that, we do get through all right, we reach the Rappahannock, and cross it, we will be reasonably safe. But we stand about one chance in five hundred of surmounting all those obstacles. Inside of an hour, or, at most, two hours, from the time we get possession of Mr. Lincoln's person, the entire country will be in a furore. The President of the United States cannot be spirited away like an ordinary citizen."

Booth said he was willing to take any chance. I believe he was a monomaniac on the subject. He had brooded over the South's wrongs so much that his mind was unsettled on the subject. He talked a good deal of ridding the country of an arch tyrant, of helping the South and of dying for his country. He was unquestionably insane when he shot Lincoln. No man in his right mind would have done that. The South lost its best friend when it lost Lincoln. He understood its conditions, and the character of its people as no man did before or since. Booth was the South's worst enemy, although he was sincere in wanting to aid her.

Surratt's Trip to Elmira

After engaging in this conversation with Booth I dismissed the matter from my mind, and supposed Booth had done the same. Going direct to Richmond I reported to Gen. Wilder, and was directed by him to go at once to Elmira, N.Y., and learn the plans of the fortifications, prison, etc., at that point, with the number of prisoners. I was in Elmira for several weeks, and as my pockets were full of Uncle Sam's gold furnished me by my government, I made hosts of friends.[1] I may add that it was a blessed good thing for me that I did, for it saved my life at my trial.

Among the people I met at that point was a Union Colonel, who was connected with the fortifications. He seemed to be suffering from a chronic state of "dead-broke," and finding that I had plenty of money and was not averse to accommodating a friend, he soon began to borrow. That was exactly what I wanted. At first it was $10 and $20 at a time. Then it was hundred and two hundred. I finally had him completely in my power. One day we were walking along the street, and he said to me, "Look here: let me ask you a question; what are you doing around here, and what do you want?" I told him that I was in Elmira because I liked the place, and I added that I was anxious to get inside of the prison to see what it looked like. He promised to get me inside, and on the following day was as good as his word. He took me all through the place, and finally left me on a tower, where I made careful plans of the place. I repeated my visit on the following day, and having gained what I wanted, I determined to go back to Richmond.

It was on my journey from Elmira to Albany that I first learned of Lincoln's assassination. I was shocked, and my conversation with Booth immediately recurred to my mind. The next day, en route from Albany to New York, I bought a New York paper and read in it that it was supposed that I was with Booth in his flight, and that a reward of $25,000 was offered for my capture, dead or alive. When I read that startling intelligence I immediately left the train and took the first one northbound that came along. Late that night I crossed into Canada, and that was the last time I saw the United States until brought back on a man-of-war two years later. I went to Montreal and then to Quebec.

His Experiences Abroad

In the latter city I was secreted in a monastery, and there remained for five months. Thinking it wiser to be out of the country on account of the angry feeling of the people I boarded a steamer and went to London. I was in London some time, and also visited Liverpool and Birmingham. I then went to Paris, and from Paris went to Rome and enlisted in the Papal Zouaves under the name of Natson [Watson]. My life while in the Papal Guards was very pleasant, but I continually longed for my native land. I eventually became a Sergeant, and in the war between the Papal states and the Garibaldians I was in my element. It was while in the ser-

---

[1] In the Rockville lecture (above, p. 428), Surratt states that $200 in gold was "the only money I ever received from the Confederate government or any of its agents." Now he reports that his pockets are full of "Uncle Sam's gold furnished me by my government" (Confederate?).

vice of Pius IX that I wrote to one of the most prominent Union statesmen in this country, telling him who and where I was, and asking him if it would be safe for me to return to the United States, and if I could get a jury trial and not undergo a drumhead court martial. He wrote back saying that, in his opinion, I could not get a jury trial and advising me to remain away from America at least three years. The Judge at my trial refused to admit those letters as evidence of my intention to return to this country voluntarily. I determined, however, to return and to take my chances of a court martial, and was on the point of doing so when I was arrested at the instance of Pope Pius IX and cast into prison.

Arrested Through Treachery

How did he learn who you were?

Through the contemptible treachery of a friend—so called—a Canadian.[2] I had shared my bread and butter, my blanket, and even my shirts, with the man, and had any one told me he was going to prove as false as he did, I would have scouted the bare suggestion. I have long since learned that no man in this world can be trusted. This man went to Cardinal Antonelli and told him my story. Antonelli went with the information to the Pope, who immediately ordered my arrest and strict confinement. I was stationed at one of the outposts between Rome and Naples, in the Italian mountains. It was a beautiful spot, and we were quartered in an old monastery. The Papal Secretary of State at once communicated with the United States Secretary of State that they had me, and our government ordered a man-of-war, then cruising in the Indian Ocean, to report to Porto Vecchio and take me aboard.

Now, as a matter of fact, our government did not want me in the United States. They were willing and anxious for me to remain abroad, and hoped I would continue to do so. While I was in London, Liverpool, and in Birmingham our Consuls at those ports knew who I was, and advised our State Department of my whereabouts, but nothing was done. Of course, when the matter was brought to the attention of the government in such an official manner and from such a source, there was nothing to do but to express thanks and take measures for having me returned to this country for trial.

In the meantime I was confined in a cell in the old monastery. The second day after my arrest, or rather the second night, a messenger arrived from Antonelli directing the officer in command of the post, the Baron de Seranpe, who you will remember married Miss Polk, of North Carolina, to have me sent to Rome under heavy guard the moment the summons was received. I was awakened at 4 o'clock A.M. by the rusty key grating in the lock of my cell, and by the light of a flickering lantern I saw that my untimely visitors were an officer and soldiers, all heavily armed. At once I knew what it meant, and when the Lieutenant in command ordered me to dress at once in order to go to Rome, I at once made up my mind that, let the consequences be what they may, I would not go to the Eternal City. While dressing I mentally arranged a plan of escape.

---

[2] Sainte Marie.

His Sensational Escape

This old monastery was built on the side of the mountain, nestling on one side and the west side was directly over a precipice over a hundred feet high. A wall four foot high guarded the court-yard. I determined to break away from my captors and go over that precipice. When I had finished dressing I was placed in the center of the guard, and we slowly ascended the stone steps of the old building, worn smooth by countless feet of many generations of monks. We reached the court-yard and turned toward the left. Just as we reached the point I had selected for my attempt, I made a break for liberty, and running quickly across the court-yard jumped on the wall. Gathering myself for the attempt, I took a long breath and jumped into space, doubling my legs slightly under me as I did so. About thirty-five feet from the top of the precipice there was a bare ledge of rock jutting out from the face of the mountain, and about four feet broad. By great good fortune I landed safely on that ledge.

Captain, it has been stated that when you broke away from your captors you made a wild jump over this precipice and landed purely by accident on that ledge. As a matter of fact, didn't you know of the existence of that ledge of rocks?

Know of it? Why, of course I knew of it. Do you think I would have been such an idiot as to jump over a hundred foot precipice to certain death in that manner? Many and many a time my comrades and myself, in hours of idleness, would lean over that precipice and wonder how many feet it was from the wall of the court-yard to the ledge, and it was an open question as to whether a man could jump from the wall and land safely on the ledge. While dressing I determined to make the attempt. It makes my blood run cold to think of it now, though. However, I managed to land on it safely and my legs doubling up under me, my head struck the bare rock with fearful force. I was knocked completely senseless.

In the meantime what a scene of confusion and what a Babel of voices there was above. The Lieutenant in command wrung his hands in anguish and swore in choice musical Italian. My break had been so sudden that every man was taken completely by surprise. They had had plenty of time to shoot me down if they had had the presence of mind. Running to the side of the precipice they looked over the wall. They must have seen me lying there unconscious, for they immediately began firing down upon me. They may have done so on a venture, however. I was brought back to my senses by the reports of their rifles from above, and the bullets flattening themselves on the bare rock unpleasantly near my head. Dizzy and sick, and shaken, I managed to gather myself together and crawl out of danger, and gradually made my way down the side of the mountain to the little town which nestled at its base. Running along the main street of the town, I ran directly into the arms of a detail of Zouaves.

Refuge Among Garibaldians

They were as much surprised as I, but I had the advantage of being on the alert. With me it was almost a matter of life and death. Doubling quickly on my tracks and expecting every moment to be hit by some of the bullets which were flying around my head, I ran like a frightened deer. Through alleys, down dark streets, and across lots I sped and managed to elude my pursuers. In the meantime the entire town was in an uproar. Every one had the alarm and all the gates were guarded. Selecting a good point, I managed to get over the wall and headed down the white Italian road toward the coast. I should have said at the beginning that all this took place during the early hours of the morning. It was 4 A.M. when I was aroused and told to dress. By the time I had left the town a few miles on the road the sun was high in the heavens and I was congratulating myself on my three escapes, when I was suddenly startled by the sharp command: "Halt! Who goes there?"

"Friend," I answered in my best Italian, recognizing that I had run into a Garibaldian camp. Glancing at my papal uniform, the outpost was by no means reassured. In the mean time I had raised my hands above my head. Bringing his rifle to his shoulder, he was pressing the trigger unpleasantly hard.

Raising my hands even higher in the air, I sang out to him: "Lower your rifle, man. Can't you see my hands are up?" Still covering me with his rifle, he ordered me to advance within a few paces of him and called out lustily for the corporal of the guard. That officer came on the run, and seeing my rig called for the sergeant of the guard. He no sooner caught a glimpse of my dress than he called for the officer of the guard. To make a long story short, I was soon surrounded by a mob of Garibaldians of all ranks and sizes. When I told them that I was an Americano, a deserter from the Papilo Guardo, and wanted to get to the coast they treated me with the greatest kindness. Brothers could not have been kinder. I shall remember these honest, red-coated men with deepest gratitude as long as I live. They entertained me for a week, and when I decided to go to Naples they made it possible for me to do so with safety.

As I was traveling under English passports I went direct to the English Consul and told him who I was. Glancing with unmingled surprise at my red fez, baggy trousers, and leggings of the Papal Zouaves, he said to me:

"Do you realize for a moment, man, the risk you run? Don't you know that Naples is in the hands of the Garibaldi and that you might have a knife run in your back at any moment?"

I told him that the Garibaldi were the very best friends I had; the only friends, in fact, and that the money I had in my pocket was given me by them. I remained in Naples several days, and the entire time I was there I was shadowed by two detectives. They never lost sight of me.

That must have been cheerful. Who did they represent?

I don't know, and as a matter of fact I did not care. Coming face to face with them on one occasion I said to them:

"You stick to me nobly, brothers. I feel deeply moved at your kind attention." They made no reply, but they did not care to arrest me in Naples in the presence of my Garibaldian friends. It became known that I was going to Alexandria [Egypt], and by a singular coincidence the very ship which took me there also carried dispatches to Consul Hale at that point to arrest me and keep me in close confinement until the arrival of Commodore Jeffrey's.[3] When we were a few days out from Naples it became known on the vessel who I was, or was suspected to be. It was reported that I had killed the President of the United States. When this became noised around the ship there was the greatest excitement at once. The Captain of the vessel came to me and said:

"Your presence is kicking up a great fuss on this ship. Who are you, anyway?"

I told him frankly the truth, and while he was most kind, he refused to land me anywhere else than Alexandria.

Surrendered at Alexandria

I was by this time completely tired of being a man without a country, and determined that on reaching Alexandria I would place no more obstacles in the way of my capture and return to the United States. Accordingly when I reached that city I went to a hotel, signed my correct name, and sat quietly on the porch smoking a cigar, waiting for some one to come to arrest me. On the afternoon of the day after my arrival, glancing down the street, I saw coming up toward the hotel an open carriage, containing one man and followed by a squad of cavalry. I knew at once who they were. The cavalcade stopped in front of the hotel and the gentleman got out—he was Col. [Charles] Hale—and coming up to me asked me if I was John H. Surratt. I told him that such was the case. He said he had orders for my arrest. When the carriage drove off there were two in it, and I was the second occupant. I was placed in the city prison, awaiting the arrival of the man-of-war, and was visited daily by Mr. Hale. He treated me as a son. While he gave me plenty of reading matter, he would never tell me when and how I was to be taken back to the United States.[4]

One day I heard a great fuss in the yard of the prison, where the common prisoners were kept. Some one was swearing like a trooper in English. I went into the yard and found a United States man-of-warsman. On my asking him what the trouble was, between his oaths he stated that he belonged to a United States war vessel, which had arrived the night before, and getting drunk he had been "jugged." Said he: "Here we have been chasing all over Europe for a fellow named Surratt, and blankety blanked if he hasn't given us a slip three times. We have come here to get him now, and blankety blank if I believe we will ever see him." I smiled grimly. He said the vessel was in command of Commodore Jeffrey. When Consul Hale called that day I asked him when I was to be delivered to Commodore Jeffrey. To say he was surprised was putting it mildly. He never learned how I found out. I was placed on board the vessel, heavily chained and hand-cuffed, and taken to Marseilles [France], where a United States fleet was lying, in command of Admiral [Louis M.] Goldsborough. When we entered the harbor and I saw that fleet of splendid vessels, with the Stars and Stripes flying from every ship, I could have cheered. I was proud of my country. The bands were playing "Star Spangled Ban-

[3] William N. Jeffers.
[4] For Hale's report on the arrest of Surratt, see above, p. 352, which is in startling contrast to Surratt's story.

449

ner," "Hail Columbia," "Maryland, My Maryland," and "Dixie." I was taken aboard the Admiral's flagship, and when he saw me he said:

"So you are the desperate fellow we have been chasing around the world. Why, you are only a beardless boy." Turning to Commodore Jeffrey he said, "Surely, Commodore, there is no occasion to iron Surratt. It is certainly unnecessary." The Commodore stated that they were his orders and there was nothing left but to obey. I was placed in a stateroom and a marine with drawn cutlass and loaded revolver placed on guard. The marine was given orders that if I attempted to escape to cut me down or shoot me down if necessary. The whole thing struck me as being a perfect farce and I laughed in the face of the officer who gave the command. He scowled at me. As I had a whole stateroom to myself, and as the marine had to march three paces forward and three paces back, I think I had the best of the bargain. The voyage was uneventful and we landed in New York, and I was taken direct to Washington.

Trial of John H. Surratt

During my trial, which lasted sixty-two days, over 200 witnesses were examined. As you may know the jury disagreed, standing eight for acquittal and four for conviction, and after being kept in the old Capitol prison for some months, I was liberated on $25,000 bail. The case was never called again, and I presume the bail has expired by limitation. My counsel were Gen. Merrick and John O. Carlisle. After that trial my nervous system was a wreck. I have never gotten over it.

How about the testimony of Lewis J. Weichmann, Captain?

That man's testimony from beginning to end was outrageously false. He lied, lied; lied from the time he took the witness stand until he left it. During the three days he was on the stand he did not dare to look me in the face. I never took my eyes off him for a moment. Gen. Merrick told me that the newspapers were commenting on the fact. I believe that if I could have caught his eye it would have ended his perjury. As I said to you at the beginning of our talk, that man has done more to bring disgrace and ruin on me and my family than anyone and everyone else, living or dead. I am convinced that if he was on his death-bed he would send for me and ask my forgiveness for the ruin and trouble he has caused me.

Do I think that his testimony was actuated by malice?

No, I do not. Moral cowardice was at the bottom of it. The morning after Lincoln's assassination, a great many people were arrested. Weichmann was one of these. It became known that he was a friend of Booth. In order to get a confession from him a rope was placed around his neck, the other end of it thrown over a beam, and he was ordered to tell what he knew. He was lifted off his feet. Under such circumstances a man will tell or say anything to get a rope from around his neck. Weichmann made up his story out of whole cloth, and when he was in safety he did not have the moral courage to contradict it, as any honest man would. He was a moral coward. He was that way as a schoolboy. At school it was forbidden to have novels. I had one in my desk, and Weichmann opened the desk and took it out. Through some chance it fell into a teacher's hands. When I accused

Weichmann of having taken it out, he swore by all that was holy that he did not do so, although I confronted him with three boys who saw him. As I said, the child is father to the man. The boys at school would not have anything to do with him. He was continually hanging around the teachers and running to them with tales.

It would have been an easy matter for Weichmann to have confessed that he was frightened into a false confession in the Capitol prison. Many men have done the same thing. I remember on one occasion, when I was traveling the "Underground Route" in Southern Maryland, in company with a number of Confederates, one of the party, a nephew of Judge Roger A. Prior, was arrested by a squad of Union troops. They put a rope around his neck, threw it over a limb of a tree, and jerked him off his feet. He confessed everything to them. Told the officer in charge exactly who we were, and as a consequence, we were all arrested. The evidence against us was without a flaw. After being liberated, this young man, realizing what he had done, went to the Judge and told him that he had lied in his so-called confession, that he was so frightened that he would have said anything. He said that he did not even remember what he had confessed. The next day we were all liberated. Look at the difference between Weichmann and this young man. The latter confessed the truth and took it back. Weichmann confessed a lie and stuck to it. When he was giving that false testimony against me, he was enjoying a position as teacher which I got him. I met him on Pennsylvania avenue one day during the war, and he told me he was in a bad way, and asked me to help him.

The cost of my trial about impoverished me, and I could not have paid for it had not two friends in Baltimore sent me money. I received from them checks for from $1,000 to $5,000 at a time. My detectives had to follow the government detectives all through the North. The latter tore a leaf out of an Albany hotel register, where I had signed the day before Lincoln was murdered. But I was able to secure other registers, where I had signed on dates which made my presence in Washington during those exciting times, impossible. I also summoned many prominent citizens of Elmira, all strong Union men, whom I had met there, and they testified to my being in that city on the dates I claimed. My counsel demanded that I give them the name of the Union Colonel who let me into the prison, but I refused. It would have ruined him, although it would have caused my acquittal. My lawyers threatened to throw up the case unless I revealed his name, but I declined.

During my trial, Gen. Merrick pointed out to me a group of men in one corner of the room, and asked me if I ever saw them before. I said I had not. He told me that they were going to swear that they drove me into Maryland the morning after Lincoln's death. They were employed by the government to swear that way. Gen. Merrick went to the *National Intelligencer,* of Washington, and exposed the entire plot. The next morning that paper came out and stated all the facts, and the men mysteriously disappeared. The government has taken good care of Weichmann. He has held a public office in Philadelphia from the day of the first trial until now.

*   *   *

Booth lies buried in beautiful Greenmount Cemetery, in this city, and is in the same grave with his father, mother, two sisters and a brother. His famous brother [Edwin Booth] never entered Washington after Lincoln's death.

No one questions in this city, where the facts of the great controversy are better known than anywhere else, but that Mrs. Surratt was officially murdered. It is generally believed that John H. Surratt had nothing to do with the crime, but it is believed that he was in the conspiracy to abduct. Of the eleven who were tried, four were hanged, five died natural deaths, and two are yet alive.

"PURSUED BY HIS FOES" [1]

Mr. Weichmann Submits Testimonials
of Character

EMINENT MEN WERE HIS FRIENDS

Judge Advocate General Holt and Hon. William Kelley Wrote Several Letters
Commending Him for His Truthfulness in Testifying at the Trial of Lincoln's
Assassins · Attempts to Oust Him from Federal Office
Because of His Testimony

Editor Post: In your issue of Sunday, April 3, 1898, you published a long article entitled "The Crime of Booth," coming from a correspondent in Baltimore. In the course of that article very serious charges are made against me because of my testimony in the conspiracy trial. These charges, if true, would rightfully stamp me as the vilest of men and as one utterly unworthy to hold his head among civilized beings. I know that they are not true, and some of them I, in common with others, now read for the first time.

In my present communication to you I shall not enter into any review of my testimony, nor shall I involve myself in any personal controversy.

It is nearly thirty-three years since the close of the conspiracy trial. During that long period I have been subjected to vile slanders and malicious misrepresentations of all sorts. Trusting to the healing influences of time and to the intelligence of my fellow-men, I have never once stepped aside from the beaten path of duty to notice these falsehoods; but now it seems that the time is here at last when I must do so.

For more than twenty years I filled an honorable position in the custom house of Philadelphia, to which I was appointed through the influence and with the approval of Secretary Stanton, Judge Holt, the able Judge Advocate General of the United States Army, and Hon. William D. Kelley, member of Congress from Philadelphia.

I shall let the letters [2] that these gentlemen have written in my behalf, and

[1] From the *Washington Post*, April 18, 1898.
[2] For the letters published in this article, see above, Chapter XXXII.

what they say of me, speak for my cause. I also submit letters from some of the members of the military commission in reference to my evidence, and by these I will ask to be judged for all future time by my countrymen. Their words are more potent and eloquent than any that I can frame. If these letters are not sufficient to place me right in the estimation of all good people, then naught that I can do or say will be of avail.

DETECTIVE DEFENDS WEICHMANN

A. C. Richards Declares That No Testimony Was Extorted from Him

Editor Post: It is my privilege to read The Post here in Florida. In your issue of the 3d instant I see the story of John H. Surratt, published over the signature of Hanson Hiss. While heretofore I have never written for publication, a word in reference to the scenes and incidents that transpired on the night of the assassination of President Lincoln, and the few days following, including my visit to the house of Mrs. Surratt a little after midnight of the memorable night of the assassination, for the reason that I do not sanction the propriety of ex-officials going into the business of exhibiting skeletons unearthed in the course of their official duties. Yet as this "story" attacks the integrity of the witness [Louis] J. Weichmann, who had the misfortune of being a boarder at Mrs. Surratt's house while the assassination plot was in process of incubation, I feel that it is due to Weichmann, whom I understand is yet living, that I vindicate him so far as I may from the charges of falsehood and perjury contained in said "story." As will be remembered, the assassination was on Friday night, and it so happened that I was in Ford's Theatre that night at the time of the assassination. It became my official duty to at once set about the discovery of the identity of the assassin. Before midnight I had information (the source of which I have not now time to narrate) that the rendezvous of the conspirators had been in Mrs. Surratt's house, and hence I visited her house soon after midnight of that night. I did not see Weichmann that night, nor the day following (Saturday), but on Sunday morning following Weichmann came to my office (Police Headquarters), and introducing himself, said he was in possession of information in regard to the operations and movements of those who by that time had become known as the conspirators, which he thought of importance in the light of the disclosures of the past few hours.

Weichmann then at once, and without hesitation, narrated to me freely, and also without request even on my part that he should do so, incidents that had transpired at the Surratt house, the names of those who had been meeting there and elsewhere, and in whose company he frequently was, and also many other matters that subsequently aided very materially in establishing the assassination plot and the conviction of those engaged therein. Weichmann came to my office voluntarily and unattended by any one, and put me in possession of such information as he had. He did not do so under the pressure of duress, for he was not under arrest, had not been arrested, and was not arrested or held under restraint of any kind thereafter. He came and went to and from my office for several days immediately subsequent to the assassination, as and when he pleased. He with others, in the course of three or four days, obtained information which led me to send officers to Montreal, Canada, in pursuit of John H. Surratt. I sent Weichmann with the officers for the purpose of identifying Surratt. They reported that Surratt had left some Catholic institution in Montreal about the time, or very soon after, they arrived in that city, which statement I note that the "story" corroborates very fully. Weichmann returned from Canada with the officers, and remained in Washington for months, and during the trial of the conspirators was a principal witness. At no time was he under restraint of his liberty.

The writer of the story makes Surratt say as follows: "The morning after Lincoln's assassination a great many people were arrested. Weichmann was one of these. It became known that he was a friend of Booth's. In order to get a confession from him a rope was placed around his neck, the other end of it thrown over a beam, and he was ordered to tell what he knew. He was lifted off his feet." Now if any one put a rope around Weichmann's neck and threw it over a beam I did it, and I say that statement is as false in fact and circumstances as it is possible for a statement to be. It was conceived in recklessness, and is a mere figment of imagination. There are other statements contained in the story that I know of my own knowledge to be untrue, but I will not dwell upon them. I write the above to show how utterly devoid of credence this story, as published, is, and in justice to Louis J. Weichmann, whom I have not seen or heard from for more than thirty years. Weichmann was then a young man of more than ordinary intelligence and attainments. In no instance was any statement in relation to the conspiracy made by him found to be false or incorrect, and very many of his statements were subsequently corroborated by undoubted testimony. I have read many statements within the past thirty years relating to incidents said to have transpired at the theatre at the time of the assassination, and immediately thereafter, purporting to have been written by eye-witnesses, which were purely imaginary and fictitious; but as they did not involve the integrity of any one I have chosen not to notice them. Such is not the case in the instance in hand, and hence this communication. If John H. Surratt had not, unwisely, as it seems to me, called public attention to his alleged connection with the assassination of President Lincoln in the nature of a public statement of self-vindication, that involves the integrity and conduct of others, I would not have felt called upon in justice to Weichmann, and, perhaps, myself, to write the foregoing. Weichmann could give, if he would, very interesting incidents relative to the attempted abduction of President Lincoln and of his visit to Surrattsville with Mrs. Surratt on the day of the assassination, but he has wisely, so far as I know, refrained from doing so. John H. Surratt should have regarded Weichmann's course in preserving silence with feelings of gratitude, instead of accusing him and others falsely with acts of infamy. His story is not worthy of a moment's consideration.

A. C. Richards

THE HARDIE-WALTER CONTROVERSY

The controversy between Father Walter and General Hardie over the spiritual aid and confession of Mary Surratt. The following memorandum and letters are from the Hardie Papers, Library of Congress, Collection No. 24869.

MEMORANDUM

by James A. Hardie

Inspector General and Brevet Brigadier General, U. S. Army

On the publication of the statement in *The Tribune* a few days ago, that the Secretary of War had interfered with the attendance of Mrs. Surratt's spiritual adviser, *The New York Times* and an obscure Philadelphia journal took occasion, without any knowledge of facts, to denounce it as a malicious fabrication. The subjoined statement was obtained from the very best authority, and neither *The Times* or the Secretary of War dare deny it.

On Thursday morning, the 6th instant, the Rev. Father Walter, pastor of St. Patrick's Church, in this city, went to the War Office to ask for a pass to visit Mrs. Surratt, ignorant of the fact that she had already been condemned to suffer death on the following day. He had never previously visited Mrs. S., nor did he know her except by reputation. On application, he was informed by Gen. Hardie, A.A.G. to Sec. Stanton, that he could not give him a pass without first consulting Mr. Stanton, who was out at the time. Father Walter returned home, and at 1 o'clock P.M. on the same day, received a pass to visit the prison, signed, by order of the Secretary of War, Gen. Hardie, A.A.G.

The messenger who brought the pass to Father Walter, being an intelligent Irishman, Father W. entered into conversation with him on the subject of the execution, firmly asserting his belief in Mrs. Surratt's innocence. In half or perhaps an hour afterward, Gen. Hardie himself called at the residence of Father Walter, and after some irrelevant conversation, said: "Father Walter, you made quite an impression on the mind of my messenger in regard to the execution of Mrs. Surratt," to which Father W. remarked that he was firmly impressed with her entire innocence. Gen. Hardie then said: "Father Walter, the pass you have will not admit you to the military prison to-morrow, because it is not signed by the Secretary of War. I want you to make me a promise to say nothing of Mrs. Surratt's innocence, and I will give you the necessary pass."

Father Walter, naturally indignant, immediately refused to accede to Gen. H.'s demand, giving him to understand in the plainest kind of language, that no official, civil or military, could enforce his silence on this point; and remarking that he knew under whose authority he (Gen. H.) was acting. Gen. Hardie—

a converted Catholic by the way—then said, patronizingly, that as yet there were no charges lodged against him, Father W., at the War Department; to which the latter rejoined that he might tell his master, Stanton, that he conscientiously believed Mrs. Surratt guiltless; that he should proclaim his belief, and that the War Department might hang him if it thought proper.

Gen. Hardie was about to go without giving Father W. the pass, when the latter said: "Gen. Hardie, I cannot suffer Mrs. Surratt to die without administering the sacrament; I say yes to your proposition; give me the pass." Gen. Hardie then drew from his pocket a pass duly filled up and signed by Edwin M. Stanton, admitting him, Father W., to the prison until after the execution.

Previous to the removal of Mrs. Surratt from the Carroll to the Military Prison, Father W. had made application to the War Office for a pass to visit her, she being very ill, but in every instance his applications were denied, and up to the very day before the execution Mrs. S. was deprived by the Secretary of War of spiritual attendants.

Referring to the above extract from the *New York Tribune* of July 17th, I beg to state that the facts in the case are as follows:

On the 6th instant the Rev. Mr. Walter called at the War Department and asked for a pass to visit Mrs. Surratt in the Military Prison, saying (if I am not mistaken) that she had expressed a desire to see him. I submitted the request to the Secretary of War, who at once said that a pass might be given. Neither the Rev. Mr. Walter nor myself then knew of the approval of the sentence of the Military Commission, in the case of Mrs. Surratt. I sent Mr. Walter a pass, but afterwards, fearing that the pass signed by myself might not, under the circumstances, be accepted by the officer in charge of the prison, in order that there might be no possibility of disappointment in the admission of a clergyman to afford the necessary spiritual services, I sent Mr. Barry, a clerk in my office, to see the Rev. Mr. Walter, and to tell him that it would be better not to go on the pass sent, but that I would again see the Secretary of War, and (as he had assented to the visit of the clergyman to the prisoner) would get a pass signed by *himself,* as otherwise there was a probability of his being put to the trouble of going to the prison without being enabled to secure admission. It was also a part of my design that Mr. Barry should impress upon Rev. Mr. Walter the necessity of good faith in the use of the pass when replaced. After thus sending Mr. Barry to Father Walter, I went to the Secretary of War and asked his own signature to a pass as referred to above; upon his signing which I said to him that I was confident the pass would be used solely for the purpose for which it was asked—a professional visit, to administer the sacraments, and to prepare the person to be visited for death.

Upon Mr. Barry's (my messenger to Rev. Mr. Walter,) return, he informed me of the violent and excited language of Father Walter with regard to the trial and its result, which he, (Mr. Walter,) it appears, had heard of after leaving the War Department. On this I went myself to see the Rev. Mr. Walter, to caution him, as his well-wisher and as a friend of the Church, and in my private capacity entirely, with regard to the use of language so inflammatory as that he had indulged in, at this, a time of great public excitement. I introduced the conversation by stating that what he had said had made an impression upon the mind of my messenger, who had repeated his remarks to me. I explained to him, as I have said above, that there might be a possibility of his not getting into the prison upon my pass, and that I therefore asked the Secretary of War for a pass signed by himself, upon giving which I had said that I was confident that it would not be used for any other purpose than that for which it was asked, and I wanted him (Mr. Walter) to be so governed as that I would be safe in the assertion I had made. Mr. Walter had displayed so much excitement and temper, that it was a duty of charity on my part, in view of all the circumstances, to endeavor to induce him to pursue a more discreet course, and to counsel him to be silent, as became his place, on these topics. I asked him in a friendly and kindly way to promise me that he would desist from talking about the matter. Mr. Walter's convictions as to the innocence of the prisoner, or the use of any proper efforts (believing her to be innocent) to avert her execution, were not made matters of objection. It was to the inflammatory character and effect of his observations, at this period, when the public mind was agitated, that my attention was directed. Unnecessary, idle and angry discussions and harangues could not but be mischievous just at this moment; and since it appeared that Mr. Walter could not approach the subject with temper and discretion, it was better he should let it alone. This was a confidential conversation between myself and Mr. Walter. As has been seen, the visit was not at all official, but entirely that of a private individual. My motives were laudable; they were to restrain imprudent and mischievous discussions, and to insure the use of the pass to be given, in the faith intended when it was signed, and thus to make my assurance good. The visit was not suggested by the Secretary of War, or even known to him until the present time. On this point, after what I had said, I do not see how Mr. Walter could have understood me as prompted by instructions in my conversation.

In replying to me, the Rev. Mr. Walter was very violent and generally denunciatory. The range of his conversation was quite wide. He harangued upon the Administration and rebellion, and dwelt with bitterness on what he called military tyranny, &c. He said probably all that he is represented in the fourth paragraph of the article in question as having said, and very much more that a prudent priest, a loyal citizen, or a man of common sense, would not have said. During all this time I was endeavoring to counsel moderation, remonstrating against his expressions, and enjoining prudence.

I do not know that I sought to *patronize* the Rev. Mr. Walter at all; and the phrases which allude to this, and the indignant rejoinder of Father W., do not bring to my mind the recollection of the scene described.

I did not tell Father Walter that he should not have a pass if he did not promise to say nothing of Mrs. Surratt's innocence. Annoyed by what he had said, I was about, however, to leave the room and to defer giving him the pass, remarking, "I will send you word as to the pass in two hours," when he said, "I promise."

I intended within the two hours to see the Secretary of War, and to say to him that I was convinced, after what had taken place, that Father Walter was not in proper disposition and frame of mind to be a suitable religious attendant upon the prisoner, and that, under the circumstances the services of another priest should be procured for her instead. When Mr. Walter said that he promised, satisfied that he had determined to be governed by the considerations of prudence I had suggested, and believing he would perform what he had undertaken, I gave him the pass. Nor did I, when I designed to withdraw from Father W. without giving him then the pass, by any means intend that this act should have the effect to deprive the prisoner of the services of the clergy. My view, on the contrary, was only that some other priest should go. In fact another priest [Father Wigget] did go, besides Mr. Walter. It has been my fortune to be the means of sending the clergy to attend many, during this war, in need of their services, and I never threw a straw in the way of any clergyman, of any faith, visiting a penitent, loyal or disloyal, living or dying, when his services were called for. I could not see or know of a person of my own creed dying, without giving any assistance in my power to secure the attendance of a priest.

With regard to the denials of passes to Mr. Walter to visit the prisoner when ill, referred to in the last paragraph of the article in question, Father Walter stated to my messenger that he had been requested by Mrs. Surratt, shortly after she was arrested, and since, to visit her, but that he had refused to do so, not wishing to have his "name connected with it until the trial was over."

I did not seek to meddle with Mr. Walter's convictions as to the innocence of Mrs. Surratt, nor did I attempt to restrain him from the use of any proper efforts to bring his convictions to notice in quarters where his representations might be of avail. So far from this, an hour or two after the conversation referred to, when he called upon me at the War Department, and told me that he could not get admittance, with the daughter of the prisoner, to the Executive Mansion, and asked me for my assistance, I gave him a card to the Acting Military Secretary of the President, asking that gentleman to see the Rev. Mr. W., trusting that this means would assist him in getting his case before the Executive.

In conclusion, I distinctly aver that the Secretary of War expressly and readily assented to the visit of a Catholic clergyman to Mrs. Surratt. He made no condition as to any conviction of the clergyman as to the guilt or innocence of the prisoner, or as to anything he might say on the subject.

Private

Baltimore, July 23, 1865.

Brig. Genl. Hardie Inspector Genl.

Dear Sir:

I have received your letter of 22 inst, with its enclosure, & I return you my thanks.

I am convinced that you acted with the best motives, & in what you believed to be the interests of the Church, of which you have been a staunch friend. While I say this, I may be permitted to express regret at your having thought it necessary to employ certain expressions in regard to Rev. Mr. Walter, which were scarcely called for by the argument. Though I have not a doubt that Father Walter also acted for what he believed the best, I had already, several days since, cautioned him to observe silence, & he promised to do so.

> I remain, very truly, yr friend
> M. J. Spalding, A.B.

Philadelphia
1240 Broad St.,
July 21, 1865.

To
Gen. Jas. A. Hardie,
War Department,
Washington, D.C.

My Dear Sir,

I *thank* you for the timely letter, which appears in this morning's papers in answer to the many attacks upon the War Department on account of its alleged treatment of the Rev. Mr. Walter.

Coming to this city on a short visit I have had many times occasion to defend the conduct of the government toward Mrs. Surratt and her spiritual advisors, and your letter comes very apropo to relieve me of much trouble. The conduct of the government towards these conspirators and their senseless sympathizers is so prudent and admirable we can afford for the future to let them go on so long as the result of their foolish course remains so harmless.

Your letter is well-written and altogether satisfactory.

Again, *I thank you for it.*

> Very Respectfully,
> Yours,
> E. Q. S. Waldron
> Pikesville, Md.

SELECTED BIBLIOGRAPHY

*Manuscripts, Microfilms, Government Documents,
and Archival Material*

Allen, J. D. *Booth's Diary*. Washington, D.C.: Lincoln Museum; National Park Service, Informational Circular V, October 24, 1968.

Doherty, E. P. Letter to W. Ward, New York, February 1, 1895, Risvold Collection.

Hardie Papers. Library of Congress, Collection No. 24869.

Holt (Judge Joseph) Papers. Library of Congress.

Impeachment Investigation: Testimony Taken before the Judiciary Committee of the House of Representatives in the Investigation of the Charges against Andrew Johnson. 2nd Session 39th Congress and 1st Session 40th Congress. Washington, D.C.: Government Printing Office, 1867.

Investigation and Trial Papers Relating to the Assassination of President Lincoln. Washington, D.C.: National Archives, Microfilm No. 599 (16 rolls).

Olszewski, George J. *House Where Lincoln Died*. Washington, D.C.: National Park Service, U. S. Department of the Interior, April 15, 1967.

39th Congress, 2nd session. *House Exec. Doc. No. 1, Diplomatic Correspondence*.

39th Congress, 2nd session. *House Exec. Doc. Nos. 9 and 25, John H. Surratt*.

Weichmann manuscript and related papers, including Richards' letters, are in the Risvold Collection.

Newspapers and Periodicals

Baker, Ray Stannard. "The Capture, Death, and Burial of J. Wilkes Booth," *McClure's Magazine*, May 1897.

Doherty, Edward P. "Captain Doherty's Narrative," *Century Magazine*, January 1890.

Ford, John T. "Behind the Curtain of a Conspiracy," *North American Review*, April 1889.

Hiss, Hanson. "John H. Surratt's Story," *Washington Post*, April 3, 1898.

Mason, Victor Louis. "Four Lincoln Conspiracies," *Century Magazine*, April 1896.

Munroe, Seaton. "Recollections of Lincoln's Assassination," *North American Review*, April 1896.

Obituary of Louis J. Weichmann, *Anderson Herald* (Anderson, Indiana), June 6, 1902.

Porter, General Horace. "Campaigning with Grant," *Century Magazine,* October 1897.

"Pursued by His Foes" (by Weichmann and A. C. Richards). *Washington Post,* April 18, 1898. Weichmann Papers, Risvold Collection.

Ruggles, Major M. B. "Major Ruggles' Narrative," *Century Magazine,* January 1890.

Speed, John and James. "The Assassins of Lincoln," *North American Review,* September 1888.

Surratt, John H. Lecture by John H. Surratt at Rockville, Maryland, *The Evening Star* (Washington, D.C.), December 7, 1870.

Townsend, George Alfred. "How Wilkes Booth Crossed the Potomac," *Century Magazine,* April 1884.

Walter, Rev. Jacob A. Remarks made before the United States Catholic Historical Society. *Church News, a Catholic Family Journal* (Washington, D.C.), August 18, 1891. Clipping in Weichmann Papers, Risvold Collection.

Wilgus, C. W. S. "The Lincoln Tragedy," *Ravenna Republican* (Ravenna, Ohio), April 19, 1906.

Books

Arnold, Samuel Bland. *Defence and Prison Experiences of a Lincoln Conspirator.* Edited by Charles F. Heartman. Hattiesburg, Miss.: The Book Farm, 1943.

Baker, Lafayette C. *History of the United States Secret Service.* Philadelphia: L. C. Baker, 1867.

Bates, David Homer. *Lincoln in the Telegraph Office.* New York: Century Company, 1907.

Bingham, John A. *Trial of the Conspirators for the Assassination of President Lincoln.* Washington, D.C.: Government Printing Office, 1865.

Campbell, Helen Jones. *The Case for Mrs. Surratt.* New York: G. P. Putnam's Sons, 1943.

——. *Confederate Courier.* New York: St. Martin's Press, 1964.

Carpenter, Francis B. *Six Months at the White House.* New York: Hurd & Houghton, 1867.

Clarke, Asia Booth. *The Elder and the Younger Booth.* Boston: James R. Osgood & Company, 1882.

——. *The Unlocked Book: A Memoir of John Wilkes Booth by His Sister.* Edited by Eleanor Farjeon. New York: G. P. Putnam's Sons, 1938.

DeWitt, David M. *The Assassination of Abraham Lincoln and Its Expiation.* New York: Macmillan, 1909.

——. *The Judicial Murder of Mary E. Surratt.* Baltimore: J. Murphy and Company, 1895.

Eisenschiml, Otto. *In the Shadow of Lincoln's Death.* New York: Wilfred Funk, Inc., 1940.

———. *Why Was Lincoln Murdered?* Boston: Little, Brown, 1937.

Guernsey, Alfred H., and Henry M. Alden. *Harper's Pictorial History of the Great Rebellion.* 2 vols.; New York: Harper and Brothers, 1868.

Hamilton, Charles, and Ostendorf, Lloyd. *Lincoln in Photographs.* Norman, Okla.: University of Oklahoma Press, 1963.

Harris, T. M. *Assassination of Lincoln.* Boston: American Citizen Company, 1892.

Heitman, Francis B. *Historical Register and Dictionary of the United States Army.* Vol. 1. Washington, D. C.: Government Printing Office, 1903.

Kunhardt, Dorothy Meserve, and Philip B., Jr. *Twenty Days.* New York: Harper and Row, 1965.

Lewis, Lloyd. *Myths After Lincoln.* New York: Harcourt, Brace, 1929.

McCarthy, Burke. *Suppressed Truth about the Assassination of Abraham Lincoln.* Philadelphia: Burke McCarthy, 1924.

Moore, Guy W. *The Case of Mrs. Surratt.* Norman, Okla.: University of Oklahoma Press, 1954.

Mudd, Nettie. *Life of Dr. Samuel A. Mudd.* New York: Neale Publishing Company, 1906.

National Cyclopedia of American Biography. Vol. IV. New York: James T. White and Company, 1897.

Nicolay, John G., and John Hay. *Abraham Lincoln: A History.* 10 vols.; New York: Century Company, 1890.

Oldroyd, Osborn H. *Assassination of Abraham Lincoln.* Washington, D.C., 1901.

Pitman, Benn. *The Assassination of President Lincoln and the Trial of the Conspirators.* New York: Moore, Wilstach and Baldwin, 1865.

Roscoe, Theodore. *The Web of Conspiracy.* Englewood Cliffs, N.J.: Prentice-Hall, 1959.

Ruggles, Eleanor. *Prince of Players: Edwin Booth.* New York: W. W. Norton, 1953.

Sandburg, Carl. *Abraham Lincoln: The War Years.* Vol. 4 of 4 vols. New York: Harcourt, Brace, 1939.

Shelton, Vaughan. *Mask for Treason.* Harrisburg, Pa.: Stackpole Books, 1965.

Stern, Philip Van Doren. *The Man Who Killed Lincoln.* New York: Literary Guild of America, Inc., 1939.

[Teillard], Dorothy Lamon (ed.). *Recollections of Abraham Lincoln.* Chicago: A. C. McClurg and Company, 1895.

Townsend, G. A. *Katy of Catoctin.* New York: D. Appleton and Company, 1886.

Trial of the Assassins and Conspirators for the Murder of President Abraham Lincoln. Philadelphia: T. B. Peterson Brothers, 1865.

Trial of John H. Surratt in the Criminal Court for the District of Columbia. 2 vols.; Washington, D.C.: Government Printing Office, 1867.

Wallace, Lew. *Lew Wallace: An Autobiography.* 2 vols.; New York, Harper and Brothers, 1906.

NOTES

CHAPTER I

[1] See below, p. 235.

[2] In spite of what Weichmann says, the conclusions of the Commission have been in controversy ever since they were made.

[3] The ancient Greek temple in the city of Ephesus which was set on fire by the Ephesian Herostratus because he wanted to immortalize his name.

[4] See below, pp. 140–1.

[5] George Franklin Edmunds was senator from Vermont. The law concerning presidential succession was enacted by the 49th Congress on January 19, 1886. It provided for succession by the Cabinet officers, starting with the Secretary of State, to act as President in case of the death, removal, or resignation of the President and the Vice-President. On July 18, 1947, the 80th Congress changed the law of succession to: first, the Speaker of the House of Representatives; second, the President pro tempore of the Senate; and then the Cabinet officers, in the following order: Secretary of State, Secretary of the Treasury, Secretary of War, Attorney General, Postmaster General, Secretary of the Navy, Secretary of the Interior, Secretary of Agriculture, Secretary of Commerce, and finally Secretary of Labor.

[6] See John G. Nicolay and John Hay, *Abraham Lincoln: A History* (10 vols.; New York: Century Company, 1890), VIII, 312–13.

[7] O'Laughlin came from a Protestant family and it is questionable whether he was a Catholic. Although contemporary sources, historians, and this book spell his name O'Laugh*lin*, his family spelled it O'Laugh*len*. According to James O. Hall, McLean, Virginia; hereafter referred to as Hall Research.

CHAPTER II

[1] John Brown, American abolitionist, was executed on December 2, 1859, for seizing the U. S. arsenal at Harpers Ferry, Virginia, with the intent to arm the slaves and instigate their freedom through rebellion.

CHAPTER III

[1] Surratt, Sr., died on or about August 19, 1862. Hall Research.

[2] Anna Surratt's name was Elizabeth Susanna Surratt, although she used Anna or

Annie. She was born in the District of Columbia on January 1, 1843, and died on October 24, 1904. Hall Research.

3 Mary Eugenia Jenkins Surratt was probably born in May or June 1823. Her middle name has always been reported as Eugenia but according to Hall she was named Elizabeth, after her mother.

4 Mrs. Surratt's mother, Mrs. Elizabeth Jenkins, died in 1878, and is buried in St. Ignatius Catholic Church cemetery, Prince Georges County, Maryland. Zadoc Jenkins is buried in Mount Olivet Catholic cemetery, Washington. Hall Research.

5 Letter from Fourth Assistant Postmaster General J. L. Bristow under date of May 6, 1898, to Weichmann. Weichmann Papers, Risvold Collection.

6 Sainte Marie was a friend of Weichmann and John Surratt but later informed on both of them.

7 Castle Thunder was a Confederate prison in Richmond where political prisoners, spies, and those accused of treason were held.

8 Both testimonials in Weichmann Papers, Risvold Collection.

9 John Surratt later became a Confederate spy and blockade runner and Weichmann was accused of giving him confidential information on prisoners of war. See Rockville lecture, above, p. 30.

10 Major General Lew Wallace, with inferior numbers, held General Jubal Early in check until reinforcements from Grant's Army of the Potomac arrived and prevented the capture of the capital.

CHAPTER IV

1 Rockville lecture, see above, p. 30. Italics added by Weichmann. Miss Anna E. Surratt testified that her brother left college in 1861 or 1862. See Benn Pitman, *The Assassination of President Lincoln and the Trial of the Conspirators* (New York: Moore, Wilstach and Baldwin, 1865), p. 131; hereafter referred to as Pitman. Pitman was the chief recorder to the Commission and owned the Phonographic Institute of Cincinnati, Ohio. He was the brother of Sir Isaac Pitman, English phonographer, who invented the Pitman method of shorthand. Pitman died on December 28, 1910, at the age of eighty-eight.

2 The exact date on which Surratt met Booth is not known. In a newspaper interview, published in the *Washington Post*, April 3, 1898, he stated that Dr. Mudd never introduced him to Booth "on the street or anywhere else." This would indicate that they knew each other previous to the December 23, 1864, meeting in the street and the National Hotel which is described in this chapter. See Hanson Hiss article, below, p. 444.

3 At the trial of the conspirators, Weichmann gave January 15, 1865, as the date of the National Hotel meeting but the date of this meeting was later established as December 23, 1864. The defense was never able to disprove this meeting—only the date was changed. For the testimony of Weichmann, see Pitman, p. 117, and for the argument of John A. Bingham, see pp. 383–4. See also *Surratt Trial*, I, 424–7.

[4] See Osborn H. Oldroyd, *Assassination of Abraham Lincoln* (Washington, D.C., 1901), p. 160; hereafter referred to as Oldroyd. At both trials Weichmann testified that Booth was introduced by Dr. Mudd as "Mr. Booth." See Pitman, p. 114, and *Surratt Trial*, I, 371. However, the point remains—Dr. Mudd did introduce Booth to Surratt on December 23, 1864, at the National Hotel, when the two already knew each other, according to John H. Surratt.

[5] At the second trial, Weichmann stated that the marks were "more like roads or straight lines than anything else." *Surratt Trial*, I, 372.

[6] The nickname for a secessionist or Southern sympathizer.

CHAPTER V

[1] By this marriage Booth, Sr., had a daughter who died in infancy, and a son, Richard Junius. See Eleanor Ruggles, *Prince of Players: Edwin Booth* (New York: W. W. Norton, 1953), pp. 8–11.

[2] Booth, Sr., was not divorced from his first wife until March 1851, and then married Mary Ann on May 10, 1851. *Ibid.*, pp. 47, 215.

[3] The other children were Rosalie, Henry, Mary Ann, Frederick, and Elizabeth. John Wilkes was the ninth child.

[4] Asia Booth Clarke, *The Elder and the Younger Booth* (Boston: James R. Osgood & Company, 1882), pp. 66–7.

[5] Richard Booth was an English lawyer.

[6] Junius Brutus Booth's body was brought to Baltimore and held in a vault until the following spring of 1853, when it was buried in Baltimore Cemetery. On June 13, 1869, Edwin Booth bought a lot in the name of Mary Ann Booth, in Greenmount Cemetery, Baltimore. On June 17, the bodies of Junius Brutus Booth and his father, Richard Booth, were taken from Baltimore Cemetery and reburied in this new lot. John Wilkes Booth's body, which had been turned over to the Booth family on February 15, 1869, was buried on June 26, along with the remains of the Booth children previously buried at Tudor Hall, the Booth farm. Hall Research.

[7] Asia Booth Clarke, *The Unlocked Book: A Memoir of John Wilkes Booth by His Sister*, edited by Eleanor Farjeon (New York: G. P. Putnam's Sons, 1938), pp. 186–7.

[8] Lewis Payne.

CHAPTER VI

[1] For testimony of Mrs. Mary Hudspeth, see Pitman, pp. 39–40.

[2] See also Samuel Bland Arnold, *Defence and Prison Experiences of a Lincoln Conspirator*, edited by Charles F. Heartman. (Hattiesburg, Miss.: The Book Farm, 1943); hereafter referred to as Arnold. In this book Arnold gives his side

of the story and admits his connection with the plot to abduct the President, but not to assassinate him.

[3] For testimony of Newman, see Pitman, p. 239.

[4] Jacob Thompson, Secretary of the Interior during Buchanan's administration, Clement C. Clay, former U. S. senator from Alabama, Beverly Tucker, a former judge in Virginia, George N. Sanders, William C. Cleary, George Young, and George Harper, among others, had been agents for the Confederacy in Canada.

[5] See also *Quebec Gazette*, June 7, 1865.

[6] For testimony of Campbell, see Pitman, pp. 45–6.

[7] Weichmann does not copy Oldroyd perfectly, but in the main the quotation is correct.

[8] The italics are Weichmann's.

[9] Not quoted word for word but with no loss of meaning. See Theodore Roscoe, *The Web of Conspiracy* (Englewood Cliffs, N.J.: Prentice-Hall, 1959), pp. 534–6.

[10] See Pitman, p. 46.

CHAPTER VII

[1] For this and the following quote, see Ward Hill Lamon, *Recollections of Abraham Lincoln*, edited by Dorothy Lamon [Teillard], (Chicago: A. C. McClurg and Company, 1895), pp. 262–3, 265–6.

[2] Unidentified; probably taken from a newspaper.

[3] *Selma Morning Despatch*, December 1, 1864.

[4] Francis B. Carpenter, *Six Months at the White House* (New York: Hurd & Houghton, 1867), pp. 62–3.

[5] For testimony of Chester, see Pitman, pp. 44–5. Not quoted word for word, but in the main it is correct. The italics are Weichmann's.

[6] Booth bought stock in oil lands in 1863–4, but never had more than six thousand dollars invested and never made a cent on the investment. In September 1864, he made two conveyances of his holdings—to his brother Junius Brutus Booth and to his business agent, Joseph H. Simonds. See Pitman, p. 45.

[7] Booth's plan to abduct Lincoln by force at Ford's Theater probably stems more from his flair for the dramatic than from sound thinking. Lincoln was a rough-and-tumble wrestler in his youth, and at fifty-six would be no easy mark.

[8] Samuel Cox helped provide food and shelter for Booth and Herold following the assassination, but he was never prosecuted by the Government for this act.

[9] For testimony of Mrs. Hudspeth, see Pitman, pp. 39–40. Not quoted perfectly, but in the main correct.

[10] Charlotte Corday was a French revolutionist who assassinated Jean Paul Marat, and paid for her crime on the guillotine, July 17, 1793.

[11] For the Selby and Leenea letters, see Pitman, p. 40. The Selby letter is not quoted word for word, but with no loss of meaning.

[12] For testimony of Bates, see *Surratt Trial*, I, 506–7.

[13] See *Surratt Trial*, II, 1306.

CHAPTER VIII

1 See Rockville lecture, below, pp. 430–1.
2 See Hanson Hiss article, below, p. 444. Surratt's Rockville lecture indicates that Booth met John Surratt before the December 23, 1864, meeting in the National Hotel.
3 For testimony of Maddox, see Pitman, pp. 75–6.
4 For testimony of McDonough, see *Surratt Trial,* I, 356–7.
5 Weichmann has not copied Martin's testimony word for word, but in the main it is correct, except for "on several occasions," which the editor has corrected to "on [one] occasion."
6 Atzerodt was born in Germany.
7 *Surratt Trial,* I, 215, and Pitman, p. 306.
8 Also known as Tee Bee, Maryland.

CHAPTER IX

1 Professional actors.
2 Doster gave the year of Payne's birth as 1845, but Weichmann has used the correct date of 1844. See Pitman, p. 308. Lewis Thornton Powell was also known as Mr. Wood, Lewis Paine, Lewis Payne, and Mosby.
3 For testimony of Howell, see Pitman, pp. 133–5. Howell testified for the defense and the following note from Pitman is in regard to Howell's testimony: *"We can not present the contradictions and prevarications of this witness without occupying many pages. In each case we give his last statements, many of them flatly contradicting those made a few moments before."*

CHAPTER X

1 Pitman gives the date of this meeting as March 3. See testimony of Norton, p. 177. See also p. 94 below, where Weichmann quotes Bingham's closing argument at the trial in which he gives the date of March 3.
2 Bessie or Lucy Hale, daughter of Senator John P. Hale of New Hampshire. Historians differ as to the first name.
3 Lieutenant John W. Westfall was a member of the Capitol police force from about 1865 to about 1878. They were under the authority of the Commissioner of Public Buildings and not connected with the Metropolitan Police Force.
4 These statements indicate that Booth was not arrested and taken away, but was pushed back into the crowd.
5 For a photograph showing Booth, and persons alleged to be Surratt, Payne, Atzerodt, and Herold, at the second inaugural, see the illustration section of this book.
6 See Pitman, p. 45. At the first trial the defense tried to establish the fact that Booth first thought of killing Lincoln on the morning of April 14, or no earlier

than the day before the assassination. Therefore, they reasoned, how could the conspirators on trial be guilty of murder? In this way, they could be guilty only of the plan to abduct, with the exception of Lewis Payne, who had made the attempt on Seward's life, and Herold, who had aided Booth in his effort to escape.

[7] See Pitman, p. 385.

CHAPTER XI

[1] See Pitman, p. 223.

[2] *Jane Shore* was presented at Ford's Theater on March 15, 1865. No other night, just once. Hall Research.

[3] For testimony of Miss Honora Fitzpatrick, see *Surratt Trial*, I, 232. Miss Fitzpatrick never gave the exact date of her evening at the theater with John Surratt, Mr. Wood, and Miss Dean. The date of March 15 was established at the first trial.

[4] For testimony of Raybold, see Pitman, pp. 109–11, and *Surratt Trial*, I, 612–19. At the trial of the conspirators Raybold testified that box No. 8 was the President's box and that when the President was in attendance the partition between it and No. 7 was removed to make a larger box. He also stated that a ticket was sold to Booth about two weeks before April 14 for box No. 4, which was changed, at Booth's request, to No. 7 or 8—he could not remember which one. No record was made at either trial as to the price of the ticket.

[5] According to Arnold, this meeting took place on March 15, 1865, with the following men present: John Wilkes Booth, John H. Surratt, Lewis Payne, George A. Atzerodt, David E. Herold, Michael O'Laughlin, and Samuel Bland Arnold. This meeting of the conspirators was dissolved at "about 5 o'clock A.M. in the morning of the 16th March 1865," according to Arnold. Thus Surratt and Mr. Wood (Lewis Payne) could have gone to the theater the evening of the 15th and still attend the meeting. See Arnold, pp. 45–7.

[6] Arnold gives March 17, 1865, as the date of the "horseback ride" of the conspirators. Herold rode to Surrattsville with weapons and did not go along. Booth had information that the President was to attend a play at an army hospital just outside Washington at the terminus of Seventh Street. They met at a restaurant near the hospital and enjoyed a social drink while Booth left to see if the President was in attendance. Upon his return, Booth was "very much excited cautioning care and discretion" and advised that the party break up and return at once as Lincoln had failed to show up. See *Arnold*, pp. 47–8.

This is confirmed by Hall, who reports an unidentified newspaper clipping in which the actor E. L. Davenport states that an afternoon performance of *Still Waters Run Deep* was given by his troupe at Campbell Hospital on March 17, and that Booth showed up—dressed to the hilt—and asked him if Lincoln was in attendance. Unidentified newspaper clipping dated August 27, 1893, Bullfinch Place, Boston.

The *National Intelligencer* reported, March 18, 1865, that *Still Waters Run Deep* was presented "yesterday"—that is, March 17, 1865—at Campbell Hospital. Also that the soldiers presented *their own* play, with soldier actors, on *Friday* night, March 16, 1865. Hall Research.

Booth played Pescara in *The Apostate* at Ford's Theater on March 18. From the above it would appear that March 17 is the correct date.

[7] For testimony of Weichmann, see Pitman, p. 118.

[8] Ella Turner made an abortive attempt to suffocate herself with chloroform. See *New York Daily Tribune*, April 17, 1865.

[9] For testimony of Anna Surratt, see Pitman, p. 131.

[10] Father Wigget was also Mrs. Surratt's confessor. He and Father Walter walked with her to the gallows.

[11] Not quoted word for word, but with no loss of meaning. See Lafayette C. Baker, *History of the United States Secret Service* (Philadelphia: L. C. Baker, 1867), pp. 562–3.

[12] Booth was born on May 10, 1838; John Surratt, on April 13, 1844; Payne, on April 22, 1844; Herold, on June 16, 1842; O'Laughlin, in June 1840; Arnold, on September 6, 1834; Atzerodt, on June 12, 1835; and Dr. Mudd, on December 20, 1833. Hall Research.

[13] For testimony of Chester, see Pitman, p. 44. For the confession of Atzerodt, see below, p. 385.

[14] For testimony of Stabler, see Pitman, p. 71.

[15] Captain D. H. L. Gleason confirmed this and did report it to the War Department. For Gleason's version, see *Magazine of History*, February 1911. See also Lloyd Lewis, *Myths After Lincoln* (New York: Harcourt, Brace, 1929), p. 231; hereafter referred to as *Myths*.

[16] The italics are Weichmann's. See Rockville lecture, below, pp. 431–2.

[17] Probably Arnold. See Arnold, pp. 46–7.

CHAPTER XII

[1] See also *Washington Star*, December 7, 1881.

[2] See Arnold, p. 25.

[3] For testimony of Thompson and Norton, see *Surratt Trial*, I, 510–17.

[4] For testimony of Lloyd, see Pitman, p. 85. See also *Surratt Trial*, I, 277–8.

[5] At the first trial Weichmann gave the date of *The Apostate* as March 24, but later corrected it to the 18th.

[6] See *Surratt Trial*, I, 381.

[7] See Rockville lecture, below, pp. 435 and 438.

[8] For testimony of Martha Murray, see Pitman, p. 154, and *Surratt Trial*, I, 246–7. Mrs. Murray testified that she did not know Mrs. Surratt and that Lewis Payne had applied directly to her for a room. She also stated that she could not remember if anyone had spoken to her about engaging a room for Payne and that

she had conversations with so many people that she could not remember "any particular circumstance of that kind." For testimony of Miss Ward, see Pitman, p. 135. Miss Ward stated that in February or March she went to the Herndon House to see if there was a vacant room but did not engage one.

[9] For testimony of Miss Fitzpatrick, see *Surratt Trial*, I, 234–5. Miss Fitzpatrick testified that Mrs. Surratt was in the Herndon House only a few minutes and that she did not say why she went in. Weichmann testified that she was in the house about twenty minutes and that she said she was going in to see Payne. The defense never gave a reason for her visit to the Herndon House. See also testimony of Mrs. Murray, Pitman, p. 154. For Weichmann's testimony, see *Surratt Trial*, I, 385.

[10] For testimony of Stabler, see *Surratt Trial*, I, 217. Not quoted word for word, but in the main correct.

[11] For "Sam" letter, see Pitman, p. 236. Not quoted word for word, but without loss of meaning.

[12] See Pitman, p. 223.

CHAPTER XIII

[1] The horse was purchased by Booth, not Mudd. Hall Research.

[2] Judah P. Benjamin, Confederate Secretary of State, and then Secretary of War during the last days of the rebellion; and Jefferson Davis, President of the Confederated States.

[3] See Rockville lecture, below, pp. 432–3; italics are Weichmann's.

[4] Confederate General Joseph E. Johnston, who surrendered to General William T. Sherman at Durham Station, North Carolina, on April 26, 1865.

[5] For testimony of Purdy, see Pitman, p. 43.

[6] For the argument of John Bingham, see Pitman, p. 387. With the exception of a few words Weichmann copies Bingham with no loss of content or meaning. He also rearranges the paragraphs with no loss of meaning.

[7] For testimony of Lloyd, see Pitman, p. 85. The italics are Weichmann's. One of the more controversial points at both trials was the conversation between Lloyd and Mrs. Surratt about the "shooting irons" at Uniontown on April 11, 1865. This controversy centered on whether Weichmann heard the conversation while sitting next to Mrs. Surratt in the buggy. Here is part of the testimony from the trial of John H. Surratt: Lloyd testified that she told him to have the "shooting irons" ready, as they would be wanted soon. He also stated that she was sitting in a high narrow buggy with the top up. When Lloyd was asked if the conversation between him and Mrs. Surratt was loud enough for Mr. Weichmann to hear, he said, "I cannot swear that Mr. Weichmann heard her." On being asked the same question again, Lloyd answered, "That I am unable to say. As I said before, Mr. Weichmann was an entire stranger to me. As far as I know he may have heard." Lloyd never insisted that Weichmann heard the conversation. See *Surratt Trial*, I, 276–302.

When Weichmann was asked why he did not hear the conversation when he was seated next to her in the buggy, he said, "She leaned her head out of the window and talked to him. I do not know anything of the conversation that passed between them." He was then asked again why he did not hear it and he said, "In the first place, I never make a habit of listening to people; and in the second place, the conversation was not loud enough for me to hear." When asked what tone of voice this conversation between Lloyd and Mrs. Surratt was carried on in, Weichmann replied, "It was in that kind of a tone that I did not hear." Asked again if he did not hear the words, he said, "No, sir. If I had heard them, I would have no hesitation in saying so." Weichmann then stated that Mrs. Surratt had a louder conversation with Lloyd's passenger, Mrs. Emma Offutt. When asked what the conversation was about, he stated, "She was speaking of a man named Howell, who had been arrested on the 24th of March and thrown into the Old Capitol Prison, as a blockade runner." See *Surratt Trial,* I, 389–90.

At the trial of the conspirators, Weichmann had testified that Mrs. Surratt spoke to Lloyd in a "whisper," whereas he called it a "tone of voice" at the Surratt trial. At this second trial, he was asked, "Do you mean to say a whisper or a tone of voice?" He replied, "Is not a whisper a tone of voice?" When told, "No, sir; not in the ordinary common acceptation. We make a distinction," Weichmann replied, "True, it is not so in the ordinary acceptation; but a whisper is nevertheless a tone of voice produced by the vocal organs." He further stated that he meant the same thing by either expression. See *Surratt Trial,* I, 446.

Later on Weichmann was questioned about a conversation he had with Lloyd, when both of them were in prison, regarding the meeting at Uniontown. Weichmann said that Lloyd was astonished and angry because Weichmann had testified that he did not hear the conversation because it was carried on in a whisper. When asked, "Did not Mr. Lloyd tell you there, that if you had sworn to a whisper, you had sworn to what was not true?" Weichmann replied, "I cannot remember what Mr. Lloyd said. I do not recall anything of that kind that he said. I am judge of my own conscience and Mr. Lloyd is not. I know what I heard, and he knows what he heard." *Surratt Trial,* I, 448.

Upon being committed to Carroll Prison, Weichmann made a verbal statement which was converted to writing by the warden, Colonel William P. Wood, under date of April 30, 1865—at least Colonel Wood claims he did, although the statement is not in Weichmann's hand and is *not signed* by him. There are no filing dates or remarks as to when and where it was received, but a copy is now in the War Department records of the National Archives.

This purported statement has been used by some writers to point out that Weichmann *did hear* the conversation between Lloyd and Mrs. Surratt at Uniontown and therefore Weichmann perjured himself when he claimed he did not. Here is the controversial part of the statement: "On or about Tuesday 11th of April, Weichmann and Mrs. Surratt drove in a buggy to Surrattsville, also to

Capt. Gwinn [Gwynn's] residence. On the road to Surrattsville, she met her Tenant Lloyd with whom she had some conversation in relation to the man Howell. Stating that she would like to have him released on taking the oath of allegiance and would see Judge Turner about it." The accuracy of this statement depends on whether Weichmann made it in the first place and whether Colonel Wood put it down in the same words and context as Weichmann gave it. It is questionable as to when it was put in writing and doubtful if Weichmann ever saw it. It could have been written after the trial and the executions when the claims for the reward money were being filed. Colonel Wood was not averse to rigging an exhibit in a court trial, as in the famous reaper case of *McCormick* vs. *Manny*, which was lost by McCormick because of a patent infringement. Colonel Wood in a statement before a notary public dated December 16, 1897, claimed that he altered the reaper blade in question, causing McCormick to lose the case. See Otto Eisenschiml, *Why Was Lincoln Murdered?* (Boston: Little, Brown, 1937), pp. 191–2.

[8] For testimony of John Nothey, see Pitman, p. 126.

[9] For testimony of Bennett F. Gwynn, see Pitman, pp. 126, 182.

[10] For testimony of Lieutenant Keim, see Pitman, p. 147.

CHAPTER XIV

[1] H. Clay Ford, known as Harry, was the brother of John T. Ford, owner of Ford's Theater.

[2] At the first trial Coyle testified that he knew Booth, but "not intimately." See Pitman, p. 83.

[3] Undated newspaper clipping from the *Washington Post*, signed in print "John F. Coyle." Weichmann Papers, Risvold Collection.

[4] For testimony of James W. Pumphrey, see Pitman, p. 72.

[5] For testimony of Anderson and Turner, see Pitman, p. 75.

[6] For testimony of Ferguson, see Pitman, p. 76.

[7] The date of the letter is the 17th; the date of the newspaper is July 18, 1867.

[8] Secretary of War Stanton did not want Lincoln to attend the theater that evening and urged him to cancel his engagement. Stanton thought it unwise to expose the President and General Grant in a public theater, as they would be too tempting a target for anyone opposed to the Government. For that reason Stanton asked General Grant to excuse himself and hoped that this might discourage Lincoln from going. When Grant asked to be excused because of personal reasons, Lincoln asked Stanton to send Major Thomas T. Eckert, chief of the War Department telegraph office, but Stanton said that Eckert had to work that evening and could not go. Lincoln then playfully asked Eckert to put off his "business" until the next day, but Eckert, knowing that Stanton was trying to discourage Lincoln, asked to be excused. Actually Lincoln, as Commander in Chief of the Army, could have ordered anyone in the military to escort him to

the theater. These are the facts as stated by David Homer Bates in his book *Lincoln in the Telegraph Office* (New York: Century Company, 1907), pp. 366–8. Bates was the manager of the War Department telegraph office.

In a newspaper interview published in the *Ravenna Republican* (Ravenna, Ohio), April 19, 1906, A. C. Richards made the following statement: "Our officers [Metropolitan Police] were on duty at the White House, but Lincoln went about without a personal guard and wanted none." Weichmann Papers, Risvold Collection.

[9] Edward Spangler, one of the conspirators, was a stagehand at Ford's Theater.

[10] For testimony of Deveny, see Pitman, pp. 38–9.

[11] For testimony of Joseph Burroughs, see Pitman, p. 74. See also letter of A. C. Richards dated June 10, 1898, below, p. 417.

[12] For testimony of Kelleher, see Pitman, p. 151.

[13] For testimony of Fletcher, see Pitman, pp. 83–4, 145.

[14] For testimony of Grillo, see *Surratt Trial*, I, 176.

[15] For testimony of Maddox, see Pitman, pp. 75–6.

[16] For testimony of Burroughs, see Pitman, p. 74.

[17] For testimony of Rhodes, see *Surratt Trial*, I, 501–6.

[18] Also known as Navy Yard Bridge.

[19] See Atzerodt's confession to J. L. McPhail, *Baltimore American*, Monday, January 18, 1869. See also the confession of Atzerodt, below, Chapter XXXI. As Weichmann points out, there is the possibility that Atzerodt had originally agreed to kill Vice-President Johnson and then lost his nerve to follow through.

[20] See Pitman, p. 145.

CHAPTER XV

[1] Schuyler Colfax was Vice-President in Grant's first term.

[2] George Ashmun was a member of Congress from Massachusetts from 1845 to 1851.

[3] Alfred H. Guernsey and Henry M. Alden, *Harper's Pictorial History of the Great Rebellion* (2 vols.; New York: Harper and Brothers, 1868), II, 783. Not quoted word for word, but with no loss of meaning.

[4] The President's personal bodyguard, Colonel William Crook, did not go to the theater because Lincoln had ordered him to stay with his little son Tad; he was replaced with John Frederick Parker of the Metropolitan Police Force. Parker became interested in the play and deserted his post. Richards preferred charges against him for neglect of duty but nothing was ever done about the matter. See Otto Eisenschiml, *Why Was Lincoln Murdered?*, Chapter 3.

[5] *Our American Cousin* was playing at the McVerick Theater in Chicago the same day that Lincoln was nominated to run for President on the Republican ticket on May 18, 1860, in that city. This little vignette of history has not been generally known. See diary of Colonel Robert Burns, 1860, in Risvold Collection.

[6] *Harper's Pictorial History of the Great Rebellion*, II, 783.

[7] For testimony of Sleichmann, see Pitman, p. 73.

[8] For testimony of Dye, see Pitman, p. 72.

[9] See *Surratt Trial*, I, 135.

[10] See *Surratt Trial*, I, 148.

[11] An extra-soft lead with very little tin.

[12] For testimony of Rathbone, see Pitman, pp. 78–9.

[13] For testimony of Withers, see Pitman, pp. 79, 104.

[14] For testimony of Stewart, see Pitman, p. 79. See also letter of A. C. Richards to Weichmann under date of June 10, 1898, in which he gives his eyewitness version of the same scene; below, p. 417. Weichmann probably did not change Stewart's version because Richards advised him to leave it "as it was" because it had no bearing on the outcome of the case.

[15] According to the U. S. Naval Observatory, Washington, D.C., the moon rose on the night of April 14, 1865, at 10:02 P.M. L.C.T. in the direction of 24 degrees south of east. Moonrise is considered to occur when the upper edge of the disk of the moon appears to be exactly on an unobstructed horizon. See letter from John R. Hankey, Capt. USN, Superintendent, U. S. Naval Observatory, to James O. Hall under date of March 9, 1971. Hall Research.

[16] Also known as Navy Yard Bridge.

[17] For testimony of Ritterspaugh, see Pitman, pp. 97–8.

[18] The house in which Lincoln died still stands at 516 Tenth Street and is now a National Historic Site open to the public.

[19] Weichmann lists twenty-four persons at Lincoln's bedside, but he could hardly mean all twenty-four at one time. The room was only about ten by fifteen feet and more than a dozen would be too many at one time.

[20] Newspaper clipping from the *Philadelphia Press*, December 12, 1885. Interview with Noble McClintock, who was in charge of his company of the 24th Veteran Reserve Corps at Ford's Theater the night of the assassination. Weichmann Papers, Risvold Collection.

[21] Edwin M. Stanton, Secretary of War; Gideon Welles, Secretary of the Navy; John P. Usher, Secretary of the Interior; Attorney General James Speed; Postmaster General William Dennison; Henry W. Halleck, Army Chief of Staff; Montgomery Meigs, Quartermaster General of the Army; Senator Charles Sumner of Massachusetts; General John Blair Smith Todd, first cousin of Mrs. Lincoln; John Hay, Lincoln's private secretary; Governor Richard J. Oglesby of Illinois; General John F. Farnsworth; Dr. Robert K. Stone, Lincoln's family physician; Neal (Weichmann must mean Dr. Charles A. Leale), a twenty-three-year-old assistant surgeon, U. S. Volunteers, who was the first doctor to reach Lincoln after the shot was fired. Also in attendance on the President were Dr. Charles S. Taft, Dr. Albert F. A. King, Surgeon General Joseph K. Barnes, his assistant, Dr. Charles H. Crane, and Hugh McCulloch, Secretary of the Treasury. Although Weichmann includes Salmon P. Chase, the former Secretary of the Treasury, and at that time Chief Justice, he did not go to the Petersen house that fateful night.

[22] It is questionable whether Stanton or anyone else made this statement, but it has become legend beyond recall.

[23] Phineas D. Gurley was pastor of the New York Avenue Presbyterian Church in Washington, the church that Lincoln attended.

[24] For testimony of Matthews, see *Surratt Trial*, II, 821–8. See also A. C. Richards' letter of June 10, 1898, below, p. 417.

[25] *National Intelligencer*, July 18, 1867.

[26] For testimony of Dr. T. S. Verdi, see Pitman, p. 157.

[27] For testimony of Seward, see *Surratt Trial*, I, 249–52.

[28] For testimony of William H. Bell, see Pitman, pp. 154–5.

[29] For testimony of Robinson, see Pitman, pp. 155–6.

[30] For testimony of Seward, see Pitman, pp. 156–7.

CHAPTER XVI

[1] It seems that Booth must have known that Mrs. Surratt was going to Surrattsville that day in order to have her deliver the packages to Lloyd for use that same night.

[2] See Pitman, p. 420, and *Surratt Trial*, I, 391.

[3] For testimony of Calvert, see Pitman, p. 126. Not quoted word for word, but with no loss of meaning.

[4] For testimony of Nothey, see Pitman, p. 126. Weichmann quotes Pitman except for the words "at Surrattsville" and "April 11th," which he has added, as well as the italics.

[5] For testimony of Bennett F. Gwynn, see Pitman, p. 126.

[6] From the testimony at both trials it would appear that no one could have heard the conversation between Lloyd and Mrs. Surratt with regard to the "shooting irons" at Surrattsville on April 14, and it is Lloyd's word against hers. Because of this, and the fact that Lloyd was a drinking man, the defense tried to prove that he was too drunk to remember anything. He was not too drunk or sick to hand the "shooting irons" over to Booth and Herold that same evening. For Lloyd's testimony, see Pitman, pp. 85–7, and *Surratt Trial*, I, 276–302.

[7] Lloyd appeared as a witness at both trials—military and civil—and did not change his testimony, although he lived for twenty-seven years after the assassination and had time to recant if he had sworn falsely.

[8] James Lusby testified for the defense that he met Lloyd at Marlboro, where he and Lloyd had a few drinks, and that Lloyd was very drunk. On cross-examination he stated that it took about two and a half hours to return from Marlboro and that neither one had a drink during that time. Lloyd drove a carriage and Lusby a small wagon. On reaching Surrattsville, Lusby went into the barroom for a drink while Lloyd had his meeting with Mrs. Surratt in the yard. The testimony ended with Lusby admitting that he drank "right smart" that day and that it was a question as to who was the drunker of the two, he or Lloyd. See Ben Perley Poore, ed., *The Conspiracy Trial for the Murder of the President*,

pp. 65–68. J. E. Tilton & Company, Boston, 1866, reprinted by Arno Press, New York, 1972.

[9] See affidavit of Weichmann in Pitman, p. 420.

[10] For testimony of Miss Ward, see Pitman, p. 135. She testified to the poor eyesight of Mrs. Surratt and to receiving the two letters from Surratt while he was in Canada. For testimony of Weichmann, see Pitman, p. 113, and *Surratt Trial*, I, 381–2, 388.

[11] Mr. and Mrs. Kirby were friends and neighbors of Mrs. Surratt. Mrs. Kirby is so mentioned in the testimony of Miss Fitzpatrick. See Pitman, p. 132. No one ever denied that someone called that evening before the assassination, but the defense never produced that person. Both Olivia Jenkins, who was visiting the Surratts, and Miss Fitzpatrick testified that someone called about 9 P.M. the night of the assassination. Miss Jenkins said it was a man by the name of Scott from the Navy with papers for her and that Anna Surratt answered the call and not Mrs. Surratt. See *Surratt Trial*, I, 715–16 and II, 746–7. The fact remains that someone did call.

[12] At the Surratt trial Misses Fitzpatrick and Jenkins both testified that they did not hear Mrs. Surratt ask Weichmann to pray for her intentions. They also testified that they were teasing Mr. Weichmann and Weichmann testified that they were "jesting and laughing." When he was asked if the conversation was loud enough for them to hear, he said, "I heard it." He was then asked, "Did she come up and whisper it?" and he replied, "No, sir; she said it right out." Asked, "Loud enough for them to hear?" he replied, "*They might not have paid attention*" (editor's italics). He further stated that it was in an audible tone loud enough for them to have heard. Shortly after this Mrs. Surratt ordered them all to go to their rooms because they were *making too much noise. Surratt Trial*, I, 450–1.

[13] James A. McDevitt, John Clarvoe, Daniel R. P. Bigley, and John F. Kelly, of the Metropolitan Police Force.

[14] For testimony of Dye, see Pitman, p. 72.

[15] See *Surratt Trial*, I, 136–7.

[16] For the letters of Richards, see below, pp. 411–12 and 421.

[17] This newspaper article also appeared in the *Washington Evening Star*, April 14, 1894. McDevitt thought the man in the street looked like John McCullough the actor but could not be sure.

[18] Weichmann did not testify to this at the trial of the conspirators and states that he did not do so "because I had too much sympathy for the poor girl." When asked why he was telling it now, he said, "Because you bring it out" and "because I have been hunted down and persecuted on account of these very people." See *Surratt Trial*, I, 454.

[19] Holohan claims that he took Weichmann to police headquarters the following morning and implies that Weichmann did not go down of his own free will. Why would he force Weichmann to go? If Weichmann was guilty in Holohan's mind and was a party to the Conspiracy, why didn't he prefer charges against him? There is no evidence that he did.

CHAPTER XVII

[1] See below, p. 393.

[2] For testimony of Eaton, see Pitman, p. 41.

[3] Known at the trial of the conspirators as the "Sam" letter. See Pitman, pp. 235–6, for testimony of Lieutenant William H. Terry and copy of the "Sam" letter.

[4] For testimony of Wharton, see Pitman, p. 241.

[5] For testimony of Horner, see Pitman, pp. 234–5.

[6] For testimony of Fletcher, see Pitman, pp. 83–4.

[7] Weichmann's account of Payne hiding out in the cemetery was taken from George A. Townsend's *Katy of Catoctin*, pp. 518–21. Townsend was a noted newspaper correspondent and columnist who established his reputation by his battle reports of the Civil War and his coverage of the assassination.

[8] For testimony of Smith, see Pitman, p. 121.

[9] General Christopher C. Augur, Department of Washington, U. S. Army.

[10] For testimony of Morgan, Wermerskirch, and Dempsey, see Pitman, pp. 122–4.

[11] For testimony of Smith, see Pitman, pp. 121–2. Mrs. Surratt's failure to recognize Payne is paralleled by Dr. Mudd's failure to recognize Booth the night of April 14. The defense claimed that Mrs. Surratt had very poor eyesight. Holohan testified on the witness stand that he never knew that she had poor eyesight. See Pitman, p. 139.

[12] Much has been made of the fact that Payne first appeared at the Surratt house as Mr. Wood and on his second visit as Mr. Payne. After he was arrested, he said his real name was Lewis Thornton Powell. It has been claimed that they were actually two different men—that Powell and Wood were one, and Payne the second person. However, the day that Payne, alias Powell or Wood, was hanged they all disappeared. There has been much confusion in identifying Payne under his various names—Wood, Payne, Paine, Powell—and it seems strange that both men would look so much alike that they could not be recognized by the conspirators as two different persons, if such were the case. See Vaughan Shelton, *Mask for Treason* (Harrisburg, Pa.: Stackpole Books, 1965), p. 202.

[13] See *Surratt Trial*, I, 340–1.

[14] See Pitman, pp. 121–4.

[15] For testimony of Bell, see Pitman, pp. 154–5.

[16] Payne was received on board the monitor *Saugus* at 5 A.M., April 18, 1865. Hall Research.

[17] For testimony of Wells, see Pitman, p. 158.

[18] For testimony of Seward, see Pitman, pp. 156–7.

[19] A cruel, uncomfortable canvas hood which covered the entire head, with only the mouth and nose exposed. It was used on male prisoners.

[20] See testimony of Samuel Smith, stable boy, Pitman, p. 151.

[21] Weichmann gives Briscoe's first name as Walter, but it is given as Washington Briscoe in Pitman, p. 145.

22 For testimony of Metz, see Pitman, p. 149, and for Somerset Leaman, p. 152.

23 For testimony of Richter, see Pitman, p. 153.

24 For details of Dr. Mudd's arrest, see below, pp. 192–3.

CHAPTER XVIII

1 Booth was challenged by the sentry at the Navy Yard Bridge at "about half-past 10 or 11 o'clock," according to the testimony of Sergeant Silas T. Cobb. See Pitman, pp. 84–5. It has been claimed that Stanton closed all exits from Washington the night of the assassination except the one Booth took—the Navy Yard Bridge. See Otto Eisenschiml, *Why Was Lincoln Murdered?* p. 96. However, the records of the 22nd Army Corps show that, as soon as the initial shock of the assassination had worn off, orders were issued to close all exits, including the Navy Yard Bridge. Hall Research. Booth was on his way south in a matter of seconds after shooting Lincoln and would have escaped before any orders could have been enforced. It has also been claimed that the military wires out of Washington were cut the night of the assassination, but the records do not bear this out. Major Eckert stated at the impeachment investigation of President Johnson that the military wires were up and operating the night of the assassination—only the commercial wires suffered interruption. See *Impeachment Investigation: Testimony Taken before the Judiciary Committee of the House of Representatives in the Investigation of the Charges against Andrew Johnson.* 2nd session 39th Congress and 1st session 40th Congress, 1867. (Washington, D.C.: Government Printing Office, 1867), p. 673.

2 For testimony of Gardiner, see Pitman, p. 85.

3 For testimony of Lloyd, see Pitman, pp. 85–6.

4 See Pitman, p. 86.

5 For testimony of Joshua Lloyd, see Pitman, p. 90.

6 For testimony of Cottingham, here and below, see Pitman, p. 124. It was at Roby's Post Office in Surrattsville that Lloyd first mentioned his conversation with Mrs. Surratt about the "shooting irons."

7 See Pitman, p. 124.

8 See Pitman, p. 169.

9 For testimony of Lovett, see Pitman, p. 87.

10 For testimony of Thompson, see Pitman, p. 178. Dr. Mudd's failure to recognize Booth, when questioned by the arresting officers, weighed heavily against him at the Conspiracy trial. In fact, his attorney, Frederick Stone, said in later years that Dr. Mudd's prevarications had almost placed him in the hands of the hangman. *New York Tribune*, June 10, 17, 1883. Booth shot Lincoln in full view of a theater audience, making no attempt to hide his identity and stopping to pose on the stage before making his exit. At the Navy Yard Bridge, he gave his correct name when challenged by the sergeant of the guard, and at Surrattsville Tavern he boasted to John Lloyd that he had shot Abraham Lincoln. After

crossing the Rappahannock River, he dramatically proclaimed to three ex-Confederate officers and the ferryman that he had just assassinated the President of the United States and that there was a large reward on his head. It seems strange that he would try to disguise himself and say nothing about the event to Dr. Mudd when he was eager to proclaim it to strangers.

[11] Jones died March 2, 1895. Hall Research.

[12] Weichmann first published Chapters 18 and 19 in the *Indianapolis Journal* under the cognomen "Occasional," on May 9, 10, 1897. Weichmann Papers, Risvold Collection.

CHAPTER XIX

[1] The ferry was owned by Champ Thornton of Port Royal and Rollins lived just across the river at Port Conway. Hall Research.

[2] "Major Ruggles' Narrative," *Century Magazine*, January 1890, p. 443. Weichmann quotes extensively from this narrative by Major M. B. Ruggles.

[3] *Ibid.*, p. 444.

[4] *Ibid.*

[5] *Ibid.* Richard H. Garrett's farm was near Port Royal, Virginia.

[6] Reverend R. B. Garrett, "Booth's Last Days," *Indianapolis Bulletin*, November 11, 1896. Reverend Garrett, the son of Richard H. Garrett, was twelve years old at the time and witnessed that fateful night at Garrett's barn. See also below, pp. 213–17.

[7] "Major Ruggles' Narrative," p. 445.

[8] Lieutenant Edward P. Doherty, "Captain Doherty's Narrative," *Century Magazine*, January 1890, pp. 446–7. Colonel Lafayette C. Baker was the chief of the War Department's secret service, which was also known as the War Department detectives. Baker was promoted to Brigadier General, U. S. Volunteers, on April 26, 1865, and died on July 3, 1868.

[9] Boston Corbett's name was Thomas P., but he changed it to Boston. See *Myths*, pp. 284–5.

[10] Lieutenant Luther B. Baker was a double cousin to Colonel Lafayette C. Baker. L. B. Baker to Weichmann, October 20, 189?. Weichmann Papers, Risvold Collection.

[11] See "Captain Doherty's Narrative," p. 448.

[12] For testimony of Jett and Conger, see Pitman, pp. 90–3.

[13] L. B. Baker, "J. Wilkes Booth's Death," *Philadelphia Press*, January 17, 1880, and reprinted from the *Lansing Republican* (Lansing, Michigan).

[14] *Ibid.*

[15] *Ibid.*

[16] There has always been the question whether Booth shot himself, but Boston Corbett claimed that he shot him.

[17] "J. Wilkes Booth's Death."

[18] *Ibid.*

[19] Booth was a Protestant, although he was known to have attended St. Mary's Catholic Church near Bryantown in November 1864.

[20] Major Rathbone.

[21] Booth's diary was never admitted as evidence at the trial of the conspirators. Because of this and the fact that eighteen pages had been cut out of the diary, it became the subject of a congressional investigation. See *Impeachment Investigation, 1867,* p. 672. Colonel Baker claimed that the pages had been cut out *after* he turned it over to the War Department. Colonel Conger claimed that *the pages were missing when he removed the diary from Booth's body* at Garrett's farm, and Secretary Stanton stated that they were missing when it was turned over to the War Department. One sentence in the diary has caused speculation: ". . . though I have a greater desire and almost a mind to return to Washington, and in a measure clear my name, which I feel I can do." Perhaps the real reason for withholding the dairy as evidence at the first trial was the Government's determination to implicate Jefferson Davis and other Confederate officials in the Conspiracy to assassinate Lincoln. Since there was nothing in the diary to confirm this or to aid in the conviction of the accused conspirators, it was not presented. The diary is now in the Ford's Theater Museum in Washington, D.C. In order to conform to the Government transcript of Booth's diary, the missing words have been bracketed on Weichmann's rendition. See J. D. Allen, *Booth's Diary.*

[22] U.S. ironclad *Montauk.* Booth's body and Herold were delivered aboard at 1:45 A.M., April 27, 1865.

[23] For testimony of Dawson, see Pitman, pp. 42–3.

[24] For testimony of Dr. John F. May, see *Surratt Trial,* I, 270–1. See also his statement made at Washington, D.C., January 10, 1887, and printed in the *Cincinnati Enquirer,* January 30, 1893.

[25] It has been claimed that Booth was not the man shot in Garrett's barn. The most publicized example of these claims was the one made by David E. George of Enid, Oklahoma, who stated in 1900 that he was Booth. See Theodore Roscoe, *Web of Conspiracy,* pp. 516–23.

In a statement signed by Edward C. Jones (dated January 29, [1897], and located in the Weichmann Papers, Risvold Collection), Christopher C. Ritter, a butcher living in Anderson, Indiana, gave the following account: After killing Lincoln, Booth and Robert E. Stinton, another actor, changed into the cast-off clothes of some plasterers in the rear of a nearby restaurant. Later, when Booth was hiding out in Lower Maryland, he ordered Stinton to return to Washington and have Edward Fox and Edward Derrole retrieve his clothes and some documents they contained, put on the clothes, and return to him. These men, including Booth, were all members of an organization known as the Knights of the Golden Circle. Fox and Derrole never reached Booth and were the two men surrounded by the soldiers in Garrett's barn. Fox, who was wearing Booth's clothes, had injured his leg when he was kicked by Derrole's horse, had a scar on his neck, and, in addition, bore a strong resemblance to Booth. Fox was shot and died; Derrole was captured and died on the gallows without confessing; Booth escaped to South America, where he married and lived out his life. A highly improbable tale.

26 The disposition of Booth's body became one of the better-kept secrets of the War Department for many years. The most popular version was published in *Frank Leslie's Illustrated Newspaper,* May 20, 1865. It contained a sketch showing Colonel L. C. Baker and Lieutenant L. B. Baker consigning Booth's canvas-wrapped body to the bottom of the Potomac River in the dead of night. The editor, Frank Leslie, stated that he was able to vouch for the truth of the representation.

On March 15, 1901, Dr. George L. Porter wrote to Weichmann: "The manner and locality where the post-mortemized remains of Booth were secreted has never been correctly described and very likely may not be until after my death. The sensational illustration and description in Baker's book [*History of the United States Secret Service*] are fables." Weichmann Papers, Risvold Collection.

In April 1911, the *Columbian Magazine* published an article by Dr. Porter in which he described the hiding place of Booth's body. He stated that it was delivered to him by the Bakers at the Old Penitentiary building on the Government arsenal grounds. It was buried with great secrecy under a warehouse floor not far from the very site where the conspirators were later hanged. In 1869, the remains were turned over to the Booth family. See *Myths,* pp. 221–2.

27 Actually June 26, 1869. See Chapter V above.

28 Undated newspaper clipping, Weichmann Papers, Risvold Collection.

CHAPTER XX

1 In the original order, Holohan's first name is given as George instead of John.

2 See Rockville lecture, below, p. 438.

3 For testimony of Du Tilly, see *Surratt Trial,* II, 856.

4 Lieutenant Bennett H. Young with twenty-five Confederates raided the town of St. Albans, Vermont, on October 19, 1864.

5 At the time of the conspiracy trial, Burnett signed his name as Brevet Colonel, although Heitman lists him as a Brevet Brigadier General. See Francis B. Heitman, *Historical Register and Dictionary of the United States Army,* vol. 1 (Washington, D. C.: Government Printing Office, 1903), p. 264.

6 Carroll Prison was an annex to the Old Capitol Prison. Mrs. Surratt was brought to Carroll annex on April 18 and placed in room 41. Weichmann was brought to Carroll on April 30 and Mrs. Surratt was taken away by Baker the same day. Weichmann could be mistaken as to which prison he saw her in. Hall Research.

7 See also Otto Eisenschiml, *In the Shadow of Lincoln's Death,* pp. 175–6.

8 For letter of Richards, see below, pp. 421–2. See also Richards' testimony, *Surratt Trial,* II, 987–8. From Richards' testimony it would seem that Weichmann was not under arrest at that time, but was under protective custody as a witness.

Richards was concerned about Weichmann falling into the hands of Baker's War Department detectives and being arrested by them.

CHAPTER XXI

[1] See Pitman, p. 17.

[2] General Hunter was the president of the Commission. General Wallace later won fame for his book *Ben Hur*. He was also the president of the Military Commission which tried and hanged Captain Henry Wirz, the former commander of the Andersonville prison. General Harris was the only member of the Commission to write a history of the assassination (T. M. Harris, *Assassination of Lincoln*, Boston, 1892). Colonel Tompkins was awarded the Congressional Medal of Honor for leading a brilliant cavalry charge and having two horses shot out from under him at Fairfax Court House, Virginia, June 1, 1861.

[3] See above, Chapter XVII, note 19.

[4] See Pitman, pp. 18–19.

[5] See Pitman, pp. 19–21.

[6] See Pitman, p. 21.

CHAPTER XXII

[1] Quoted almost word for word, with no loss of meaning.

[2] Peterson reports 361 examined—198 for the prosecution and 163 for the defense. See *Trial of the Assassins and Conspirators for the Murder of President Abraham Lincoln* (Philadelphia: T. B. Peterson Brothers, 1865), p. 16.

[3] Herold did not go with the conspirators on the so-called "horseback ride"—he went to Surrattsville with weapons.

[4] Also known as Anacostia Bridge and Navy Yard Bridge. Anacostia Creek is the eastern branch of the Potomac River.

[5] At the first trial Colonel H. H. Wells testified that the boots taken from Payne had "a broad ink-stain on them on the inside," which was later identified to be "J. W. B—th." Spencer M. Clark of the Treasury Department testified that, while part of it was indistinct, the "J.W." was very plain and that he was sure that the name was Booth. See Pitman, pp. 158–9.

[6] For argument in defense of Lewis Payne, by William E. Doster, see Pitman, pp. 308–17.

[7] For testimony of Lieutenant W. R. Keim, see Pitman, p. 147.

[8] For argument in defense of George A. Atzerodt, by William E. Doster, see Pitman, pp. 300–7. The date of March 18 as given by Doster is in conflict with both Weichmann and Arnold. Arnold states that the so-called "horseback ride" took place on March 17, whereas Weichmann says that it was on the 16th. However, they both agree that the ride did take place. See above, p. 101.

[9] See Pitman, p. 307.

[10] See Pitman, pp. 382–3.

[11] For testimony of Norton, see Pitman, p. 177.

[12] For testimony of Evans, see Pitman, p. 174.

[13] For testimony of Jarboe, see Pitman, pp. 213–16.

[14] For testimony of Elzee Eglent, see Pitman, p. 171.

[15] Colonel H. H. Wells testified at the trial of the conspirators that he had three interviews with Dr. Mudd the week subsequent to the assassination—two were oral and one was in writing. "Dr. Mudd's manner was so extraordinary, that I scarcely know how to describe it. He did not seem unwilling to answer a direct question; he seemed embarrassed, and at the third interview alarmed, and I found that, unless I asked direct questions, important facts were omitted." At the last interview, Colonel Wells advised Dr. Mudd that "he seemed to be concealing the facts of the case, which would be considered the strongest evidence of his guilt, and might endanger his safety." He also told Wells that he first met Booth in November of 1864 and had not seen him again until the Saturday morning following the assassination. He made no mention of his meeting with Booth, Surratt, and Weichmann in the National Hotel on December 23, 1864. See Pitman, pp. 168–9.

[16] For affidavit of Dutton, see Pitman, p. 421.

[17] For testimony of Horner, see Pitman, pp. 234–5, 241.

[18] For testimony of Wharton, see Pitman, p. 241.

[19] For argument of John A. Bingham, see Pitman, pp. 351–402. The quotes for the balance of this chapter are from Bingham.

[20] Lewis Payne.

[21] For testimony of Samuel Street, see Pitman, p. 224.

CHAPTER XXIII

[1] See Pitman, p. 86.

[2] See Pitman, pp. 121–3.

[3] Not recorded in Pitman since it was not part of the testimony.

[4] See Pitman, pp. 393–4.

[5] Johnson, a distinguished lawyer and senator from Maryland, argued the legality of the Commission to try the case in a military court. The Attorney General had ruled that the Military Commission had jurisdiction and the Commission denied Johnson's argument, which was made before the Commission on June 16, 1865. See Pitman, pp. 251–62. Johnson apparently withdrew from active participation in the case because General Harris objected to his presence on the grounds that Johnson did not recognize the moral obligation of an oath as an obligation of loyalty, although he did withdraw his objection after some discussion of the matter.

[6] *Investigation and Trial Papers Relating to the Assassination of President Lincoln* (Washington, D.C.: National Archives, Microfilm No. 599, 16 rolls, Roll No. 8).

7 See Pitman, p. 42.

8 See Pitman, pp. 47–63.

9 See Pitman, pp. 45–6.

10 For testimony of Bates, see Pitman, pp. 46–7. Pitman gives the date as the 11th of April.

CHAPTER XXIV

1 For the following findings and sentences of the Commission, see Pitman, pp. 247–9.

2 See below, pp. 296–315.

3 See Pitman, p. 249.

4 See Pitman, p. 249.

5 See Pitman, p. 250.

6 See Pitman, p. 250.

7 For Father Walter's story, see below, pp. 316–27.

8 The trap was sprung at 1:26 P.M.; they were pronounced dead at 1:44 P.M., and they were cut down at 1:54 P.M. See *The Case of Mrs. Surratt*, p. 61.

9 On July 15, 1865, President Johnson changed the orders of imprisonment from the penitentiary at Albany, New York, to Fort Jefferson, Dry Tortugas, Florida. Dr. Mudd, Arnold, and Spangler were given a full pardon by President Johnson after serving about four years. O'Laughlin died from yellow fever while in prison and before the others were pardoned.

CHAPTER XXV

1 See Father Walter, below, pp. 318–19.

2 General Hunter died on February 2, 1886, at the age of eighty-three.

3 General Ekin died on March 27, 1891, at the age of seventy-one.

4 General Kautz died on September 4, 1895, at the age of sixty-seven.

5 Colonel Clendenin died on March 5, 1895, at the age of sixty-four.

6 General Howe died on January 25, 1897, at the age of seventy-eight.

7 General Harris died on September 30, 1906, at the age of eighty-nine.

8 General Wallace died on February 15, 1905, at the age of seventy-seven.

9 General Foster died on March 3, 1903, at the age of sixty-nine.

10 Colonel Tompkins died on January 18, 1915, at the age of eighty-four.

11 President Johnson died on July 31, 1875, at the age of sixty-six.

12 Secretary Stanton died on December 24, 1869, at the age of fifty-five.

13 Brophy issued a strong statement against Weichmann for testifying against Mrs. Surratt. See *The Case of Mrs. Surratt*, pp. 62–4, where it is reproduced in full. Weichmann answered Brophy's charges in a letter to the editors of the *Sunday*

Despatch, Philadelphia, July 15, 1865, in which he gives Brophy a rough going over. He states that Holahan went to Canada "whole heartedly" in pursuit of Surratt and wonders why Mrs. Surratt's lawyers, Aiken and Clampitt, did not bring out the charges of Brophy on the witness stand. Weichmann claims that Brophy was "summoned twice—once for the defense and once for the prosecution—but according to his own (Brophy's) wishes he never appeared on the stand." *Lincoln Obsequies Scrapbook* (newspaper clippings) (Library of Congress, Rare Book Room), pp. 151–3.

[14] General Winfield Scott Hancock died on February 9, 1886, at the age of sixty-two.

[15] John F. Hartranft died on October 17, 1889, at the age of fifty-eight.

[16] Printed in the *Washington Daily Morning Chronicle,* September 19, 1873.

[17] John A. Bingham died on March 19, 1900, at the age of eighty-five.

[18] General Burnett died on January 4, 1916, at the age of seventy-seven.

CHAPTER XXVI

[1] This paper was printed in full by T. M. Harris, *Assassination of Lincoln,* pp. 407–19. Not quoted word for word, but with no loss of meaning.

[2] Harlan, U. S. senator from Iowa, was a close associate of Lincoln, and his daughter Mary was married to Robert T. Lincoln. He became Secretary of the Interior in 1865 and resigned in 1866 because of a disagreement with President Johnson over Reconstruction policy. He died at Mount Pleasant, Iowa, October 5, 1899.

[3] General Kautz, in a reminiscence he wrote, stated that five of the nine judges, including himself, signed a clemency plea for Mrs. Surratt, because they did not think it "wise or expedient to hang her." He also stated that President Johnson was not very sincere when he attempted to shift the responsibility by claiming that he had never seen the plea, although the recommendation with the names of those who signed it was published in the newspapers within a day or two of the adjournment of the Commission on June 30. See Charles F. Cooney, ed., "At the Trial of the Lincoln Conspirators: The Reminiscences of General August V. Kautz," *Civil War Times Illustrated* (Gettysburg, August 1973), pp. 22–31, where it is published for the first time. The *New York World,* for example, under date of July 6, 1865, reported in its columns that four judges of the Commission had signed a recommendation for mercy for Mrs. Surratt and that the rumor was going the rounds in Washington.

[4] Floyd, Secretary of War under Buchanan, is referred to as a traitor because he resigned as Secretary of War in 1860 over the military occupation of Fort Sumter by Major Robert Anderson, which he considered a breach of faith to South Carolina. He was also accused of transferring arms to the South, while Secretary of War, but this was investigated by Congress in February 1861 and the charges were found to be groundless.

[5] President Johnson died July 31, 1875, and Holt probably thought that Speed would now reveal the truth of the matter.

[6] Attorney General Speed's refusal to reveal what was said in a meeting of the Cabinet officers in the White House reminds one forcibly of Watergate 1973. If anyone was ever left "hanging in the wind—to slowly twist and turn," it was Judge Joseph Holt by Speed's refusal to speak up on the clemency plea for Mrs. Surratt.

CHAPTER XXVII

[1] Father Jacob Ambrose Walter, born in Baltimore, December 7, 1827, and died April 5, 1894.

[2] In March 1865, Hardie received the brevets of brigadier and major general. After the war he reverted to the rank of colonel and was one of four inspector generals in the regular army.

[3] Also published in *The New York Times,* July 21, 1865, and directed "To The Agent of The Associated Press." Hardie's views on the matter are quite different from those of the *New York Tribune* article and Father Walter's statement. See below, p. 455.

[4] According to this statement, Father Walter was not under official orders to remain silent on the confession of Mary Surratt. However, Archbishop Martin John Spalding advised Hardie, under date of July 23, 1865, that he had cautioned Father Walter to observe silence and that Father Walter had promised to do so, but it is questionable when he told him, before or after the execution. Spalding died on February 7, 1872. Hardie Papers, Library of Congress, Collection No. 24869. See below, p. 458.

[5] James R. and H. Clay Ford were brothers of John T. Ford.

[6] Some writers have viewed the failure to convict John H. Surratt in the trial of 1867 as a vindication of his mother, Mary E. Surratt—how could she be guilty if he wasn't? Under date of August 12, 1900, Dr. George L. Porter wrote the following to Weichmann in regard to John H. Surratt: "I have no doubt of his guilt, nor of the fact that the failure of the jury to agree was due to religious and political influences and not to the lack of legal proof." Weichmann Papers, Risvold Collection.

CHAPTER XXVIII

[1] Certified copy of original letter is in Weichmann Papers, Risvold Collection.

[2] John McGill, appointed bishop of the Richmond diocese July 23, 1850, serving until his death, January 14, 1872.

[3] Those critical of Weichmann have claimed that this was his reward for his testimony at the trial of the conspirators.

[4] The fifth, and successful, attempt to lay the transatlantic cable was made by the steamship *Great Eastern* in 1866. This vessel arrived off Newfoundland with the cable July 28, 1866.

[5] For testimony of Dr. Lewis J. A. McMillan, see *Surratt Trial*, I, 461–84. Weichmann draws heavily from McMillan's testimony.

[6] For testimony of Charles H. Blinn, see *Surratt Trial*, I, 174–6.

CHAPTER XXIX

[1] 39th Congress, 2nd session, *House Exec. Doc. No. 1*, p. 129. Hereafter referred to as *Diplomatic Correspondence*. Letter is dated at the "Legation of the United States, Rome, April 23, 1866."

[2] *Ibid.*, p. 131. Weichmann has corrected the date of 1853 to 1863 and does not copy word for word, but with no loss of meaning.

[3] *Ibid.*, pp. 131–2.

[4] The U. S. Government knew of Surratt's presence in England and Italy, but for some unexplained reason did not act to arrest him. Much has been made of this fact, with the implication that the Government did not want him back, or, more pointedly, that they were afraid to bring him back and let him talk in a civil court of law. The fact remains that they did bring him back and he did have his day in court—sixty-two days.

[5] See *Diplomatic Correspondence*, No. 1, p. 139.

[6] *Ibid.*, p. 140.

[7] Published in 1865 by Moore, Wilstach and Baldwin, New York.

[8] See *Diplomatic Correspondence*, No. 1, pp. 140–1; "Legation of the United States."

[9] 39th Congress, 2nd session, *House Exec. Doc. No. 9, John H. Surratt*, p. 20.

[10] *Ibid.*, pp. 20–1.

[11] *Ibid.*, p. 21.

[12] *Ibid.*, p. 28. Weichmann has filled in the name "St. Marie," which is deleted from the official record.

[13] *Ibid.*, pp. 28–9.

[14] Weichmann's account of Surratt's escape is taken from Hanson Hiss, "John H. Surratt's Story," almost word for word, except that it has been changed from the first person to the third. See below, p. 447.

[15] See *Diplomatic Correspondence*, No. 1, pp. 143–4. Letter is dated at the "Legation of the United States, Rome, November 19, 1866."

[16] 39th Congress, 2nd session, *House Exec. Doc. No. 25, John H. Surratt*, pp. 2–3.

[17] *Ibid.*, pp. 13–14.

[18] *Ibid.*, p. 23.

[19] The *Swatara* landed at Washington, D.C., on February 19, 1867.

[20] A. C. Richards took charge of Surratt, when he landed, and turned him over to the U. S. marshal. See Richards' letter of June 2, 1898, below, p. 416.

CHAPTER XXX

[1] The trial of John H. Surratt amounted to a rehash of the first trial with additional evidence and witnesses on both sides. The Government produced several witnesses who testified that Surratt was in Washington on April 14, and Sainte Marie testified that Surratt told him that he left Washington the night of the assassination. See *Surratt Trial*, I, 492. However, the jury was not convinced that Surratt had been in Washington on April 14 and the trial ended in "no process." Perhaps the real reasons were that no one really had the heart to convict him because of the public indignation over the hanging of his mother; moreover, the jury voted pretty much along party lines—four Northerners for conviction and five Southerners and one from New York for acquittal.

[2] *Surratt Trial*, I, 117.

[3] *Ibid.* Weichmann does not quote perfectly, but with no loss of meaning.

[4] For testimony of Kent, see *Surratt Trial*, I, 123–5.

[5] Ezra B. Westfall, not Westfield. See testimony of in *Surratt Trial*, II, 935–41.

[6] Morris Drohan, not Martin. See *Surratt Trial*, II, 924–5.

[7] For testimony of Sainte Marie, see *Surratt Trial*, I, 492–3. His full name was Henri Beaumont de Sainte Marie and he was also known as Henry Benjamin Sainte Marie.

[8] For testimony of Charles H. M. Wood, see *Surratt Trial*, I, 494–8.

[9] For testimony of Reed, see *Surratt Trial*, I, 158–62, and for that of Theodore Benjamin Rhodes, see pp. 501–6.

[10] For testimony of Vanderpoel, see *Surratt Trial*, I, 240–6.

[11] For testimony of Cleaver, see *Surratt Trial*, I, 204–13.

[12] For testimony of Dye, see *Surratt Trial*, I, 135, and for that of Susan Jackson, see pp. 162–5.

[13] For testimony of Carroll, see *Surratt Trial*, II, 732–45. For Atkinson, see pp. 729–32, and for Stewart, see I, 723–4. Atkinson and Stewart stated that they saw Surratt on the 13th or 14th but could not say which day it was.

[14] For testimony of Bissell, see *Surratt Trial*, II, 863–92.

[15] For testimony of Cass, see *Surratt Trial*, I, 724–28; II, 729.

[16] See *Surratt Trial*, II, 767–8.

[17] See *Surratt Trial*, II, 768–9.

[18] For testimony of Blinn, see *Surratt Trial*, I, 174–6.

[19] For testimony of Chapin, see *Surratt Trial*, I, 236–40.

[20] For testimony of Hobart, see *Surratt Trial*, I, 169–74.

[21] The maiden name of Susan Jackson. She was married two weeks after the assassination. See *Surratt Trial*, I, 162.

[22] See Rockville lecture, below, pp. 434–8.

[23] For testimony of Roccofort, see *Surratt Trial*, II, 838–40.

[24] See letter of A. C. Richards under date of October 5, 1899, below, p. 423.

[25] For argument of District Attorney Carrington see *Surratt Trial*, II, 1073–1151.

26 For argument of Merrick, see *Surratt Trial*, II, 1155–1212.

27 For argument of Judge Pierrepont, see *Surratt Trial*, II, 1247–1366.

28 For Judge Fisher's charge to the jury, see *Surratt Trial*, II, 1368–78.

CHAPTER XXXI

1 These are Weichmann's italics.

2 If Atzerodt is correct in this statement, then John Surratt was in Washington the night of the assassination, April 14.

CHAPTER XXXII

1 Weichmann copies Oldroyd almost word for word with no loss of meaning.

2 Spangler died on February 7, 1875. His first name was Edman, according to George S. Bryan in his book *The Great American Myth* (New York: Carrick and Evans, 1940), which is in agreement with Hall. However, the records of St. Peter's Catholic Church at Beantown give his first name as Edmund. Regardless of the above, it is apparent that he used the name Edward.

3 Weichmann is wrong. Samuel B. Arnold was living at the time and did not die until September 21, 1906.

4 Unidentified newspaper clipping.

5 Boston Corbett's final demise still remains a mystery. It has been established that he became a salesman in Oklahoma, traveling out of Enid, but it is not known when and where he died (George W. Martin, Secretary, Kansas State Historical Society, to Weichmann, August 22, 1901, Risvold Collection). One rumor has it that his relatives brought him back to Boston, where he died in an asylum and is buried in a Boston cemetery. Booth's sister Asia Clarke stated that Boston Corbett saved her beloved brother from an ignominious death (on the gallows) by shooting him at Garrett's barn. See *The Unlocked Book*, p. 140.

6 William A. Petersen died on June 18, 1871.

7 Ford died on March 14, 1894. Father Walter died on April 5, 1894.

8 Lloyd died on December 18, 1892.

9 Henri Beaumont de St. Marie, also known as Henry Benjamin Sainte Marie, died on September 8, 1874. *The New York Times* reported on September 12, 1874, that he died *"suddenly in the street in Philadelphia"* from heart disease at the age of forty-one.

10 June 9, 1893.

11 See Oldroyd, pp. 87–8.

12 Under date of August 29, 1901, William H. Seward, Jr., wrote to Weichmann: "Mrs. Seward died June 21, 1865, immediately following the partial recovery of Mr. Seward and my brother Frederick. My sister, Frances, who was in poor health at the time, did not die until the following year, both deaths I have no

doubt, were hastened by the shock of the attempted assassination." Weichmann Papers, Risvold Collection. Miss Frances J. Seward (Fannie) died on October 29, 1866.

[13] Mary Todd Lincoln passed away July 15, 1882, at the age of sixty-four. Mary Lincoln died believing the rumor, which originated in the wake of the assassination, that President Johnson had hired Booth and the conspirators to kill her husband so he could become President. Almost a hundred years later, a similar rumor followed in the wake of the Kennedy assassination—that Lyndon Johnson had hired the assassin so he could be President.

[14] Major Henry Reed Rathbone died on August 14, 1911, at Hildesheim, Germany, in an asylum for the criminally insane.

[15] These letters to Weichmann were published by him in the *Washington Post*, April 18, 1898.

INDEX

i

A NOTE ABOUT THE EDITOR

———

Floyd E. Risvold was born in Milltown, Wisconsin, in 1912 and grew up in Minneapolis. In the 1930's and '40's he worked as a government surveyor in the geodetic service in the West and Alaska. He is now president of the firm of O. E. Risvold and Sons, distributors of infants wear and accessories. His private collection on American history, of which the Weichmann manuscript is a part, includes letters, books, maps, philatelic Americana, and is unique in the international fur trade of North America. Mr. Risvold is married and lives in Edina, Minnesota.

A NOTE ON THE TYPE

———

The text of this book was set on the Linotype in a typeface called Scotch. Though there is a divergence of opinion regarding its exact origin, a cutting of such a face was undertaken and recorded by Messrs. Miller and Richard, of Edinburgh, in 1808. The original Linotype version of Scotch was cut in 1902 by Theodore L. DeVinne. The essential characteristics of Scotch are sturdy capitals, full-rounded lower-case letters, the graceful fillet of the serifs, and a general effect of crispness through sharply contrasting "thicks and thins."

The book was designed by Betty Anderson and was composed, printed, and bound by American Book-Stratford Press, New York, New York.